Tom Schorn

COMPUTER ENGINEERING

A DEC VIEW OF HARDWARE SYSTEMS DESIGN

C. GORDON BELL · J. CRAIG MUDGE · JOHN E. McNAMARA

DIGITAL PRESS

Printed in U.S.A.

1st Printing, September 1978
Documentation Number JB066-A
Library of Congress Catalog Card Number 77-91677
ISBN 0-932376-00-2

The manuscript was created on a DEC Word Processing System and, via a translation program, was typeset on Digital's DECset-8000 Typesetting System.

Cover and display pages designed by Elliott N. Hendrickson.

To the people at Digital, especially the engineers, and Ben

FOREWORD

The progress which has brought the number of computers in use in the world from dozens to millions within a generation has not been the result of a single discovery or the work of a single inventor or company. Rather, men and women from fields as diverse as semiconductor physics and mechanical engineering have studied long hours and worked with various measures of inspiration and perspiration to make the discoveries and develop the technologies needed to advance the state of the art in computer technology.

There are several aspects of the progress in computer technology which have made it an exceptionally exciting and rewarding field for the people involved. First of all, a great many of the major steps forward, such as the invention of the transistor, have taken place within our lifetimes. Secondly, there has been an opportunity to associate with many fine colleagues whose brilliance, courage of conviction, and capacity for endless work have been a great inspiration. Finally, there has been the great promise of computers – their ability to free men's minds of repetitive and boring tasks, their ability to reduce the cost of producing goods, their ability to improve the lives of so many people in so many ways – and the fun and excitement of working with them.

In the chapters of this book, various authors relate some of their experiences in the past twenty years, draw some conclusions about how computer technology got to where it is, and project into the future from some of the trends they have seen. While it is impossible in a single book to capture all of the excitement and challenge of these years, they have done an admirable job for which they are to be commended. Hopefully, this glimpse into the past and present will encourage the students of the future to enter the computer engineering field and bring with them ideas, ambition, and courage.

Kenneth H. Olsen
President
Digital Equipment Corporation

FOREWORD

PREFACE

This book has been written for practicing computer designers, whether their domain is microcomputers, minicomputers, or large computers, and for those who by their contact with computer are students of design - users, programmers, designers of peripherals and memories, and students of computer engineering and computer science.

Computer engineering is a collage of different activities and disciplines, only one of which - the technical aspects (multiplier design, the behavior of synchronizer circuits, and series/parallel tradeoffs, for example) - is covered by conventional texts. This book uses the case study method to show how all the different factors (technology push, the marketplace, manufacturing, etc.) form the real-world constraints and opportunities which influence computer engineering.

Computer engineering can be thought of as a multivariable mathematical problem in which the engineer searches for an optimum within certain constraints. Unfortunately, an optimum in one variable is rarely an optimum in another, and thus a major portion of computer engineering is the search for reasonable compromises. A common method used to aid the search is to assign weights to various system variables and to seek a weighted optimum. The weights vary with the intended application. In one situation, speed might receive the maximum weight; in another, instruction set compatibility might be the most important; and in yet another, reliability might be paramount. The number of dimensions to the problem is large, and the meaningful measures for them are few. For example, the cost variable is multidimensional and includes manufacturing, development, and field support costs. In addition, there are numerous interdependencies among the variables such as the relationships between instruction set, machine organization, logic design, and circuit design. These relationships and the contraints that control the weighting of the variables change with time. For example, the cost function changes when different subsystems use different technologies, and this influences the relationships. In addition, constraints such as maintainability and compatibility vary in importance from year to year. Finally, while some of the relationships, such as the time-space tradeoff in adder design, are well understood, others, particularly those involving marketing factors, are not.

Because no theory exists to undergird this multidimensional design problem, we believe that there is no substitute for an extensive, critical understanding of the existing examples of designed and marketed systems. Therefore, this book uses the case study approach. For examples, we have used the thirty DEC computers that have been built over the twenty years that the company has existed, plus some PDP-11-based machines built at Carnegie-Mellon University. Carnegie-Mellon's machines explore interconnect structures that we feel will form the basis of future generations.

The association between DEC and Carnegie-Mellon has produced not only some interesting machines to examine but also some of the written material for this book. People in universities can and do write, whereas engineers directly involved in design work are less inclined or encouraged to publish their work.

A substantial portion of the material contributed by DEC authors is historical. We strongly believe that historical information is worth the expense in terms of writing, reading, and learning; machine design principles and techniques change slowly. In fact, the machines currently being designed are based on principles that have been understood and used for years, and we are often asked, "Are we running out of design issues?" Yes, we feel technology provides the forcing function for new designs, not new principles.

Learning about design is always important. Although new designs often appear to be a reapplication of old principles, in the process of being reapplied they change and go beyond their first application. Design is learned by examining and emulating previous designs plus incorporating general principles, new use, and new technology. Indeed, the microcomputer developments draw (or should draw) extensively from the minicomputers. As we build new structures, we should be able to avoid the pitfalls of the immediate past design.

We have intentionally restricted our scope to DEC computers. The reason is obvious: we can speak with first-hand knowledge. If we had used other companies' designs, our data would have been less accurate, and some factors, e.g., design styles, would have been omitted. The main reason, however, is a key part of the philosophy of the book. To understand machine design evolution, the effects of changes in the underlying technologies, and time-invariant principles, we must analyze a family beginning at birth and follow it over several generations of technology. Four series of DEC computers allow such an analysis. DEC computers also provide an opportunity to study another dimension of computer engineering – the coexistence of complementary (and sometimes competing) products. Particular design efforts must compete for resources (design talent, manufacturing-plant capacity, and software, marketing, and sales support). DEC computers have, in general, been designed to be complementary and to avoid overlapping or redundant products. Thus, another set of constraints can be seen at work in the design space.

The book concerns itself with general purpose computers which are intended to be widely available commercially. The engineering of computers for highly specialized applications, for which only a few copies are built, is not treated. Moreover, because not all major principles of computer architecture and computer engineering are embodied in the DEC computers, the reader may want to examine other designs, as well. For example, the reader cannot learn about descriptor architectures, array processors, list-processing machines, or general purpose emulators from this book.

At one time consideration was given to postponing the publication of a book until 1982, at which time DEC will celebrate its twenty-fifth anniversary. This idea was rejected because another five years would further impede the collection of data about the early machines. More importantly, the twenty-year period of DEC modules and computers (1957–1977) has extended from the early second generation to the fourth generation. Today, the processor of several DEC computers occupies a single large-scale integrated circuit consisting of several thousand transistors, whereas in 1957 only one transistor could be fabricated on a single piece of germanium. In another five years, the design, manufacture, and distribution of computers will be radically different – so much so as to merit a new book.

We expect an increasingly larger number of people to be involved in computer engineering and hence students of this material, because we expect computers as we know them today will disappear within ten years! With the processor-on-a-chip, the number of computer *systems* designers (users) has risen by several orders of magnitude.

In the area of large computer systems, the buyers and users are also clearly the computer designers: they select components (from the set of available components) and interconnect them to form specific structures. It is essential for us all to have a model of the price, performance, and reliability parameters and how they vary with time. Previous generations have focused first on the invention of the computer, next on the understanding of price/performance tradeoffs, and most recently on manufacturing – especially the fabrication of the semiconductors that now drive computer evolution. In the next five years, design will focus on applications: conventional applications will be more efficient, computers will be extended to reach new applications, and life-cycle costs will receive more attention. For the computer engineer, the evolution of DEC machines provides an excellent perspective on the influence of applications on design. For those of us who must deal with design goals, constraints, and objective functions to improve reliability, availability and maintainability, it is imperative that we first clearly understand previous design problems.

For the programmers who use computers and are a part of the computer design process, understanding this material is mandatory in order to know the rules of the game. We say comparatively little about software, other than how it has influenced hardware design. The increasing role of software functions in the hardware domain is a clear process that has allowed (and forced) computer architecture to change. The engineering of DEC software will be treated in subsequent volumes, perhaps one on language translators and one on operating systems. We hope also that future volumes will be devoted to mass storage devices, terminals, and applications.

Two notations, ISP and PMS, were introduced in the book, *Computer Structures* [Bell and Newell, 1971]. We continue to use them in this book, especially since they have left the realm of notations and have become working design tools. ISP was introduced to describe the instruction set processor of a computer – the machine seen by the program (and programmer). ISP is now used for machine description, simulation, verification of diagnostics, microprogramming, automatic assembler generation, and the comparison of computer architectures. The evolution and improvement of ISP is principally due to needs of the Army/Navy Computer Family Architecture (CFA) project and the work of Mario Barbacci. The latest version, ISPS, is being used within DEC for implementing processors, simulators, etc. ISPS language descriptions of current DEC machines (PDP-8, PDP-10, PDP-11, VAX-11) and several terminals have been made. We hope that these will be made widely available and so further stimulate the use of machine-description languages. The widespread application of good languages would help alleviate two current design problems: first, that of hand-crafted design tooling keeping up with the rate of introduction of new technologies and second, the problem of managing the ever-increasing complexity of computer structures. The PDP-8 description presented in Appendix 1 has been verified by machine diagnostics, in contrast to conventional descriptions.

PMS (processor-memory-switch) notation (given in Appendix 2) has not yet been widely used in formal methods to aid design. It has, however, been used extensively to describe computer structures. A prototype system which recognizes PMS and performs several performance analysis functions was constructed by Knudsen [1972]. Currently, ISPS is being extended to include the interconnection of computational blocks so that PMS and ISPS form a single system describing structure and behavior. In this book, we use PMS to describe functional blocks. However, all PMS components are enclosed to form a block diagram, unlike the original stick notation.

The book begins with three introductory chapters. The first presents the major themes to be illustrated by the book. We show that computer evolution has been based primarily on semiconductor and magnetic recording technologies. These technologies determine costs, and therefore price, performance, reliability, size, weight, power, and other dimensions which constitute the physical characteristics of the machines. The major theme of the book is that technology has enabled (or forced) three types of computers to be built:

1. Machines with constant performance and decreasing cost.
2. Machines with contant cost and increasing performance.
3. Radically new (large or small) structures, often research machines, which create new computer classes outside the evolution possibilities.

Chapter 2 traces the evolution of memory and logic technology. Engineering is firmly rooted in economics and inherently practical. Packaging (including component interconnections) is covered in Chapter 3 for a very pragmatic reason: of the total product cost of a small computer system, 50 percent is due to packaging and power, and these costs are rising. To further emphasize the practical aspects of engineering in Chapter 3, a section on high-volume manufacturing is included; the result of a designer's creativity must not only work but be buildable by production-line methods.

Following the introductory chapters are five parts:

I. In the Beginning

II. Beginning of the Minicomputer

III. The PDP-11 Family

IV. The Evolution of Computer Building Blocks

V. The PDP-10 Family

The introductions to each part describe what to look for in the evolution of each machine: its interaction with designers, technology, and use (marketplace). More importantly, we have tried to point out the classic (timeless – so far) design principles. Data that has become available since the original papers were published is also included.

Part I describes modules, the product on which DEC was initially founded. Chapter 5 shows how modules evolved and assimilated semiconductor technology in order to build computers.

The PDP-1 and other 18-bit machines and the PDP-8 began the minicomputer phenomenon as described in Part II. Although six computers form the 18-bit family, there is only one chapter devoted to them, primarily because there has been a dearth of written papers; this chapter was written for *Computer Engineering*. Chapter 7 shows the historical development of the 12-bit machines, and Chapter 8 explores the structure of the PDP-8 in detail.

Part III, nearly two-thirds of the book, is based on the PDP-11. The PDP-11 has been implemented with multiple technologies and multiple design goals at a given time, i.e., a set of machines to span a performance range. Because of cost and performance goals, a number of problems have had to be solved to permit subsetting (for the LSI-11) and supersetting (for the larger memory PDP-11/70 and for VAX-11).

Part IV is devoted to module set evolution. Chapter 18 describes the Register Transfer Modules (RTMs, also called PDP-16), a set of modules for building digital systems. Although these modules were unsuccessful in the marketplace, they were the forerunner of the bit-slice approach now widely used for implementing mid-range processors and special-purpose digital systems. Chapter 20 describes a set of modules based on the PDP-11 computer, called Computer Modules, which grew out of the original RTM research and were used to construct Cm*, a multi-microprocessor system.

Part V covers the PDP-10. Prior to the publication of the paper reproduced here as Chapter 21, very little had been published at the engineering level. The published literature had emphasized operating systems, languages, networks, and applications.

Computer Engineering is modeled after *Computer Structures* [Bell and Newell, 1971] and is intended to complement the subject matter therein. *Computer Structures* treats the design of instruction set architectures; *Computer Engineering* treats the design of machines which *implement* instruction sets. *Computer Structures* covers a broad range of ISP structures and PMS structures, from early stack machines and bit-serial machines, through list processors and higher level language machines, to supercomputers. By giving the seminal Burks, Goldstine, and von Neumann paper and the Whirlwind paper, it reaches far back into history. *Computer Engineering* on the other hand, takes a much narrower set of ISPs (four) and examines their implementations in detail. Instruction set design is mentioned only as it interacts with implementation. We focus on four computer families from both the designer and the historical viewpoint. In particular, we emphasize the lower level technological, economic, organizational, and environmental forces affecting the evolution of DEC computer families.

Although this book is principally for designers and students, it will also be of interest (as an historical record) to DEC employees who have been involved in the design, manufacture, distribution, and servicing of the computers.

Our recommendations for the use of this text in university curricula are based on teaching experience, requests from academic colleagues for material to teach design, and our participation in curriculum development. The book directly addresses the philosophy of the IEEE Computer Society Task Force on Computer Architecture [Rossman *et al.*, 1975]: "To appreciate how the architectures of computer systems develop, one must analyze complete systems." As such, *Computer Engineering* serves to complement Buchholz [1962], Bell and Newell [1971], and Blaauw and Brooks [in preparation] in a course on computer architecture, for example, IEEE course CO-3.*

For undergraduate courses on computer organization, such as IEEE CO-1* and the ACM courses I3 and A2†, we believe that the book could be used as a supplementary text. In a course on computer engineering, using the style given in

*"A Curriculum in Computer Science and Engineering-Committee Report," Model Curricula Subcommittee, IEEE Computer Society, EH0119-8, January 1977.
†"Curriculum 68," Commun. ACM, *11*, 3, pp. 151–197, March 1968.

the syllabus of CO-2* (I/O and Memory Systems) as a model, this could be a primary text, provided that material on other manufacturers' computers is made available to show different viewpoints.

ACKNOWLEDGEMENTS

We gratefully acknowledge our contributing authors, whose insights have greatly enhanced the scope of this book, and our colleagues at DEC, who assembled information, and provided subject matter expertise and advice.

We would like to thank R. Eckhouse, R. Glorioso, S. Fuller, J. Lipovski, and P. Jessel whose critiques of the preliminary drafts of the introductory chapters and book outline proved very helpful. We would also like to thank J. Cudmore, R. Doane, R. Elia-Shaoul, S. Fuller, L. Gale, L. Hughes, R. Peyton, and S. Teicher, who provided data for Chapter 2 and valuable critiques of earlier drafts. We also acknowledge the reviewers of the second draft of the manuscript, to whose criticisms we have especially tried to respond. We received instructive comments and evaluations from D. Aspinall, G. Blaauw, R. Clayton, D. Cox, J. Dennis, P. Enslow, D. Freeman, J. Grason, J. Gray, W. Heller, G. Korn, J. Lipcon, J. Marshall, E. McCluskey, C. Minter, M. Moshell, E. Organick, W. Schmitt, B. Schunck, I. Sutherland, J. Wakerly, and J. Wipfli. We would like to extend special thanks to H. Stone for his extensive and particularly useful review comments.

We are also indebted to many for their support in producing *Computer Engineering*. We are particularly indebted to Heidi Baldus of Digital Press who coordinated the production of *Computer Engineering* and whose encouragement kept us going through a number of difficult times. For their expertise and patience, we thank the Technical Documentation group, especially Denise Peters. We also thank Mary Jane Forbes and Louise Principe for their constant support in the course of this book's development and production. The manuscript creation and preparation on the DEC Word Processing System, followed by transmission to the DECset-8000 Typesetting System, permitted numerous drafts and rapid creation of the final typeset material.

C.G.B.
J.C.M.
J.E.M.

August 1978

ACKNOWLEDGEMENTS

C.G. Bell, J.C. Mudge, and J.E. McNamara: Seven Views of Computer Systems. C.G. Bell, Digital Equipment Corporation and Carnegie-Mellon University; J.C. Mudge and J.E. McNamara, Digital Equipment Corporation.

C.G. Bell, J.C. Mudge, and J.E. McNamara: Technology Progress in Logic and Memories. C.G. Bell, Digital Equipment Corporation and Carnegie-Mellon University; J.C. Mudge and J.E. McNamara, Digital Equipment Corporation.

C.G. Bell, J.C. Mudge, and J.E. McNamara: Packaging and Manufacturing. C.G. Bell, Digital Equipment Corporation and Carnegie-Mellon University; J.C. Mudge and J.E. McNamara, Digital Equipment Corporation.

K.H. Olsen: Transistor Circuitry in the Lincoln TX-2. Copyright © 1957 by AFIPS. Reprinted, with permission, from the *Proceedings of the Western Computer Conference,* 1957, pp. 167–171. This work was supported jointly by the U.S. Army, Navy, and Air Force under contract with M.I.T. K.H. Olsen, Lincoln Laboratory M.I.T. (currently with Digital Equipment Corporation).

R.L. Best, R.C. Doane, and J.E. McNamara: Digital Modules, the Basis for Computers. R.L. Best, R.C. Doane, and J.E. McNamara, Digital Equipment Corporation.

C.G. Bell, G. Butler, R. Gray, J.E. McNamara, D. Vonada, and R. Wilson: The PDP-1 and Other 18-Bit Computers. C.G. Bell, Digital Equipment Corporation and Carnegie-Mellon University; G. Butler *et al.,* Digital Equipment Corporation.

C.G. Bell and J.E. McNamara: The PDP-8 and Other 12-Bit Computers. C.G. Bell, Digital Equipment Corporation and Carnegie-Mellon University; J.E. McNamara, Digital Equipment Corporation.

C.G. Bell, A. Newell and D.P. Siewiorek: Structural Levels of the PDP-8. Revised and updated version of Chapter 5, "The DEC PDP-8," *Computer Structures: Reading and Examples,* C.G. Bell and A. Newell, McGraw-Hill Book Co., New York, 1971. C.G. Bell, Digital Equipment Corporation and Carnegie-Mellon University; A. Newell and D.P. Siewiorek, Carnegie-Mellon University.

C.G. Bell *et al.:* A New Architecture for Minicomputers – The DEC PDP-11. Copyright © 1970 by AFIPS. Reprinted, with permission, from the *Proceedings of the Spring Joint Computer Conference,* 1970, pp. 657–675. C.G. Bell, Digital Equipment Corporation and Carnegie-Mellon University. Those who have contributed subject matter expertise include R. Cady, H. McFarland, B.A. Delagi, J.F. O'Loughlin, R. Noonan, and W.A. Wulf.

W.D. Strecker: Cache Memories for PDP-11 Family Computers. Copyright © 1976 by the Institute of Electrical and Electronics Engineers, Inc. Reprinted, with permission, from the *Proceedings of the 3rd Annual Symposium on Computer Architecture,* 1976, pp. 155–158. W.D. Strecker, Digital Equipment Corporation.

J.V. Levy: Buses, The Skeleton of Computer Structures. J.V. Levy, Digital Equipment Corporation (currently with Tandem Computers, Inc.).

M.J. Sebern: A Minicomputer-Compatible Microcomputer System: The DEC LSI-11. Copyright © 1976 by the Institute of Electrical and Electronics Engineers, Inc. Reprinted, with permission, from the *Proceedings of the IEEE,* June 1976, Vol. 64, No. 6. Manuscript received by IEEE on October 10, 1975; revised December 12, 1975. M.J. Sebern, Digital Equipment Corpoation (currently with Sebern Engineering, Inc.).

J.C. Mudge: Design Decisions for the PDP-11/60 Mid-Range Minicomputer. Copyright © 1977 by the Computer Design Publishing Corp. Reprinted, with permission, from *Computer Design,* August 1977, pp. 87–95. Appears under title "Design Decisions Achieve Price/Performance Balance in Mid-Range Minicomputers" in *Computer Design* issue. J.C. Mudge, Digital Equipment Corporation.

E.A. Snow and D.P. Siewiorek: Impact of Implementation Design Tradeoffs on Performance: The PDP-11, A Case Study. Copyright © 1978 by Edward A. Snow and Daniel P. Siewiorek. This research was supported in part by the National Science Foundation under grant GJ-32758X and by an IBM fellowship. Engineering documentation was supplied by the Digital Equipment Corporation. E.A. Snow (currently with Intel Corp.) and D.P. Siewiorek, Carnegie-Mellon University.

R.F. Brender: Turning Cousins into Sisters: An Example of Software Smoothing of Hardware Differences. R.F. Brender, Digital Equipment Corporation.

C.G. Bell and J.C. Mudge: The Evolution of the PDP-11. Chapter includes material from "What Have We Learned From the PDP-11?" by C.G. Bell, in *Perspectives on Computer Science:* From the 10th University Symposium at the Computer Science Department, Carnegie-Mellon University, A. Jones (Ed.), Academic Press, Inc., 1978. C.G. Bell, Digital Equipment Corporation and Carnegie-Mellon University; J.C. Mudge, Digital Equipment Corporation.

W.D. Strecker: VAX-11/780: A Virtual Address Extension to the DEC PDP-11 Family. Copyright © 1978 by American Federation of Information Processing Societies, Inc. Reprinted, with permission, from the *Proceedings of the National Computer Conference,* June 1978, pp. 967–980. W.D. Strecker, Digital Equipment Corporation.

C.G. Bell, J. Eggert, J. Grason, and P. Williams: The Description and Use of Register Transfer Modules (RTMs). Copyright © 1972 by the Institute of Electrical and Electronics Engineers, Inc. Reprinted, with permission, from the *IEEE Transactions on Computers,* May 1972, Vol. C-21, No. 5, pp. 495–500. Manuscript received by IEEE February 19, 1971; revised May 11, 1971. C.G. Bell, Digital Equipment Corporation and Carnegie-Mellon University; J. Eggert, Digital Equipment Corporation (currently with Eggert Engineering); J. Grason, Carnegie-Mellon University (currently with Bell Laboratories); P. Williams, Digital Equipment Corporation (currently with Data Terminal Systems, Inc.).

T.M. McWilliams, S.H. Fuller, and W.H. Sherwood: Using LSI Processor Bit-Slices to Build a PDP-11 – A Case Study in Microcomputer Design. Copyright © 1977 by AFIPS. Reprinted, with permission, from the *Proceedings of the National Computer Conference,* 1977, pp. 243–253. This work was partially supported by the Advanced Research Projects Agency (ARPA) of the Department of Defense under contract F44620-73-C-0074, monitored by the Air Force Office of Scientific Research. T.M. McWilliams, Carnegie-Mellon University (currently with Stanford University and Lawrence Livermore Laboratory, University of California); S.H. Fuller, Carnegie-Mellon University (currently with Digital Equipment Corporation); W.H. Sherwood, Carnegie-Mellon University (currently with Digital Equipment Corporation).

S.H. Fuller, J.K. Ousterhout, L. Raskin, P. Rubinfeld, P.S. Sindhu, and R.J. Swan: Multi-Microprocessors: An Overview and Working Example. Copyright © 1978 by Institute of Electrical and Electronics Engineers, Inc. Reprinted, with permission, from the *Proceedings of the IEEE,* February 1978, Vol. 61, No. 2, pp. 216–228. Manuscript received by IEEE November 11, 1977. This work was supported in part by the Advanced Research Projects Agency of the Department of Defense under Contract F44620-73-C-0074, which is monitored by the Air Force Office of Scientific Research, and in part by the National Science Foundation under Grant GJ 32758X. The LSI-11s and related equipment were supplied by Digital Equipment Corporation. S.H. Fuller, Carnegie-Mellon University (currently with Digital Equipment Corporation); J.K. Ousterhout *et al.*, Carnegie-Mellon University.

C.G. Bell, A. Kotok, T.N. Hastings, and R. Hill: The Evolution of the DECsystem-10. Copyright © 1978 by the Association for Computing Machinery. Reprinted, with permission, from the *Communications of the ACM*, January 1978, Vol. 21, No. 1, pp. 44–63. C.G. Bell, Digital Equipment Corporation and Carnegie-Mellon University; A. Kotok, T.N. Hastings, and R. Hill, Digital Equipment Corporation.

M. Barbacci: Appendix 1 – An ISPS Primer for the Instruction Set Processor. M. Barbacci, Carnegie-Mellon University.

J.C. Mudge: Appendix 2 – The PMS Notation. J.C. Mudge, Digital Equipment Corporation.

C.G. Bell, J.C. Mudge, and J.E. McNamara: Appendix 3 – Performance. C.G. Bell, Digital Equipment Corporation and Carnegie-Mellon University; J.C. Mudge and J.E. McNamara, Digital Equipment Corporation.

TRADEMARKS

The following trademarks appear in *Computer Engineering: A DEC View of Hardware Systems Design.*

Company	**Trademark**	
Computer Automation Corporation	Naked Mini	
Digital Equipment Corporation	DEC	DECsystem-10
	DECSYSTEM-20	DECtape
	DECUS	DDT
	DIBOL	DIGITAL
	Fastbus	Flip Chip
	FOCAL	LSI-11
	Massbus	PDP
	RSTS	RSX
	TOPS-10	TOPS-20
	Unibus	
Fairchild Camera and Instrument Corporation	Macrologic	
Friden Company – A Division of Singer Company	Flexowriter	
Gardner-Denver Company	Wire-wrap	
Teletype Corporation	Teletype	
Xerox Corporation	Xerox 6500 color graphics printer	

CONTENTS

1

Seven Views of Computer Systems

C. GORDON BELL, J. CRAIG MUDGE,
and JOHN E. McNAMARA

A computer is determined by many factors, including architecture, structural properties, the technological environment, and the human aspects of the environment in which it was designed and built. In this book various authors reflect on these factors for a wide range of DEC computers - their goals, their architectures, their various implementations and realizations, and occasionally on the people who designed them.

Computer engineering is the complete set of activities, including the use of taxonomies, theories, models, and heuristics, associated with the design and construction of computers. It is like other engineering, and the definition that Richard Hamming (then at Bell Laboratories) gave is especially appropriate: engineers first turn to science for answers and help, then to mathematics for models and intuition, and finally to the seat of their pants.

In the few decades since computers were first conceived and built, computer engineering has come from a set of design activities that were mostly seat-of-the-pants based to a point where some parts are quite well understood and based on good models and rules of thumb, such as technology models, and other parts are completely understood and employ useful theories such as circuit minimization.

In this chapter, seven views are presented that the authors have found useful in thinking about computers and the process that molds their form and function. They are intentionally independent; each is a different way of looking at a computer. A computer scientist or mathematician sees a computer as levels-of-interpreters. An engineer sees the computer on a structural basis, with particular emphasis on the logic design of the structure. The view most often taken by a buyer is a marketplace view. While these people each favor a particular view of computers, each typically understands certain aspects of the other views. The goals of Chapter 1 are to increase this understanding of other views and to increase the number of representations used to describe the object of study and, hence, improve on its exposition. Thus, "The Seven Views of Computer Systems" forms a useful background for the subsequent chapters on past, present, and future computers.

VIEW 1: STRUCTURAL LEVELS OF A COMPUTER SYSTEM

In *Computer Stuctures* [Bell and Newell, 1971], a set of conceptual levels for describing, understanding, analyzing, designing, and using computer systems was postulated. The model has survived major changes in technology, such as the fabrication of a complete computer on a single silicon chip, and changes in architecture, such as the addition of vector and array data-types.

As shown in Figure 1, there are at least five levels of system description that can be used to describe a computer. Each level is characterized by a distinct language for representing the components associated with that level, their modes of combination, and their laws of behavior. Within each level there exists a whole hierarchy of systems and subsystems, but as long as these are all described in the same language, they do not constitute separate levels. With this general view, one can work up through the levels of computer systems, starting at the bottom.

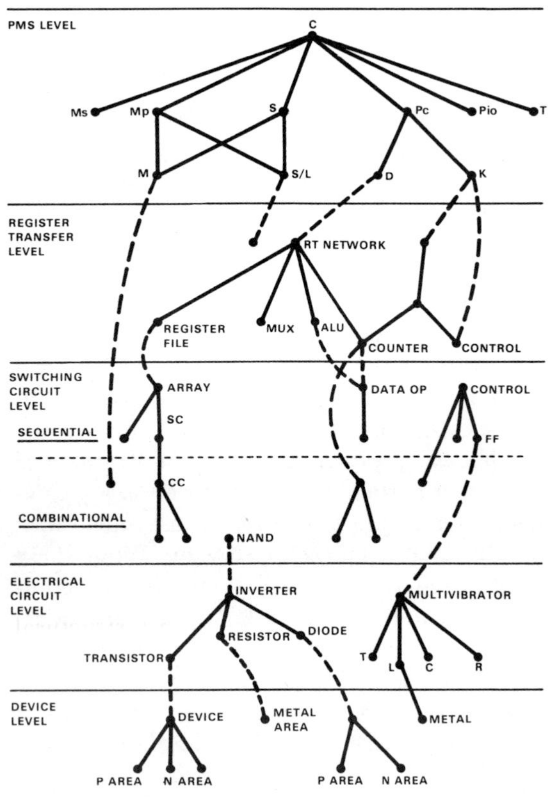

Figure 1. Hierarchy of computer levels, adapted from Bell and Newell [1971].

The lowest level in Figure 1 is the device level. Here the components are p-type and n-type semiconductor materials, dielectric materials, and metal formed in various ways. The behavior of the components is described in the languages of semiconductor physics and materials science.

The next level is the circuit level. Here the components are resistors, inductors, capacitors, voltage sources, and nonlinear devices. The behavior of the system is measured in terms of voltage, current, and magnetic flux. These are continuously varying quantities associated with various components; hence, there is continuous behavior through time, and equations (including differential equations) can be written to describe the behavior of the variables. The components have a discrete number of terminals whereby they can be connected to other components.

Above the circuit level is the switching circuit or logic level. While the circuit level in digital technology is very similar to the rest of electrical engineering, the logic level is the point at which digital technology diverges from electrical engineering. The behavior of a system is now described by discrete variables which take on only two values, called 0 and 1 (or + and −, true and false, high and low). The components perform logic functions called AND, OR, NAND, NOR, and NOT. Systems are constructed in the same way as at the circuit level, by connecting the terminals of components, which thereby identify their behavioral values.

After a system has been so constructed, the laws of Boolean algebra can be used to compute the behavior of the system from the behavior and properties of its components.

In addition to combinational logic circuits, whose outputs are directly related to the inputs at any instant of time, there are sequential logic circuits which have the ability to hold values over time and thus store information. The problem that the combinational level analysis solves is the production of a set of outputs at time t as a function of a number of inputs at the same time t. The representation of a sequential switching circuit is basically the same as that of a combinational switching circuit, although one needs to add memory components. The equations that specify sequential logic circuit structure must be difference equations involving time, rather than the simple Boolean algebra equations which describe purely combinational logic circuits.

The level above the switching circuit level is called the register transfer (RT) level. The components of the register transfer level are registers and the functional transfers between those registers. The functional transfers occur as the system undergoes discrete operations, whereby the values of various registers are combined according to some rule and are then stored (transferred) into another register. The rule, or law, of combination may be almost anything, from the simple unmodified transfer ($A \leftarrow B$) to logical combination ($A \leftarrow B \wedge$ (AND) C) or arithmetic combination ($A \leftarrow B +$ (PLUS) C). Thus, a specification of the behavior, equivalent to the Boolean equations of sequential circuits or to the differential equations of the circuit level, is a set of expressions (often called productions) that give the conditions under which such transfers will be made.

The fifth and last level in Figure 1 is called the processor-memory-switch (PMS) level. This level, which gives only the most aggregate behavior of a computer system, consists of central processors, core memories, tapes, disks, input/output processors, communications lines, printers, tape controllers, buses, teleprinters, scopes, etc. The computer system is viewed as processing a medium, information, which can be measured in bits (or digits, characters, words, etc.). Thus, the components have capacities and flow rates as their operating characteristics.

The program level from the original set of levels shown in Bell and Newell has been dropped because it is a functional rather than a structural level.

Many notations are used at each of the five structural levels. Two of the less common ones are the processor-memory-switch (PMS) and instruction set processor (ISP) notations. A complete description of these notations is given in Bell and Newell [1971: Chapter 2]. Those aspects of PMS that are used in this book are described in Appendix 2. The ISP notation has evolved to the ISPS language, which is described in Appendix 1.

VIEW 2: LEVY'S LEVELS-OF-INTERPRETERS

In contrast to the Structural View, this view is functional. According to this view, presented by John Levy [1974], a computer system consists of layers of interpreters, much like the layers of an onion.

An interpreter is a processing system that is driven by instructions and operates upon state information. The basic interpretive loop, shown in Figure 2, is most familiar at the machine language level but also exists at several other levels.

To formalize the notion of Levels-of-Interpretation, one can represent a processing system by the diagram in Figure 3.

The state information operated on by an interpreter is either internal or external. This can best be understood by considering the "onion skin" levels of the five processing systems that form a typical airline reservation system. These levels are listed in Table 1.

The Level 0 system is the logic that sequences the Level 1 micromachine. The Level 1 system is a microprogrammed processor implemented in real hardware. It is the machine seen by the logic designer. The Level 2 system is the central processing unit (CPU). It is the machine seen by the machine language programmer. The Level 3 system shown here is a FORTRAN language processing system. The Level 4 system is an airline reservation system. Four of these five systems form the hierarchy shown in Figure 4, where each system is an interpreter that sequences through multiple steps in order to perform a single operation for the next level interpreter. The highest level system, the airline reservation system, is an interpreter operating on messages received from outside of the system. It tests and modifies states and generates messages to send back outside the system, thus performing a single operation for the outermost interpreter.

In practice, few systems are levels of pure interpreters, although layers are present. Deviations from the model have occurred for both hardware and software reasons. In the hardware deviation case, the micromachine shown in Level 1 is often not present, but rather the Level 2 central processing unit is implemented directly using Level 0 sequential controllers. This practice of skipping Level 1 was initially due to the lack of adequate read-only memories but is now generally limited to the case of very high speed machines such as the Cray 1 and the Amdahl V6 which cannot tolerate the fetch and execute cycle times associated with a control store.

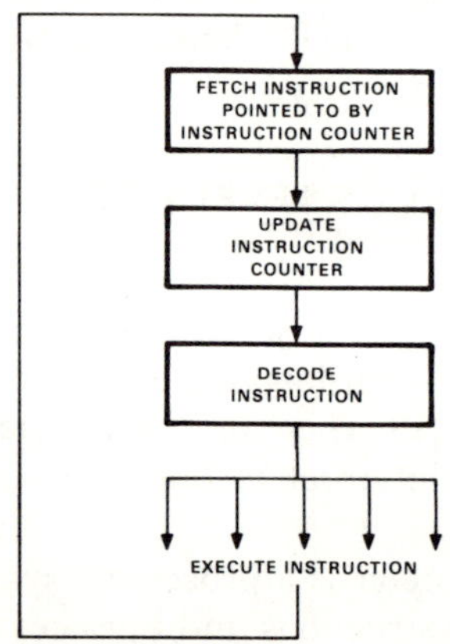

Figure 2. The basic interpretive loop [Levy, 1974].

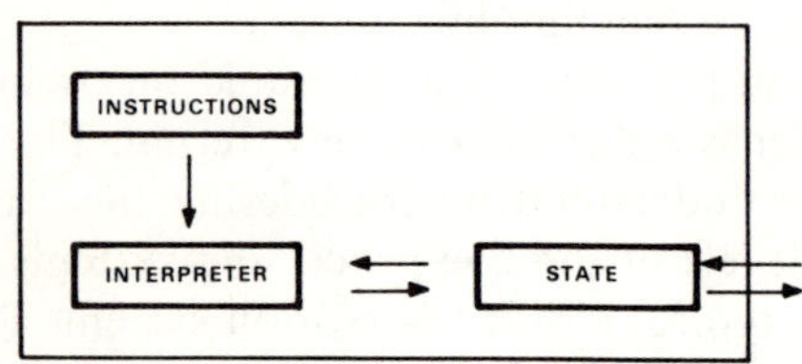

Figure 3. A processing system [Levy, 1974].

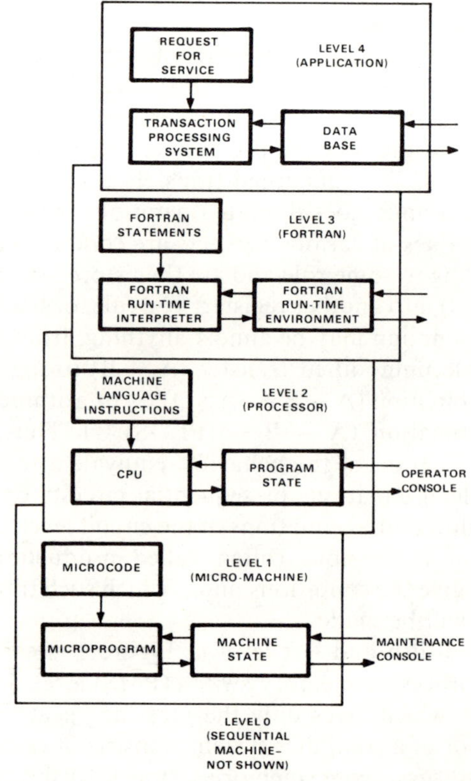

Figure 4. A hierarchy of interpreters [Levy, 1974].

Table 1. Five Levels-of-Interpreters for an Airline Reservation System [Levy, 1974]

Level		
Level 4	Instruction:	Seat allocation request message
	Interpreter:	Airline reservation system
	Internal state:	Number of requests pending at this moment Location of passenger list on a disk file Number of lines connected to system
	External state:	Number of reserved seats on a given flight Airline name for a given flight
Level 3	Instructions:	FORTRAN statement codes
	Interpreter:	FORTRAN execution system
	Internal state:	Memory management parameters User name Main storage size Location of disk files Interrupt enable bits Expression evaluation stack Dimensions of arrays
	External state:	Subroutine names Values of data in arrays Statement number Program size Value of an expression DO-loop variable value Printed characters on line printer
Level 2	Instructions:	Machine language instructions
	Interpreter:	Processor
	Internal state:	Program registers Condition codes Program counter
	External state:	Data in main memory Disk controller registers
Level 1	Instructions:	Microcode
	Interpreter:	Micromachine
	Internal state:	Instruction register Flip-flops holding error status Stack of microprogram subroutine links
	External state:	Program registers Condition codes Program counter
Level 0	Instructions:	Hardwired combinational network
	Interpreter:	Sequential machine controlling the micromachine
	Internal state:	Clock, counters, etc., controlling micromachine timing
	External state:	Micromachine, console

There are two primary software driven departures from the pure interpreter model: (1) high level languages are usually executed by a compiler rather than by an interpreter, and (2) some layers are bypassed when more ideal primitives exist at deeper levels. Figure 5 illustrates this bypassing process. A pure interpreter implementation of FORTRAN would use an object time system (OTS) for all FORTRAN *C* operations designated in the figure. The object time system would require an operating system (OPSYS) for the interpretation of some of its operations, and the operating system in turn

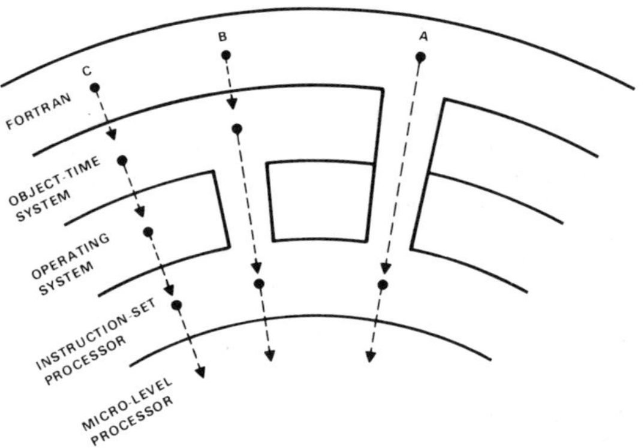

Figure 5. Levels-of-interpreters with "pipes" that bypass levels. FORTRAN operation *C* is interpreted by an OTS function which in turn is interpreted by the operating system which is interpreted by the ISP. FORTRAN operation *A* has a pipe directly to the ISP interpreter.

would be interpreted by the instruction set interpreter (ISP interpreter). However, the *A* operations in the figure would be directly interpreted by the instruction set interpreter.

In the final analysis, the number of levels is just another tradeoff. Performance considerations lead to the deletion of levels; complexity leads to the addition of levels. Having presented the pure interpreter model, one can now return to the Onion-Skin-Layered Model to better understand how the different layers relate.

The macromachine hardware can be thought of as a base level interpreter. It is most often extended upward with an operating system. There may be several operating system levels so that the machine can be built up in an orderly fashion. A kernel machine might manage and diagnose the hardware components (disks, terminals) and provide synchronizing operations so that the multiple processes controlling the physical hardware can operate concurrently. Next, more complex operations such as the file system and basic utilities are added, followed by policy elements such as facilities resource management and accounting. As viewed through the operating system, one sees a much different machine than that provided by the basic instruction set architecture. In fact, the resultant machine is hardly recognizable as the architecture most usually given by a symbolic assembler. It includes the basic machine but has more capable I/O and often the ability to be shared by many programs (or tasks).

Operating systems designers believe all these facilities are necessary in order to implement the next higher level interpreter – the standard language. The language level may include interpreters or compilers to translate back to the machine architecture for ALGOL, BASIC, COBOL, FORTRAN, or any of the other standard languages and their dialects.

VIEW 3: PACKAGING LEVELS-OF-INTEGRATION

This is a structural view that packages the various components (hardware and software) into levels. The levels for DEC computers in 1978 were as follows:

9 Applications
8 Applications components
7 Special languages
6 Standard languages

5 Operating systems
4 Cabinets (to hold complete hardware systems)
3 Boxes
2 Modules (printed circuit boards)
1 Integrated circuits

This view is the most important in the book, because it shows how computer systems are actually structured and, hence, how their costs are structured. As a structural view of the object being sold, however, it is completely a function of the technology, the organization building the system, and the marketplace, all of which are changing so rapidly that the view could better be titled "Dynamic Levels-of-Integration." There are three major changes taking place:

1. Changes in the hardware levels, where the shrinking in physical size of functions has three effects:
   a. Lower levels subsume higher levels.
   b. The semiconductor component supplier is forced to assume higher and higher level design responsibilities.
   c. Levels disappear.
2. Changes in the software levels, again with three effects:
   a. Each level grows in size as more functionality is added over time.
   b. More levels are added as minicomputers are applied to a broader range of applications.
   c. Functions migrate downward from level to level.
3. Changes in the hardware/software interface, where software functions migrate into hardware for higher performance.

For the first of these areas of change, hardware levels, it is interesting to note that interconnection and packaging now constrain and limit design more than any other factor, excluding the basic lowest level component (semiconductor) technology.

The constraint caused by the interconnection and packaging takes place because most manufacturing costs are associated with the physical structure. As interconnection levels must be introduced to build complex structures, many usually undesirable side effects occur. Electrical interconnection requires cables which require space and interfere with cooling airflow. Long interconnections increase signal transmission delays, and these reduce performance. Signal transmission not only makes the computer susceptible to electromechanical interference but also may radiate electromagnetic waves that need to be controlled.

Figure 6 shows the costs of various levels-of-integration versus time for small computers. The cost depends partly on implementation and architecture word length. As the word length is made shorter, there are some savings, particularly for very small computers, because some levels-of-integration cease to exist. For example, most hand-held calculators are implemented using 4-bit, stored program computers with fixed programs that occupy a single integrated circuit. There are associated modules, backplanes, boxes, and cabinets – but all are contained in a single package that fits in the hand.

Semiconductors, the lowest level of technology, have had the greatest price decline (Figure 6). Modules have a lesser price decline because they are a mix of integrated circuits, printed circuit boards, component insertion labor, and testing labor. The price decline for the integrated circuit portion of the module cost is moderated by the labor-intensive nature of module fabrication, thus producing a price decline for modules that is markedly less than that for integrated circuits. At the box level-of-integration, power supplies and metal or plastic boxes are also labor-intensive and further moderate the price decline provided by the integrated circuits. Finally, as boxes are integrated (by people) and applied at a system

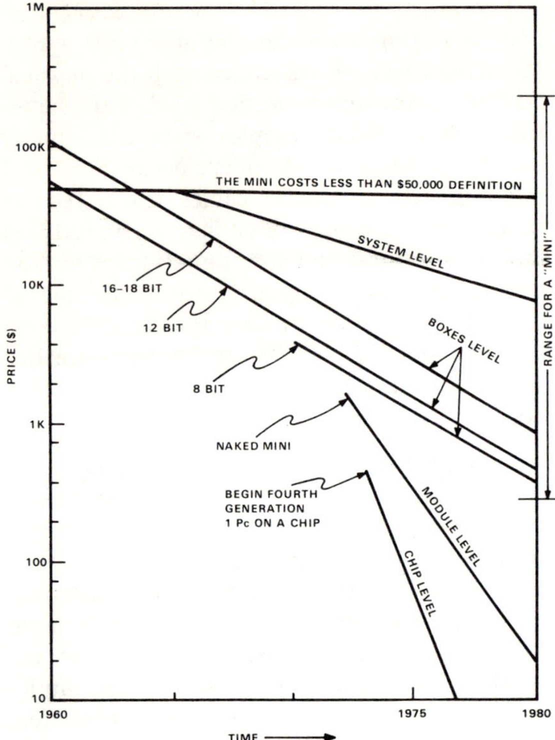

Figure 6. Machine price for various levels-of-integration versus time.

level (by people), the price decline almost disappears.

Many of the cost improvements brought about by new technology are derivative. They are by-products of using less power and less space, thus avoiding the labor-intensive levels of packaging integration.

An astute marketing-oriented person might ask, "How, with all the technology, can we do something unique so that we can maximize the benefit from the technology without having to pay so much for labor-intensive items such as packaging?" One answer: "Reduce prices by not providing a power supply and mounting hardware. Let the user provide all added-on parts and mount the computer as needed. In this way, the price, though not necessarily the total cost to the user, is reduced. We'll sell at the board level." Computer Automation followed this philosophy when it introduced the Naked Mini so that users could supply more added value (packaging and power technology).

A similar effect can be seen in the PDP-11 series since the PDP-11/20's introduction in 1970. At that time, the 4,096-word PDP-11/20 (mounted in a box) sold for $9,300. In 1976, the boxed version of an LSI-11 cost $1,995, reflecting a factor of 4.7 improvement over the PDP-11/20. The 4,096-word core memory module used in the PDP-11/20 sold for $3,500, while a 16,384-word metal-oxide semiconductor (MOS) memory module for an LSI-11 sold for $1,800, reflecting a factor of 7.8 improvement.

The changing levels-of-integration have also changed the domain of the semiconductor suppliers. In the early 1970s, Intel, North American Rockwell, and other semiconductor companies began to use the higher semiconductor densities to reduce the number of levels-of-integration by packaging a complete processor-on-a-chip. These organizations had assimilated logic design, but were frustrated because their customers could really not identify higher functionality units (beyond memory) requiring on the order of 1,000 gates on a chip. Also, the speed of these high density units was quite low.

They discovered that the best finite state machine to make was just a simple computer, because it provided the finite state machine plus the useful functions that were not covered by switching circuit theory. It was "simply a small matter of programming" to do something useful. Whereas programs for these simple computers cost $1 to $100 per instruction to write, the prices for processors-on-a-chip have followed a very steep decline of up to 50 percent price reduction per year.

Robert Noyce of Intel developed Figure 7 in October 1975. It illustrates what has been happening in the semiconductor industry and has been modified slightly to show the technology

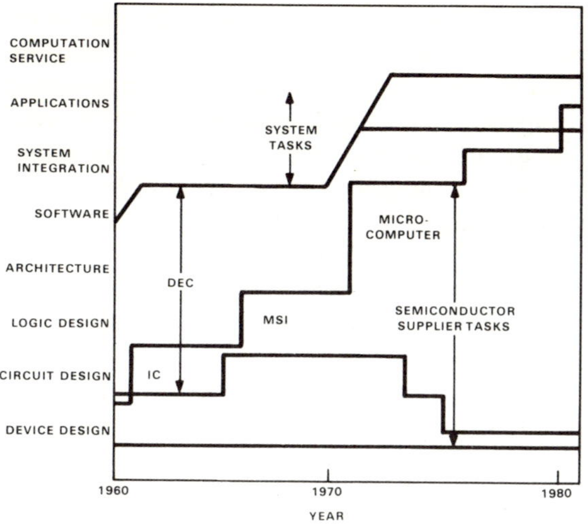

Figure 7. Semiconductor (Noyce) manufacturer's levels-of-integration versus time.

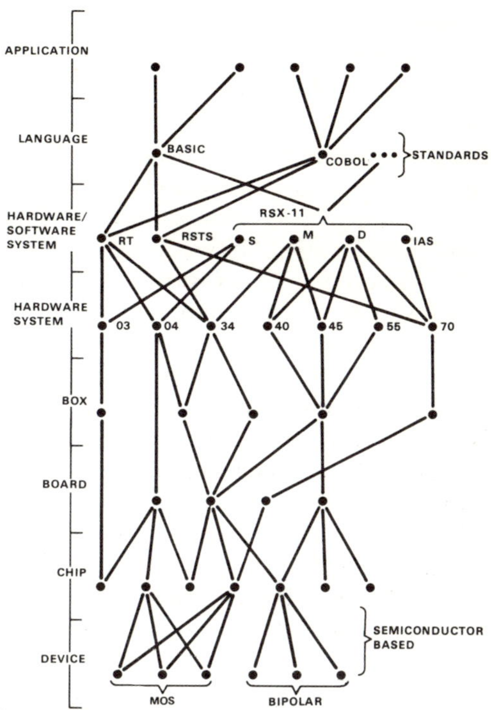

Figure 8. A computer system is a network, not just a tree-structured hierarchy of eight distinct levels.

that DEC has assimilated with time. It indicates the breadth that semiconductor manufacturers now have in technology, starting from the semiconductor device level, through Noyce's view of the various levels-of-integration, and continuing into end-user applications.

The Levels-of-Integration View can be summarized as components of one level being combined into a system at the next highest level in a hierarchy. A level denotes a single conceptual design discipline or set of interacting disciplines which determine the function, structure, performance, and cost of the constituent level. "Level" is a deceptive word, because as Figure 8 shows, the structure is actually a lattice, or network, style of hierarchy rather than the classical tree style of hierarchy. In Figure 8 various standard languages can be used on any of several different hardware/software systems, which in turn can be implemented on several different processors. Each processor is available in several different boxes.

VIEW 4: A MARKETPLACE VIEW OF COMPUTER CLASSES

Because it is the complete marketplace process that produces the computer, this view is the most complex. In terms of marketability, a computer can be characterized as a function of price, performance, and time of introduction in what might appear to be a commodity-like environment.

Because various computers operate at different performance rates and at various costs, computation can be purchased in multiple ways, and price/performance ratios will thus affect marketability. For example, computation can be supplied by a shared large, central batch computer; each organizational entity can own and operate a shared minicomputer; an individual can operate a single desk-top system; or each individual can operate a programmable calculator.

The price/performance ratio is not the sole factor determining marketability, however. Program compatibility with previous machines is important. Compatibility considerations are based on the economic necessity of using a common software base. The computer user's investment in software dwarfs that of the computer manufacturer, if the machine is successful. For example, if there is only one man-year of software investment associated with each of the 50,000 PDP-11s, and each man-year costs about $40,000 and produces something on the order of 5,000 instructions, there is then a cumulative investment of $2 billion and 250 million lines of program for the PDP-11. This investment is roughly the same scale as the original hardware cost.

Thus, while rapidly evolving technology permits new designs to be more cost-effective – even radical – in a price/performance sense, there must be backward (in time) compatibility in order to build on and preserve the user's program base. The user must be able to operate programs unchanged to take advantage of the improvements brought about by technology changes.

In a similar way, compatibility over a range of machines at a given time allows a user to select a machine that matches his problem set while having the comfort that the problems can change and there will be a sufficiently large or small machine available to solve the new problems.

For these reasons, nearly all modern computer designs are part of a compatible computer family which extends over price and time. Technology provides basic improvements with each new generation at approximately six-year intervals, and most new designs usually provide increased performance at constant price.

The influence of technology on the computers that are built and taken to the marketplace is so strong that the four generations of computers have been named after the technology of their components: vacuum-tubes, transistors, integrated circuits (multiple transistors packaged together), and large-scale integrated (LSI) circuits.

Each electronic technology has its own set of characteristics, including cost, speed, heat dissipation, packing density, and reliability, all of which the designer must balance. These factors combine to limit the applicability of any one technology; typically, one technology is used until either a limit is reached or another technology supersedes it.

Design Alternatives

When an improved basic technology becomes available to a computer designer, there are four paths the designs can take to incorporate the technology:

1. Use the newer technology to build a cheaper system with the same performance.
2. Hold the price constant and use the technological improvement to get an increase in performance.
3. Push the design to the limits of the new technology, thereby increasing both performance and price.
4. Find a drastically new structure using the computer as a basic archetype (e.g., calculators) such that the design can be considered off the evolutionary path.

Figure 9 shows the trajectory of the first three design alternatives. In general, the design alternatives occur in an evolutionary fashion as in Figure 10 with a first (base) design, and subsequent designs evolving from the base.

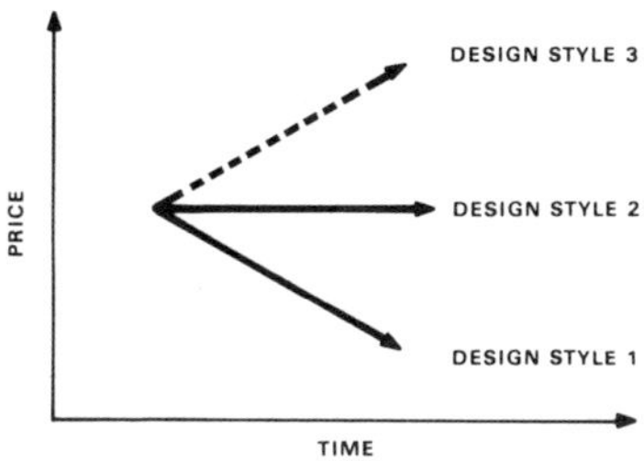

Figure 9. Three design styles on the evolutionary path.

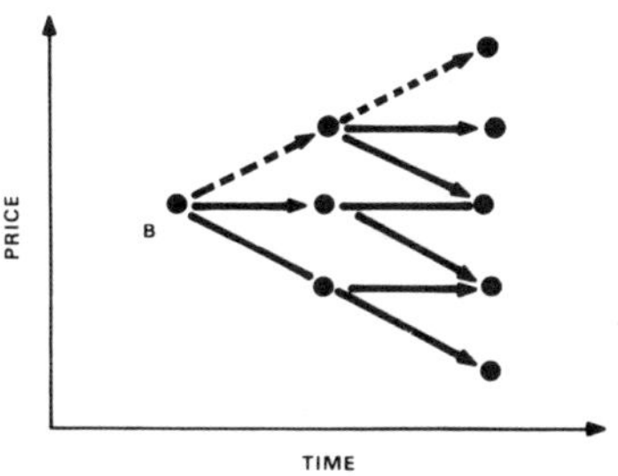

Figure 10. Evolution from the base design *B*.

In the first design style, the performance is held constant, and the improved technology is used to build lower price machines which attract new applications. This design style has as its most important consequence the concept of the *minimal computer*. The minimal computer has traditionally been the vehicle for entering new applications, since it is the smallest computer that can be constructed with a given technology. Each year, as the price of the minimal computer declines, new applications become economically feasible.

The second, constant cost alternative uses the improved technology to get better performance at a constant price and will usually yield the best increase in total system cost and effectiveness, for reasons which will be discussed shortly.

The third alternative is to use the new technology to build the most powerful machine possible. New designs using this alternative often solve previously unsolved problems and, in doing so, advance the state-of-the-art. This design alternative must be used cautiously, however, because going too far in price or performance (i.e., building beyond the technology) is dangerous and can lead to a zero performance, high-cost product. There are usually two motivations for operating at this leading edge: preliminary research motivated by the knowledge that the technology will catch up; and national defense, where an essentially infinite amount of money is available because the benefit – avoiding annihilation – is infinite.

Table 2 shows the effect of pursuing the two design strategies of: (1) constant performance at decreased price, and (2) constant price at increased performance. The first column gives the base case at a given time t. Because this is the base case, the price, performance, and price/performance ratio of the computer are all 1. As the computer is applied to a particular environment, operational overhead is added at a cost of 2 to 4 times the original cost of the computer; the total cost to operate the computer becomes 3 to 5 times higher, and the performance/total cost ratio is reduced to between 0.33 and 0.2 (depending on the total cost).

Now assume the same operating environment, with the same fixed (overhead) costs to operate, at a new time $t + 1$, when technology has improved by a factor of 2. Two alternative designs are carried out; one is at constant price/higher performance, and the other is at constant performance/lower price (columns 2 and 3). The application is constant in three cases (columns 1–3), and a new application is discovered for the fourth case (column 4). Both the constant-cost and constant-performance designs give the same basic performance/cost improvement – when only the cost of the computer is considered. However, when one

Table 2. Using New Technology for Constant Price and Constant Performance Designs

Introduction (generation)	Time t	t + 1	t + 1	t + 1
Design style	Base case	Constant price/ increased performance	Constant performance/ decreased price	Constant performance/ decreased price
Application	Base	Base	Base	New base
Computer price	1	1	0.5	0.5
Operating costs (range)	2–4	2–4	2–4	1–2
Total cost	3–5	3–5	2.5–4.5	1.5–2.5
Performance (and improvement)	1	2	1	1
Improvement (in total cost)	1	1	0.83–0.9	0.5
Performance/price (computer only and improvement)	1	2	2	2
Performance/ total cost	0.33–0.2	0.66–0.4	0.4–0.22	0.66–0.4
Improvement (in performance/total cost)	1	2	1.21–1.1	2

considers the high fixed overhead costs associated with the application (columns 1–3), there is a relatively small improvement in performance/cost, although there has been a cost savings of 17 to 10 percent. The greatest gains come in applying the computer with greater performance and getting the attendant factor of 2 gain in performance and in price/performance ratio.

To summarize, the constant price/increased performance design style gives a better gain because operating costs remain the same. Its gain can only be equalled by the constant-performance design style when operating costs are halved upon its application. This only occurs when a new application is tackled, such as that shown in column 4.

Computer Classes

Applying the three design styles shown in Figure 9 over several generations produces the plot given in Figure 11. These figures lead to one of the most interesting results of the Marketplace View, which is that computer classes can be distinguished by price and named as follows: *submicro* (to come in the next generation – say by 1980), *micro*, *mini*, *midi*, *maxi*, and *super*. The classes midi and maxi are sometimes referred to by the single, nondescriptive name, *mainframe*.

When one distinguishes computer classes by price, a new range of price can be made possible by new technology and create a new class. The

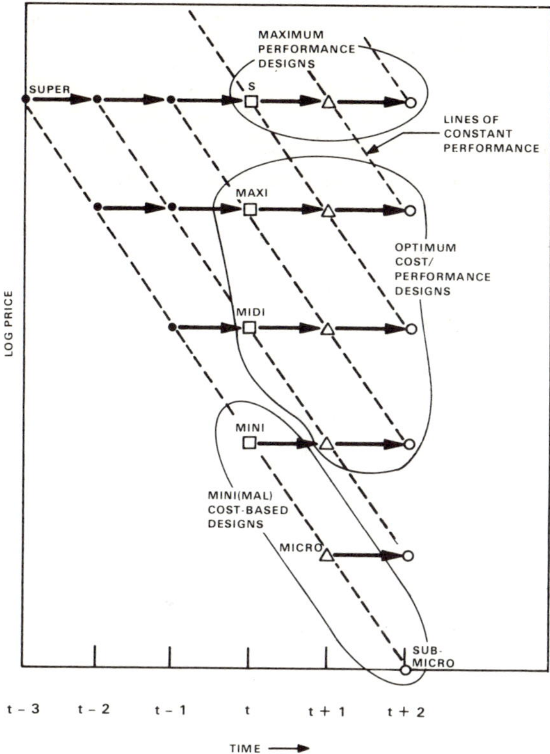

Figure 11. Price versus time for each machine class.

new class appears at the low end of the price scale where the minimal computer is introduced at a significantly lower price level than existing computers.

The measure used to define a new class is price, whereas the measure defining an established class is performance. This is because once a new class has become established in the marketplace, the users become familiar with what computers of that class can do for their applications and tend to characterize that class on a performance basis. The characterization of existing classes on a performance basis is important to this discussion because at each new technology time, performance increases by one category, and midi performance becomes available on a mini, for example.

The effect of technology upon computer classes can be summarized in the following thesis:

> Continual application of technology via the two major design styles results in: (1) price declines creating new classes of computers, (2) new classes becoming established classes, and (3) established classes being encroached upon.

Some question may arise as to how much of a price reduction is necessary to create a new class. The continuity implied by the thesis is deceptive in that it suggests that new classes come about by the continual application of the constant performance/decreasing cost style of design. Viewing the industry as a whole, this is true. However, a new class is usually not created by the same organization that is designing computers in existing classes. A new company, or new organization within a company, is usually required to provide the requisite fresh viewpoint needed to create a new class. It is the fresh viewpoint and not some arbitrary amount of price reduction that creates a new class.

For both the minicomputer and microcomputer, a fresh organization broke out. A fresh viewpoint was needed because existing organizations, like most human organizations, act to preserve the status quo, and adopt the increased performance/constant price design alternative for the existing customer base, as indicated by the analysis given in the discussion of Table 2. A new organization with a fresh viewpoint goes after new applications and new customers with a new minimal computer that establishes a new class.

As a by-product of the use of new technology, conflicts occur within the established computer classes. An established computer class, which is defined on the basis of performance, is encroached upon by constant cost/higher performance successors from the class below it. Moreover, suppliers within a class are, by their dominant constant price/higher performance evolution, operating to move up out of their class.

While movement by computer designs and computer suppliers between and among the various classes may be encouraged by price and performance trends, the speed with which that movement occurs is moderated by the software compatibility considerations discussed earlier. The computer class thesis is not meant to imply that each class implements the same instruction set processor and processor-memory-switch configurations with the only difference being speed. Rather, much specialization occurs in each class, and many of the attributes of the higher performance machines appear in substantially less degree in the lower performance classes. For example, there are more data-types in the larger machines, their address spaces (both physical and virtual) are larger, and the software support is generally broader. Resources devoted to increasing reliability and availability are more common in the higher priced machines. The PDP-11 Family, from the LSI-11 up to the VAX-11/780, exemplifies these functionality differences.

Definition of the Minicomputer

The concept of computer classes that can be distinguished by price and named submicro, micro, mini, midi, maxi, and super may be of assistance in finding a definition for the minicomputer, a definition which has thus far been rather elusive. While the classes suggest that minicomputers are those computers whose prices fall between microcomputers and midicomputers, and thus somewhere near the middle of the range of computers available, earlier definitions [Bell and Newell, 1971a] use the term mini to denote minimal.

The Marketplace View defines new computer classes according to price and established computer classes according to performance. This would suggest that a definition of the minicomputer should include some historical data on price and some comments on performance, or at least some indication of performance by a discussion of applications and configurations. In 1977 Gordon Bell provided such a hybrid definition for the Director of Computer Resources, U. S. Air Force. The definition was as follows:

> MINICOMPUTER: A computer originating in the early 1960s and predicated on being the lowest (minimum) priced computer built with current technology. From this origin, at prices ranging from 50 to 100 thousand dollars, the computer has evolved both at a price reduction rate of 20 percent per year and has also evolved to have increased functionality and a slightly higher price with increasing functionality and performance.
>
> Minicomputers are integrated into systems requiring direct human and process interaction on a *dedicated* basis (versus being configured with a structure to solve a wide set of problems on a highly general basis).
>
> Minicomputers are produced and distributed in a variety of ways and levels-of-integration from: printed circuit boards containing the electronics; to boxes which hold the processor, primary memory, and interfaces to other equipment; to complete systems with peripherals oriented to solving a particular application(s) problem. The price range(s) for the above levels-of-integration, in 1978, are roughly: 500 to 2,000; 2,000 to 50,000; and 5,000 to 250,000.

This discussion of the Marketplace View has been a qualitative explanation of the effect of technology on the computer industry. It is an engineering view, rather than one that would be given by technology historians or economists. The 20 years described in this book and the individual cost and performance measures surely invite analysis by professionals. The studies reported in Phister [1976] and Sharpe [1969] are a good departure point.

VIEW 5: AN APPLICATIONS/ FUNCTIONAL VIEW OF COMPUTER CLASSES

Because of the general purpose nature of computers, all of the functional specialization occurs at the time of programming rather than at the time of design. As a result, there is remarkably little shaping of computer structure to fit the function to be performed.

The shaping that does take place uses four primary techniques.

1. **PMS level configuration**. A configuration is chosen to match the function to be performed. The user (designer) chooses the amount of primary memory, the number and types of secondary memory, the types of switches, and the number and types of transducers to suit his particular application.
2. **Physical packaging**. Special environmental packaging is used to specialize a computer system for certain environments, such as factory floor, submarine, or aerospace applications.
3. **Data-type emphasis**. Computers are designed with data-types (and operations to match) that are appropriate to their tasks. Some emphasize floating-point arithmetic, others string handling. Special-purpose processors, such as Fast Fourier Transform processors, belong in this category also.
4. **Operating system**. The generality of the computer is used to program operating systems that emphasize batch, time sharing, real-time, or transacting processing needs.

Current Dimensions of Use

In the early days of computers, there were just two classifications of computer use: *scientific* and *commercial*. By the early 1970s, computer use had diversified to seven different functional segmentations: *scientific*, *business*, *control*, *communication*, *file control*, *terminal*, and *timesharing*. Since that time, very little has changed in terms of functional characterization, but two points are worthy of mention. First, file control computers still have not materialized as mainstream separate functional entities, despite isolated cases such as the IBM 3850 Mass Storage System; second, terminal computers have evolved to a much higher degree than expected.

The high degree of evolution in terminals has been due to the use of microprocessors as control elements, thus providing every terminal with a stored program computer. Given this generality, it has been simple to provide the terminal user with facilities to write programs. In turn, this phenomenon has affected the evolution of timesharing (when using the term to denote close man-machine interaction as opposed to shared use of an expensive resource).

Functional segmentation into categories with labels such as *business*, *control*, *communication*, and *file control* reflects a naming convention rooted in the old two-category scientific/commercial tradition. An alternative classification, more useful today, is the segmentation scheme shown in Table 3. It is based on the intellectual disciplines and environment (e.g., home based) that use and develop the computer systems. It shows the evolving structures in each of the disciplines, permitting one to see that nearly all the environments evolve to provide some form of direct, interactive use in a multiprogrammed environment. The structures that interconnect to mechanical processes are predominately for manufacturing control. Other environments, such as transportation, are also basically real-time control. Another feature of discipline-based functional segmentation is that each of the disciplines operates on different symbols. For example, commercial (or financial) environments hold records of identifier names for entities (e.g., part number) and numbers which are values for the entity (e.g., cost, number in inventory).

Table 3. Discipline/Environment-Based Functional Segmentation Scheme

Commercial environment
- Financial control for industry, retail/wholesale, and distribution
- Billing, inventory, payroll, accounts receivable/ payable
- Records storage and processing
- Traditional batch data entry
- Transaction processing against data base
- Business analysis (includes calculators)*

Scientific, engineering, and design
- Numbers, algorithms, symbols, text, graphs, storage, and processing
- Traditional batch computation*
- Data acquisition
- Interactive problem solving*
- Real time (includes calculators and text processing)
- Signal and image processing*
- Data base (notebooks and records)

Manufacturing
- Record storage and processing
- Batch*
- Data logging and alarm checking
- Continuous real-time control
- Discrete real-time control
- Machine based
- People/parts flow

Communications and publishing
- Message switching
- Front-end processing
- Store and forward networks
- Speech input/output
- Terminals and systems
- Word processing, including computer conferencing and publishing

Transportation systems
- Network flow control
- On-board control

Education
- Computer-assisted instruction
- Algorithms, symbols, text storage, and processing
- Drill and practice
- Library storage

Home using television set
- Entertainment, record keeping, instruction, data base access

*Implies continuous program development

The scientific, engineering, and design disciplines use various algorithms for deriving symbols or evaluating values. Texts, graphs, and diagrams, the major ways of representing objects, have to be processed. For these environments, the computer has changed from a calculator (it was initially funded to do trajectory calculations for ballistic weapons) to a sophisticated notebook for keeping specifications, designs, and scientific records. Whereas the minicomputer was initially only used as a transducer to collect data to be analyzed on larger machines, it has since evolved to direct recording and analysis of time-varying signals and images and even to direct analysis and control. With minicomputers taking on such additional capabilities, connections to larger computers are used solely in a network fashion to handle graphic display and control functions.

The function of computers in both the manufacturing and the commercial environments has evolved from simple record keeping to direct on-line human control.

Process control computers have evolved from their initial use of assisting human operators (controllers) with data logging and alarm condition monitoring to full control of processes with either human or secondary computer backup. The structure of the computer and the control task vary widely depending on whether the process is continuous (e.g., refinery, rolling mill) or discrete (e.g., warehouse, automotive, appliance manufacturing).

Transportation applications for aircraft, trains, and eventually automotive vehicles are forms of real-time control that use both discrete and continuous control. Control is carried out in two parts: on board the vehicle and in the network (airspace, highway) that carries the vehicles. The transportation control function dictates three unique characteristics for the computer structure:

1. Very high reliability. Society has placed such a high value on a single human life

that all computers in this environment cannot appreciably raise the likelihood of a fatality.

2. Very small size for on-board computers.
3. Extreme operating and storage temperature range for on-board computers – especially for automotive vehicles.

Communications and message-based computers have evolved from telephone switching control, message switching, and front ends to other computers to become the dominant part of communications systems. With these evolving systems, the communications links have changed from analog-based transmission to sampled-data, digital transmission. By using digital transmission, data and voice (and video) can ultimately be used in the same system.

Word processing (i.e., creation, editing, and reproduction) together with long term storage and retrieval and transmission to other sites (i.e., electronic mail) have evolved from several systems:

1. Conventional teletypewriter messages and torn-tape message switching (e.g., TWX, Western Union, Telex).
2. Terminals with local storage and editing (e.g., Flexowriters, Teletype (with paper tape reader and punch), magnetic card/magnetic tape automatic typewriters, and the evolving stand-alone word processing terminals for office use).
3. Large, shared text preparation systems for centralized documentation preparation, newspaper publication, etc.
4. Large systems with central filing and transmission (distribution). These will negate the need for substantial hard copy. With these systems, text can be prepared either centrally with the system or with local intelligent word processing systems.
5. Computer conferencing. People can sit at terminals and converse with others without leaving their office.

The education-based environment implies a system which is a combination of transaction processing (for the human interaction part), scientific computation as the computer is required to simulate real world conditions (i.e., physical/natural phenomena), and information retrieval from a data base. These systems are evolving from the simple drill-and-practice systems which use a small simple algorithm, through simulation of particular real world phenomena, to knowledge-based systems which have a limited, but useful, natural language communications capability.

Home-based computers are beginning to emerge. The dominant use to date is in providing entertainment in the form of games that model simple, real world phenomena, such as ping-pong. Appliances are beginning to have embedded computers that have particular knowledge of their environments. For example, computer-controlled ranges can cook in fairly standard ways. Alternatively, cooking can be controlled by embedded temperature sensors. Simple calculators to record checkbooks have existed for quite some time. These will soon evolve to provide written transactions for recording and control purposes. Many domestic activities are in essence scaled-down versions of commercial, scientific, educational, and message environments.

With the evolution of each computer class, one can see several cases of machine structures which begin as highly specialized and evolve to being quite general. This evolution is driven by applications in accordance with the Applications/Functional View of Computer Classes.

The applications-driven evolution toward generality applies to both hardware and software. As a hardware example, consider the case of a computer installations using large, highly general computers, where minicomputers are applied to offload the large computers. The first application of the minicomputer is thus on a well-defined problem, but then more problems are added, and the minicomputer system is soon performing as a general computation facility with the help of a general purpose operating system. A similar effect occurs in software, where operating systems take on multiple functions as they evolve with time because users specify additional needs, and operating systems designers like to add function. Thus, a COBOL run-time environment might be added to a simple FORTRAN-based real-time operating system. At the next stage, a comprehensive file system might be added. In the hardware system, the next step in the evolution is usually offloading the minicomputer; in the software case, the next step is often the development of a new small, simple, and fast operating system.

Part of this evolution is due to the inherent generality of a computer, and part is a consequence of constant-cost design philosophy. The evolution is observable in computers of all classes, including calculators. The early scientific calculators evolved from just having logs, exponentials, and transcendental functions to include statistical analysis, curve fitting, vectors, and matrices.

Machines, then, evolve to carry out more and more functions. Since a prime discriminant is data-type, Figure 12 is presented to show an estimate of data-type usage for various applications, using mostly high level data-types, e.g., process descriptions. The estimates shown are very rough, because attempts to measure such distributions to date have not shown marked differences across applications (except for numerical versus non-numerical) because the data-types have not been of a sufficiently high level.

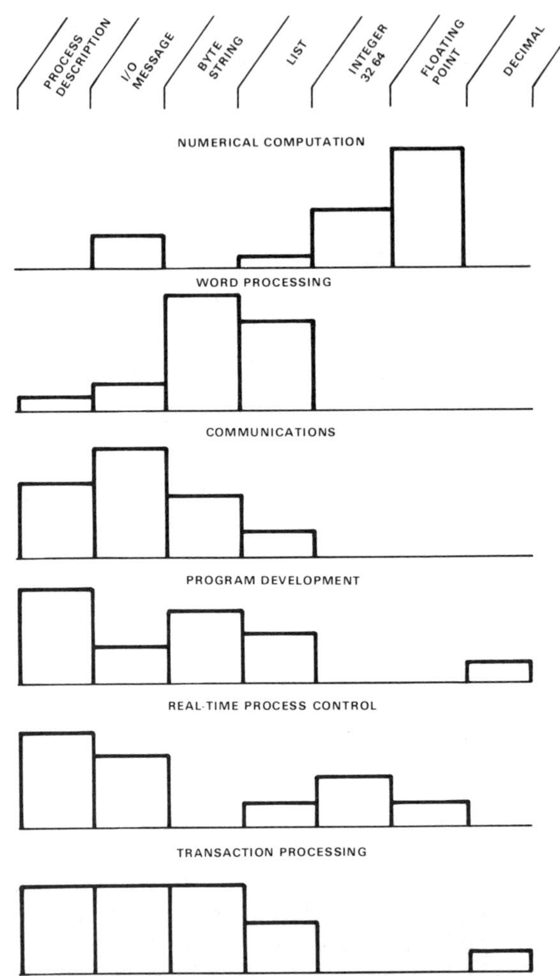

Figure 12. Data-type usage by application.

VIEW 6: THE PRACTICE OF DESIGN

Whereas previous views emphasized the object being designed, this is a view of the design process which gives rise to the object. Two models of design, those of Asimow and Simon, are presented, followed by some remarks on factors that particularly influence computer design.

In *Introduction to Design* [1962], Asimow gives a general perspective of engineering design and how the formal alternative generators and evaluating procedures are used. He also indicates where these formalisms break down and where they do not apply. He defines engineering design as an activity directed toward fulfilling human needs, based on the technology of our culture.

Asimow distinguishes two types of design: design by evolution and design by innovation.

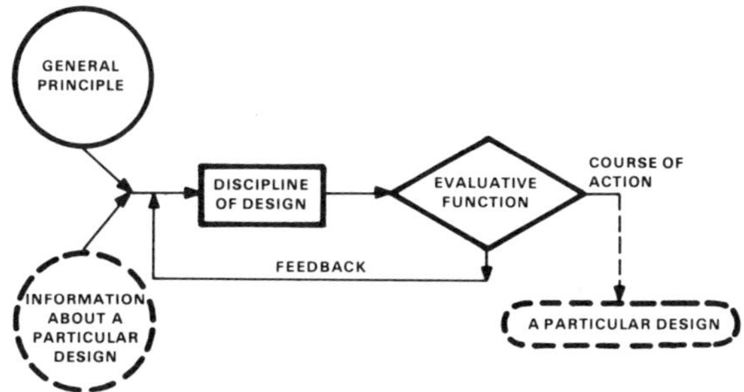

Figure 13. Philosophy of design. The feedback becomes operable when a solution is judged to be inadequate and requires improvement. The dotted elements represent a particular application [Asimow, 1962:5].

While there are examples of both in this book, design by evolution predominates both in this book and in the computer industry. Asimow's first diagram (Figure 13), called Philosophy of Design, shows the basic design process. Asimow lists the following principles [Asimow, 1962: 5–6].

1. **Need**. Design must be a response to individual or social needs which can be satisfied by the technological factors of culture.
2. **Physical realizability**. The object of a design is a material good or service which must be physically realizable.
3. **Economic worthwhileness**. The good or service, described by a design, must have a utility to the consumer that equals or exceeds the sum of the proper costs of making it available to him.
4. **Financial feasibility**. The operations of designing, producing, and distributing the good must be financially supportable.
5. **Optimality**. The choice of a design concept must be optimal among the available alternatives; the selection of a manifestation of the chosen design concept must be optimal among all permissible manifestations.
6. **Design criterion**. Optimality must be established relative to a design criterion which represents the designer's compromise among possibly conflicting value judgments that include those of the consumer, the producer, the distributor, and his own.
7. **Morphology**. Design is a progression from the abstract to the concrete. (This gives a vertical structure to a design project.)
8. **Design process**. Design is an iterative problem-solving process. (This gives a horizontal structure to each design step.)
9. **Subproblems**. In attending to the solution of a design problem, there is uncovered a substratum of subproblems; the solution of the original problem is dependent on the solution of the subproblem.
10. **Reduction of uncertainty**. Design is a processing of information that results in a transition from uncertainty about the success or failure of a design toward certainty.
11. **Economic worth of evidence**. Information and its processing has a cost which must be balanced by the worth of the evidence bearing on the success or failure of the design.
12. **Bases for decision**. A design project (or subprobject) is terminated whenever confidence in its failure is sufficient to warrant its abandonment, or is continued when confidence in an available design solution is high enough to warrant the commitment of resources necessary for the next phase.
13. **Minimum commitment**. In the solution of a design problem at any stage of the process, commitments which will fix future

design decisions must not be made beyond what is necessary to execute the immediate solution. This will allow the maximum freedom in finding solutions to subproblems at the lower levels of design.

14. **Communication**. A design is a description of an object and a prescription for its production; therefore, it will have existence to the extent that it is expressed in the available modes of communication.

Asimow goes on to define the phases of a complete project.

1. **Feasibility study**. The purpose is to determine some useful solutions to the design problem. It also allows the problem to be fully defined and tests whether the original need which initiated the process can be realized. Here the general design principles are formulated and tested.
2. **Preliminary design**. This is the sifting, from all possible alternatives, to find a useful alternative on which the detailed design is based.
3. **Detailed design**. This furnishes the engineering description of a tested and producible design.

While the above are the primary design phases, there are four succeeding phases resulting from the need for production and consumption by the outside world.

4. **Planning the production process**. This is really another design process which is simply a special case of design. The goal is to design and build the system that will produce the object.
5. **Planning for distribution**. This activity includes all aspects related to sales, shipping, warehousing, promotion, and display of the product.
6. **Planning for consumption**. This includes maintenance, reliability, safety, use, aesthetics, operational economy, and the base for enhancements to extend the product life.
7. **Retirement of the product**.

Obviously all of these activities overlap one another in time and interact as the basic design is carried out. Phister [1976] posits a model of this process (Figures 14 and 15) and gives the amount of time spent in each activity (Figure 16) for a hardware product.

Simon uses a more abstract model of design for human problem solving, which he calls *generate and test*. In *The Sciences of the Artificial*, Simon [1969] discusses the science of design and breaks the problem into representing the design problem alternatives, searching (i.e., generating alternatives), and computing the optimum. When it is too expensive to search for the optimum, as is often the case, satisfactory alternatives (which Simon calls *satisficing* alternatives) must be selected and tested. For most parts of computer design, the design variables are selected on the basis of satisfactory rather than optimal choice. Simon also discusses the tools

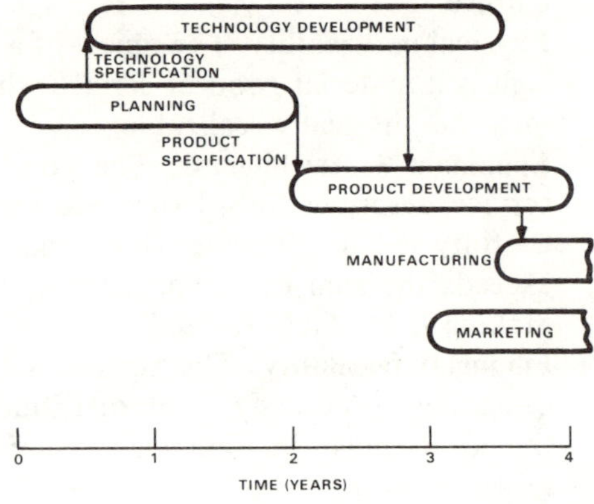

Figure 14. Hardware product development schedule I, comprehensive view [Phister, 1976].

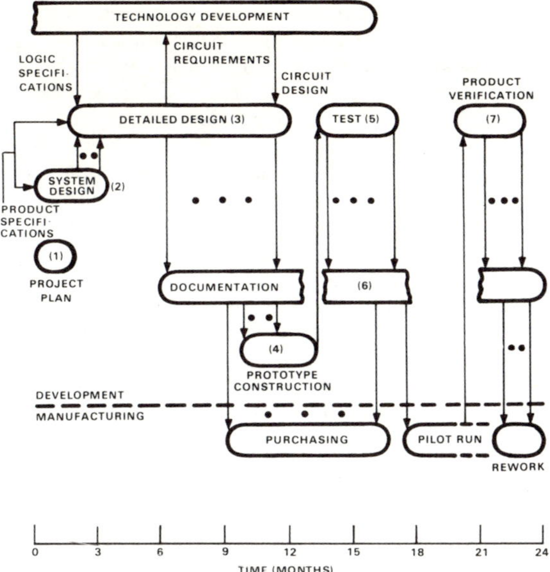

Figure 15. Hardware product development schedule II, development organization details [Phister, 1976].

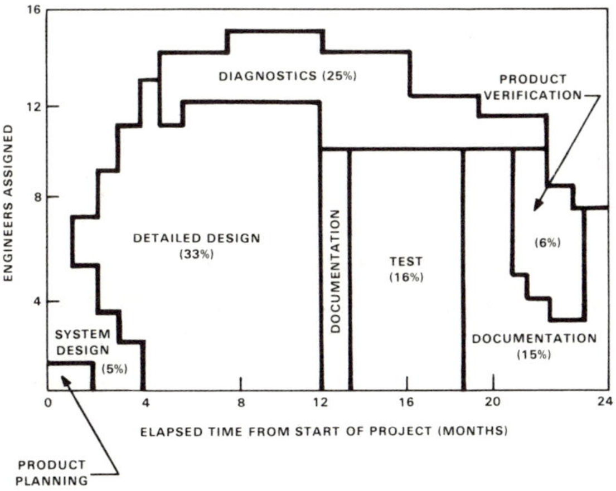

Figure 16. Hardware development costs for developing a $50,000 processor in 1974 [Phister, 1976].

of design, including the use of simulation both as an alternative to building the complete system and as a method to evaluate the behavior of various alternatives.

In addition to his contribution of the generate and test design model to the Practice of Design View, Simon's work has also contributed indirectly to the first three views discussed earlier in the chapter. In his discussion of the importance of the design hierarchy, Simon introduced the notion of *architecture of complexity*.

In the search for design optima, whether it be by generate and test or some other algorithm, the problem of design representation is often encountered. The more representations one has, the larger the number of design problems that can be tackled and, hence, the closer one can get to a global optimum. Most disciplines have at least two representations: schematic and visual. In chemical engineering, heat balance is obtained by thermodynamic equations, not from a plant piping diagram. In the design of power supplies, transformer design is accomplished using equivalent circuits, not by using physical representations. In the design of computer buses, most designers work with timing diagrams, although state diagrams and Petri nets are alternative representations.

In general, the importance of alternative representations in computer engineering is not well understood. The large number of representations that exist at the programming level is deceptive. There are many different algorithmic languages, but they differ mostly in syntax, not in semantics.

It is too simplistic to think that computer design should be a well-defined activity in which mathematical programming can be employed to obtain optimum solutions. There are major problems, five of which are listed below:

1. The cost function is multivariable.
2. The primary measure, performance, is not well understood.

3. The objective function that relates cost and performance is not understood.
4. Objectives are not as objective as they look.
5. There is a dynamic aspect (because the technology changes rapidly) which is hard to quantify.

These problems are explored in the following extract from a discussion of design given in Bell *et al.,* [1972a:23–24].

> Objectives can often be stated as maximizing or minimizing some measure on a system. A system should be as reliable as possible, as cheap as possible, as small as possible, as fast as possible, as general as possible, as simple as possible, as easy to construct and debug as possible, as easy to maintain as possible – and so on, if there are any system virtues that have been left out.
>
> There are two deficiencies with such an enumeration. First, one cannot, in general, maximize all these aspects at once. The fastest system is not the cheapest system. Neither is it the most reliable. The most general system is not the simplest. The easiest to construct is not the smallest, and so on. Thus, the objectives for a system must be traded off against each other. More of one is less of another and one must decide which of all these desirables one wants most and to what degree.
>
> The second deficiency is that each of these objectives is not so objective as it looks. Each must be measured, and for complex systems there is no single satisfactory measurement. Even for something as standardized as costs there are difficulties. Is it the cost of the materials – the components? Does one use a listed retail cost or a negotiated cost based on volume order? What about the cost of assembly? And should this be measured for the first item to be built, or for subsequent items if there are to be several? What about the costs of design? That is particularly tricky, since the act of designing to minimize costs itself costs money. What about cost measured in the time to produce the equipment? What about the cost of revising the design if it isn't right; this is a cost that may or may not occur. How does one assign overhead or indirect costs? And so on. In a completely particular situation one can imagine an omniscient designer knowing exactly which of these costs count and being able to put dollar figures on each to reduce them all to a common denominator. In fact, no one knows that much about the world they live in and what they care about.
>
> The dilemma is real: there is no reducing the evaluation of performance in the world to a few simple numbers. The solution is to understand what systems objectives are: they are guides to understanding and assessing system behavior in various partial aspects. Various measures for each type of objective are developed, and each shows something useful. Since all measures are partial and approximate (even conceptually), rough and ready measures that are easy to make, display and understand are often to be preferred to more exact and complex measures. Standard measures are to be developed and used, even if not perfect. Experience with how a measure behaves on many systems is often to be preferred to a better, but unique, measure with which no experience exists.

Although this book does not systematically treat all the different system measures, many of them are illustrated throughout the book. Table 4 provides a guideline, listing in one place the components that contribute to overall cost and performance.

The following list points out some tradeoffs, taken from experience, among the various activities.

System Cost Versus Component Cost. DEC sells products at each of the packaging levels-of-integration – from chips to turnkey application systems. Because each product is constructed from lower packaged levels, and because the levels model (View 3: Packaging

Table 4. Cost and Performance Components for a System [Bell et al., 1972a:24]

Cost Components

Arising from the design effort
- Specifying
- Designing (drawing, checking, verifying)
- Prototyping
- Packaging design
- Describing (documenting)
- Production system design
- Standardizing

Arising from production
- Buying (parts)
- Assembling
- Inspecting
- Testing

Arising from selling and distribution
- Understanding
- Configuring (i.e., user designing)
- Purchasing
- Applying
- Operating in the environment (heat, humidity, vibration, color, power, space)
- Repairing
- Remodeling
- Redesigning
- Retiring

Performance Components

Arising from designing, producing, and selling environment
- For a single task
- For a set of tasks
  - operation times
  - operation rate
  - memory size and utilization
- Reliability, availability, maintainability, and error rate
  - mean time between failures (MTBF)
  - availability (percent)
  - mean time to repair (MTTR)
  - error rate (detected, undetected)

Levels-of-Integration) strictly applies, it is very difficult to have designs that are optimally competitive at every level. For example, if DEC sold just hardware systems (cabinet level) it would not need a boxed version of its central processors. The box level could then be deleted and the price of the systems product would be proportionately lower. When primitives are to be used as building blocks, there is a cost associated with providing generality. For example, some boxes have too much power for most of their final applications because the powering was designed for the worst possible configuration of modules within the box. (Some boxes have too little power because increased logic density was accompanied by increased power density, permitting new worst-case configurations in existing boxes.)

Initial Sales Price Versus User Life Cycle Cost. There is a cost associated with parts that break and have to be repaired and maintained. Nearly every part of the computer can be improved over a range of a maximum of a factor of 10 to provide increased reliability (extended mean time between failure) for a price. To the extent that these costs are added, the product will be less competitive in terms of a higher purchase price. However, if the total life cycle costs are considered, the product may still be better even at the higher initial cost.

Reliability, Availability, Maintainability (and Producibility) Versus Performance. By designing to take advantage of the fastest components and operating them at the limit of their capability, one is able to have increased performance. In doing so, the tradeoff is clear: producibility, reliability (error rate), and maintainability (ease of fixing) all generally suffer.

Performance Versus Cost. This is the most traditional design tradeoff. In addition to the conventional product selection, the planning of a computer family further increases the selection/tradeoff process.

Early Shipment Versus Product Life and Quality. Delivering products before they are fully engineered for manufacture is risky. If faults are found that have to be corrected in the factory or field, the cost far outweighs any early product availability.

Length of Time to Design Versus Product Life. By allowing more time for design, a product can be designed in such a way that it is easier to enhance. On the other hand, if prospective customers, especially new customers, are faced with a choice between the competitor's available nonoptimum product and your unavailable optimum product, they may not be willing to wait.

Operating Environment Versus Cost. Here there are numerous tradeoffs even within a conventional environment. In each of the packaging dimensions (heat, humidity, altitude, dust, electromagnetic interface (EMI), etc.), there are similar tradeoffs that may appeal to unique markets or may simply translate to increased reliability in a given setting. The Norden 11/34M is an example of packaging to provide a PDP-11 for the aerospace environment.

The principles of computer design and the optimization efforts associated with those principles are parts of computer science and electrical engineering, the responsible disciplines. From computer science come many of the technical aspects (such as instruction set architecture), much of the theory (such as algorithms and computational complexity), and almost all of the software design (such as operating systems and language translators) applied in the practice of computer engineering. However, in their construction, computers are electrical; and the discipline that has fundamental responsibility is electrical engineering. Thus, discussion of the Practice of Design View concludes with Table 5, a set of maxims compiled by Don Vonada, an experienced DEC engineer. Many other engineers in many other companies have developed similar sets of maxims.

VIEW 7: THE BLAAUW CHARACTERIZATION OF COMPUTER DESIGN

Another view is based on the work of Blaauw [1970]. He distinguishes between *architecture*, *implementation*, and *realization* as three separable levels in the construction of anything, including computer structures.

The architecture of a computer system defines its functionality (behavior) as it appears to the machine level programmer and can be characterized by the instruction set processor (ISP). The implementation of a computer system is the actual hardware structure – the register transfer (RT) level behavior and data-flow organization. This also includes various algorithms for controlling a machine as it interprets an architecture. Realization encompasses the actual

Table 5. Vonada's Engineering Maxims

1. There is no such thing as ground.
2. Digital circuits are made from analog parts.
3. Prototype designs always work.
4. Asserted timing conditions are designed first; unasserted timing conditions are found later.
5. When all but one wire in a group of wires switch, that one will switch also.
6. When all but one gate in a module switches, that one will switch also.
7. Every little pico farad has a nano henry all its own.
8. Capacitors convert voltage glitches to current glitches (conservation of energy).
9. Interconnecting wires are probably transmission lines.
10. Synchronizing circuits may take forever to make a decision.
11. Worse-case tolerances never add – but when they do, they are found in the best customer's machine.
12. Diagnostics are highly efficient in finding solved problems.
13. Processing systems are only partially tested since it is impractical to simulate all possible machine states.
14. Murphy's Laws apply 95 percent of the time. The other 5 percent of the time is a coffee break.

technologies used and includes the kind of logic and how it is packaged and interconnected. Realization includes all the details associated with the physical aspects of the machine.

Modern architectures (ISPs) usually have multiple (RT) implementations. For example, the LSI-11, PDP-11/40, and PDP-11/60 are different implementations of the same basic PDP-11 instruction set. Sometimes, although rarely, a particular implementation has more than one realization. For example, the IBM 7090 has the same architecture and implementation (i.e., the same ISP and RT structure) as the IBM 709. The difference lies in realization: the 709 used vacuum tubes, the 7090 transistors. For a more recent example, two models of the PDP-11 architecture that share the same implementation are the DEC PDP-11/34 and Norden's 11/34M. The realization differs, however, as the latter uses militarized semiconductor components and component mountings, and a different packaging and cooling system. Table 6 attempts to clarify the distinguishing characteristics of architecture, implementation, and realization.

This book concentrates on the realization and implementation columns in Table 6. Instruction set architecture is discussed only insofar as it interacts with the other two characteristics. There are also some differences between the views of Blaauw and Brooks [in preparation] and those expressed in this book. It is important to try to reconcile these differences, because everyone engaged in computer engineering uses the words "architecture," "implementation," and "realization" - quite often to mean different things. This book will not limit the definition of architecture to just a machine as seen by a machine language programmer. Instead, it will use architecture to mean the ISP associated with any of the machine levels described in View 2, Levels-of-Interpreters. Therefore, architecture standing alone will mean the machine language, the ISP. This book will also use *architecture of the microprogrammed machine* as seen by a microprogrammed machine's microprogrammer, *architecture of the operating system* as the combined machine of operating system and machine language, and *architecture of a language*

Table 6. Characteristics of Design Areas [Blaauw and Brooks, in preparation: Chapter 1]

	Architecture	Implementation	Realization
Purpose	Function	Cost and performance	Buildable and maintainable
Product	Principles of operation	Logic design	Release to manufacturing
Language	Written algorithms	Block diagram, expressions	Lists and diagrams
Quality measure	Consistency	Broad scope	Reliability
Meanings (used herein)	ISP Machine ISP	RT level machine; microprogrammed sequential machine (at logic level)	Physical realization; physical implementation

for each language machine. For example, ALGOL, APL, BASIC, COBOL, and FORTRAN all have as separate and distinct architectures as a PDP-10 and a PDP-11 do. This use of architecture, because it describes behavior, is quite consistent with that of Blaauw. Moreover, when applied to software structures, Blaauw's framework fits well. There are two implementations, FORTRAN IV-PLUS (an optimizing compiler) and the initial FORTRAN IV of the one ANSI FORTRAN architecture. Moreover, different implementations use different realization techniques: some use BLISS, others use assembler language.

Although Blaauw and Brooks define implementation and realization clearly, these definitions are not widely used. The main problem is that both terms are sensitive to technology changes and, hence, interact closely. Computer engineers tend to overuse and intermix them so that the two words are used interchangeably. This is reflected in this book, where they are used to have roughly the same meaning (e.g., "The KI10 processor for the PDP-10 was implemented using high-speed (H-Series) transistor-transistor logic."). In Table 6, definitions are given for the two words so that the reader may further relate descriptions back to these definitions. "Implementation" is the register transfer level machine, roughly the microprogrammed machine; "realization" is the physical realization, the physical implementation in terms of packaging and technology.

The most useful distinction is between architecture, on the one hand, and implementation (subsuming realization), on the other. Seeing the distinction clearly enables one to preserve architectural compatibility between machine models, and this is crucial if users' and manufacturers' software investments are to be preserved. Implementation can then be as dynamic as desired, being continually changed by technology. Architecture must remain static for long periods (10 years is a common goal).

In 1949 Maurice Wilkes, only one month after his EDSAC computer was operational and before *any* stored program computers in the United States were operating, had already perceived the value in having a series, or set, of computers share the same instruction set:

> When a machine was finished, and a number of subroutines were in use, the order code could not be altered without causing a good deal of trouble. There would be almost as much capital sunk in the library of subroutines as the machine itself, and builders of new machines in the future might wish to make use of the same order code as an existing machine in order that the subroutines could be taken over without modification.

2

Technology Progress in Logic and Memories

C. GORDON BELL, J. CRAIG MUDGE, and JOHN E. McNAMARA

It is customary when reviewing the history of an industry to ascribe events to either market pull or technology push. The history of the auto industry contains many good examples of market pull, such as the trends toward large cars, small cars, tail fins, and hood ornaments. The history of the computer industry, on the other hand, is almost solely one of technology push.

Technology push in the computer industry has been strongest in the areas of logic and memory, as the case studies in the following chapters indicate. Where the following chapters give examples of the effects of the technology push in these areas, this chapter explores individual elements of that push, with particular emphasis on the role of semiconductors.

Semiconductor devices are discussed from the viewpoint of the user because, until recently, DEC has always bought its semiconductors (especially integrated circuits) from semiconductor manufacturers, and its engineers (users of integrated circuits) have viewed the integrated circuit as a black box with a carefully defined set of electrical and functional parameters. Most design engineers will probably continue to hold that view (and be encouraged to do so), even though some integrated circuits will be supplied by an in-house design and manufacturing facility. The advantages and disadvantages of in-house integrated circuit design will be discussed later in the chapter.

The portion of the discussion dealing with semiconductors begins by presenting a family tree of the possible technologies, arranged according to the function each carries out and showing how these have evolved over the last two or three generations to affect computer engineering. The cost, density, performance, and reliability parameters are briefly reviewed; the application of semiconductors, using various logic design methods, is then discussed with particular emphasis on how the semiconductor technology has pushed the design methods.

The discussion of the use of semiconductors in logic applications is followed by a section on memories for primary, secondary, and tertiary storage. While semiconductors have been a dominant factor in technology push within the computer industry for both logic and memory applications, magnetic recording density on disks and tapes has evolved rapidly, too, and must be understood as a component of cost and as a limit of system performance.

The section on memory is followed by a section containing some general observations about technology evolution: how technology is measured, why it evolves (or does not), cases of it being overthrown, and a general model for how its use in computers operates and is managed.

SEMICONDUCTOR LOGIC TECHNOLOGY

A single transistor circuit performing a primitive logic function within an integrated circuit is among the smallest and most complex of man-made objects. Alone, such a circuit is intrinsically trivial, but the fabrication process required for a set of structures to form a complete integrated circuit is complex. For users of digital integrated circuits there are several relevant parameters:

1. The function of an individual circuit in the integrated circuit, the aggregate function of the integrated circuit, and the functions of a complete integrated circuit family such as the 7400-series.
2. The number of switching circuit functions per integrated circuit. This quantity and density is a measure of the capability of the integrated circuit and the ingenuity of the designers.
3. Cost.
4. The speed of each circuit and the speed of the integrated circuit and set of integrated circuits within a family. The semiconductor device family (transistor-transistor logic = TTL, Schottky TTL = TTL/S, emitter-coupled logic = ECL, metal oxide semiconductor = MOS, complementary MOS = CMOS, silicon on saphire = SOS, integrated injection logic = I^2L) usually determines this performance.
5. The number of interconnections (pins) to communicate outside the integrated circuit.
6. The reliability. This is a function of the circuit technology, the density, the number of pins, the operating temperature, the use (or misuse), and the maturity (experience) of the manufacturing process.
7. Power consumption and *speed-power product*. A frequently used metric is the speed-power product, where the delay through a typical gate is multiplied by the power consumption of the gate. For a particular technology, the speed-power product tends to be constant because short gate delays usually are accompanied by high power consumption. A technical advance that lowers the speed-power product is considered noteworthy.

Figure 1 shows a family tree (taxonomy) of the most common digital integrated circuits. The least complex functions are in the upper portion of the figure, and the most complex are at the bottom. In addition, the circuits are ordered by generation, starting with the second generation on the left side of the figure and progressing to the fifth generation on the right side. The circuits are clustered roughly by the regularity of the function and whether memory is associated with the function. Circuit regularity is important in large-scale integrated circuits because it is desirable to implement regular structures to minimize area-consuming interconnections and, thus, to simplify layout and understanding and to aid testing.

As indicated in Figure 1, the branching of the integrated circuit family tree began in earnest at the beginning of the third generation. At that time, advances in integrated-circuit technology permitted collections of basic logic primitives (AND, NAND, etc.) and sequential circuit components (flip-flops, registers, etc.) to occupy a single integrated circuit rather than an entire module. This had the benefit of providing a drastic reduction in size between the second and third generation computer designs, as

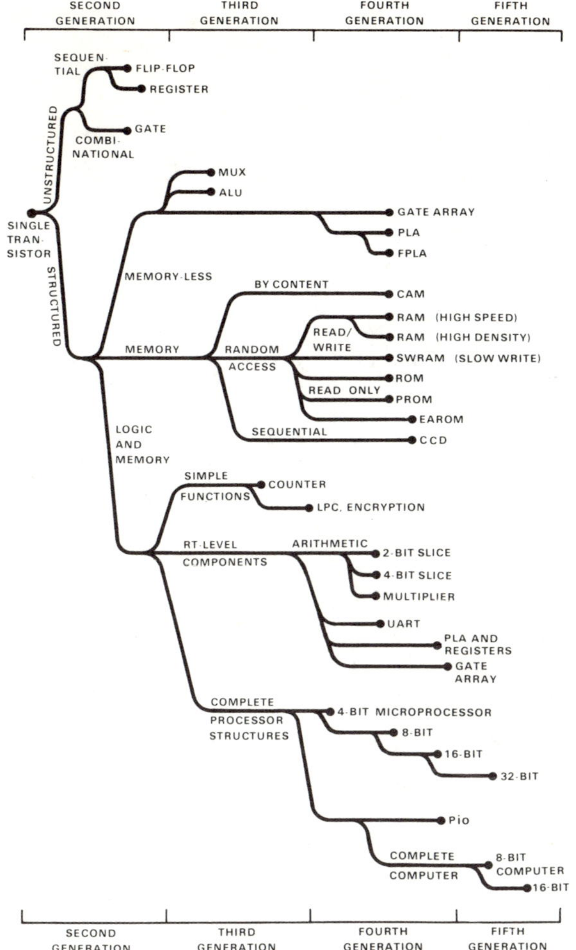

Figure 1. Family tree of digital integrated circuit functions.

shown most vividly by comparing the PDP-9 and PDP-15 (Chapter 6), but it also had the drawback that modules contained a wide variety of functions and were thus specialized.

As the densities began to approach 100 gates, the construction of complete arithmetic units on a single chip became possible. The earliest and most famous function, the 74181 arithmetic logic unit (ALU) shown in Figure 2, provided up to 32 functions of two 4-bit variables. By the fourth generation, it became possible to construct on a single chip very large combinational circuits, such as a complete 16 × 16-bit multiplication circuit (e.g., the TRW Corp. multiplier) requiring about 5,000 gates.

Progress during the fourth and fifth generations has not been without its problems, however. Without well defined functions such as addition and multiplication, semiconductor suppliers cannot provide high density products in high volume because there are few large-scale, general purpose universal functions. The alternative for users is to interconnect simple logic circuits (AND gates, flip-flops), but that does not permit efficient use of the technology, and the cost per function remains high (about that of the third generation) because the printed circuit board and integrated circuit packaging costs (pins) limit the cost reduction.

To address these problems, two methods of effectively customizing large-scale integrated circuit logic are included in Figure 1 and discussed in greater detail later in the chapter. These are the programmable logic array (PLA) and the gate array (also called master slice). The programmable logic array (PLA) is an array of AND-OR gates that can be interconnected to form the sum-of-products terms in a combinational logic design. Gate arrays are simply a large number of gates placed on the chip in fixed locations where they can be interconnected during the final metalization stages of semiconductor manufacture.

There is a special branch of the tree shown in Figure 1 purely for memory functions. Memory is used in the processor as conventional memory, but it can also be used as an alternative to conventional logic for performing combinational logic functions. For example, the inputs to a combinational function can be used as an address, and the output can be obtained by reading the contents of that address. Memory can also be used to implement sequential logic functions. For example, it can be used to hold state information for a microprogram. Because

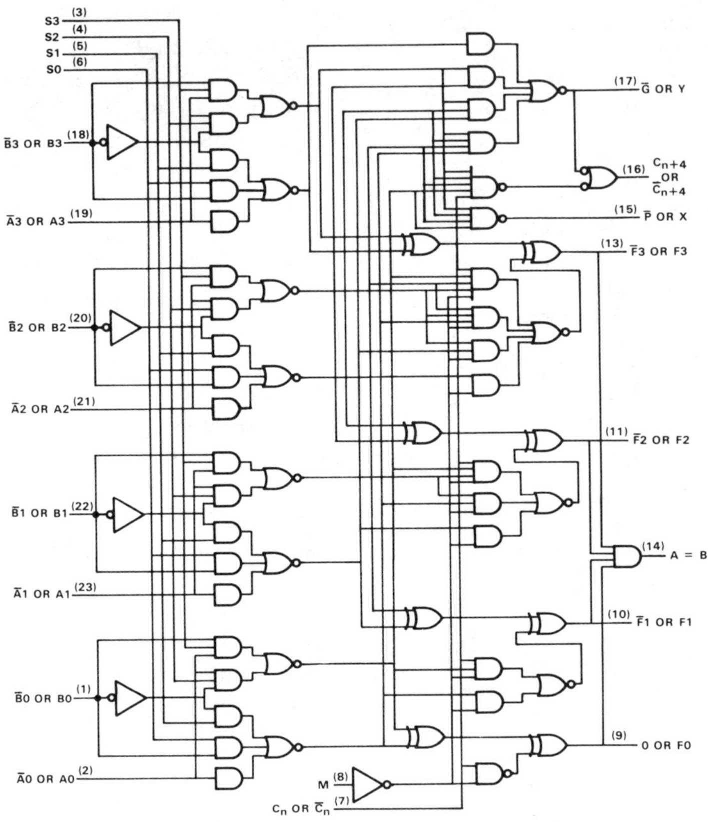

Table 1

Selection				Active Low Data		
				M = H	M = L; Arithmetic Operations	
S3	S2	S1	S0	Logic Functions	C_n = L (No Carry)	C_n = H (With Carry)
L	L	L	L	$F = \overline{A}$	F = A minus 1	F = A
L	L	L	H	$F = \overline{AB}$	F = AB minus 1	F = AB
L	L	H	L	$F = \overline{A} + B$	F = $A\overline{B}$ minus 1	$F = A\overline{B}$
L	L	H	H	F = 1	F = Minus 1 (2's comp.)	F = Zero
L	H	L	L	$F = \overline{A + B}$	F = A plus $(A + \overline{B})$	F = A plus $(A + \overline{B})$ plus 1
L	H	L	H	$F = \overline{B}$	F = AB plus $(A + \overline{B})$	F = AB plus $(A + \overline{B})$ plus 1
L	H	H	L	$F = \overline{A \oplus B}$	F = A minus B minus 1	F = A minus B
L	H	H	H	$F = A + \overline{B}$	$F = A + \overline{B}$	F = $(A + \overline{B})$ plus 1
H	L	L	L	$F = \overline{A}B$	F = A plus (A + B)	F = A plus (A + B) plus 1
H	L	L	H	$F = A \oplus B$	F = A plus B	F = A plus B plus 1
H	L	H	L	F = B	F = $A\overline{B}$ plus (A + B)	F = $A\overline{B}$ plus (A + B) plus 1
H	L	H	H	F = A + B	F = (A + B)	F = (A+B) plus 1
H	H	L	L	F = 0	F = A plus A*	F = A plus A plus 1
H	H	L	H	$F = A\overline{B}$	F = AB plus A	F = AB plus A plus 1
H	H	H	L	F = AB	F = $A\overline{B}$ plus A	F = $A\overline{B}$ plus A plus 1
H	H	H	H	F = A	F = A	F = A plus 1

*Each bit is shifted to the next more significant position.

Table 2

Selection				Active High Data		
				M = H	M = L; Arithmetic Operations	
S3	S2	S1	S0	Logic Functions	$\overline{C}_n$ = H (No Carry)	$\overline{C}_n$ = L (With Carry)
L	L	L	L	$F = \overline{A}$	F = A	F = A plus 1
L	L	L	H	$F = \overline{A + B}$	F = A + B	F = (A + B) plus 1
L	L	H	L	$F = \overline{A}B$	$F = A + \overline{B}$	F = $(A + \overline{B})$ plus 1
L	L	H	H	F = 0	F = Minus 1 (2's complement)	F = Zero
L	H	L	L	$F = \overline{AB}$	F = A plus $A\overline{B}$	F = A plus $A\overline{B}$ plus 1
L	H	L	H	$F = \overline{B}$	F = (A + B) plus $A\overline{B}$	F = (A + B) plus $A\overline{B}$ plus 1
L	H	H	L	$F = A \oplus B$	F = A minus B minus 1	F = A minus B
L	H	H	H	$F = A\overline{B}$	F = $A\overline{B}$ minus 1	$F = A\overline{B}$
H	L	L	L	$F = \overline{A} + B$	F = A plus AB	F = A plus AB plus 1
H	L	L	H	$F = \overline{A \oplus B}$	F = A plus B	F = A plus B plus 1
H	L	H	L	F = B	F = $(A + \overline{B})$ plus AB	F = $(A + \overline{B})$ plus AB plus 1
H	L	H	H	F = AB	F = AB minus 1	F = AB
H	H	L	L	F = 1	F = A plus A*	F = A plus A plus 1
H	H	L	H	$F = A + \overline{B}$	F = (A + B) plus A	F = (A + B) plus A plus 1
H	H	H	L	F = A + B	F = $(A + \overline{B})$ plus A	F = $(A + \overline{B})$ plus A plus 1
H	H	H	H	F = A	F = A minus 1	F = A

*Each bit is shifted to the next more significant position.

Figure 2. A functional block diagram of the 181 arithmetic logic unit (courtesy of Texas Instruments, Inc., from *TTL Data Book*, 2nd edition, 1976, p. 7–273, 7–280).

memories have so many uses, this branch is discussed separately in the memory section of this chapter.

The remainder of the interesting logic functions include combinations of logic and memory. There are various special functions such as linear predictive coding algorithms for use in real-time applications and data encryption algorithms for use in communication systems. One of the most useful communications functions, and the first one to use large-scale integration, is the Universal Asynchronous Receiver/Transmitter (UART).

There is a special branch for bit-slice components that can be combined to form data paths of arbitrary widths. These are being used to construct most of today's high speed digital systems, mid-range computers, and computer peripherals. Although there have been several bit-slice families, the AMD Corp. 2900-series whose register transfer diagram is shown in Figure 3 has become the most widely used. Note that all the primitives of this series were present in the Register Transfer Module Family (Chapter 18), including the microprogrammed control unit referred to as the Programmed Control Sequencer.

The final branch of the tree in Figure 1 is the most complex and is used to mark the fourth (microprocessor-on-a-chip) generation of technology and the beginning of the fifth (computer-on-a-chip) generation. The fourth generation is marked by the packaging of a complete processor on a single silicon die; by this standard, the fifth generation has already begun since a complete computer (processor with memory) now occupies a single die. The evolution in complexity during each generation simply permits larger word length processors or computers to be placed on one chip. At the beginning of the fourth generation, a 4-bit processor was the benchmark; toward the end of the fourth generation, a complete 16-bit processor such as the PDP-11 could be placed on a single chip.

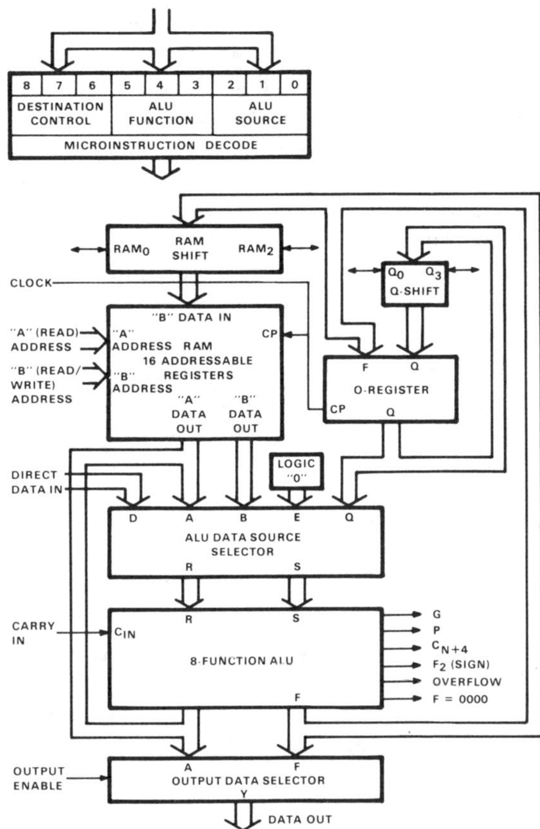

Figure 3. AMD2900 four-bit microprocessor slice block diagram (registers and data path).

Gates per Chip

The function performed by a chip is clearly dependent on the number of gates that can be placed on a chip. Thus, density in gates per chip is the single most important parameter determining chip functionality. By this measure, one can predict the functions likely to be implemented by just following the tree. It should be noted that the whole tree is relatively alive and has dense areas of new branches everywhere except at the top, where unconnected gate and register structures have been relatively static. In the growing areas, as density increases sufficiently, a new branch grows. For example, the processor-on-a-chip started out as a 4-bit processor (or rather as 2 chips for a single processor) and then progressed to 8-bit and then 16-bit processors on a single chip. Similar effects can be observed with the arithmetic logic unit and with memories.

The number of gate circuits per chip not only determines chip functionality, it also is the measure of density as seen by a user (Figure 4). This metric is the product of the circuit area and the number of circuits per unit area. Progress in lithography has led to a reduction of conductor linewidths and a corresponding reduction of circuit size to yield higher speeds and higher densities. Linewidths have decreased from 10 microns in early large-scale integrated circuit chips to 6 microns in the LSI-11 chips, and more recently to 3 or 4 microns in Intel's 8086. Linewidths of less than a micron have been achieved at the research level, but they require electron beam techniques instead of present photographic methods of production. The processing techniques to create semiconductor materials have also been improved for better manufacturing yields (and lower costs). Circuit and device innovation (such as reducing the number of transistors per memory cell) have also contributed to density and yield increases.

The result given in Figure 4 is exponential and indicates that the number of bits per chip for a metal oxide semiconductor (MOS) memory doubles every two years according to the relationship:

$$\text{Number of bits per chip} = 2^{t-1962}$$

There are separate curves, each following this relationship, for read-only memories in prototype quantities, read-only memories in production quantities, read-write memories in prototype quantities, and read-write memories in production quantities. Thus, depending on the product and the maturity of its production process, products lead or lag behind the above

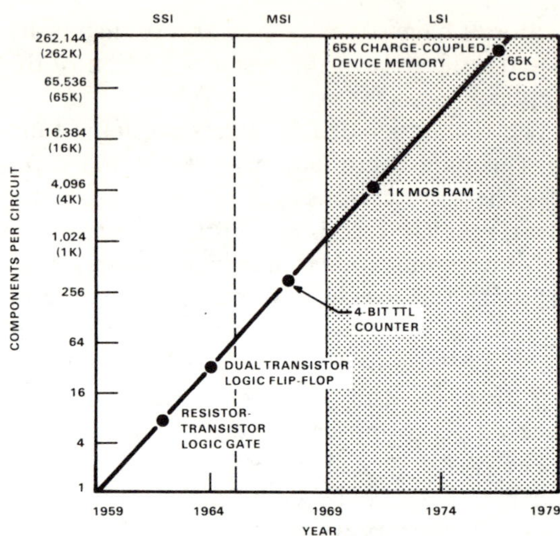

Figure 4. Components per single integrated circuit die versus time. Number of components per circuit in the most advanced integrated circuits has doubled every year since 1959, when the planar transistor was developed. Gordon E. Moore, then at Fairchild Semiconductor, noted the trend in 1964 and predicted that it would continue (from [Noyce, 1977:67]; courtesy of *Scientific American*).

state-of-the-art time line by one to three years according to the following rules:

- Bipolar read-write memories lag by two to three years.
- Bipolar read-only memories lag by about one year.
- MOS read-only memories lead by one year.

This model gives the availability of various sizes of semiconductor memories as shown in Figure 5. The significance of various size memory availabilities is that they determine (technology push) when certain architectures and implementations can occur. The chapter discussing the PDP-11 (Chapter 16) uses this model to show how semiconductors accomplish this push.

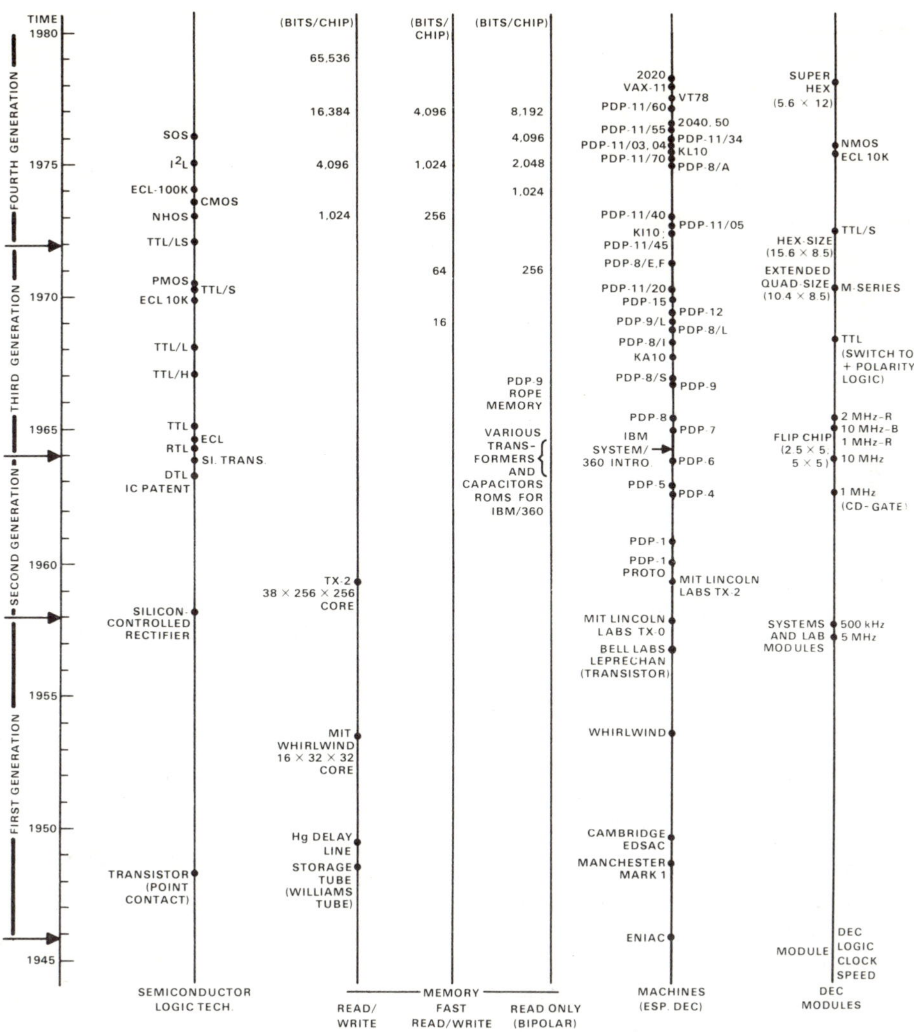

Figure 5. Logic and memory technology evolution timeline.

Cost

After density, the most important characteristic of integrated circuits is cost. The cost of integrated circuits is probably the hardest of all the parameters to identify and predict because it is set by a complex marketplace. For circuits that have been in production for some time, and for memory arrays, the price is set in essentially the same way as the price of a commodity like eggs or bacon is set; and users generally consider these integrated circuits as very similar to commodities, with the attendant benefits, costs, and problems (having a sufficient supply). In low volumes, integrated circuit prices are proportional to the die cost (which is proportional to the die area); but at higher volumes, assembly, testing, packaging, and distribution become the dominant cost factors. Furthermore, for those low volume circuits that have not yet reached commodity status, the prices also depend on the strategy of the supplier – whether he is willing to encourage competition.

Two curves are presented to reflect the price of various components (transistors) implemented in integrated circuits. Figure 6 shows the price per gate for MOS and TTL circuits as a function of time and scale of integration. Table 1 gives some idea of how circuit density (in elements) relates to actual function.

The cost history of integrated circuits is reflected very dramatically in the cost history of a special class of integrated circuits, semiconductor memory. The semiconductor memory cost curves, given in Figure 7, are also interesting because of the important role of memory in past and future computer structures. As shown in the figure, the 1978 cost per bit was roughly 0.08¢ and 0.07¢ per bit for the 4-Kbit and 16-Kbit integrated circuit chips, respectively, giving costs of $3.30 and $11.50.

Two factors influence the cost of integrated circuits: density in bits per integrated circuit and cost per bit. The two factors have not had equal influence in reducing costs because, while chip density has improved by a factor of 2 each year (Figure 4) [Noyce, 1977], the cost per bit (at the integrated circuit level) has not declined by a factor of 2 every two years. The equation for the line drawn in Noyce's [1977] Figure 7 is:

$$\text{Cost/bit } (¢) = 0.3 \times 0.72^{t-1974}$$

It is interesting to note that the cost decline compares favorably with the price decline in core memory over the period since 1960–1970 for the 18-bit computers (Chapter 6), and with the memory price declines in both the PDP-8 (Chapter 7) and the PDP-10 (Chapter 21).

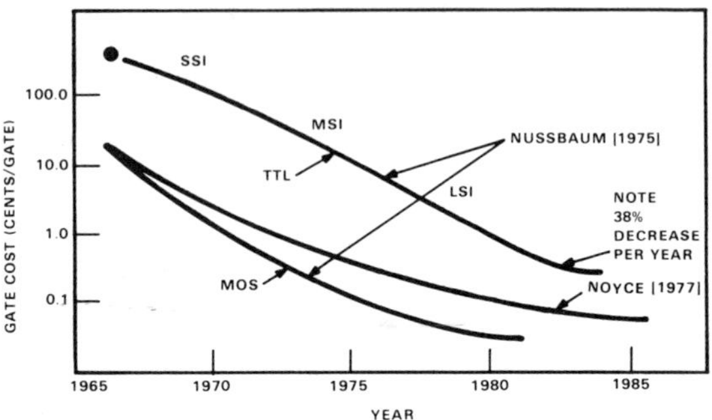

Figure 6. Price per gate versus time.

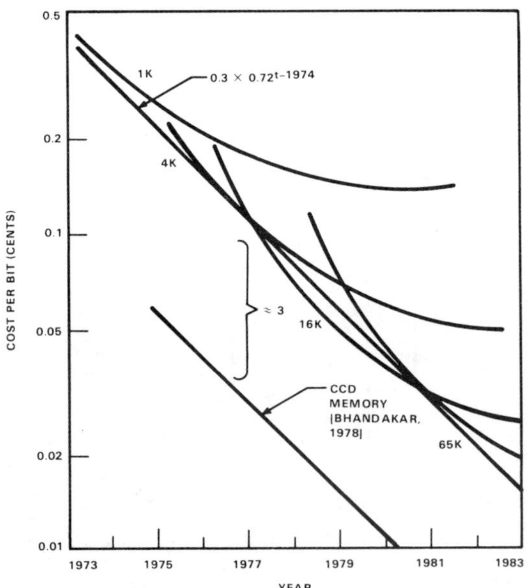

Figure 7. Cost per bit of integrated circuit memory versus time. Cost per bit of computer memory has declined and should continue to decline as is shown here for successive generations of random-access memory circuits capable of handling from 1,024 (1 K) to 65,536 (65 K) bits of memory. Increasing complexity of successive circuits is primarily responsible for cost reduction, but less complex circuits also continue to decline in cost (adapted from [Noyce, 1977: 69]; courtesy of *Scientific American*).

Table 1. The Number of Areal Elements to Implement Logic Functions in Different Technologies

	MOS			Bipolar		
Function	**NMOS**	**PMOS**	**CMOS**	**ECL**	**TTL**	**I^2L**
Inverter	2	2	2	7	3	1
2-input gate	3	3	3 or 4	8	3	1
8-input gate	9	9	9 or 16	14	3	2
R/S latch	6	6	6 or 8	12	6	2
Memory cell (dynamic)	2	2	2	–	–	2
Memory cell (static)	6	6	6	4–6	4–6	4
D flip-flop	20	20	20 or 28	28	20	9
JK flip-flop	20	20	20 or 36	–	26	11

Performance

The performance for each semiconductor technology evolves at different rates depending on the cumulative learning associated with the design and manufacturing processes together with marketplace pressure to have higher performance for the particular technology. One may hypothesize that each technology can be looked at as being relatively appealing or relevant to the particular design(er) styles associated with various computer marketplaces. One would then expect the evolution to continue along the lines shown in Table 2.

DEC's use of the various integrated circuit technologies shown in Table 2 is probably typical of most of the computer industry: TTL for mid- and high-sized minicomputers; ECL for the larger scale machines (PDP-10); MOS for memories, microprocessors, and specialized high density circuits; and CMOS for special microcomputers, especially those intended for battery operation.

Some of the lesser used technologies such as I^2L (integrated-injection logic) and SOS (silicon on saphire) have been omitted from the table. I^2L features high density and very low power consumption, but it is slow as initially implemented. SOS MOS enhances CMOS speed by removing stray capacitance, making it comparable with low power Schottky (TTL/LS) speed while retaining MOS complexity capabilities. Both I^2L and SOS have been touted as replacements for various technologies shown in the table. But, if an entrenched technology has evolved for some time and continues to evolve, it is difficult for alternative technologies to displace it because of the investment in process technology and understanding. Semiconductors appear to be characteristic of other technologies in that usually only a single technology is used for a given problem.

The early technologies, RTL (resistor transistor logic), TRL (transistor resistor logic), and DTL (diode transistor logic) have also been omitted from the table. These technologies are important historically because they were used in the first integrated circuits. However, many manufacturers, including DEC, did not use them in computers (RTL was used in DEC industrial control modules) because they did not represent a sufficient advance over the discrete transistor circuits already being used. In addition, early circuits were packaged in flat packages and metal cans rather than in the dual in-line package used today, and automated manufacture using the components was thus not economically feasible.

Table 3 gives the speed-power product and the gate delay, the two most useful measures of

Table 2. Characteristics of Dominant (1978) Semiconductor Technologies

Type	Evolution	Use
TTL (transistor-transistor logic)	TTL	Logic, bus interfacing
	TTL/Schottky	Higher speed than TTL
	TTL/LS	Same speed as TTL, but low power
ECL (emitter-coupled logic)	MECL II, III	High and higher performance
	MECL 10 K, 100 K	Easier to work with
		Evolving to gate array design
MOS (metal oxide semiconductor)	p-channel	Low cost
	n-channel	Greater densities, cost
		Evolving to performance (memory)
		Evolving to shorter channels: HMOS, DMOS, VMOS
CMOS (complementary MOS)	CMOS	Low power, higher speed
		Better noise immunity

Table 3. Gate Delay of Various Semiconductor Technologies [Luecke, 1976:53]*

Year	Type of Logic	Gate Delay (nanoseconds)	Power Dissipation (milliwatts)	Speed-Power Product (picojoules)
[1963	DTL	–	–	200]
[1964	RTL	–	–	180]
1965	TTL	10	10	100
1967	TTL/H-series	5	20	100
1968	TTL	30	1	30
1970	TTL (Schottky)	3	20	60
1972	TTL (low power Schottky)	10	2	20
1967	ECL	2	30	60
1974	ECL	0.7	43	30
1970	PMOS	200	0.1	20
1973	NMOS	100	0.1	10
1973	CMOS	30	1.0	30
1974	SOS	15	0.05	7.5
[1976	NMOS	4	1	4]
[1978	HMOS	0.9	1	0.9]
1975	I^2L	35	0.085	3.0
1976	I^2L	20	0.05	1.0

*The four entries in brackets have been added by the authors.

performance, for the various technologies as they have evolved with time. The speed-power product metric for a technology at a given time indicates what performance versus power tradeoffs the user can make. There are limits to this tradeoff. Only about one watt can be dissipated by the off-the-shelf integrated circuit package, and tradition in integrated circuit package design has been strong. The table was formulated by Jerry Luecke of Texas Instruments (TI) at a time when I^2L technology had just been introduced (October, 1975) by TI.

Reliability

Over the past 15 years, the failure rate for standard integrated circuits has been reduced by two orders of magnitude to the neighborhood of 0.01 percent per 1,000 hours. This corresponds to 10^7 hours (about a millenium) mean time to failure (MTTF) per component. Figure 8, from a recent survey article by Hodges [1977:63], shows the trend. The lower curves show the higher reliability obtained when more extensive testing and screening are employed. The improved MTTF of between 10^8 and 10^9 are obtained at a cost increase of 4 to 100 times per component.

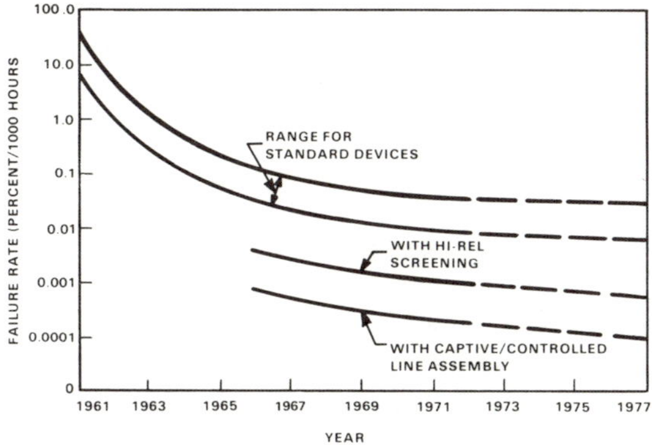

Figure 8. Failure rate of silicon integrated circuits. (Rate of 0.0001 percent per 1,000 hours is 10^9 hours mean time to failure.) [Hodges, 1977:63]

I/O Connections

The number of pins per integrated circuit package has risen relatively slowly because of the mechanical handling equipment (e.g., sorters, bonders, testers, inserters) to the point where 48 pins has just become accepted in 1978. The packages of the 1980s will no doubt go beyond 100 with the ability for multiple die per package.

The Large-Scale Integrated Circuit Dilemma

As indicated in the discussion of Figure 1, a dilemma involving a search for universal circuits has developed in the manufacture of large-scale integrated (LSI) circuits. The economics of the LSI industry make it essential that integrated circuit suppliers produce circuits with a high degree of universality. This is because the learning curve of a manufacturing process causes cost to be inversely proportional to volume, and for a design to be sold in high volume, it must be usable in a large number of applications. However, the trend in circuit complexity, which allows semiconductor manufacturers to put more transistors on a constant die area each year, tends to increase specialization of function, lowering the volume and raising the price.

The LSI product designer is therefore continually in search of universal primitives or building blocks. For a certain class of applications, such as controller applications, the microprocessor is a fine primitive and has been so exploited [Noyce, 1977]. For other applications, circuit complexity can embrace even higher functionality at the processor-memory-switch level. The Intel 827X is an interesting example: two processors, a 1.25-microsecond byte-processor and a 250-nanosecond bit-processor, are combined in one large-scale integrated circuit [Louie *et al.*, 1977].

Moore [1976] discusses the LSI dilemma in a paper on the role of the microprocessor in the evolution of microelectronic technology. He points out that a similar situation existed when integrated circuits were first introduced. Users were reluctant to relinquish the design prerogative they had when they built circuits from discrete components. It was not until substantial price reductions were made that the impasse was broken. Then the cost advantages were sufficient to force users to adopt the new technology circuits.

The first high functionality, high universality circuit that comes to mind is the microprocessor-on-a-chip. For many applications, including most computer systems, the microprocessor-on-a-chip is not a cost-effective building block, and other solutions to the dilemma are used. For example, microprogramming is a highly general way of generating control signals for data path elements, and table lookup using read-only memories is a highly general technique. Both methods are attractive because they use memory, an inherently low cost LSI circuit. Microprogramming, however, does have limitations. The extra level of interpretation extracts a performance penalty, and some potential data path parallelism is often given up to reduce cost. A more subtle, but practical, limitation is the development cost of microcode. Assuming the writing rate to be 700 microwords per man-year for wide-word, unencoded (horizontal) micromachines, a desire to limit the effort to 20–24 man-years would limit the maximum control store size to about 16 Kwords. This maximum will tend to increase in the future, when the use of better microprogramming tools increases the microcode writing rate beyond 700 microwords per man-year.

At the register transfer level, the standard microprogramming design method is (conservatively) twice as expensive per instruction as conventional programming. Moreover, because microinstructions are usually not as powerful as conventional instructions, more microinstructions than conventional instructions are usually required to solve a given problem. These two factors, more expense per instruction and more instructions, cause a microprogram to be five to ten times as expensive as a conventional program to solve the same problem. However, the instruction execution speeds of a microprogrammed controller are at least 10 times faster than the instruction execution speeds of a conventional mini.

The characteristics of microprocessor and read-only memory design methods of creating customized results from universal large-scale integrated circuits are summarized, along with the characteristics of a number of other methods, in Table 4.

Table 4. Design Techniques for Various LSI Building Blocks

Building Block	Technique for Varying Function	Degree of Generality	Permanence of Change
Computer module	Program	Very high	None
Micro-processor	Program	High	Low to medium
Bit-slice	Microprogram	Medium	Medium
ROM	Factory mask change	Very high	Irreversible
PROM	Field change	Very high	Irreversible
EAROM, EPROM	Field change	Very high	Low
PLA	Factory mask change	Medium	Irreversible
FPLA	Field change	Medium	Irreversible
Gate array	Factory mask change	Medium	Irreversible
RAM	Write	Very high	None

The increased basic circuit functionality available at each new generation has not only been an important part of semiconductor design, but has also caused design methods to change with the generations. This book provides examples, as summarized in Table 5.

The design of most relatively high speed digital systems (including low- to mid-range minicomputers) is carried out using standard register transfer integrated circuits complete with data path and memory. For higher performance computers, there is no alternative to using either tightly packed standard integrated circuits or building a unique set of integrated circuits using some form of customization. The high performance IBM and Amdahl machines, for example, use custom ECL circuits or gate arrays to improve packaging. Although Seymour Cray continues to build his high speed computers (the CDC 6600, 7600 and Cray 1) with no custom logic, he does so by using impressively dense modules with high density interconnection and freon cooling.

The current spectrum of integrated circuits and their use is summarized in Table 6.

The Changing Nature of System Design

With the advent of the processor-on-a-chip, digital system design has been, or soon will be, converted completely to computer system design (design at the processor-memory-switch level of Chapter 1, View 1). Problems such as controlling a CRT, controlling a lathe, building

Table 5. Design Method versus Generation

Design Method	Generations: First	Second	Third	Fourth	Fifth	Examples in this Book
Combinational and sequential; use of "standard" modules, integrated circuits	s	s	s	–	–	18-bit; PDP-8
Read-only memory and PLA; microprogramming	–	–	s	m	–	PDP-9; PDP-11
Microprogramming with standard RT elements (high performance) minor logical design	–	–	–	s	m	CMU-11
Programming using micros and logic for interfaces	–	p	p	s	x	LSI-11
PMS design using completely specified and predesigned microcomputer components	–	–	–	–	s	Cm*
Customized chip design and standard (logic) design (high performance)	–	–	m	m	m	LSI-11

s - The standard method for most digital systems
m - Done by manufacturers of basic equipment
x - Also used
p - Prelude to micros, also done using minis

Table 6. Integrated Circuit Organization and Use in Various Computers

Organization	Technology	Unique Chips	Performance (MIPS)	Cost	Examples
Microcomputer	MOS, very large-scale integration (VLSI)	1	0.1	Lowest	Intel 8048, MOSTEK 3870
Microprocessor	MOS	1			Intel 8080, Zilog Z80, Motorola 6800
Microprocessor	MOS	2–4			DEC LSI-11, Fairchild F-8
Microprocessor	MOS	>4			Burroughs B80, National IMP 16
Bit-slice (micro-programmed)	TTL	Few			DEC 11/34 Floating-Point Processor
Gate array	TLL	Most			Raytheon RP16, IBM Series 1
Medium-scale integration	TTL	Few			DEC VAX 11/780, 11/70, HP 3000
Gate array	ECL	All			IBM 370/168, Amdahl 470/v6
Small-scale integration	ECL	Std.	80	Highest	CRAY 1

a billing machine, or implementing a word processing system become computer system design problems similar to those attacked over the first three generations. The hardware part of the design, the interface to the particular equipment, is straightforward. The major part of the design is the programming. Since the late 1940s, three generations have learned about computer design, especially programming. The first generation discovered and wrote about it. Then it was rediscovered and applied to minicomputer systems. This time, it is being learned by everyone who must use and program the microcomputer. Each time, for each individual or organization, the story is about the same: people start off by programming (using binary, octal, or hexadecimal codes) small tasks, using no structure or method of synchronizing the various multiple processes; the interrupt mechanism is learned, and the symbolic assembler is employed; and finally some more structured system, possibly an operating system, is employed. Occasionally, users move to high level languages or macroassemblers.

In view of this cyclical history, it seems likely that current digital systems design practice, which consists of building simple hardware interfaces to relatively poorly defined buses together with programming the application, will be relatively short lived. The design method of the future (fifth generation) will be at the PMS level component, although at the moment there are several factors that prevent this from being done reliably and cheaply by large numbers of engineers.

One factor which impedes this progress to the fifth generation is the (fundamental) interconnect problem. Currently, many small-scale integration components are required to handle the mismatch between microprocessor chips and memory and I/O subsystems. Furthermore, buses are hard to specify, as will be discussed in Chapter 11.

Another impediment is that system level behavior (the interaction of processors, memories, and transducers via switches and links) is less understood than is interaction at the register transfer level.

Of substantial assistance in easing the transition to the fifth generation would be base level operating systems that were embedded in hardware. These should be placed in read-only memory to give a feeling of permanence so that users would be less likely to embark on the expensive, unreliable rediscovery path.

In summary, standard components must be built that can be interfaced to a wide range of external systems, via clearly defined links, using parameters that are specified by a field programming method (instead of using logic design and building with interconnection on modules). In this way, the complexity of individual integrated circuits can be increased; and with a standard method for interconnection, higher volume and lower costs will result.

Design Costs versus Unit Costs

Before discussing the alternatives associated with integrated circuit design, it is important to characterize the various costs. Figure 9 shows, at a crude level, what the relative design costs might be for various inter- and intra-integrated circuit design methods. The design cost is highly variable depending on the project size, its goals, the manufacturing volumes expected, and most important, the computer aided design programs that are available.

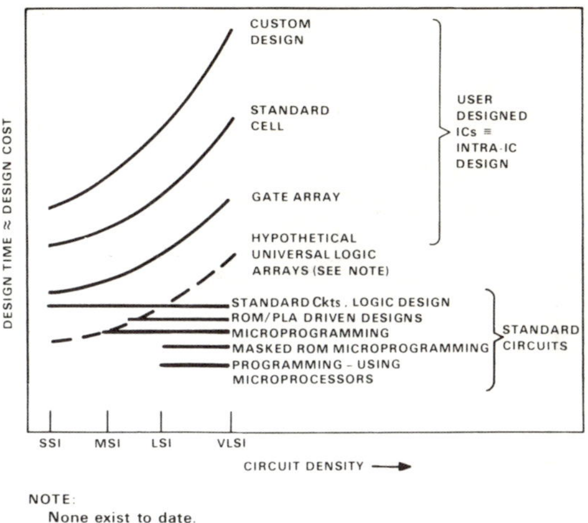

Figure 9. Current design cost (or time) versus circuit density using various design methods.

The lowest design cost is achieved by staying completely away from modifying the integrated circuits, except for programming read-only memories. There are two elements to the cost of read-only memories, programming cost and parts cost. The programming cost has already been discussed, so this discussion is limited to parts cost. There are two kinds of read-only memories, the programmable read-only memory (PROM) and the masked read-only memory (ROM). PROM chips have a higher initial cost than ROMs, but they provide some inventory advantages in a manufacturing environment because a common stock of unprogrammed parts can be divided into various programmed parts rather than stocking a full supply of each required part. In many high volume applications, however, the cost of the extra testing steps involved in the common stock approach, plus the extra piece part costs for PROMs, make masked ROMs preferable.

The design costs discussed in the preceeding paragraphs are summarized in Figure 10, which shows the costs for conventional programming, costs for microprogramming, and the design

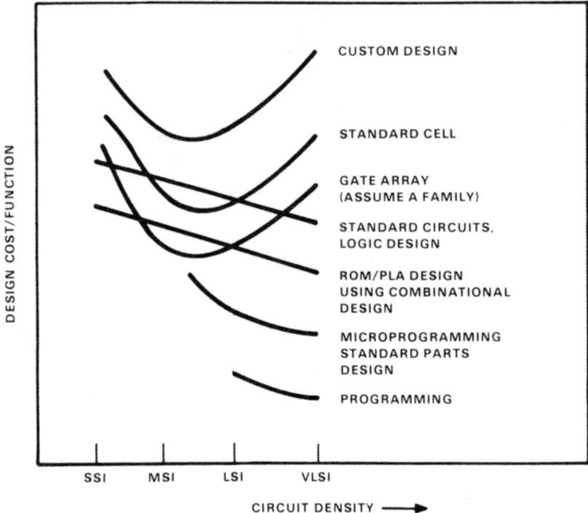

Figure 10. Manufacturing costs versus LSI circuit density for various design techniques.

costs for methods which use combinational techniques rather than programming techniques. These latter methods, employing read-only memories and programmable logic arrays, will be discussed shortly. The most costly approach of all shown in Figure 10, excluding intra-IC design, is design using standard circuits and associated design techniques.

Design of Integrated Circuits (Intra-IC Design)

Despite the prospects of higher design cost with custom integrated circuits than with standard integrated circuits, and, in some cases, higher manufacturing cost, there are numerous reasons that a designer is often forced to design integrated circuits. These are summarized in Table 7.

There are some drawbacks to custom integrated circuit design. These are listed in Table 8.

The use of custom integrated circuits to reduce the number of discrete components or to reduce the total number of integrated circuits in a machine improves the reliability because the reliability of a system is mostly a function of the number of explicit physical connections, including the bonds to the semiconductor die. Thus, the anticipated reliability of two equal functionality designs can be compared by counting discrete circuit pins, integrated circuit pins, module pins, and connector pins.

Gate Array Design

The most straightforward and extensively used intra-integrated circuit design method is to modify an existing design. If this approach cannot be used, the next most straightforward method is to use arrays of gates and interconnect them to form the desired function. Design with gate arrays occurs in a completely defined environment because there is only one circuit from which the gate is formed and the gate can be completely characterized. The manufacture of gate arrays is fairly simple because the fabrication technique of all but the last few semiconductor processing steps is identical for all designs. The customization, accomplished by interconnection of the gates by metal, is carried out last. Interconnection is a well understood aspect of logic design and is used to form the more complex macrostructures (various flip-flop types, adders, etc.) and then to form the higher levels of design by using arrays of gate arrays. A disadvantage of gate arrays is that gate array design methods do not permit the high density possible with the more custom methods because device placement is fixed.

It should be noted that gate array design is not a new idea brought about by the need for a simple method of customizing large-scale integrated circuits. Instead, it was one of the design philosophies advocated in the first few generations. The concept then was to have a single module containing a set of gates, and all subsequent logic design would be done in terms of that module. For example, flip-flops would be constructed by interconnecting the gates. A design predicated on a single module type immensely simplifies the spare stocking and servicing aspects, and it is possible to troubleshoot

Table 7. Reasons To Do Custom Integrated Circuit Design

1. A performance advantage can be gained.
2. Product life cycle costs can be lower if diagnosability and reliability features are added.
3. Diagnostic labor can be a high percentage of printed circuit board manufacturing cost. Diagnosis to the chip level can be sped up by features within the chip, and by a lower chip count, with a resultant lower manufacturing cost.
4. Data buses can be absorbed entirely within a chip to avoid bus interface costs. Even shortening a data bus from multi-board to single-board length may reduce cost and/or improve performance by reducing stored energy and its attendant drive/speed penalties.
5. Innovations concealed within a chip are difficult for competitors to study and duplicate.
6. Performance barriers may be breakable only through custom large-scale integration. In central processor design especially, and perhaps for certain memory interface applications, a custom integrated circuit approach may be the only practical way to get around conflicting issues of size, power, capacitance, etc.
7. In some engineering environments there are extremely small amounts of space or very little power.

Table 8. Reasons Not To Do Custom Integrated Circuit Design

1. For designs in the 100–500 equivalent gate complexity range, it may take up to a year to do the design with primitive design tools.
2. For designs in the 100–500 equivalent gate complexity range, it may take up to $100,000 to do the design.
3. Unless substantial product volumes are obtained, the chip cost will be high relative to off-the-shelf chips.
4. A decision will have to be made whether to have the design done by an outside vendor or within the company. This can be a very complicated and expensive decision.
5. The logic design and logic partitioning for large-scale integrated circuit design is different from that of conventional logic design, and designers used to dealing with conventional design will have to assimilate new knowledge to design large-scale integrated circuits themselves or even to talk with integrated circuit designers.

a problem by simply replacing circuits according to a pattern. Designers did not find these advantages important enough at that time, however, so the gate array concept was set aside until it was rediscovered by integrated circuit designers.

A representative gate array is a Raytheon RA-116. It has 300 TTL Schottky gates, of two cluster configurations, each repeated twelve times within the 160 mil × 160 mil chip:

Type 1
- 3 external driver gates (4-input NAND)
- 5 internal driver gates (3-input NAND)
- 5 internal expansion gates (3-input NAND)

Type 2
- 2 external driver gates (4-input NAND)
- 5 internal driver gates (3-input NAND)
- 5 internal expansion gates (3-input NAND)

Within each cluster, the expansion gates may be combined with the driver gates to form 7 or 8 input NAND gates and AND-OR-INVERT circuits with up to six product terms. The gates have a typical propagation delay of 5–6 nanoseconds and dissipate 5.5–6 milliwatts per driver and 1 milliwatt per OR expander. Two metal layers are used for interconnect, and the resulting circuitry can be connected to the outside world by means of 56 external pins, including power and ground.

Because the use of integrated circuit gate arrays is recent, data on package count reduction is scarce, but one informal study for the Raytheon RP-16 aerospace computer measured a nine to one replacement ratio and an overall improvement by a factor of 2 over a system constructed with standard components [Parke, 1978].

A 920-gate MOS array of 3 input NOR gates has been reported by Nakano *et al.*, [1978]. Its 3-nanosecond gate delay illustrates the performance potential as the metal oxide semiconductor process continues to progress toward smaller, faster gates. For truly high speed applications, an ECL gate array can be used. These devices, with subnanosecond speeds, exploit the inherent properties of current mode logic to obtain a particularly flexible element [Gaskill *et al.*, 1976].

Standard Cell Design

An alternative to gate array design is standard cell design. Standard cell design is identical to the logical design of the first few generations because there is a previously designed, well characterized set of primitive components (AND gates, flip-flops) in which the design is carried out. The advantage of the standard cell design methods is that special functions can be mixed on the chip in greater variety. There may also be a density advantage over gate arrays. However, in some schemes each cell occupies a different space and has a fixed shape. Careful planning of the cell arrangements is necessary to minimize loss of space. Hence, the improvement in packing density is not as substantial as direct comparisons between standard cell technology and gate array technology might at first indicate. In addition, if there are a large number of circuit types, their interconnection rules may not be characterized well enough to achieve a quick, cheap design that works the first time.

Custom Design

Custom design is in some ways a variant of the standard cell because designers typically have a set of favorite circuits which they interconnect to create designs for specified applications. With custom design, the designer can (theoretically) specify a circuit for each use within a particular logic design. For example, upon observing that a particular gate or flip-flop only drives a certain load, the designer can modify that gate or flip-flop to provide only the appropriate driving capability. Therefore, with custom design, the whole integrated circuit can theoretically be an optimum size, since each part is no larger than it need be. The advantages are clearly size, cost, and speed. The design costs are high because each part can, in principle, be customized. The quality of the circuit design is totally dependent on the designer, who must analyze each circuit geometry in terms of his expectation of performance, operating margins, etc. To the extent that this analysis is carried out, the circuit is clearly optimal.

Universal Logic Arrays, PROMs, and ROMs

Also shown in Figure 9 is a hypothetical line for universal logic arrays. For at least 15 years, academicians have studied the possibility of designing a single array of logical design elements, or a collection of such arrays, that could be interconnected on a custom basis to carry out a given function. The gate array can be looked at as the simplest example of this type of design. While many are skeptical that such a device exists, a line representing it is placed on the graph as a target for those who search for the one truly universal logic array.

Both programmable read-only memories and masked read-only memories are commonly used, but trivial, forms of the truly universal arrays, because they can be used in a table lookup fashion to create several functions of a number of input variables. For example, a 1,024 word read-only memory arranged in a 256 × 4-bit fashion can generate 4 independent functions of 8 variables. This is a distinct alternative for using a conventional gate structure to carry out combinational functions. A disadvantage of this method is that the required read-only memory size doubles for each additional input variable.

Programmable Logic Arrays

The progammable logic array (PLA) is a combinational circuit which remedies the disadvantages of the read-only memory implementation of combinational functions by allowing the use of product terms rather than completely decoding the input variables. Figure 11 shows a typical circuit, which consists of separate AND and OR arrays. Inputs are connected to the AND array, and outputs are drawn from the OR array. Each row in the programmable logic array can implement an AND function of selected inputs or their complements, thus forming a Boolean product term, and the OR array can combine the product terms to implement any Boolean function.

A simple application is operation-code decoding. For the PDP-11, the 16-bit Instruction Register could be directly connected to a programmable logic array and the output thereof used to specify the address of the microprogram that executed that instruction. Three different types of operation-code decoding are customarily applied to PDP-11 instructions: source mode decoding, destination mode decoding, and instruction decoding. With a programmable logic array implementation, a PLA could be used for each of these decoding operations, and only three chips would be required. A read-only memory implementation, on the other hand, would require 128 K × 8 bits for address mode decoding and 64 K × 8 bits for instruction decoding. Using 2 K × 8-bit read-only memories, 33 chips would be required. For this reason, modern minicomputers, such as the PDP-11/34, use programmable logic arrays rather than read-only memories or combinational logic for instruction decoding. The technique is also extended downward into microcomputers such as the LSI-11, where programmable logic arrays are used to conserve the die area used by the microcomputer control units.

The programmable logic array becomes an even more useful building block when it is made field programmable – the FPLA. The programmable connectors shown in Figure 11 are fusible nichrome links that are burned out when the unit is programmed.

When a register is added to the outputs of the programmable logic array and incorporated in the same integrated circuit, a simple sequential machine is obtained in one package. Since register circuit packages are pin intensive, adding registers to programmable logic arrays (or to read-only memories) permits about a factor of 2 package count reduction in typical applications.

The first programmable logic arrays had propagation times of the order of 150 nanoseconds and were thus suitable building blocks for slow, low-cost computers. Propagation times of 45 nanoseconds are quite common today, and the programmable logic array is now more widely used. An attractive application with these higher speed components is the replacement of the small-scale integration and

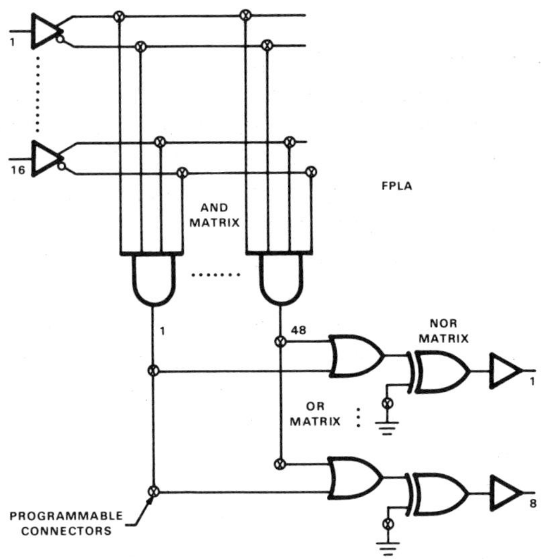

Figure 11. Signetics field programmable logic array (FPLA) (courtesy of Signetics Corporation, from *Signetics Field Programmable Logic Arrays – An Applications Manual,* February 1977; copyright © 1977 by Signetics Corporation).

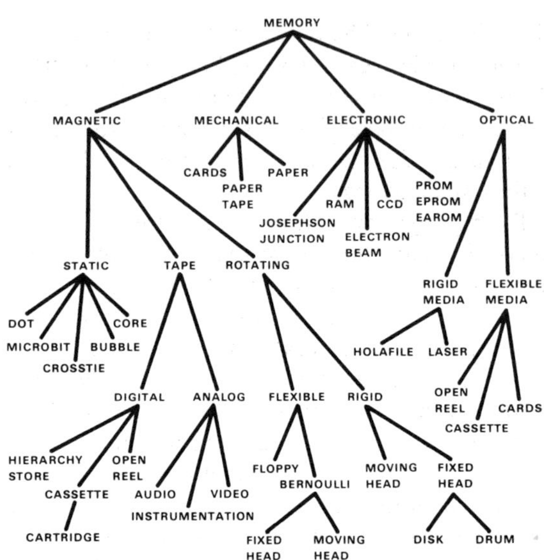

Figure 12. Family tree of memory technology (courtesy of Memorex Corporation and S.H. Puthuff, 1977).

medium-scale integration packages used to implement the control logic for Unibus arbitration in PDP-11 computers.

A more complex application than instruction decoding has been documented [in Logue *et al.*, 1975]. An IBM 7441 Buffered Terminal Control Unit was implemented using programmable logic arrays and compared with a version implemented with small- and medium-scale integration. The programmable logic array design included two sets of registers fed by the OR array (PLA outputs): one set fed back to the AND array (PLA inputs); the other set held the PLA outputs. A factor of 2 reduction in printed circuit board count was obtained with the programmable logic array version. The seven programmable logic arrays used in the design replaced 85 percent of the circuits in the small- and medium-scale intregration version. Of these circuits, 48 percent were combinational logic and 52 percent were sequential logic.

MEMORY TECHNOLOGY

The previous section discussed the use of memory for microprogramming and table lookup in logic design, but that is not the principal use of memory in the computer industry. The more typical use of memory components is to form a hierarchy of storage levels which hold information on a short-term basis while a program runs and on a longer term basis as permanent files. Figure 12 shows the various technologies employed in these memory applications. Although the principal focus of this section is on core and semiconductor memories, slower speed electromechanical memories (drums, disks, and tapes) are considered superficially, as their performance and price improvements have pushed the computer evolution. Because the typical uses for memory usually require read and write capabilities, write-once or read-only memory such as video disks is excluded from the discussion.

Measurement Parameters

Because memory is the simplest of components, it should be possible to discuss memory using a minimal number of measurement parameters. One of the most important parameters is the state of development of the memory technology at the time the other parameters are measured, relative to the likely life span of that technology. Unfortunately, this is one of the most difficult parameters to quantify, although its effects are readily observable, principally in the rate of change of the other parameters associated with that technology. Thus, in new technologies many of the parameters vary rapidly with time. This is particularly true of semiconductor memory price, which has declined at a compound rate of 28 percent per year (which amounts to about 50 percent in two years). The price is expressed only as price/bit, but it is important to know the price (or size) of the total memory system for which that price applies. To get the lowest price per bit, a user may be forced to a large system because of economy of scale.

Performance for cyclical memories, both the electromechanical types such as disks and the electronic types such as bubbles, is expressed in two parameters: the time to access the start of a block of memory and the number of bits that can be accessed per second after the transfer begins. Other parameters, such as power consumption, temperature sensitivity, space consumption, and weight, affect the utility of memories in various applications. In addition, reliability measures are needed to see how much redundancy must be placed in the memory system to operate at a given level of availability and data integrity.

In summary, the relevant parameters for a given memory are:

1. State of development of the technology at the time the measurements are taken relative to the likely life span of the technology.
2. Price per bit.
3. Total memory size or total memory price.
4. Performance.
   a. Access time to the first word of the block.
   b. Time to transfer each word (data rate) in the block.
5. Operational power, temperature, space, weight.
6. Volatility.
7. Reliability and repairability.

As indicated by the rapidity of the parameter changes, a good example of a technology that is young relative to its expected total lifetime is semiconductor memory. Figure 7 gives past prices and expected future prices of semiconductor memory. As mentioned above, these memories have declined in price every two years by 50 percent, and that rate of decline is expected to continue well into the 1980s because of continued increases in semiconductor densities. Figure 13, a graph by Dean Toombs of Texas Instruments, shows memory size versus performance with time for random-access memories, and cyclically accessed charge-coupled devices (CCDs) and magnetic bubbles.

Core and Semiconductor Memory Technology for Primary Memory

The core memory was developed early in the first generation for Whirlwind (1953) and remained the dominant primary memory component for computers until it began to be superseded by semiconductor technology. The advent of the 1-Kbit memory chip in 1972 started the demise of core as the dominant primary memory medium, and the crossover point occurred for most memory designs with the availability of the 4-Kbit semiconductor chip in 1974.

Over the period since the early 1960s, the price of core memory declined roughly at a rate

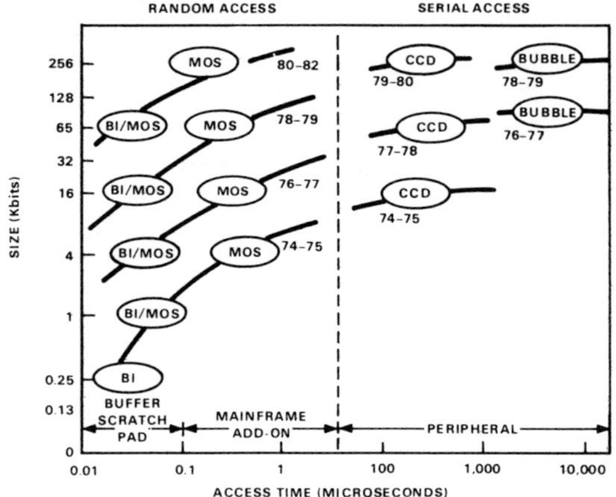

Figure 13. Memory size versus access time for various memories and yearly availability (courtesy of Dean Toombs, Texas Instruments, Inc.).

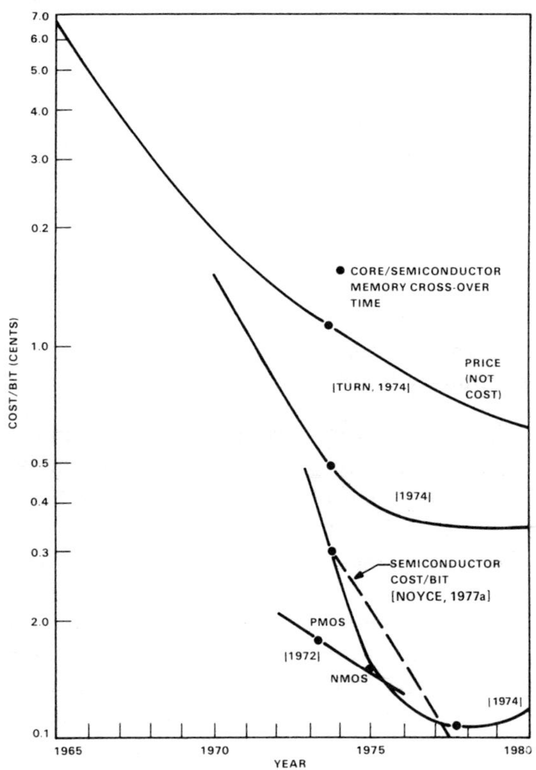

Figure 14. Cost per bit of core memory estimated by various market surveys and future predictions.

of 19 percent per year. This decline can be seen in the DEC 12-bit machine memory prices, the DEC 18-bit machine memory prices, and in the IBM 360/370 memory prices (since 1964). The price of PDP-10 memory has declined at 30 percent per year, although it is unclear why. A possible reason is that the modular memory structure had a high overhead cost; with subsequent implementations, the memory module size was increased, thereby giving an effective decrease in overhead electronics and packaging costs and a greater decrease in the cost per bit.

The cost of various memories was projected by several technology marketing groups in the period 1972–1974. Each study attempted to analyze and determine the core/semiconductor memory crossover point. Three such studies are plotted in Figure 14 along with Turn's [1974] memory price data and Noyce's [1977a] semiconductor memory cost (less overhead electronics) projection. Most crossover points were projected to be in 1974, whereas one study showed a 1977 crossover. Even though all studies were done at about the same time, the variation in the studies shows the problem of getting consistent data from technology forecasts.

While these graphs of core and semiconductor prices and performance permit an understanding of trends in the principal use areas for these devices, additional information is needed for disk and tape memory in order to complete the collection of memory technologies that can be used to form a single memory hierarchy.

Disk Memories

Disk memories are a significant part of most systems costs in the middle-range minicomputer systems; in larger systems, they dominate the costs.

Although access time is determined by the rotational delays and the moving head arm speed, the single performance metric that is most often used is simply memory capacity and the resultant cost/bit. In the subsequent section on memory hierarchies, it will be argued that performance parameters are less important than cost because more higher speed memory can be traded off to gain the same system level performance at a lower cost.

Memory capacity is measured in disk surface areal density (i.e., the number of bits per in^2) and is the product of the number of bits recorded along a track and the number of tracks of the disk. Figure 15 shows the progress in areal recording densities using digital recording methods. Figure 16 shows the price of the state-of-the-art large, multiple platter, moving head disks. Note that the price decline is a factor of 10 in 9 years, for a price decline of 22 percent per year.

Figure 17 shows the performance plotted against the price per bit for the technology in 1975 and 1980.

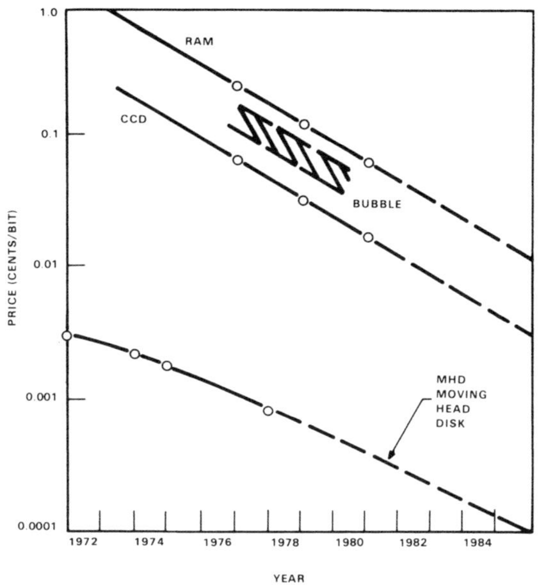

Figure 16. Price per bit of large, moving head disks and semiconductor memories (courtesy of Memorex Corporation, 1977).

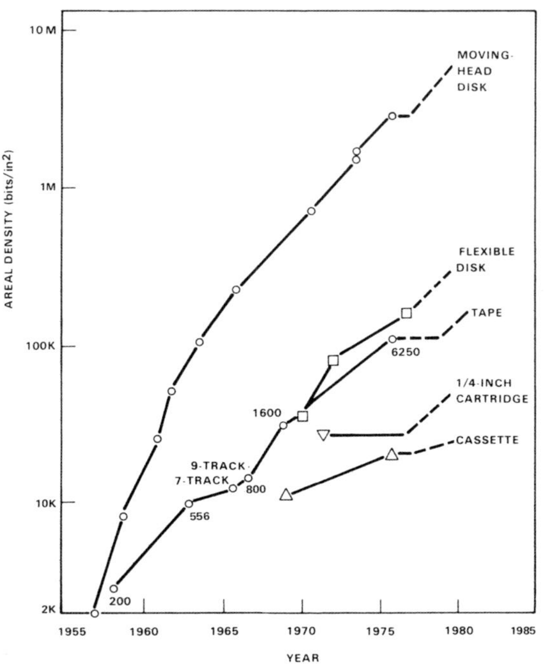

Figure 15. Areal density of various digital magnetic recording media (courtesy of Memorex Corporation, 1978).

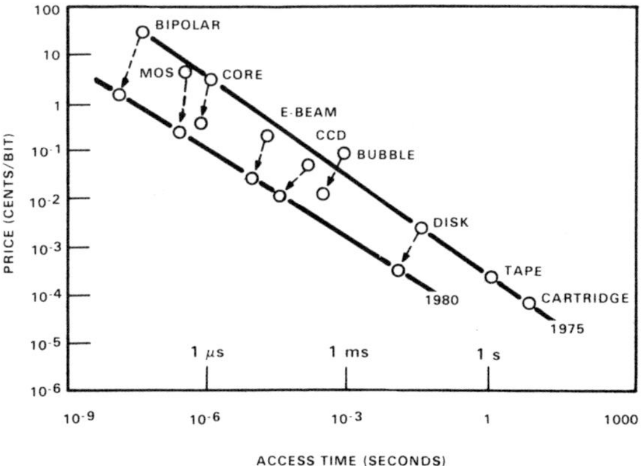

Figure 17. Memory trends, 1975–1980 (courtesy of Memorex Corporation, 1978).

Magnetic Tape Units

Figure 18 shows the relevant performance characteristics of magnetic tape units. The data is for several IBM tape drives between 1952 and 1973. It shows that the first tape units started out at 75 inches per second and achieved a speed of 200 inches per second by 1973. Although this amounts to only a 5 percent improvement per year in speed over a 21-year period, this is a rather impressive gain considering the physical mass movement problems involved. It is akin to a factor of 3 improvement in automobile speed.

The bit density (in bits per linear inch) has improved from 100 to 6,250 in the same period, for a factor of 62.5, or 23 percent per year. With the speed and density improvements, the tape data rate has improved by a factor of 167, or 29 percent per year.

Tape unit prices (Figure 19) are based on the various design styles. Slow tape units (minitapes) are built for lowest cost. The most cost effective seem to be around 75 inches per second (the initial design), if one considers only the tape. High performance units, though disproportionately expensive, provide the best system cost effectiveness.

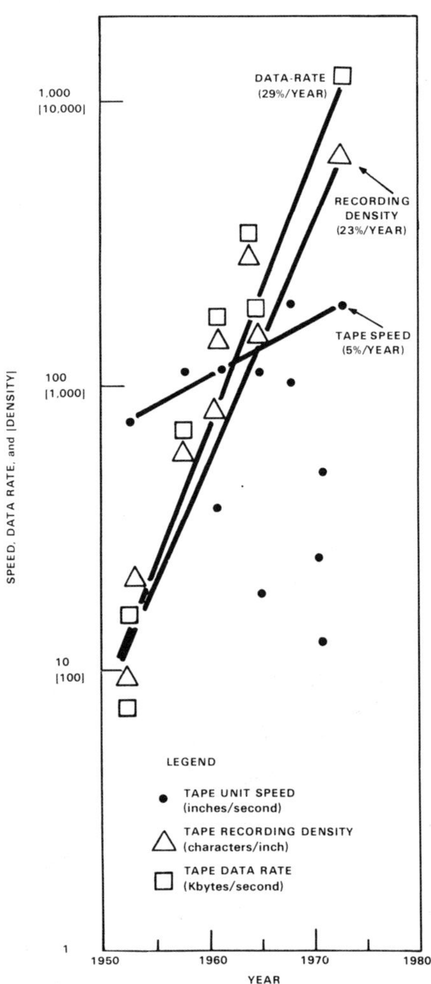

Figure 18. Characteristics of various IBM magnetic tape units versus time.

Memory Hierarchies

A memory hierarchy, according to Strecker [1978:72], "is a memory system built of a number of different memory technologies: relatively small amounts of fast, expensive technologies and relatively large amounts of slow, inexpensive technologies. Most programs possess the property of locality: the tendency to access a

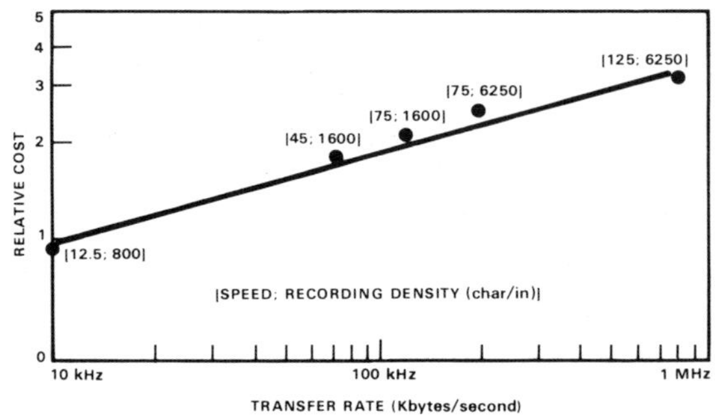

Figure 19. Relative cost versus transfer rate for various tape drives and controllers (1978).

small, slowly varying subset of the memory locations they can potentially access. By exploiting locality, a properly designed memory hierarchy results in most processor references being satisfied by the faster levels of the hierarchy and most memory locations residing in the inexpensive levels. Thus, in the limit a memory hierarchy approaches the performance of the fastest technology and the per bit cost of the least expensive technology."

The key to achieving maximum performance per dollar from a memory hierarchy is to develop algorithms for moving information back and forth between the various types of storage in a fashion that exploits locality as much as possible. Two examples of hierarchies which depend on program locality for their effectiveness are the one level store (demand paging), first seen on the Atlas computer [Kilburn *et al.*, 1962], and the cache, described by Wilkes [1965] and first seen on the IBM 360/85 [Liptay, 1968]. Because both of these are automatically managed (exploiting locality), they are transparent to the programmer. This is in contrast to the case where a programmer uses secondary memory for file storage: in that case, he explicitly references the medium, and its use is no longer transparent.

Table 9 lists, in order of memory speed, the memories used in current-day hierarchies.

Table 9. Computer System Memory Component and Technology

Part	Transparency (To Machine Language Programs)	Characteristics on Which Its Use Is Based
Microprogram memory	Yes	Very fast
Processor state	No	Very small, very fast register set (e.g., 16 words)
Alternative processor state context	Yes	Same (so speed up processor context swaps)
Cache memory	Yes	Fast. Used in larger machines for speed.
Program mapping and segmentation	Yes	Small associative store
Primary (program) memory	No	Relatively fast, and large depending on processor speed
Paging memory	Yes	Can be electromechanical, e.g., drum, fixed head disk, or moving head disk. Can be CCD or bubbles.
Local file memory	No	Usually moving head disk, relatively slow, low cost.
Archival files memory	Yes (preferably)	Very slow, very cheap to permit information to be kept forever.

There is a continuum based on need together with memory technology size, cost, and performance parameters.

The following sections discuss the individual elements of the heirarchy shown in Table 9.

Microprogram Memories. Nearly every part of the hierarchy can be observed in the computers in this book. Part III describes PDP-11 implementations that use microprogramming. These microprogram memories are transparent to the user, except in machines such as the PDP-11/60 and LSI-11 which provide user microprogramming via a writable control store. Mudge (Chapter 13) describes the writable control storage user aspects associated with the 11/60 and the user microprogramming.

In retrospect, DEC might have built on the experience gained from the small read-only memory used for the PDP-9 (1967) and exploited the idea earlier. In particular, a read-only memory implementation might have produced a lower cost PDP-11/20 and might have been used to implement lower cost PDP-10s earlier.

In principle, it is possible to have a cache to hold microprograms; hence, there could be another level to the hierarchy. At the moment, this would probably be used only in high cost/high performance machines because of the overhead cost of the loading mechanism and the cache control. However, like so many other technical advances, it will probably migrate down to lower cost machines.

Processor State Registers. To the machine language program, the number of registers in the processor state is a very visible part of the architecture. This number is solely dictated by the availability of fast access, low cost registers. It is also occasionally the means of classifying architectures (e.g., single accumulator based, general register based, and stack based).

In 1964, even though registers were not available in single integrated circuit packages, the PDP-6 adopted the general register structure because the cost of registers was only a small part of the system cost. In Chapter 21 on the PDP-10, there is a discussion of whether an architecture should be implemented with general registers in an explicit (non-transparent) fashion, or whether the stack architecture should be used. Although a stack architecture does not provide registers for the programmer to manage, most implementations incur the cost of registers for the top few elements of the stack. The change in register use from accumulator based design to general register based design and the associated increase in the number of registers from 1 to 8 or 16 can be observed in comparisons of the 12-bit and 18-bit designs with the later PDP-10 and PDP-11 designs.

Alternative Processor State Context Registers. As the technology improved, the number of registers increased, and the processor state storage was increased to provide multiple sets of registers to improve process context switching time.

Cache Memory. In the late 1960s, the cache memory was introduced for large scale computers. This concept was then applied to the latest PDP-10 processor (KL10). It was applied to the PDP-11/70 in 1975 when the relatively large (1 Kbit), relatively fast (factor of 5 faster than previously available) memory chip was introduced. The cache is described and discussed extensively in Chapter 10. It derives much power by the fact that it is an automatic mechanism and is transparent to the user. It is the best example of the use of the principle of memory locality. For example, a well designed cache of 4 Kbytes can hold enough local computational memory so that, independent of program size, 90 percent of the accesses to memory are via the cache.

Program Mapping and Segmentation. A similar memory circuit is required to manage (map) multiprogrammed systems by providing relocation and protection among various user programs. The requirements are similar to the cache and may be incorporated in the caching structure. The PDP-10 models with the KI10 processor use an associative memory for this mapping function, and the VAX 11/780 uses a 64-entry, 2-way associative memory.

Paging Memory. The Atlas computer [Kilburn, *et al.*, 1962] was designed to have a single, one level, large memory. This structure ultimately evolved so that multiple users could each have a large virtual address and virtual machine. The paging mechanism works because of the locality exhibited by program references. Denning pointed out the clustering of pages for a given program at a given time and introduced the notion of the working set [1968]. For most programs, the number of pages accessed locally is small compared with the total program size. Initially, a magnetic drum was used to implement the paging memory; but as disk technology began to dominate the drum, both fixed head and moving head disks (backed up with larger primary memories) were used as the paging memories. Denning's tutorial article [1970] is an excellent discussion of this section of the memory hierarchy. In the next few years, the relatively faster and cheaper charge coupled device semiconductor memories and bubble memories are clearly the candidates for paging memories. Hodges [1975] compares the candidates for paging memory in terms of reliability, power, cost per bit, and packaging.

Local File Memory and Archival File Memory. For local file memory in medium-sized to large-scale systems there is no alternative to disks. Archival files, however, are usually kept on magnetic tapes, which permit files to be stored cheaply on an indefinite basis. There are usually fewer memory technologies used in smaller systems than in larger systems because the smaller systems cannot afford the overhead costs (disk drives, tape drives, etc.) associated with the various technologies. At most, two levels of storage would probably exist as separate entities in smaller systems.

Alternatively, one might expect a combination of floppy disk, low cost tape, and magnetic bubbles to be used to reduce the primary memory size and to provide file and archival memory. Currently, the floppy disk operates as a single level memory. Here there are two alternatives for technology tradeoff using parts in the hierarchy: a tape or floppy disk can be used to provide removability and archivability, whereas bubbles or charge-coupled devices can be used to provide performance. The Strecker paper [1978] quoted at the beginning of this section on memory hierarchies elaborates on these concepts.

MEASURING (AND CREATING) TECHNOLOGY PROGRESS

The previous sections have presented technology in terms of exponentially decreasing prices and/or exponentially increasing performance. This section presents a basis for this constant change rate. The progress of a particular technology as a function of time, $T(t)$, has been classically observed to be:

$$T(t) = K \times e^{ct}$$

where K = the base technology at the beginning of the time frame, and c = a learning constant.

This can be converted to a yearly improvement rate, r, by changing the base of the exponential to:

$$T(t) = T \times r^{t-t0}$$

where T = the base technology at $t0$, and r = yearly increase (or decrease) in the technology metric.

This is the same form used for declining (or increasing) cost from base c:

$$C = c \times r^{t-t0}$$

Clearly there are manufactured goods that neither improve nor decrease in price exponentially, although many presumably could with the proper design and manufacturing tooling investments. The notion of price decline is completely tied to the cumulative learning curves of: (1) people building a product for a long time, (2) process improvement based on learning to build it better, and (3) design improvement by engineers learning from the history of design. Production learning *per se* is inadequate to drive cost and prices down because, after an extremely long time in production, more units contribute little to learning. With inflation in labor costs, the costs actually rise when the learning is flat. In order to provide a base for predicting the inflationary effect, the consumer price index has been plotted in Figure 20.

Learning curves do not appear to be understood beyond intuition. They are (empirical) observations that the amount of human energy, En, required to produce the nth item is:

$$En = K \times n^d$$

where K and d are learning constants. Thus, by producing more items, the repetitive nature of a task causes learning, and the time (and perhaps cost) to produce an item decreases with the number produced and not with the calendar time in which an object is produced.

In his study of technology progress, Fusfeld [1973] took six items, chose a measure of progress in the production thereof, and plotted that measure against cumulative units produced. In each case, he found a relationship of the form:

$$Ti = a \times i^b$$

where i is the number of units produced and Ti is the value of his selected technology progress measure at the ith unit – the same as the learning curves would predict.

The graph for turbojet engines, where he used fuel consumed per pound as the technology measure, is reproduced in Figure 21. The results for all six items studied are shown in Table 10.

Where two values are given for the technology progress constant, a second rate of progress was observed after a significant shift in the industry occurred. For example, such a shift occurred in the automobile industry in the late 1920s when the acceptance of the automobile, the development of a new tire, and the expansion of the public road network operated concurrently to change the nature of the industry.

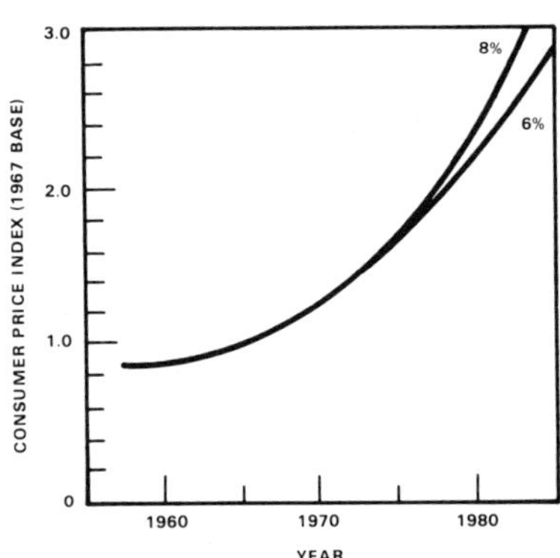

Figure 20. Consumer Price Index using 1967 as base.

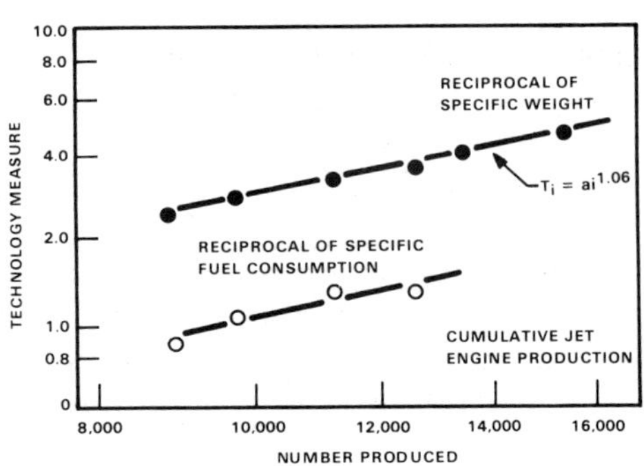

Figure 21. Technology progress functions for turbojet engines [Fusfeld, 1973].

Examination of the table will reveal substantial variations in the technology progress constant from item to item. This is probably because most of the technologies represented above are mechanically oriented with associated physical limits. Computer technology is electronically oriented and has not yet reached its limits. In essence, the table is comparing systems constrained by Newton's Laws with those constrained by Maxwell's Equations.

Using the two formulas,

$$T(t) = K \times e^{ct}$$

and

$$Ti = a \times i^{b}$$

Fusfeld [1973] related the unit learning curve concept to the more conventional, timely view of technology progress when the number of units produced increases exponentially with time, that is, relations expressed in the first two formulas are equivalent when the condition expressed by the following formula holds:

$$i = e^{c/b \times t}$$

This previous formula indicates that the production rate is a constant fraction of the total production to date – i.e., production occurs with exponential growth.

While the Fusfeld information shows interesting results, it does not explain why technology improves exponentially, nor does it explain why cost declines exponentially. Learning curves and an exponential increase in the quantity of items produced may depress cost, but simple production learning does not account for the rapid technology changes in the integrated circuit, for example, where totally different production processes have been evolved to support the greater technology.

In the computer industry, the mobility of technical personnel from company to company has certainly been a significant factor in technology innovation. The strongest force toward technology innovation in the computer industry, however, has been the computer users. They have been doing a significant portion of the inventing, both in hardware development and in software development. Although the case studies in this book indicate several specific places where users have influenced hardware design, it would be a substantial oversight not to mention the profound effect users had on the creation of PL/1 and COBOL. Furthermore, all applications work is done first by users and then developed by manufacturers at a later date along the lines of the above model.

The Influence of Technology Innovation on Cost

The cost of computing is the sum of the costs which correspond to the various levels-of-integration described in Chapter 1, plus the operational costs. The levels are integrated circuits,

Table 10. Fusfeld's [1973] Measures of Technology Progress

Item	Measure, Ti	Quantity Produced (i)	Technology Progress (b)	Change Observed In Study	Total Change
Light bulbs	Lumens/bulb	10^{10}	0.04; 0.19	33	80
Automobiles	Vehicle h.p.	3×10^{7}; 10^{8}	0.11; 0.74	10	6; 13
Titanium	Psi/$/16	3×10^{8}	0.3; 1; 1.04	10	350
Aircraft	Maximum speed	2×10^{5}	0.33–1.2	6	56
Turbojet engines	Fuel consumed, weight	1.6×10^{4}	1.06	2	2.9×10^{4}
Computers	Memory size × rate	10^{5}	2.51	10^{9}	3.5×10^{12}

boards, boxes, cabinets, operating systems, standard languages, special languages, applications components, and applications. In practice, each additional level-of-integration is often looked at as overhead. Using standard accounting practice, the basic hardware cost, at the lowest level, is then multiplied by an overhead factor at each subsequent outer level. While an overhead-based model may work operationally for a stable set of technologies, such a model will not adequately allow for rapidly evolving technologies or the elimination of levels. By examining each level, observations can be made about the use and substitution of technology. More importantly, conclusions can be drawn about how structures are likely to evolve.

Cost, Performance, and Economy of Scale

For most technologies used in the computer industry, there is a relationship between cost, performance, and economy of scale:

$$\text{Performance} = k \times \text{cost}^{s} \times r^{t}$$

where k = base case performance, s = economy of scale coefficient, r = rate of improvement of technology, and t = calendar time.

There are four possibilities for the effect of economy of scale on the production of any device. These are:

1. Economy of scale holds. A particular object can be implemented at any price, and the performance varies exponentially with price.
   $\text{Performance} = k \times \text{price}^{s}; s > 1$
2. Linear price performance relationship.
   a. $\text{Performance} = k \times \text{price}$
   b. $\text{Performance} = \text{base} + K \times \text{price}$
3. Constant performance, price independent.
   $\text{Performance} = k$
4. Only a particular device has been implemented. The performance (or size) is a linear sum of such devices.
   $\text{Performance} = n \times (k \times \text{price})$

Sometimes, economy of scale effects are observed in situations where they would not normally be expected. For example, assume a performance improvement feature exists that costs the same whether it is added to a large computer or added to a small computer. Adding that feature to a product that is already high priced will have a modest effect (say 5 percent) on the cost but a substantial effect (say 100 percent) on the performance. Adding the same constant cost feature to a lower cost product will have a substantial effect (say 200 percent) on the cost but only a performance effect (again 100 percent) similar to that obtained with the higher cost system. This condition is especially true in disks and computer systems. Use of a particular recording method employing costly logic for encoding/decoding, or addition of a cache memory, is often employed to the high priced systems first. With time and learning, the technique can then be applied to lower cost systems. For example, cache, a nearly perfect example of the constant cost add-on, first appeared in such large machines as the IBM 360/85 in 1968 and later migrated down to large minicomputers such as the PDP-11/70 in 1975. On a research basis, cache even reached the small minicomputer, the cache-based PDP-8/E at Carnegie-Mellon University (Chapter 7).

In Figure 22, the cost of the lowest price unit is kept to a minimum and decreases, while the cost of the mid-range product continues to increase. The cost of the highest performance product increases the most, because it can afford the overhead costs. Looking at the basic technology metric, there are really three curves, as shown in Figure 23. The first curve represents the application of new technology to a high cost/high performance product to get a substantial performance improvement. With time, the technology evolves and is reapplied to the mid-range products (the first level copy), and finally, several years later, the technique becomes commonplace and is applied to low cost

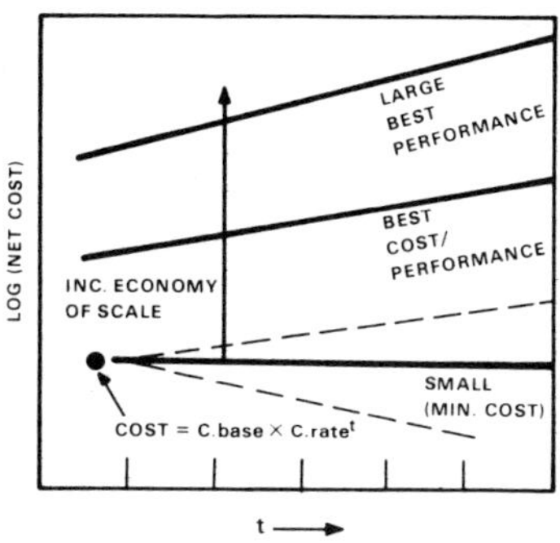

Figure 22. Cost versus time.

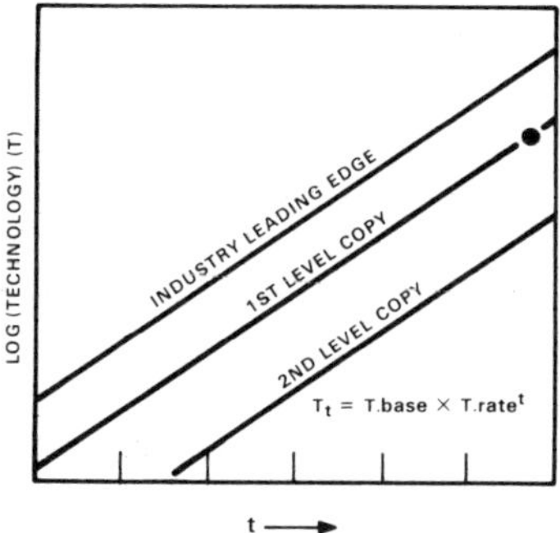

Figure 23. Technology versus time.

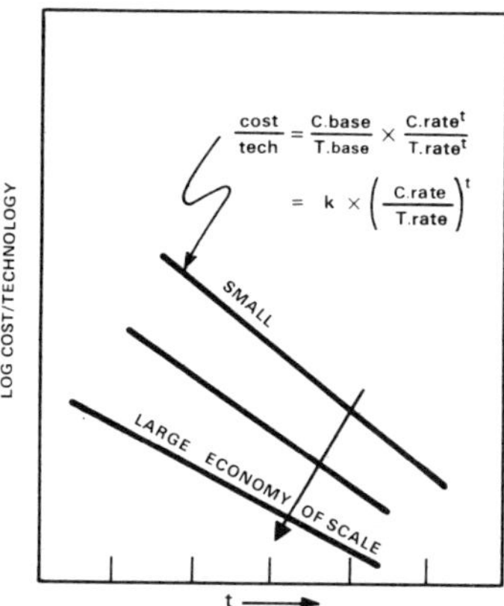

Figure 24. Cost/technology versus time.

products (second level copies). The resultant cost/performance ratios are shown in Figure 24.

The management of technology by applying it to products in various price and performance ranges occurs in a more or less ordered fashion in most industries, but has not occurred to the extent that it has in the computer industry. This is probably because no other industries have evolved in the same rapid and broad fashion as have the computer and semiconductor industries. The computer industry is fundamentally driven by the semiconductor technology push on the one hand, and by IBM on the other. IBM follows the strategy of applying technology on an economy of scale basis. This permits the technology to be first tested at the high performance/high price lower volume systems before being introduced in higher volume production. The following examples (from IBM) show this at work. In printing, the high price/low volume to low price/ high volume introduction cycle was followed in the use of dot matrix printing, chain printing, ink-jet printing, and computer printing as a precursor to systems products using xerography. In magnetic storage, the cycle saw the basic technology for large disks as a precursor to the use of similar technology on smaller disks.

Technology Substitution

The cost and performance of a computer system are roughly the additive and multiplication functions, respectively, of the parts. The technologies represented in those parts each evolve at their own rates. Usually, when one component begins to dominate the cost (e.g., packaging) or constrain the performance, then pressure occurs to more rapidly change and improve the associated technology to avoid the cost or performance bottleneck. Sometimes a slowly evolving technology is just eliminated as a substitute is found. The following is a list of some of the substitutions that have occurred:

1. Semiconductor memories are now used in place of core memories. Since the latter has evolved more slowly in terms of price decline, semiconductors are now used to the exclusion of cores. (This has not occurred where information must be retained in the memory during periods of time without power.)
2. Read-only semiconductor memories are now substituted for semiconductor logic elements.
3. In a similar way, programmable logic arrays can be potentially substituted for read-only memories, and true content addressable memories can replace various read-write and read-only memories.
4. The judicious use of charge-coupled devices or bubble memories can cause drastic reduction (and quite possibly the elimination) of the use of MOS random-access memories for primary memory. The fixed head disk could be eliminated at the same time.
5. For small systems, the main operational memories could be completely nonelectromechanical; electromechanical memories (e.g., tape cassettes and floppies) would be used for loading files into the system and for archives. For even lower cost systems, semiconductor read-only memories could replace cassettes and floppies for program storage, as in programmable calculators.

After a while those components of computer system cost which are decreasing less rapidly than other components, remaining static, or are rising (like the packaging and power) may become a significant fraction of the total cost. Because costs are additive, the exponential decrease in some costs, such as those for semiconductor logic and memories, will cause the costs that are not similarly decreasing to be more evident. This causes pressure for structural change and may cause new packaging, for example, to become an especially important attribute of a new design. For instance, although the PDP-8 is normally considered to be the first minicomputer, it postdates the CDC 160 (1960) and DEC's PDP-5 (1963). However, the PDP-8 was unique in its use of technology because:

1. It eliminated the full frame cabinets used by other systems. This also presented a new computer style such that users could embed the computer in their own cabinets. A separate small box held the processor, memory, and many options.
2. Automatic wire-wrap technology was used to reduce printed circuit board interconnection cost. This also eliminated errors and reduced checkout time.
3. Printed circuit board costs were reduced by using machine insertion of components.
4. The Teletype Corporation Model 33 Automatic Send Receive (ASR) teleprinter (also used on PDP-5) was connected as the peripheral. It had a combined printer, keyboard, and paper tape I/O device (for program loading). It eliminated the paper tape reader and punch.

Technology Progress, Product Development, and the State-of-the-Art Line

If there were no such thing as technological progress, there would be no such thing as an obsolete product. In such a situation, it would not matter when a product was introduced into the market, as it would be technically equal to the other products available. In the computer industry, this is far from the case: for computer processors, peripherals, and systems, there is a state-of-the-art line that indicates the average technological level at which present products are being offered. Since higher technology has generally meant better price/performance, new products introduced in the market must have a proper relationship to the state-of-the-art line. The following paragraphs elaborate on the interaction between technology progress, product development, and the state-of-the-art line.

The complete development process can be envisioned as a pipeline process with the following stages: research, applied research, advanced development (product breadboard), development, test, sell/build, and use. In this model, ideas and information flow through the various organizations in a process-like fashion, culminating in a product. Each product type has a different set of delays associated with the parts of the pipeline. At the end of the pipeline, the "education of use" delay occurs while the prospective customers are taught how the product meets their needs; this delay culminates in market demand. For well defined, commodity-like products such as disks and primary memory, the education of use delay is zero, as each user "knows" the product. For a new language, on the other hand, there is a large education of use delay, and the market demand usually develops slowly.

The disk supply process is a good example of the pipeline nature of the development process. The technology (as measured by the number of bits per areal inch) doubles about every two years (i.e., the density improves 41 percent per year). IBM is estimated to invest about 100 million dollars per year in the development and associated manufacturing process pipelines. Because of this massive investment, the IBM disks essentially establish the state-of-the-art line in a structure that is typified by Figure 23. Using the pipeline development process, development of competitive disks by other companies would lie somewhere about four to six years behind the state-of-the-art line. This can be seen by looking at the development process and taking into account the delays through each stage. To be more competitive, the disk industry short circuits various delays by engaging in reverse engineering; this results in only two-year lags. In reverse engineering, the tools are micrometers and reverse molds. At the time of the first shipment of a new product by the technology leader, the product is purchased by competitors and basically copied on a function per function basis. The more successful designs use pin for pin compatibility to take maximum advantage of the leader's design decisions.

From the process, it is also easy to see how merely copying competitive products guarantees products that will be at least two years behind leadership products and lagging behind the state-of-the-art. Nonetheless, if there is a strong market function which operates to define products based on existing product use, and if the design and manufacturing process at the copying company is quite rapid, such a strategy can be effective. The copying process can also be very effective for software products because, while there are no delays associated with manufacture, the time to learn about the product provides a time window in which copiers can catch up with the leaders.

A high technology, exponentially increasing (volume) product is denoted by:

1. Exponential yearly cost improvement (price decline) rates through product technology improvements as measured by price decline of greater than 20 percent (e.g., disk price this year = 0.8 last year's disk price, CPU = 0.79, primary memory = 0.7).
2. Short product life (less than 4 years).
3. Various types of learning curves. Some products require very little learning, while others require a great deal of learning or require re-learning because of personnel turnover or the frequent hiring of additional personnel.

The Product Problem (Behind the State-of-the-Art)

Typical product situations, including competitive "problems," can be seen in Figure 25. When a product is introduced to the market, it has a relationship to the state-of-the-art line. There are five possible situations:

1. Ideal (on the state-of-the-art line).
2. Advanced (moves below the line).
3. Late (slip in time to the right).
4. Expensive (more than expected in cost, straight above the line).
5. Late and expensive (to the right and above the line).

Situations 3, 4, and 5 are product problems because they are behind the state-of-the-art line and, hence, less competitive. This implies increased sales costs, lower margins, loss of sales, and so on. Note that a late product could be acceptable if somehow the cost were lower. Similarly, an expensive product is acceptable if it appears earlier in time.

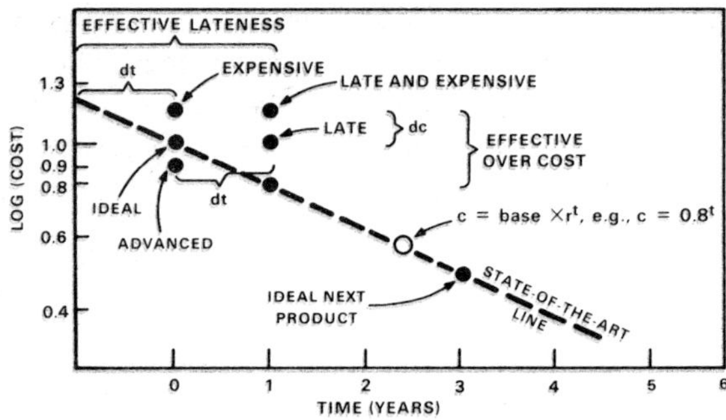

Figure 25. Use of the state-of-the-art line to model product cost problems and timing problems.

Time Is Money (and vice versa)

Thus, product problems can be solved by either:

1. Movement in time (left) to get on the line.
2. Movement in cost (straight down) to get on the line.

With exponential price declines, a family of products over a long time will follow a cost curve, c:

$$c = b \times r^t$$

where c = cost at time, t (in years), b = base cost, and r = rate of price decline.

With dc = change in cost above (or below) to get back to the state-of-the-art line and dt = delay (or advance) in time to get back to the state-of-the-art line, let:

$f = dc/c$ = fraction of cost away from line
$f = 1 - r^{dt}$ = (poor cost, expressed as project slip)

and:

$dt = \ln(1 - f)/\ln(r)$ = (poor timing, expressed as poor cost)

These formulas permit the interchange of time and money (cost). For example, in disks or central processors where $r = 0.8$ and $\ln .8 = 0.22$, note:

$$f = 1 - 0.8^{dt}$$

A one-year slip is equal to a 20 percent cost overrun.

$$dt = -4.45 \times \ln(1 - f)$$

A 10 percent cost increase is equal to a 0.47-year slip.

Engineering, Manufacturing, and Inflation Effects

Engineering, by establishing the product direction, has the greatest effect on the product. However, since most product problems may have multiple components, it is worth looking at each.

1. **Timing.**
   a. **Engineering.** Schedule slips translate into a competitive cost problem as a sub state-of-the-art, late product.
   b. **Manufacturing.** Building up the learning curve base quickly by making many units before the design is mature is risky, but it has a high payoff when considering the apparent cost and/or delay.

2. **Cost.**
   A number of components and organizations contribute to the total product cost in an evolutionary fashion, as shown in Figure 26.

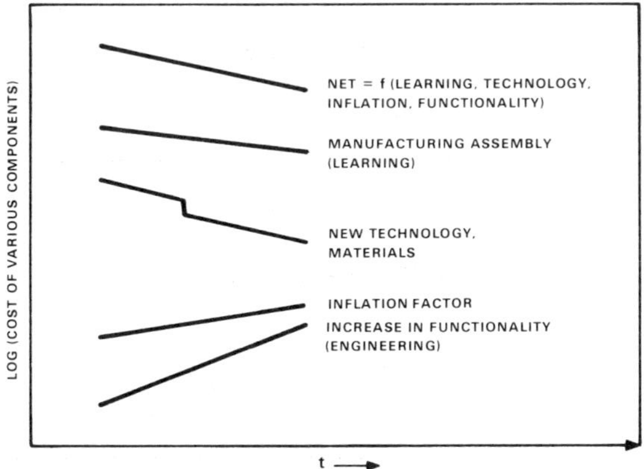

Figure 26. The various components that contribute to product cost.

   a. **Engineering.** Perhaps the major determinant of cost by the product design – number of parts, ease of assembly, etc. The most common cost problems occur by continued product enhancement during the design stage to provide increased functionality (called "one-plussing the design"). One-plussing often occurs because the market had not been modeled before the design was begun, and without a model of the market, engineering is a ship without a rudder.
   b. **Manufacturing.** Direct labor and manufacturing overhead really matter when determining productivity. Making major changes in the design of a product or the location of manufacture for a product starts a new learning curve and serves to stretch the production time out, and the increased costs associated therewith put false pressure on engineering to design new products. One curve in Figure 26 shows the direct costs associated with manufacturing assembly. Some learning should take place as long as product volumes increase exponentially, to get a net lower cost. New technology materials show the greatest cost improvement for computers, assuming that semiconductors and other electronic materials continue to improve with time. By capital equipment investment (tooling), there can be stepwise cost reductions in materials costs.
   c. **Inflation.** While not a direct cost function, it combines with labor cost to negate the downward cost trends that were obtained from learning effects.

d. **Compound Cost.** The costs are taken altogether. In terms of a sub state-of-the-art product, the costs are compound.

3. **Manufacturing learning.** Learning curves and forgetting curves really matter. Left alone, a typical product may go down three alternative paths (Figure 27):
   a. $c = b \times 0.95^t$
   (a decrease of 5 percent/year)
   b. $c = b$
   (staying constant with little attention)
   c. $c = b \times 1.06^t$
   (increasing with inflation as little learning occurs after many units are produced)

   Where c = cost at time, t (in years), and b = base cost.

Mid-Life Kicker for Product Rejuvenation

By enhancing an existing product (the "mid-life kicker"), one can improve the cost/performance metric of a given product. This is non-trivial, and for certain products must be inherent (i.e., designed in). Under these conditions, improvements in cost go immediately to get the product back onto the state-of-the-art line. For example, a factor of 2 in performance halves cost/performance. The effect of doubling the density of a disk is to move the product back to the state-of-the-art line by a time shift. The preceding formula gives:

$$dt = 4.45 \times \ln (0.5) = 3.1 \text{ years}$$

This situation is shown in Figure 28 and is compared with a 5 percent per year learning curve.

SUMMARY

The discussions above have attempted to show how technology progress, particularly in the areas of semiconductor logic, semiconductor memories, and magnetic memory media, have influenced progress in the computer industry and have provided choice and challenge for computer design engineers.

As was implied in the Structural Levels-of-Integration and Packaging Levels-of-Integration Views of Chapter 1, computer engineering is not a one-dimensional undertaking and is not simply a matter of taking last year's circuit schematics and this year's semiconductor vendor catalogues and turning some kind of design process crank. Instead, it is much more complicated and includes many more dimensions.

Two additional dimensions with which a discussion of computer engineering must deal, before going on the DEC computers as case studies, are packaging and manufacturing. These are discussed in Chapter 3.

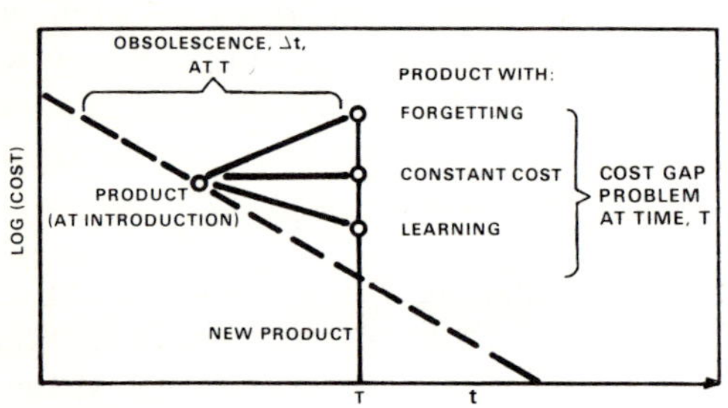

Figure 27. Product cost versus time within manufacturing learning.

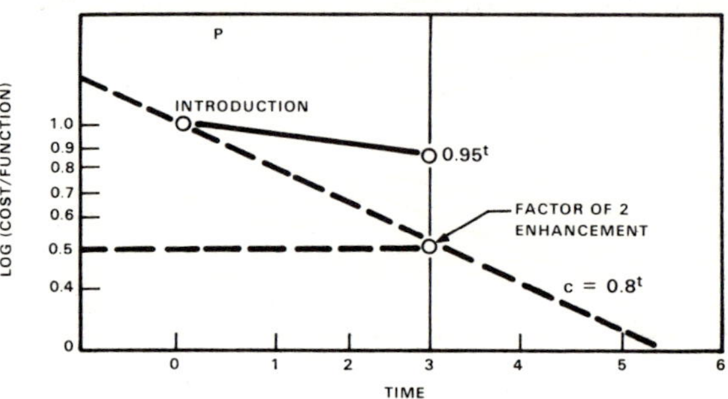

Figure 28. Product cost improvement by enhancement of cost/function.

3

Packaging and Manufacturing

C. GORDON BELL, J. CRAIG MUDGE,
and JOHN E. McNAMARA

As indicated in the previous chapter, computer engineering is more complicated than simply applying new technology to existing designs or designing new structures to exploit new technology. To design a successful new computer, the engineer must often deal with issues of packaging, manufacturing, software compatibility, marketing, and corporate policy. Some of these issues have been briefly referred to in the first two chapters, and some are beyond the scope of this text. However, two issues that can and should be discussed before exploring the case studies are packaging and manufacturing. Both of these are crucial to DEC, as well as to the computer industry in general.

GENERAL PACKAGING

Packaging is one of the most important elements of computer engineering, but also one of the most complex. The importance of packaging spans the size and performance range of computers from the super computers (CDC 6600, CDC 7600, Cray 1) to the pocket calculator. Seymour Cray, the designer of the super computers cited, has described packaging as the most difficult part of the computer designer's job. The two major problems he cites are heat removal and the thickness of the mat of wires covering the backplane. (The length of the wires is also important.) His rule of thumb indicates that with every generation of large computer (roughly five years), the size decreases by roughly a factor of 5, making these problems yet worse. In his latest machine, the Cray 1, the C-shaped physical structure is an effort to reduce the time-consuming length of backplane wires while providing paths for the freon cooling system by having wedge-shaped channels between the modules.

At the opposite end of the size and performance range, pocket calculators are also greatly influenced by packaging. In fact, they are determined by packaging. The first hand-held scientific calculator, the Hewlett-Packard HP35, was simply a new package for a common object, the calculator, which had been around for about a hundred years. It was not until semiconductor densities were high enough to permit implementation of a calculator in a few chips, and not until those chips could be repackaged in a particular fashion, that the hand-held calculator came into existence. Currently this embodiment is synonymous with the calculator name, but other forms are appearing. The calculator watch, the calculator pencil, the calculator alarm clock, and the calculator checkbook have all been advertised.

Between the two extremes of super computers and calculators, packaging has also been important in minicomputers and large computers. In particular, packaging seems to be the dominant reason for the success of the PDP-8 and the minicomputer phenomenon, although marketing, the coining of the name, and the ease of manufacture (also part of packaging) are alternative explanations. The principal packaging advantage of the PDP-8 over predecessor machines was the half-cabinet mounting which permitted it to be placed on a laboratory bench or built into other equipment, both locations being important to major market areas.

The Packaging Design Problem

The importance of packaging is equalled only by its complexity. The complexity stems from the range of engineering disciplines involved. Packaging is the complete design activity of interconnecting a set of components via a mechanical structure in order to carry out a given function. To package a large structure such as a computer, the problem is further broken into a series of levels, each with components that carry out a given function. Figure 1 shows the hierarchy of levels that have evolved in the last twenty years for the DEC computers. There are eight levels which describe the component hierarchy resulting in a computer system.

For each packaging level there is a set of interrelated design activities, as shown in Figure 2. The activities are almost independent of the level at which they are carried out, and some design activities are carried out across several levels.

While the initial design activities indicated in Figure 2 are each aimed at solving a particular problem, the solving of one problem in computer engineering usually creates other problems as side effects. For example, the integrated circuits and other equipment that do information processing require power to operate. Power creates a safety hazard and is provided by power supplies that operate at less than 100 percent efficiency. These side effects create a need for designing insulators and providing methods of carrying the heat away from the power supply and the components being powered. In this way, cooling problems are created. Cooling can be accomplished by conducting heat to an outside surface so that it may be carried away by the air in a room. Alternatively, cooling can be done by convection: a cabinet fan draws air across the components to be cooled and then carries the heated air out of the package into the

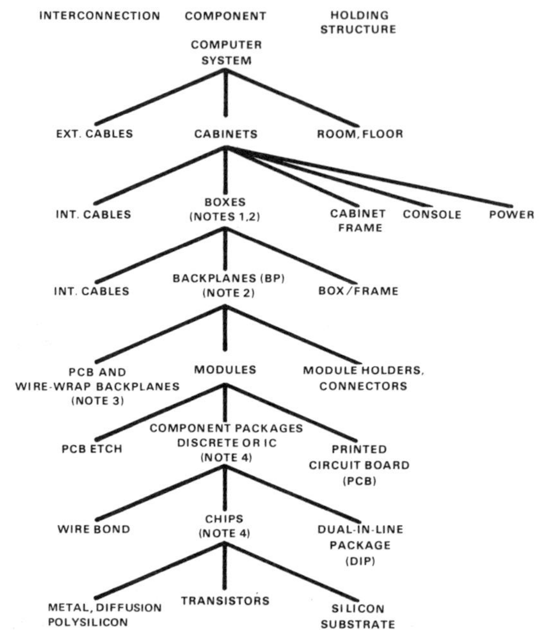

NOTES
1. Not present in second generation
2. Can be taken together as a single level in later generations
3. Sometimes hand wired
4. Third and fourth generations only

Figure 1. Eight-level packaging hierarchy for second to fourth generation computer systems.

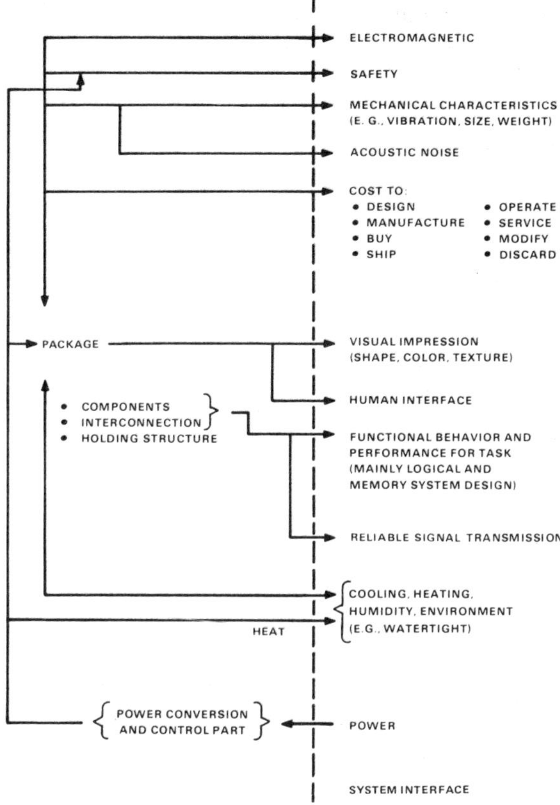

Figure 2. Packaging – a set of closely interrelated design activities.

room. In either case, the air conditioning system is left with the problem of carrying the heat away, and the fans associated with that system are added to the fans associated with the computer to create acoustical noise pollution in the room, making it more difficult for people to work. Furthermore, if the computer is used in an unusually harsh environment, a special heat exchanger is required in order to avoid contamination of the components within the computer by the pollutants present in the cooling airflow.

Finally, the mechanical characteristics of a particular package such as weight and size directly affect manufacturing and shipment costs. They determine whether a system can be built and whether it can be shipped in a certain size airplane or carried by a particular distribution channel such as the public postal system. The mechanical vibration sensitivity characteristics determine the type of vehicle (ordinary or special air ride van) in which equipment can be shipped.

It is also necessary to examine the particular design parameter in order to determine whether it is a constraint (such as meeting a particular government standard), a goal (such as minimum cost), or part of a more complex objective function (such as price/performance). Table 1 lists the various kinds of design activities and constraints, goals, or parts of more complex objective functions that they determine. The table also gives the dimensions of various metrics (e.g., cost, weight) available to measure the designs; many of these metrics are used in subsequent comparisons.

Given the basic design activities, one may now examine their interaction with the hierarchy of levels (i.e., the systems) being designed (see Table 2). This is done by looking at each level and examining the interaction of the design activities for that level with other design activities (e.g., function requires power, power requires cooling, cooling requires fans, fans create noise, and noise requires noise suppression).

Computer Systems Level. The topmost level in Table 2 is the computer system, which for the larger minicomputers and PDP-10 computers consists of a set of subsystems (processor, memories, etc.) within cabinets, housed in a room, and interconnected by cables. The functional design activity is the selection and interconnection of the cabinets, with a basic computer cabinet that holds the processor, memory, and interfaces to peripheral units. Disks, magnetic tape units, printers, and terminals occupy free standing cabinets. The functional design is usually carried out by the user and consists of selecting the right components

Table 1. Design Activities, Metrics, and Environment Goals and Constraints

Design Activity	Environment and [Metrics]
Primary function and performance (e.g., memory)	Market, the consumer of the system [Memory size in bits, operation rate in bits/sec]
Human engineering	Human factors criteria, competitive market factors
Visual/aesthetics	Market, other similar objects, the environment in which the object is to exist
Acoustic noise	Government standards, operating environment, market [Decibels in various frequency bands]
Mechanical	Shippability by various carriers, handling, assembly/disassembly time [Weight, floor area, volume, expandability, acceleration, mechanical frequency response]
Electromagnetic radiation	Government standards, must operate within intended environment [Power versus frequency]
Power	Operating environment, market [watts, voltage supply range]
Cooling and environment	Market, intended storage and operating environment, government standards [Heat dissipation, temperature range, airflow, humidity range, salinity, dust particle, hazardous gas]
Safety	Government standards
Cost Cost/metric ratios	[Cost/performance (its function) – cost/bit and cost/bit/sec, cost/weight, cost/area, cost/volume, cost/watt]
Density metrics	[Weight/volume, watts/volume, operation rate/volume]
Power metrics	[Operation rate/watt; efficiency = power out/power in]
Reliability	[Reliability – failure rate (mean time between failures), availability – mean time to repair)

to meet cost, speed, number of users, data base size, language (programming), reliability, and interface constraints. Aside from the functional design problem, cooling and power design are significant for larger computers. For smaller computers, accessibility, acoustic noise, and visual considerations are significant because these machines become part of a local environment and must "fit in."

Cabinet Level. Since the cabinet is the lowest level component that users interface to and observe, physical design, visual appearance, and human factors engineering are important design activities. For the computer hardware designer, on the other hand, the component mounted in the cabinet is usually the largest system. Functional design efforts ensure that the various components (i.e., boxes) that make up a

Table 2. Interrelationship of Hierarchy of Levels and Design Activities

Design Activity	Chip	Chip Carrier	Module	Backplane	Box	Cabinet	Computer System
	Level of Packaging						
Functional	Logic electrical →					Configuration options	Selection of right components by user
	Circuit design physical layout		Physical layout	Physical layout	What fits and operates	Boxes and operable configurations	
Human Interface						Location of console, size for use	Placement for use
Visual					Visible, bought for integration	Determines system appearance	Set of cabs, attractive place to be
Acoustic				Airflow vibration →			Quiet for operators and users
Mechanical	Buildable and signal transmission		Shippable and serviceable →				Floor load room size
Electromagnetic interface	Noise coupling and rejection of radio frequency interference (RFI)		Inter/intra-module noise coupling, RFI containment and shielding		RFI → containment, external RFI shield		Away from RFI input (outside operating range)
Power	Special on-chip		Dist. and regulation	Dist. and regulation	Control, dist. and regulation	Interconnect with computer system	By user special power supplies for high availability
Cooling and other environment	Chip to cooling special environment	IC module cooling special environment	IC to cooling	Module	Cooling and covering	Source	Interbox coupling to room air environment
Safety			Power for various systems →		Determines safety if used at this level	Determines user safety	
Dominant design activities	Circuit logic	Logic →			Mechanical, power, cooling, EMI, acoustic	Configuration visual, shipping EMI, safety	User configuration design

The box and backplane levels can be considered as a single level (alternatively, the box level may be eliminated in large systems).

cabinet level system will operate correctly when interconnected. Safety and electromagnetic interference characteristics are important because the cabinet serves as the outermost place in which shielding can be installed. Cooling and power distribution must be considered, since a number of different boxes may be mounted within the same cabinet. Finally, the mechanical structure of a cabinet must be designed to maintain its physical integrity when shipped.

Box Level. Box level functional design consists of taking one or more backplanes, the power supplies for the box, and any user interface such as an operator's console and interconnecting them mechanically (see Figure 3). For systems that are not sold at the box level, no separate box is required, and the power supply and backplanes are mounted directly in a cabinet (see Figure 4) or other holding structure such as a desk or terminal case, so that box and backplane design merge. If systems are sold at the box level, then the visual characteristics may be important; otherwise, the design is basically mechanical and consists of cooling, power distribution, and control of acoustic noise. The structure must be sound to protect the unit during shipment.

Of all the dimensions to consider in the design, perhaps the most important is how the box (or module mounting structure) is placed in a cabinet. This placement affects airflow, shippability, configurability, cable placement, and serviceability, and is a classical case of design tradeoffs. The scheme that provides the best metrics, such as packaging density and weight, may have the poorest access for service and the most undesirable cable connection characteristics. These characteristics are given in Table 3.

Table 3. Fixed, Drawer, and Hinged Box/Cabinet Mounting

Mounting	Service Access	Cabling	Density	Cooling	Applicability
Fixed	Good for either backplane or module, but not both unless a thin cabinet is used	Best (i.e., shortest)	Good for thin or rear cabinet power supply mounting	Best (known)	Box not needed; box can be used
Drawer	One-side access	Long and movable	Very high	Can be cooled*	High density, self-contained
Drawer (with tilt) for service	Good	Longer and more movable than non-tilt version	Very high	Can be cooled*	
Drawer vertical mounting modules	Very good	Long and movable	High		
Hinged (module backplane)	Very good	Short	Medium	Good (if fans are fixed to cage)	Separate box is awkward

* Density restricts cabinet airflow.

REMOVABLE SIDE PANEL
REMOVABLE TOP COVER
SLIDE GUIDE
DECORATIVE PANEL
CONSOLE

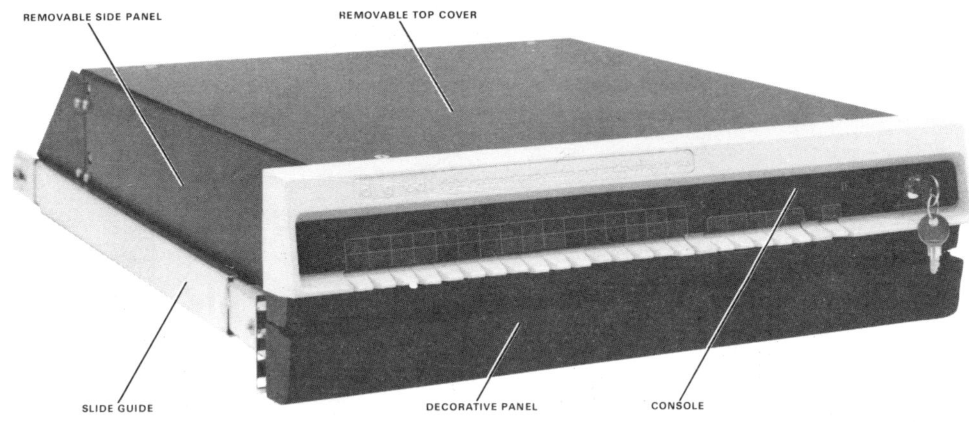

(a) Front view (with top cover).

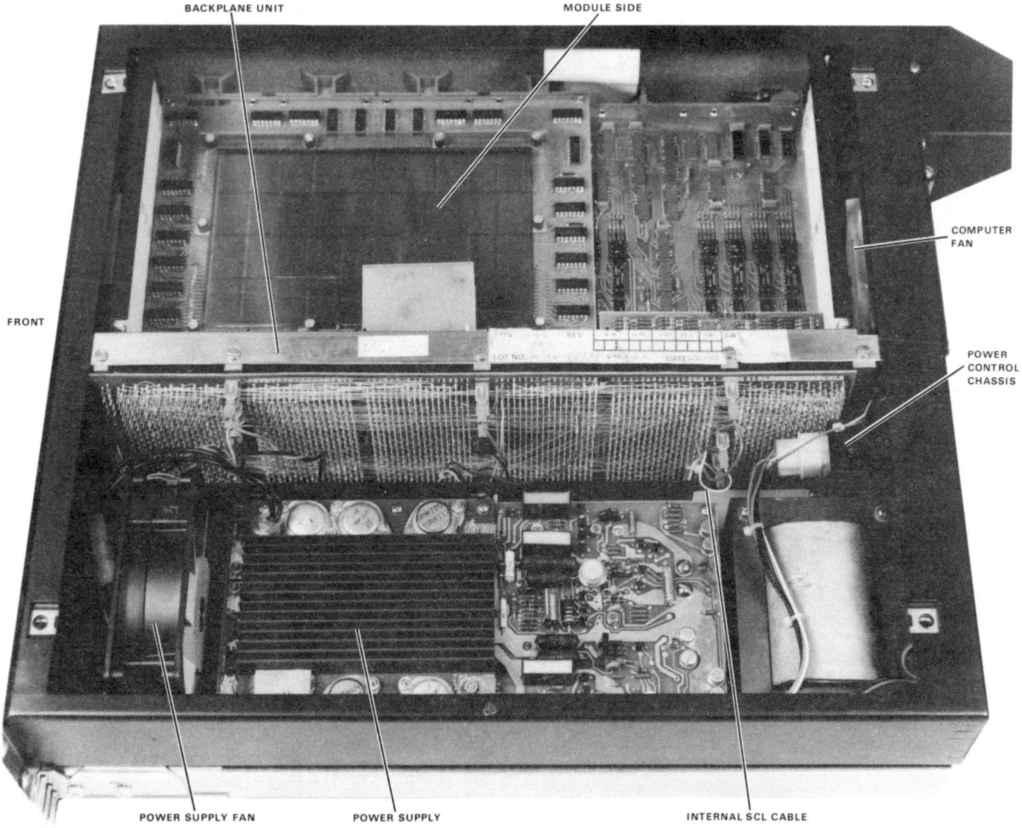

BACKPLANE UNIT
MODULE SIDE
COMPUTER FAN
FRONT
POWER CONTROL CHASSIS
POWER SUPPLY FAN
POWER SUPPLY
INTERNAL SCL CABLE

(b) Side view (with top cover removed).

Figure 3. PDP-11/05 computer box.

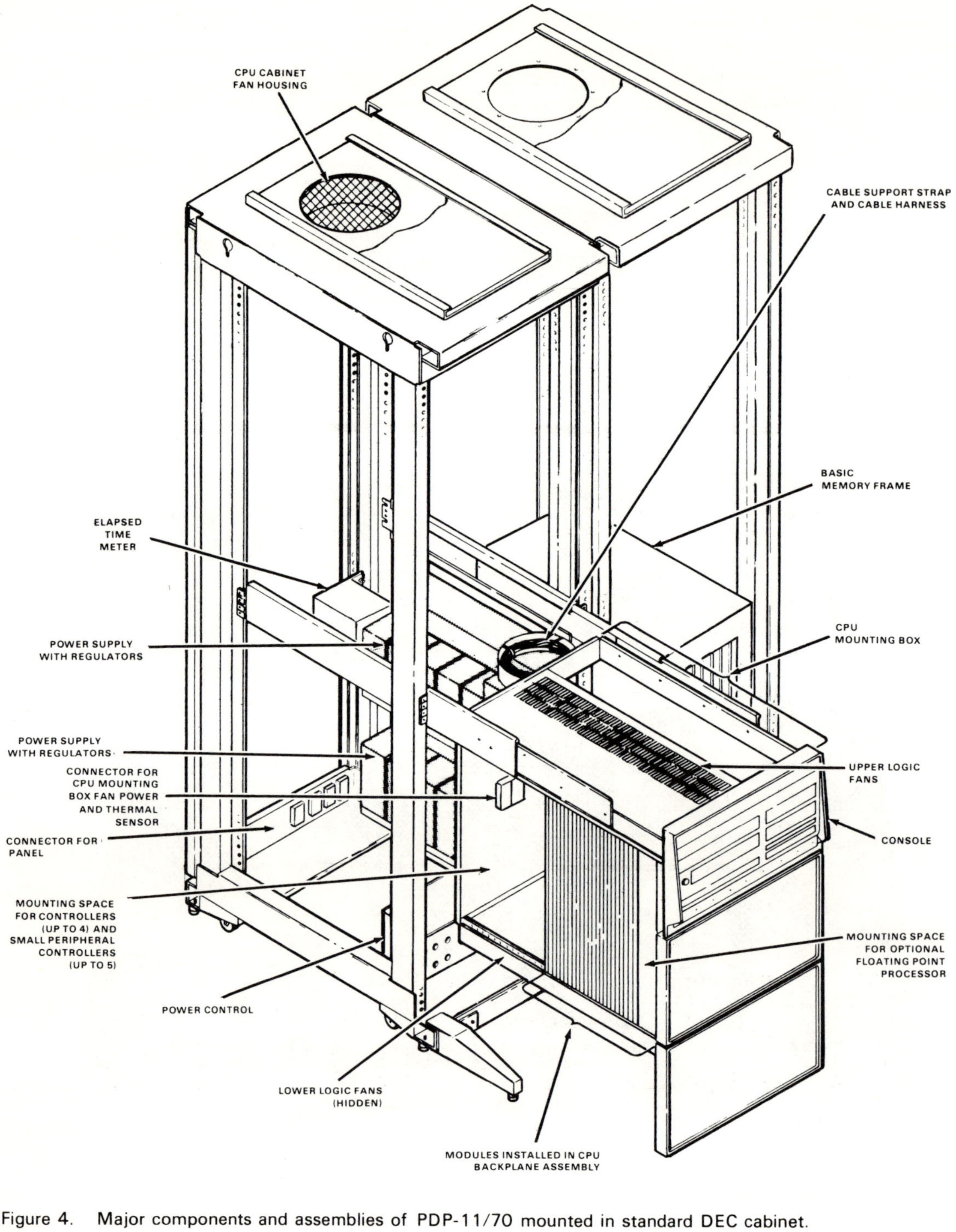

Figure 4. Major components and assemblies of PDP-11/70 mounted in standard DEC cabinet.

Backplane Level. This level of design is the final level of interconnection for the computer components that are designed to stand alone, such as a basic computer disk or terminal. Backplane design is part of the computer's logical design. In second generation machines such as the PDP-7 (Figure 24*a*, Chapter 6), the backplane was wire-wrapped. In the early 1970s printed circuit boards were used to interconnect modules (Figure 5). Secondary design activities include holding, powering, and cooling the modules so they will operate correctly. Since the signals are transmitted on the backplane, there is an electromagnetic design problem. For industrial control systems whose function is to switch power mains voltages, additional safety problems are created.

Module Level. In the second generation, module level design was a circuit design activity taking discrete circuits and interconnecting them to provide a given logic function. In the third and fourth generations, this interface between circuit and logic design moved within chip level design, so that module level design became the process of dealing with the physical layout problems associated with logic design. Module level design is basically electronic, so power, cooling, and electromagnetic interference (cross talk) considerations dominate.

Integrated Circuit Package and Chip Level. Most integrated circuits used in the computer industry today are sold in a plastic or ceramic package configuration that has two rows of pins and is called a dual inline package (DIP). The majority of the integrated circuits in the module shown in Figure 6 are 16-pin DIPs. Because of the popularity of this packaging style, the terms "integrated circuit," "chip," and "DIP" are often used interchangeably. This is not strictly correct; an integrated circuit is actually a 0.25- × 0.25-inch portion of semiconductor material (die or chip) from a 2- to 4-inch diameter semiconductor wafer. Except for cases where multiple die are packaged within a single DIP, the integrated circuit, chip, and DIP can be discussed as a single level.

Design considerations at the integrated circuit level include power consumption, heat dissipation, and electromagnetic interference. Because some integrated circuits are designed to operate in hostile environments, there is considerable mechanical design activity associated

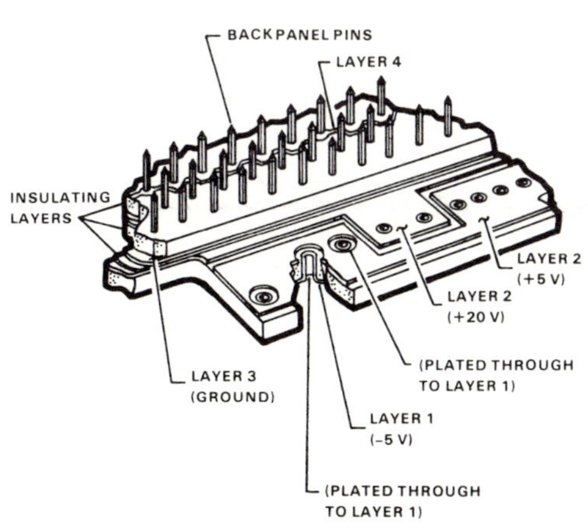

Figure 5. Cross-section of a printed circuit backplane.

Figure 6. LSI-11 processor with 8 Kbytes of memory and microcode for commercial instruction set.

with packaging, interconnection, and manufacturing.

The Packaging Evolution

Figure 7 shows the relation of packaging and the computer classes for the various computer generations. For each new generation there is a short, evolutionary transition phase. Ultimately, however, the new technology is repackaged such that a complete information storage or processing component (bit, register, processor) occupies a small fraction of the space and costs a small fraction of the amount it did in the prior generation. Discrete events mark packaging characteristics of each generation, starting from 1 bit per vacuum tube chassis in the first generation and evolving to a complete computer on a single integrated circuit chip in the fifth generation. Not only the size of the packaging changed, but also the mounting methods. In the first generation, logic units were permanently mounted in racks, where they were removable for ease in servicing in later generations.

While the timeline of Figure 7 shows the packaging evolution of a complete computer, Table 4 shows how a particular component,

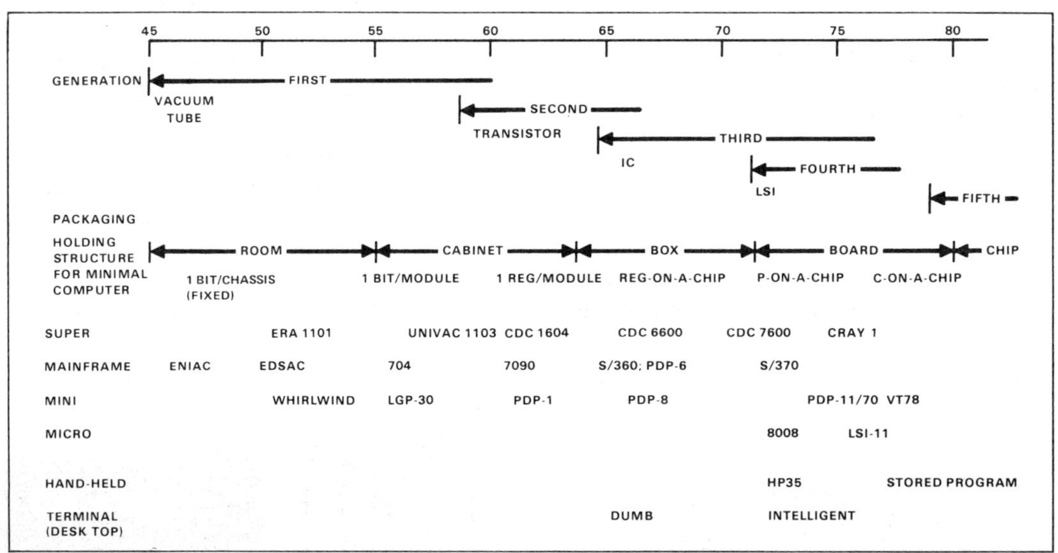

Figure 7. Timeline evolution of packaging.

Table 4. Packaging Hierarchy Evolution for Universal Asynchronous Receiver/Transmitter (UART) Telegraph Line Controller

Generation				
Early Second	**Late Second**	**Early Third**	**Late Third**	**Late Fourth**
Backplane, Modules, Discrete Circuit	2 modules Discrete Circuit	Module, IC, Chip	IC, Chip	Chip area

now called the Universal Asynchronous Receiver/Transmitter (UART), has evolved.

The UART logic carries out the function of interfacing to a communications line that carries serial data and transforms the data to parallel on a character-by-character basis for entry into the rest of the computer system. The UART has three basic components: the serial/parallel conversion and buffering, the interfaces to both the computer and to the communication line, and the sequential controller for the circuit.

The UART is probably the first fourth generation computer component, since it is somewhat less complex than a processor yet rich enough to be identifiable with a clean, standard interface.*

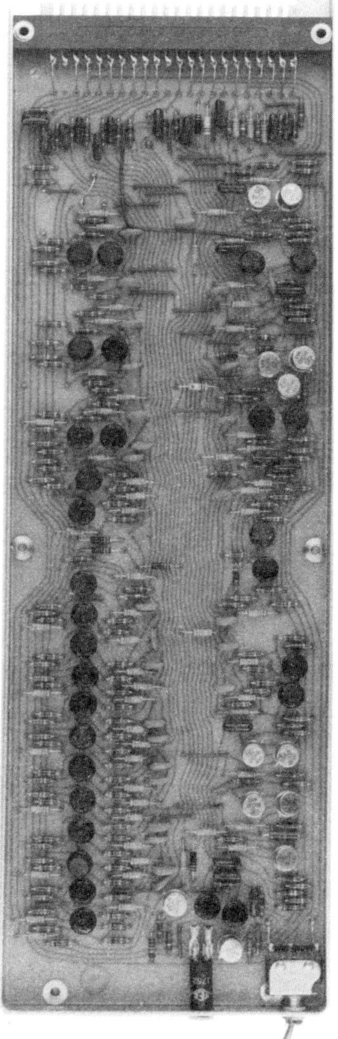

Figure 8. 4707 transmitter line unit of the late second generation.

THE DEC COMPUTER PACKAGING GENERATIONS

With this general background on packaging, one can examine the DEC packaging evolution more specifically and against the general archetype of Figure 1. Figure 9 shows how the hierarchies have changed with the technology generations. The figure is segmented into the different product groupings. A product is identified as being at a unique level if it is sold at the particular packaging level. The first DEC computers (i.e., PDP-1 to PDP-6) were sold at the cabinet level as complete hardware systems. Although the PDP-8 was available at the cabinet level for complete systems, it was significantly smaller than the previous machines and was principally sold at the mechanical box level.

* Historically, DEC played a significant part in the development of the UART technology. With the PDP-1, the first UART function was designed using 500-KHz systems modules and was used in a message switching application as described in Chapter 6. The interface was called a line unit and was subsequently repackaged in the late second generation as two extended systems modules (Figure 8). The UART function was also built into the PDP-8/I using two modules that were substantially smaller than those for the PDP-1. In the 680/I, a PDP-8/I-driven message switch, the UART function was accomplished by programmed bit sampling. Late in the third generation (or at the beginning of the fourth generation), some designers from Solid State Data Systems of Long Island, N.Y., worked with Vince Bastiani at DEC and developed a UART that occupied a single chip. This subsequently evolved into the standard integrated circuit and is used throughout the industry.

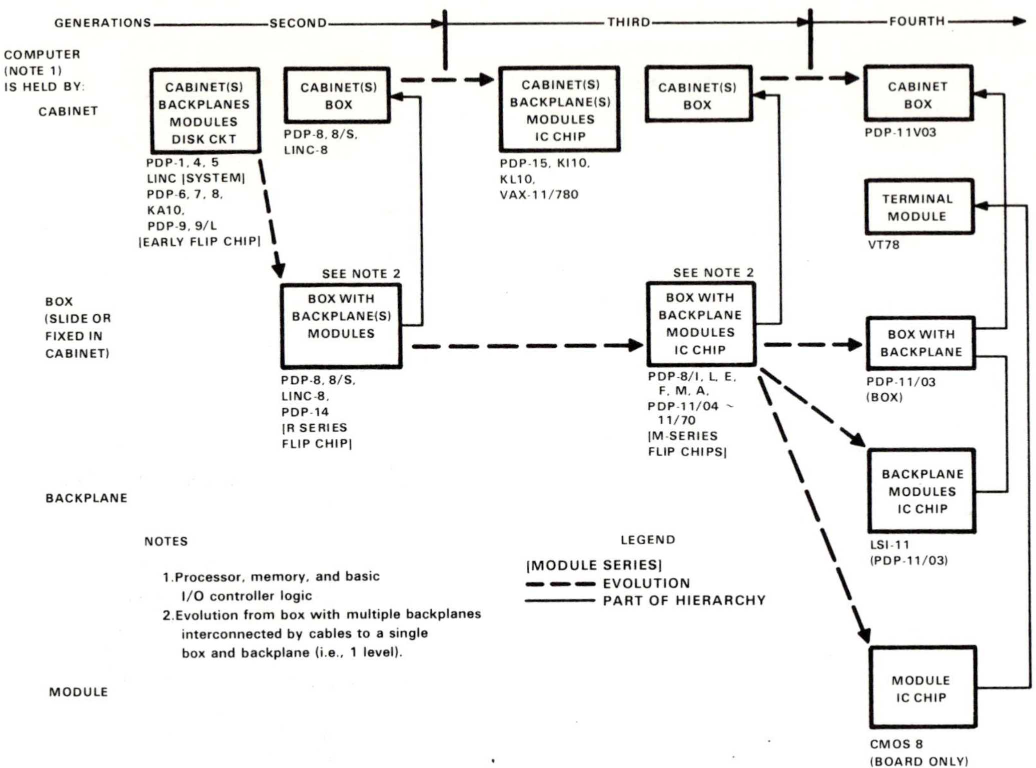

Figure 9. DEC physical structure (packaging) hierarchies by technology generation.

Subsequently, computer systems became available at the backplane level (LSI-11), and at the module level (CMOS-8).

The original packaging hierarchy for most of DEC's second generation computers used a relatively common packaging scheme based on the PDP-1. The most significant change occurred late in the second generation when Flip Chip modules (Figure 9) were introduced so that backplanes could be wire-wrapped automatically.

The change to wire-wrap technology not only reduced costs and increased production line throughput, it also enabled the box-level production of computers. The change to wire-wrap and two level products (box and cabinet) is clear in the second generation. The offering of products at these two levels continued into and through the third generation.

With the advent of the fourth generation, large-scale integration permitted the construction of a complete minicomputer processor on a single module. Although components are sold as separate modules (e.g., processor, communications line interfaces, additional primary memory), a complete system requires a backplane; thus, the lowest level for the product is the backplane. For larger systems, a power supply is combined and placed in a metal box. A typical example of such a product is the LSI-11, which is marketed at three levels as shown in Figure 9.

The late fourth generation has brought the processor-on-a-chip, and another packaging level to the price list. An example of the processor-on-a-chip is the CMOS-8, described in Chapter 7. The new packaging level offered to the customer is the CMOS-8 module, which is a single-board complete computer with processor, 16-Kword memory, and all the optional controllers to directly interface up to five peripheral options.

DEC Boxes and Cabinets

Since the function of the cabinet and box is to hold backplanes that in turn hold modules that in turn hold circuit level components, the metric of electronic enclosures is the number of printed circuit boards they hold. The earliest DEC method of mounting was to place the backplanes directly in a 6-foot-high cabinet which held 19-inch-wide equipment in a 22- × 30-inch floor space and weighed about 185 pounds. Figure 10 shows the top view of the various cabinets used to hold module backplanes and boxes for minicomputers since 1960. The changes to the basic DEC 6-foot cabinet have mainly been for improved producibility. The latest (circa 1973) was to use riveted upright supporting members so the cabinet could be assembled easily without requiring bulk space for shipment and storage.

The original cabinet used the entire cabinet as an air plenum so that air was forced between the modules and out the front doors. When the PDP-7 used the same cabinet and the module mounting frame cut off the airflow, it was necessary to add fans to the back doors to blow air at the modules. Since cooling was one of the weak points in the PDP-7, the PDP-9 used a self-contained mounting and cooling structure in which air was circulated between the modules with air pulled in from outside without going through the cabinet.

A second, later packaging method, initiated with the PDP-8, packaged the metal-boxed minicomputer inside the 6-foot cabinet. Figure 11 shows the significant boxes that have been used to package minicomputers both within the 6-foot cabinet and freestanding. The box packaging history begins with the PDP-8. The rows of Figure 11 indicate the four ways that are available to access the circuitry (fixed, book, slides, and tilt for access). The PDP-8 design was followed by the PDP-8/S design which oriented the modules with the pins up for access to the backplane. By tilting (rotating) the box, the handle side of the modules could be accessed. For the PDP-8/I (not shown), modules were mounted in a vertical plane.

Several fixed backplane module mounting structures were formed beginning with the PDP-8/A (1975), which was the first DEC minicomputer since the PDP-5 to be mounted in a fixed structure in a cabinet.

DEC Backplanes

Backplanes provide the next level-of-integration packaging below cabinets and boxes; they are used to hold and interconnect a set of modules which form a computer or an option (e.g., processor, memory, or peripheral controller). Figure 12 gives the relative cost of interconnecting backplane module pins. Here the cost per interconnection is roughly the same as with a printed circuit module interconnection (Figure 13). This can be somewhat misleading because backplanes require a negligible cost for testing and few failures occur during testing.

Figure 12 shows various kinds of interconnection technologies. Even though there are exponential increases in quantities produced, the cost continues to increase in the long run with only occasional downward steps. The greatest cost decline occurred when interconnections were carried out using automatic wire-wrap machinery, but the PDP-8/E was equally significant by being the first DEC computer to use a completely wave-soldered backplane. Figure 12 also shows how effectively the module pins were used (i.e., whether all available pins were used).

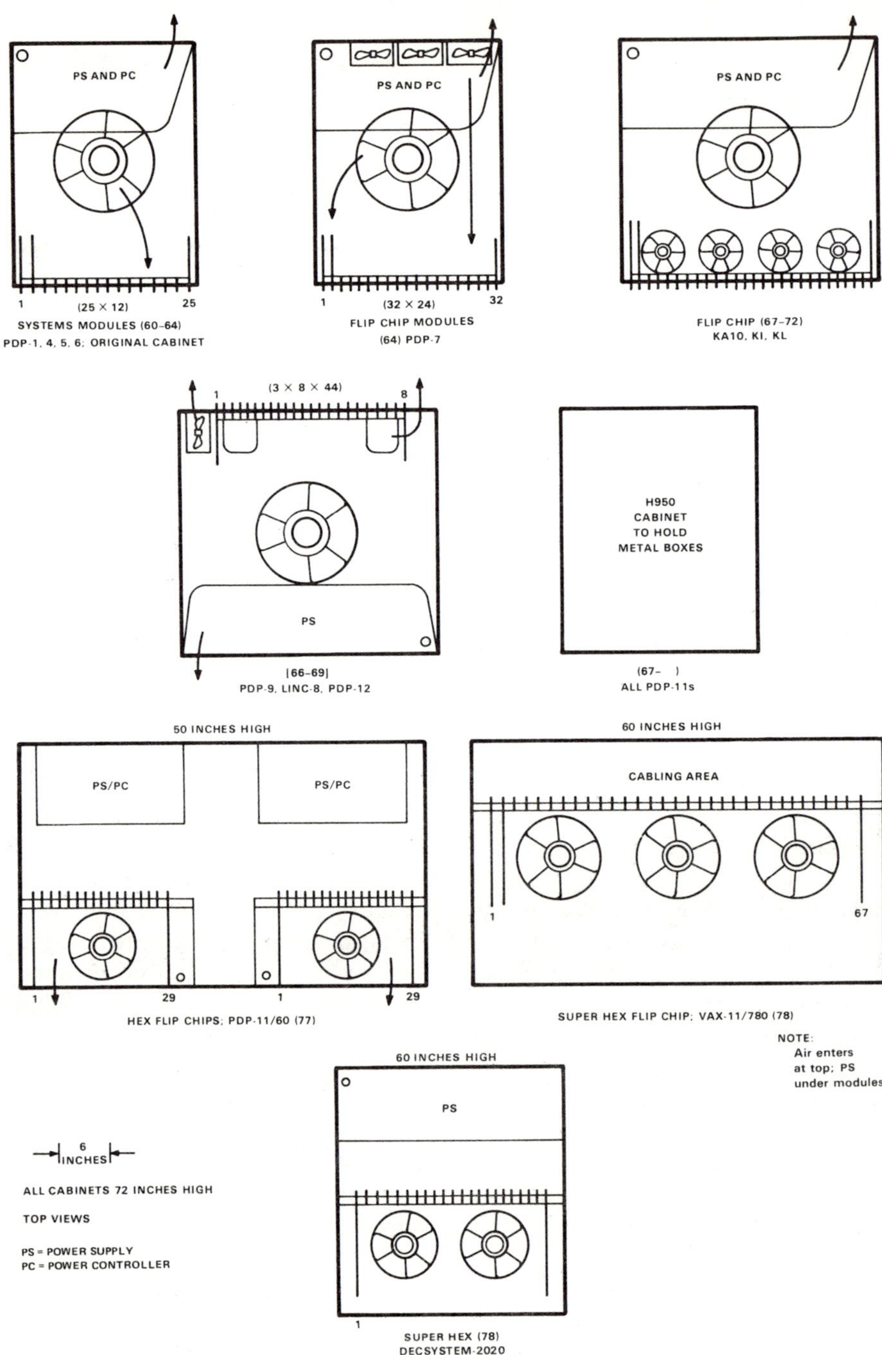

Figure 10. Cabinets used to hold various DEC computers (in fixed, book, and box configurations).

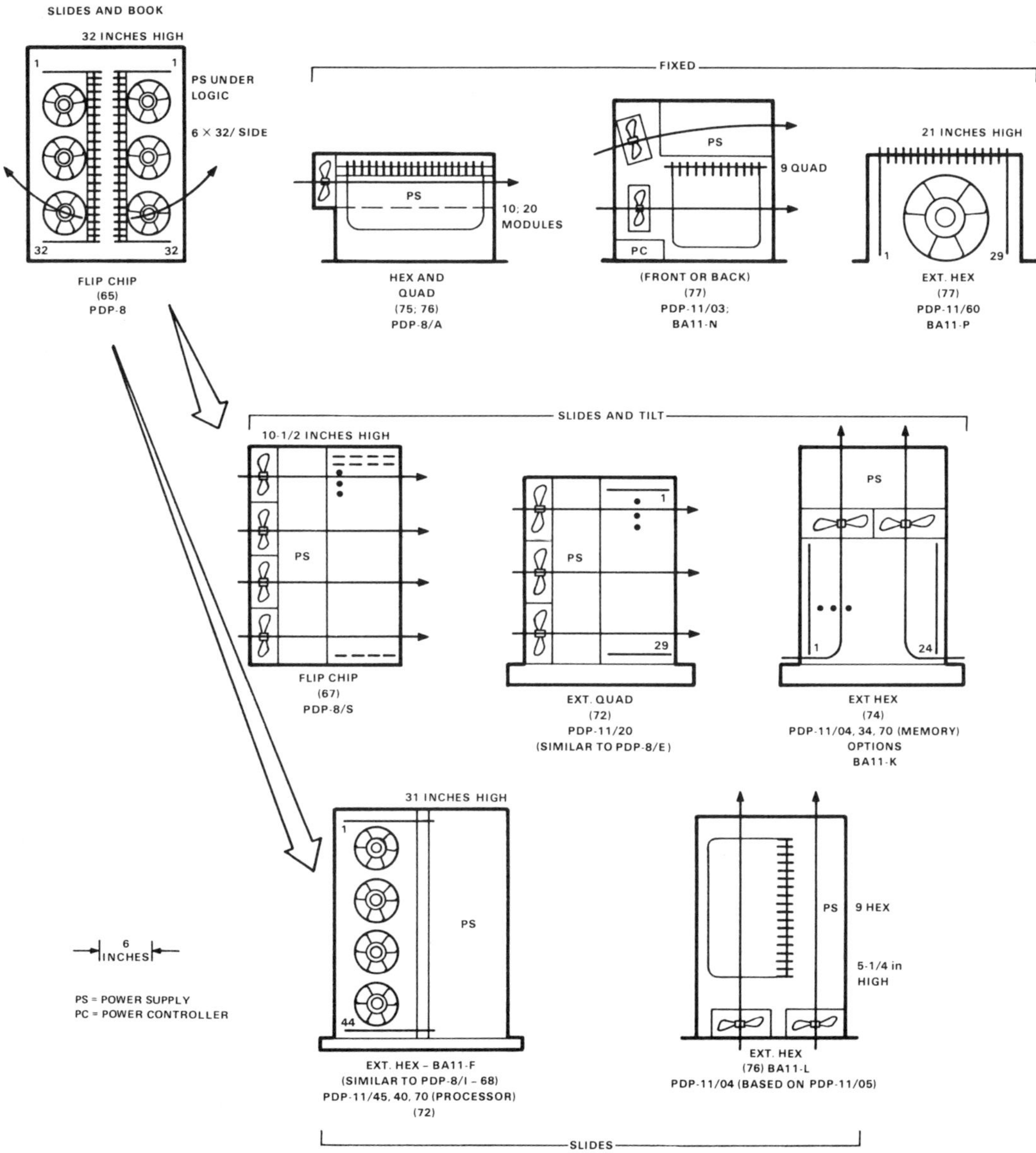

Figure 11. Boxes used to hold various DEC PDP-8 and PDP-11 series minicomputers.

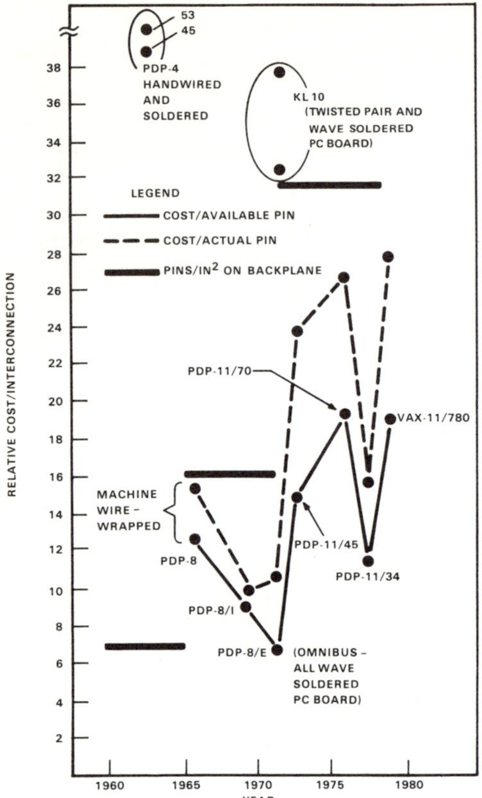

Figure 12. Relative cost per possible and actual interconnection versus time for various DEC computer backplanes; also pin density (in pins per in²) versus time.

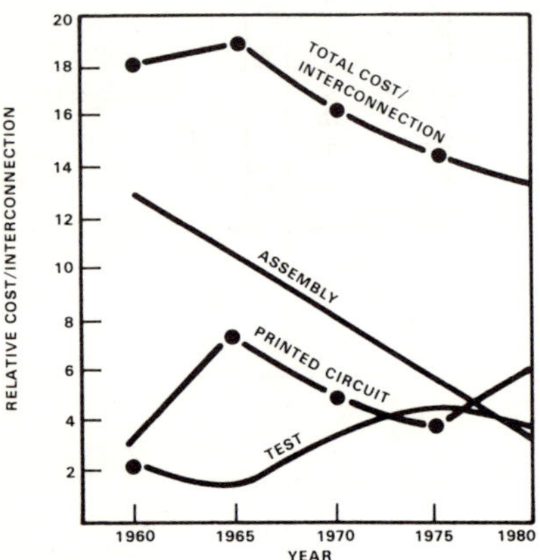

Figure 13. Relative cost per interconnection on DEC printed circuit board modules versus time.

DEC Modules

Since the function of modules is to interconnect and hold components, the metrics for modules are the area for mounting the components and the cost of each circuit interconnection. For minicomputers, the emphasis has been to have larger modules with more components packed on a module as a means to lower the interconnection cost. Figure 14 shows the area of DEC modules and the number of external pins per module versus time. Because integrated circuit densities have been increasing, in effect providing lower interconnection costs, a given module automatically provides increased interconnects simply by packaging the same number of integrated circuits on a module. Obviously, one does not want to credit this effect to improved module packaging. By increasing the components per module, the cost per interconnect can be reduced provided the cost to test the module increases less rapidly than the increase in components. The emphasis on module size is usually most intense for larger systems, where a relatively large number of modules are needed to form a complete system.

Until recently, the increase in module area was accompanied by increases in the number of pins available to interconnect to the backplane. In the case of the VAX-11/780 and the DECSYSTEM 2020, the number of pins did not increase significantly over previous designs, although the board area was 50 percent larger. In these cases, the number of integrated ciruits that could be cooled limited the density. In other cases, either the number of pins or the module size limited the module's functionality. There are similar effects throughout the generations.

In the early second generation Systems Module designs, the number of pins and the circuit board area (in square inches) were about the same. Components were fairly large and loosely packed on modules. With the Flip Chip series, circuits were modified to pack a larger number

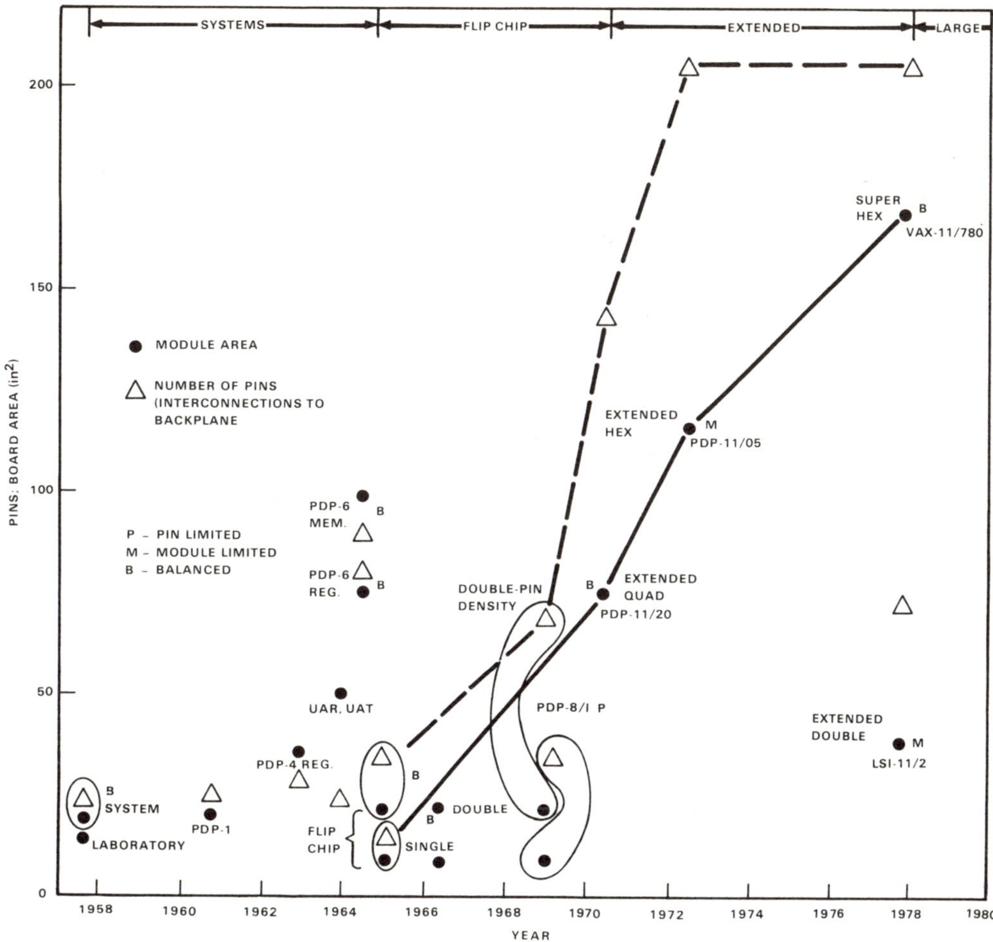

Figure 14. Module printed circuit board area and number of pins per module versus time for DEC modules.

of smaller components on a single module, using automatic component insertion equipment, and some of the space-consuming components (e.g., pulse transformers) of the earlier circuits were removed so that a module design was a better balance between area and pins. As a result, the early second generation Flip Chip modules had higher packing densities than comparable Systems Modules.

With the beginning of the third generation, the need for more printed pins to the backplane was clear because so many interconnections were made on the computer's backplane. The PDP-8/I was the first DEC integrated circuit computer, and the packaging philosophy strictly followed that of the second generation. As a result, the sudden increase in component functions meant that the modules were drastically lacking in pins. By putting pins on both sides of the module, the number of pins for a double-height module (20 in^2) was increased from 36 to 72, which was still inadequate. Assuming that each integrated circuit has 14 signal pins and a module has 70 signal pins, only 5 integrated circuits could be placed on a board and still have pins brought out to the backplane pins, although the 20-in^2 area of the module could potentially hold 20 integrated circuits.

Although the 8/I was packaged using the 20-in^2 72-pin modules, it was clear that another packaging scheme was necessary to utilize integrated circuits, modules, pins, and backplanes. Thus, when the PDP-11/20 and the PDP-8/E were designed (about 1970), they used larger modules in order to carry the large number of intramodule interconnections required when many integrated circuits were placed on a single module.

It is interesting to note that in a recent case of a processor using high density integrated circuits, the LSI-ll/2, the module area was too large to have a single option on a module, and since the LSI-11 Bus only required a few signals, the number of pins was more than adequate. Here, the modules were functionality limited rather than pin limited. Figure 14 indicates situations in which either pins or modules limited the design.

Although the size of the module is important in determining the systems that can be built, how they are serviced, and how they are manufactured, the important module metric is the cost per interconnection on the printed circuit board (and remainder of the system). Figure 13 shows how this has varied with time. Here one can see that the introduction of Flip Chip modules initially increased costs (because learning had to start almost anew).

Interconnection costs consist of the costs of the printed circuit board, the insertion of the components on the module, and the testing of the module. Printed circuit board costs have been decreasing with time, reflecting benefits both of learning and of placing more integrated circuits on a single module, giving a compound economy-of-scale effect. The cost to assemble the components on the module have decreased rapidly, reflecting the increasing use of automatic component insertion machines. Testing has not been a significant cost component in module manufacturing, although it does represent a substantial cost by the time the module has been integrated into a system and delivered to the customer's site. The total cost per interconnection has been decreasing, but the trend may either remain constant or even increase as greater use of large-scale integration decreases the number of total connections in a system but makes the remaining interconnections more expensive to assemble and test.

Many of the important problems in packaging, specifically heat and electromagnetic interference, originate not from a computer's logic but rather from the power supplies that power the logic.

POWER SUPPLIES

Although logic functions can be performed using small quantities of electrons and can thus be accommodated in very small physical structures, the power to move those electrons at useful speeds comes from power supplies which do not scale down in size as readily as the logic functions they support. Power supply technology has not provided the impressive increases in capability per dollar or capability per cubic foot that semiconductor technology has. Power supplies involve such materials properties as voltage breakdown limits, dielectric constants, magnetic permeability, and heat conductivity. Since these properties vary with physical dimension, increased capabilities in terms of voltage breakdown rating, capacitance, inductance, or heat dissipation are gained by making the component physically larger.

The performance criteria for power supplies are predominantly determined by the application for which they are designed. These criteria are given in terms of various efficiencies of volume, weight, power conversion, and cost. It is somewhat difficult to compare the various supplies because all are available at different

Table 5. Characteristics of Power Supply Types

	Processor and Memory	Disk and Tape	Terminal
Power (watts)	250–2500	100–500	0–150
Use	Logic	Very low noise for head electronics; high current for servos	High voltage for CRT; high current for mechanical motions
Quantity in system	Low to medium	Medium	High
Cost sensitivity	Low	Medium	High
Size	Important, especially in boxed computers	Not important	Very important
Weight	Relatively unimportant	Not important	Very important
Reliability	Very important	Important	Important
Features	Power line sensing, battery backup		

times, produced in different quantities, designed for different reliabilities, and available with different features.

For the computer industry, power supplies can be divided into three main categories: processor and memory power supplies, disk and tape power supplies, and terminal power supplies. Each of these product categories has a unique set of requirements, which are summarized in Table 5.

Three of the four efficiency measures, cost (in relative cost per watt), weight (in watts per pound), and volume (in watts per in^3), are plotted for processor power supplies in Figures 15 and 16. The plots in Figure 15 use a time axis; those in Figure 16, a watts-of-output axis. The fourth efficiency measure, power conversion (watts out per watts in), is given in Figure 17 using a time axis.

The cost of a power system is very dependent on the unit's electrical size and technology. The features required on the units such as power line monitoring (ac low, dc low), battery backed-up power, and servicing aids also significantly influence the cost. Since the cost is size dependent, a relative metric, dollars per watt, is chosen for processor power supplies.

In the cost characteristics the different bands of cost curves are technology dependent: they span new, mature, and obsolete technologies. For example, the cost of power supply technology until just recently depended on iron and copper prices and labor costs. Now, costs of power supply technology tend to track semiconductor costs as a result of the widespread use of line switching power supplies. Bands within the cost curves represent the size dependency; larger power supplies are the most cost-effective, with one exception (Figures 15*a* and 16*a*).

The size of power supplies for minicomputers has been important, especially for the boxed versions. The volume occupied by logic has decreased for the constant functionality computer; however, power requirements have declined far less than logic volume, and hence

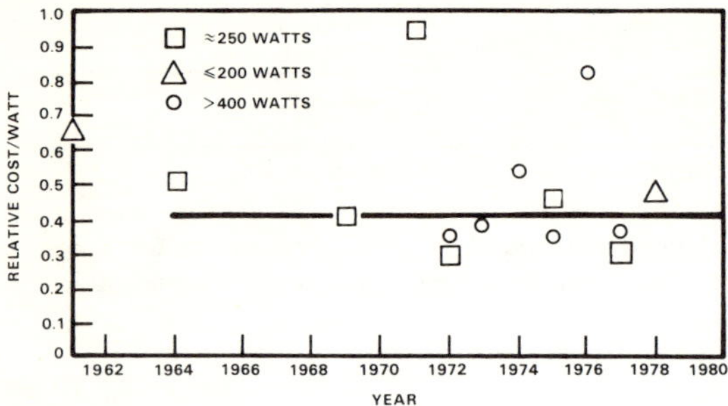

(a) Cost efficiency (in relative cost per watt).

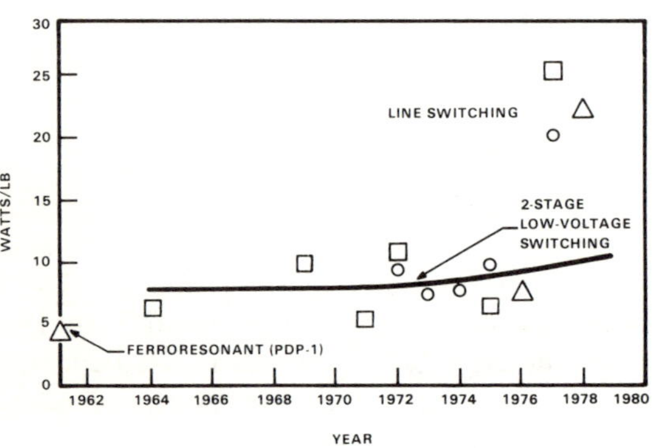

(b) Weight efficiency (in watts per lb).

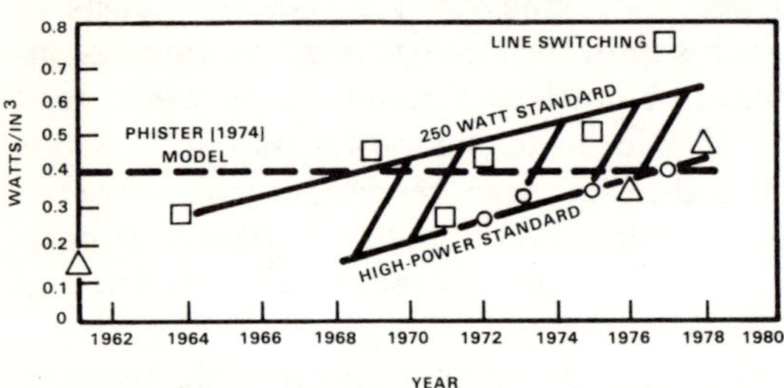

(c) Volumetric efficiency (in watts per in^3).

Figure 15. Cost, weight, and volumetric efficiencies versus time for various DEC computer power supplies.

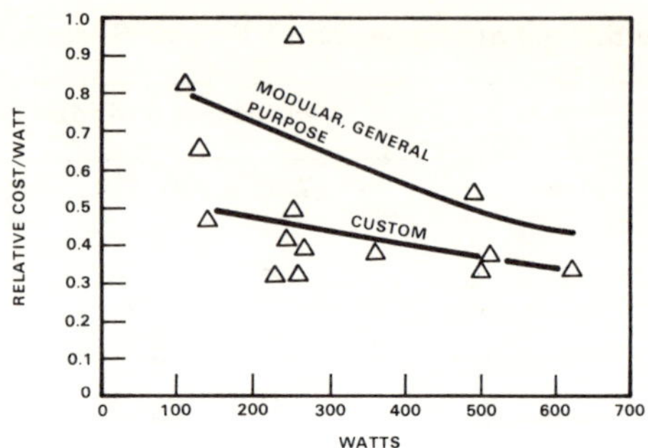

(a) Cost efficiency (in relative cost per watt).

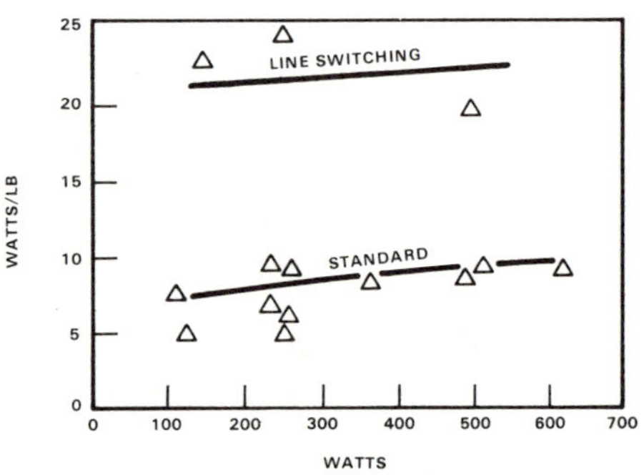

(b) Weight efficiency (in watts per lb).

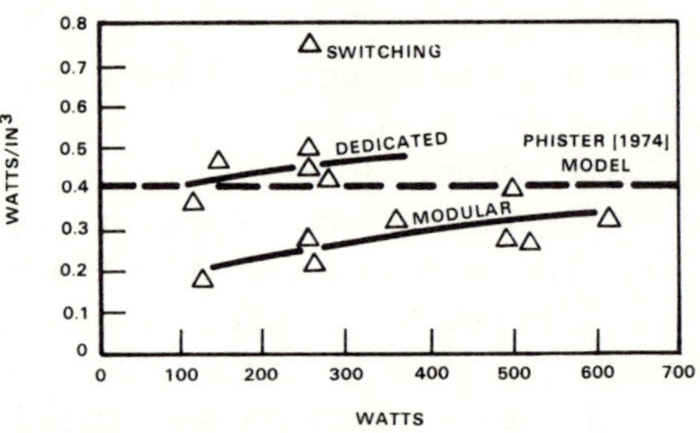

(c) Volumetric efficiency (in watts per in^3).

Figure 16. Cost, weight, and volumetric efficiencies versus size for various DEC computer power supplies.

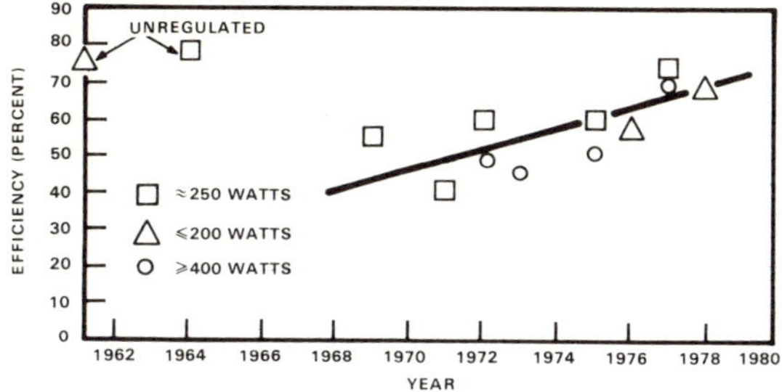

Figure 17. Power supply efficiency (watts out per watts in) versus time for various DEC computer power supplies.

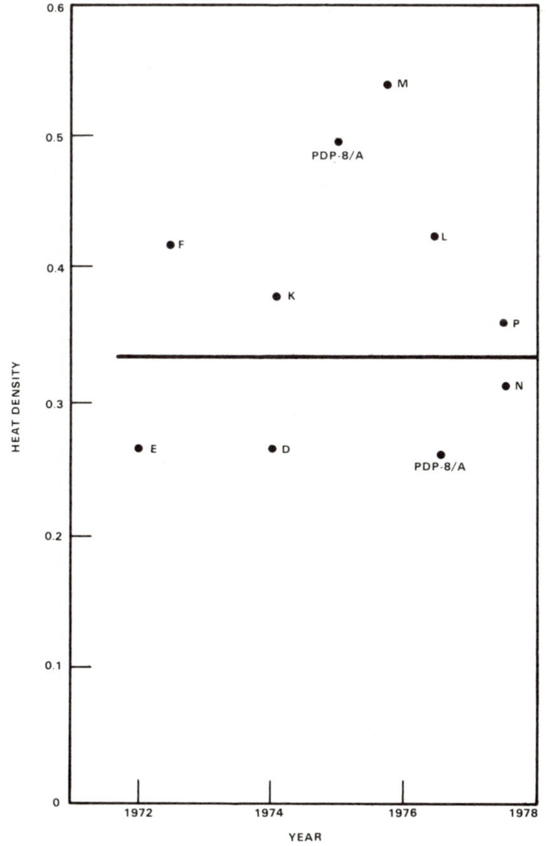

Figure 18. Heat density (kilowatts per ft^3) of various DEC computer boxes.

power densities have increased. Where 250 watts used to suffice for a 10.5 × 19 × 25-inch box, 800 watts is now required, and the space for the power supply has barely increased. This has put substantial constraints on the weight and efficiency of power systems; and, at times, space utilization has been (inadvertently) traded for cost, manufacturability, and serviceability.

In response to these space pressures, there has been a constant gain in volumetric efficiency (Figure 15*b*) over the years with the highly dense power supplies on the top of the band and the modular packaged units on the bottom. With the introduction of line switching power supplies, this curve made a quantum jump. The increase in volumetric efficiency, plotted relative to time in Figure 15*b*, is plotted relative to power output in Figure 16*b*.

Power supply technology determines not only volumetric efficiency but also the weight of the unit. Here again the use of high frequency line switcher technology rather than low frequency transformer technology has produced marked results – in this case, two distinct curves.

The weight efficiency (watts per pound) has been fairly constant over time but has shown a slight improvement as larger supplies were built (Figure 16*c*).

Finally, Figure 17 shows how power supply efficiency is improving with time. Note that with direct line switching, efficiencies of 70 percent are expected. This efficiency permits the increase in volumetric efficiency because there is less heat to dissipate.

HEAT

Although the volumetric measures of module area and the size of the cabinet are also important, the amount of heat that the enclosure is capable of dissipating is the most important metric of reliability. Table 6 gives some of the important metrics of several of the recent DEC computer boxes.

Figure 18 gives the heat density for the various boxes. The amount of heat dissipated by the

Table 6. Expansion Box Characteristics

Box Model	Used On	Year	Weight (lb)	Size (ft^3)	Modules	Module Volume ft^3	Heat In (kW)	Heat Density (kW/ft^3)	Space Efficiency
BA11-D	11/35	1974	100	2.6	24 hex	0.93	0.7	0.27	0.35
BA11-E	11/45	1972	100	2.6	27 quad	0.7	0.7	0.27	0.27
BA11-F	11/40*	1972	260	5.3	44 hex	1.7	2.2	0.42	0.32
BA11-K	11/04†	1974	110	2.6	24 hex	0.93	1.0	0.38	0.36
BA11-L	11/04	1976	50	1.3	9 hex	0.35	0.55	0.43	0.27
BA11-M	11/03	1975	25	0.5	4 quad	0.1	0.25	0.54	0.24
BA11-N	11/03	1977	40	1.0	9 quad	0.23	0.24	0.31	0.22
BA11-P	11/60	1977	100	3.0	29 hex	1.1	1.1	0.36	0.22
BA8-CA	8/A	1975	117	2.4	20 quad	0.52	1.2	0.50	0.22
H9300	8/A	1977	55	1.1	10 quad	0.26	0.3	0.26	0.24
H9500‡	11/780	1978	344	43.4	67 ext hex	3.7	6.0	0.15	0.10

*Also 11/45 and 11/70.
†Also 11/34 and 11/70 memory.
‡Actually a cabinet.

box (in kilowatts per cubic foot) has been relatively constant with time. There has been great variation about the norm, and the very high heat dissipation of the first PDP-8/A (due to high packing density and a relatively inefficient power supply) resulted in the next design being of lower density. The space utilization follows a similar path, although the efficiency appears to be declining (Figure 19). This decline is hardly noticeable and is even surprising in light of more efficient power supplies which make it possible to place more components in a given enclosure. The cost-effectiveness of the average enclosure, as measured by the material cost, is declining with time as measured by the relative cost of materials per cubic foot of modules held (Figure 20).

The time chart gives a completely erroneous view of the situation because economy of scale is not considered. Figure 21 shows how the relative cost of box materials varies with the volume (in number of hex modules). Here the upward trend of the previous figure is not apparent, but it merely occurs because later packages are for smaller numbers of modules.

AN OVERVIEW OF MANUFACTURING

Although the result of a design project is an entity which is manufactured, very little is written about manufacturing in the computer engineering literature. Such literature generally discusses algorithms, logic design, and circuit technology. Yet for a computer to be commercially successful, it must be manufacturable, economically operable, and serviceable. Moreover, for most of the computer engineering discussed in this book, because the designs are intended for volume production, engineering costs are small (1 to 10 percent) compared with other product and life cycle costs. The product cost is determined by the price of the components and the manufacturing process; the life cycle cost includes the purchase price, the operational costs, and service costs.

For production, machines must be easy to assemble and test, repair must be rapid, engineering changes must be introduced smoothly, and the production line cannot be held up because of shortages of components – all parts of traditional manufacturing considerations.

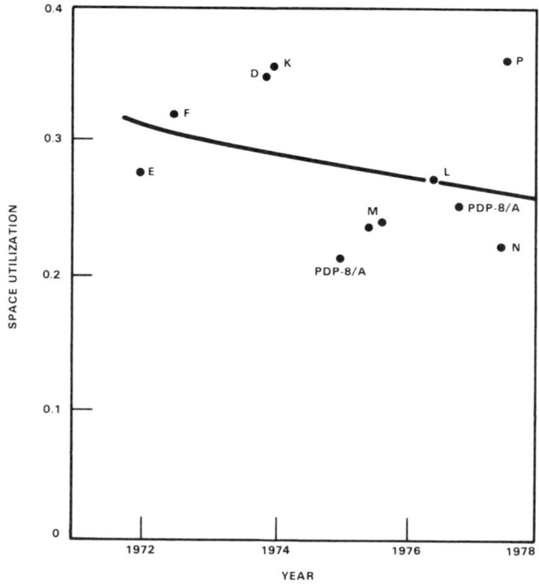

Figure 19. Space utilization (ft³ of modules per cubic foot) of various DEC computer boxes.

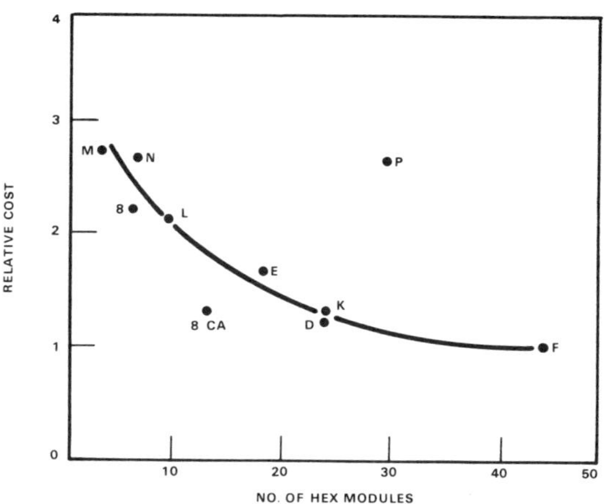

Figure 21. Relative cost of box materials versus number of hex size modules for various DEC minicomputer boxes.

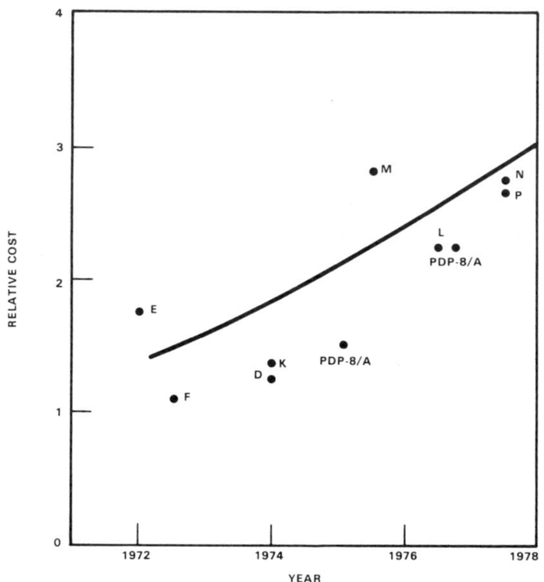

Figure 20. Cost payload (relative cost of materials per ft³ of modules held) of various DEC computer boxes.

The Life Cycle of a Product

Figure 22 shows a simplistic process flow for the major phases and milestones in the life of a product. In reality, planning and designs for many of the phases go on concurrently. The early research, advanced development, and definitional phases are not shown. Often, products proceed from the idea stage to the engineering breadboard and are then terminated because they do not meet original goals or because better ideas arise.

To facilitate changes, the engineering breadboard is usually built with wire-wrapped rather than printed circuit boards if the circuit technologies used permit the long wire lengths characteristic of wire-wrapped boards. At or before the breadboard stage, manufacturing start-up schedules are made. Other organizations formulate and execute plans: systems engineering, for product test/verification; software engineering, for special software and verification; marketing, for promotion and product distribution; sales, for training; field service, for training and parts logistics; and software support.

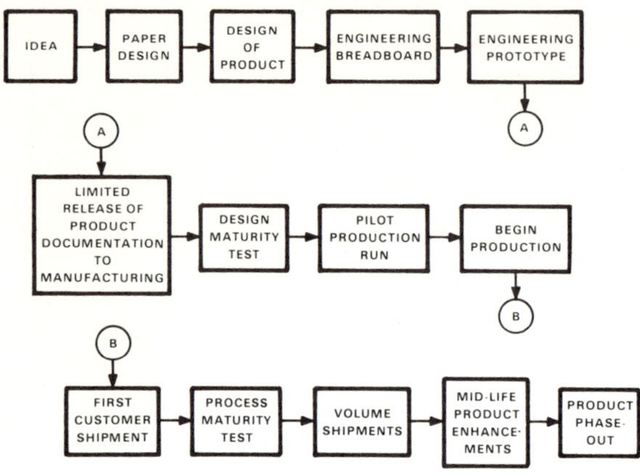

Figure 22. A simplified process flow for the major phases and milestones in the life of a product.

After the engineering breadboard has been debugged, construction of engineering prototypes begins. The engineering prototypes test the design using the actual printed circuit modules that will be used in manufacturing. Usually a number of prototypes are constructed, the number varying from 10 to 100 depending on the complexity, cost, and anticipated product volume. All processors and peripherals in the planned systems configurations are tested in conjunction with the prototypes. The complete system must meet the product specifications and must run all of the system software.

The requirement that all of the system software be run is an excellent supplement to the normal testing of prototypes. It is especially useful when the product being designed is a processor with a mature architecture because more system software is then available. Because the number of possible states and state sequences in a computer system is very large, a diagnostic test which exercises every one is impractical. Diagnostic programs and microdiagnostics therefore test a judiciously chosen subset of all states. Such programs are not perfect in their coverage, however, and system software is run as well. Thus, the more software that is available to test a prototype, the less likely it is that a design error will go unfound. The general problem of testing requires much more work before it can be considered mature. One would like to see, for example, the automatic generation of verification programs from an ISP description of the architecture being built.

Design maturity testing with a number of engineering prototypes verifies the design and justifies the risk of releasing the design to manufacturing. Tests for reliability and functionality are conducted. Environmental tests for shock, temperature, humidity, static discharge, radiation, power interrupt, and safety are also conducted at this stage.

The release to manufacturing is a major milestone. The product is placed under formal engineering change control to ensure that everyone knows what version of the documentation is current; specifications and documentation are available for the product and manufacturing process. For the integrated circuits, sources of supply and testing procedures are in place. Process control tapes are ready for the numerically controlled machine tools, such as component insertion, backplane wiring, and printed circuit board drilling machines. Any special tooling for the mechanical packaging has been obtained. Testing at all levels has been specified; test programs for computer-controlled testers have been written, special test equipment has been built, and diagnostic programs are ready.

For some products, particularly processors, a pilot run is manufactured. The pilot run shakes down and verifies the actual manufacturing process by building a small number of units, using the product, and processing documentation at the manufacturing plant.

Product announcement usually occurs during the design maturity testing period but can occur at any time – often as early as when the breadboard works or as late as the first customer shipment, depending on the marketing strategy. This strategy is clearly a function of the volume, novelty, and competitive needs.

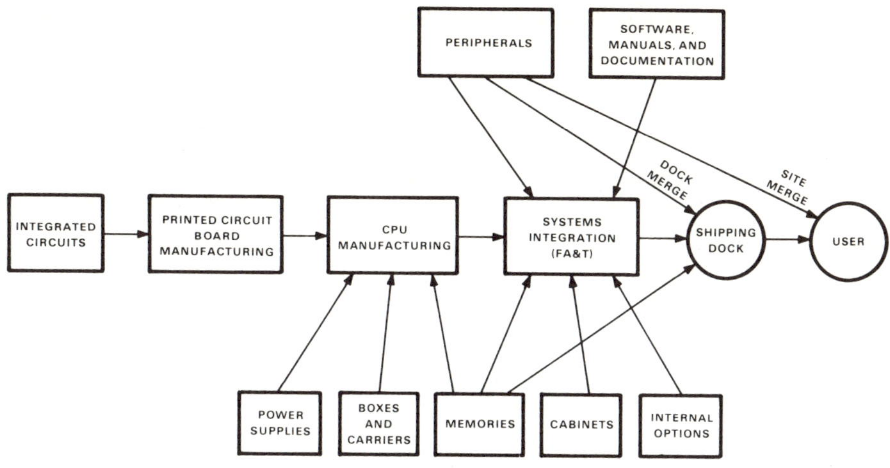

Figure 23. Overview of manufacturing computer system flow.

Process maturity testing verifies that the product is being manufactured with the desired cost, quality, and production rate. After process maturity testing, the steady state phase of manufacturing continues (with possible perturbations due to the introduction of product enhancements, engineering change orders, or process changes to lower product costs) until the product is phased out.

Manufacturing Process Flows

An overview of a manufacturing process is given in Figure 23 which shows how a product moves through the various factories. There are often different plants for boards, peripherals, memories, and central processors. Integration from the other stages and stock storage occurs at the stage called "final assembly and test" (Figure 24). Here, the software system that is to be run, operations manuals, and other documentation are also integrated and tested.

Figure 25 gives the complete flow for a typical volume manufacturing line, the PDP-11/60 central processor facility in Aguadilla, Puerto Rico.

Testing

Since testing occurs at each stage in the manufacturing process, dedicated logic must be added to the design to provide physical access probes for the test equipment. To test a particular function, it must be specifiable, invokable, and observable. For example, the function of an adder can be clearly specified, but it cannot be easily invoked or observed if its inputs and outputs are etch runs on a printed circuit board. Several testing strategies are used: add signal lines from the adder to the backplane where there are adequate probe access points, probe directly onto the module etch or pins, and subsume the adder in a function whose inputs and outputs can be more easily controlled and observed. The problems of observation and control exist at all levels-of-integration. Examples of observation points at each level for the PDP-11/60 are given in Table 7.

The problem of testability must be addressed at design time. Providing access for testing always incurs added product cost (extra logic and module pins or circuit pins) but lowers manufacturing cost and field service costs. As gate

Table 7. Examples of Observation Points at Each Structural Level for the PDP-11/60

Level in Computer Hierarchy	Observation Point	Stage in Manufacture of Computer	Example
Electrical circuit	Transistor contacts on metallization layer	Semiconductor fabrication	Wafer test with microprobe
Switching circuit	Leads on IC package	Incoming inspection of ICs	IC tester
Register transfer	Etch run	Module	Probe on module (module-specific tester)
Register transfer	Backplane	Module	Memory exerciser for cache
Central processor	Unibus	Central processor	Unibus voltage margin tester
Central processor	Contents of memory	Central processor	Diagnostic programs at subsystem level, e.g., memory management unit or processor instruction set tests
Computer	Contents of memory	System integration	Peripheral diagnostic programs
Computer	Unibus	System integration	Bus exerciser

Figure 24. Final assembly and test (FA&T) for computer systems.

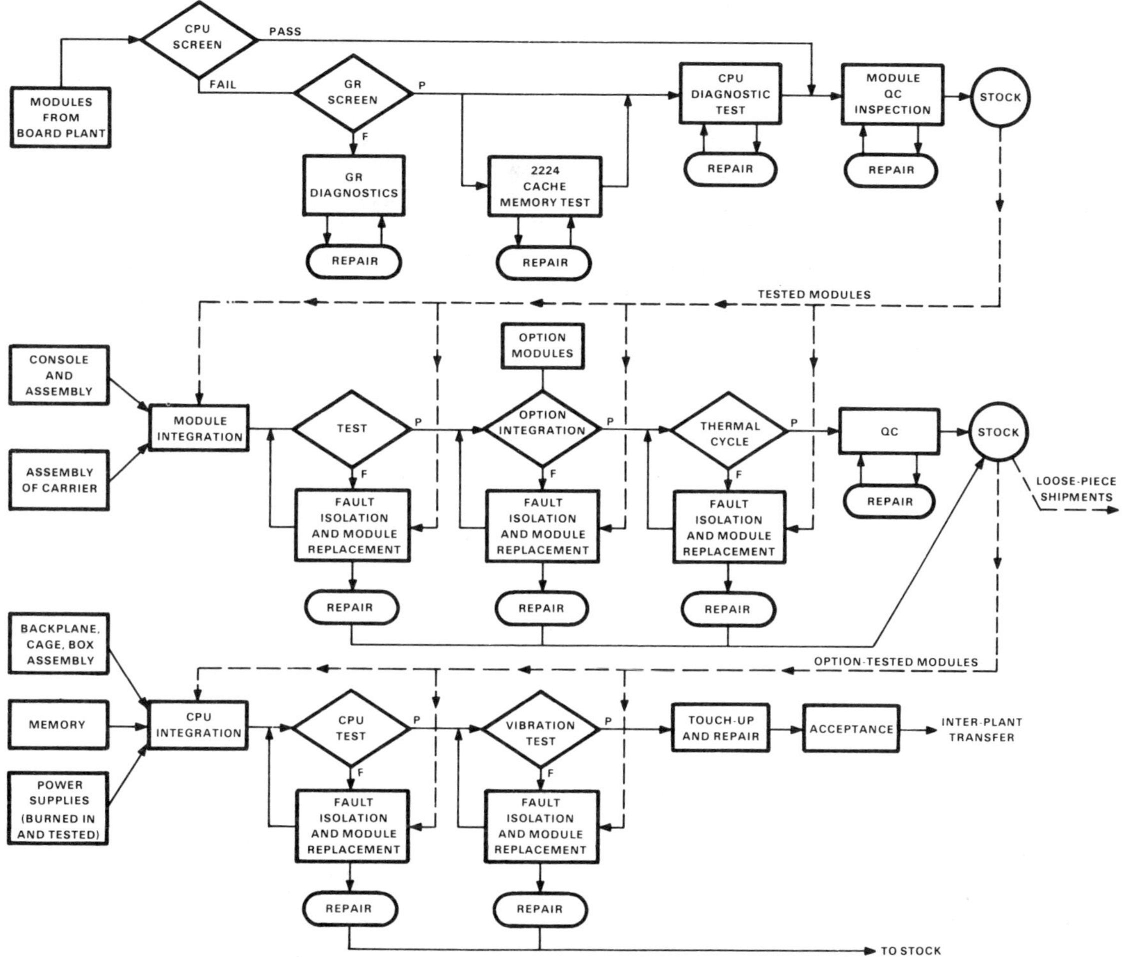

Figure 25. The process flow for the PDP-11/60 manufacturing plant in Aguadilla, P.R.

density per chip continues to increase, the problem worsens. One solution, which is economical in I/O connections, is to design every storage element as a shift register which can be loaded in parallel (normal mode) or serially loaded (with an invoking state) or serially read (with the state to be observed). Eichelberger and Williams [1977] report on such a scheme for gate array designs. The individual shift register latches are connected to form one or more independent shift registers which are connected to the leads of the gate array package.

The testing which occurs at the various stages of the manufacturing process can be classified into three types according to the different failure modes anticipated. Type 1, a static test, is intended to find process-related faults. Examples are solder shorts, open-circuit etch connections, dead components, and incorrectly valued resistors. Figure 26 shows a GenRad

Figure 26. GenRad Corp. (GR) tester for modules.

Figure 27. Quick-Verify (QV) station to verify that tested modules operate within a system.

Figure 28. Chambers for thermal cycling operating modules.

Corp. (GR) tester of the type first used (Figure 25) to detect this type of fault. A module-specific program in the tester guides the operator through a fault-finding procedure. Approximately 95 percent of all Type 1 failures are diagnosed and repaired at this step.

Type 2 is dynamic. It seeks to detect faults which are caused by timing parameters being out of specification range, by logic incompatibilities, and by other functional problems. Figure 27 shows a tester (Figure 25) performing this type of test.

Type 3 is the reliability or burn-in test. The manufacturing process includes extensive thermal cycling to ensure that component "infant mortality" cases are discovered early during manufacturing because it is more expensive to find defective components at the later, more integrated systems level. For some components, notably integrated circuits, thermal cycling is done when the components are received from the vendor. In addition, thermal cycling and burn-in are done near the end of the production process for entire processors and options. The temperature/humidity environmental chambers used, which house twelve or sixteen processors each, are shown in Figure 28. Test chambers to heat entire computer systems are also used.

ACKNOWLEDGEMENTS

We gratefully acknowledge the following colleagues who provided data for this chapter and valuable critiques of earlier drafts: Jim Cudmore, Russ Doane, Sam Fuller, Lorrin Gale, Dick Gonzales, Jim Scanlan, Henk Schalke, Joe Smith, Steve Teicher, and Dave Widder.

Opposite:

- DEC Systems Modules.

PART I

IN THE BEGINNING

In the Beginning

Because modules were DEC's first product, and for many years their major product, it is appropriate to study the history of DEC's modules and the influence of technology on their development. The history of modules is a subset of the history of computers, and many of the views of computers expressed in Chapter 1 apply as readily to modules. In particular, the Structural View and the Packaging Levels-of-Integration View plainly apply. Further, a study of module history shows the effects of progress in semiconductor technology, as discussed in Chapter 2, and demonstrates on a small scale many of the packaging and manufacturing concepts discussed in Chapter 3.

With the advent of microprocessors, the distinction between a module and a computer has become blurred, and complete computer systems have become available at the printed circuit board/module level of packaging integration. The structural levels (Chapter 1, Figure 1) found on a single module have changed from solely circuit level to logic level, then to register transfer level, and finally to processor-memory-switch level. These developments will be explored more fully in Part IV, "The Evolution of Computer Building Blocks"; the discussion here is limited to the simpler modules that characterized the first 18 years of DEC's computers.

The two chapters in this part consist of a 1957 paper by Ken Olsen and a historical review by Dick Best. Both of these papers, but in particular the Olsen paper, give a glimpse of how early computer design was heavily weighted toward the electrical circuit level shown in Figure 1 of Chapter 1. As indicated above, the capability of modern technology to package complete switching circuit level and register transfer level systems into single chips has been a motivating force moving computer design toward the PMS level. There has also been increased activity "downward" however, as is also shown in Figure 1 of Chapter 1. To fit the modern, more complex systems into chips, increased attention to the lowest level (the device level) has also been required. Since this has been more the domain of the materials scientist than the computer scientist, it is not discussed in detail here.

While module design and computer design have evolved a great deal in the past 18 to 20 years, certain aspects of the Olsen paper reflect design methods which have counterparts today. In particular, convenient maintenance was plainly one of the important goals in the TX-2 circuit design effort. The use of a single, standard type of flip-flop and the use of a minimum number of different plug-in units were important elements in meeting that goal. These features simplified the design, simplified maintenance training, and reduced the variety of spare modules that needed to be stocked. A voltage adjusting (margining) system for identifying marginal circuits was another important feature of the TX-2 circuit design.

Today, computer engineers generally try to use a limited number of flip-flop types (or RAM types, etc.) because they have certain favorites whose characteristics they understand well and because the cost of bringing new parts into a company is very high. The old reasons – to simplify design, training, and stocking of spares – continue to apply as well. Even though keeping the number of different plug-in units (modules) to a minimum continues to have these advantages, this cannot be done as easily as it once was, principally because the increased functionality now available has customized modules to such a great degree. For example, in the case of an LSI-11, the computer is a single module.

Modern designs do not use margining except in special cases where the refresh clock cycles of dynamic memories are altered to detect failures. However, special maintenance logic is often included in current designs. The idea of built-in maintenance features is in some ways similar to the old margining idea: in other ways it is a substantial deviation because additional parts are required, and the old designers were extremely careful of the parts count. The emphasis on low component cost and parts count expressed in these chapters may seem odd to modern designers, but the gradual lessening of this concern (as discussed in Chapter 4) serves as an excellent example of the declining cost of electronic technology and of semiconductor technology in particular.

In summary, the modules chapters which follow form a starting point, both in time and in technology, for a study of how the views, concepts, and trends described in the first two chapters have applied in the development of DEC modules and computers.

4

Transistor Circuitry in the Lincoln TX-2

KENNETH H. OLSEN

CIRCUIT CONFIGURATIONS

Only two basic circuits are needed to perform most of the logical operations in the TX-2 computer: a saturated transistor inverter and a saturated emitter follower. To the logical designer who works with them, these circuits can be considered as simple switches that are either open or closed.

The schematic diagram of an emitter follower and the symbol used by the logical designers is shown in Figure 1. With a negative input, the output is "shorted" to the -3 V supply as through a switch. When several of these emitter followers are combined in parallel, as in Figure 2, any one of them will clamp the output to -3 V. We then have an OR circuit for negative signals and an AND circuit for positive signals. The transistor inverter is shown in Figure 3 with its logic symbol. Basic AND, OR circuits result from the connection of these simple switches in series or parallel (Figures 4 and 5). More complex networks like the TX-2 carry circuit use these elements arranged in series-parallel (Figure 6).

In Figure 3 the resistor R_1 is chosen so that under the worst combinations of stated component and power supply variations, the drop

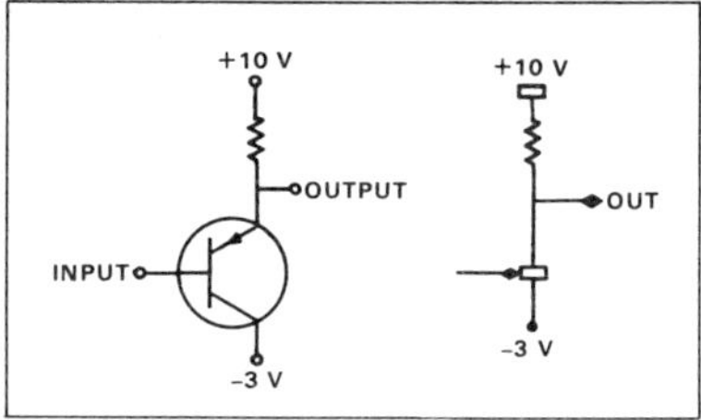

Figure 1. Emitter follower.

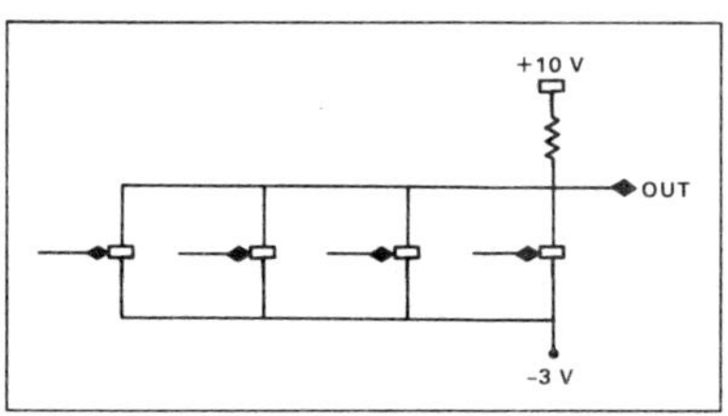

Figure 2. Parallel emitter follower.

across the transistor will be less than 200 mV during the "on-condition." R_2 biases the transistor base positive during the off condition to provide greater tolerance to noise, I_{OO}, and signal variations. Capacitance C was selected to remove all of the minority carriers from the base when the transistor is being turned off. The effect of C on a test circuit driven by a fast step is shown in Figure 7. Note that the delay due to hole storage is only a few millimicroseconds.

We run the circuits under saturated conditions to achieve stability and a wide tolerance to parameters without the need for clamp diodes. Unlike vacuum tubes, which always need an appreciable voltage across them for operation, a transistor requires practically no voltage across it. In spite of the delay in turning off saturated transistors, these circuits are faster than most vacuum tube circuits. Faster circuit speed is not due to the fact that the transistors are faster than vacuum tubes, but because they operate at much lower voltage levels. A vacuum tube takes several volts to turn it from fully "on" to fully "off"; a transistor takes less than 1 V.

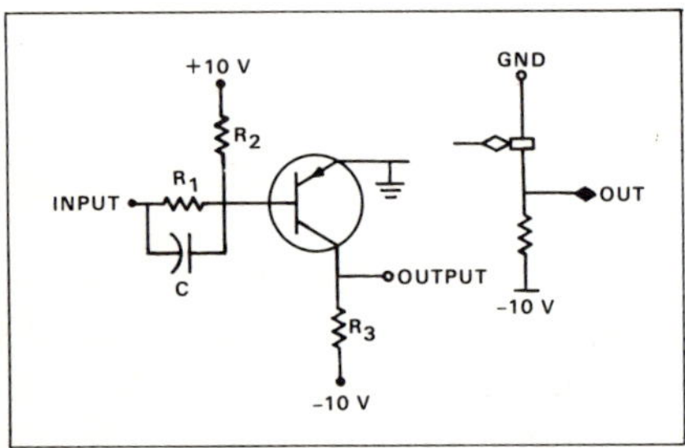

Figure 3. Inverter.

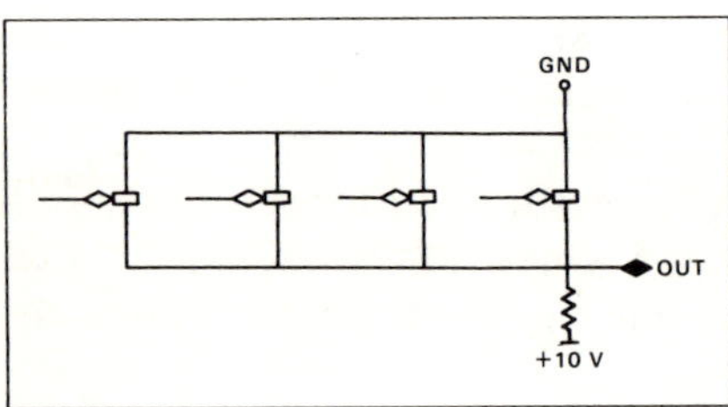

Figure 4. Parallel inverters.

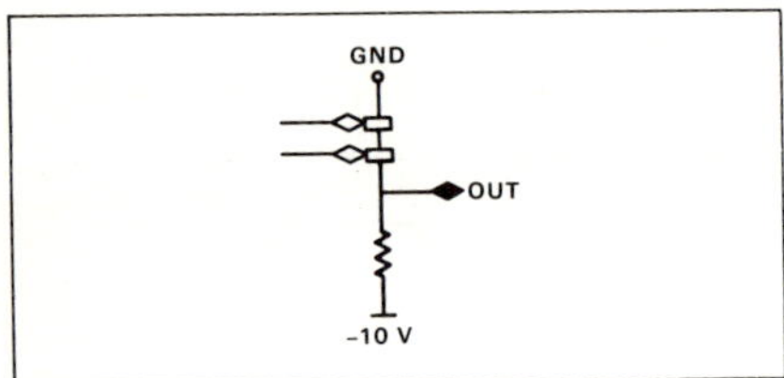

Figure 5. Series inverters.

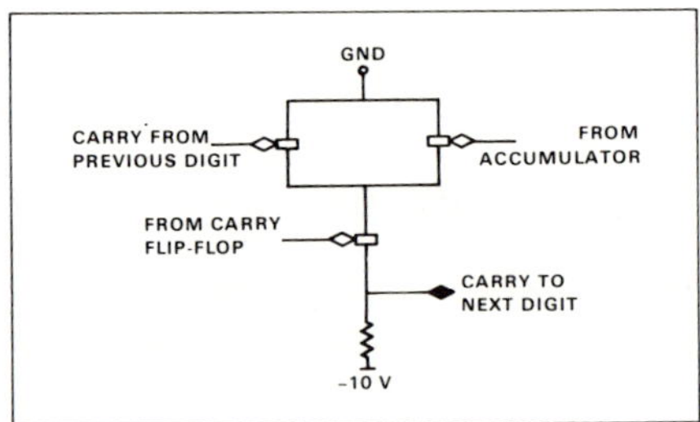

Figure 6. TX-2 carry circuits.

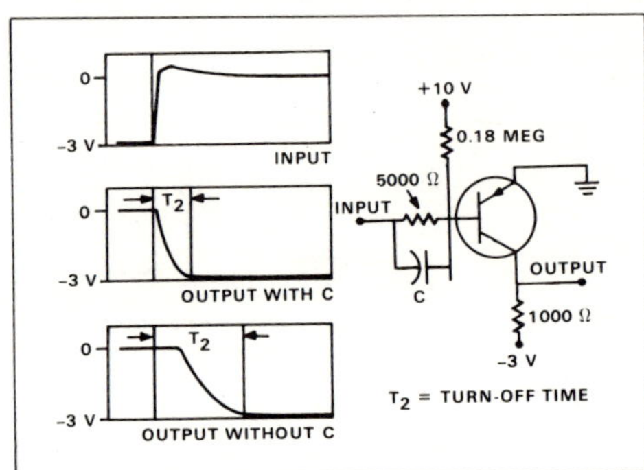

Figure 7. Turn-off time.

FLIP-FLOP

On the basis of previous experience, we decided that the advantages of having one standard flip-flop were worth some complication in TX-2 circuitry. The circuit diagram of the flip-flop package in Figure 8 is basically an Eccles-Jordan trigger circuit with a 3-transistor amplifier on each output. The input amplifiers isolate the pulse input circuits and give high-input impedance. The amplifiers give enough delay to allow the flip-flop to be set at the same time that it is being sensed. Figure 9 shows the waveforms of this flip-flop package when complemented at a 10-megapulse rate. The rise and fall times, about 25 millimicroseconds, are faster than one normally sees in a single inverter or an emitter follower because on each output there is an inverter that pulls to ground and an emitter follower that pulls to –3 V. Figure 10 is a plot of the pulse amplitude necessary to complement the flip-flop at various frequencies. Note the independence of trigger sensitivity to pulse repetition rate. This circuit will operate at a 10-megapulse rate, twice the maximum rate at which it will be used in TX-2.

The TX-2 circuits reproduced most often were designed with a minimum number of components to achieve economies in manufacture and maintenance. The design of less frequently reproduced circuits made liberal use of components – even redundancy – to achieve long life and broad tolerance to component variations. The goal was system simplicity and high performance with a lower total number of components than might otherwise be possible. For

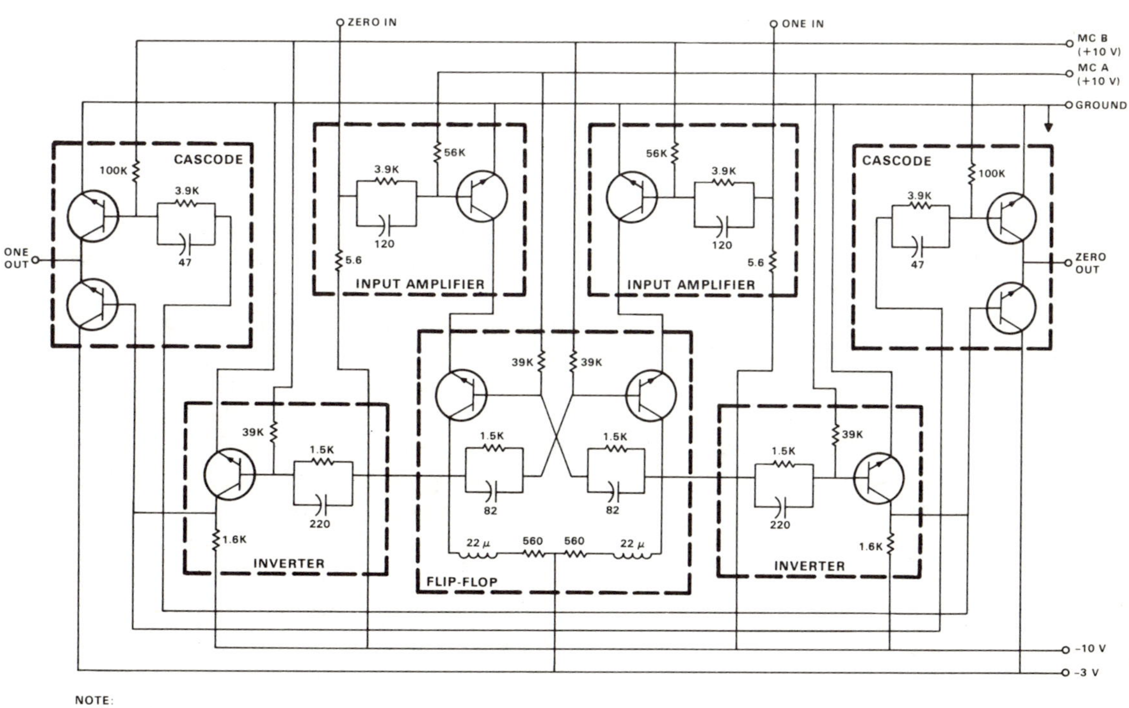

Figure 8. TX-2 flip-flop.

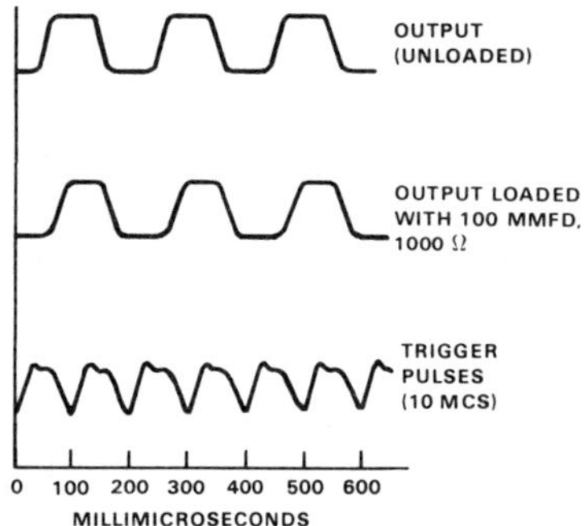

Figure 9. Flip-flop waveforms.

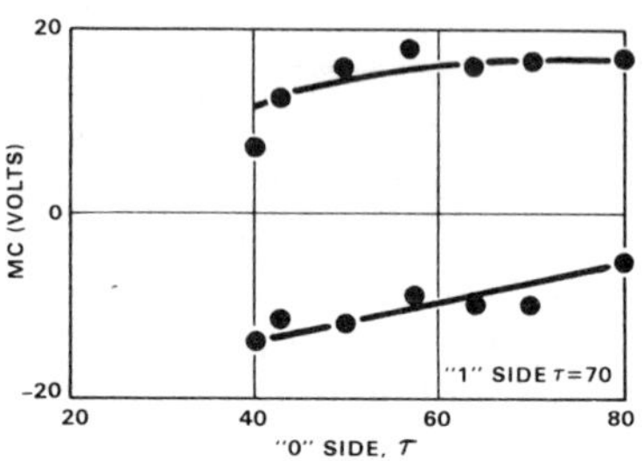

Figure 11. Tau margins.

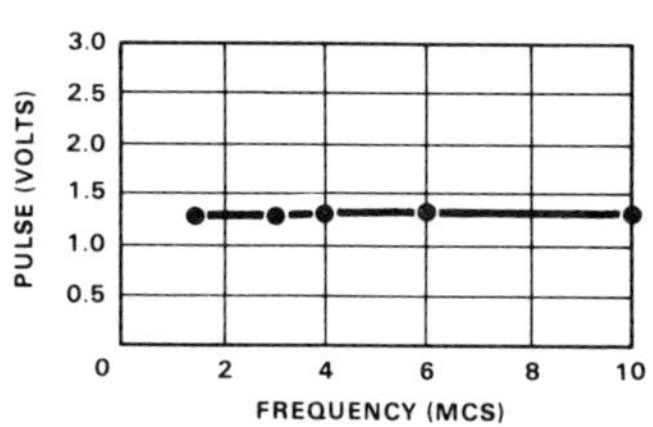

Figure 10. Trigger sensitivity.

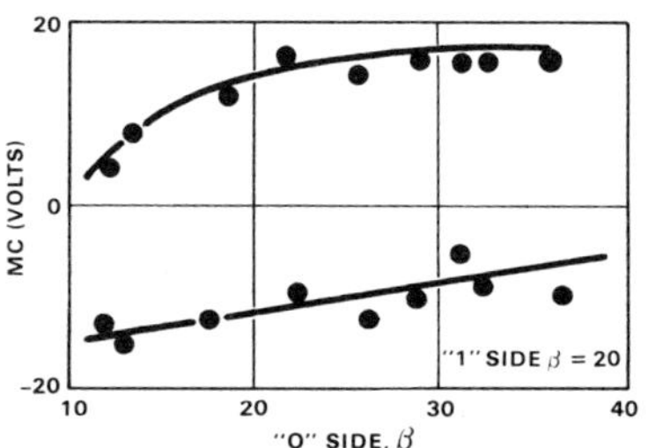

Figure 12. Beta margins.

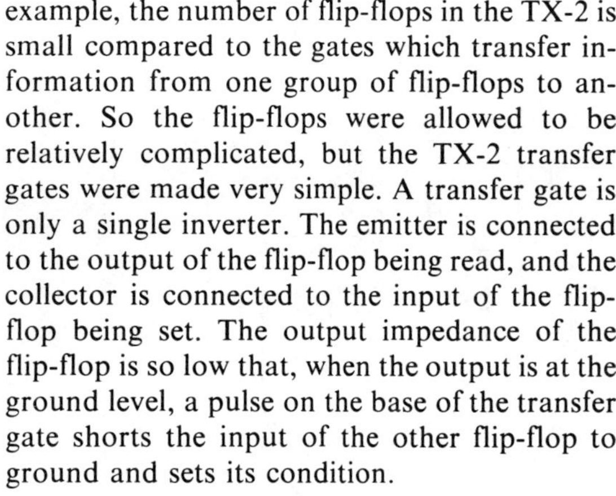

example, the number of flip-flops in the TX-2 is small compared to the gates which transfer information from one group of flip-flops to another. So the flip-flops were allowed to be relatively complicated, but the TX-2 transfer gates were made very simple. A transfer gate is only a single inverter. The emitter is connected to the output of the flip-flop being read, and the collector is connected to the input of the flip-flop being set. The output impedance of the flip-flop is so low that, when the output is at the ground level, a pulse on the base of the transfer gate shorts the input of the other flip-flop to ground and sets its condition.

MARGINAL CHECKING

We planned, of course, to incorporate marginal checking in the design of these circuits so that, under a program of regularly scheduled maintenance, deteriorating components could be located before they caused failure in the system. We also found it practical to use the technique during the design of the circuits to locate the design center of the various parameters and to indicate the tolerance of circuit performance to these parameters. A further application of marginal checking has been found in other systems during shakedown and initial operation to pinpoint noise and other system faults not serious enough to cause failure and therefore very difficult to isolate by other means.

The operating condition of the inverters is indicated by varying the +10 V bias. In the flip-flop schematic in Figure 8, the inverters were divided into two groups for marginal checking, and the two leads labeled MCA and MCB were

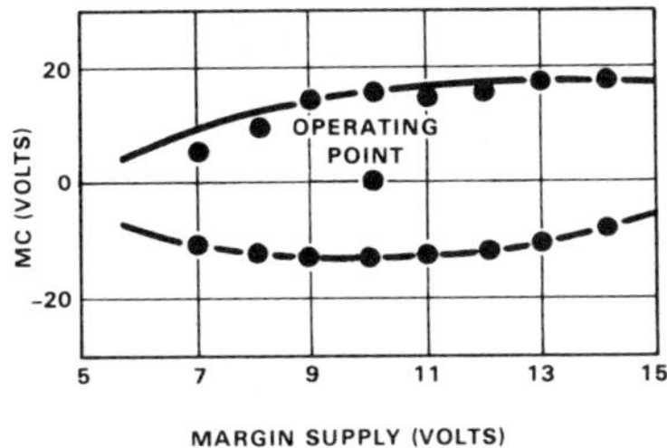

Figure 13. −10 V supply margins.

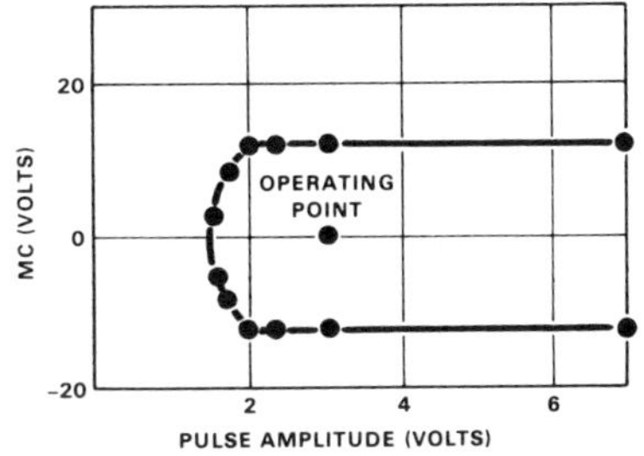

Figure 16. Pulse margins.

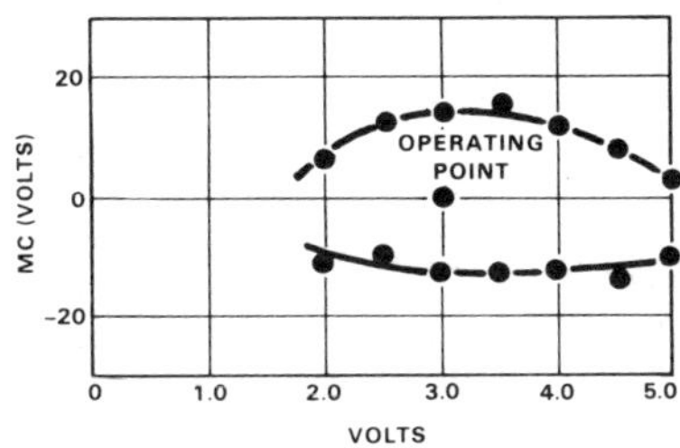

Figure 14. −3 V supply margins.

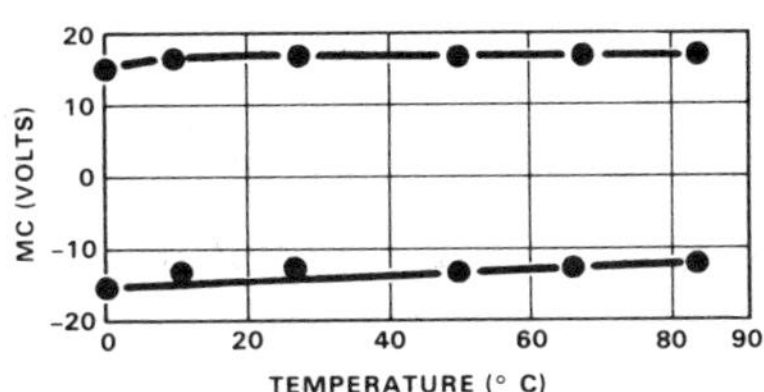

Figure 15. Temperature margins.

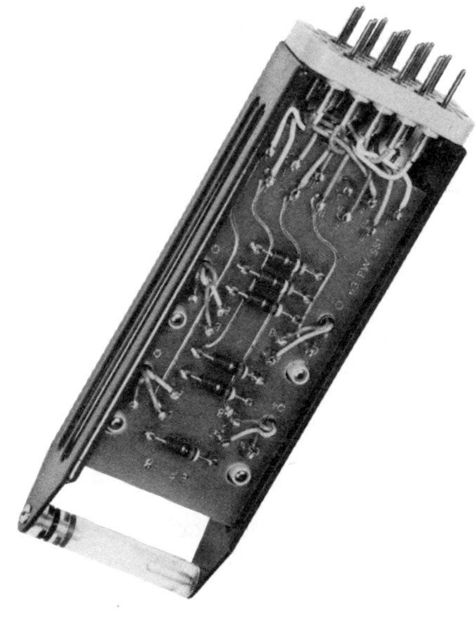

Figure 17. TX-2 plug-in unit.

varied one at a time for most critical checking of the circuit. The following curves show the locus of failure points for various parameters as a function of the marginal checking voltage. Figure 11 shows the tolerance to tau, a measure of hole storage, and Figure 12 shows the tolerance to beta, the current gain. Operating margins for supply voltages, temperature, and pulse amplitude are shown in Figures 13 through 16.

PACKAGING

The number of types of plug-in units was kept small for ease of production and to keep the number of spares to a minimum. The circuits are built on dip-soldered etched boards, and the components are hand soldered in solid turret lugs. The boards are mounted in steel shells shown in Figure 17 to keep the boards

Figure 18. TX-2 back panel.

from flexing. The male and female contacts are machined and gold plated. The sockets are hand wired and soldered in panels (Figure 18).

CONCLUSION

The result of these design considerations is a 5-megapulse control and arithmetic element that will take less than 40 square feet of space and dissipate less than 800 watts of power. The simplicity of the circuits has encouraged a degree of logical sophistication that would not have been chanced before.

ACKNOWLEDGEMENTS

A number of people took part in the work reported here. Major contributions were made by B. M. Gurley, J. R. Fadiman, R. A. Hughes, K. H. Konkle, and M. E. Petersen.

5

Digital Modules, The Basis for Computers

RICHARD L. BEST, RUSSELL C. DOANE, and JOHN E. McNAMARA

The circuits and design concepts described in Chapter 4 were the basis for the subsequent development of DEC modules. In Chapter 5, the discussion of this development is broadened to include not only circuits and design concepts but also packaging and the effects of progress in semiconductor technology. DEC modules are important because the progress in semiconductor technology that has formed the major element of the technology push driving the computer industry is evident in the history of DEC modules on a scale convenient for close examination and understanding.

The first modules produced by DEC were called Digital Laboratory Modules and were intended to sit on an engineer's workbench or be mounted in a scientist's equipment rack. To facilitate the rapid construction of logic systems using these modules, interconnection was accomplished with simple cords equipped with banana plugs. As shown in Figure 1, the modules were mounted in aluminum cases 1-3/4 × 4-1/2 × 7 inches in size. All of the logic signals were brought out to the front of the case, where they appeared on miniature banana jacks mounted in a schematic diagram of the logic function performed by the module. The modules were offered in three speed ranges with compatible signal levels. The three speed ranges were 5 MHz (1957), 500 kHz (1959), and 10 MHz (1960).

The Digital Laboratory Module product line was supplemented by the Digital Systems Modules. These modules, samples of which are

Figure 1. Digital Laboratory Modules.

Figure 2. Digital System Modules.

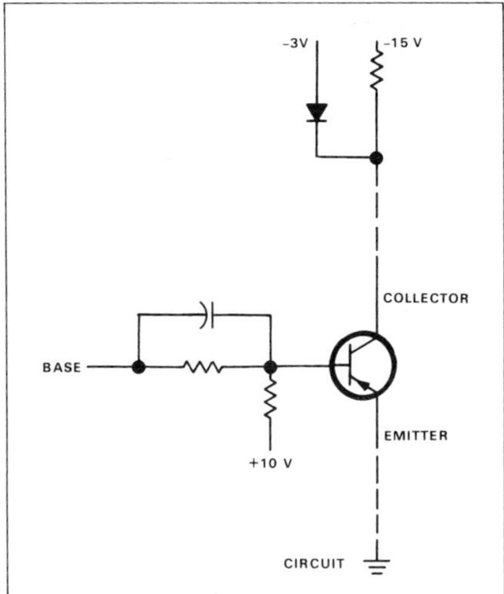

Figure 3. Schematic drawing of an inverter used in digital system modules.

shown in Figure 2, were identical to the Laboratory Modules in circuitry, signal levels, and speed range, but they had a different packaging scheme. The System Module packaging was designed for rack mounting and used 22-pin Amphenol connectors at the backs of the modules rather than banana plugs at the front. The 22-pin connectors were originally available only in a soldered connection version, but a taper pin version was later offered. The System Module mounting method was chosen for the PDP-1 computer, as it permitted a wired panel of 25 modules to be mounted in a 5-1/4-inch section of standard 19-inch rack.

The circuits used in both module series were based on the M.I.T. Lincoln Laboratory TX-2 computer circuits described in Chapter 4. All of the TX-2 basic circuits were used, except those gates which used emitter followers. The emitter follower gates were not short circuit proof, and it was felt that misplaced patch cords in Laboratory Module configurations or slipping scope probes in System Module configurations would cause a high fatality rate for those circuits.

What follows is a brief review of some of the circuits to indicate how much present day logic design differs from the logic design of 20 years ago. Today designers deal with arithmetic logic units and microprocessors as units, whereas in the early 1960s, single gates and flip-flops were units.

In the early module designs, most logical operations were performed using saturating PNP germanium transistors. While the use of transistors in radios and television sets relies on the linear relationship between base current and emitter-to-collector current to provide the amplification of radio frequency and audio frequency signals, the use of transistors in computer circuits (except those using emitter-coupled logic (ECL)) relies primarily on the behavior of transistors in either the saturated state or the cutoff state. The use of transistors in such circuits can best be appreciated from the simple example shown in Figure 3.

Figure 3 is a schematic drawing of an inverter. When the emitter is at ground and the base lead is brought to a sufficiently negative voltage, the resulting base current will saturate the transistor, effectively connecting the emitter to the collector. If, on the other hand, the base is grounded, then no base current flows, no emitter-to-collector current flows, and the transistor is in the cutoff state. The collector would then assume the voltage of the negative voltage

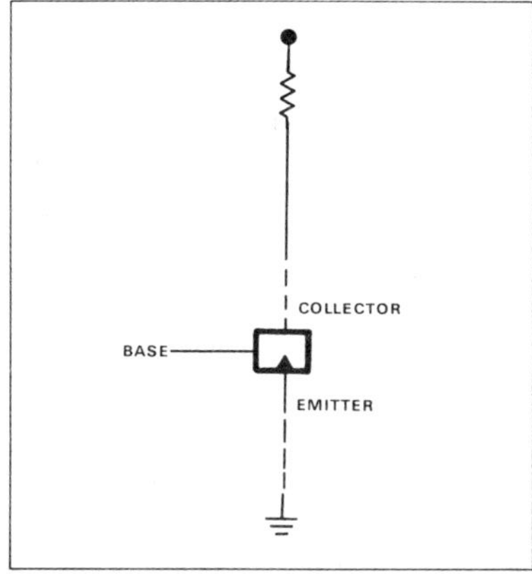

Figure 4. Symbolic drawing of an inverter.

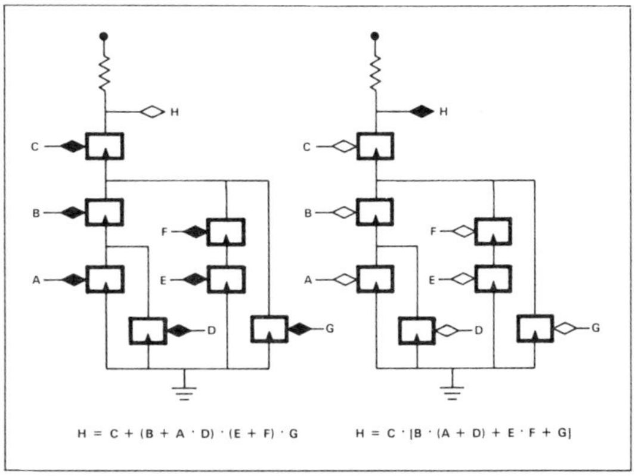

Figure 5. Sample circuits using series and parallel arrangements of inverters.

source, were it not for the clamp diode which limits the voltage of the collector to −3 volts.

To facilitate maintenance, the +10-volt bias supply shown in Figure 3 was adjustable for margin checking, a feature which had been used in the TX-2 and which is discussed in Chapter 4.

To simplify the logic drawings, a symbolic drawing like that in Figure 4 was customarily used to represent the inverter circuit. Note that neither Figure 3 nor Figure 4 shows the emitter directly connected to ground or the collector directly connected to the negative supply. Rather, a dotted line is used on the drawings to indicate that Laboratory Modules and System Modules often used a series connection of up to three inverter gates between the negative supply and ground to accomplish various logic functions. Parallel and series-parallel arrangements were also used, as shown in the sample circuits in Figure 5.

The Digital Laboratory Modules and the Digital System Modules used a dual polarity logic system employing both levels and pulses. The logic voltage levels were −3 volts and ground. Correspondence between the logic state, ONE or ZERO, and the voltage levels of −3 and ground were indicated at each point in the logic diagram by a diamond. The diamond defined the necessary voltage level for the action desired. A solid diamond denoted that a −3-volt level was an assertion, and a hollow diamond indicated that a ground level was an assertion. This convention gave two signal names to one physical signal: if a given asserted signal *A* was passed through an inverter, four signals resulted, as shown in Figure 6.

A logic function lower in cost yet equivalent to both the series and parallel inverter arrangements used diodes added to the circuit of Figure 3 to form AND or OR gates, as shown in Figures 7 and 8.

Except for very small amounts of delay, the inputs and outputs of these circuits changed simultaneously; thus, no information was stored. The storage of information was accomplished by bistable devices called "flip-flops" whose state was controlled by the application of pulses. Before discussing the construction of flip-flops, it is therefore necessary to briefly describe pulses, which were an important type of logic signal.

A pulse, as the name implies, was a very well controlled, short event in which a logic signal was asserted. Pulses were used for computer clocks and for carrying out the register transfer operations between the registers. Pulses were

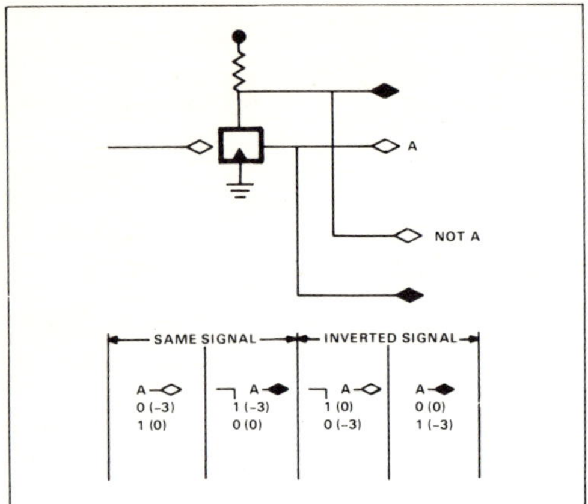

Figure 6. Signal naming convention for DEC dual polarity logic.

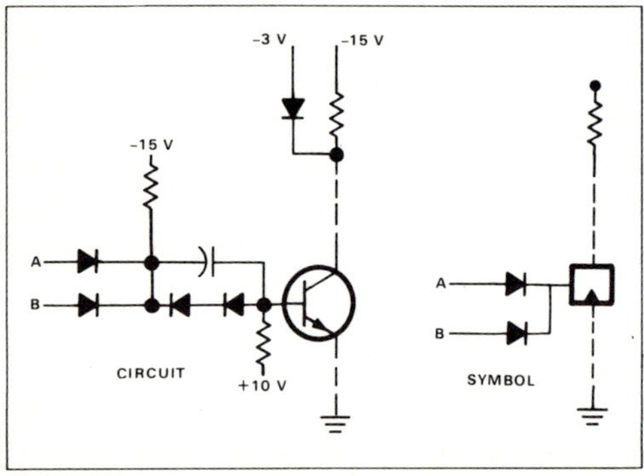

Figure 7. AND gate for negative signals.

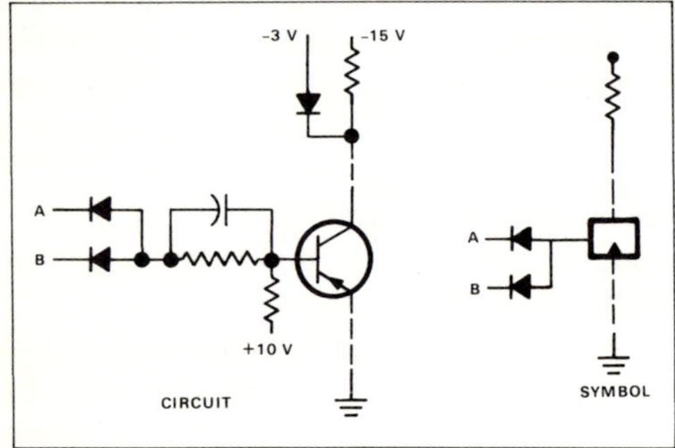

Figure 8. OR gate for negative signals.

generated by pulse amplifiers which were blocking oscillator circuits employing pulse transformers. The pulse transformer had both terminals of its secondary winding available so that either positive or negative pulses could be obtained, depending upon which terminal was grounded. A negative pulse (ground to −3 volts and back to ground) was represented in the logic drawings by a solid triangle, and a positive pulse (ground to +3 volts and back to ground) was represented by a hollow triangle. These signals were normally distributed on twisted pair and could travel the long distances needed in large digital systems like the PDP-1 without degradation.

Pulse amplifiers were important elements because they produced high energy (high fan-out), standardly shaped pulses which could be used to gate a complete 18-bit register as a single logical signal. The use of pulses and buffered/delayed output flip-flops is emphasized because the concept of gating a pulse at the source and using the gated pulse to transfer data from register to register on a parallel basis used a minimum of logic compared to other methods in use at that time. Some other methods used a common clock and dual rank flip-flops for register output delays or used clocked serial logic and delay lines to store register contents.

Returning to the discussion of gates and flip-flops, a primitive flip-flop can be obtained by interconnecting two grounded emitter inverters as shown in Figure 9. When one inverter is cut off, its output is negative. This holds the other inverter on, which in turn holds the first inverter off. If another inverter circuit is added to the circuit in Figure 9, the circuit in Figure 10 is obtained.

The application of a negative pulse to the input of the additional inverter changes the state of the flip-flop. In the actual implementations of DEC Laboratory Module flip-flops, buffer amplifiers were added to the outputs to permit a single flip-flop to drive the inputs of many other

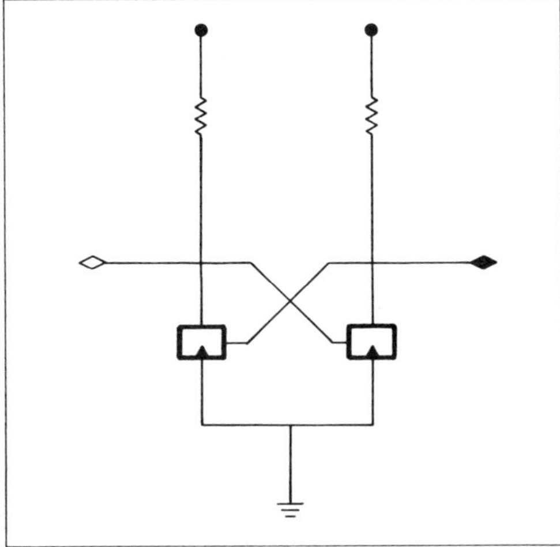

Figure 9. Primitive flip-flop.

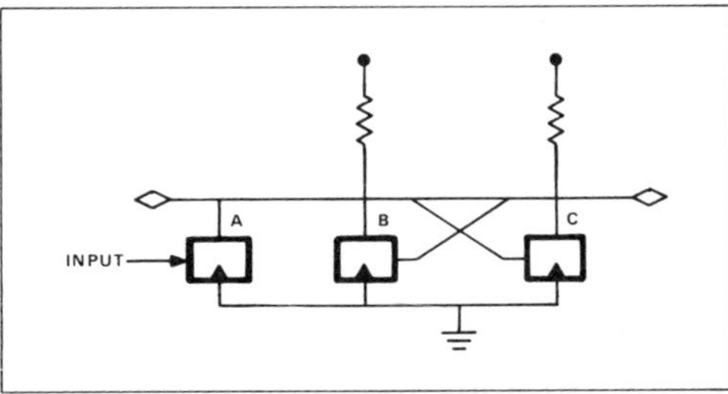

Figure 10. Primitive flip-flop with inverter.

gates. The buffer amplifiers also provided delays at the outputs of the flip-flops such that the output did not change until after the activating pulse was over. This permitted the state of the flip-flop to be sensed while the flip-flop was being pulsed, a necessary feature for the simple implementation of shift registers, simultaneous data exchange between two registers, counters, and adders.

Collections of the inverters, gates, and flip-flops just described were packaged in appropriate quantities (i.e., as many as would fit within the module size and pin constraints) and sold as Laboratory Modules and System Modules. There were a relatively small number of module types available in the Laboratory Module Series. For example, the first product line, the 100 Series, included:

- 103 6 inverters
- 110 2 6-input negative diode NORs
- 201 1 buffered flip-flop
- 302 1 one-shot
- 402 1 clock pulse generator
- 406 1 crystal clock
- 410 1 Schmitt trigger circuit pulse generator
- 501 3 level standardizers
- 602 2 pulse amplifiers
- 650 1 tube pulser (15 volt, 100 nanosecond pulses)
- 667 4 level amplifiers (0 to −15 volts)
- 801 1 relay

By contrast, there were many System Module types developed. With their higher packing density, lower cost, and fixed backplane wiring, they were used for computers, memory testers, and other complex systems of logic.

It is interesting to note that a large percentage of the modules on the above list were designed for generating and conditioning of the pulses and levels used in the relatively small number of logic circuits. Reference to a present day integrated circuit catalog reveals few pulsing and clocking circuits but a great many logic circuits. The emphasis on pulses was one of economy, as previously noted.

Register transfer level structures and the System Module logic diagrams can easily be corollated, both because of the use of pulse amplifiers to evoke operations and because of the buffered/delayed flip-flops. Figure 11 shows in simplified form the interconnection of two PDP-1 registers and lists some of the register transfer commands that could be used in conjunction with these registers. Typical examples of such register arrangements in the PDP-1 were the Accumulator (AC), which was the

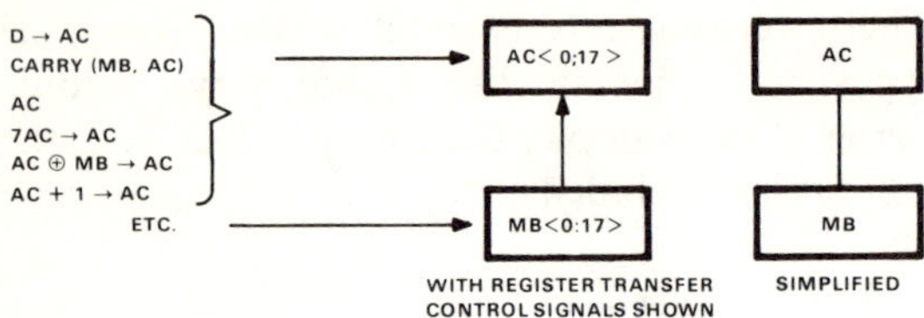

Figure 11. Register transfer representation of PDP-1 Accumulator (AC).

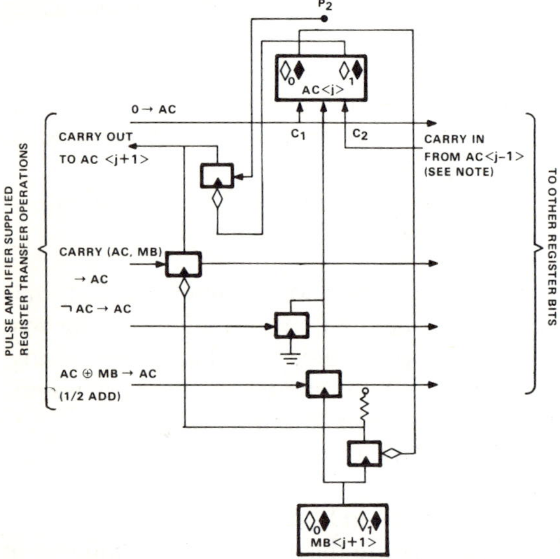

Figure 12. Logic diagram of PDP-1 Accumulator bit, AC<j>.

basic register in which all arithmetic operations were carried out, and the Memory Buffer (MB) register.

Figure 12 shows the logic diagram for one bit of the Accumulator and Memory Buffer for operations given in the register transfer diagram. The operation to clear the Accumulator is carried out by a pulse amplifier connected to all 18 bits of the Accumulator, with logic at the input of the pulse amplifier to specify the conditions under which the Accumulator is to be set to ZERO. Complementing the Accumulator is done by a transistor at one of the complementing inputs, *C1*, which receives a negative control pulse. Addition is a two-step process in which the Accumulator and Memory Buffer are half-added to the Accumulator using an exclusive-OR operation (where an Accumulator bit is complemented if the corresponding Memory Buffer bit is a ONE), and then the carry operation is performed. A carry at a given bit position is initiated to the next bit if the Memory Buffer is ONE and the Accumulator is ZERO. Once a carry is started as a bit, it will continue to propagate if each bit of the Accumulator is a ONE. The propagation is done via a standard pulse at the propagation output P2. In a similar way, a ONE can be added to the Accumulator by pulsing the least significant bit of the Accumulator which, if it is a ONE, will create a carry that will propagate along all the digits that are ONE, complementing each bit of the Accumulator to ZERO as it propagates.

In 1960 DEC began building modules with slightly different circuitry than that described above. While transistor inverters, buffered/delayed flip-flops, and their associated pulse logic were the best choice for 5- and 10-MHz logic, capacitor-diode (C-D) gates and unbuffered flip-flops were found to be preferable for low speed logic because greater logic density and lower cost could be achieved.

A positive capacitor-diode gate is illustrated in Figure 13. With both the level input and the pulse input at ground for sufficent time to allow the capacitor charge to reach 3 volts, a negative level change or a negative pulse at the pulse input will cause a positive pulse to appear at the output. Such gates could drive the direct set input of any flip-flop which required a positive pulse and were built into some unbuffered flip-flop inputs to be used for shifting and counting, using the capacitor as a delay element. Often one inverter would drive many capacitor-diode combinations in the same module.

A negative capacitor-diode gate is illustrated in Figure 14. With the level input at −3 and the capacitor input at ground for a sufficient time to allow the charge on the capacitor to become stable, a negative level change or a negative pulse at the capacitor input will cause the transistor to conduct. The conducting transistor grounds the output for an amount of time determined by the gate time constant or the input pulse width, whichever is shorter. Gates of this type could be used to set and clear unbuffered flip-flops by momentarily grounding the correct flip-flop outputs in a fashion similar to the inverter gate that was added to Figure 9 to obtain Figure 10.

The principal advantages of the capacitor-diode gates were:

1. The level input to the gate was used to charge a capacitor and was isolated from the rest of the circuit by a diode. Thus, no dc load was presented to the circuit driving the level input of a capacitor-diode gate.
2. The resistor-capacitor time constant of the gate required that the conditioning level be present a certain amount of time before the pulse input occurred. This introduced a delay between the application of a new gate level and the time the gate was conditioned, and allowed the sampling of unbuffered flip-flop outputs at the same time that the flip-flop was being changed.
3. The resistor-capacitor combination differentiated level changes, permitting a level change to create a pulse.

The use of saturating micro alloy diffused transistor (MADT) transistors and toroidal pulse transformers appeared to be nearing an operating limit at 10 MHz. The pulses needed to operate the circuits shown in the previous diagrams were 40 percent of the cycle time of 10-MHz logic (40 nanoseconds), which tightly constrained transformer recovery time and made it difficult to design circuits that were not excessively sensitive to repetition rate. Furthermore, gate delays were large enough to prevent some needed logic configurations from propagating within the 100 nanosecond interval implied by the 10-MHz rating.

A major break with previous circuit geometries appeared necessary. The use at IBM (in the IBM 7030 "STRETCH" machines) of non-saturating logic encouraged an exploration in

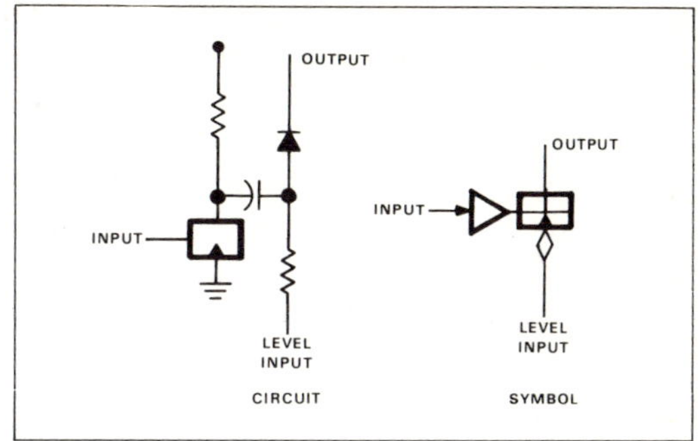

Figure 13. Positive C-D gate.

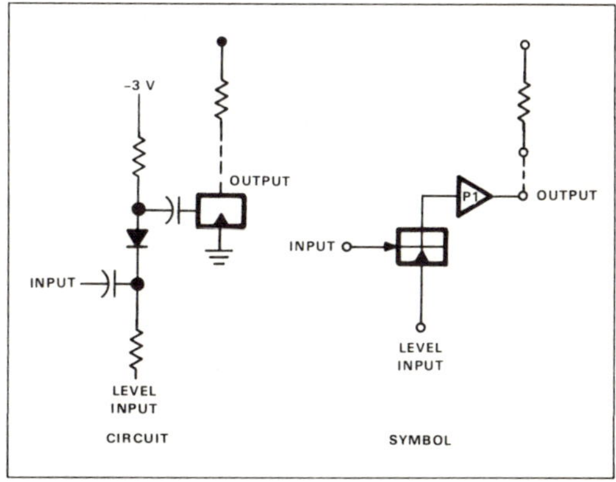

Figure 14. Negative C-D gate.

that direction. The project was called the "VHF Logic" project because operation at 30 MHz or better (the bottom end of the very high frequency (VHF) radio band) was the goal.

The complex 30-MHz flip-flops were packaged one to a module (Figure 15), with the result that a great many interconnections were needed to implement logic functions. In systems designed for 30-MHz operation, the use of leads longer than a few centimeters was expected to require special care; hence, it was thought essential for ease of use that a satisfactory transmission line hookup medium be available. A new solid wall coaxial cable had just been introduced, the 50-ohm impedance version of which was chosen to hook up the VHF modules. It appeared to have a strong enough center conductor for practical hookup between modules without being too bulky for easy hand-bending.

Due to the low impedance needed for the coaxial cable connections, substantial driving current was necessary to achieve adequately high signal voltages, and considerable power had to be dissipated. The ability to drive a load at any point along the transmission line was deemed necessary for practical hookup, and 3-volt swings had to be available to insure compatibility with existing modules. These needs were met by choosing a 60-milliampere output current, producing a 1.5-volt swing on a double-terminated 50-ohm line and a 3-volt swing with a 50-ohm load when interfacing to existing slower logic. These voltage and current levels required the addition of heat sinks to the output transistors. This was accomplished by installing spring clips that fastened the cases of the transistors directly to the connector pins, exploiting the connectors as heat sinks and at the same time providing a minimum inductance connection from the transistor collector (common to the case) out of the module.

The VHF modules contained a novel delay line implementation which has reappeared in recent days in the emitter-coupled logic boards used in the latest PDP-10 processor (KL10). Flip-flop output delay was provided by a 10-nanosecond stripline etched onto the printed circuit board. A meander pattern was selected with a degree of local coupling between the loops to achieve a 7 to 1 delay-to-risetime ratio. Both the delayed and undelayed ends of this 50-ohm stripline were made available at the module pins. The undelayed outputs switched simultaneously with the flip-flop outputs, allowing a subsequent gate to subtract a delayed flip-flop output from the undelayed complement output side of the flip-flop and produce a 10-nanosecond pulse when the flip-flop changed state.

The performance of the VHF modules was rated at 30 MHz, which was the limit of the module testers used on the production floor. Bench testing demonstrated 40-MHz capability with the promise of 50-MHz performance if adequate testing apparatus could be found. Risetimes were better than 1 nanosecond.

Modules delivered to customers were used to build satisfactory high performance systems, but the need for such high performance was not widespread. In addition, the product development cycle was, by the standards of the time, quite long (two years) and enthusiasm for the VHF modules among DEC engineers waned, further slowing product momentum. Despite their failure as a product, with only eight modules in the series, the VHF modules eventually made a contribution to computer progress. To produce timesharing systems, the PDP-6 needed a way of comparing relocated addresses at very high speed. A high speed register comparator was quickly designed using current mode logic similar to that in the VHF modules.

As a series of general purpose products for engineers to use, the VHF modules were too costly and their wiring too inconvenient. Further developments in general purpose logic modules were to lie in the opposite direction: toward cheaper, more compact, easier to use, and slower units.

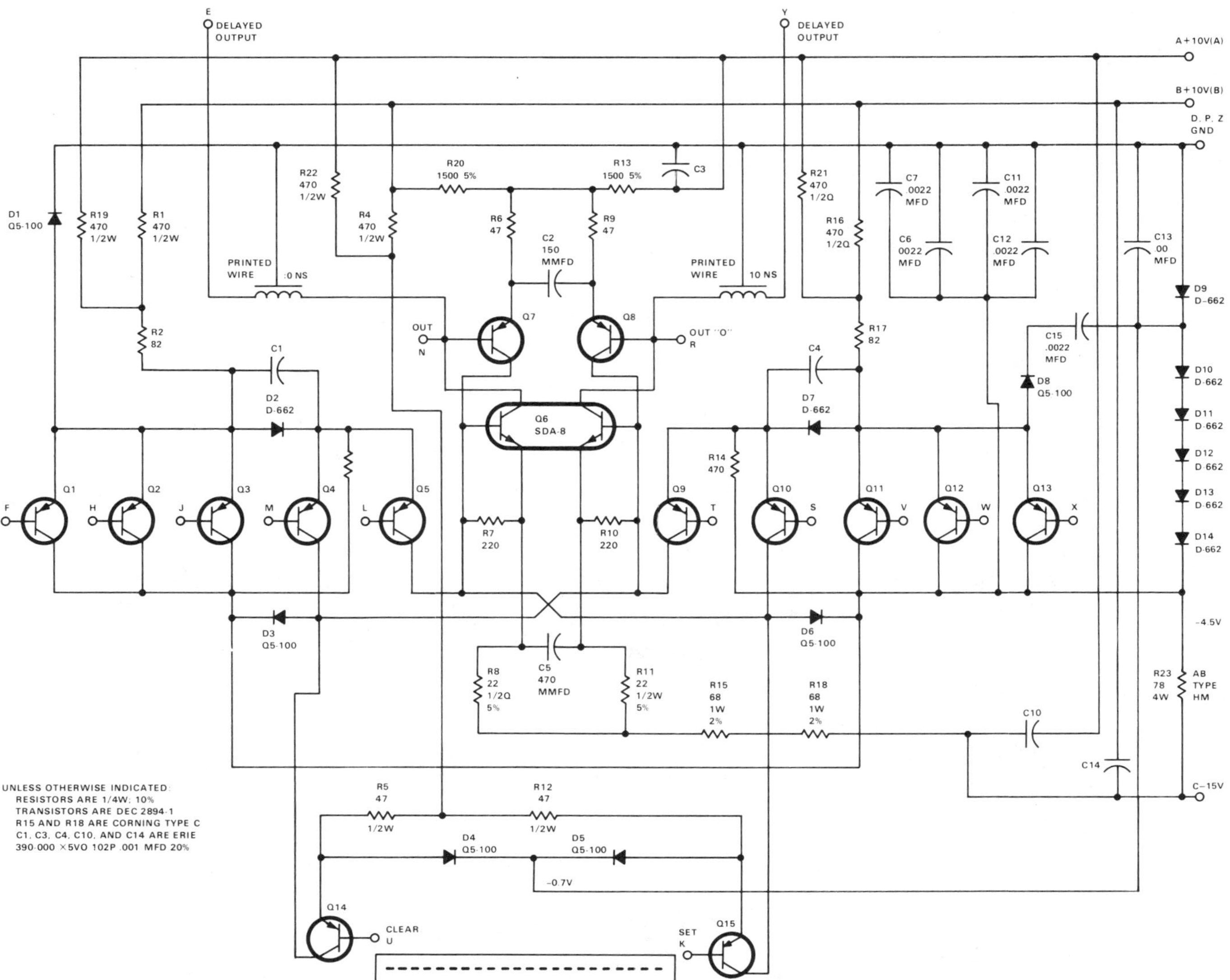

Figure 15. 30-MHz VHF flip-flop module.

By 1964, because of the decreasing cost of semiconductors during the early 1960s, the cost of System Module mounting hardware and of wiring had become a significant portion of the total system cost. In response to this trend, a new type of module was developed which was a 2.5- × 5-inch printed circuit card with a color-coded plastic handle (Figure 16). The printed circuit card provided its own mechanical support – there was no metal frame around it as there had been in the System Module design. The new modules, called Flip Chip modules, plugged into 144-pin connector blocks that could support eight such modules, providing 18 pins per module. While the improvements in the cost of module mounting hardware realized with the new modules were important, the major advantage of the new Flip Chip modules was that automatic Gardner-Denver Wire-wrap equipment could be used to wire the module mounting blocks.

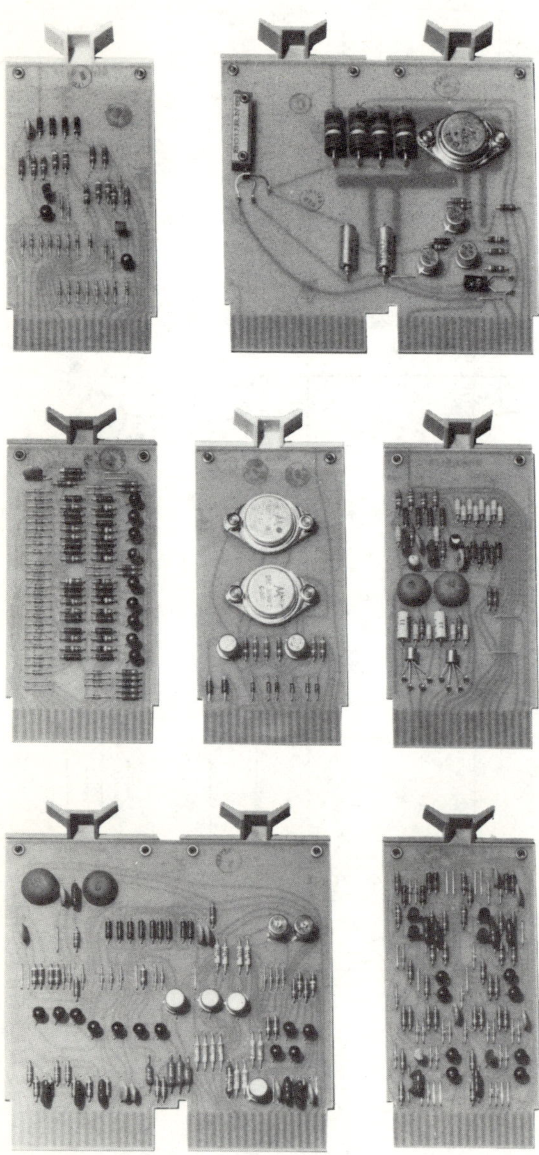

Figure 16. Single and double Flip Chip modules used in PDP-7 and PDP-8.

The first series of the new modules was designated the R-Series and was identified by using red handles. The R-Series circuits were a reaction to the rather complicated set of rules developed for using the previous products. The goal was to make these modules easy to use and inexpensive. Integrated circuits were not used because they were more expensive than discrete components, and the computer industry had not yet decided on the type of integrated circuit to use. The building block for R-Series logic was the diode gate, an example of which is shown in Figure 17. The other basic circuit was the diode-capacitor-diode (D-C-D) circuit shown in Figure 18. The diode-capacitor-diode gate was used to standardize inputs to active devices such as flip-flops and to produce the logic delay necessary to sense and change flip-flops at the same time.

A second series of the new modules was developed for the first PDP-8s. This series was called the S-Series, although it also had red handles. The S-Series modules used the same circuits as their R-Series counterparts, but with variations in the values of the load resistors and diode-capacitor-diode gate storage capacitors to obtain greater speed.

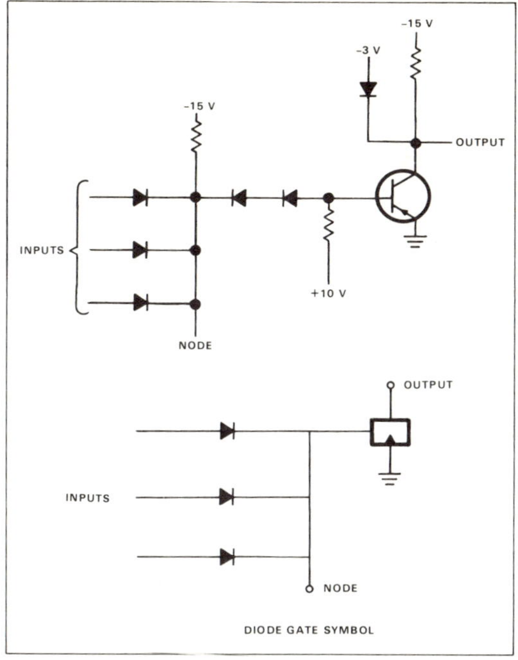

Figure 17. Diode gate.

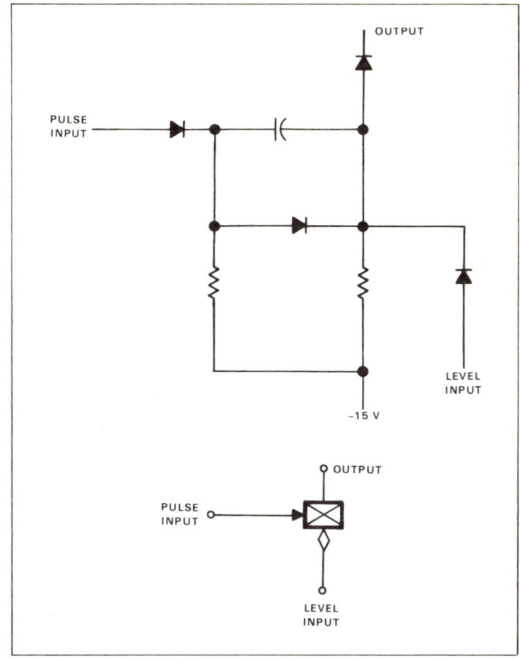

Figure 18. D-C-D gate.

The B-Series with blue handles was essentially the same as the 6000 Series of 10-MHz System Modules, except that it was repackaged on new 2.5- × 5-inch cards and used silicon transistors rather than germanium transistors. The new silicon transistors were a mixed blessing. While they had temperature sensitivity characteristics superior to those of the germanium transistors, and their voltage drop characteristics permitted the elimination of the bias resistor to +10 volts, they did not saturate as well as the germanium transistors. Because they did not saturate well, the voltage between the collector and the emitter in the saturated state was not as low as it was with germanium transistors. This meant that the series arrangement of three inverters discussed in conjunction with the dotted lines in Figure 4 could not be used. Instead, only two of the silicon transistor inverters could be connected in series if the output was intended to drive another inverter. The first computer to use the B-Series modules was the PDP-7, and the series was heavily used and extended by the first PDP-10 processor (KA10).

Analog applications were the target market for the A-Series modules, which had amber handles. This series, still being manufactured today, includes analog multiplexers, operational amplifiers, sample and hold circuits, comparators, digital-to-analog converters, reference voltage supplies, analog-to-digital converters, and various accessory modules. The development rate of analog modules peaked in 1971 with 38 new types and declined to 5 new types in 1977.

While all of the preceding modules had been designed as user-arrangeable building blocks, the green handled G-Series was intended for modules that would be sold only as part of a system. For example, all of the DEC core memory circuits have been in the G-Series because a core memory system is sufficiently complex that a cookbook approach using a standard series of modules is not appropriate. The G-Series is still actively used today for circuits other than logic, generally in peripheral devices such as disks, tapes, and terminals.

Like the A-Series and G-Series, the W-Series (white handle) is still manufactured and is used to provide input/output capability between Flip Chip modules and other devices. Lamp drivers, relay drivers, solenoid drivers, level converters, and switch filters are included in this family, but the only modules used widely today are those modules which include cable termination modules and blank boards upon which the user can mount integrated circuits and wire-wrap them together.

While the W-Series modules provided a variety of interface capabilities, their circuitry was still too fast for typical industrial applications. Computer logic, by its very nature, is high speed and provides noise immunity far below that required in small-scale industrial control systems located physically close to the process they control.

Unfortunately, industrial electrical noise is not predictable to the nearest order of magnitude. Thus, attempts to solve noise problems with high level logic, whose voltage thresholds were merely a few times greater than computer logic thresholds, did not work well.

A new series of modules was developed, the K-Series (with blac(K) handles), which relied on a combination of voltage, current, and time thresholds to protect storage elements such as flip-flops and timers from false triggering. Since industrial controls typically interact with physically massive equipment which moves slowly relative to electronic speeds, time thresholds are particularly attractive. There are four ways of exploiting these:

1. Using basic 100 KHz slow-down circuits everywhere.
2. Making optional 5 KHz slow-down circuits available.
3. Providing transition-sensitive (edge-detecting) circuits with hysteresis to allow additional discrete capacitor loading of the input when all else fails.
4. Replacing the conventional monostable multivibrator or "one-shot" circuit with a timing circuit which has both a low impedance and hysteresis at the input.

The hardware for the K-Series was specifically designed to fit the NEMA (National Electrical Manufacturers Association) enclosures traditionally used with relay implemented industrial controls. The K-Series used the same connectors as the other Flip Chip modules, however. Sensing and output terminals were provided with screw terminals and indicator lights, and appropriate arrangements were made to interface with 120-volt ac devices. Wire-wrap terminals were protected from external voltages but were available for oscilloscope probes. Magnetically latched reed relays and diode arrays that could be programmed by snipping out diodes were provided as memory elements that would retain data during power failures.

Gating in early K-Series modules was accomplished with discrete diode-transistor circuits such as that shown in Figure 19. Other K-Series modules used integrated circuits for the logic functions. In these designs the inputs to the integrated circuits were protected with filter/trigger circuits which filtered out the noise and then restored the fast risetimes required by the integrated circuits. Outputs were protected from output-induced noise and converted to standard K-Series signals by circuits similar to those used in the discrete logic gates.

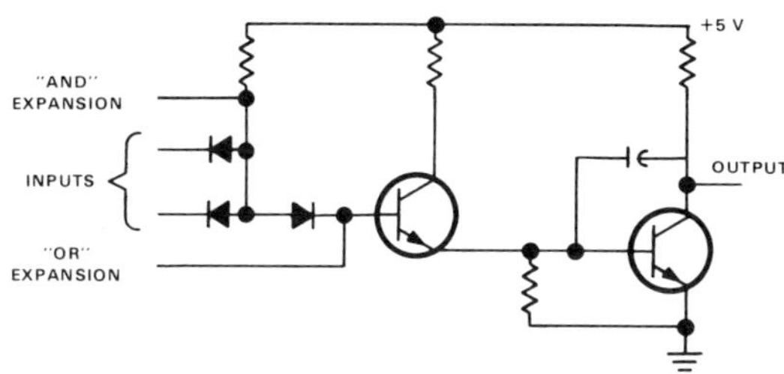

Figure 19. K-Series circuit.

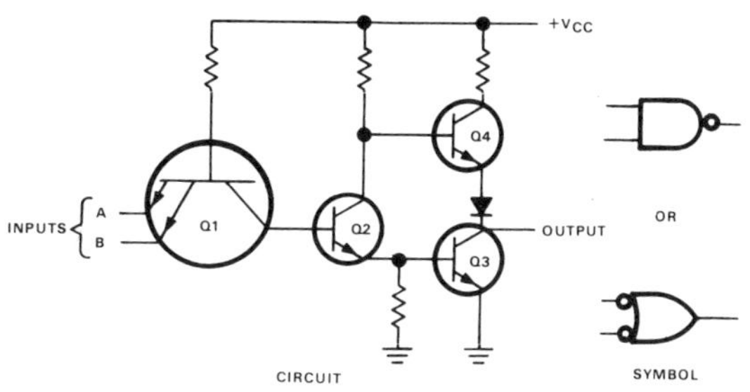

Figure 20. Basic TTL NAND gate circuit.

Unlike other DEC modules, the K-Series modules were not directly useful for constructing computers or computer data processing subsystems due to their low speed and high cost. They did play an important part in bringing digital logic into industrial applications, and the noise protection techniques developed for these modules were useful in the design of the PDP-14 Industrial Controller (Chapter 7).

By 1967 the electronics world had settled on transistor-transistor logic (TTL) and the dual in-line package (DIP) as the technology and package of choice for integrated circuits. In addition, the cost for logic functions implemented in TTL integrated circuits had dropped below that of discrete circuit implementations. With much more logic fitting into the same printed circuit board area, a single Flip Chip card could now accommodate much more complicated functions. However, there were not enough connector pins available to get the necessary signals on and off the card. The answer to the problem was to keep the cards the same size, but to have etch and associated contacts on both sides of the printed circuit board. This increased the number of contacts from 18 to 36, and a new series with magenta handles (the M-Series) was born. Subsequently, some G-Series and W-Series modules were also designed with integrated circuits and double-sided boards.

The advent of transistor-transistor logic brought the first power supply and signal level change in DEC's history. The −15-volt and +10-volt supplies were no longer required. Only a single +5-volt supply was needed to supply the logic signals which were now O and +3 volts. The packaging was kept consistent, however, as the old single-sided modules could be plugged into the new connector blocks. Careful attention to pinning arrangements allowed half of the circuits of a double-sided module to be used in a single-sided block.

The basic TTL circuit is the NAND gate shown in Figure 20. Since the change to TTL logic brought a change in logic symbols, a sample of the new symbology is also shown in Figure 20.

The input of the TTL gate is a multiple emitter transistor. If either input is at or near ground (0 to 0.8 volts), transistor *Q1* becomes saturated, bringing the base voltage of transistor *Q2* low, turning off transistor *Q3* while turning on transistor *Q4*, and making the output high (+2.4 to +3.6 volts). If both inputs are high (above 2 volts), *Q2* has base current supplied to it through the collector diode of *Q1*, turning *Q2* on. This in turn provides base current to *Q3*, saturating it and cutting off *Q4*, making the output low (0 to 0.4 volts).

Like the transistor inverter circuits discussed in conjunction with System Modules, TTL NAND gates can be cross-connected to form flip-flops.

The first generation of M-Series modules was used in a redesign of the PDP-8, called the PDP-8/I. The circuits used in these modules used TTL integrated circuits which were called 7400 series integrated circuits because of a growing tendency in the semiconductor industry to standardize part numbers for TTL circuits, calling a package of 4 NAND gates a 7400, a package of 6 inverters a 7404, etc. Soon there was a need in the computer industry for higher speed circuits. This need led to the development of the 74H00 series. The 74H00 circuits were similar to those in the earlier 7400 series, but they were faster and used much more power. The first PDP-11 (the PDP-11/20), the second PDP-10 processor (KI10), and the PDP-8/E used both 7400 and 74H00 series integrated circuits. The PDP-11/45, designed between 1970 and 1972, used Schottky TTL, a circuitry with such rapid switching speeds and high power consumption that four-layer boards had to be used such that the inner layers of power and ground etch could provide both shielding and an adequate supply of power and ground.

In 1972 work began on a new PDP-10 processor, the KL10. This used current switching nonsaturating logic from several vendors, including the MECL (Motorola Emitter Coupled Logic) 10,000 series. This line of circuits is in some ways an integrated circuit version of the VHF modules. The basic gate is shown in Figure 21.

In the circuit shown in Figure 21, transistor *Q6* has a temperature compensated, internally generated reference voltage of −1.3 volts on its base. The outputs drive 50-ohm terminated transmission lines returned to −2 volts. There is a complementary pair of outputs so that the circuit is both an OR and a NOR gate. At 25 degrees Celsius the upper level will be between −0.81 and −0.96 volts, while the lower level will be between −1.65 and −1.85 volts. The circuits, like the Schottky circuits, are so fast that multi-layer boards are required. In addition, a great deal of care in signal line termination is required. As with the previous logic families studied, flip-flops can be created. The ECL master-slave flip-flops are quite complex, typically requiring 32 transistors and 7 diodes.

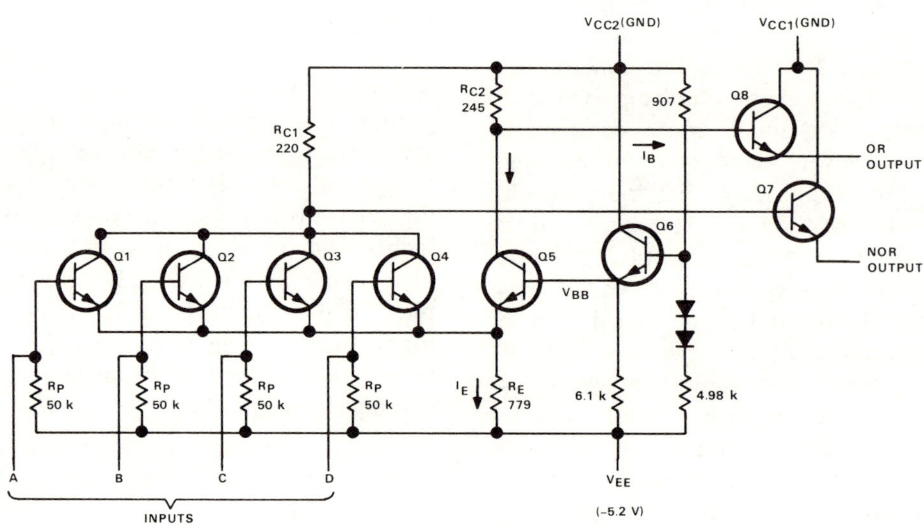

Figure 21. ECL circuit.

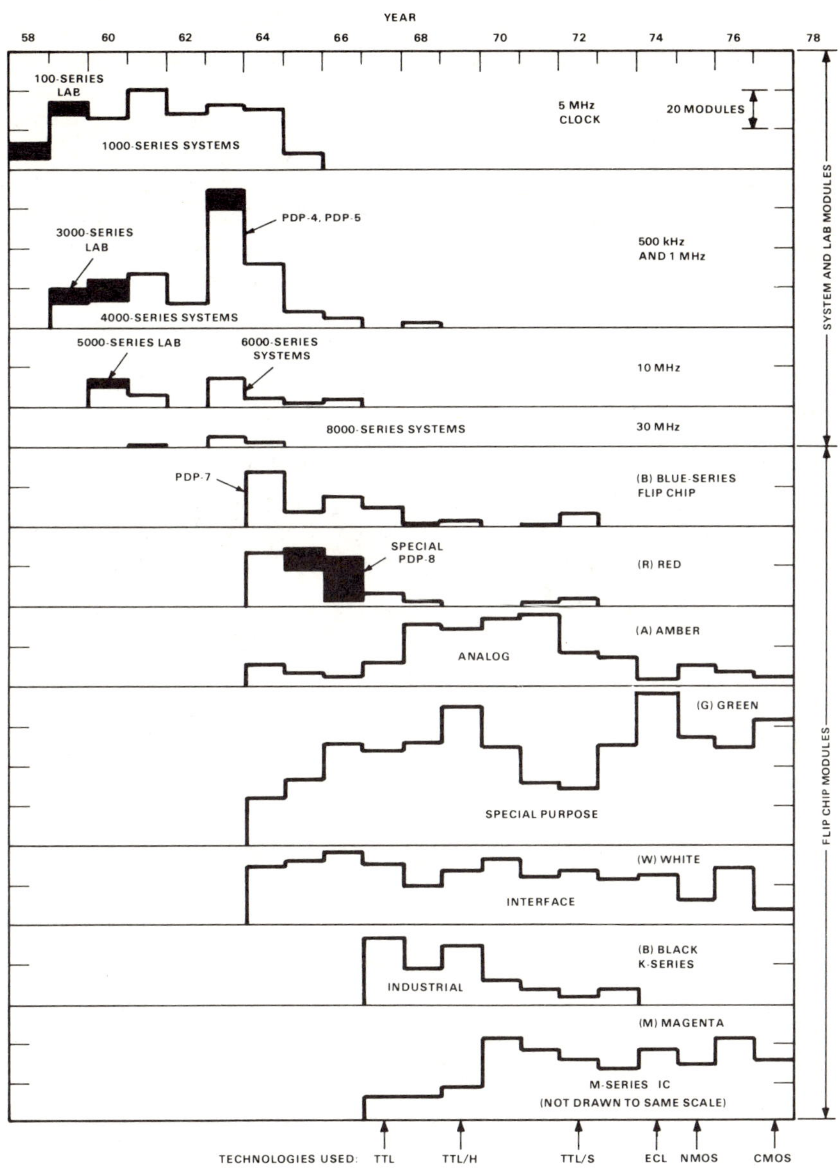

Figure 22. Modules introduced each year at DEC.

As the various module circuit technologies developed, more logic functionality fit in a given space, and the space provided on individual logic modules was increased. The modules used in the PDP-8/I, PDP-8/L, PDP-10 (KI10 processor), and PDP-15 were single (2.5 × 5-inch) and double (5 × 5-inch) general purpose modules, and these machines had relatively low packing densities because most interconnections were carried out on the wired backplane. The PDP-8/E (and, to a lesser extent, the PDP-11/20) used 8.5 × 10.4-inch "extended quad" modules which were functionally specialized and eliminated many of the backplane connections required in previous designs. By 1973, the "hex" module (8.5 × 15.6 inches) was widely used, principally in the PDP-11 family. By 1978 two DEC computers, the VAX 11/780 (1977) and the DECSYSTEM 2020 (1978), were using 12 × 15.6-inch "super hex" modules to further reduce interconnection cost by placing more logic on a single module.

An evolution in circuits has continued as the technology has changed. As integrated circuits have become more functional by the reduction of the size of their active elements, each new computer introduced is smaller, faster, and less costly than its predecessor. While only DEC examples have been mentioned here, the trend toward smaller, faster, and less costly computers has been consistent for all computer manufacturers.

The chart in Figure 22 shows the number of module types introduced each year from 1957 to 1977.

ACKNOWLEDGEMENTS

We gratefully acknowledge the review assistance offered by Allan Kent, Tom Stockebrand, Phil Tays, and Don White.

Opposite:

- PDP-8.

PART II

BEGINNING OF THE MINICOMPUTER

Beginning of the Minicomputer

In November 1960, the first PDP-1 computer was delivered. This machine and the 49 other PDP-1s that followed established Digital Equipment Corporation in the computer business. Four and a half years later, in April 1965, the first PDP-8 was delivered. This machine, and the 40,000 PDP-8s that followed, established the concept of minicomputers, leading the way to a multibillion dollar industry. In the chapters of Part II, the development of DEC's 12-bit and 18-bit computers are explored in detail, with special attention paid to the factors influencing their development, the technology used in their implementation, and the reception of each machine in the marketplace. Sections of these chapters were co-authored by the designers or key project team members of the machine where possible. This permits a glimpse into the thoughts of the designers as they recollect and critique the designs in the light of subsequent developments.

Chapter 6 begins with a discussion of the PDP-1, showing the influence of various M.I.T. machines and exploring the design goals of the PDP-1, many of which are only speculations at this late date. The discussion of the PDP-1 is followed by brief discussions of the PDP-4, PDP-7, and PDP-9. The PDP-15, the most significant of the 18-bit machines in terms of longevity, number in use, and product range, is also discussed. The architectural changes that made the PDP-15 substantially different from the PDP-4, 7, and 9 are not included in the PDP-15 discussion, but an interesting retrospective view of the design goals and decisions is included. Thus, this section provides a good model of how design should be carried out and reviewed – hopefully, on an *a priori* basis.

The final section of Chapter 6 on 18-bit machines compares them in terms of cost, performance, and physical metrics. This section can be read independently of the machine design descriptions. Here, it is important for designers to realize that there is a continuity to design and that subsequent designs have to be better along one or more of the evaluation dimensions. Ignoring or not understanding the dimensions can lead to failure in the marketplace.

Chapter 7 describes the PDP-5 and the PDP-8 Family of 12-bit machines. The original PDP-8 is described, along with the various implementations of the same instruction set that occurred over the following fifteen years. Included is a brief discussion of the latest implementation, a computer on a single 40-pin chip. The chapter concludes with a discussion of the technology, price, and performance of the 12-bit computers, including a number of charts.

Chapter 8 is a top-down, hierarchical description of the implementation of the PDP-8 computers; it is based on material from *Computer Structures* by Bell and

Newell [1971]. This chapter includes some use of ISP and PMS notation, and readers who are unfamiliar with these notations are advised to study Bell and Newell, read Appendices 1 and 2, or scan this chapter lightly.

ACKNOWLEDGEMENTS

Although the reviewers of Part II are credited elsewhere, Wes Clark and Dan Siewiorek deserve special thanks. Wes reviewed the draft for historical content and contributed various early memos and technical reports, and Dan did a great deal of work revising and clarifying the PDP-8 hierarchical description.

6

The PDP-1 and Other 18-Bit Computers

C. GORDON BELL, GERALD BUTLER, ROBERT GRAY,
JOHN E. McNAMARA, DONALD VONADA,
and RONALD WILSON

THE PDP-1

Although Digital Equipment Corporation was formed in 1957 with the explicit goal of constructing computers, the company's first computer, the PDP-1, was not demonstrated until almost two years later. The principal backer of DEC, American Research and Development headed by General Georges F. Doriot, was somewhat skeptical that a computer company could be successful. They were enthusiastic, however, about the business possibilities in logic modules for laboratory and system use, and they felt that the plan to build computers should be conditional upon building a solid base in the module business.

After a year of operation, DEC met its profit and sales goals and was permitted to move on to the construction of computers. However, Ken Olsen felt it would be worthwhile to wait an additional year to obtain more business experience and to build a larger customer and financial base. Thus, it was not until the summer of 1959 that an engineer, Ben Gurley, was hired to design and build the PDP-1. Ben headed computer engineering until he left in 1962. In addition to logic and computer design, he specialized in complex analog circuitry, including the circuits for core memories and displays. The displays (including high precision and color point plotting) were pivotal to DEC's success, and many of the display circuits that he designed remained unchanged until the 1970s. His death in 1963 was a tragic loss to computer engineering and the industry.

Ben Gurley and other engineers* at DEC had worked at the Massachusetts Institute of Technology (M.I.T.) Computer Laboratory on Whirlwind and had then gone on to develop computers at the M.I.T. Lincoln Laboratory. As a result, the machines constructed at the M.I.T. campus and at Lincoln Laboratory greatly influenced the design and construction of the PDP-1. In fact, the DEC System Modules

*Harlan Anderson, Dick Best, Ken Olsen, Stan Olsen, and Bob Savell.

that formed the basis of the PDP-1 were directly patterned after the circuits of the TX-0 and the TX-2 computers at M.I.T., as discussed in Chapter 5.

The TX-0 and TX-2 computers were among the most advanced machines of their time and were the offspring of M.I.T.'s Whirlwind [Everett, 1951; Redmond and Smith, 1977], a computer that was operational in 1950. Whirlwind (Figure 1) was an important ancestor of the TX-0, the PDP-1, and modern minicomputers because of the short word length (16 bits), because of the high speed operation, and because of the people involved in its development. The high speed operation was accomplished by using an M.I.T.-developed random-access storage tube rather than a drum for primary memory. Subsequently, performance was further upgraded by using the core memory that was developed by Jay Forrester at M.I.T. in 1951 [Forrester, 1951].*

To test the Whirlwind core memory, a special computer called the Memory Test Computer (MTC) was developed by a design team headed by Ken Olsen, a recent M.I.T. graduate. The core memory worked so well that it was immediately moved to Whirlwind. A 4-Kword memory was built for MTC, permitting MTC to be operated as a special purpose computer for several years.

MTC is shown in Figure 2 as it was first assembled and operated in a factory building near M.I.T. Its word length was selected to be 16 bits because that was the size of the Whirlwind memory being tested and because 16 bits were adequate to represent the data for M.I.T.'s Project Lincoln air defense applications.

The MTC turned out to be a useful training ground for the designers (especially K. Olsen) when they went to Project Lincoln's new facility, Lincoln Laboratory in Lexington, Massachusetts. The MTC packaging, circuits, and toggle switches influenced the subsequent TX-0 design. The MTC packaging used various standard radio relay racks and had a somewhat homely appearance; this encouraged the designers to be more concerned about appearance in the future. The MTC circuits used significantly smaller modules than those in Whirlwind and used a gated pulse delay line clock for control rather than the synchronous clock used in Whirlwind. In addition, MTC used a dc bus for gating registers to one another that was carried out on an open-wired bus (versus coaxial cable) that ran the entire length of the computer. The MTC toggle switches formed a memory of 32 registers. As it turned out, when the 512 toggle switches were put together, they formed about the most unreliable part of the computer. At the time, lifetesting in large batches was not done; hence, the experience with the MTC toggle switches formed the basis for significant improvement of switch designs in the TX-0.

Although the speed of the MTC was about the same as the speed of Whirlwind, it was not fully used, perhaps because it lacked the software and peripherals.

Like the MTC, the TX-0 was designed as a test device. It was designed to test transistor circuitry, to verify that a 256 × 256 (64-Kword) core memory could be built [Mitchell and Olsen, 1956] and to serve as a prelude to the construction of a large-scale 36-bit computer, the TX-2. The transistor circuitry being tested featured the new Philco SBT100 surface barrier transistor, costing $80, which greatly simplified transistor circuit design. The work on the 256 × 256 core memory, using vacuum-tube drivers,

*Whirlwind was dismantled in 1959 and moved to Wolf Research and Development where it was reassembled and operated until the 1970s. Whirlwind is now part of the Digital Distributed Museum Project, although the first core memory module and other parts have been given to the British Science Museum, the Smithsonian, and other museums.

Figure 1. M.I.T. Whirlwind computer (courtesy of M.I.T. Lincoln Laboratory).

Figure 2. M.I.T. Memory Test Computer (MTC) used to test first core memory (courtesy of M.I.T. Lincoln Laboratory).

was done by William Papian and Dick Best [Best, 1957] and proceeded independently of work on the computer.

The original TX-0 (Figure 3) had a number of I/0 devices. After it was moved to M.I.T., the largest device was a 12-inch point-plotting cathode ray tube (designed by Ben Gurley) and light pen console, giving the TX-0 some physical resemblance to Whirlwind. In addition to the cathode ray tube, there was a high speed (300 characters per second) Ferranti paper tape reader and a Friden Flexowriter that was used as both a typewriter and paper tape punch. There was also a large bank of toggle switches, some of which formed the two program accessible registers and some of which formed the

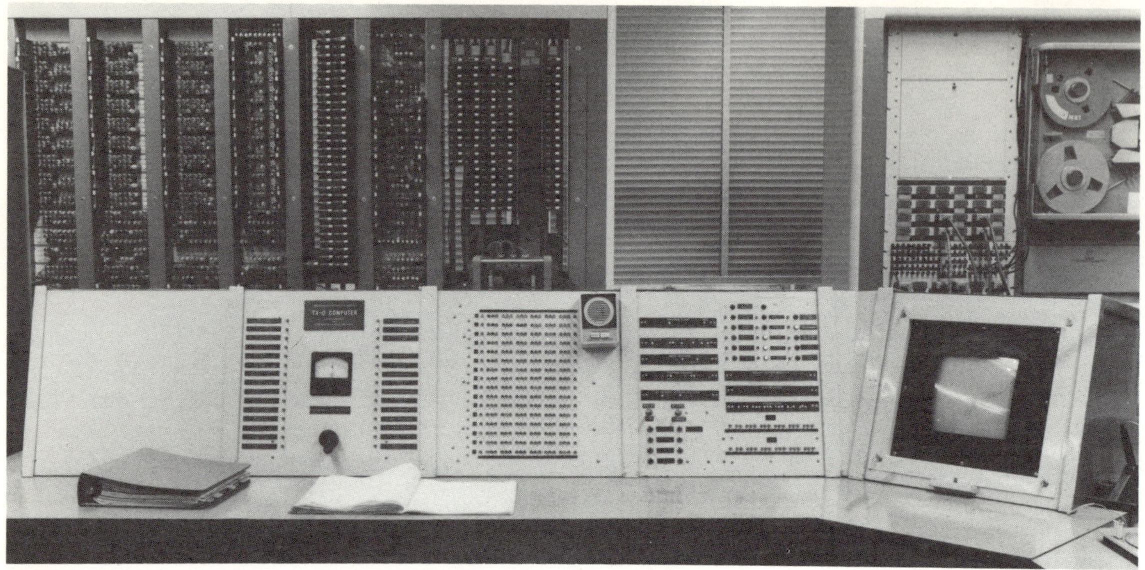

Figure 3. Lincoln Laboratory TX-0 computer (courtesy of M.I.T. Lincoln Laboratory).

first 16 memory locations, permitting direct entry of variables. However, despite the multiple I/O devices, the TX-0 had no program interrupt mechanism.

The two program accessible registers were called the Accumulator and the Live Register. The Accumulator was used for logic functions and the Live Register was used for controlling and buffering transfers to various I/O equipment. The initial version of the TX-0 had only four instructions encoded in two bits, leaving sixteen bits to access the large, 64-Kword memory. Three of the instructions accessed memory: "store in location," "add from location," and "transfer if Accumulator is negative to location." The fourth instruction, "operate," was for program controlled I/O transfers and included commands that could be combined to produce a large number of instructions. The combining process was called "microprogramming" because bits in the instruction specified particular register transfer operations and could be programmed. Among the instructions that could be created were "clear the right half of the Accumulator," "cycle the Accumulator right one position," and "start the paper tape reader." The operations encoded in the instruction could occur at any one of six possible times during the instruction; thus, a multifunction instruction could be formed, such as one to display a point on the screen and to generate a new pseudo-random point.

In 1958 the TX-0 was transferred (by Earl Pugh and John MacKenzie) from Lincoln Laboratory to the M.I.T. campus for laboratory experiment control and for teaching. The memory size was reduced from 64 Kwords to 4 Kwords but used one of the first all-transistor driven core memories. A second memory stack was later added to provide 8 Kwords. In 1960 Professor Jack Dennis assumed the management of TX-0 and extended the architecture in an up-

Figure 4. Lincoln Laboratory TX-2 computer (courtesy of M.I.T. Lincoln Laboratory).

ward compatible fashion to include an index register and more instructions.*

Following the completion of the original TX-0 at Lincoln, work began on what became the TX-2 [Clark, 1957; Frankovich and Peterson, 1957]. The TX-2 was a large machine, using 22,000 transistors compared to the 3,600 in the TX-0 (Figure 4). A principal design goal of the new machine was to create an I/O organization that would be far more efficient than that of existing machines. To accomplish this, the idea of a separate I/O processor was rejected, and a minimum buffering scheme with direct transfers to memory was chosen instead. Additional program sequences with associated program counters were provided to facilitate the I/O transfers, using the processing facilities of the central processor to effect the I/O transfers. This I/O system [Forgie, 1957] formed much of the basis for the PDP-1 Sequence Break System and nearly all subsequent DEC computer designs.

In addition to the I/O system improvements, the TX-2 featured increased parallelism. There were separate adders for indexing, program counter incrementation, and instruction execution. The increase in word length from 18 bits for the TX-0 to 36 bits for the TX-2 permitted the construction of a 36-bit arithmetic unit that could be reconfigured dynamically and in-

*The TX-0 remained in service at M.I.T. until 1975, when it was purchased by DEC for display in the Digital Distributed Museum Project.

cluded 4 × 9-bit, 2 × 18-bit, 9/27-bit, and 36-bit arithmetic.*

By the time the PDP-1 was designed in 1959, most of the important ideas of logical organization, such as addressing, address modification, sequencing control, arithmetic, and I/O control, had been invented. However, the major advances in the hardware realizations of these concepts were yet to come. Machines were just entering the second (transistor) generation. A review of the state of the art in logical organization is given in [Beckman *et al.*, 1961]. A review of the state of the hardware art in core memories is given in Rajchman [1961], and examples of the transistor circuitry used at the time are given in Chapter 4.

There is no record of the goals, constraints, and objectives of the PDP-1 design. It is clear that the PDP-1 instruction set processor was a reaction to the TX-0, but it is unclear whether an effort to make the PDP-1 compatible to the TX-0 was ever considered. It seems unlikely because there was little software when TX-0 arrived at M.I.T. As it turned out, it is fortunate that no such effort was pursued because the TX-0 was continuously extended, making compatibility a difficult goal to achieve. Instead of being program compatible with the TX-0, the PDP-1 was oriented toward being producible by a commercial enterprise and usable by a variety of programmers. To this end, it had more instructions than the TX-0 and a simpler I/O structure for ease in interfacing. In contrast to the existing large-scale scientific and business computers, the PDP-1 had a much shorter word length (18 bits) and a simpler instruction set (28 instructions). The I/O structure included a sequence break option (the name given to the sixteen channel interrupt mechanism) and a high speed channel (now called Direct Memory Access). The hardware implementation of the machine used DEC's 5 MHz 1000-series system modules and a 4-Kword memory which was later expanded to 64 Kwords. The processor and memory occupied four cabinets.

The registers and functional units of the PDP-1 are shown in Figure 5, a diagram taken from the original PDP-1 programming manual. The PDP-l registers were named after those of

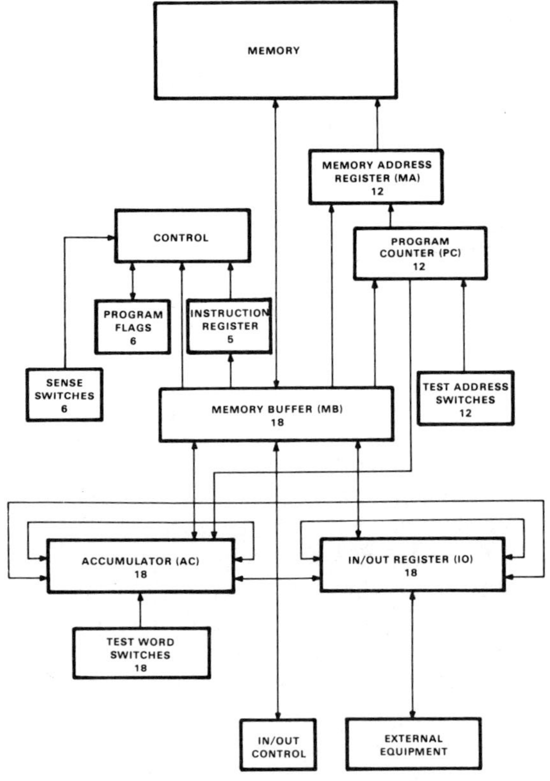

Figure 5. PDP-1 processor register transfer diagram.

*TX-2 operated until 1977, when it was dismantled. In the last decade of its use, it was modified and operated as a multiprogrammed timesharing system [Forgie, 1965]. The machine was used for a variety of applications. Two notable works included Sutherland's Sketchpad [1963], an interactive graphic design program, and the first computer network experiment between Lincoln Laboratory and the System Development Corporation computer [Marill and Roberts, 1966].

the TX-0, except for the TX-0's Live Register, which was renamed the Input-Output Register. The I/O register was also used as the Multiplier-Quotient register when used as an accumulator extension. An appreciation of the relatively high cost of logic at the time of the PDP-1's design can be obtained from the fact that an index register was rejected because of the high cost.

Even more important than the cost of logic was the cost of memory, which had a major impact on the machine's price. Since the cost of memory so strongly determined the machine's price, a 4-Kword minimum was selected for the PDP-1, although a 1-Kword system also appeared in the price list.

The instruction format used the 18 bits in a fashion quite different from the 2 bits for instruction/16 bits for address method of the original TX-0. In the PDP-1, five bits were used to encode the instruction, one bit was used for indirect addressing, and twelve bits were used for addressing the 4-Kword memory. Because the machine was oriented to control applications and low cost was a goal, the only data-types which were included were word, integer, and Boolean vector (logical). Hence, just seven data operators (+, −, ×, /, AND, OR, and EXCLUSIVE OR) for the one accumulator structure and some control instructions were required.

The first description of the PDP-1 order code by Harlan Anderson, DEC's Vice President, appeared in a company memorandum dated October 27, 1959. That two-page memo assigned the order code and the instruction names for the 24 instructions that were used in the initial design. A few instructions were later added to improve subroutine calling; thus, 28 instructions were eventually used in production machines. The instruction set description of the PDP-1 is given in Figure 6, and the corresponding description for the PDP-4 is also shown for purposes of comparison.

To make it a commercially viable machine, the PDP-1 had not only more instructions than the TX-0, but also a simplified I/O structure to permit various I/O devices to be easily interfaced to the computer. One of the first user manuals was the *Input-Output Systems Manual,* which described the methods available for interfacing. These methods, now standard in mini-computer and microcomputer design, included:

1. Program controlled transfers.
2. Program controlled transfers using the Sequence Break System (now called an interrupt system).
3. Multiple channel interrupt programmed control.
4. High speed channel data transmission (now called Direct Memory Access).

The first method, program controlled transfers, was a well established method, but the second method was a unique capability. The Sequence Break System permitted a program to handle much of the processing associated with I/O devices instead of using special hardwired controllers. Each time that an I/O device had information to be transferred to memory, it caused an interrupt to the processor and the processor handled the transfer. This was a marked change from the large computers that used extensive (and expensive) I/O processors, such as the IBM 7090 channels. A single IBM channel was more expensive than a PDP-1.

The I/O character rates for devices such as magnetic tapes and drums exceeded the rates which could be handled by the program, so information was transmitted directly to the PDP-1's memory in blocks under the control of the device. Inter-block control was handled by the interrupt facility, however. This basic scheme is still in use in today's DEC computers.

A block diagram of the magnetic tape control unit used on the PDP-1 is shown in Figure 7.

```
pdp1 :=
Begin {oc}          ! One's Complement

** Processor.State **

AC\Accumulator<0:17>,
IO\Input.Output.Register<0:17>,
PC\Program.Counter<6:17>,
OV\Overflow<>,
PF\Program.Flags<1:6>,
RUN< >

** Memory.State **

M\Memory[0:4095]<0:17>,

** Console.State **

TWS\Test.Word.Switches<0:17>,
SS\Sense.Switches<1:6>,
AS\Address.Switches<0:15>,

** Instruction.Format **

i\instruction<0:17>,
op<0:4>      := i<0:4>,      ! Operation Code
ib< >        := i<5>,        ! Indirect Bit
y<6:17>      := i<6:17>,     ! Address
cli< >       := i<6>,        ! Clear IO
lat< >       := i<7>,        ! OR AC and Test Switches
cma< >       := i<8>,        ! Complement AC
hlt< >       := i<9>,        ! Halt
cla< >       := i<10>,       ! Clear AC
lap< >       := i<11>,       ! Load PC
stf< 0:3>    := i<14:17>,    ! Set Program Flags
clf<0:3>     := i<14:17>,    ! Clear Program Flags
spi< >       := i<7>,        ! Skip if Positive IO
szo< >       := i<8>,        ! Skip if Zero OV
sza< >       := i<9>,        ! Skip if Zero AC
spa< >       := i<10>,       ! Skip if Positive AC
sma<>        := i<11>,       ! Skip if Negative AC
szs<0:2>     := i<12:14>,    ! Skip if Zero Switches
szf<0:2>     := i<15:17>,    ! Skip if Zero Flags

** Effective.Address **

z<6:17> :=
Begin
z = y Next
Repeat Begin                 ! indefinite indirect
       If Not ib => Leave z Next

       z = ib@y = M[y]<5:17>
       End
End,
```

```
pdp4 :=
Begin {tc}          ! Two's Complement

** Processor.State **

AC\Accumulator<0:17>,

PC\Program.Counter<5:17>,
L\Link< >,

RUN< >

** Memory.State **

M\Memory[0:8191]<0:17>,

** Console.State **

ACS\AC.Switches<0:17>,

AS\Address.Switches<0:12>,

** Instruction.Format **

i\instruction<0:17>,
op<0:3>      := i<0:3>,      ! Operation Code
ib< >        := i<4>,        ! Indirect Bit
y<5:17>      := i<5:17>,     ! Address
cla< >       := i<5>,        ! Clear AC
cll< >       := i<6>,        ! Clear L
rt< >        := i<7>,        ! Rotate Twice
hlt< >       := i<12>,       ! Halt
rar< >       := i<13>,       ! Rotate Right
ral< >       := i<14>,       ! Rotate Left
oas< >       := i<15>,       ! OR AC and Switches
cml< >       := i<16>,       ! Complement L
cma< >       := i<17>,       ! Complement AC
is< >        := i<8>,        ! Invert Sense of Skip
szl< >       := i<9>,        ! Skip if Zero Link
snl< >       := i<9>,        ! Skip if Non-Zero Link
sna< >       := i<10>,       ! Skip if Non-Zero AC
sza< >       := i<10>,       ! Skip if Zero AC
spa< >       := i<11>,       ! Skip if Positive AC
sma< >       := i<11>,       ! Skip if Negative AC

** Effective.Address **

z<5:17> :=
Begin
z = y Next

If Not ib => Leave z Next
If z Eqv #0001? => M[z] = M[z] + 1 Next
z = M[z]<5:17>

End,
```

Figure 6. PDP-1 and PDP-4 ISPS description (courtesy of Mario Barbacci) (part 1 of 5).

```
** Instruction.Interpretation **

interp :=
Begin
Repeat Begin
        If Not RUN => Stop( ) Next
        i = M[PC] Next
        PC = PC + 1 Next
        execute( )
        End
End,

execute :=
Begin
Decode op =>
        Begin
! Load and Store Group
lac  :=AC = M[z( )],               ! Load Accumulator
lio  :=IO = M[z( )],               ! Load I/O Register
law  :=AC<= ib@y,                  ! Load Immediate (sign extension)
dac  :=M[z( )] = AC,               ! Deposit Accumulator
dio  :=M[z( )] = IO,               ! Deposit I/O Register
dap  :=M[z( )]<6:17> = AC<6:17>, ! Dep. Address Part
dip  :=M[z( )]<0:5> = AC<0:5>,! Deposit Instruction Part
dzm  :=M[z( )] = 0,                ! Deposit 0 in Memory

! Arithmetic and Logical Group
add  :=Begin
        OV@AC = AC + M[z( )] Next
        If AC Eqv #777777 = > AC = 0
        End,
sub  :=Begin
        OV@AC = AC - M[z( )] Next
        If AC Eqv #777777 = > AC = 0
        End,
mus  :=Begin                       ! Multiplication Step
        If IO<17> => AC = AC + {us} M[z( )] Next
        AC@IO = (AC@IO) Sr0 1 Next
        If AC Eqv #777777 => AC = 0
        End,
dis  :=Begin                       ! Division Step
        AC@IO = AC<1:17>@IO@(Not AC<0>) Next
        If IO<17> => AC = AC - {us} M[z( )] Next
        If Not IO<17> => AC = AC + {us M[z()] + 1 Next
        If AC Eqv #777777 => AC = 0
      End,
and. :=AC = AC And M[z( )],
ior  :=AC = AC Or M[z( )],
xor. :=AC = AC Xor M[z( )],
! Program Control Group
jmp  :=PC = z( ),                  ! Jump
jsp  :=Begin                       ! Jump and Save PC
        AC = OV@'00000@PC Next
        PC = y
        End,
```

```
** Instruction.Interpretation **

interp  :=
Begin
Repeat Begin
        If Not RUN => Stop( ) Next
        i = M[PC] Next
        PC = PC + 1 Next
        execute( )
        End
End,

execute :=
Begin
Decode op =>
        Begin
! Load and Store Group
lac  :=AC = M[z( )],

dac  :=M[z( )] = AC,

dzm  :=M[z( )] = 0,

! Arithmetic and Logical Group
add  :=Begin
        L@AC = AC + {oc} M[z( )] Next
        If AC Eqv #777777 => AC = 0
        End,
tad  :=L@AC = AC + {tc} M[z( )],

and. :=AC = AC And M[z( )],

xor. :=AC = AC Xor M[z( )],
! Program Control Group
jmp  :=PC = z( ),
jms :=  Begin
        M[z( )] = L@'0000@PC Next
        PC = z + 1
        End,
```

Figure 6. PDP-1 and PDP-4 ISPS description (courtesy of Mario Barbacci) (part 2 of 5).

```
cal.jda  :=Begin
         Decode ib =>
                   Begin
         cal   :=Begin              ! Subroutine Call
                   M[#100] = AC Next
                   AC = OV@'00000@PC Next
                   PC = #101
                   End,
         jda   :=Begin              ! Jump and save AC
                   M[z( )] = AC Next
                   AC = OV@'00000@PC Next
                   PC = y + 1
                   End
                   End
         End,
idx   :=Begin                       ! Index
         AC = M[z( )] + 1 Next
         If AC Eqv #777777 => AC = 0 Next
         M[z] = AC
         End,
isp   :=Begin                       ! Increment and Skip if Positive
         AC = M[z( )] + 1 Next
         If AC Eqv #777777 => AC = 0 Next
         M[z] = AC;
         If AC Geq 0 => PC = PC + 1
         End,
sad   :=If AC Neq M[z( )] => PC = PC + 1, ! Skip if AC Differs
sas   :=If AC Eql M[z( )] => PC = PC + 1, ! Skip if AC is Same
xct   :=Begin                       ! Execute
         i = M[z( )] Next
         Restart exec
         End,
iot   :=undefined( ),
sft   :=shift.rotate.group( ),
skp   :=skip.group( ),
opr := operate.group( ),



Otherwise := RUN = 0                ! Undefined Operations
          End
End,

skip< >,                            ! Result of Condition Tests

skip.group :=
Begin
skip = 0 Next
Decode ib =>
          Begin
          0     :=Begin             ! True Test
                  If szo And (OV Eqv 0) => (skip = 1; OV = 0);
                  If sza And (AC Eql 0) => skip = 1;
                  If spa And (AC Geq 0) => skip = 1;
                  If sma And (AC Lss 0) => skip = 1;
                  If spi And (IO Geq 0) => skip = 1;
                  Decode szs =>     ! Test Sense Switches
                          Begin
                  #0    :=No.Op( ),
                  #7    :=If SS Eql 0 => skip = 1,
                  Otherwise := If SS<szs> Eqv 0 => skip = 1
                          End;
```

```
cal   :=Decode ib =>
        Begin
          0 :=    Begin
                  M[#20] = L@'0000@PC Next

                  PC = #21
                  End,
          1 :=    Begin
                  M[M[N20]C = L@'0000@PC Next

                  PC = M[N20] + {us} 1
                  End
          End,



isz   :=Begin   ! Increment and Skip if Zero
          M[z] = M[z( )] + 1 Next


          If M[z] Eql 0 => PC = PC + 1
          End,
sad   :=If AC Neq M[z( )] => PC = PC + 1,

xct   :=Begin
          i = M[z( )] Next
          Restart exec
          End,
iot   :=Undefined( ),


opr.law := Decode ib =>
                  Begin
          0\opr := operate.group( ),
          1\law := AC <= y
                  End,
Otherwise := RUN = 0
          End
End,

skip< >,          ! Result of Condition Tests

skip.group :=
Begin
skip = 0 Next
Decode is =>
          Begin
          0 :=    Begin                                  ! True Test
                  If snl And (L Xor 0) => skip = 1;
                  If sza And (AC Eql 0) => skip = 1;

                  If sma And (AC Lss 0) => skip = 1
                  End,
```

Figure 6. PDP-1 and PDP-4 ISPS description (courtesy of Mario Barbacci) (part 3 of 5).

```
                Decode szf =>        ! Test Program Flags
                        Begin
                #0    := No.Op( ),
                #7    := If PF Eql 0 => skip = 1,
                Otherwise := If PF<szf> eqv 0 => skip = 1
                        End
                End,
        1       := Begin             ! Reverse Test
            If szo And (OV Xor 0) = > (skip = 1; OV = 0);
                If sza And (AC Neq 0) => skip = 1;
                If spa And (AC Lss 0) => skip = 1;
                If sma And (AC Geq 0) => skip = 1;
                If spi And (IO Lss 0) => skip = 1;
                Decode szs =>        ! Test Sense Switches
                        Begin
                #0    :=             No.Op( ),
                #7    :=             If SS Neq 0 => skip = 1,
                Otherwise := If SS<szs> Xor 0 => skip = 1
                        End;
                Decode szf =>        ! Test Program Flags
                        Begin
                #0    :=             No.Op( ),
                #7    :=             If PF Neq 0 => skip = 1,
                Otherwise := If PF<szf> Xor 0 => skip = 1
                        End
                End
        End Next
If skip => PC = PC + 1 ! Skip
End,
operate.group :=
Begin
If hlt => RUN = 0;

If cla => AC = 0;
If cli => IO = 0;

Decode clf =>
        Begin
        #01:#06 := PF<clf<1:3>> = 0,
        #07 := PF = #00,
        Otherwise := No.Op( )
        End;
Decode stf =>
        Begin
        #11:#16 := PF<stf<1:3>> = 1,
        #17 := PF = #77,
        Otherwise := No.Op( )
        End Next
If lat => AC = AC Or TWS Next
If lap => Begin
        AC<0> = AC<0> Or OV;
        AC<1:5> = 0;
        AC<6:17> = PC
        End Next
If cma => AC = Not AC

End,

! Shift and Rotate Operations

hardware function ones(x<0:8>)<0:3>,     ! Count Number of 1's in x
```

```
1 :=    Begin                                ! Reverse Test
        If szl And (L Eqv 0) => skip = 1;
        If sna And (AC Neq 0) => skip = 1;

        If spa And (AC Geq 0) => skip = 1
        End

        End Next
If skip => PC = PC + 1                       ! Skip
End,
operate.group :=
Begin
If hlt => RUN = 0;
skip.group( ) Next
If cla => AC = 0;
If cll => L = 0;
If rt => shift.rotate.group( ) Next

If oas => AC = AC Or ACS;

If cma => AC = Not AC;
If cml => L = Not L;
shift.rotate.group( )
End,

! Shift and Rotate Operations
```

Figure 6. PDP-1 and PDP-4 ISPS description (courtesy of Mario Barbacci) (part 4 of 5).

```
shift.op<0:3>  := i<5:8>,                              ! Shift Conditions

shift.n<0:8>   := i<9:17>,                             ! Shift Count

shift.rotate.group :=                                                          shift.rotate.group :=
Begin                                                                          Begin
Decode shift.op =>
        Begin
! Rotates
#01\ral   := AC = AC Slr Ones(shift.n),                ! AC Left               If ral => L@AC = (L@AC) Slr 1;
#11\rar   := AC = AC Srr Ones(shift.n),                ! AC Right              If rar => L@AC = (L@AC) Srr 1
#02\ril   := IO = IO Slr Ones(shift.n),                ! IO Left
#12\ril   := IO = IO Srr Ones(shift.n),                ! IO Right
#03\rcl   := AC@IO = (AC@IO) Slr Ones(shift.n),        ! AC@IO Left
#13\rcr   := AC@IO = (AC@IO) Srr Ones(shift.n),        ! AC@IO Right
! Shifts
#05\sal   := Decode AC<0> =>
           Begin ! AC Left
        0 := AC = AC Sl0 Ones(shift.n),
        1 := AC = AC Sl1 Ones(shift.n)
           End,
#15\sar   := AC = AC Srd Ones(shift.n),                ! AC Right
#06\sil   := Decode IO<0> =>
                Begin                                  ! IO Left
        0 := IO = IO Sl0 Ones(shift.n),
        1 := IO = IO Sl1 Ones(shift.n)
                End,
#16\sir   := IO = IO Srd Ones(shift.n),                ! IO Right
#07\scl   := Decode AC<0> =>
                Begin                                  ! AC@IO Left
        0 := AC@IO = AC@IO Sl0 Ones(shift.n),
        1 := AC@IO = AC@IO Sl1 Ones(shift.n)
                End,
#17\scr   := AC@IO = (AC@IO) Srd Ones(shift.n),        ! AC@IO Right
Otherwise := Undefined( )
        End
End                                                                            End

End                          ! End of Description                              End                         ! End of Description
```

Figure 6. PDP-1 and PDP-4 ISPS description (courtesy of Mario Barbacci) (part 5 of 5).

This controller, which operated under program control, used a minimum of hardware, but it used 100 percent of the processor's time when it was reading or writing data. For high speed operation, the various tape movement signals were connected directly into the program flags. To minimize hardware, there were no word buffers in the controller; instead, characters were assembled in the processor's I/O register. While a controller that requires 100 percent of a $120,000 computer's attention would not be designed today, this structure is identical to modern day microprocessor-based controllers that occupy 100 percent of a much cheaper processor's time. Thus, each computer generation goes exactly through all the stages of evolution of the predecessor generations. (A similar concept, the "wheel of reincarnation," is discussed in the Chapter 7 description of displays.)

The PDP-1 engineering prototype (1/A) is shown in Figure 8. It was first shown in Boston at the Eastern Joint Computer Conference in December 1959. The cathode ray tube was integrated into the console, as shown in Figure 9,

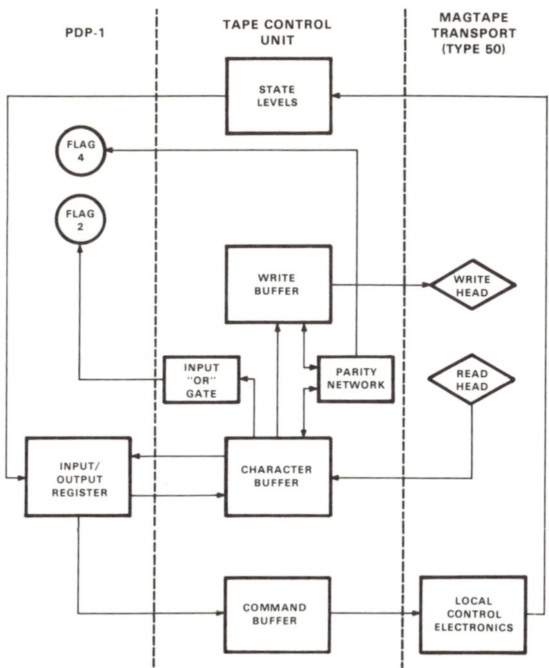

Figure 7. Program control-based magnetic tape control from PDP-1 register transfer diagram.

Figure 8. PDP-1/A prototype (circa 1960).

Figure 9. PDP-1/A CRT console.

Figure 10. PDP-1/B at BBN (circa 1960).

but this design was subsequently dropped for cost reasons. The use of a cathode ray tube integrated into the console never returned to the DEC main line of computers, except briefly in a few PDP-6s and in the LINC and PDP-12 laboratory computers. In modern fourth generation (large-scale integration) computers, the entire computer is integrated into the cathode ray tube housing.

Bolt, Beranek, and Newman (BBN), a consulting firm in Cambridge, Massachusetts, purchased the first production machine (1/B) for delivery in November 1960. This machine is shown in Figure 10. A third machine, similar to

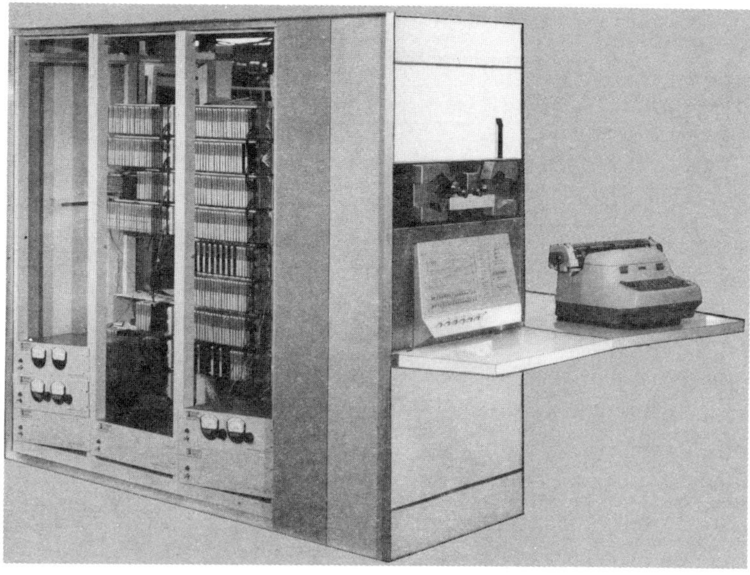

Figure 11. PDP-1/C production version (circa 1961).

the 1/A and 1/B, was constructed for internal use.

After building the first three machines, it was clear that modifications were needed to improve producibility, lower production costs, and improve reliability. The separate console required many cables, and the connectors between the console and the computer were unreliable. For this reason, the final design (called the PDP-1/C) used an operator/maintenance console integrated into the cabinets, as shown in Figure 11. The cabinets were produced by DEC and were designed as air plenums to improve air flow by having air enter at the bottom of the cabinet and flow past all the modules. The PDP-1/C cabinet design and module mounting scheme were used directly in the PDP-4 and PDP-5 computers and have remained relatively unchanged (except for airflow direction) through the years. They are being used in housings of the smaller metal-boxed minicomputers and in options of the third (integrated circuit) and the fourth (large-scale integrated circuit) generations.

The PDP-1/C design used four cabinets instead of the three cabinets of the earlier versions and preassigned the space in those cabinets for improved producibility and configuration control. Each of the multiply-divide, sequence break, memory extension control, and high speed channel options had an assigned location. Figure 12 shows the numerous options that were offered for the PDP-1. Figure 13 shows a side view of a typical cabinet and shows the space for interconnecting to other options. Expansion was accommodated by adding bays to the basic four-bay mechanical structure and by interconnecting stand-alone options via cables. Rather than the bused connection scheme commonly used today, the PDP-1 used a radial interconnect system. The radial design of the I/O structure and the free-standing controllers for the magtape, displays, card equipment, printer, and other devices made cabling relatively easy.

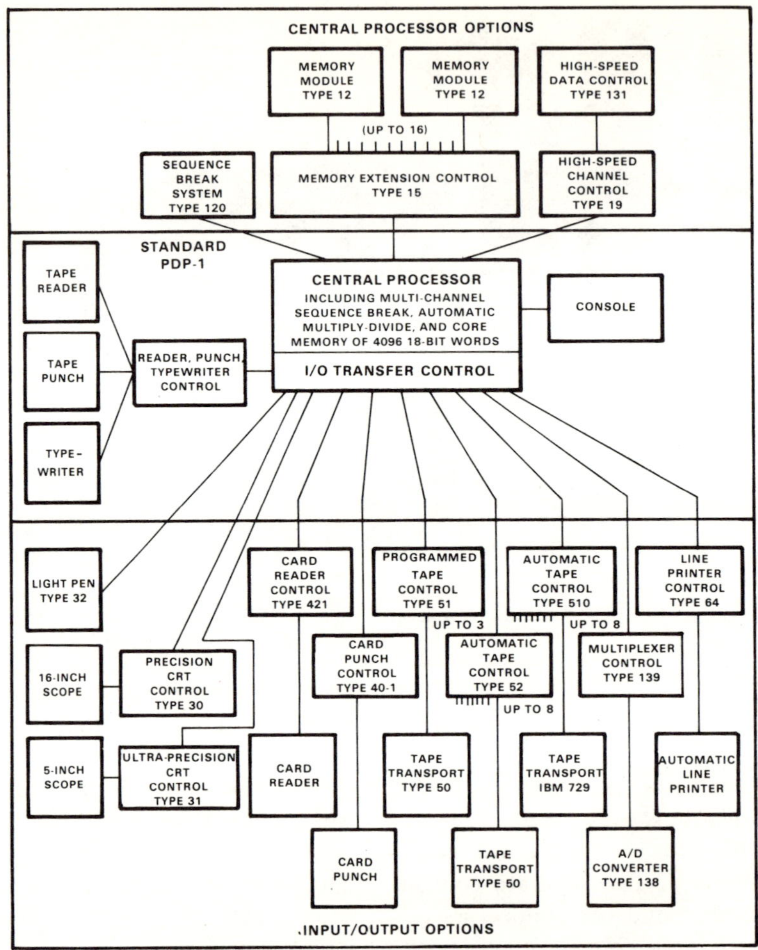

Figure 12. PDP-1 system block diagram.

As with device controllers, history is repeating itself today in this area, as new fourth generation designs are returning to radial interconnect due to the decreased cost of logic, the high cost of interconnect, and the need to bound the system.

The additional year of module design between American Research and Development's permission to construct computers and DEC's actual commencement of computer construction had permitted more low speed (500 KHz) modules to be designed. These newer modules used the same circuit techniques as their predecessors, but they used less expensive, slower transistors. These new modules were used for the I/O equipment. The PDP-1 was built from only 34 module types, including memory modules. Each module type was fully general purpose, except the five module types that were used for the analog memory circuitry. The module types are shown in Table 1.

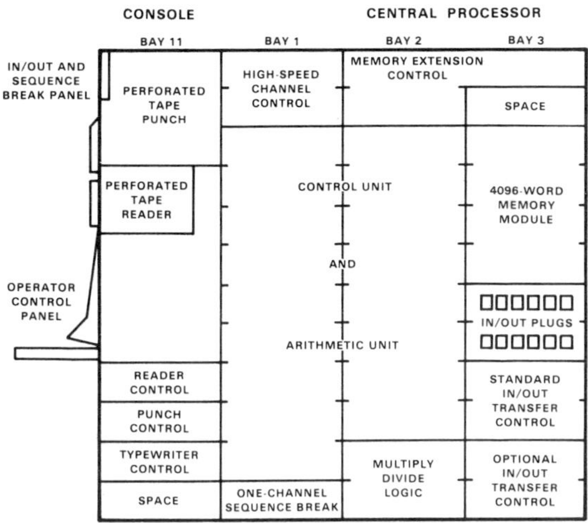

Figure 13. PDP-1/C logic layout diagram.

Table 1. PDP-1 Modules

Circuit Type	High Speed 5 MHz Clock	Low Speed 500 KHz Clock
Inverters, gates, decoders	7	5
Pulse amplifiers, delay lines	4	2
Flip-flop configurations	2	3
Special drivers, signal conditioning	4	2
Core memory circuits	5	–
	22	12

Because of its short word length and high speed, the PDP-1 was particularly suited to the laboratory and scientific control applications that were to emerge later in the second generation. The small, scientific computers from Bendix (G-15) and Librascope (LGP-30) had longer word lengths and cost less than the PDP-1, but they were slower because of their serial design which was dictated by the use of a drum as primary memory. This slow speed limited the utility of these machines in computation, control, and laboratory applications.

There were some market credibility problems which inhibited PDP-1 sales. It was an unorthodox machine in that it had high speed, a short word length, and no built-in floating-point arithmetic. Also, potential buyers doubted that a company with only 100 employees and less than a million dollars in sales could be a reliable and long-lived computer supplier.

The first few PDP-1s were sold for the anticipated applications in scientific computation and real-time control. Users directly interacted with the computer via its typewriter, cathode ray tube, and console. Customers included: Lawrence Livermore Laboratory (for peripheral support processing to their large scientific calculators and for graphics I/O); Bolt, Beranek and Newman (for psycho-acoustics and general computer science research); and Atomic Energy of Canada Limited (for pulse height analysis and van de Graaf generator experiment control). The most important sale in terms of DEC's future was to International Telephone and Telegraph (ITT), which used PDP-1s in message switching systems.

Nearly half of the PDP-ls constructed were used, as the ADX 7300, for the ITT message switching application. The application was, in essence, the automation of a torn tape switching center. In a torn tape switching center, messages are received punched on tape, and the tapes are hand carried to a tape reader appropriate to the message's destination. In the computerized version, up to 256 teleprinter lines could be switched under program control in a store and forward scheme on a character-by-character basis using the interrupt facility of the PDP-1. The PDP-1 was uniquely suited for this application because of its high speed and high performance Sequence Break System which permitted low cost teleprinter line interfaces.

Aside from the experience gained from having to produce computers that could run unattended and without service, the most important result of the ITT order was that it allowed DEC to build a number of identical machines without special engineering. This in turn provided a production base with decreased costs (as described in Chapter 3) and a discipline to be less special systems oriented. The first few machines ordered by other customers had been nearly all different, requiring DEC to build options that were sold only a few times. In addition, many of those machines had interfaces that were unique to the applications.

It should be noted that because the hardware for the PDP-1 was relatively inexpensive, DEC could afford to stock an ample supply of basic modules for building special interfaces. Constructing interfaces and specialized hardware was relatively easy compared to modern day hardware design. Also, design errors could be corrected with simple wiring changes – a much easier process than that demanded by the modern day, where expensive printed circuit boards have fine etch lines to be cut and read-only memories to be changed. Finally, the special interfaces and controllers for the PDP-1 were quite simple compared to modern designs.

While the ITT sale was important to DEC's future, the Bolt, Beranek, and Newman (BBN) sale was important to the future of the entire computer industry because it was one of the events leading to the development of timesharing. A number of computer scientists at M.I.T. and BBN believed that it was necessary to provide interactive access to computers. The only way to make this economically viable was to simultaneously share the computer among the users. Three experiments were carried out to demonstrate its feasibility: the IBM 7090 system at M.I.T. [Corbato *et al.*, 1962] which later became the Compatible Time Sharing System (CTSS), the multiuser PDP-1 at M.I.T. [Dennis, 1964] which was operational in 1963, and the shared PDP-1 at BBN [McCarthy *et al.*, 1963].

Batch multiprogramming [Strachey, 1959] was an important part of the design of the Stretch computer [Buchholz, 1962] and the Atlas computer [Kilburn *et al.*, 1962]. They were oriented toward hardware efficiency in that they aimed for high utilization of all components. Timesharing, on the other hand, was concerned with the efficiency of the people trying to use the computer – the efficiency of the man-computer interaction [Corbato *et al.*, 1962].

A set of requirements was identified for a timesharing system. Unless the workload was restricted to programs that were specially designed to run concurrently and to programs that were error-free, one needed the following:

1. Memory protection.
2. Program and data relocatability.
3. A supervisor program.
4. A timed return to the supervisor.
5. Interpretive execution of the I/O instructions.

The BBN timesharing system began operation in September 1962. Five teleprinter users shared the upper 4 Kwords of memory; the lower 4 Kwords held the supervisor program, called the "channel 17 routine." The modifications to the PDP-1 to effect timesharing were embodied in the "restricted mode" of operation. They matched the above requirements in the following way:

1. **Memory protection.** Switching between the two 4-Kword areas required the use of an I/O instruction.
2. **Program and data relocatability.** Because only one user was resident at one time, this was not needed.
3. **A supervisor program.** The channel 17 clock routine fulfilled this function.
4. **A timed return to the supervisor.** The channel 17 clock generated an interrupt every 20 milliseconds.

5. **Interpretive execution of I/O instructions.** Whenever the PDP-1 was in restricted mode, an attempt to obey an I/O instruction caused a sequence break.

The TYC Control Language, a debugging aid adapted from the DDT language devised for the PDP-1 and its predecessor languages, was regarded as important because it allowed direct language program debugging. The "restricted mode" modifications, a high speed swapping drum, and the use of the new multiport memory designed for the PDP-6 formed the PDP-1/D design. Timeshared computers were built and operated at BBN, Stanford, and M.I.T. These timesharing efforts later influenced the use of timesharing in the PDP-6 (Chapter 21).

THE PDP-4

About two years after the PDP-1 was first shown, the notion of a much smaller machine developed during discussions of process control applications with Foxboro Corporation and various other customers. A machine called the DC-12 Digital Controller was proposed. This would be a 12-bit computer oriented toward process control data collection and laboratory data processing. During the preparation of the proposal, the CDC 160 was studied, and the DEC engineers briefly considered building a copy or version of the 10-bit L-1 computer designed by Wes Clark at Lincoln Laboratory. However, the principal idea input for the Digital Controller came from another Wes Clark computer, the Laboratory Instrument Computer (LINC).

The DC-12 Digital Controller was never built by that name; instead, it became the PDP-5 (Chapter 7). Some of the ideas studied in the LINC and L-1 were used in other DEC machines, including the machine that became the PDP-1 successor, the PDP-4 (Figure 14). The PDP-2 designation was saved for a possible 24-bit machine, but none was ever built. DEC also never built a PDP-3, although one was designed on paper as a 36-bit machine.*

The decision to make the next machine an 18-bit machine, rather than a 12-bit machine, was taken very lightly when it was made in December of 1962. In retrospect, it may have been a poor decision, but the reasoning went somewhat as follows.

Based on the programming experience of the TX-0, Gordon Bell felt that an 18-bit machine significantly simpler than the PDP-1 could be built and that simple machines with few instructions for a given number of data-types would perform nearly as well as those with more instructions. This feeling was based on the use of Whirlwind, TX-0 as it evolved through its various versions, and the PDP-1. This was later proven to be true, as the PDP-4 was implemented in less than half the space of the PDP-1 and provided 5/8 the performance for 1/2 the price. There is some question, however, as to how much of the size reduction was due to the simpler architecture, how much to the substantially better logic design implementation, and how much to the increased logic packing density.

Gordon Bell had conceived the idea of auto-incrementing memory registers. This allowed vectors to be accessed easily instead of using index registers. The auto-incremented memory registers performed about as well as index registers and were much less expensive to implement.

The PDP-1 had used one's complement arithmetic, which was especially poor for the fast multiple precision operations and floating-point arithmetic that DEC's customers needed.

*In 1960 a customer (Scientific Engineering Institute, Waltham, Massachusetts) built a PDP-3. It was later dismantled and given to M.I.T.; as of 1974, it was up and running in Oregon.

Figure 14. PDP-4.

Multiple precision operations required the detection of carry or borrow and the ability to add or subtract the result into the next most significant word. One's complement (especially as implemented on PDP-1) did not conveniently provide this capability, whereas two's complement arithmetic did. Therefore, the PDP-4 was designed to use two's complement arithmetic and to use the Link bit idea from the Lincoln Laboratory L-1 design to permit the efficient programming of multiple precision arithmetic operations.

Two control instructions were changed so that they would not affect the Accumulator and interfere with arithmetic instructions. The "jump to subroutine" instruction was changed to store the return link in the program area. This convention would not be used today because it destroys the state of subroutines, thus precluding reentrant programming, and it makes the use of read-only memory difficult. The other change was that the "index and skip" instruction operated on memory only.

Those PDP-1 features that cost logic but added little to performance were eliminated. Among these were program flags, sense switches, and the wired-in program (read-in mode) that controlled the automatic reading of paper tape.

The PDP-1 had used 4-Kword memory with memory bank switching, an arrangement that was common when the useful software required

8 Kwords of memory. It was felt that 8 Kwords of directly addressable memory would be ideal. The corollary to Parkinson's Law that programs expand to fill any physical memory size was clearly not understood. However, it turned out that most PDP-4s stayed within the 8-Kword constraint, although the machine could operate with up to 32 Kwords of memory.

It was decided that the goal was to build a modular design such that the optional equipment cost would be associated with the option rather than wired into all of the machines. It was also decided that the Teletype Corporation Model 28 should be used instead of a modified IBM Model B typewriter such as that used on the PDP-1. It was felt that this would provide a lower failure rate, less time to repair, and lower cost.

The logic design of the PDP-1, although quite straightforward, was optimized in the PDP-4 by eliminating redundant terms and encoding the instructions in ways that would simplify the implementation. (The only way to get a significantly smaller machine was to start over with a new instruction set processor.) However, the existing peripherals and memories for the PDP-1 could be used immediately to assist the implementation of the new machine. This was another important factor in favor of building a new 18-bit machine rather than going to a 12-bit design.

In addition to the hardware design considerations, software offerings were an important consideration. The PDP-1 users and the prospective customers for the new machine were adamant about writing process control applications in a high level language. The designers at DEC briefly considered providing ALGOL 60, but decided that it would be better to provide a FORTRAN II for the new machine. It turned out that FORTRAN was used somewhat for computation, but most users stayed with assembly language programming, especially where real-time programming was concerned.

The designers had a fairly clear idea of the intended market for the new machine. Like its predecessor, the PDP-1, the PDP-4 was to be used predominately for process control, with some use in the laboratory for pulse height analysis, data gathering, and other similar applications. In fact, during the planning for the PDP-4, meetings were being held with Foxboro Corporation about applications at Nabisco for baking control and with Corning Glass about the control of a glass tube manufacturing process. The meetings with Foxboro may have been another factor in the 12-bit versus 18-bit decision, as Foxboro favored the longer word length due to their previous experience with a 24-bit RCA control computer. When the PDP-4 machines were produced, both Foxboro and Corning bought them.

The simplifications achieved in the PDP-4 can best be appreciated by comparing the PDP-1 and PDP-4 ISPs, as shown in Figure 6, and the register transfer structures, as shown in Figures 5 and 15.

As with the PDP-1, the major design goal of the I/O system was that users be able to connect equipment easily. The use of an I/O bus structure such as party line or daisy chain was not considered for the PDP-4, although one was developed one year later for the PDP-5. Instead, the design effort focused on improving the existing radial scheme to achieve greater peripheral compatibility. The I/O section, called the Real-Time Control (Figure 16), included the ability to interface with PDP-1 peripherals. There was a small taper pin patch panel where cable drivers and input gates could be patched to the cables which radiated out to the peripherals from the main computer cabinets. The input capabilities were somewhat better than the cable drive capabilities, as the process control operations of that day were really more process monitoring than process control, a reflection of industry's distrust of the reliability of computers for actual control applications. The simplicity of the I/O distribution contributed a

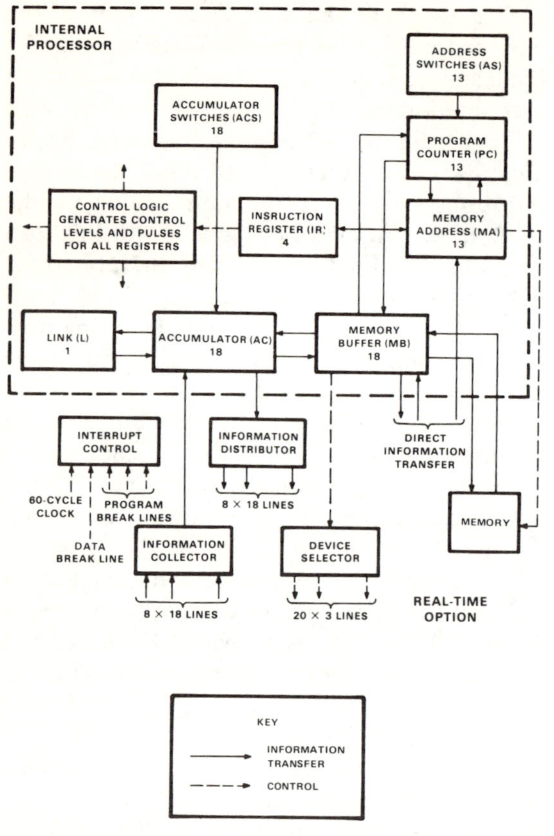

Figure 15. PDP-4 processor/real-time option register transfer diagram.

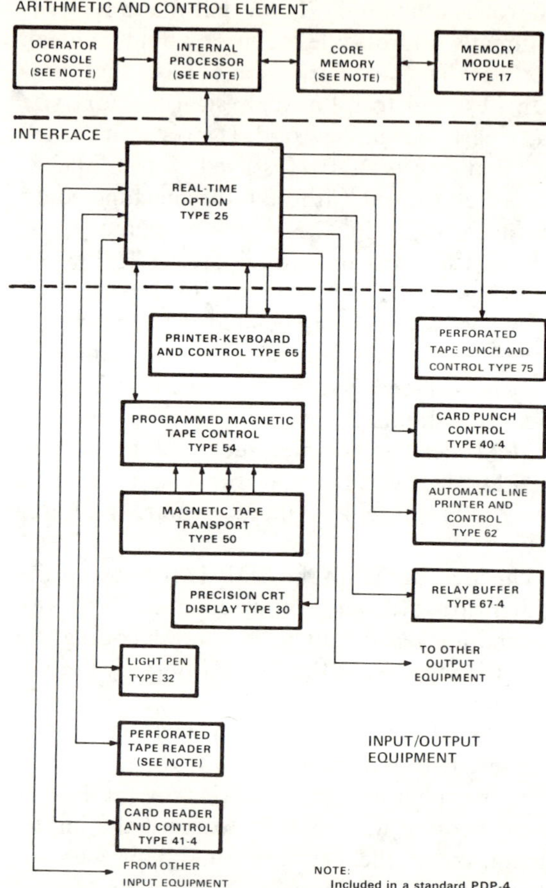

Figure 16. PDP-4 block diagram.

great deal to the compactness of the PDP-4. A complete PDP-4 with card reader, magnetic tape, display, and other options required three bays, but many systems could fit within the two standard bays (Figure 17), making PDP-4 systems less than half the size of comparable PDP-1 systems.

In addition to the physical aspects of the I/O system, the logical design of the I/O system included some new features. One of these was the ability to count events. Event counting was important in scientific applications such as pulse height analysis, and the first customer to express a need for it was the Columbia University Physics Department. It was also important in process control applications such as metering flows and counting discrete items. Options such as the 16-channel clock implemented the event counting feature by having the option access a memory cell and then rewrite its contents plus one, thus changing the contents of memory as it was rewritten. Counting could occur at event rates up to the 125-KHz memory rate.

This method of event counting lead to the design of a relatively low cost, high performance Direct Memory Access feature called the Three

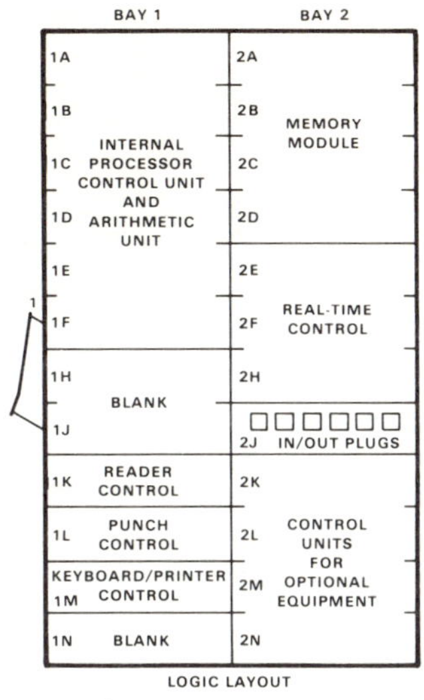

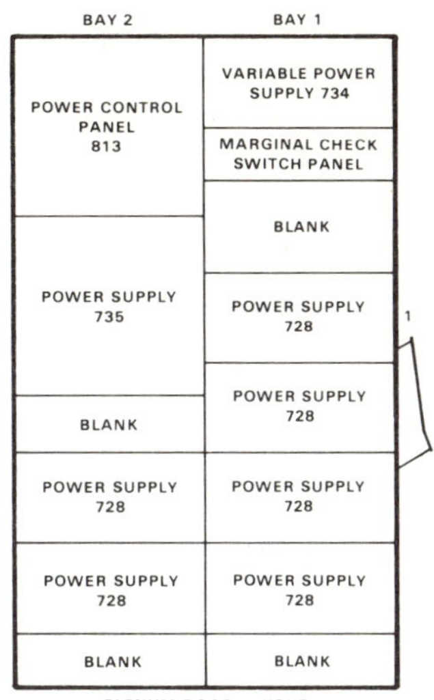

1. Operator Control Panel.

Figure 17. PDP-4 logic layout diagram.

Cycle Data Break. This feature was first used in the magnetic tape controller that was designed for the PDP-4, and it has been used extensively since then in PDP-8 options (Chapter 7). The Three Cycle Data Break method of Direct Memory Access works as follows:

1. During the first cycle, the word count (stored as a word in memory) is incremented. The word count is the negative of the length of the block to be transferred, and the incrementation step indicates that the present transfer is reducing the number of words left to be transferred by one.
2. During the second cycle, the current address pointer (also stored as a word in memory) is incremented. The current address pointer indicates the memory address to which or from which the data transfer is to take place.
3. During the third cycle, the actual data transfer between the memory and the I/O device takes place.

In addition to changes in the instruction set processor and the I/O system, the PDP-4 differed from the PDP-1 in the module technology used, as was discussed in Chapter 5. During the manufacture of the PDP-1, DEC had been extending its main business, the sale of logic modules, by extending the lower cost, slower speed 500-KHz versions of the 5-MHz modules that were used in the PDP-1. The new 500-KHz modules, evolving to 1 MHz, were 50 percent less expensive to build than the 5-MHz modules because they used germanium alloy transistors rather than micro alloy diffused transistor (MADT) transistors. They were also substantially easier to use and more reliable because of their lower data rate and wider clock pulses. Two additional circuit design techniques reduced the cost and increased reliability by reducing the number of active elements. Rather than use a transistor per gate as in the earlier designs, a diode-transistor logic design was used. In addition, capacitor-diode gates were used for the AND gates associated with register transfers.

The changes in the technology not only permitted lower cost, greater noise immunity, and greater reliability, they also permitted greater densities. This made it possible, in some cases, to design entire device controls on a single module. Because the modules had only 22 pins (18 pins for signals), the increased densities could not be applied directly to the more complicated logic functions. To solve this problem, a 10-pin connector was added on the back of each module for the register transfer gating signals. In this way, bit-slice architecture could be used, packaging one bit of the Accumulator register and all of the associated input gates on a single module (Figure 18).

An interesting device with multiple stable states was devised to simplify the control section of the PDP-4. It was a generalization of the flip-flop to n stable states, using n NAND gates in a cross-coupled way with each NAND gate having n-l inputs. A patent was awarded for this circuit, and it was subsequently used in other computers and in the module product line.

Maintenance did not represent such a high portion of the product cost as it does today, and the designers of the PDP-4 did not feel that the fraction of the total system represented by the memory justified such present day features as parity memory. Nonetheless, maintenance was a major consideration in the PDP-4 design, motivating the simplicity of architecture, straightforwardness of implementation, care in logic design, and clarity of the maintenance documentation. The machine instruction set description occupied only one letter-size page. The logic design flow chart (a state diagram) occupied only one D-size (22 × 34 inch) drawing, and the design drawings for the processor occupied seven D-size sheets. To facilitate understanding the machine operation, each signal name on the drawings had a mnemonic prefix identical to the drawing name (e.g., AC) indicating from which of the seven drawings that signal originated. This convention has been carried forward through many other DEC machines.

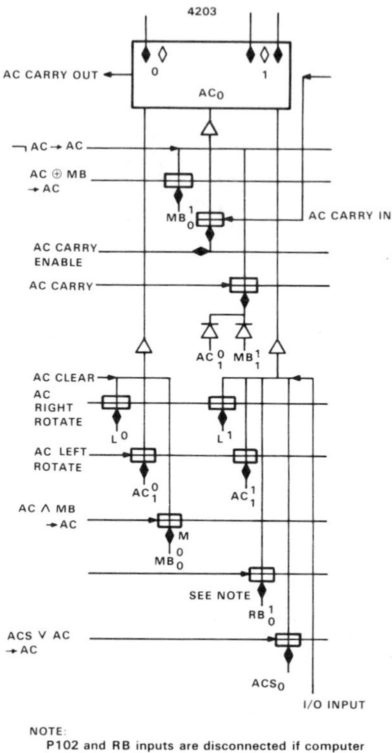

Figure 18. PDP-4 Accumulator bit-slice register transfer diagram.

The operator's console, shown in Figure 19, included several functions to assist maintenance. The console switches (Read, Read Next, Write, Write Next, Start, Continue) could be repeated at a clock rate varied by a speed control

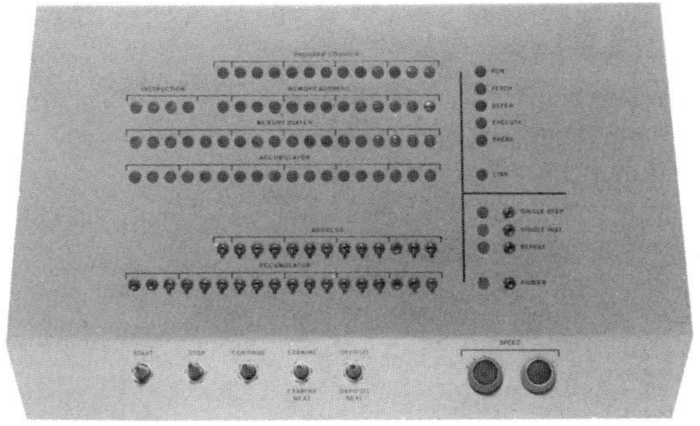

Figure 19. PDP-4 operator console.

on the console. This simplified testing by permitting easy use of an oscilloscope. In addition, simple checks on memory could be performed by using the console Read and Write switches and observing the results on the console lights.

Because the PDP-1 had been generally used in dedicated applications, the users had written their own programs. M.I.T., for example, had contributed a good macroassembler, linking loader, and interactive debugging program – DDT. BBN had contributed various subprograms. DEC had invested very little in PDP-1 software and thus had no concern for the cost of writing system software or for the concept that a new machine should capitalize on previous systems programming. It was easy for people at DEC to believe that a small part of the savings achieved by building a simpler machine could be used to pay for the writing of new software for that machine.

In the present day, designers of new computers realize that program compatibility is a constraint and that any new machine must be on an improving cost/performance line. (This is discussed in greater detail in Chapters 2 and 15.) At the time that compatibility decisions were being made with regard to the PDP-4, about 20 PDP-1s had been installed out of an eventual population of 50. Looking back from today's vantage point, a compatible machine might have been built that would have interpreted most of the PDP-1 programs and offered the same improved cost/performance ratios as the PDP-4 did, but still not have been very much larger than the original PDP-4.

The PDP-4 was a limited success. While it met the corporate profit standard, it did not sell as well as had been expected. The market demands were not as completely elastic as they had been for the PDP-1, and 5/8 of the performance for 1/2 the price was not good enough. According to the evolution model discussed in the final section of this chapter, a machine with a lower price should have had the same performance as the PDP-l, or else it should have been priced much less than the PDP-1 to compensate for the relatively poor performance. In summary, the PDP-4 was not aggressive enough in performance or in price. There is an additional reason for the poor financial showing of the PDP-4. Experience with other machines that were the first of a series, such as the PDP-5, PDP-6, LINC-8, PDP-14, and PDP-11/20, indicates that the financial performance of the first machine is always the poorest of the series, largely because of the lack of a software and hardware option base. The PDP-7, 9, 9/L, and 15 were necessary successors that used the software and hardware option base created by the PDP-4.

THE PDP-7

In many ways the original concept of the PDP-7 (or what was finally named the PDP-7) started with the design of the PDP-1/D. The initial plans were to simply repackage the PDP-1, using some higher density systems modules, and to reduce the processor cycle time. The goal was to use these changes to produce a lower price machine with much better performance. This goal was met quite well in the PDP-7, as it had a greater performance/price gain over its predecessors than any other DEC 18-bit computer.

The plan to simply repackage the PDP-1 was abandoned when consideration was given to the relative sizes of the existing software and peripheral option bases of the PDP-1 and the PDP-4. The PDP-4 had more extensive software than the PDP-1, including an operating system and a FORTRAN compiler. The PDP-4 also had a much larger peripheral hardware option base than the PDP-1. Therefore, the goal of program compatibility with the PDP-4 was added to the goal of a substantial performance/price improvement, and the I/O interface scheme for the new machine was constrained to match the timing and structure of the past computers. Although sounding quite broad, these goals were rather restrictive, especially the requirements for program and peripheral compatibility. The sales goal was truly broad, however. That goal was to sell 120 systems, more machines than the total of all other DEC computer systems sold to date.

To sell all those systems, a substantial advance in performance would be required. Thus, the performance goal was to decrease the cycle time from 8 microseconds to 1.75 microseconds, the practical limit of core memories at the time. This was a rather ambitious goal and required designing a new core memory system and a new set of modules, the B-Series, which were Flip Chip modules based on the 10-MHz systems modules (Chapter 5). These new modules were used for the central processor and memory. Originally, they were also used in the I/O section of the system, but that was subsequently redesigned to use primarily 2-MHz R-Series modules, as will be described near the end of this section. (Note the similarity to the PDP-1, where cheaper, lower speed, 500-KHz modules were used in the I/O.)

Program compatibility between the PDP-7 and the PDP-4 was maintained generally, but was slightly modified in the I/O section to facilitate the introduction of the ASCII 8-level code. The PDP-4 console teleprinter had been a Teletype Corporation Model 28 KSR teleprinter that used Baudot (5-level) code. A shift to ASCII (8-level) code had already started in the industry, so the PDP-7 was designed to use the Teletype Corporation Model 33 KSR. This change necessitated that all programs determine whether they were running on a PDP-4 or on a PDP-7 so that they could determine how to interpret the characters typed on the console teleprinter. Other than this, an upward compatibility was maintained. Downward compatibility was not maintained, as the PDP-7 had some additional instructions, a trap feature, and a multilevel interrupt option to allow multiuser environments. In addition, the program read-in mode of PDP-l days returned to the console. This feature permitted the user to press a key and cause a paper tape, punched in a special format with address and data or terminating address, to be loaded into the computer's memory. (Figure 20 shows the PDP-7 operator console.)

The structure of the processor with its registers and the interfaces to I/O and memory are shown in Figure 21. Note that the structure and style of the design was essentially the same as that used in the earlier designs, but modified for the higher speed technology. The PDP-7 and the PDP-4 had identical architectures and similar implementations, but they had radically different realizations. Although the I/O section and the new options were designed to operate at the 1.75 microsecond cycle rate, to use the slower PDP-4 compatible I/O equipment, special pulses were used to implement a slow cycle of 8 microseconds.

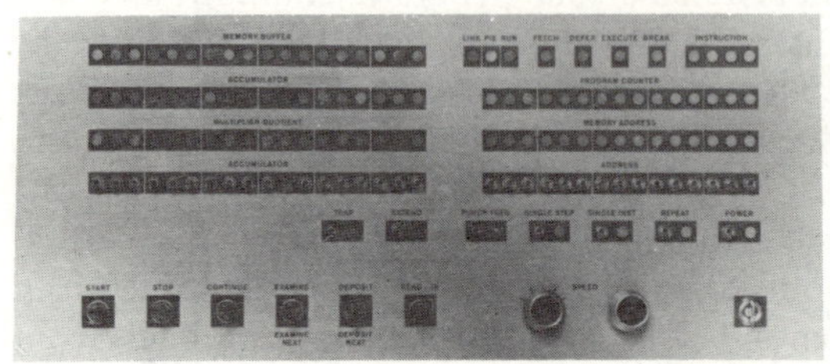

Figure 20. PDP-7 operator console.

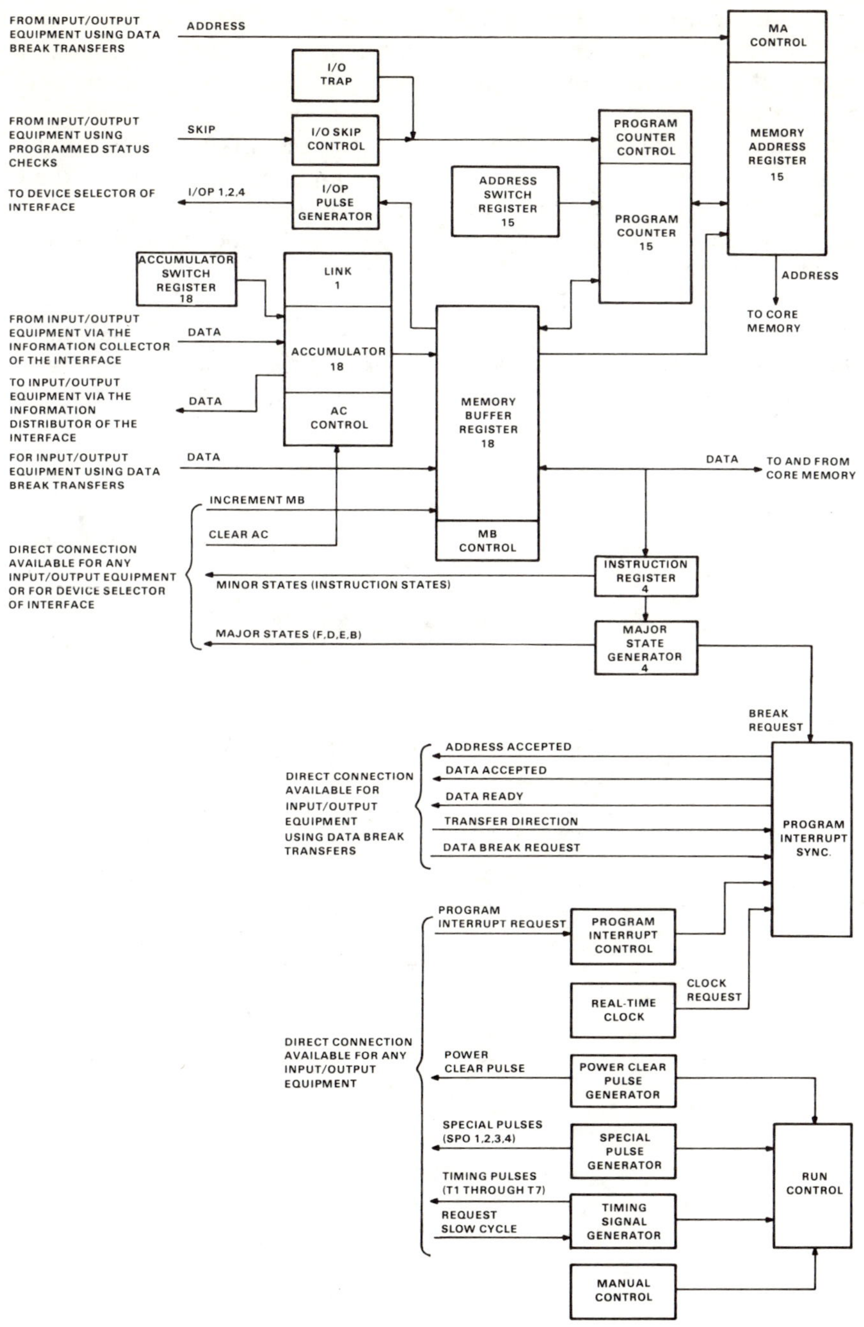

Figure 21. PDP-7 processor and I/O section register transfer diagram.

The system diagram of the PDP-7 (Figure 22) shows the options and the general interconnection scheme. It was fundamentally the same structure as its predecessors and was designed for use with many of the earlier peripheral controllers.

Physically, the PDP-7 was larger than the PDP-4 because the console was mounted on the side plane to facilitate maintenance instead of on the end as in PDP-1 and PDP-4. This permitted a service man to both look at a scope and operate the console. Also, the paper tape I/O equipment, which had been on an extra table in the PDP-1 and PDP-4, was now housed in the third bay of the main computer cabinets. Figure 23 shows that the number of logic panels for the processor of the PDP-7 was the same as that for the PDP-4, even though the circuit board area of the modules in the PDP-7 (3,348 in^2) was slightly larger than that in the PDP-4 (3,300 in^2). Although it does not show in the diagrams or in the photos, a significant portion of the volume of the PDP-4 was cable connectors to various subassemblies. The PDP-7 improved the cabling by having all of the connectors in the backplane so that all of the wiring

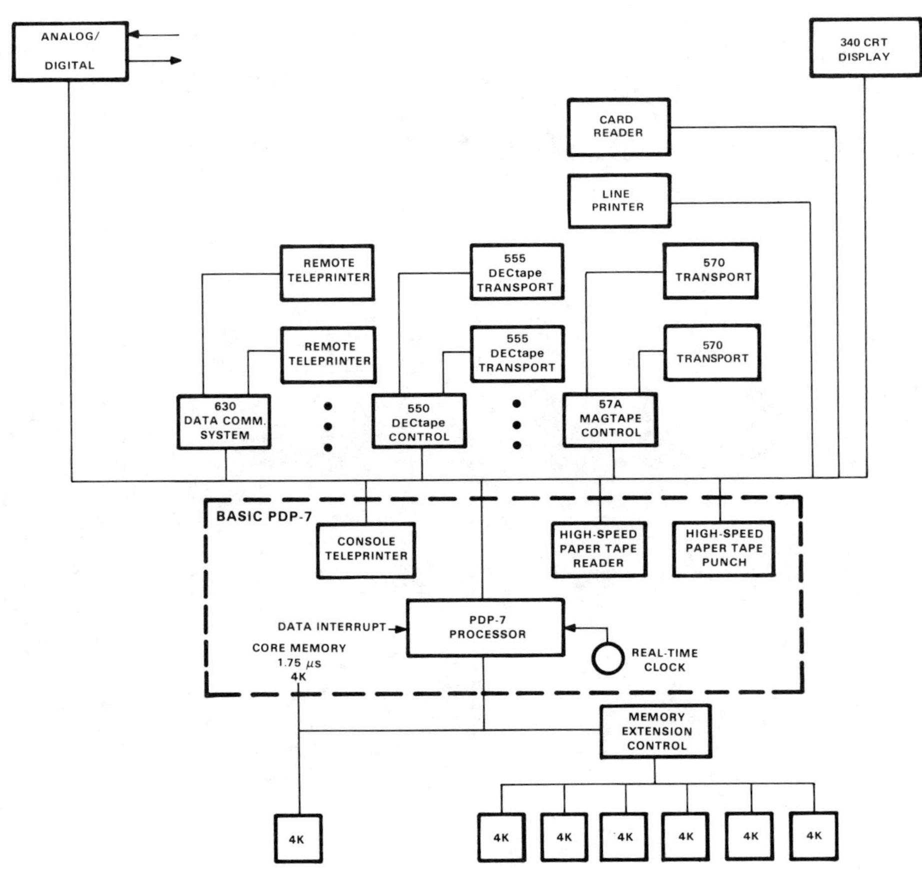

Figure 22. PDP-7 system block diagram.

could be done in a single wiring operation. The PDP-7 was thus the first DEC computer designed for automated wire-wrapping. Mechanical block holders were designed to mount the connector blocks for the modules and cable connectors in the cabinets and a semi-automatic wire-wrapping technique was developed to allow a much higher speed production of wire-wrapped backplanes. Also, a Gardner-Denver fully automatic Wire-wrap machine was ordered and programs to control it were developed.

The PDP-7 (shown in Figure 24) was a successful product. The design costs, excluding module and labor costs, were less than $100,000 from the start of the project to completion of the first prototype. Time was considered a very important factor in the design of the PDP-7. The project started on April 1, 1964, and the first production system was delivered on December 22 of the same year. The entire logic implementation was undertaken by Ron Wilson and one assistant, Jack Williams. Later, a Field Service representative, Don Zereski, literally hand-built the first production system to be delivered to Bell Laboratories. The memory control and stack were designed by a memory design engineer, Derrick Chin, who coordinated his design with the processor logic design. Despite the hand-building of the first unit, the production of the PDP-7 was the beginning of several mass production techniques at DEC, and it was an important machine in the history of DEC 18-bit computers.

The development problems that were overcome were quite formidable. A complete new

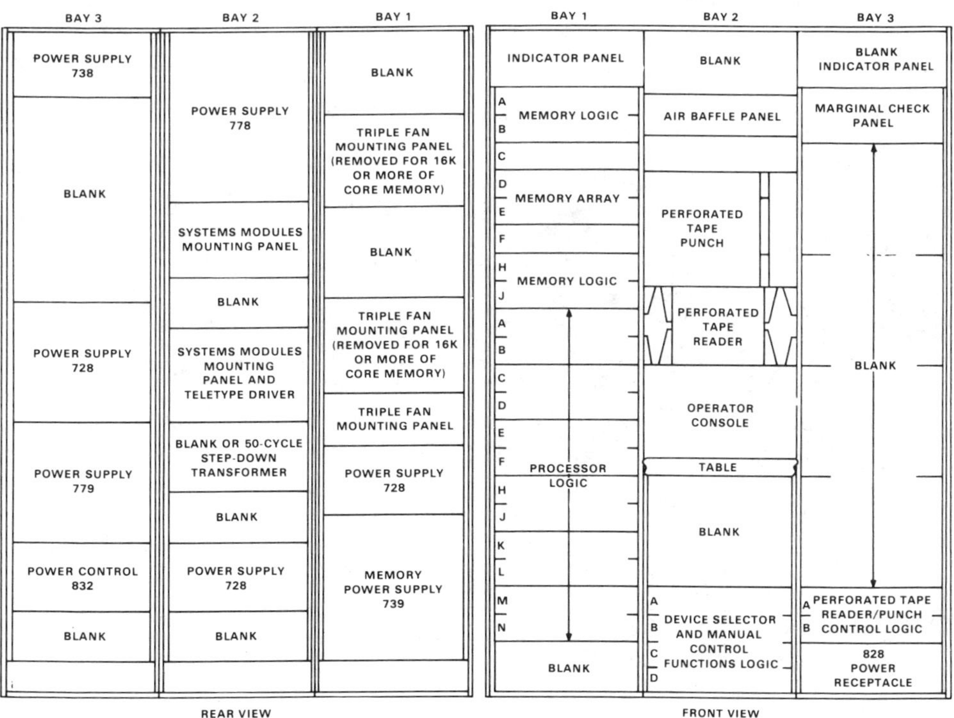

Figure 23. PDP-7 front and back logic layout.

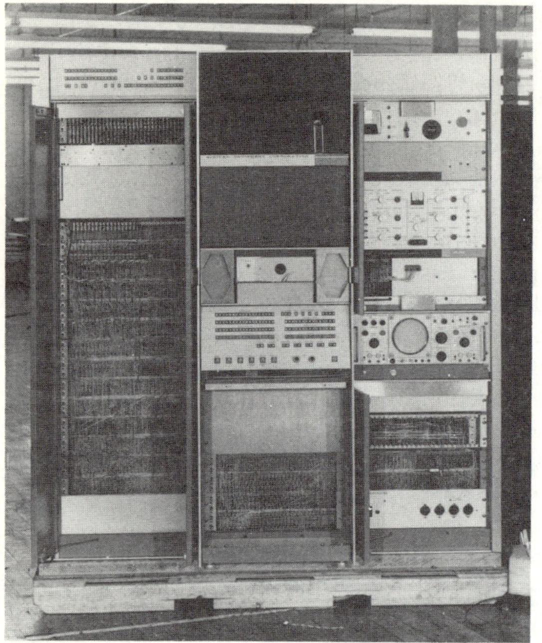

(a) Front.

(b) Rear.

Figure 24. PDP-7.

line of modules, the Flip Chip series, was developed (although 10-MHz circuits had been tested in the PDP-6). New connector blocks had to be obtained to hold the modules, a design effort that was concurrent with similar efforts for the PDP-8. New wire-wrap techniques had to be devised to ease the labor requirements so that systems could be wired faster. Toward this end, a program was ultimately developed for the PDP-4 to do wire-routing and to control the Gardner-Denver machine. System layouts had to be developed to facilitate wire-wrapping. The mechanical packaging and cooling had to be altered to accommodate the new wiring panels, as the existing PDP-1, PDP-4, and PDP-5 air plenum scheme was completely blocked by the new connector blocks. The memory performance goals (1.75 microseconds) were difficult to achieve, as the best memory performance to date was that of the PDP-6, which was 2 microseconds. All of the above had to be done within the cost goals.

As the design phase of the PDP-7 neared an end and production models were being delivered, two developments occurred that suggested the possibility of an improved production model. One of these was the R-Series module developments. These modules were lower speed than the B-Series modules that formed the processor, but they were lower in cost and more complete in the range of functions available. After analyzing the configurations that the customers were ordering, the designers came up with a new I/O panel that used R-Series modules as much as possible and was prewired for several of the most popular peripheral controls, thus reducing the amount of special wiring required to produce a system. This improved system was called the PDP-7/A.

With the PDP-7/A completed, the designers contemplated the possibilities of a next generation system that would use the new tools that were now in place, such as the Gardner-Denver fully automatic Wire-wrap machine. The design criteria for the new machine would be that it be completely wire-wrappable using the automatic machine and that a system with 8 Kwords of memory sell for approximately $35,000. The new machine was called the PDP-7/X.

To meet the goals set for the new machine, a new cabinet design was started that would mount the wire-wrap panels on door-type frames. These frames opened to allow access either to the connector side for oscilloscope tracing or to the module handle side for module replacement. The new cabinets also dealt with two problems involving the air flow. One of these was that the air flow needed to be increased due to the high density of the new logic, and the second was that the existing air flow method pulled air from the floor, which was sometimes dirty. To solve these two problems, a horizontal air flow system was implemented.

To control the system costs, which were becoming a major factor, the computer was divided both logically and physically into three divisions: memory, central processor, and input/output logic. This was done to permit the calculation and control of costs more accurately and to divide the computer into the largest single panels that the Gardner-Denver machine could wrap.

The cabinet design and system partitioning completed, the logic design moved ahead smoothly. At this time, Larry Seligman, who had designed the Extended Arithmetic Element for the PDP-7, took over the project from Ron Wilson. By this time, the project had changed its name from PDP-7/X to PDP-9.

THE PDP-9

The basic logic and hardware for the PDP-9 (Figure 25) were the same as that used in the PDP-7. Although some integrated circuits were available, no standards had yet been set, and there were no cost or speed advantages to be gained. Therefore, the logic used discrete PNP

Figure 25. PDP-9.

transistor, capacitor-diode circuitry operating with signal levels of −3 volts and ground. The modules were about 2.5 × 5 inches or 5 × 10 inches and were plugged into an assembly of 144-pin connector blocks interconnected by 24-gauge wire-wrap.

The major technology advance of the PDP-9 over the PDP-7 was in memory. A new memory had been designed that used a 2-1/2 D driving/sense structure. The 2-1/2 D system required only three wires through each core in the stack, rather than the four wires used in earlier, coincident current designs such as that used in the PDP-8 memory. The new memory obtained a cost advantage by being oriented in an 8-Kword organization rather than a 4-Kword organization. The costs of the discrete component logic in the machine were still high compared to those of memory, so the cost advantage was not as exciting as the second advantage of the new memory, which was speed. The new memory had a cycle time of 1 microsecond as opposed to 1.75 microseconds for the memory in the PDP-7. Because memory speed limited system performance, the new memory would permit the system performance of the PDP-9 to be 1.75 times better than that of the PDP-7.

The structure of the PDP-9 processor is shown in Figure 26. It was a great deal simpler than earlier designs and used a general data path through the adder rather than the *ad hoc* register structure of the earlier machines. The basic PDP-9 implemented the PDP-4 instruction set processor and the Extended Arithmetic Element option using microprogrammed control. It was the first DEC computer to use this technique.

In addition to being a technological advancement, the PDP-9 was an interesting precursor of things to come. A 64-word, 36-bit, 212-nanosecond read-only, transformer-coupled, rope memory was used as the microprogrammed control store. The design allowed for easy bench modification in the event that the microcode required changing. It was originally intended that the control words be arranged for unary encoding, or what is now called horizontal microprogramming. In such an arrangement, each bit in the microinstruction denotes an action and can be specified independently of other microinstructions. This behavior is similar to the operate class of instructions in the 12-bit and 18-bit computers. However, the intention of using horizontal microprogramming

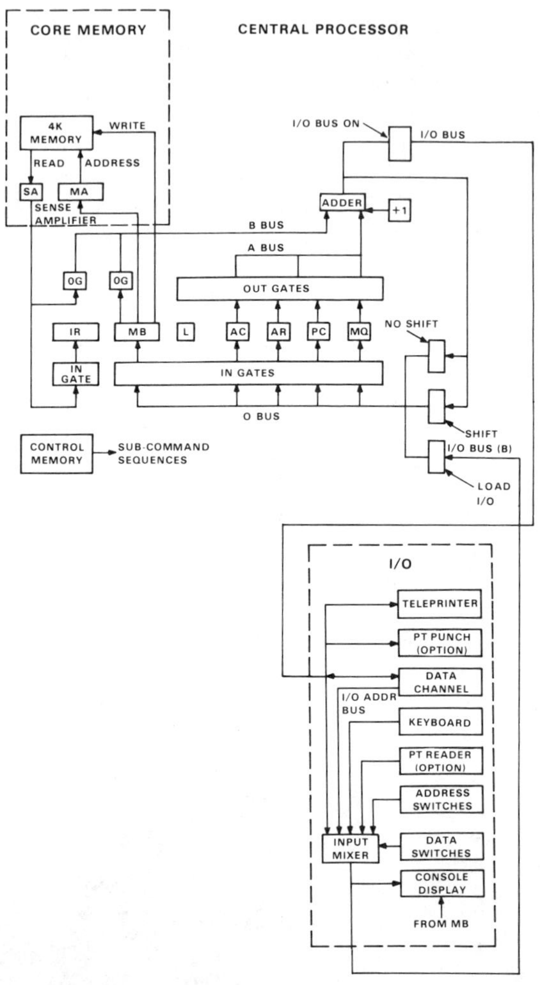

Figure 26. PDP-9 central processor register transfer diagram.

was soon lost in the complexities of design, and the bits were encoded to reduce the width of the control words. This eliminated the possibility of providing special purpose machines by a simple read-only memory change, a feature that the designers had originally hoped to include.

The necessity of staying within the size constraints of the read-only memory also constrained the extendability and use of the microprogram control, in that floating-point arithmetic could not be included due to space limitations. There were not enough words, a problem all too familiar when programming either macro or micromachines. The Extended Arithmetic Element was included in the microprogram-controlled portion of the machine. The Extended Arithmetic Element demonstrated the power of the control store technique because this option, a 36-bit multiply/divide option, was implemented in only six single height (5 × 2.5 inch) Flip Chip modules. The processor occupied about 320 module slots, for a total printed circuit board area of 3,100 in^2. This was not only less than the 3,348 in^2 for a PDP-7, but it also included both the optional arithmetic element and much of the I/O control. Thus, when functionality is considered, the PDP-9 was about half the size of earlier machines.

Interesting sidelights of the processor design effort included the discovery of an error in the PDP-1 signed integer divide algorithm and Richard Sogge's design of a discrete carry adder which would develop the carry over 18 bits in under 30 nanoseconds. This was an especially impressive circuit since ECL technology is required even today to obtain this speed.

Figure 26 shows a register transfer level diagram of the processor together with I/O and memory interface lines. The I/O control extended the features of earlier machines by implementing an eight level nested automatic priority interrupt facility and a data channel transfer facility. The Automatic Priority Interrupt had four levels of hardware interrupt capability at the I/O Bus and four levels of software priority. The Data Channel Transfer Facility was the same as a Direct Memory Access channel, but used the Three Cycle Data Break System pioneered in the magnetic tape control for the PDP-4 (page 144).

The Direct Memory Access channel was the most disappointing part of the I/O bus concept because the speed requirement dictated the use of an extra set of data and address lines which were carried between the DMA device and the memory bus multiplexer via an extra set of cables. In addition, a second port to memory was required. A clean bus cabling scheme for high speed transfer devices could not be implemented because of the extra lines required, and the only alternative, slowing down the machine to handle the transfers, was not acceptable.

Logic for the PDP-9 was mounted in three sections, each capable of holding eight rows of forty modules (Figure 27). Each of the three sections had self-contained cooling and final power regulation.

A system block diagram of the PDP-9 (Figure 28) shows the evolution of the I/O and memory bus structured computer. This scheme, derived from the PDP-5 and PDP-6, was in contrast to the radial structure of the earlier 18-bit computers and provided greater modularity and a major cost improvement. The new bus was daisy-chained from device to device using twisted pair cables. This technique provided uniformity in I/O backplane wiring compared with the PDP-7, which was customized for each option. The daisy-chain method allowed independent development, manufacturing, and test of I/O options and simplified the field installation of options. Also, it allowed costs to be associated with each option rather than being initially higher as in the radial scheme where all options had to be planned for in the central processor. The new bus structure was a mixed blessing in that it created the illusion that systems of unlimited size could be built.

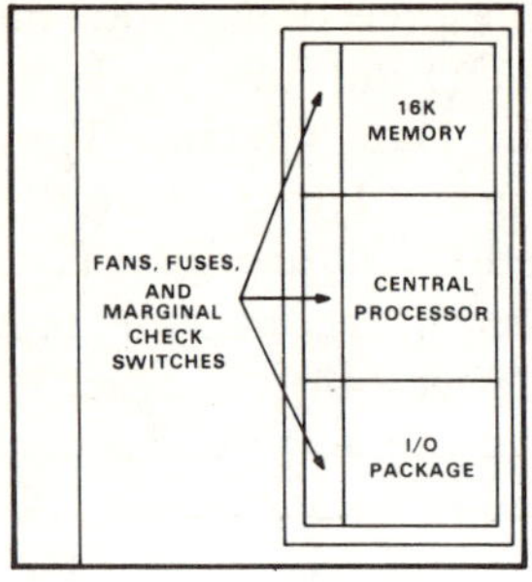

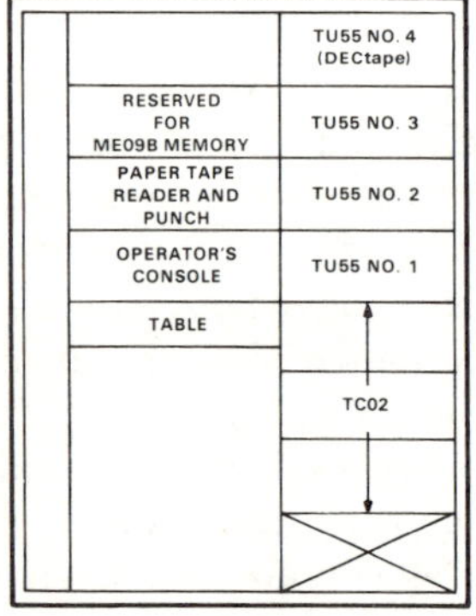

Figure 27. PDP-9 front and back logic layout.

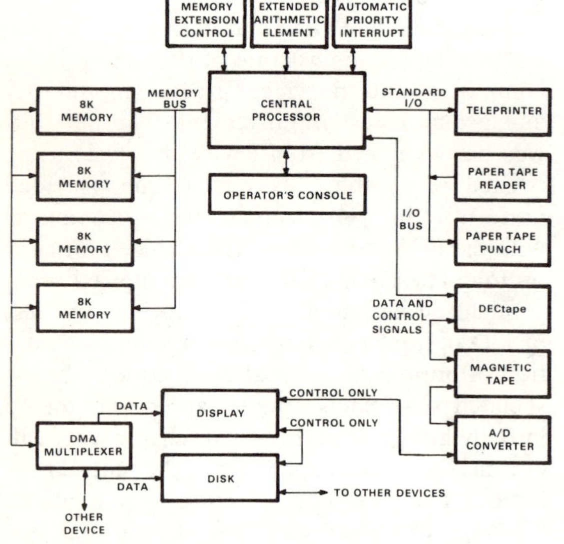

Figure 28. PDP-9 system block diagram.

Except for the 300 wire field change on the first ten processor backplanes, the PDP-9 enjoyed a good reputation for performance and up time. It was followed by a less costly version, the PDP-9/L. The cost reduction was accomplished by using a new (and somewhat cumbersome) power supply design and by offering a 4-Kword minimal system with lower cost paper tape equipment. The 4-Kword memory planes were borrowed from the PDP-8 line and adapted to provide half the memory in half the space. To provide lower cost paper tape capability, the PDP-9/L used a teleprinter equipped with paper tape reader and punch instead of a separate, heavy-duty paper tape reader and punch. The product life of the PDP-9/L was relatively short; it was soon made obsolete by the PDP-15.

THE PDP-15

Unlike its predecessors, the PDP-15 was designed to provide a range of systems with both hardware and software. While early 18-bit machines had evolved to include several configurations, the notion of a planned range for PDP-15 systems was explicit from the start. As it turned out, the PDP-15 evolved too, and over a considerably larger range than was anticipated. Table 2 shows the range of systems that eventually developed; of these, only the models up through 15/40 were in the original plan.

As in the past, the goal for the new machine was to provide better performance/cost than the predecessor. The PDP-7 to PDP-9 transition had provided a performance improvement, but not a big cost improvement. The new semiconductor technology, transistor-transistor logic (TTL) available in dual inline packages, could provide the cost improvement required. The 7400 and 74H00 series of TTL integrated circuits permitted clock speeds of 10 to 20 MHz and lower costs and higher packing densities than did the discrete circuits used in the PDP-9. Not only did the higher packing densities lower the packaging costs, but they also permitted the

Table 2. The PDP-15 Family of 18-Bit Computer Systems

Model	Hardware	Software
PDP-15/10 (basic paper tape system)	Central processor 4-Kword memory Teleprinter	Assembler Editor Debugger Utilities
PDP-15/20 (keyboard monitor using DECtape file system)	Central processor 8-Kword memory Extended arithmetic Paper tape DECtape Teleprinter	Keyboard monitor FORTRAN IV FOCAL PIP* Utilities
PDP-15/30 (background/foreground)	Central processor 16-Kword memory Extended arithmetic Automatic Priority Interrupt Memory protection Clock Paper tape DECtape 2 teleprinters	B/F monitor FORTRAN IV FOCAL PIP* Utilities
PDP-15/35	(PDP-15/30 with disks)	
PDP-15/40 (Disk based background/ foreground)	Central processor 24-Kword memory Extended arithmetic Automatic Priority Interrupt Memory protection Clock Paper tape DECtape 524-Kword fixed head disk 2 teleprinters	Disk B/F monitor FORTRAN IV FOCAL PIP* Utilities
PDP-15/50	16-Kword memory	
PDP-15/76	15/40 plus PDP-11	11-based file and I/O device management

*PIP = Peripheral (Data) Interchange Program

basic PDP 15/10 (Figure 29) to be the smallest of the 18-bit series, while providing a number of options and additional features including an additional instruction set with an index and limit register for multiprogramming. The new TTL technology had one substantial drawback, however. Where the old discrete transistor technology had used −3 volt and ground signals, the new technology used +5 and ground. Thus, to permit the use of both existing peripherals

Figure 29. PDP-15/10.

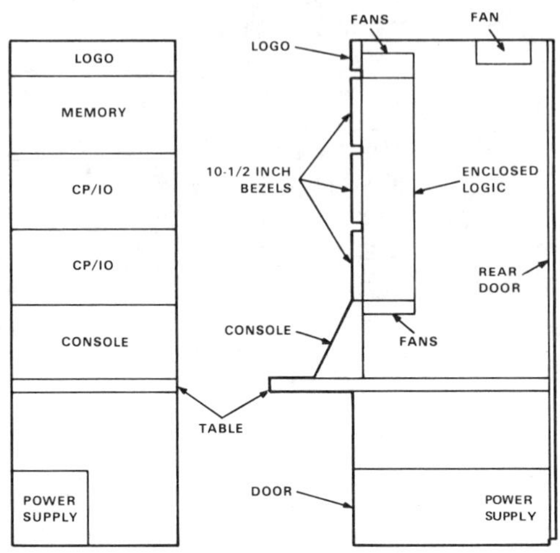

DEC 19-INCH CABINET DEMENSIONS:
30 INCHES DEEP; 21-11/16 INCHES WIDE; AND
71-7/16 INCHES HIGH.

Figure 30. PDP-15 side/front logic layout.

and new peripherals, level converters on the I/O Bus were required.

In addition to the cost improvements anticipated from the use of integrated circuits, it was also hoped that new memory systems available would offer both cost and performance improvements. The PDP-15 memory is contrasted with the PDP-1 memory in Table 3.

With the new memories and changes in addressing capabilities through the Index Register and relocation options, memory size could be expanded to 131 Kwords. A separate control unit, called the I/O Processor, handled the bookkeeping for the I/O channels and I/O Bus. Figure 30 shows a typical PDP-15 system. The two processors (main processor and I/O Processor) occupied only a third of the cabinet space of a comparable PDP-9 system, yet were faster and had more capability. While on the subject of cabinets, note that the packaging for the PDP-15 reverted to the simplicity of the earlier PDP-1, PDP-4, and PDP-7 cabinets by using a fixed mounting structure rather than having the module connector blocks mounted on a door.

The goals for the PDP-15 were to obtain an 850 nanosecond cycle time, to be compatible with the PDP-9, to have a low manufacturing cost, to improve priority interrupt latency, to fit the basic system in one cabinet, to extend the length of the I/O Bus, and to improve maintainability. The success in meeting these goals varied.

The goal of achieving an 850-nanosecond cycle time was exceeded, as the PDP-15 was shipped with an 800-nanosecond cycle time. It was particularly gratifying that this goal was met and exceeded because there had been a number of obstacles to overcome. The central processor, memory, and I/O had been made asynchronous to reduce I/O latency, but this required synchronizing logic that resulted in significant circuit delays. A dc (round-trip) interlocked memory bus had been designed so that speed independent memories could be used, but this caused communications delays. Finally, to minimize cabling, a single set of lines had been used for communicating address and data information to the memory. This caused further communications delays.

Table 3. Comparison of PDP-1 and PDP-15 Memories

	PDP-1	PDP-15	PDP-15 (Late)
Year	1960	1968	1972
Stack size	4 Kwords	4 Kwords	24 Kwords
Cycle time	5 μs	800 ns	960 ns
Words/cabinet	12 Kwords	48 Kwords	96 Kwords
Electronics	1/3 cabinet	1/12 cabinet	1/24 cabinet
Configuration	3D stack	5 planes	
		4 bits/plane	20 bits/plane
		Planar stack	Planar stack
Core size	30 mil	18 mil	18 mil
Wires/core	4	3	3

The PDP-9 instruction compatibility was achieved with three minor exceptions about which no complaints were received. Compatibility for I/O devices was achieved by changing the receiver/driver modules to provide the required conversions back and forth between the older peripherals and the new PDP-15 I/O Bus.

To meet the manufacturing cost goals, a number of things were considered. The PDP-15 was one of the first DEC computers to use integrated circuits extensively. Because each logic type used in the machine would have to be specified, purchased, delivered, and tested, it was important to minimize the number of logic types. (Note the similarity of this concern to that expressed in Chapter 4 with regard to minimizing the number of flip-flop types in the TX-0.) The PDP-15 was designed with 21 semiconductor types, including integrated circuits, transistors, and diodes. All of them were available from multiple suppliers. To simplify manufacturing and field installation of options, the PDP-15 had fixed configuration rules. This was a mixed blessing because the fixed configuration rules resulted in higher costs from the greater number of partially filled cabinets. Margin testing for the PDP-15 was planned using a combination of varying logic timing and temperature. Special test equipment was constructed for the PDP-15 production line to permit rapid heat cycling of central processors and memories. In addition, a fast program loader system was designed using a PDP-8 with multiple DECtape units. This system permitted programs to be loaded into the memory of a unit being tested by merely pressing a button. This saved considerable checkout time compared to the previous methods of loading diagnostics via paper tape.

It was originally planned that manufacturing costs would also be reduced by using subassembly replacement. The concept was that if a processor, memory, power supply, or other logic assembly failed to work when it was integrated into a system, the entire subassembly would be replaced and sent back to its appropriate test line, rather than repairing it in the final assembly area. This process, planned for both the PDP-9 and PDP-15, did not work because the production line was never filled with enough material to allow the subassembly substitution to take place.

The manufacturing cost goals were not met during the production of the first 50 units, so an examination was made to determine which items were most costly. It was determined that most of the cost difficulty was in the mechanical packaging, and that the cabling, in particular, was costing more than anticipated. Sights were set on reducing the cabling complexity by using a single power harness that could be built and tested on a jig. The cabling was reduced to one console cable, one teleprinter cable, one I/O bus cable assembly, and two memory bus cables. In trying to limit console cabling, a time division multiplex communication scheme was designed to get the signals to the lights and from the switches. In this scheme, a number of signals were transmitted on the same wires on a timeshared basis, and the console lamp filaments were used as storage elements. While this scheme was clever enough to gain the PDP-15's only patent, it was generally unsatisfactory. It made the console logic so complex that when it failed, it was harder to fix than the processor.

The goal of reducing interrupt latency to two microseconds was not achieved. With the parity, memory protect, and memory relocation options implemented, and with adder and synchronizing delays added in, the latency could only be reduced to four microseconds; but that was acceptable.

The goal of packaging the basic system (central processor, I/O processor, console, and 32 Kwords) in one cabinet was met; it was a close fit, and there were virtually no spare module slots. Since few small systems were sold, it is not clear that this emphasis was warranted.

The goal of extended I/O bus length was achieved by switching from an unterminated, diode-clamped I/O bus such as the PDP-9 used, to a new, terminated I/O bus. A new set of bus transceiver modules was designed to provide greater speed and less bus loading. The new bus design, with cleaner signals and no reflections, combined with the new bus transceiver modules, permitted the I/O bus to be extended to 75 feet. The penalty paid was higher power consumption and greater power supply cost than in the PDP-9.

The goal of better maintainability was partially achieved by equipping the logic with a means of monitoring 400 signal points. This feature was combined with a single step feature which permitted troubleshooting from the console without the use of an oscilloscope. As it turned out, the single step feature was used infrequently because of the training required to use it properly.

Figure 31 shows the register transfer structure of the PDP-15 processor. It was based on elements and features used in earlier designs and had a basic data path which permitted the results from any of the 11 registers to be read into the arithmetic unit and then back into the registers. In order to achieve high speed operation, a number of separate registers (such as the Step Counter, the Program Counter, and the Multiplier-Quotient registers), operated in

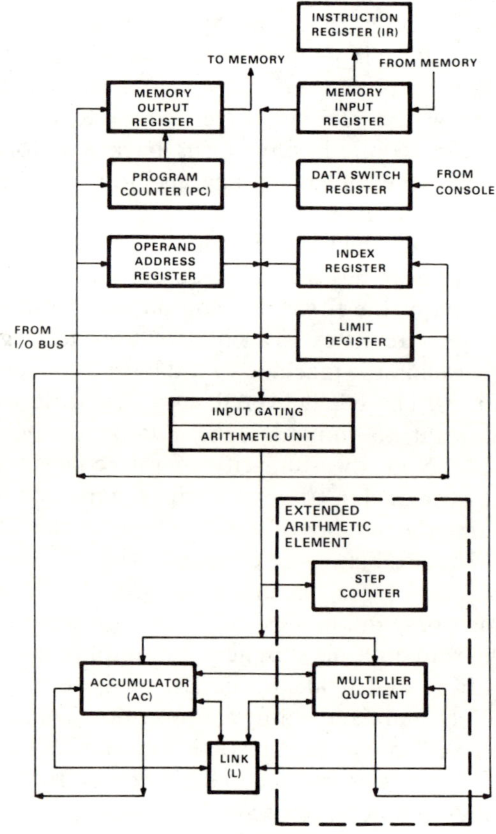

Figure 31. PDP-15 processor register transfer diagram.

parallel with the basic data path. In this way, significant overlap occurred, permitting the 800-nanosecond cycle time. The contrast between this design and the PDP-4 design is noteworthy. The PDP-4 had only four registers in the basic machine, but the use of integrated circuits in the PDP-15 permitted more registers to be used without so much concern for cost.

The first major extension of the PDP-15 was the addition of the Floating-Point Processor (Figure 32) to enable it to perform well in the scientific/computation marketplace using FORTRAN and other algorithmic languages. With the addition of the Floating-Point Processor, the time for a programmed floating-point operation was reduced from 100-200 microseconds to 10-15 microseconds, giving nearly a factor of 10 increase in FORTRAN performance – depending on the mix of floating-point

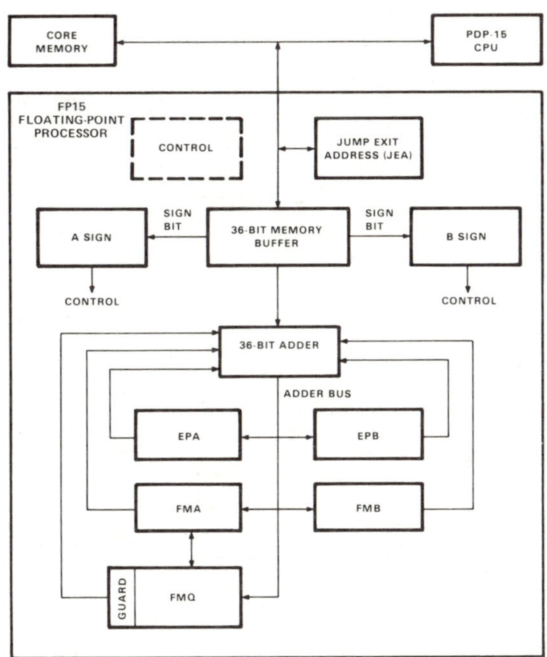

Figure 32. PDP-15 Floating-Point Processor register transfer diagram.

operations. For most machines, the difference between built-in and programmed data-types is higher; but, because the machine was originally designed to operate effectively without hardwiring, the difference is quite low. Table 4 gives a summary of the performance improvements offered by the floating-point option.

The addition of the floating-point unit required that a number of instructions be added to the machine. The irony of this extension is that the PDP-11 and nearly all minicomputer instruction set extensions exactly follow this evolution.

A low cost multi-user protection system was added in the form of a relocation register and a boundary register. Because this was marketed as an add-on option, it degraded the machine performance more than necessary. However, the minimum machine cost maintained the performance/cost target.

The first PDP-15 was shipped in February 1970, 18 months after the project had started. A number of difficulties had been encountered, including personnel turnover, that caused a two-month slip. However, the project at first customer ship was within the budget and, by 1977,

Table 4. Floating-Point Computation Times

Program Type	Without Floating-Point Option	With Floating-Point Option	Improvement
Matrix Inversion	12.0 sec	5.0 sec	2.4
Fourier Transform	16.9 sec	2.9 sec	5.8
Least Squares Fit	5.1 sec	0.7 sec	7.3
Test of all FP Functions	11.4 sec	1.4 sec	8.1
A Physics Application	37.0 sec	3.0 sec	12.3

790 machines had been shipped – more than the total of all other DEC 18-bit machines.

Two of the PDP-15 models are of special interest. A dual central processor version and the PDP-15/76. These are treated separately below.

DUAL CENTRAL PROCESSOR PDP-15

In 1973 the PDP-15 product line proposed and sold a system that was a dual processor. From the dual processor project came a dual port memory, which eventually was transferred to the PDP-15 standard product line. The dual port memory also expanded memory to the full 128 Kwords built into the PDP-15 addressing structure. The unit occupied a single rack and used the M-Series logic modules. Because there was space to add a third port within the rack unit, the dual port memory was actually built to be a three port device. At the time, the laboratory breadboard was an impressive array of three cabinets containing 128 Kwords of memory and two processors.

The logic included what went unrecognized as a "synchronizer" problem for two months, despite reviews by some senior engineers. The synchronizer problem, first described by Chaney and Molnar [1973] of Washington University, is a classical logic design problem that is theoretically unsolvable. When synchronizing (detecting) the presence of an event occurring at a random time relative to a fixed clock event, a small amount of energy is available to set the flip-flop. When the flip-flop is triggered with such a small signal, it can go into an undecided (metastable) state for a relatively long (even indeterminant) period of time. The problem occurred in the dual port memory design because the three inputs (2 ports and the memory clock) needed to be synchronized. Despite the theoretical lack of a solution, the practical solution is usually to wait longer (e.g., two clock times) or to improve the circuit by unbalancing it. Once the problem was recognized, the design went to a quick completion.

PDP-15/76

Of the systems listed in Table 2, the PDP-15/76 was one of the most interesting. A simplified block diagram of the final evolved state of the PDP-15/76 is shown in Figure 33. The diagram is referred to as an evolved design because the PDP-11 connection and the floating-point arithmetic features were not part of the original PDP-15 design.

The design of the PDP-15/76, also referred to as the Unichannel 15/76, began as a problem: find the most cost-effective way to attach a new moving head, removable platter disk to the PDP-15. After a review of the problem, it became clear that the correct way to solve the problem was to use a PDP-11 processor and the controller that had been designed for the PDP-11. The key reason for this was not the cost of designing a controller for the PDP-15, but rather the cost of writing a new set of disk diagnostics in PDP-15 code. (By that time, it was clear to all designers that hardware costs were swamped by software costs.)

As the system design progressed, it became clear that the PDP-11 could be used to run the other PDP-11 family peripherals that were the object of most of DEC's development and production efforts. The list of new peripherals quickly grew to include communications lines, plotters, printers, and card equipment. Figure 34 shows the options available for the PDP-15/76.

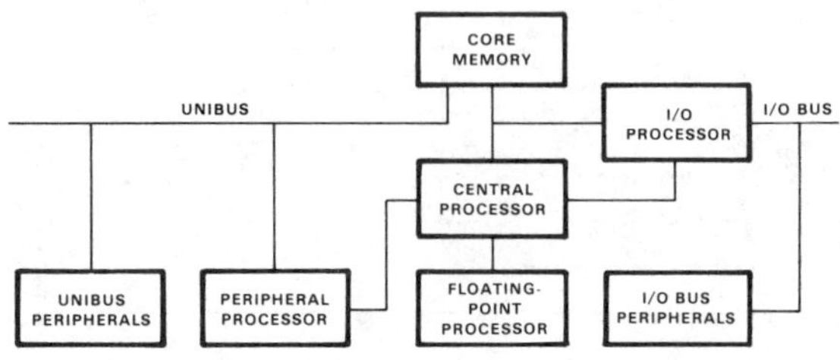

Figure 33. PDP-15/76 simple system block diagram.

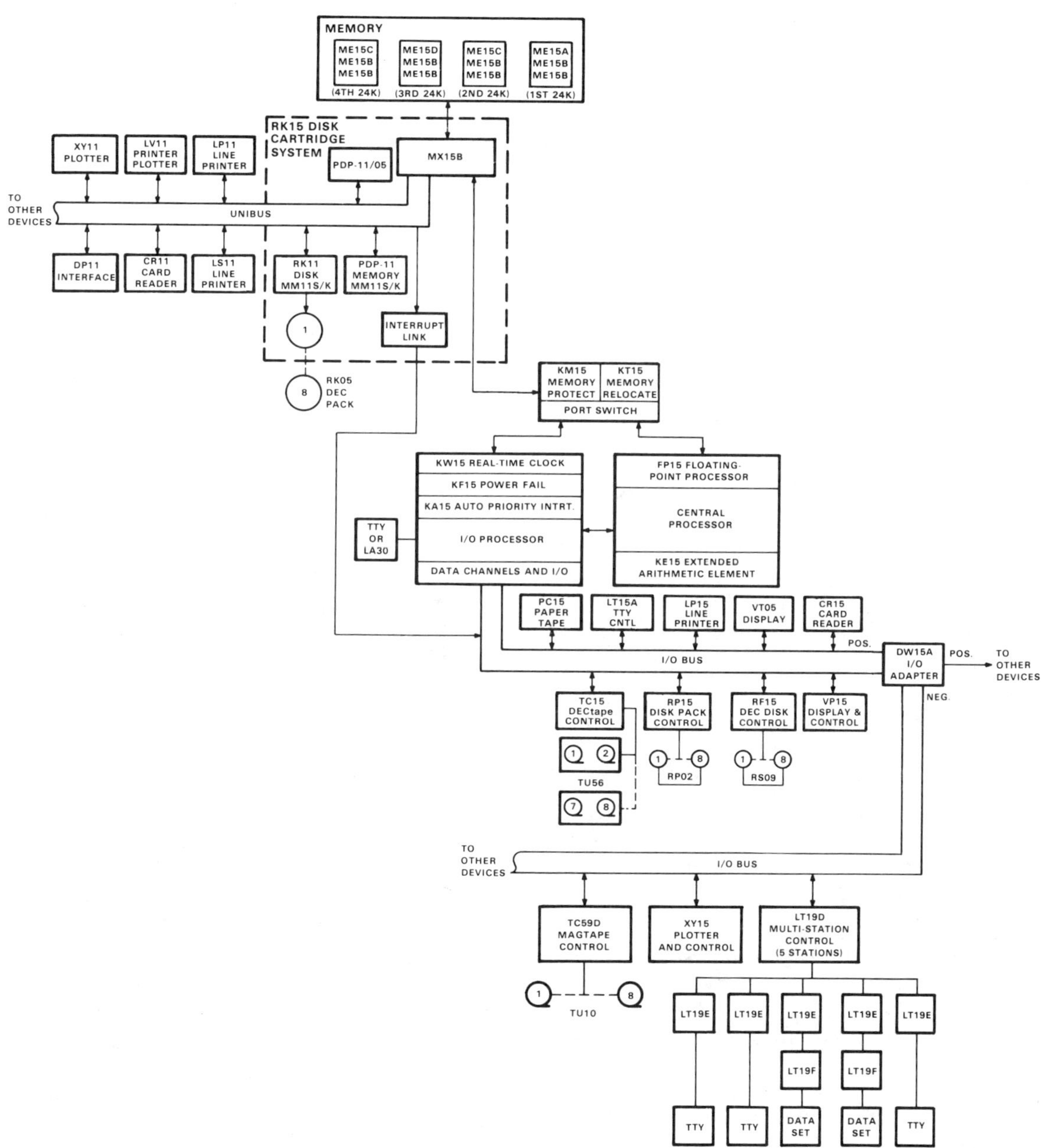

Figure 34. PDP-15/76 (XVM) system block diagram.

The project had a very small but excellent staff, and the hardware part of the program went very smoothly. Al Helenius did much of the logic design for the memory multiplexer device, using existing M-Series logic modules, and the prototype was operational in early November 1972. The complexity and size of the software task was clearly underestimated. However, the successful system operation depended on having more software. Rick Hully proposed an operating system structure that, for the era and application, was elegant, advanced, and yet straightforward. The reality was that the PDP-15/76 was a "multiprocessor" system, and today's terms "back-end processor" and "file processor" apply to what was accomplished on this machine in the early 1970s. Also, this structure was used by IBM in the coupled 7090/7044 system and the 360 Attached Support Processor.

From an application point of view, the PDP-15/76 dual processor system was extremely effective, especially in the following applications:

1. **Computer-aided design.** With the PDP-15 processor handling figures and computation while the PDP-11 processor handled an input digitizer, high speed plotter, and printer; with the PDP-11 and PDP-15 sharing memory and the new disk.
2. **Batch processing.** With the PDP-15 and the floating-point option handling computation while the PDP-11 handled spooling to printers, input from card readers, and terminals.

THE SERIES AND ITS EVOLUTION

It is useful to compare the five 18-bit computers that were designed over the course of roughly 10 years. The series began in the early second (transistor) generation and extended to the early part of the third (integrated circuit) generation. Had the series been extended to the fourth (large-scale integrated circuit) generation, a version of the PDP-15 could have been easily implemented on a single silicon chip. The paragraphs which follow each summarize the important characteristics of one or two members of the series, and Table 5 gives the technical information.

Contributions of Individual Machines to Series Development

The PDP-1 had a number of innovations over its laboratory predecessors, the Whirlwind and TX-0. It contributed extremely straightforward I/O interfacing capability together with a multichannel interrupt structure and Direct Memory Access capability which enabled a high I/O data rate. These characteristics made it ideal for high performance laboratory applications. The PDP-1 also represented a major stepping stone in the early days of timesharing computers. The message switching application contributed significantly to its market success and motivated the design of good communication interfaces in subsequent computers. Because the PDP-1 served as a thorough test vehicle for the circuitry of the 1000-series system modules, these modules were more suitable for their general application in building digital systems.

The PDP-4 contributed in small ways: there were minor improvements in the instruction set processor; and, because the PDP-4 was oriented to a much lower cost, some of the modules were refined. The simplified logic design of the PDP-4 was a major influence on the implementation style of subsequent computers. It also contributed the fundamental minicomputer notion that successor machines should be lower cost. Moreover, the PDP-4 extended the marketplace to industrial control, which had not been possible at PDP-1's price levels, and further improved the ease of I/O interfacing.

The PDP-7 and PDP-9 Families exploited a significant refinement in the wire-wrap packaging technology. Although the circuits were

Table 5. Characteristics of DEC's 18-Bit Computers

	PDP-1	PDP-4	PDP-7	PDP-9; 9/L	PDP-15
Project start; first ship	8/59; 11/60	11/61; 7/62	4/64; 12/64	8/66 – 12/68	5/68; 2/70
Goals	Cost; short word length; speed	Cost	Speed; cost	Speed; cost; producibility	Cost; range of machines, hardware/software systems
Applications	Lab control; message switching; time-sharing	Process control; industrial testing	Improved time-sharing	Graphics	Numerical computation; graphics processing
Innovations/ improvements	Circuit use; package; ISP; interrupts; Direct Memory Access; I/O interfacing	Functional (bit-slice) modules; ISP trend to mini; 3 Cycle DMA; I/O interfacing	Package; modules; performance	Micro-programming; I/O Bus	Integrated circuits; floating-point; multi-processor
Price (K$) with paper tape reader/punch, Typewriter, 4-Kwords	120	65.5 (56.5)	45	25+; 24.4 (19.9)	19.8 (16.2)
Price/word ($)	7.32	3.66	3.99	2.19; 1.95	1.71; 1.32
MTBF (hours)	2800	–	–	–	5400
Memory cycle time (μs)	5	8	1.75	1; 1.5	0.8
Memory accesses/sec (millions)	0.2	0.125	0.57	1; 0.67	1.25
Multiply/ divide time (μs)	25/40	–	4.4/9	4.5–12.5/12.5	4.5/4.5
Memory size (Kwords)	1,4,...165	1,4,8,...,32	4,...,32	8,4,...,32	4,...,131
Bits accessed per sec per $	30 (0.033)	34.5 (0.029)	227 (0.0044)	714 (0.0014)	1135 (0.00088)
Perf./price improve*	–	1.1	6.6	3.1	1.7

*Uses previous model as base for improvement.

Table 5. Characteristics of DEC's 18-Bit Computers (Cont)

	PDP-1	PDP-4	PDP-7	PDP-9; 9/L	PDP-15
Price improve*	–	1.8	1.45	1.8	1.3 (1.5)
Perf. improve*	–	0.62	4.57	1.75	1.25*
Product life (years)	4	3	4	4	7
Number produced	50	45	120	445	790
Power (W)	2160	1125	2100	2000	2875
Weight (lb)	1350	1030	1150	790	750
Size (69 × 21 × 28 inch bays)	4	2	3	1.5 (special)	1
Volume (ft^3)	94	47	70.5	36	23.5
Power density (W/ft^3)	22.9	23.9	29.8	55.5	122.3
Weight density (lb/ft^3)	14.4	21.9	16.3	21.9	31.9
Watts/$	0.018	0.017	0.046	0.08	0.15
Lb/$	0.011	0.016	0.026	0.032	0.038
Kbits accessed per W	1.6	1.1	4.9	9.0	7.8
Kbits accessed per lb	2.6	2.2	8.9	22.8	30.0
Kbits accessed per Kft^3	38.3	47.9	146.0	500.0	957.0
Logic technology	Saturating MADT transistors	Capacitor-diode gates; diode transistors	Saturating transistors	–	7400, 74H00 series integrated circuits
Module series	1,000	4,000	B	–	M
Logic speed (MHz)	5, 0.5	1, 0.5, 5	10, 1, 0.5	10, 1	10, 20

*Uses previous model as base for improvement.

Table 5. Characteristics of DEC's 18-Bit Computers (Cont)

	PDP-1	PDP-4	PDP-7	PDP-9; 9/L	PDP-15
Module size	5.25 × 4	5.25 × 4	2.25, 5 (× 3.875)	2.25, 5, 10 (× 3.875)	Same
Modules/types	544/34	236/41	614/39	644/44	300/54
Transistors, diodes, ICs	3.5 K, 4.3 K	–	–	–	350, 200, 3.4 K
Power supply/ types	8/4	4/2	9/4	1/1	1/1
Modules space processor	18 × 25	6 × 25	12 × 32	8 × 44	4 × 32
Modules space, I/O interface	3 × 25	3 × 25	–	–	4 × 32
Modules space, reader, punch, typewriter	3 × 25	3 × 25	8 × 32	8 × 44	7
Modules space, 4-Kword memory	4 × 25	4 × 25 (8 K)	3 × 32	3 × 44	4 × 32
Pc, Mp, I/O logic area (in^2 × K)	11.9	5.2	5.3	5.6	3.4
Processor logic area (in^2 × K)	8.9	3.3	3.3	3.1	2.1
Logic prints	18	16	27	44/2 = 22	75/2

*Uses previous model as base for improvement.

based on the early PDP-6 10-MHz circuits, the more cost-effective and producible Flip Chip package was used. Both machines had significant performance gains over all predecessors. Using the number of words or bits accessed by the processor per unit time as the performance measure, the PDP-7:PDP-4 ratio was 4.57 and the PDP-9:PDP-7 ratio was 1.75. Both gains were due to the use of faster core memories. The PDP-9 used microprogrammed control, even though the simple instruction set processor probably did not necessitate the high entry cost. A large microprogram store could have changed the performance (and history) of successor minis. The change to an I/O bus structure, pioneered in the PDP-5, entered the 18-bit series with the PDP-9. It distributed the I/O interface to each option and so further reduced the basic cost.

The PDP-15's use of integrated circuits provided an 18-bit series improvement. At last there was a significant reduction in size, although the power consumption increased. The board area in the processor decreased by a factor of three over previous implementations, where it had been relatively constant at about 3,000 in^2. The two major contributions of the PDP-15 were the notion that systems include both hardware and software and that the machine would span a range of sizes. Finally, to extend the life of the machine, a number of improvements (e.g., in memory, PDP-11 I/O) were later made to reduce price and to increase performance (floating-point, multiple processors).

Project Development Times and Product Lifetimes

The duration of the projects generally increased with time, reflecting the longer tooling time for increased production volumes. The PDP-4 is an exception; it had the shortest design time because the circuits and mechanical packaging were based on the PDP-1. In addition to increased development times with passing years, later members of the series had longer product lifetimes; hence, longer times elapsed before re-implementations occurred. The time between the first few implementations was only about two years. The final implementation, the PDP-15, was produced for seven years. The early (too frequent) implementations were per haps indicative of the attention paid to low hardware cost and performance, rather than to application and software enhancements to increase the market life.

Price

Figure 35 shows that the price for a basic "bare-bones" system declined by more than 19 percent per year. The price of the typical midsize system has never been properly analyzed, but roughly speaking, the average price declined from an initial cost of $250K for a PDP-1 to $65K for a PDP-9. For a given processor, however, the size of typical systems purchased

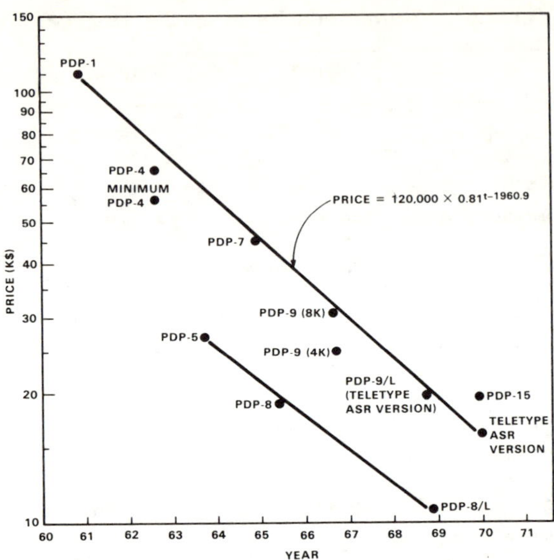

Figure 35. Price versus time for 18-bit computers with paper tape I/O, typewriter, and 4-Kword memory.

grew with time. For example, early PDP-15 systems were sold at an average price of $75K, while the final average price was about $125K.

Not all price reductions were the result of cheaper logic technology or better manufacturing techniques on the part of DEC. Some prices, particularly system prices, were influenced strongly by the prices of peripherals. For example, the Teletype Corporation Model 33 ASR teleprinter with built-in paper tape reader and punch helped reduce the price of the minimum configurations of later 18-bit computers by as much as any other component price reduction.

The primary memory price decline (Figure 36) of only 16 percent per year can be attributed to the fact that each subsequent machine needed higher performance memories. Memories were always implemented at relatively constant price with increasing performance. Again, the PDP-4 is an exception; it shows the effect of building a low performance memory versus the fastest memory. While the first PDP-4s were

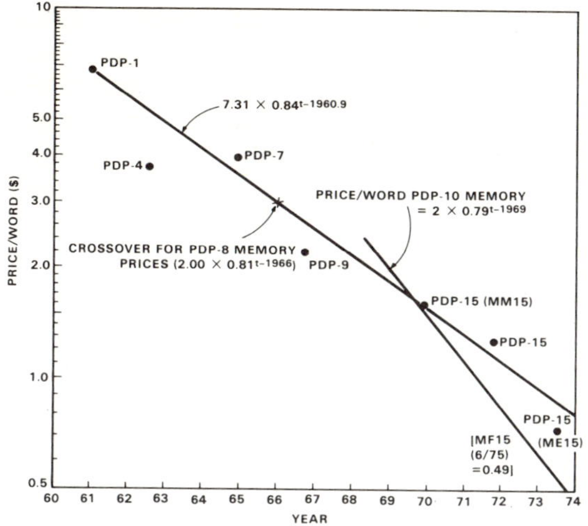

Figure 36. Price/word of 18-bit memory versus time.

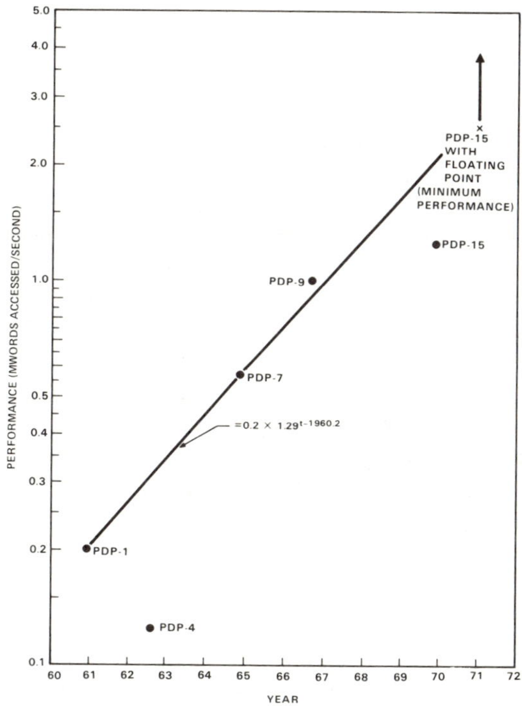

Figure 37. Performance of 18-bit computers versus time.

shipped with PDP-1 memory, the next machines had 8-Kword memory systems that cost about half that of the PDP-1. The price of the 18-bit memory systems decreased at a rate slightly less than that of the 12-bit or 36-bit computers. One possible explanation would be an economy of scale in quantity shipped in the 12-bit case and an economy of scale in word length in the 36-bit case.

Performance

Performance (in millions of words accessed per second by the processor) is shown in Figure 37 and exhibits a 29 percent yearly increase. Neither the PDP-15 nor PDP-4 fall on the line because both were oriented to lower price rather than to increased performance. In reality, the PDP-15 later evolved to have much greater effective performance when built-in floating-point arithmetic was added. Then its real performance (a factor of 2 to 10 better for FORTRAN programs involving floating-point) exceeded the line position. Midlife extensions of this sort were generally missing on the other 18-bit computers, as design resources went into developing new processors.

Price/Performance

The performance/price ratio, a reasonable index for simple systems, is shown in Figure 38. This ratio has improved by 52 to 69 percent per year over the 10-year period. A variant of this plot is shown in Figure 39, where price is plotted against the performance (in millions of accesses per second by the processor).

The lines of constant performance/price are separated by a factor of 2. In this representation, any measure which changes by 41 percent per year takes two years to move from one line to another. A yearly improvement of 26 percent takes three years to double, and a yearly improvement of 19 percent takes four years to double.

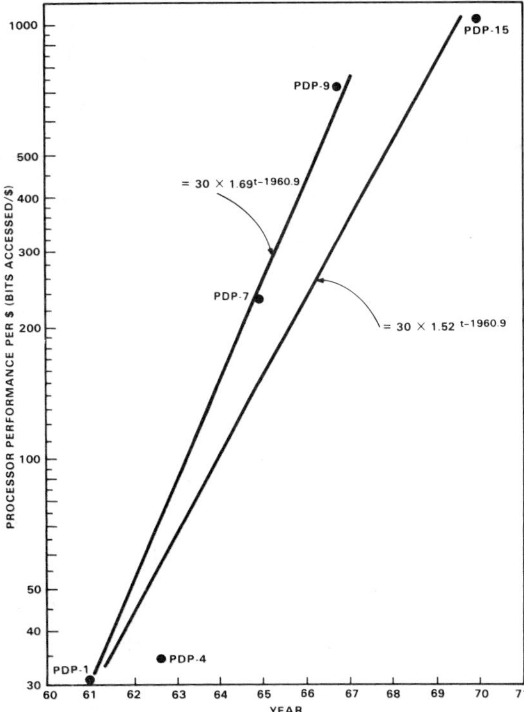

Figure 38. Processor performance per $ versus time of 18-bit machines.

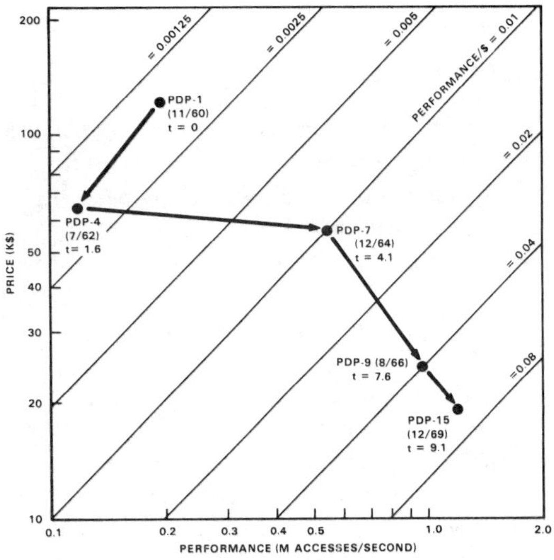

Figure 39. Price versus performance of 18-bit machines.

Since the gain in price/performance is at least 52 percent per year, the 9.1 year evolution crosses five factor of 2 lines. Only the PDP-4 stands out as being on a line of constant performance/price. It was either overpriced by a factor of 2 or should have performed better by a factor of 2 for the same price.

Market Demand

In order to speculate on a theory of demand for small computers, two demand curves are given. Figure 40 is the classic demand curve: price of the unit versus quantity. If one ignores the PDP-1 anomaly, it appears that there is complete price elasticity of demand. There are two possible reasons for the PDP-1 anomaly. Twenty of the PDP-1s are accounted for by a single, perhaps fortuitous, order for the ADX 7300 systems. By subtracting this amount from the PDP-1 quantity, one obtains the second conjecture: sales were higher than the model projection because the PDP-1 was first into the market.

An alternative to the demand model is given in Figure 41 where price per unit of performance is plotted against quantity. This model is based on the thesis that computers are like power generators (or tractors): demand is based on the amount of work they can do per unit of cost. (This would explain why roughly the same number of PDP-1s and PDP-4s were sold.) Note that more PDP-9s and PDP-15s were sold than the curve would have predicted. Because both machines had longer lives before successors were introduced, a better ordinate might be the maximum number shipped in any one year, which would take into account other marketplace limits.

Other Characteristics

Table 5 has other data that has not been plotted. The input power (with the exception of PDP-4) is constant over all implementations. The weight is correlated with size, reflecting a relatively constant weight per bay. The volume has declined, which reflects consistent improve-

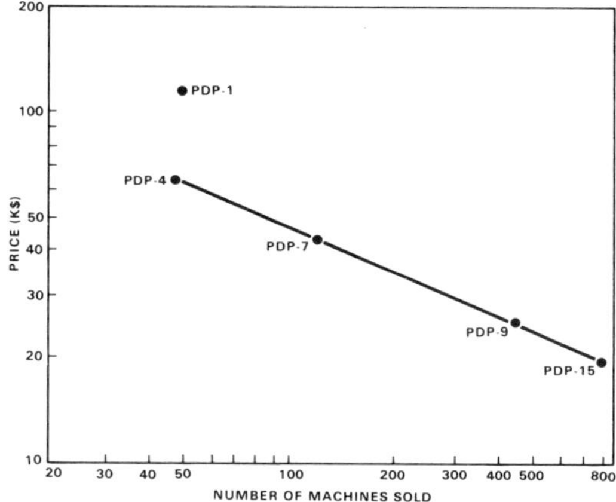

Figure 40. Price versus number of 18-bits machines sold.

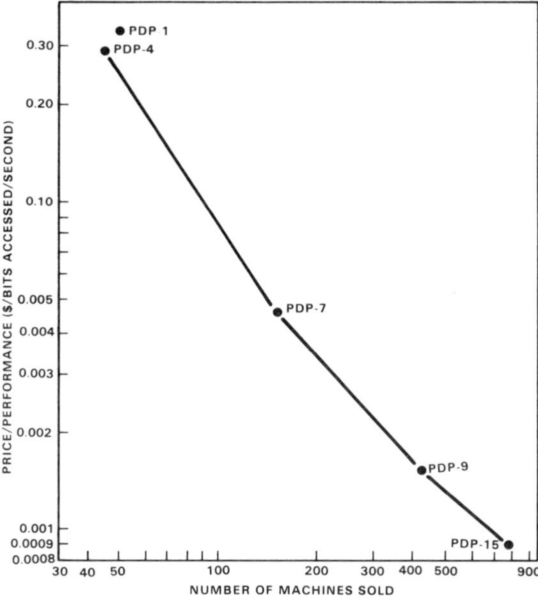

Figure 41. Price/performance versus number of 18-bit machines sold.

ments in packing density. In this respect, the PDP-4 was a better implementation than the PDP-1. The PDP-7 was even better in packing density and provided a great performance improvement. The PDP-9 improvements were in memory performance and packaging for manufacturing, rather than in logic-related performance or packaging, as it used the same logic (10 MHz) as the PDP-7. The PDP-15 achieved its size reduction using integrated circuit technology. The weight/price appears to have risen and almost seems to be correlated with inflation. Power and weight density measurements are given in the table together, as are several ratios involving cost, weight, power, and performance. Note that performance changes most as a direct result of core memory speed improvements. The calculated mean time between failures has declined by over a factor of 2 between the PDP-1 and PDP-15.

The reader should compare the implementations. With the exception of PDP-1 and PDP-15, all computers required about 5,000 in^2 of printed circuit board area for the processor, memory, and basic I/O. The bit-slice approach of the PDP-4 made possible a major reduction in backpanel interconnections by using two specialized modules. All subsequent implementations used the bit-slice approach with a few special purpose modules. Of special interest is the number of logic module types and power supply types. All but the PDP-15 had about 40 different logic types. The PDP-15 had 54 types because the advent of integrated circuits enabled higher packing density per module which resulted in lower generality per module given the limitation of the pins on each module. This small number of module types and relatively low cost per module meant that the cost of a complete package of spare modules for a computer represented a small fraction of the computer's price. This is in contrast to the fourth and fifth generations, where a single module contains the whole computer and the cost of spare modules is therefore a large fraction of the computer's price.

Options

Table 6 shows the options available for the various machines. Note that PDP-1 had quite a complete set of options, including both high

Table 6. Options for DEC's 18-Bit Computers*

	PDP-1	PDP-4	PDP-7	PDP-9	PDP-15
Multiply/Divide	Std.	[18] EAE	[177]	–	EAE opt., floating-point opt.
Priority interrupt	1 ch. std.; [120] – 16 ch.; also 256 ch.	1 ch. std.	1 ch. std. [172] 16 ch.	1 ch. std; 8 opt.	1 ch. std; 8 opt.
Direct Memory Access	[19] 3 ch.	1 std.; 3 opt.	[173] 3 ch.	+1 to mem. (std.)	Up to 64
Clock	Yes	1 std.; [132] 16 ch.	Opt.	Opt.	Opt.
Power failure	N/A	Std.	–	–	Opt.
Memory protect	4-Kword core images	None	[KA70A] base and bounds	[KA70A]	[KA70A]
Secondary Memory					
Magtape (prog. control)	[51] – [50] 200 b/i	[54] – [50] 200 b/i	–	–	–
Magtape (DMA)	[52] – [50] [510] – [IBM 729]	[57A] – [50 or 570] 556 b/i	[57A] – [50 or 570]	[TC59] – [TU20]	[TC59] – [TU20 or TU30]
Drums	[23]	[24] 16 Kw...65 Kw	[24] 32 Kw...131 Kw	32 Kw...524 Kw	–
Fixed disks	N/A	–	–	[RS09] 1 Mw	[RS09] – 262 Kw...2 Mw
Disk Pack	–	–	–	–	[RP02] – 10 Mw
DECtape	N/A	[550] – [555]	[550A] – [555]	[TC02[– [TU55]	[TC02] – [TU55]
Links					
Inter-Computer	–	–	[195] DB97	DB98, 99	DB98, 99
To 7090	[150] 10 Kw/s	–	–	–	–
Commu-nications	8 ch. up to 256	–	[630] 64 ch. [634] 8 ch.	[630] 64 ch. [LT09] 5 ch.	[LT19]
To other computer buses	–	–	–	To PDP-7	[DW15] to PDP-15

*The DEC-assigned option number is given in square brackets, e.g., [177].

Table 6. Options for DEC's 18-Bit Computers (Cont)*

	PDP-1	PDP-4	PDP-7	PDP-9	PDP-15
Transducers					
Paper tape reader	Std. 400 c/s	Std. 300 c/s	Std. 300 c/s	Std. 300 c/s	Std. 300 c/s
Paper tape punch	Std. 63 c/s	[75] 63 c/s	[75] 63 c/s	[PC09] 50 c/s	[PC15] 50 c/s
Typewriter	Std. 10 c/s	[65] 28 KSR, 10 c/s	[643] 33 KSR	33 KSR, ASR	33, 35, ASR, KSR
CRTs					
Point plotting	[30] 16 in. 1 K × 1 K points 21 in. color	[30D] [340] vector plot	[30D] [340C]	[30D]	[VP15]
Storage	[34] Tektronix storage	[34]	[34]	[34H]	–
DMA	–	–	–	[339] P. display with 340	[VT15]
Precision	[31] 5 in. 4 K × 4 K points	–	–	–	–
Alphanumeric	–	–	–	–	[VT05]
Card reader	[421] 200 c/m	[41] 200 c/m	[421] 200 or 800 c/m	[CR0IE] 100 or 200 c/m	[CR033] 200 c/m
Card punch	[40] 100 c/m	[40] 100 c/m	[410] 100 c/m	–	–
Line printer	[64] 300 l/m	[64] 300 l/m	[64] 300 l/m	[647] 300 or 600 l/m	[647] 300 or 1000 l/m
Plotter	–	–	[350] to Calcomp	[350]	[350], [x415]
Relays	[140] 18 ch.	[140] 18 ch.	[140] 18 ch.	[DR09A]	DR09A
A/D converter	[138/139] 64 ch.	[138/139]	[138/139]	64 ch. 1000 ch.	[AF02] 64 ch. [AF04] 1000 ch.
D/A converter	–	–	–	–	AFC 15-analog UDC 15-digital

*The DEC-assigned option number is given in square brackets, e.g., [177].

precision and color cathode ray tubes. The PDP-1, 4, and 7 were relatively compatible in terms of I/O interconnection and evolved to have about the same set of options. PDP-9 changed to an I/O bus structure, requiring new option interfaces. Although PDP-15 used that same I/O bus structure and signals, the voltages were different; again, new option interfaces were required.

Displays have been major options throughout the series. Moving head disks were first available on the PDP-15. Although a number of card handling options were available, few were sold, reflecting the real-time, laboratory, and multiprogrammed (timesharing) use.

Evolution

This chapter concludes by relating the 18-bit series evolution to the model of minicomputer evolution presented in Chapter 1. Three design styles are distinguished in the model, as can be seen in Figure 42. Chapter 7 shows the 12-bit family (PDP-8) evolving mostly along the constant performance/decreasing price curve. The 16-bit PDP-11 family, presented in the chapters of Part IV, evolved based on all three design styles.

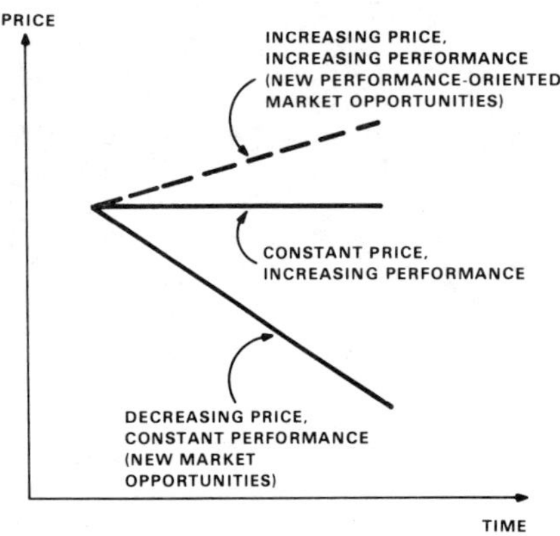

Figure 42. Three design styles.

For a family to evolve in more than one design style, design resources must be available for parallel development efforts. While the PDP-11 family had the multiplicity of designers and architects to do this, the 18-bit series did not. Each new implementation was designed by a member of a previous implementation team. For such a single-thread approach to be successful, it appears that one of the three design styles of the evolution model must be chosen and consistently followed. With the exception of PDP-4, the 18-bit series has followed the middle style: constant price/increased performance.

It appears that a clear identity is needed to guide design decisions. Consider the physical packaging of the last of the 18-bit machines, the PDP-15. Although a comparable speed/performance PDP-11 required more integrated circuits to implement (the PDP-11 has more modes of addressing, more instructions, and more data-types), the PDP-15 implementation cost more. The PDP-15 remained packaged in a large cabinet, used smaller modules, and the component density per module was lower than that of the PDP-11. Had the evolution been guided by a consistently lower cost goal, metal box packaging rather than cabinet packaging would have been used. As it was, the PDP-15 had to compete against the PDP-11 with the handicap of an extra level-of-integration in its physical packaging.

ACKNOWLEDGEMENTS

Several people helped gather the data for this chapter and critiqued its design: Dick Best, Earl Cain, Wes Clark, Dick Devlin, Craig Mudge, Carl Noelcke (reliability calculations), Ed Rawson, Jack Shields, Dan Siewiorek, Don White, and Don Zereski. Mary Jane Forbes and Louise Principe deserve thanks for typing the numerous drafts.

7

The PDP-8 and Other 12-Bit Computers

C. GORDON BELL and JOHN E. McNAMARA

THE LINC

Since the Laboratory Instrument Computer (LINC) was one of the machines that had a great influence on the design of the PDP-4 and the PDP-5, a discussion of the DEC 12-bit machines must start with the LINC.

The LINC was designed by Clark and Molnar [Clark and Molnar, 1964; 1965], who were in turn influenced by Control Data Corporation's (CDC) 160, designed by Seymour Cray. The relationship of these early computers is shown in Figure 1. The first version of the LINC was built at the M.I.T. Lincoln Laboratory where it was demonstrated in March 1962 (Figure 2). In 1963 the LINC was redesigned for production at a special M.I.T. laboratory, the Center Development Office.

While the LINC contributed to DEC history primarily as a forerunner of the PDP-4 and PDP-5, it also generated a number of other developments. The LINC tape unit and the system ideas that permitted a user to have personal files were later incorporated directly into the DECtape design and programs. The tape system and a powerful CRT-based console made possible the first complete personal computer available to a user, in this case the researcher, at a reasonable price. The LINC machines had been constructed mainly from DEC Systems Modules, a convenience when DEC subsequently manufactured LINC machines directly from the 1963 design. Later, Wes Clark with Dick Clayton designed the LINC-8, a two-processor machine (LINC + PDP-8) which executed both instruction sets in parallel. Clayton also designed the PDP-12, a single physical processor that executed either PDP-8 or LINC instructions sequentially by switching modes.

Some of the characteristics of the LINC Family machines are given in Table 1, and photographs appear in Figures 3, 4, and 5. Note that the size remained essentially constant at one cabinet throughout the life of this computer family.

On machines prior to the LINC, DEC had been stressing design flexibility and modularity, providing many ways to interconnect computer components in order to create a variety of structures. This detracted from having a base system configuration complete with software. In contrast, the LINC was quite constrained, with

Table 1. LINC Family Characteristics

	LINC	LINC-8	PDP-12
Project start	1961	Summer 1965	6/67
First shipment	3/62	8/66	6/69
Withdrawn	12/69	12/69	6/75
Number produced	50 (21 by DEC)	143	1,000
Price (minimum)	$43,600	$38,500	$28,100
Goals and features	Complete system for laboratory user (including file system and scope)	Low cost, speed, PDP-8 software/hardware, compatibility	Larger scope, bus compatible with PDP-8/I
Size (in inches)	69 X 32 X 30 plus separate tape, keyboard, console, and interconnection boxes	69 X 32 X 33	76 X 35 X 33
Memory-processor accesses (per second)	125 K	667 K (PDP-8 memory)	667 K (PDP-8/I memory)
Power (watts)	1,000	2,000	<2,000
Cathode ray tube	Originally 2 oscilloscopes; later only 1	1	1

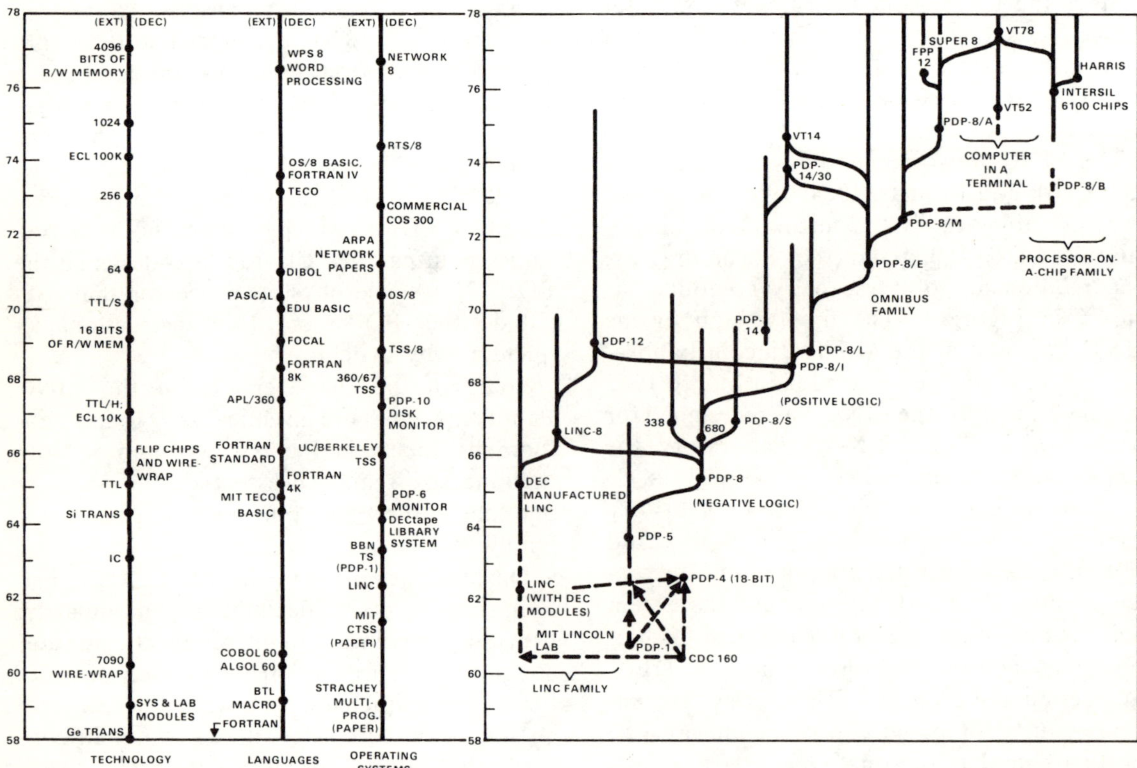

Figure 1. Family tree of 12-bit machines with associated timelines for technology, languages, and operating systems.

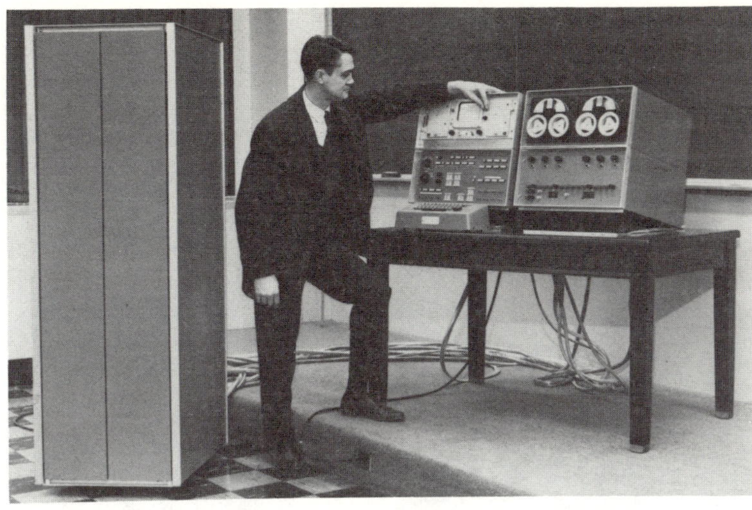

Figure 2. The LINC (Laboratory Instrument Computer) is a small stored program digital computer designed to accept analog as well as digital inputs directly from experiments, to process data immediately, and to provide signals for the control of experimental equipment. The LINC system comprises five physically distinct subassemblies which include four console modules connected by separate cables to a remote cabinet containing the electronics and power supplies. The control module contains indicator lights, push buttons, and switches used in operating the LINC. A second module provides for display oscilloscopes, while a third module holds two magnetic tape transports of special design. The last module is provided with sockets, jacks, and terminals for interconnecting the LINC and other laboratory equipment. This photograph shows the prototype version demonstrated on March 27, 1962, at the M.I.T. Lincoln Laboratory (courtesy of M.I.T. Lincoln Laboratory, from Clark and Molnar [1964]).

Figure 3. The production version of the LINC.

Figure 4. The LINC-8.

Figure 5. The LINC-12.

only 1 Kword or 2 Kwords of primary memory available, two LINC tapes, and one CRT. By bounding the system to a single configuration, it was possible to provide a complete computing environment including software and to provide for convenient interchange of user software.

THE PDP-5

As indicated in Chapter 6, discussions with Foxboro Corporation in the fall of 1961 led to the design, using many LINC ideas, of a 12-bit digital controller called the DC-12. Instead of building the DC-12, DEC built the 18-bit PDP-4 and sold one to Atomic Energy of Canada Limited. AECL used the PDP-4 for a reactor control computer system at Chalk River, an application requiring an elaborate analog monitoring system as a front-end. To reduce the complexity of the analog system, a special front-end computer was needed. The Wes Clark 10-bit L-1 design was considered but rejected because the encoded analog values required words longer than 10 bits, and because the size and complexity of the program seemed too great for such a small computer. After visiting Chalk River in the winter of 1962, DEC engineers decided that a 12-bit design based on the DC-12 would be excellent for such a front end in PDP-4 process control applications. The instruction set for the new machine, the PDP-5, was specified in detail by Alan Kotok and Gordon Bell, and the logic design was carried out by Edson DeCastro, the applications engineer responsible for building the analog front end at Chalk River.

The intent of the design was to simplify the system so that it would take no longer to design the PDP-5 than it had taken to design the analog front end that it would be replacing. The machine used the standard modules developed for the PDP-4, including the concept of bit-slice

Figure 6. The PDP-5.

construction for the Accumulator, Memory Address, and Memory Buffer registers. The analog nature of the initial application was addressed by building an analog-to-digital converter into the Accumulator, thus providing this capability at extremely low cost. The other part of the design that addressed cost was the use of an I/O Bus instead of the radial structure that had been used in the 18-bit designs. The I/O Bus permitted equipment options to be added incrementally from a zero base instead of having the pre-allocated space, wiring, and cable drivers that characterized the radial structure. This lowered the entry cost of the system and simplified the later reconfiguring of machines in the field.

Although the design was optimized around the 4-Kword memory, the PDP-5 ultimately evolved to 32-Kword configurations using a memory extension unit. Similarly, although the base machine design did not include built-in multiply and divide functions, these were added later in the form of an Extended Arithmetic Element. While the PDP-5 was designed for real time and control, the aspirations for it to be used generally in a system can be clearly seen in an early photograph (Figure 6).

THE PDP-8

While the PDP-5 had been a reasonably successful computer, it soon became evident that a new machine capable of far greater performance was required. A new series of modules, the Flip Chip series, was being developed for the PDP-7 and for the new version of the PDP-5. The new logic promised a substantial speed improvement, and new core memory technology was becoming available that would permit the memory cycle time to be shortened from 6 microseconds in the PDP-5 to 1.6 microseconds in the new machine. In addition, the cost of logic was now low enough so that the program counter could be moved from the memory to a separate register, substantially reducing instruction execution times. The new machine was called the PDP-8 (Figure 7).

Figure 7. The PDP-8.

In a fashion similar to the technical developments that marked the 18-bit family, the new 12-bit machine was physically smaller than its predecessor. This time, however, the change was more than simply a change from three cabinets to two or from two cabinets to one. It was a change from one cabinet to a half cabinet. The new small size meant that the PDP-8 was the first true minicomputer. It could be placed on top of a lab bench or built into equipment. It was this latter property that was the most important, as it laid the groundwork for the original equipment manufacturer (OEM) purchase of computers to be integrated into total systems sold by the OEM.

The improvements in logic density permitted by the new Flip Chip modules also influenced packaging and manufacturing methods. The PDP-8 logic modules were mounted in connector blocks, which were in turn mounted in frames. The two frames were each the maximum size that could be accommodated in the new Gardner-Denver automatic Wire-wrap machine. Automatic wire-wrapping was very important to the mass production success of the PDP-8 because it was both fast and accurate. The two wire-wrapped frames hung vertically and were hinged about a vertical axis at the rear of the computer cabinet. In some ways they resembled the pages of a book, with the wire-wrap pins on the surfaces that faced each other. The swinging gate backplane permitted access by maintenance personnel to both the connection pins and the modules.

Like its predecessor the PDP-5, the PDP-8 was a single-address 12-bit computer designed for task environments with minimum arithmetic computing and small primary memory requirements. Typical of these environments were process control applications and laboratory applications such as controlling pulse height analyzers and spectrum analyzers.

In addition to the originally envisioned applications, the PDP-8 was used for innumerable other applications. One of the most interesting was message switching. The PDP-8 message switching hardware assembled characters by bit sampling, checking the status of teleprinter lines at 5 times the anticipated bit rate to accurately recover data. Another interesting application was the TSS/8 small-scale general purpose timesharing system developed by Carnegie-Mellon University and DEC [van de Goor *et al.*, 1969]. While only a hundred or so systems were sold, TSS/8* was significant because it es-

*TSS/8 was designed at Carnegie-Mellon University with graduate student Adrian van de Goor, in reaction to the cost, performance, reliability, and complexity of IBM's TSS/360 (for their Model 67). Although the TSS/360 was not marketed, it eventually worked and contributed some ideas and trained thousands for IBM. At Carnegie-Mellon (CMU), a TSS/8 operated until 1974 when the special swapping disk expired. The cost per user or per job tended to be about 1/20 of the TSS/360 system CMU ran.

tablished the notion that multiprogramming applied even to minicomputers. Until recently, TSS/8 was the lowest cost (per system and per user) and highest performance/cost timesharing system. A major side benefit of TSS/8 was the training of the implementors, who went on to implement the RSTS timesharing system for the PDP-11 based on the BASIC language.

The PDP-8 was the first of the "8 Family." A subset, called "Omnibus 8" machines, is introduced later when the PDP-8/E, PDP-8/M, and PDP-8/A machines are discussed. Finally, computers which implement the PDP-8 instruction set in a single complementary metal oxide semiconductor (CMOS) chip will be referred to as "CMOS-8" based systems.

The PDP-8, which was first shipped in April 1965, and the other 8-Family machines that followed it achieved a production status formerly reserved for IBM computers, with about 50,000 machines produced, excluding the CMOS-8 based computers. During the 15 years that these machines have been produced, logic cost per function has decreased by orders of magnitude, permitting the cost of entire systems to be reduced by a factor of 10. Thus, the 8 Family offers a rare opportunity to study the effect of technology on implementations of the same instruction set processor.

The PDP-8 was followed in late 1966 by the PDP-8/S, a cost-reduced version (Figure 8). The PDP-8/S was quite small in size, scarcely larger than a file cabinet drawer. It achieved its low cost by implementing the PDP-8 instruction set in serial fashion. This did reduce the cost, but it so radically reduced the performance that the machine was not a good seller.

In 1968, the PDP-8/I (Figure 9) was produced, using medium-scale integration (MSI) integrated circuits to implement the PDP-8 instruction set with better performance than the PDP-8, and at two-thirds the price. For those customers wishing a package with less option mounting space but the same performance, the PDP-8/L (Figure 10) was introduced later the same year.

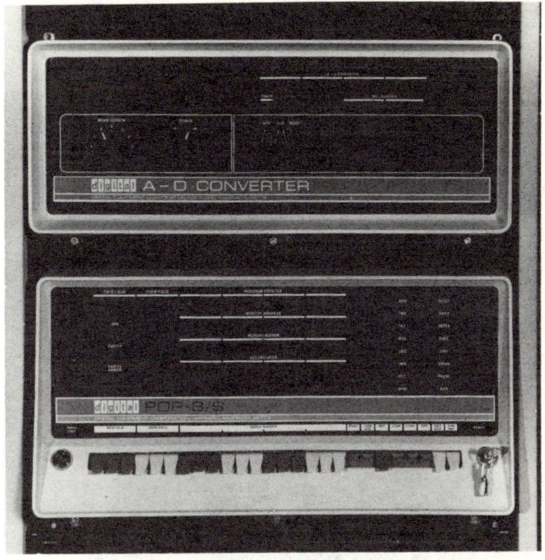

Figure 8. The PDP-8/S.

Figure 9. The PDP-8/I.

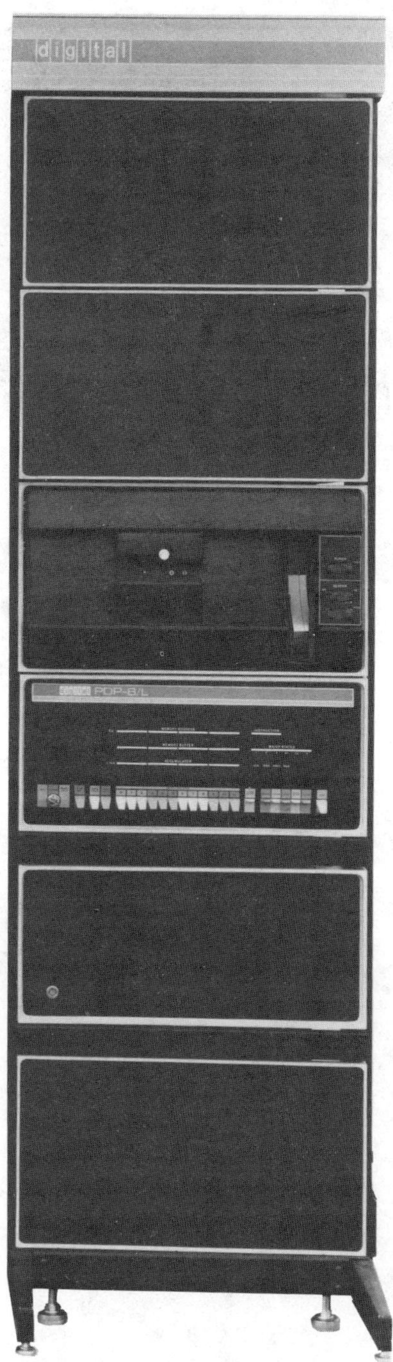

Figure 10. The PDP-8/L.

The PDP-8/S, PDP-8/I, and PDP-8/L are mentioned only briefly here because their characteristics were basically dictated by the cost and performance improvements made possible by the emerging integrated circuit technology. The cost and performance figures for these machines are examined in greater detail in the charts at the end of this chapter.

THE PDP-8/E, PDP-8/M, AND PDP-8/A

Shortly after the introduction of the PDP-8/L, it became evident that customers wanted a faster and more expandable machine. The continuing technological trend toward higher density logic and some new concepts in packaging made it possible to satisfy both of these requirements but to still produce a new machine that would be cheaper than its predecessor. The new machine was the PDP-8/E (Figure 11).

A block diagram of a complete PDP-8/E computer system is shown in Figure 12. Note that the lower half of the drawing shows an adapter for interconnecting the positive bus family (PDP-8/I and PDP-8/L) I/O devices. In addition, signal converters were available to convert a step further to the older negative bus family (PDP-5, PDP-8, and PDP-8/S) I/O devices. In this way, the new machine could capitalize on the existing hardware option base. It

Figure 11. The PDP-8/E.

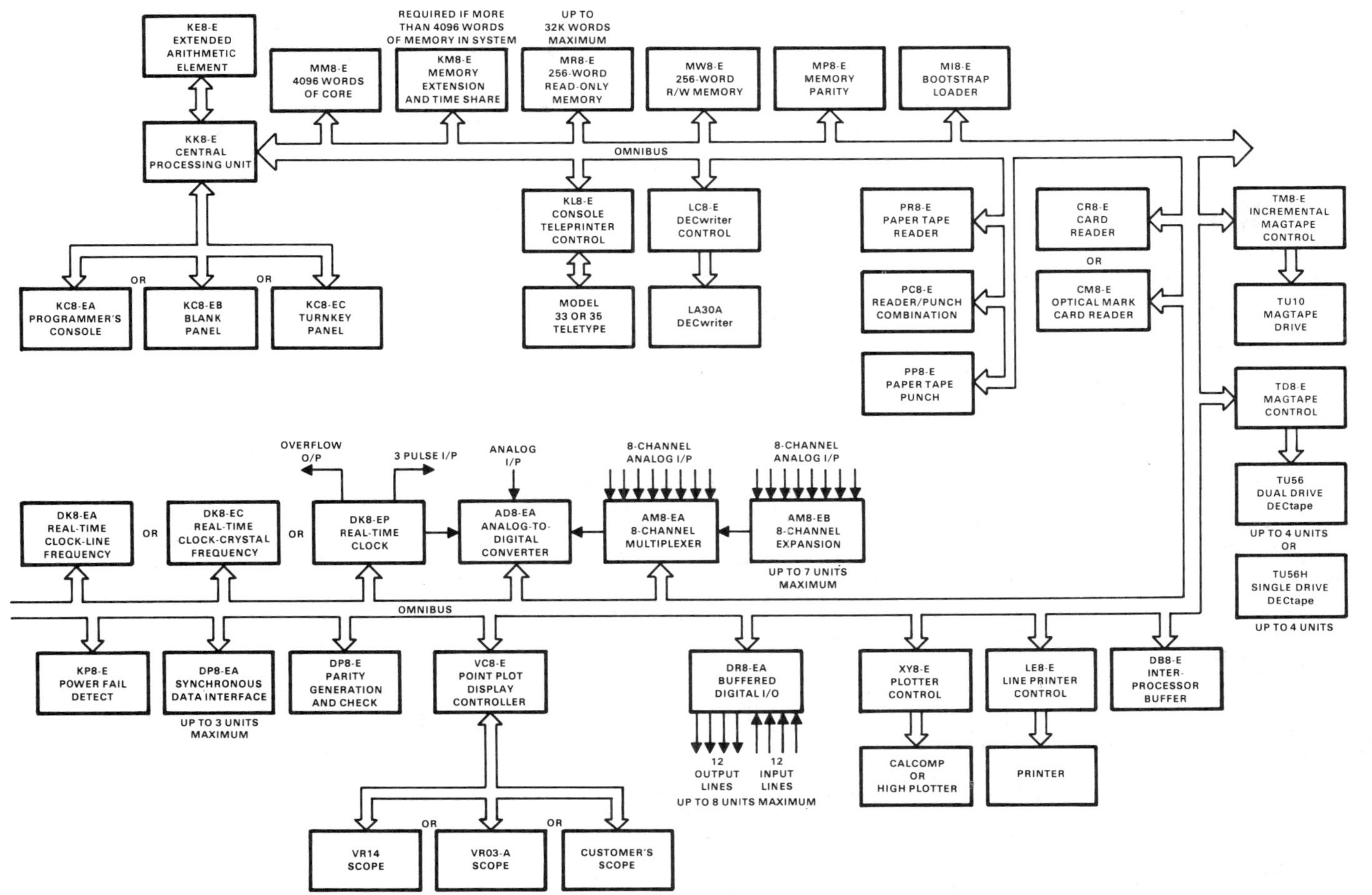

Figure 12. PDP-8/E system block diagram (part 1 of 2).

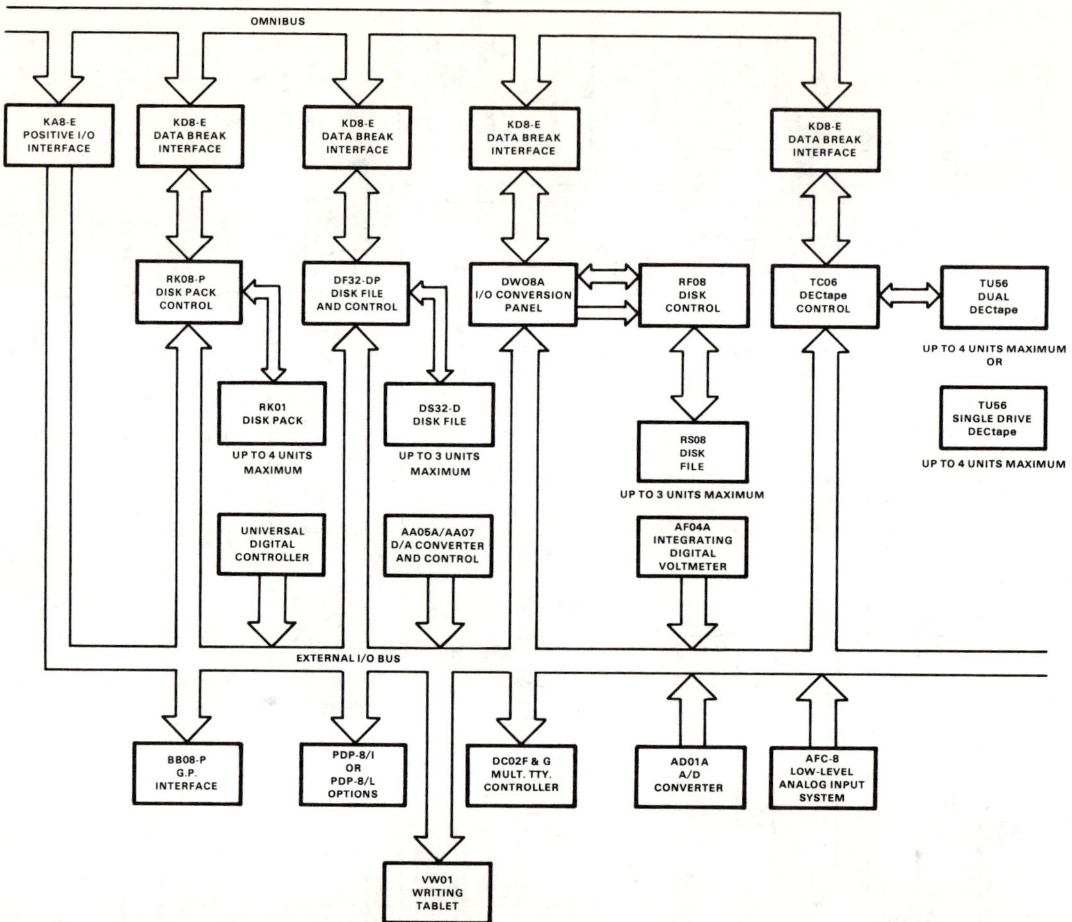

Figure 12. PDP-8/E system block diagram (part 2 of 2).

would not be necessary to design a complete new set of options at the time the machine was introduced, and existing customers could upgrade to the new computer without having to buy new peripherals.

The reason for using an adapter to connect to existing I/O devices was that the PDP-8/E featured a new unified-bus I/O Bus implementation related to the Unibus that was being designed for the PDP-11. The electrical design of the I/O Bus for both the previous negative logic and positive bus machines had been straightforward, but the mechanical packaging and cabling had not. A new implementation was needed which would simplify the packaging and cabling and solve the problems created by the Direct Memory Access channel, which had not been bused in previous designs. Don White, who was leading the design team, conducted a contest to name the new bus. After discarding such entries as "Blunderbus," the name "Omnibus" was chosen.

The Omnibus, which is still in use in the PDP-8/A, has 144 pins, of which 96 are defined as Omnibus signals. The remainder are power and ground. The large number of signals permit a great number of intraprocessor communications links as well as I/O signals to be accommodated. The Omnibus signals can be grouped as follows:

1. Master timing to all components.
2. Processor state information to the console.
3. Processor request to memory for instructions and data.
4. Processor to I/O device commands and data transfer.
5. I/O device to processor, signaling completion (interrupts).
6. I/O Direct Memory Access control for both direct and Three Cycle Data Break transfers.

The approximately 30 signals in groups 4 and 5 provide programmed I/O capability. There are about 50 signals in group 6 to provide the Direct Memory Access capability. These 80 signals are nearly equivalent in quantity and function to the preceding PDP-8 I/O Bus design, making the conversion from Omnibus structure to PDP-8/I and PDP-8/L I/O equipment very simple.

The complement of signals is quite different from that in the PDP-11 Unibus, which is more strictly an I/O bus, and the PDP-8/E processor handled many more of the Direct Memory Access and interrupt control functions than does the PDP-11 processor. One specific signaling structure that differs between the two machines is the interrupt system, which in a PDP-11 Unibus passes a Bus Grant signal through the I/O options to be propagated further or absorbed by the option. There are no such pass-through signals on the Omnibus; hence, any option can occupy any slot, and intervening slots between installed options can be left vacant. A by-product (or perhaps goal) of the Omnibus structure is that there are a fixed number of slots. The lack of cabling between options means that the electrical transmission characteristics are well defined.

The processor for the PDP-8/E occupied three 8 × 10-inch boards; 4 Kwords of core memory took up three more boards; a memory shield board, a terminator board, a teleprinter control board, and the console board completed the minimum system configuration. Thus, a total of ten 8 × 10-inch boards formed a complete system. The three-board PDP-8/E processor, occupying 240 in^2, was in striking contrast to the 100-board PDP-5 processor, which occupied 2,100 in^2.

The PDP-8/E implementation was determined by the availability of integrated circuits. Multiplexers, register files, and basic arithmetic logic units performed the basic operations in a straightforward fashion using a simple sequential controller. Microprogrammed control was not feasible because suitable read-only memories were not available. The read-only rope magnetic memory of the PDP-9 was too expensive and was unsuitable for PDP-8/E packaging. Integrated circuit read-only memories available at that time were too small, holding only about 64 bits.

There was some problem partitioning the processor logic among the three modules. Figure 13 shows the final arrangement, which was to place timing and interrupt on one module, the data path on a second, and the control on the third. Even with this partitioning, more pins were required between the data and control modules than were available through the Omnibus. To provide the necessary connections, additional connectors were installed on each module on the edge opposite the Omnibus connection.

The PDP-8/E was mounted in a chassis which had space and power to accommodate two blocks of Omnibus slots. Thirty-eight modules could be mounted in the slots, allowing space for the processor and almost 30 peripheral option controllers. Many customers wanted to build the PDP-8/E into small cabinets and have it control only a few things. They found the large chassis and its associated price to be more than they wanted. To reach this market, the PDP-8/M was designed.

The PDP-8/M was essentially a PDP-8/E cut in half. The cabinet had half the depth of a PDP-8/E, and the power supply was half as big. There were 18 slots available, enough for the basic processor-memory system and about eight options. The processor was the same as that for a PDP-8/E.

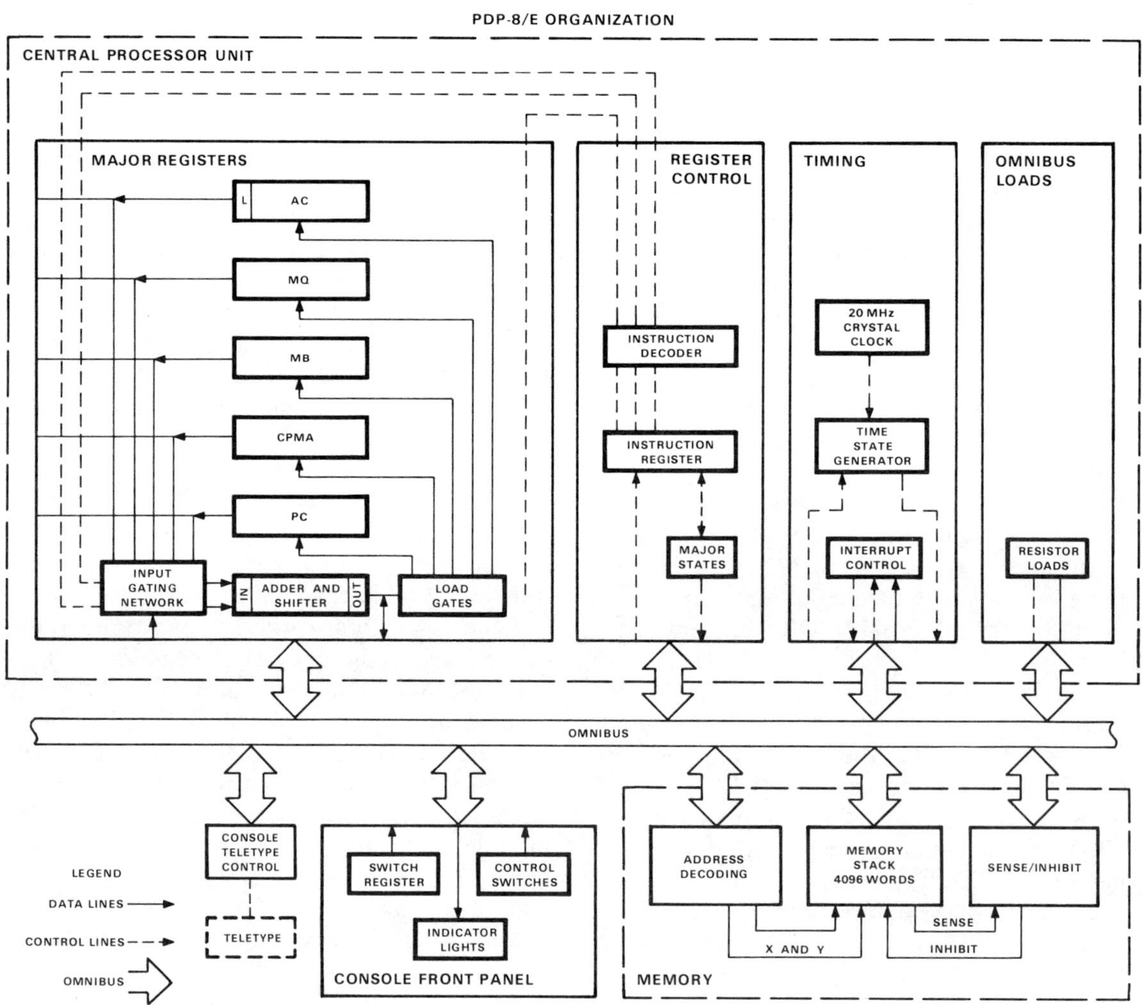

Figure 13. PDP-8/E basic system block diagram.

By 1975, DEC had been building "hex" size printed circuit boards for the PDP-11/05 and PDP-11/40 for at least two years. The hex boards were 8 × 15 inches, half again as big as the "quad" boards used in the PDP-8/E and PDP-8/M, which were 8 × 10 inches. The dimensional difference was along the contact side of the board. A hex board had six sets of 36 contacts while the quad board had only four sets. Semiconductor memory chips had also become available, so a new machine was designed to utilize the larger boards and new memories to extend the PDP-8/E, PDP-8/M to a new, lower price range. The new machine was the PDP-8/A. The PDP-8/A processor and register transfer diagram is shown in Figure 14 and the 8/A processor in Figure 15.

The hex modules permitted some of the peripheral controller options that had occupied several boards in the PDP-8/E to fit on a single board in the PDP-8/A (Figure 16). The availability of hex boards and of larger semiconductor read-only memories permitted the PDP-8/A processor to use microprogrammed control and fit onto a single board. It should be noted here that when a logic system occupies more than one board, a lot of space on each board is used by etch runs going to the connectors. This was particularly true of the PDP-8/E and PDP-8/M processor boards, due to the contacts on two edges of the boards. When an option is condensed to a single board, more space becomes available than square inch comparisons would at first indicate because many of the etch lines to the contacts are no longer required.

The first PDP-8/A semiconductor memory took only 48 chips (1 Kbit each) to implement 4 Kwords of memory. Memories of 8 Kwords and 16 Kwords were also offered. In 1977, only 96 16-Kbit chips were needed to form a 128-Kword memory. With greater use of semiconductor memory, especially read-only memory, a scheme was devised and added to the PDP-8/A to permit programs written for read-write memory to be run in read-only memory. The scheme adds a 13th bit to the read-only memory to signify that a particular location is actually a location that is both read and written. When the processor detects the assertion of the 13th bit, the processor uses the other 12 bits to address a location in some read-write memory which holds the variable information. This effectively provides an indirect memory reference.

In 1976, an option to improve the speed of floating-point computation was added to the PDP-8/A. This option is a single accumulator floating-point processor occupying two hex boards and compatible with the floating-point processor in the PDP-12. It supports 3- or 6-word floating-point arithmetic (12-bit exponent and 24- or 60-bit fraction) and 2-word double precision 24-bit arithmetic. As a completely independent processor with its own instruction set processor, it has its own program counter and eight index registers. The performance, approximately equal to that of an IBM 360 Model 40, provides what is probably the highest performance/cost ratio of any computer.

More Omnibus 8 computers (PDP-8/E, PDP-8/M, PDP-8/A) have been constructed than any of the previous models. The high demand for this model appears to be due to the basic simplicity of the design, together with the ability of the user to easily build rather arbitrary system configurations.

In the fall of 1972, DEC began the design of a single chip P-channel metal oxide semiconductor (MOS) processor to execute the PDP-8 instruction set. This processor was to be called the PDP-8/B, and it was hoped that production chips could be obtained by the spring of 1974 for systems to be shipped in the fall of 1974. The designers had progressed through the design tradeoffs in partitioning a PDP-8 for a single 40-pin chip when the project was stopped in the summer of 1973. The key reasons for stopping the project included the industry trend

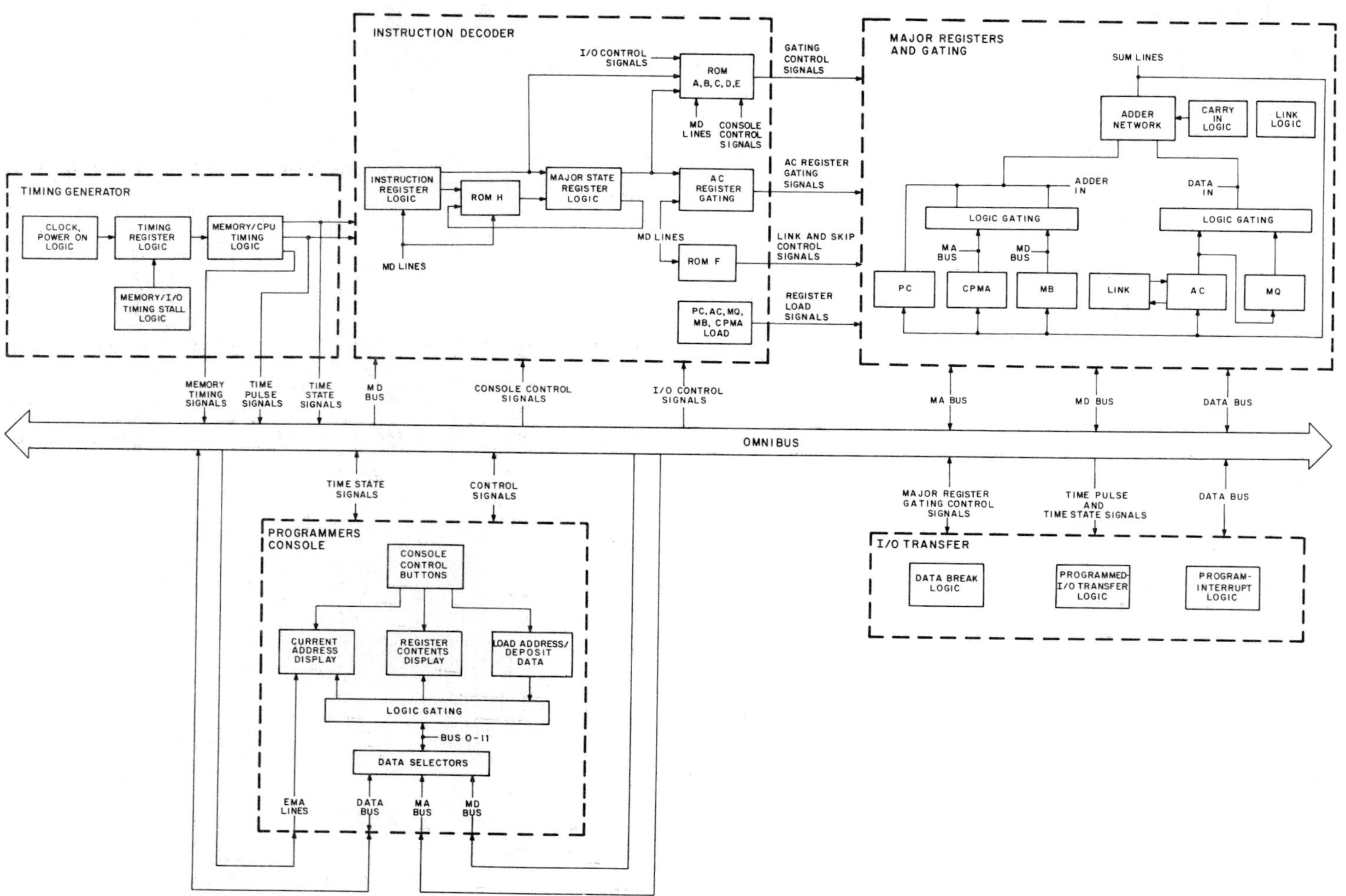

Figure 14. PDP-8/A processor and register transfer diagram.

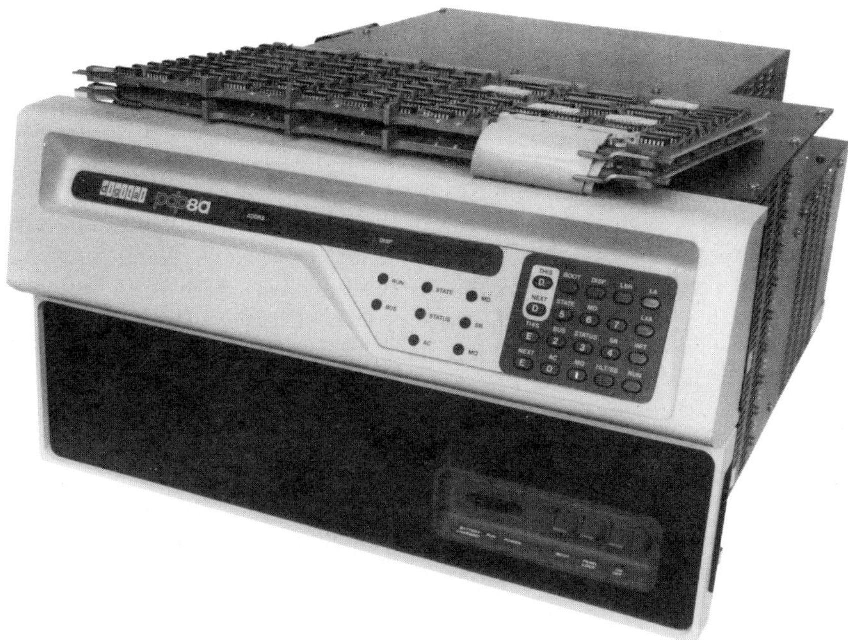

Figure 15. PDP-8/A processor.

Figure 16. PDP-8/A processor (interior).

from P-channel to N-channel and the fact that the Omnibus did not lend itself to cost reductions with large-scale integrated circuit technology. While the Omnibus was ideal for medium-scale integration and ease of interfacing, it was not as cost-effective as the buses that microcomputers used, which multiplexed address and data on the same leads at different times. The percentage of system cost and complexity represented by the processor in an Omnibus-8 system was too low to make the move to large-scale integrated (LSI) processor attractive at that time. For these reasons, it was decided to apply the newer N-channel process to a system in which the processor was a more complex and costly part of the system – the PDP-11 Family. Thus, in the summer of 1973, a project started in cooperation with Western Digital Corporation to build a PDP-11 on one or more N-channel LSI chips.

In 1976, Intersil offered the first PDP-8 processor to occupy a single chip, using CMOS technology. DEC verified that it was a PDP-8 and began to apply it to a product in the fall of 1976. In the meantime, in addition to Intersil, Harris Semiconductor became a second source of chip supply for DEC. The two manufacturers each have their own designation for these chips, but in the discussion below they will be called "CMOS-8" chips. A microphotograph of the chip is shown in Figure 17.

The CMOS-8 processor block diagram is given in Figure 18. Not surprisingly, it looks very much like a conventional PDP-8/E processor design using medium-scale integrated circuits. It has a common data path for manipulating the Program Counter (PC), Memory Address (MA), Multiplier-Quotient (MQ), Accumulator (AC), and Temporary (Temp) registers. The Instruction Register (IR), however, does not share the common arithmetic logic unit (ALU). Register transfers, including those to the "outside world," are controlled by a programmable logic array (PLA), as indicated by the dotted lines in the figure. CMOS-8 is an example of the use of programmable logic arrays for instruction decoding and for control purposes, as discussed in Chapter 2.

While the CMOS-8 is the first DEC processor to be built on a single chip, the most interesting thing about it is the systems configurations that it makes possible. It is not only small in size (a single 40-pin chip), but it also has miniscule power requirements due to its CMOS construction. Thus, some very compact systems can be built using it. The block diagram in Figure 19 shows a system built with a CMOS-8 and compatible components. In contrast to those of past systems, some of the other components in this system now represent more dollar cost and more physical space than the processor itself. Among these are the random-access read-write memory, the read-only memory, and the Parallel Interface Elements associated with the I/O devices. The Parallel Interface Elements enable interrupt signals to be sent back to the processor and decode the In-Out Transfer (IOT) commands that control data transfers. Also shown in Figure 19 are some specific I/O devices such as the Universal Asynchronous Receiver/Transmitter (UART) chips that do serial/parallel conversions and formatting for communication lines.

An excellent example of the use of a CMOS-8 as part of a packaged system is the VT78 video terminal shown in Figure 20. The goals for this terminal were to drastically reduce costs by including the keyboard, cathode ray tube, and processor in a single package the size of an ordinary terminal. The CMOS-8 chip and high density RAM chips made this possible. To form a complete, stand-alone computer system that supports five terminals, mass storage was added. Because the mass storage was floppy disks, it was not in the terminal but in a small cabinet. Even without the mass storage, however, the VT78 forms an "intelligent terminal." An intelligent terminal is usually defined to in-

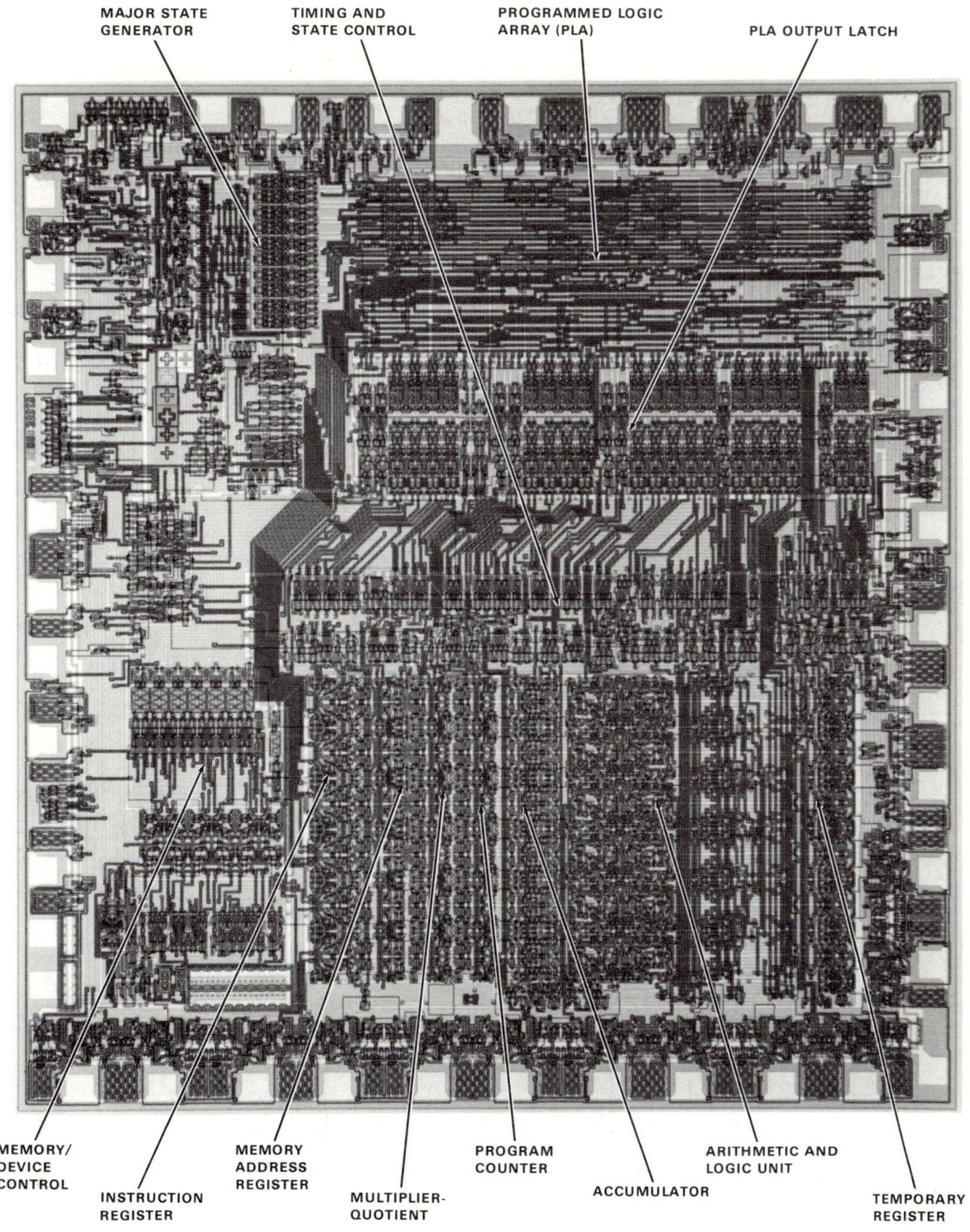

Figure 17. Microphotograph of the CMOS-8 chip (courtesy of Intersil Corporation).

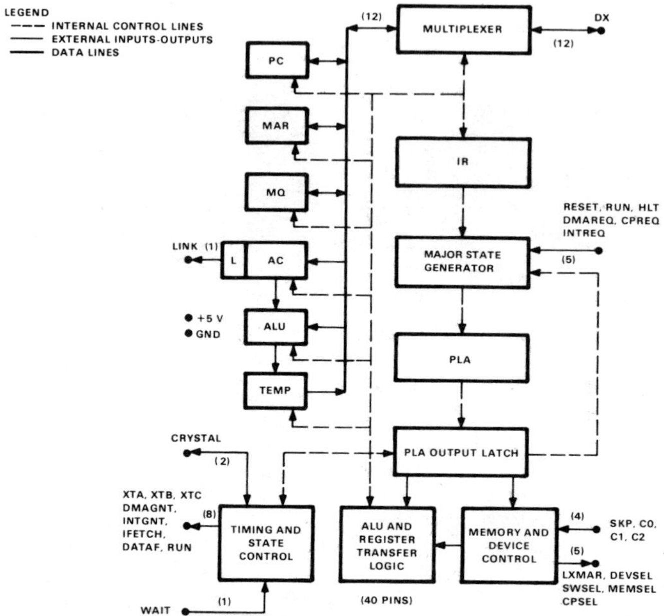

Figure 18. Block diagram of CMOS-8.

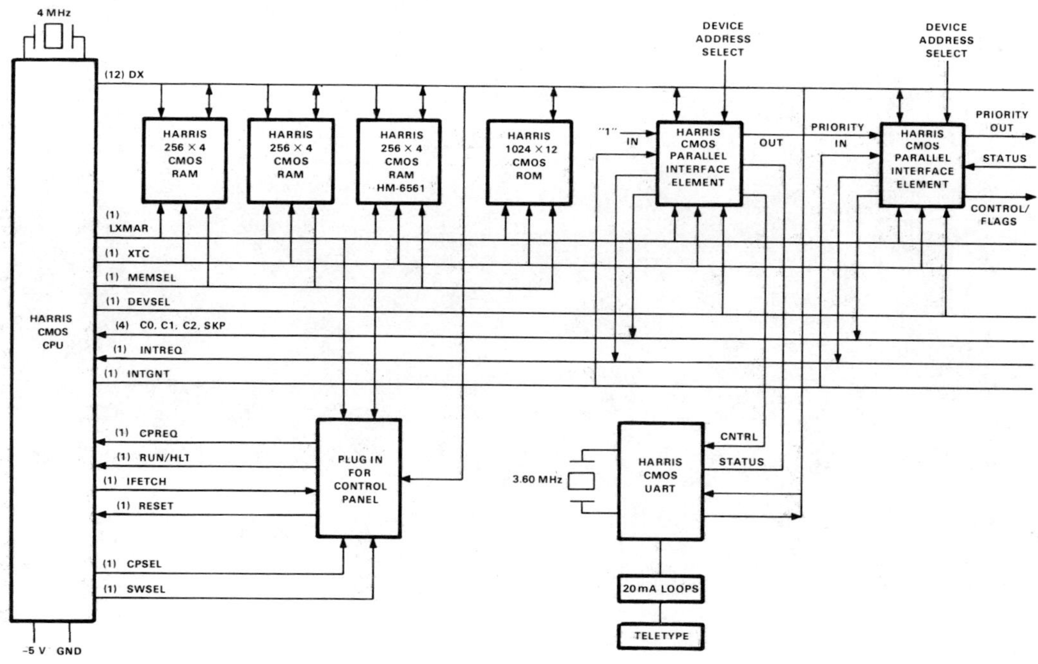

Figure 19. CMOS-8 based system.

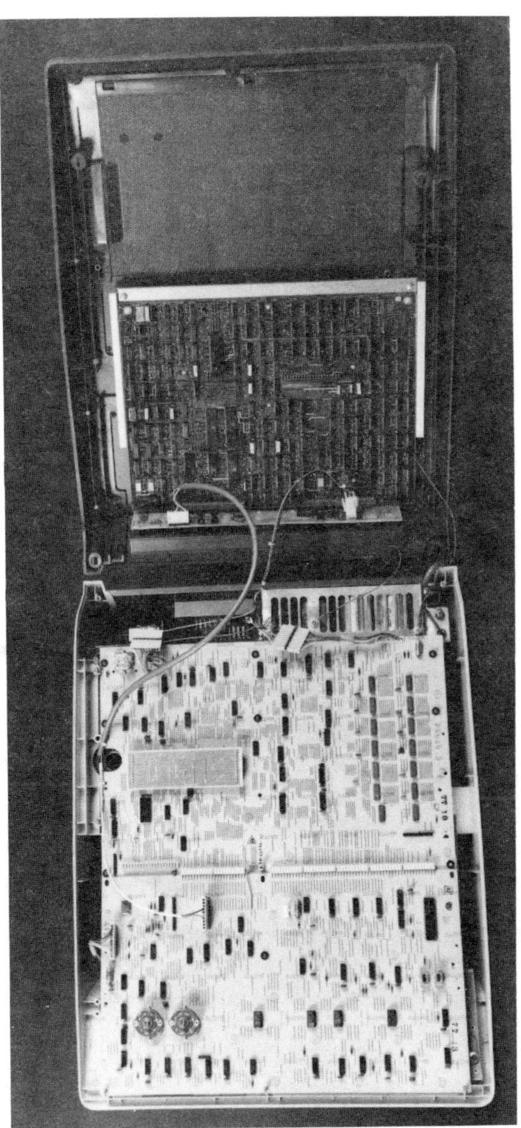

Figure 20. The VT78 video terminal.

clude a computer whose program can be loaded (usually via a communication line) to take on a variety of characteristics – i.e., it can learn. Figure 21 is a block diagram of a VT78 system terminal.

An intelligent terminal can be used either as part of a network or as a stand-alone computer system. In the former case, the application is determined by the network to which the terminal is attached, but in the latter case, the terminal functions as a desk-top computer running various PDP-8 software.

TECHNOLOGY, PRICE, AND PERFORMANCE OF THE 12-BIT FAMILY

The PDP-8 has been re-implemented 10 times with new technology over a period of 15 years. The performance characteristics of these implementations are given in Figure 22. As discussed in Chapter 1, new technology can be utilized in the computer industry in three ways: lower cost implementations at constant performance and functionality, higher performance implementations at constant cost, implementation of new basic structures. Of these three ways, the PDP-8 Family has primarily used lower cost implementations of constant performance and functionality.

The points in Figures 23 and 24 are arranged to show the cost trends of three configurations. The first configuration is merely a central processor with 4 Kwords of primary memory. The second configuration adds a console terminal, and the third configuration adds DECtapes or floppy disks for file storage. Note that the basic system represented in the first configuration has declined in price most rapidly: 22 percent per year in the early days and 15 percent per year in recent years. The price of primary memory, on the other hand, has declined at the rate of 19 percent per year, as seen in Figure 25.

The price and performance trajectories for the PDP-8 family of machines are plotted in

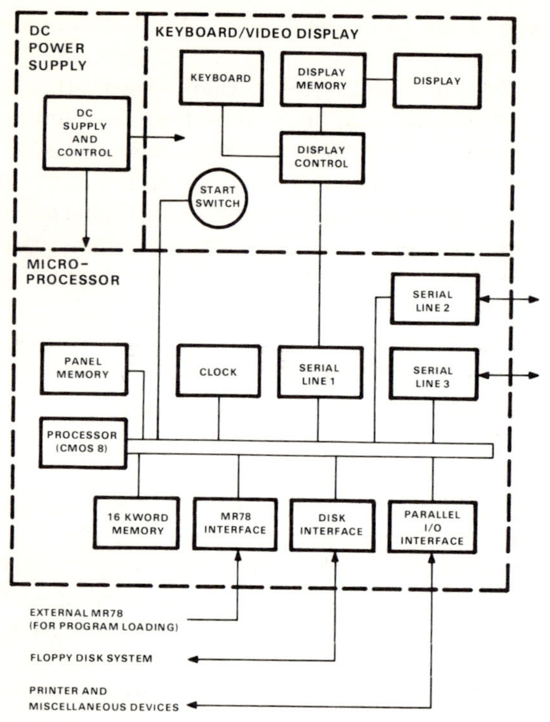

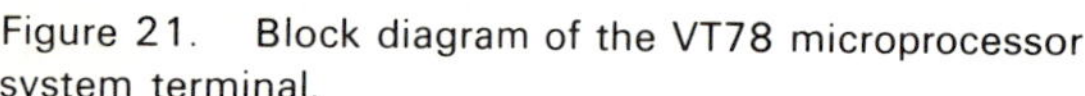

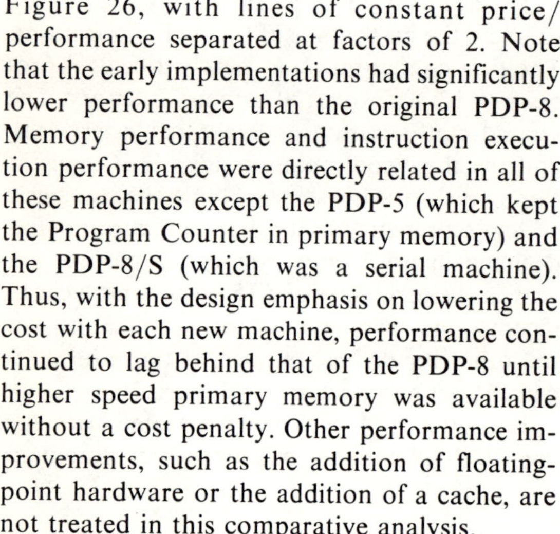

Figure 21. Block diagram of the VT78 microprocessor system terminal.

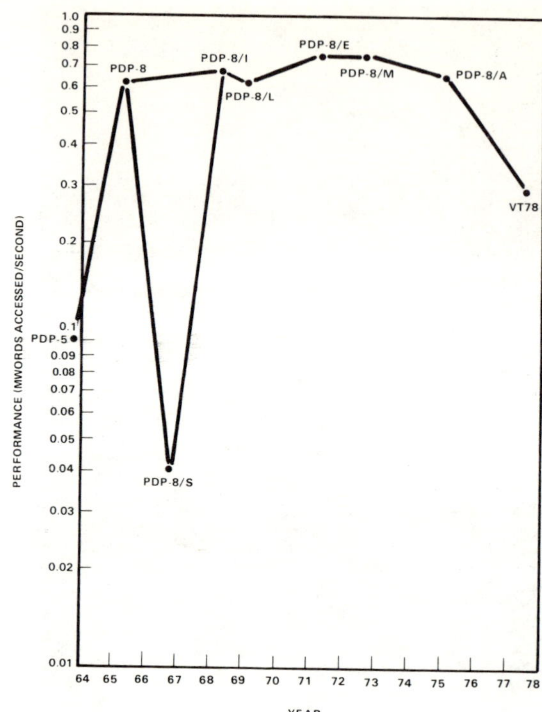

Figure 22. Performance of DEC's 12-bit computers versus time.

Figure 26, with lines of constant price/performance separated at factors of 2. Note that the early implementations had significantly lower performance than the original PDP-8. Memory performance and instruction execution performance were directly related in all of these machines except the PDP-5 (which kept the Program Counter in primary memory) and the PDP-8/S (which was a serial machine). Thus, with the design emphasis on lowering the cost with each new machine, performance continued to lag behind that of the PDP-8 until higher speed primary memory was available without a cost penalty. Other performance improvements, such as the addition of floating-point hardware or the addition of a cache, are not treated in this comparative analysis.

Figure 27 gives the performance/price ratio for the PDP-8 Family machines, and it can be directly compared with that of other machines described in this book. The 18-bit machines improved at a rate of 52 percent to 69 percent per year over a short time, as indicated on the graph. Setting aside the PDP-5 design point, the improvement for the 12-bit machines was similar during the same period but has since slowed to only 22 percent per year.

Rather than try to fit a single exponential to the performance/price data points in Figure 27, it might be better to try two independent exponentials. The reason for this is that the data points really mark the transition between two generations. The PDP-5 was a mid-second (transistor) generation machine, and the PDP-8

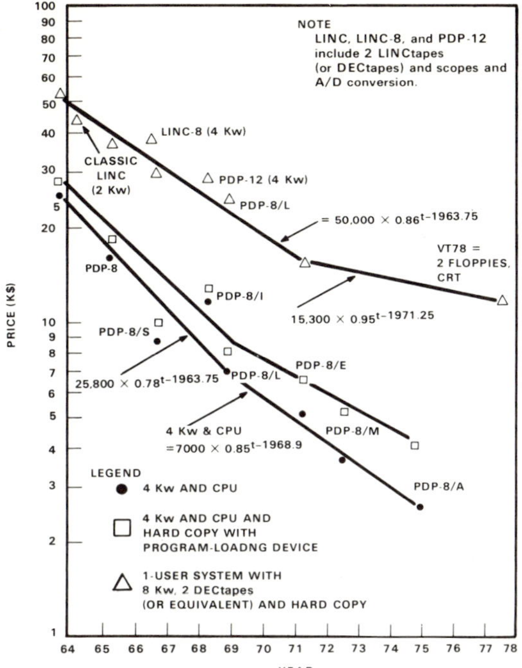

Figure 23. Price of DEC's 12-bit computers versus time (log).

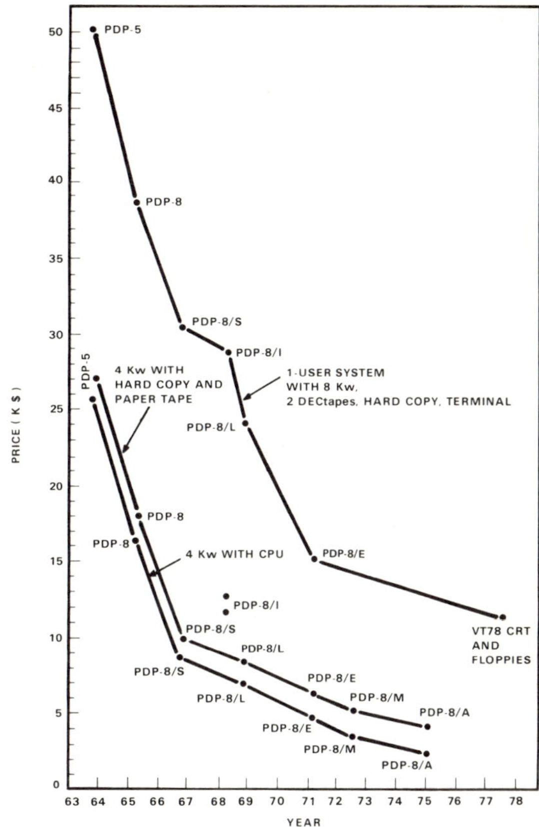

Figure 24. Price of DEC's 12-bit computers versus time (linear).

represents a late second generation machine. The PDP-8/I and PDP-8/L were beginning third (integrated circuit) generation designs. These four machines represent a relatively rapid evolution from 1963 to 1968. After the PDP-8/L, the evolution slows somewhat between 1968 and 1977, as medium-scale integrated circuits continued to be the implementation technology, and the cost of packaging and connecting components continued to be controlled by the relatively wide bus structure.

During their evolution, the DEC 12-bit computers have significantly changed in physical structure, as can be seen from the block diagrams in Figure 28. The machines up through the PDP-8/L had a relatively centralized structure with three buses to interface to memory, program-controlled I/O devices, and Direct Memory Access devices. The Omnibus-8 machines bundled these connections together in a simpler physical structure. The CMOS-8 avoids the wide bus problem by moving the bus to lines on a printed circuit board. The number of interconnection signals on the bus is then reduced by roughly a factor of 4 to about 25 signals which can be brought into and out of the chip within the number of pins available.

Figures 23 and 24 and Table 2 illustrate the price/performance oscillating history of the design evolution summarized below:

1. While the PDP-5 was designed to keep price at a minimum, the PDP-8 had additions to improve the performance

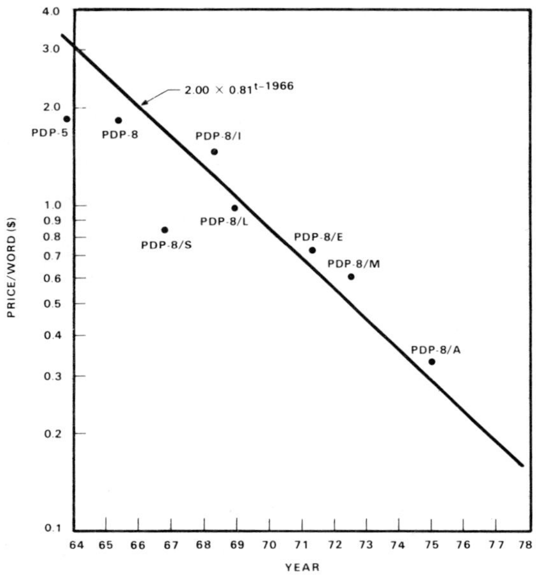

Figure 25. Price per word of 12-bit memory versus time.

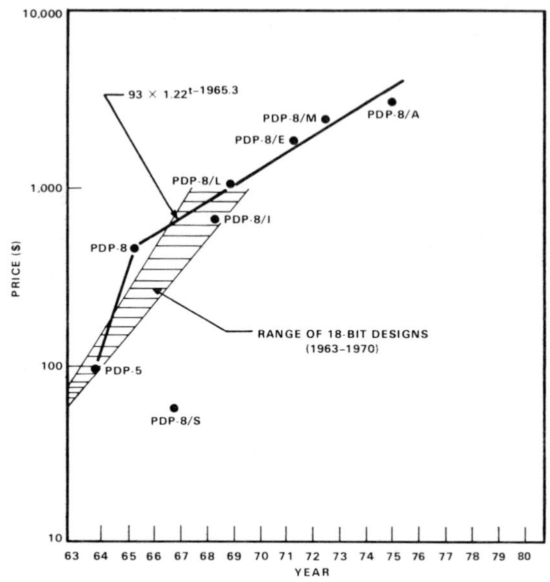

Figure 27. Bits accessed by the central processor/sec/$ versus time (for 4 Kword + processor systems).

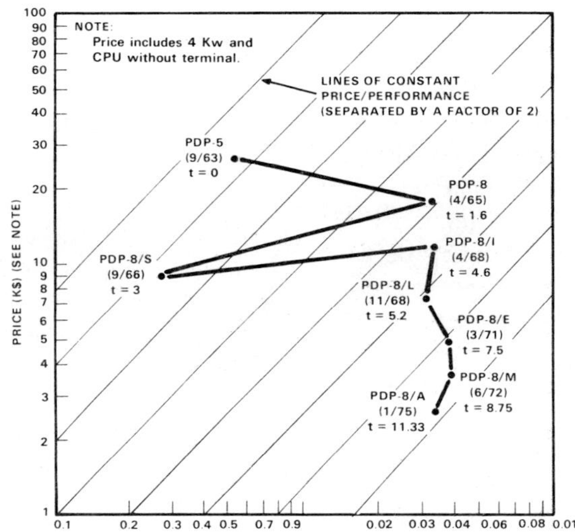

Figure 26. Price versus performance for DEC's 12-bit computers.

while not increasing price significantly over that of a slower speed design. The cost per word was modestly higher with the PDP-8 than with the PDP-5, but the PDP-8 had 6 times the perfomance of a PDP-5. Thus, the PDP-8 crosses three lines of constant price/performance in Figure 26.

2. The PDP-8/S was an attempt to achieve a minimum price by using serial logic and a minimum price memory design. However, the performance of the PDP-8/S was slow.
3. The market pressures created by PDP-8/S performance probably caused the return to the PDP-8 design, but in an integrated circuit implementation, the PDP-8/I.
4. The PDP-8/I was relatively expensive, so the PDP-8/L was quickly introduced to reduce cost and bring the design into line with market needs and expectations.
5. The PDP-8/E was introduced as a high performance machine that would permit the building of systems larger than those possible with the PDP-8/L.
6. The PDP-8/M was a lower cost, smaller cabinet version of the PDP-8/E and was intended to meet the needs of the OEM market.

The design goal of machines subsequent to the PDP-8/M has been primarily one of price reduction. The PDP-8/A was introduced to further reduce cost from the level of the PDP-8/E and PDP-8/M, although some large system configurations are still built with PDP-8/E machines. The CMOS-8 chips represent a substantial cost reduction but also a substantial performance reduction. The CMOS-8 performance is one-third that of a PDP-8/A, so a standalone system using a CMOS-8 is less cost-effective than an PDP-8/A when the central processor is used as the only performance criterion.

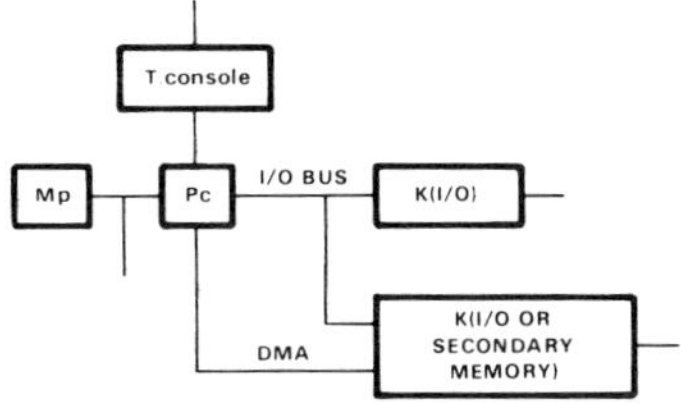

(a) Negative (PDP-5, 8, 8/S) and positive (8/I, 8/L) logic families.

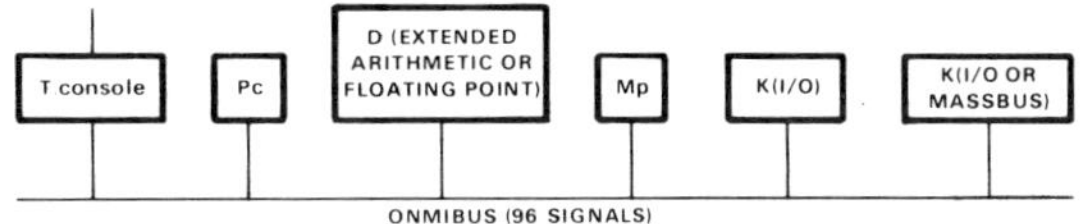

(b) Omnibus family (PDP-8/E, 8/F, 8/M, 8/A).

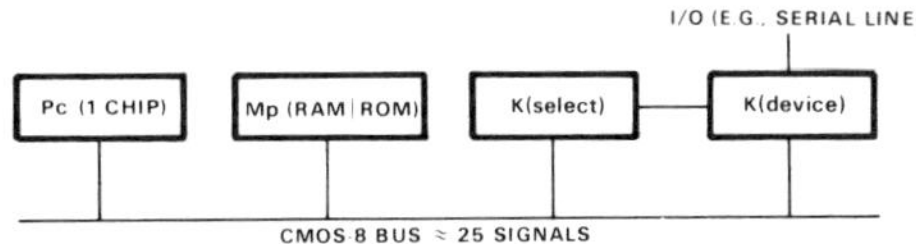

(c) CMOS-8 (6100) processor-on-a-chip family.

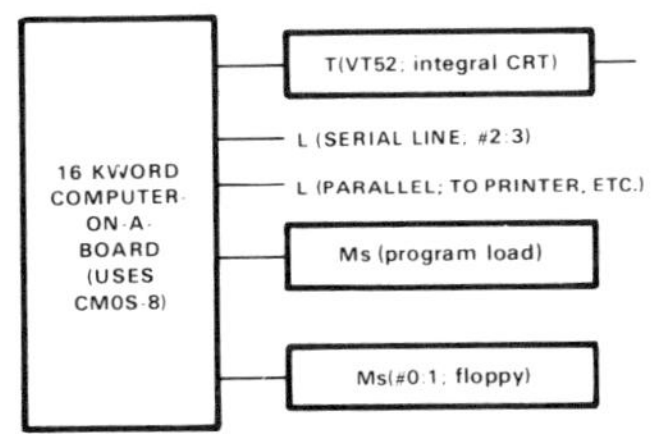

(d) VT78 computer-in-a-terminal.

Figure 28. Evolution of PDP-8 Family PMS structures.

The main reason for using large-scale integration is the reduced cost and smaller package rather than performance. Obviously, the next step is increased performance or more memory, or both more performance and more memory on the same chip.

Table 2. Characteristics of PDP-8 Family Computers

	PDP-5	PDP-8	PDP-8/S	PDP-8/I	PDP-8/L	PDP-8/E	PDP-8/M	PDP-8/A	VT78
Project start, first ship	9/63	4/65	9/66	4/68	11/68	3/71	6/72	1/75	6/77
Goals	Lowest cost computer, interface-ability	Cost, much greater performance	Cost; tabletop	Better cost, more function than 8	Lower cost	Easy to configure; more functions better performance	Lower cost, limited system	Lower cost higher density	Cost; complete system in a terminal
Applications	Process control monitoring; laboratory	+message switch control Lab.processing for instruments	Standalone calculator	Remote job entry station, TSS/8		+Business data processing, testing;		Computer-in-a-desk	Word processing; desk-top computer, terminal
Innovations/improvements	I/O bus; ISP	Wire-wrap; producible; low cost bit-sample communications controller	Serial implementation	Integrated circuits	Less package	Omnibus		Semiconductor memory; floating-point processor	Processor-on-a-chip; low power
Processor + 4 Kword memory (K$)	25.8	16.2	8.79	11.6	7.0	4.99	3.69	2.6	NA
Same + terminal (K$)	27.0	18.0	9.99	12.8	8.5	6.49	5.19	4.1	NA*
Price/memory word ($)	1.83	1.83	0.73	1.46	0.98	0.73	0.61	33.0	NA
Processor + 8 Kword + terminal + mass storage	51.1	38.8	30.4	28.9	24.1	15.3	-	-	11.6
Memory cycle time	6.0	1.6	8.0	1.5	1.6	1.3	1.3	1.5	3.6
Processor Mwords accessed/s	0.1	0.63	0.04	0.67	0.63	0.76	0.76	0.67	0.28
Processor bits accessed/s /$	93	466	55	651	1080	1828	2472	3092	-

Table 2. Characteristics of PDP-8 Family Computers (Cont)

	PDP-5	PDP-8	PDP-8/S	PDP-8/I	PDP-8/L	PDP-8/E	PDP-8/M	PDP-8/A	VT78
Performance/price improvement (over predecessor)	-	5.0	0.12	11.8	1.65	1.69	1.35	1.25	-
Price Improvement	-	1.6	1.84	0.76	1.66	1.4	1.35	1.42	-
Performance Improvement	-	6.3	0.06	16.75	0.94	1.23	1.0	0.87	0.42
Product life (years)	3	5	3	3	3	7+	5+	2+	-
Power (watts)	780	780	350	780	250	500	450	400	25
Weight (lbs)	540	250	75	190	70	90	40	55	2
Volume (ft^3)	24	8	3.2	8	2	2.2	1.8	1.2	0
Price density (lb/$)	0.02	0.015	0.009	0.016	0.01	0.018	0.011	0.021	-
Density (lb/ft^3)	22.5	31.3	23.4	23.75	35.0	40.9	22.2	45.8	-
Printed circuit board average price ($)	2100		1600			240	240	120	20
Board size	5.25X4	2.25X3.875	5X38	2.25X3.875		8X10	8X10	8X15	12X15
Programmed I/O Bus	49	49	43 + Bus	40	30	96	8E	8E	5 connectors
DMA I/O Bus	49	49	49	50	50	-	-	-	-

Figure 29 and Table 2 present the power requirements, weight, and volume of the 12-bit machines. In general, the power requirements have remained relatively constant. This is both because each package must house a fixed number of devices and because each device has a relatively high overhead power cost associated with driving the Omnibus. However, the limited configuration, lack of an Omnibus, and low power requirements of CMOS make the VT78 an exception to this rule. The weight and volume have declined significantly with time as the design has moved from two cabinets to a half cabinet, and then from a half cabinet to being embedded in a terminal.

SPECIAL DEVICES BASED ON THE PDP-8

The PDP-8/A and the products which incorporate the CMOS-8 chip are the current 12-bit product offerings, so the discussion of the

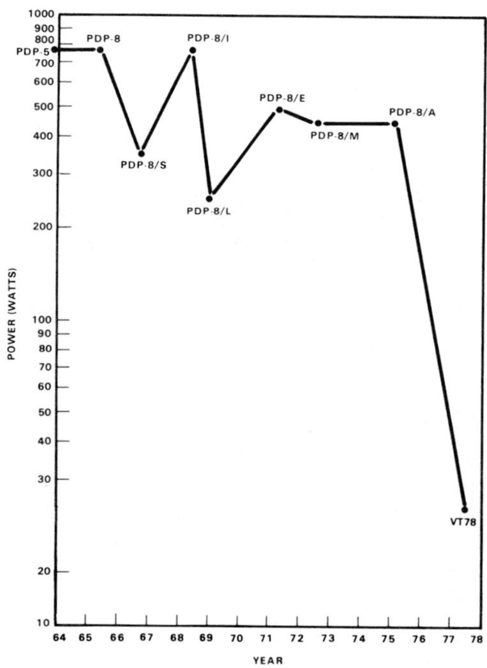

(a) Power versus time.

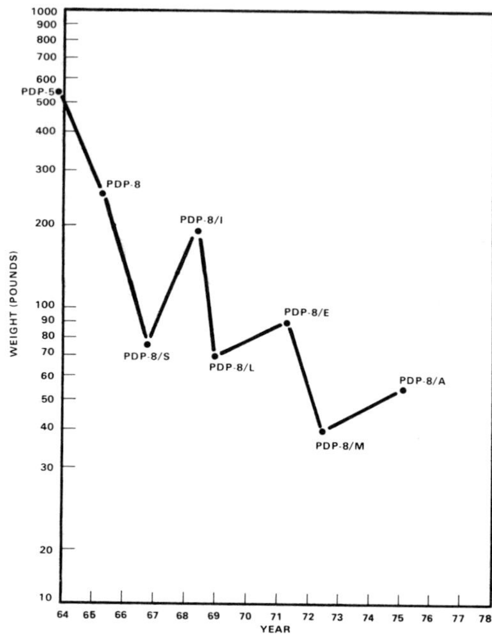

(b) Weight versus time.

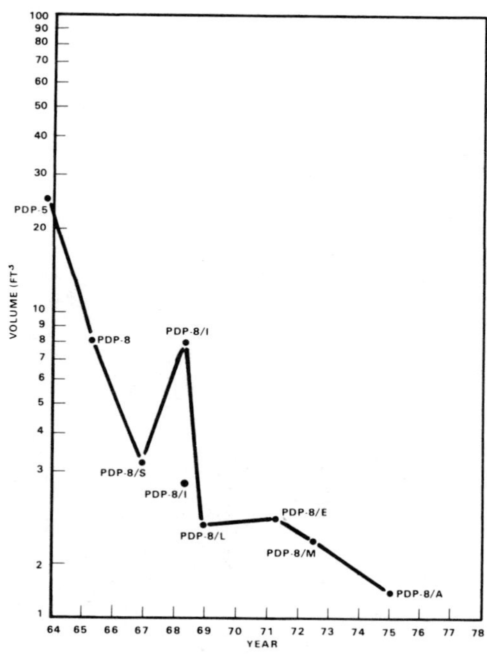

(c) Volume versus time.

Figure 29. Power, weight, and volume for DEC's 12-bit computers versus time.

development of DEC's 12-bit computers in chronological order must stop here. However, during the development of the main line of 12-bit computers, some interesting systems based on DEC 12-bit processors have been developed, both by DEC and by others. Among these are the DEC 338 Display Computer, the cache-based PDP-8, and the PDP-14 Programmable Controller (a 1-bit machine similar in its instruction set to the PDP-8 and using Omnibus packaging concepts).

DEC 338 Display Computer

The 338 display, a variant of the PDP-8, is interesting for its historical importance [Bell and Newell, 1971: Chapter 25]. It was one of the earliest display processor-based computers – if not possibly the first. The problem of displaying data on a cathode ray tube clearly shows how the application need drives a complete change in hardware in order to interpret the necessary data-type (in this case, a graphic picture).

The 338 display idea was extended and applied to the displays used with the PDP-9, PDP-15, and the PDP-11 series. Although the 338 had the right general capabilities, it did not have the refinements of later display processors for the PDP-15 and PDP-11 (GT40 and GT60).

An observation that display and other specialized processors evolve in a fashion called the "wheel of reincarnation" [Myer and Sutherland, 1968] is diagrammed in Figure 30. As the figure shows, the process starts with a very simple basic design – here, to have graphics picture output for a computer. The trajectory around the wheel follows:

Position 1: Point-plotting. The computer includes a single instruction display controller which can plot a picture on a point-by-point basis under command of the central processor. For most displays, except storage scopes, the processor can barely calculate the next point fast enough to keep the display refreshed. Hence, the system is processor bound, and the display may be idle. The original PDP-1 display is typical of this position, and a display of this type is offered on most DEC minicomputers.

Position 2: Vector-plotting. By adding the ability to plot lines (i.e., vectors), a single instruction to the display processor will free some of the processor and begin to keep all but the fastest display busy.

Position 3: Character-plotting and alphanumeric plotting. With the realization that characters are a major part of what is displayed, commands to display a character are added, further freeing the processor. Many of the point-plotting displays were extended to have character generation capability.

Position 4: General figure and character display. In reality, a picture does not consist of just characters and vectors; each element of the picture is actually a string of characters and a set of closed or open polygons to be displayed starting at a particular point. By providing the control display with a Direct Memory Access channel, the display can fetch each string of text and generate polygons without involving the central processor.

Position 5: Display processors. With the ability to put up sub-pictures with no processor intervention, it is easy for the whole picture to be displayed by linking the elements together in some fashion. This merely requires "jump" and "subroutine" call instructions so that common picture elements do not have to be re-defined. The 338 and other display processors have roughly this capability.

Position 6: Integrated display and central processor. Now, all the data paths and states are present for a fully general purpose processor so that the central processor need never be called on again. This requires a slightly more general purpose interpreter. By minor perturbations, the processor design can be refined in such a way as to execute the same instruction set as the original host computer because the cost of incompatibility is too great. Two processors require two compilers, diagnostics, manuals, and support for use. This state provides the same capability as that shown in Position 1.

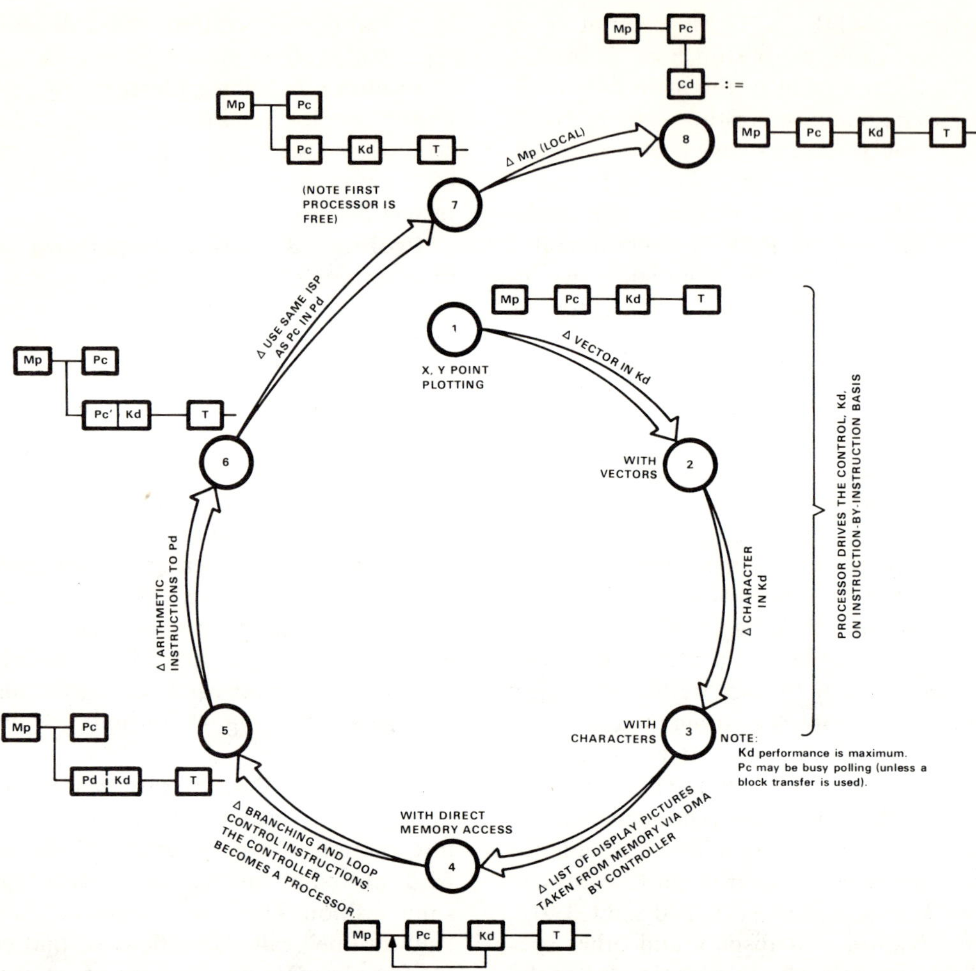

Figure 30. The wheel of reincarnation.

The original processor is completely free, and there is a display processor with the capability of executing both the original instruction set and the display instruction set.

Position 7: Two computer structures. Alternatively, the processor can be isolated as a separate computer and reconnected in some fashion to the central processor-primary memory pair in Position 1. Such a structure is just a basic computer with the addition of a general figure and character display (Position 4).

Position 8: A separate computer. A separate computer is formed solely for display, and the options available for picture processing can be decided again from the "wheel of reincarnation."

The Cache-Based PDP-8

This structure uses a small, fast memory to hold the results of recent references to primary memory. The structure has been subsequently

Table 3. Performance/Cost Comparison of 8/E and 8/E with Cache

Model	Configuration Cost			Performance	Performance/Cost Ratio		
	Minimum	Average	Large	Factor	Minimum	Average	Large
PDP-8/E	$ 5K	$10K	$35K	1.0	1.0	1.0	1.0
PDP-8/E with cache	$10K	$15K	$40K	5.0	2.5	3.3	4.3

used in the latest PDP-10 processor (KL10), in the PDP-11/60, and in the PDP-11/70.

A PDP-8 with cache was designed and constructed by Professor David Casasent at Carnegie-Mellon University [Bell and Casasent, 1971; Bell *et al.*, 1974]. Initially, the project was proposed to explore the desirability and feasibility of using emitter-coupled logic for designing fast computers (including PDP-10s). As the investigation proceeded, the need for a large, fast memory emerged. Such a memory turned out to be so costly that a computer so equipped could not be feasibly marketed. It turned out that the easiest way to build a cost-effective, fast minicomputer was to use a cache structure in order to reduce the cost of primary memory. Also, instead of designing a very fast PDP-8, which ECL logic would have provided, the goal was modified to be less fast, much less costly, and potentially marketable. This caused TTL Schottky to be used in the design even though the logic family was just beginning to evolve.

In order to make the prototype more marketable without completely redesigning it, the project was constrained to use the PDP-8/E Omnibus backplane and parts. The prototype did not become operational as quickly and cleanly as possible and was therefore not used to stimulate a market. Thus, instead of further pursuing marketing goals, the design was carried forward with the goals of testing the cache applicability, circuitry, and associated techniques for building faster computers. The difficulty in stimulating market interest was typical of products that are substantially different from those already in existence.

A number of discoveries emerged from the research on the cache-based PDP-8. A 100-nanosecond PDP-8 processor with 512-word cache and standard PDP-8/E core memory had the characteristics shown in Table 3. Note that the performance/cost ratio approaches 5 as the system price increases. This argues for always incorporating incremental performance improvements in the most expensive machines.

The work on the cache-based PDP-8 illustrates the use of the 8 Family as an experimental vehicle for understanding a design in terms of program behavior. It also allows one to observe the flow of ideas from research through advanced development to the production of machines. Finally, it shows how, by rather minor perturbations, a design can be kept compatible with its predecessors while providing rather dramatic performance and performance/cost ratio improvements, as shown in Table 2.

The PDP-14

The PDP-14 was designed expressly as a controller for complex electromechanical machinery such as transfer machines, conveyors, and simple milling machines. The need for such a controller was first recognized when General Motors expressed its need to control a large machine which handled engine blocks by a sequence of operations (transfers). The design of a controller evolved from the use of standard DEC K-Series industrial modules (see Chapter 5) for sequential circuits. These modules provided increased reliability and replaced electromechanical control components such as relays by using solid state sensing and switching. The new controller, designated the PDP-14, represented a cost reduction over controllers composed strictly of industrial modules. It did this by using time-multiplexing so that one control structure in memory – the processor – could serve as the interconnection (and processing) structure, as opposed to physically interconnecting the modules together to behave as a controller. This tradeoff is a good example of how computers are used instead of hardwired logic to carry out a task. In terms of the Levels-of-Interpreters View explained in Chapter 1, an algorithm (machine) can be made entirely at the lowest level (Figure 31), or alternatively, a higher level interpreter can carry out the same algorithm.

The design requirements that the PDP-14 had to meet were as follows:

1. Be lower priced (with lower life-cycle costs) and easier to operate than existing control alternatives.
2. Solve the control problem and be programmable by users who have solved problems using a different representation (e.g., relay ladder diagrams).
3. Operate in a high electrical noise environment.
4. Operate in the physical environment characteristic of the machine it controlled.
5. Have the appropriate I/O interfaces to sense contacts and to control power relays.

Although a PDP-8/I might have been programmed to carry out the task, it was either not considered or rejected because the cost was perceived to be too great, and there was some perception that a conventional stored program computer could not solve the problem. In addition, the PDP-8/I circuits did not appear to have adequate noise margins to operate in the anticipated environment, and there was inadequate I/O capability.

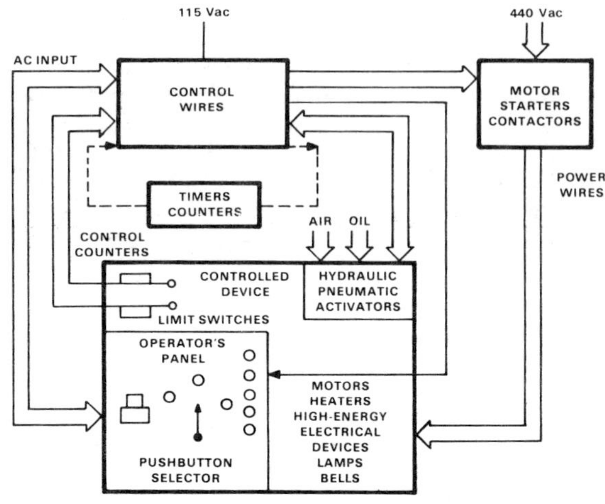

Figure 31. Hardwired machine for industrial control.

As a result, the PDP-14 was proposed and designed expressly to solve the problem and cost less than the PDP-8/I which was just going into production. The PDP-14 had no data operations except on a single Boolean value using a 1-bit accumulator called TEST. Even with so little arithmetic capability, the machine's structure and processor state were roughly equivalent to those in a PDP-8 design. Ultimately, the processor state was extended beyond that of a PDP-8 as the problem changed (e.g., when communication was required with host processors), but these extensions will not be discussed here.

In order to solve the Boolean equations that a conventional relay controller solves in parallel, the PDP-14 had to solve equations sequentially at a rate of approximately 30 Hz – fast enough to give the illusion that the equations were being solved in parallel.

To operate in an environment with high electrical noise, the circuit logic was slowed down to improve noise margins. It was felt that core memory did not have adequate noise immunity, so a braided wire, read-only rope memory was used. To battle the effects of the poor physical environment, the unit was housed in a dust-proof enclosure. To sense contacts and control

```
PDP14 :=                ! original pdp-14, not 14/30
Begin

** Memory.State **

Mp\Primary.Memory[0:4095]<0:11>,

** Processor.State **

PC\Program.Counter<0:11>,
SR\Subroutine.Return.Register<0:11>,
Test\One.Bit.Accumulator<>,
IR\Instruction.Register<0:11>,
        Op\Operation.Code<0:3>        := IR<0:3>,
        Z\Effective.Address<4:11>     := IR<4:11>,

** Input.Output.State **

I\Input.Contacts[0:255]< >,
O\Output.Relays[0:255]< >,

** Instruction.Cycle **

IExec\Instruction.Execution :=
        Begin
        Decode Op =>
                Begin
                                        ! Test input for ON
        '0101\TXN := If Not Test And I[Z] => Test = 1,
                                        ! Test input for OFF
        '0100\TXF  := If Not Test And Not I[Z] => Test = 1,
                                        ! Test output for ON
        '0011\TYN := If Not Test And O[Z] => Test = 1,
                                        ! Test output for OFF
        '0010\TYF  := If Not Test And Not O[Z] => Test = 1,
                                        ! Jump if Test ON
        '1011\JFN := (If Test => PC<4:11> = Z; Test = 0),
                                        ! Jump if Test OFF
        '1010\JFF   := (If Not Test => PC<4:11> = Z; Test = 0),
                                        ! Set Output ON
        '0111\SYN := O[Z] = 1,
                                        ! Clear Output
        '0110 := (If Z Neq #377 => O[Z] = 0; If Z Eql #377 => O[0:255] = 0 ),
                                        ! Jump
        '1000\JMP := If Z Eql #224 => PC = Mp[PC],
                                        ! Jump to Subroutine
        '1001\JMS := If Z Eql #245 => (SR = PC next PC = Z),
                                        ! Return from Subroutine, Skip
        '0000 := (If Z Eql #154 => PC = SR; If Z Eql #144 => PC = PC + 1),
        Otherwise := No.Op( )
                End
        End,

ICycle\Interpretation.Cycle :=
        Begin
        Repeat (IR = Mp[PC] next PC = PC + 1 next IExec( ))
        End
End
```

Figure 32. ISP description of the PDP-14 (courtesy of Mario Barbacci).

power relays, appropriate I/O interfaces were designed.

The instruction set of the PDP-14, shown in Figure 32, was among the smallest, most trivial instruction sets that could be found. Technically, the PDP-14 was called a computer because it could perform computation in the same way a Turing machine can – without an arithmetic unit. However, it encoded the Boolean data operators for which it was designed more efficiently than nearly any other computer, provided the equations were simple enough.

There were four instructions to take values from input switches or relay outputs and to compute new output values (the right side of a Boolean equation). Therefore, the PDP-14 also could simulate a sequential machine (state diagram or flowchart). Two additional instructions sensed the value of intermediate results (stored in TEST) and were used to eliminate the need to completely evaluate an equation each time. To direct program flow, there were four more instructions: "jump," "skip," "jump to subroutine" (a single level) and "return from subroutine." To handle the "accessories box," there was special I/O rather than having this carried out internally to a program. This I/O included up to 16 Boolean variables for timers consisting of external one-shot multivibrators, and control memory bits.

A good way to understand the PDP-14's operation is to start with the application. Figure 33 shows a combinational relay logic network that evaluates a Boolean expression (in parallel). When this network is implemented with the PDP-14, the inputs and outputs are simply connected, and the program forms the interconnection which constitutes the solution of the equation (Figure 33*b*). Figure 33*c* gives the Boolean expression for the network in Figure 33*a*. To evaluate this equation using a PDP-14 requires a sequential program (Figure 33*d*). This program requires between 120 microseconds and 200 microseconds to compute the output value, *y*8, since each instruction requires 20 microseconds. The speed of a computerized controller compared to that of relay operations is phenomenal. Heavy duty industrial control relays typically operate at a 30 Hz rate (33 milliseconds). If the PDP-14 can solve each equation with 4 terms in approximately 150 microseconds, the PDP-14 can solve 222 such equations in the time necessary to operate the relay. The memory requirements to solve the 222 equations are not large either. This equa-

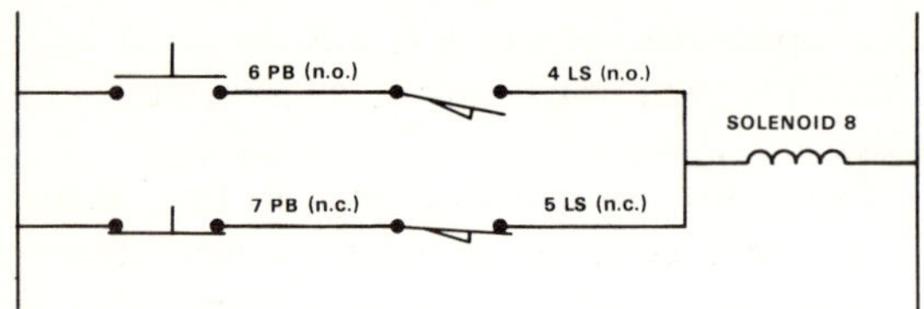

(a) Ladder diagram representation of a solenoid activated by two push buttons and two limit switches.

$$y8 = (X6 \wedge X4) \vee (\neg X7 \wedge \neg X5)$$

(b) Boolean equation expressing behavior of ladder diagram.

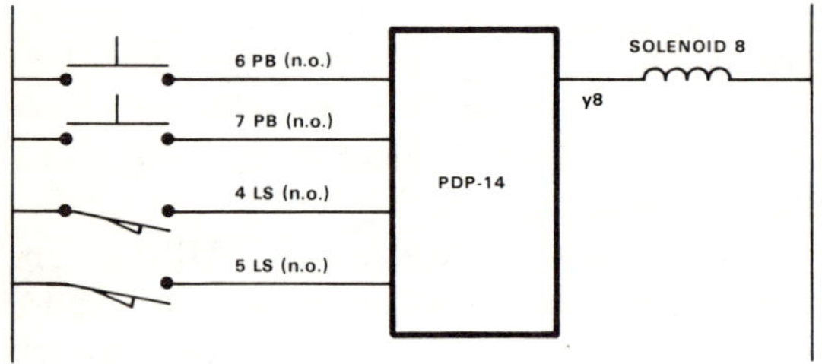

(c) Contact input (using normally open contacts) and solenoid output connections to PDP-14.

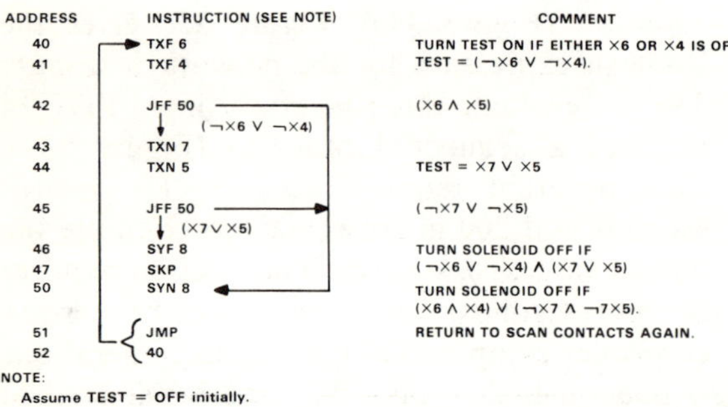

ADDRESS	INSTRUCTION (SEE NOTE)	COMMENT
40	TXF 6	TURN TEST ON IF EITHER X6 OR X4 IS OFF.
41	TXF 4	TEST = (¬X6 V ¬X4).
42	JFF 50	(X6 ∧ X5)
	(¬X6 V ¬X4)	
43	TXN 7	
44	TXN 5	TEST = X7 V X5
45	JFF 50	(¬X7 V ¬X5)
	(X7 V X5)	
46	SYF 8	TURN SOLENOID OFF IF
47	SKP	(¬X6 V ¬X4) ∧ (X7 V X5)
50	SYN 8	TURN SOLENOID OFF IF (X6 ∧ X4) V (¬X7 ∧ ¬7X5).
51	JMP	RETURN TO SCAN CONTACTS AGAIN.
52	40	

NOTE:
Assume TEST = OFF initially.

(d) PDP-14 program to simulate solenoid network by sequentially (and repeatedly) solving Boolean equation (33b).

Figure 33. Combinational network representations for solving Boolean equations.

tion required 12 locations; hence, 222 such equations require about 2.5 Kwords.

A number of PDP-14s were built and installed for the intended applications over the period 1970 to 1972. Programming was carried out in languages supported by compilers that operated on PDP-8. The languages allowed users to:

1. Write ordinary assembly programs (resembling PDP-8 programs).
2. Express a problem directly as a set of Boolean equations.
3. Express ladder diagrams (in effect, these are a set of Boolean equations).
4. Write a program as a flowchart, i.e., as a sequential machine that goes state by state and tests and branches on various input values to create output state, permitting both combinational (Boolean equations) and sequential circuits to be implemented.
5. Simulate the behavior of the program and system.

As the PDP-14 and contemporary machines were used, the demand arose for a second generation controller. By 1972, the additional requirements included lower cost, higher speed, an easily changed read-only memory, and the ability to load programs via a communications line or connected console. In addition, the controllers were required to connect in a network fashion and report back status and results to a supervisory computer at the next level of a hierarchy. The second generation controller should be capable of recording events such as counting the number of parts processed. It also needed timers which could be used as part of the control equations. The new unit should operate over an even wider environmental range than existing PDP-14 and have a more complete set of I/O interfaces.

From these requirements, the PDP-14/30 evolved (Figures 34 and 35). The initial read-only memory was replaced by an 8-Kword core

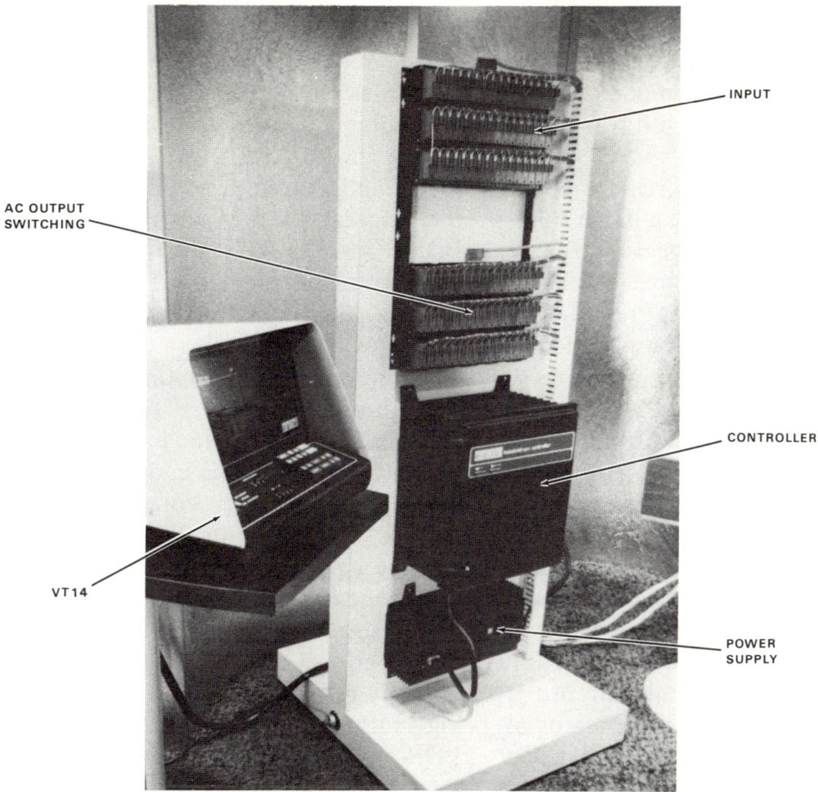

Figure 34. The PDP-14/30.

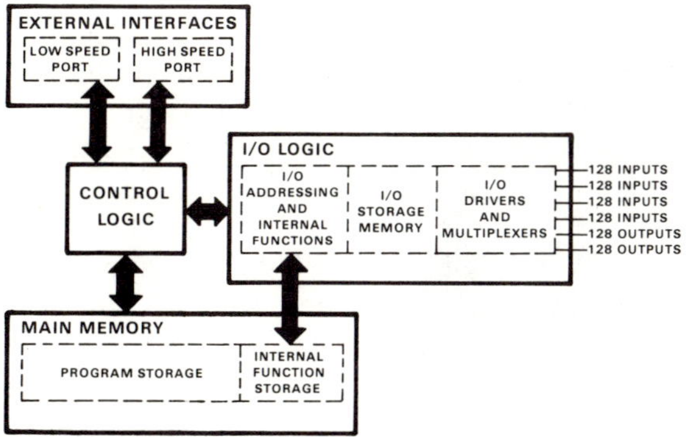

Figure 35. Block diagram of PDP-14/30.

memory. In this way, the programs could be easily changed rather than having to be returned to DEC for manufacturing. Because the original PDP-14 was so slow compared to the capability of the logic from which it was made, the instruction time was reduced from 20 microseconds to 2.5 microseconds to achieve better frequency response and to handle a larger number of equations. Additionally, because a large number of special registers had been added to hold numeric values (the shift registers, timers and counters), an arithmetic unit was added to the PDP-14/30 in an *ad hoc* fashion. All these additions forced the instruction set processor to change. The PDP-14/30 extensions could not be made in such a way as to have binary compatibility; thus, software changes were also required.

An interesting offshoot of PDP-14 development was the creation of a special terminal for a programming, program load and observation console. This terminal consisted of a CRT and PDP-8 mounted in a portable housing. Since the PDP-14/30 could report the status of its input and output variables, the terminal also had the ability to display the status of ladder diagrams (i.e., relay and contact position). A typical screen display is shown in Figure 36.

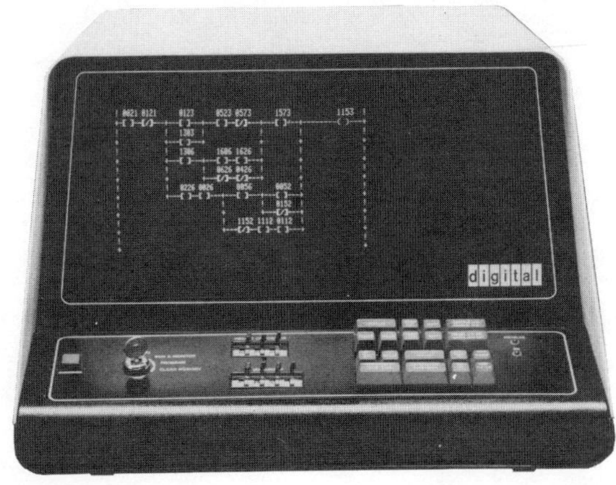

Figure 36. Typical screen display.

At the time when the PDP-14/30 was proposed, there were some who felt that it should not be built because a standard 8 Family computer was cheaper to build, and more production volume and lower costs could be obtained by not constructing a special unit. In addition, the 8 Family machine could be extended to have the original PDP-14 instruction set; and the PDP-8 instruction set would be available for evolving tasks, such as self-diagnosis, more extensive counting and timing functions, and dealing with non-Boolean data such as time, or non-discrete events including angular position. The more powerful PDP-8 instruction set would also be useful for handling general control in both the analog and the digital domains communicating with computer networks requiring protocol control for intelligent and error-free communication, and using algorithms to encode the control function instead of relatively large program state methods with no ability to perform computation.

Many of the previous arguments against using PDP-8s had now lost their merit. Since the PDP-14/30 was proposed to be built using the same circuit family as that of the PDP-8s, the electrical noise margins arguments no longer held. Furthermore, the PDP-8 could be packaged in a proper cabinet for the physical environment, and there could be adequate interfaces built. Besides, the proposed PDP-14/30 would incorporate a PDP-8 anyway, and two computers were obviously more expensive than one. In addition, adding the necessary cabinet and interface enhancements to the PDP-8 would have greatly improved the marketability of PDP-8 for all industrial applications. Although the design group did not buy the arguments that the PDP-14/30 should become a PDP-8 with appropriate extensions and packaging, some PDP-8 parts were used in the PDP-14/30 design.

ACKNOWLEDGEMENTS

The authors were pleased to have Wes Clark and Dick Clayton read and critique this chapter.

8

Structural Levels of the PDP-8

C. GORDON BELL, ALLEN NEWELL,
and DANIEL P. SIEWIOREK

The history of the DEC 18-bit and 12-bit computers, summarized briefly in the previous two chapters, was basically that of a recursive process in which new technology was applied and re-applied to the same basic designs to obtain improved price/performance ratios. In the late 1960s, the availability of relatively inexpensive integrated circuits made logic cost a less pressing concern. Computer engineering, and architectural issues of elegance, flexibility, and expandability, grew more important as the importance of architecture to total system price/performance became more evident. The PDP-11 papers in Part III elaborate on these issues, but first the hierarchical nature of computer systems design will be explored by examining the PDP-8 from the top down to lay the basic groundwork for future architectural discussions. The description of the PDP-8 will use some of the processor-memory-switch (PMS) and instruction set processor (ISP) notations introduced in *Computer Structures* [Bell and Newell, 1971]. These compact and straightforward notations are useful in comparing and analyzing computer architectures, and their use in the PDP-8 context should be helpful to the reader when encountering these notations in other papers.

A map of the PDP-8 design hierarchy, based on the Structural Levels View of Chapter 1, is given in Figure 1, starting from the PMS structure, to the ISP, and down through logic design to circuit electronics. These description levels are subdivided to provide more organizational details such as registers, data operators, and functional units at the register transfer level.

The relationship of the various description levels constitutes a tree structure, where the organizationally complex computer is the top node and each descending description level represents increasing detail (or smaller component size) until the final circuit element level is reached. For simplicity, only a few of the many possible paths through the structural description tree are illustrated. For example, the path showing mechanical parts is missing. The descriptive path shown proceeds from the PDP-8 computer to the processor and from there to the arithmetic unit or, more specifically, to the Accumulator (AC) register of the arithmetic unit. Next, the logic implementing the register transfer operations and functions for the *j*th bit of

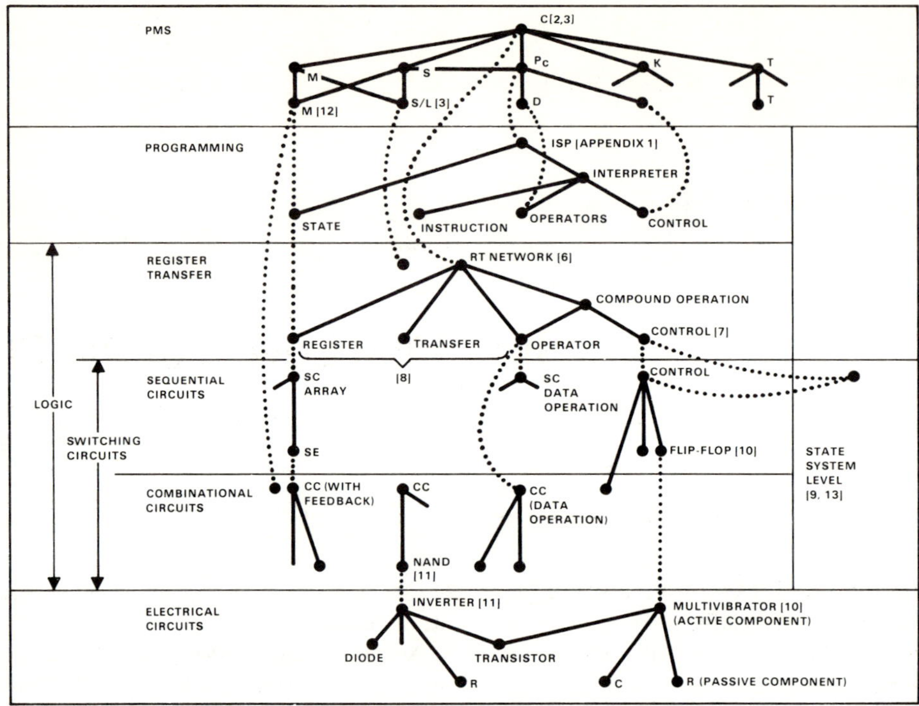

Figure 1. PDP-8 hierarchy of descriptions.

the Accumulator is given, followed by the flip-flops and gates needed for this particular implementation. Finally, on the last segment of the path, there are the electronic circuits and components from which flip-flops and gates are constructed.

ABSTRACT REPRESENTATIONS

Figure 1 also lists some of the methods used to represent the physical computer abstractly at the different description levels. As mentioned previously, only a small part of the PDP-8 description tree is represented here. The many documents which constitute the complete representation of even this small computer include logic diagrams, wiring lists, circuit schematics, printed circuit board photo etching masks, production description diagrams, production parts lists, testing specifications, programs for testing and diagnosing faults, and manuals for modification, production, maintenance, and use. As the discussion continues down the abstract description tree, the reader will observe that the tree conveniently represents the constituent objects of each level and their interconnection at the next highest level.

THE PMS LEVEL

The PDP-8 computer in PMS notation is:

C('PDP-8; technology:transistors; 12 b/w;
descendants:'PDP-8/S, 'PDP-8/I, 'PDP-8/L,
'8/E, '8/F, '8/M, '8/A, 'CMOS-8;
antecedents: 'PDP-5;
Mp(core; #0:7; 4096 words; tc:1.5 μs/word);

Pc(Mps(2 to 4 words);
instruction length:1 | 2 words;
address/instruction:1;
operations on data:(=, +, Not, And, Minus (negate), Srr 1(/2), Slr 1 (×2), +1)
optional operations:(×,/,normalize);
data-types:word,integer,Boolean vector;
operations for data access:4);
P(display; '338);
P(c; 'LINC);
S('I/O Bus; 1 Pc; 64 K);
Ms(disk, 'DECtape, magnetic tape);
T(paper tape, card, analog, cathode-ray tube)

As an example of PMS structure, the LINC-8-338 is shown in Figure 2; it consists of three processors (designated P): Pc('LINC), Pc('PDP-8), and P.display('338). The LINC processor described in Chapter 7 is a very capable processor with more instructions than the PDP-8 and is available in the structure to interpret programs written for the LINC. Because of the rather limited instruction set being interpreted, one would hardly expect to find all the components present in Figure 2 in an actual configuration.

The switches (S) between the memory and the processor allow eight primary memories (Mp) to be connected. This switch, in PMS called S('memory Bus; 8 Mp; 1 Pc; time-multiplexed; 1.5 μs/word), is actually a bus with a transfer rate of 1.5 microseconds per word. The switch makes the eight memory modules logically equivalent to a single 32,768-word memory module. There are two other connections (a switch and a link) to the processor excluding the console. They are the S('I/O Bus) and L('Data Break; Direct Memory Access) for interconnection with peripheral devices. Associated with each device is a switch, and the I/O Bus links all the devices. A simplified PMS diagram (Figure 3) shows the structure and the logical-physical transformation for the I/O Bus, Memory Bus, and Direct Memory Access link. Thus, the I/O Bus is:

S('I/O Bus duplex; time-multiplexed; 1 Pc; 64 K; *Pc controlled, K requests*; t:4.5 μs/w)

The I/O Bus is nearly the same for the PDP-5, 8, 8/S, 8/I, and 8/L. Hence, any controller can be used on any of the above computers provided there is an appropriate logic level converter (PDP-5, 8, and 8/S use negative polarity logic; the 8/I and 8/L, positive logic). The I/O Bus is the link to the controllers for processor-controlled data transfers. Each word transferred is designated by a processor in-out transfer (IOT) instruction. Due to the high cost of hardware in 1965, the PDP-8 I/O Bus protocol was designed to minimize the amount of hardware to interface a peripheral device. As a result, only a minimal number of control signals were defined with the largest portion of I/O control performed by software.

A detailed structure of the processor and memory (Figure 4) shows the I/O Bus and Data Break connections to the registers and control in the notation used in the initial PDP-8 reference manual. This diagram is essentially a functional block diagram. The corresponding logic for a controller is given in Figure 3 in terms of logic design elements (ANDs and ORs). The operation of the I/O Bus starts when the processor sends a control signal and sets the six I/O selection lines (IO.SELECT<0:5>) to specify a particular controller. Each controller is hardwired to respond to its unique 6-bit code. The local control, K[k], select signal is then used to form three local commands when ANDed with the three IOT command lines from the processor. These command lines are called IO.PULSE.1, IO.PULSE.2, and IO.PULSE.4. Twelve data bits are transmitted either to or from the processor, indirectly under the controller's control. This is accomplished by using the AND/OR gates in the controller for data input to the processor, and the AND gate for data input to the controller. A single skip input is used so that the processor can test a status bit in the controller. A controller communicates back to the processor via the interrupt request line. Any controller wanting attention simply ORs its request signal into the interrupt request

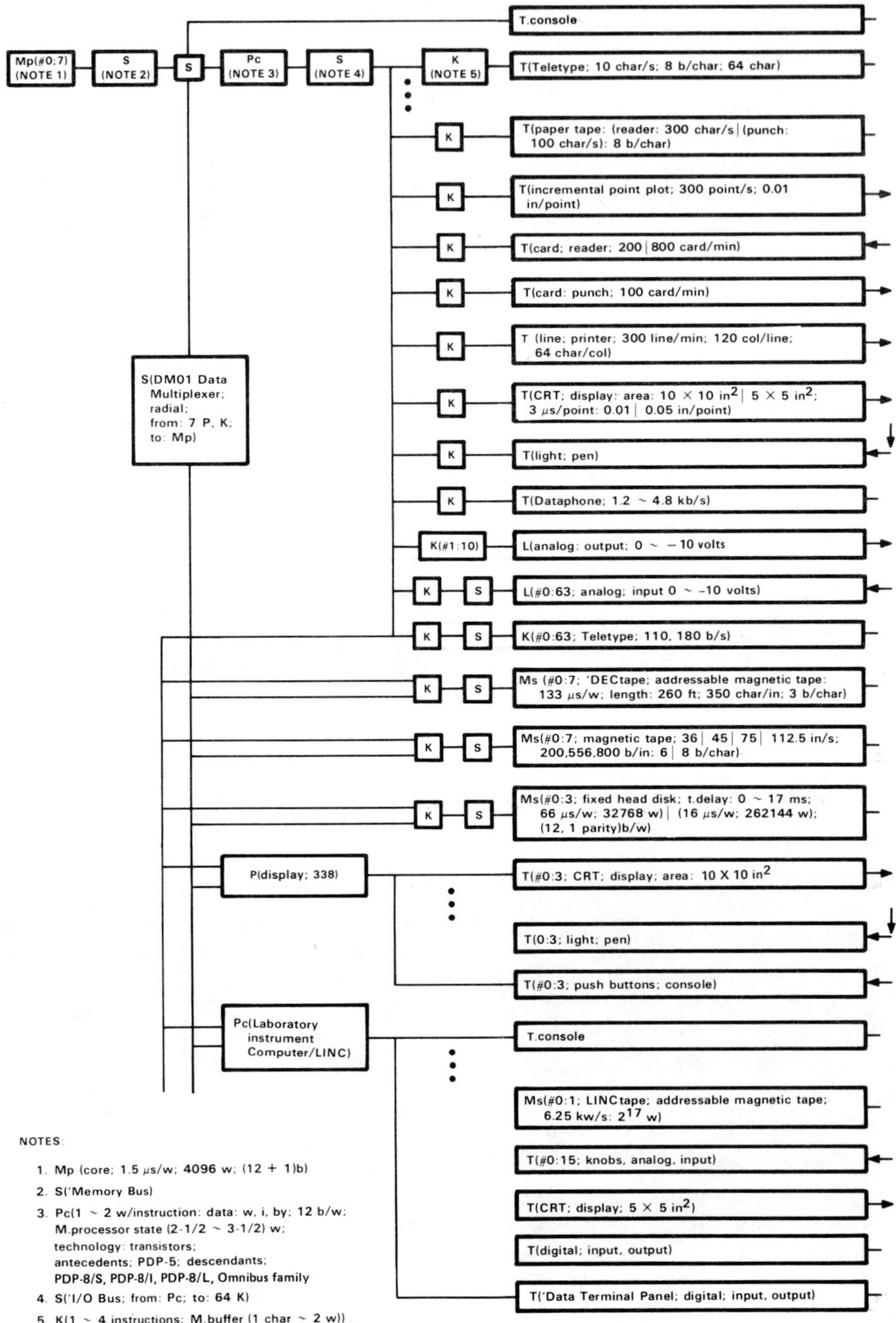

Figure 2. LINC-8-338 PMS diagram.

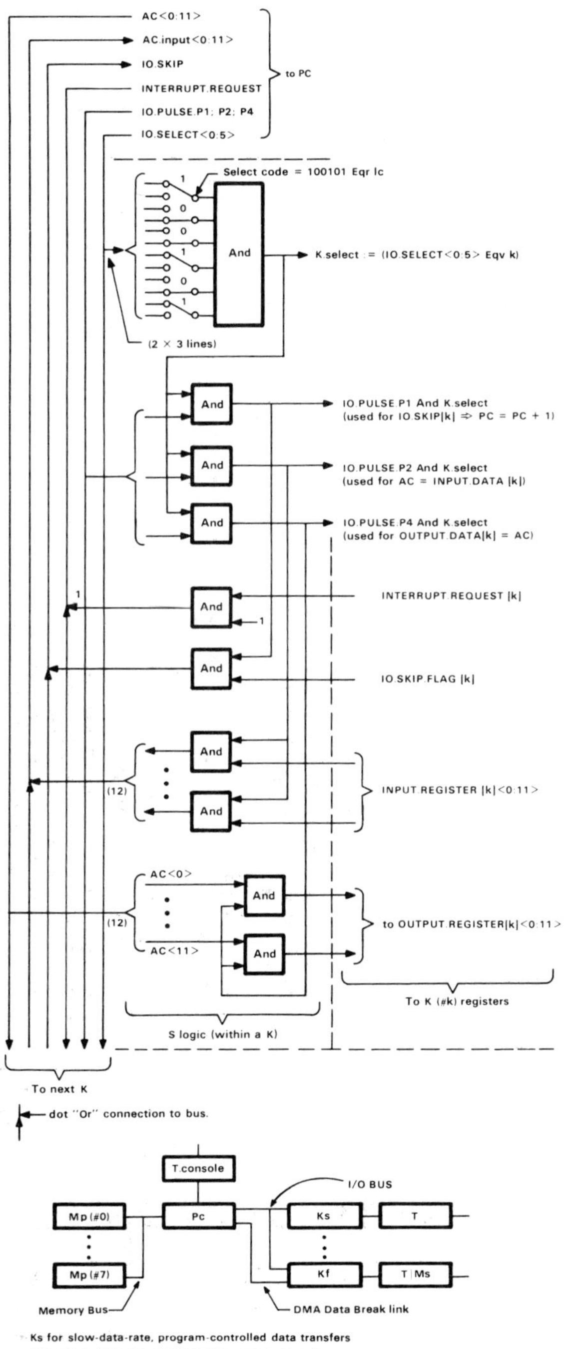

Figure 3. PDP-8 S('I/O Bus) logic and PMS diagrams.

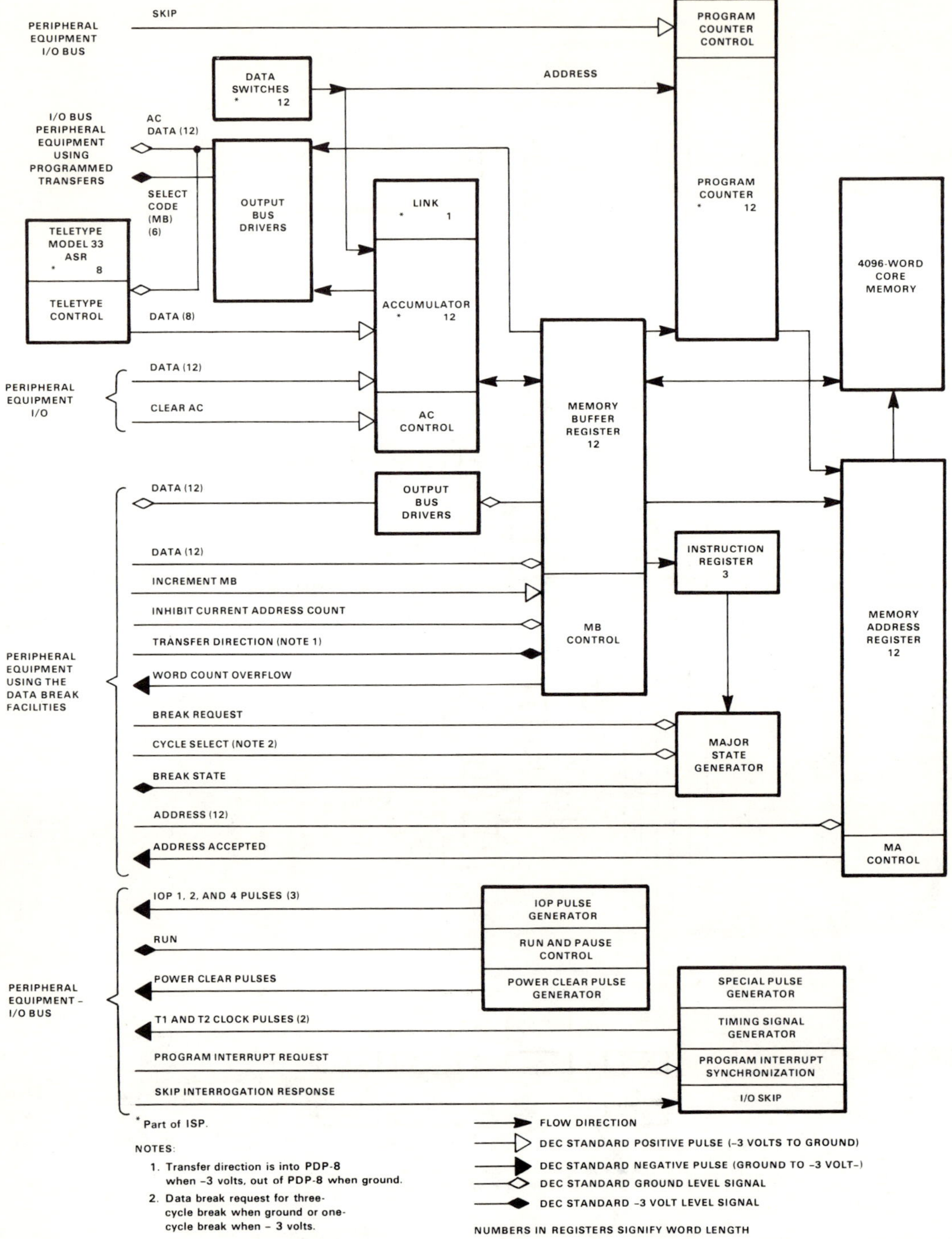

Figure 4. PDP-8 processor block diagram.

signal. Normally, the controller signal causing an interrupt is also connected to the skip input, and skip instructions are used in the software polling that determines the specific interrupting device.

The Data Break input for Direct Memory Access provides a direct access path for a processor or a controller to memory via the processor. The number of access ports to memory can be expanded to eight by using the DM01 Data Multiplexer, a switch. The DM01 port is requested from a processor (e.g., LINC or Model 338 Display Processor) or a controller (e.g., magnetic tape). A processor or controller supplies a memory address, a read or write access request, and then accepts or supplies data for the accessed word. In the configuration (Figure 1), Pc('LINC) and P('338) are connected to the multiplexer and make requests to memory for both their instructions and data in the same way as the PDP-8 processor. The global control of these processor programs is via the processor over the I/O Bus. The processor issues start and stop commands, initializes their state, and examines their final state when a program in the other processor halts or requires assistance.

When a controller is connected to the Data Break or to the DM01 Data Multiplexer, it only accesses memory for data. The most complex function these controllers carry out is the transfer of a complete block of data between the memory and a high speed transducer or a secondary memory (e.g., DECtape or disk). A special mode, the Three Cycle Data Break (described in Chapter 6), allows a controller to request the next word from a block in memory.

The DECtape was derived from M.I.T.'s Lincoln Laboratory LINCtape unit, as indicated in Chapter 7. Data was explicitly addressed by blocks (variable but by convention 128 words). Thus, information in a block could be replaced or rewritten at random. This operation was unlike the early standard IBM format magnetic tape in which data could be appended only to the end of a file.

PROGRAMMING LEVEL (ISP)

The ISP of the PDP-8 processor is probably the simplest for a general purpose stored program computer. It operates on 12-bit words, 12-bit integers, and 12-bit Boolean vectors. It has only a few data operators, namely, =, +, minus (negative of), Not, And, Slr 1(rotate bits left), Srr 1 (2 rotate bits right), (optional) ×, /, and normalize. However, there are microcoded instructions, which allow compound instructions to be formed in a single instruction.

The ISP of the basic PDP-8 is presented in Appendix 1 of this book. The 2^{12}-word memory (declared M[0:4095]<0;11>) is divided into 32 fixed-length pages of 128 words each (not shown in the ISPS description). Address calculation is based on references to the first page, Page.Zero, or to the current page of the Program Counter (PC\Program.Counter). The effective address calculation procedure, called eadd in Appendix 1, provides for both direct and indirect reference to either the current page or the first page. This scheme allows a 7-bit address to specify a local page address.

A 2^{15}-word memory is available on the PDP-8, but addressing more than 2^{12} words is comparatively inefficient. In the extended range, two 3-bit registers, the Program Field and Data Field registers, select which of the eight 2^{12}-word blocks are being actively addressed as program and data. These are not given in the ISPS description.

There is an array of eight 12-bit registers, called the Auto.Index registers, which resides in Page.Zero. This array (Auto.Index[0:7]<0 :11>:=M[#10: #17]<0:11>) possesses a useful property: whenever an indirect reference is made to it, a 1 is first added to its contents. (That is, there is a side effect to referencing.) Thus, address integers in the register can select the next member of a vector or string for accessing.

The processor state is minimal, consisting of a 12-bit accumulator (AC\Accumulator

<0:11>), an accumulator extension bit called the Link (L\Link), the 12-bit Program Counter, the RUN flip-flop, and the INTERRUPT.ENABLE bit. The external processor state is composed of console switches and an interrupt request.

The instruction format can also be presented as a decoding diagram or tree (Figure 5). Here, each block represents an encoding of bits in the instruction word. A decoding diagram allows one more descriptive dimension than the conventional, linear ISPS description, revealing the assignment of bits to the instruction. Figure 5 still requires ISPS descriptions for the memory, the processor state, the effective address calculation, the instruction interpreter, and the execution for each instruction. Diagrams such as Figure 5 are useful in the ISP design to determine which instruction operation codes are to be assigned to names and operations, and which instructions are free to be assigned (or encoded).

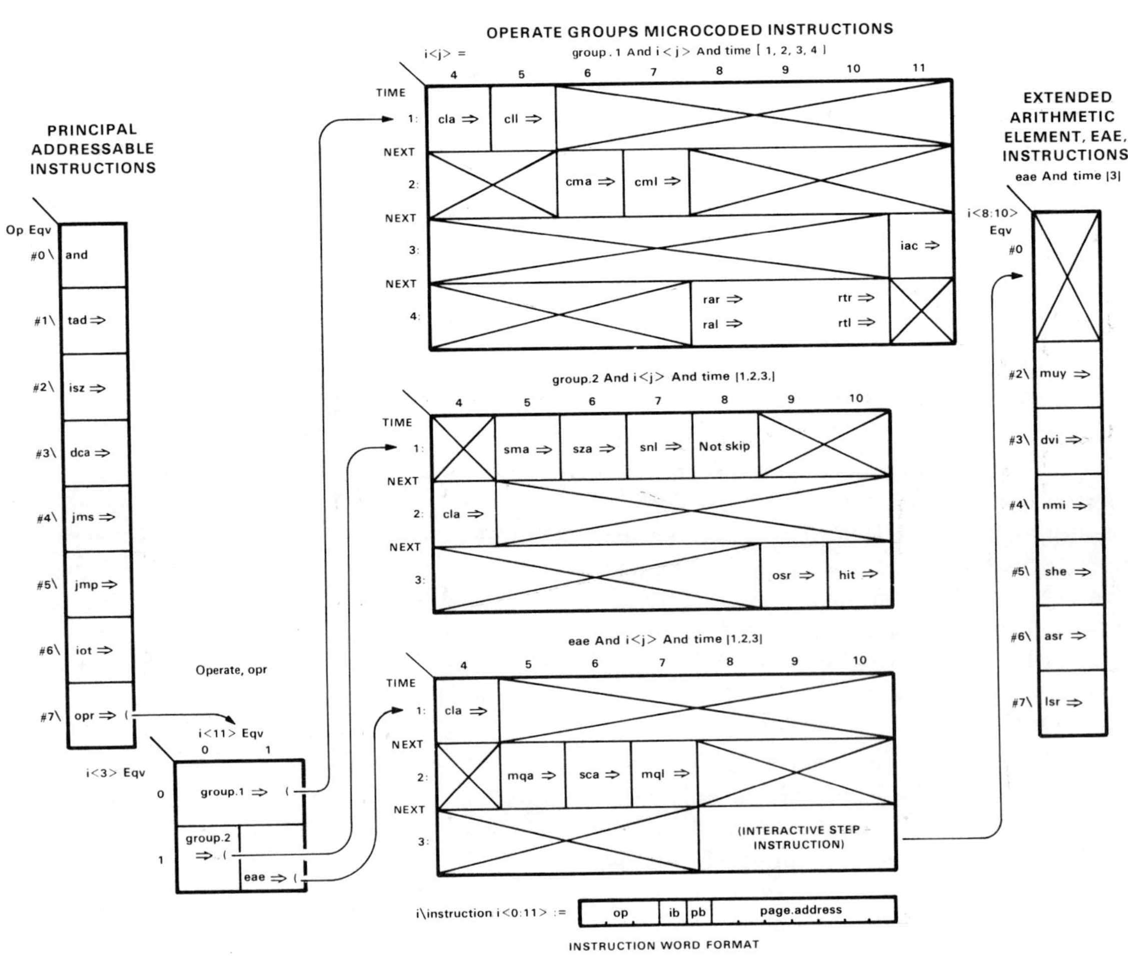

Figure 5. PDP-8 instruction decoding diagram.

There are eight basic instructions encoded by 3 opcode bits of the instruction, that is, op<0:2> := i<0:2>. Each of the first memory reference six instructions, where the opcode is less than or equal to 5, has four addressing modes (direct Page.Zero, direct Current.Page, indirect Page.Zero, and indirect Current.Page). The first six instructions in the following four categories are:

1. **Data transmission.**
   "deposit and clear Accumulator" (dca). (Note that the add instruction, tad, is used for both data transmission and arithmetic.)
2. **Binary arithmetic.**
   "two's complement add to the Accumulator" (tad).
3. **Binary Boolean.**
   "and to the Accumulator" (and).
4. **Program control.**
   "jump/set Program Counter" (jmp); "jump to subroutine" (jms); "index memory and skip if results are zero" (isz).

The subroutine calling instruction, jms, provides a method for transferring a link to the beginning (or head) of the subroutine. In this way arguments can be accessed indirectly, and a return is executed by a "jump indirect" instruction to the location storing the returned address. This straightforward subroutine call mechanism, although inexpensive to implement, requires reentrant and recursive subroutine calls to be interpreted by software rather than by hardware. A stack for subroutine linkage, as in the PDP-11, would allow the use of read-only memory program segments consisting of pure code. This scheme was adopted in the CMOS-8.

The "in-out transfer" instruction, opcode 6, IOT (op Eqv #6), uses the remaining nine bits of the instruction to specify instructions to input/output devices. The six IO.SELECT bits select 1 of 64 devices. Three conditional pulse commands to the selected device, IO.PULSE.1, IO.PULSE.2, and IO.PULSE.4, are controlled by the IOT, io.control<0:2> operation code bits. The instructions to a typical I/O device are:

1. Testing a Boolean Condition of an IO Device.
   If IO.PULSE.1 ⇒
   (If IO.SKIP.FLAG[IO.SELECT] ⇒
   PC = PC + 1)
2. Output data to a device from Accumulator.
   If IO.PULSE.4 ⇒
   (OUTPUT.REGISTER[IO.SELECT] = AC)
3. Input data from a device to Accumulator.
   If IO.PULSE.2 ⇒
   (AC = INPUT.REGISTER[IO.SELECT])

There are three microcoded instruction groups selected by (op<0:2> Eqv #7), called the operate instructions. The instruction decoding diagram (Figure 5) and the ISP description show the microinstructions which can be combined in a single instruction. These instructions are: operate group 1 ((op<0:2> Eqv #7) And Not ib) for operating on the processor state; operate group 2 ((op<0:2> Eqv #7) And ib<3> And i<11>) for testing the processor state; and the Extended Arithmetic Element group (op<0:2> Eqv #7 And i<3> And i<11>) for multiply, divide, etc. Within each instruction the remaining bits, <4:10> or <4:11>, are extended instruction (or opcode) bits; that is, the bits are microcoded to select additional instructions. In this way, an instruction is actually programmed (or microcoded, as it was originally named before "microprogramming" was used extensively). For example, the instruction, "set link to 1," is formed by coding the two microinstructions, "clear link" followed by "complement link."

```
If ((op <0:2> Eqv #7) And (group Eqv 0)) ⇒ (
    If i<5> ⇒ L = 0; Next
    If i<7> ⇒ L = Not L )
```

Thus, in operate group 1, the instructions "clear link, complement link, and set link" are formed by coding i<5,7> = 10,01, and 11, respectively. The operate group 2 instructions are used for testing the condition of the processor state. These instructions use bits 5, 6, and 8 to code tests for the Accumulator. The AC skip conditions are coded as never, always, AC Eql 0, AC Neg 0, AC Lss 0, AC Leq 0, AC Geq 0 and AC Gtr 0. The optional Extended Arithmetic Element (EAE) includes additional Multiplier Quotient (MQ) and Shift Counter (SC) registers and provides the hardwired operations "multiply," "divide," "logical shift left," "arithmetic shift," and "normalize." If all the nonredundant and useful variations in the two operate groups were available as separate instructions in the manner of the first seven (dca, tad, etc.), there would be approximately 7 + 12 (group 1) + 10 (group 2) + 6 (eae) = 35 instructions in the PDP-8.

THE INTERRUPT SCHEME

External conditions in the input/output devices can request that the processor be interrupted. Interrupts are allowed if the processor's interrupt enable flip-flop is set (If INTERRUPT.ENABLE Eqv 1). A request to interrupt (i.e., INTERRUPT.REQUEST=1) clears the interrupt enable bit (INTERRUPT.ENABLE = 0), and the processor behaves as though a "jump to subroutine" 0 instruction (jms 0) had been executed. A special IOT instruction (i<0:11> Eql #6001) followed by a "jump to subroutine indirect" to 0, and instruction (i<0:11> Eql #5220) returns the processor to the interruptable state with INTERRUPT.ENABLE a 1. The program time to save the processor state is six memory accesses (9 microseconds), and the time to restore the state is nine memory accesses (13.5 microseconds).

Only one interrupt level is provided in the hardware. If multiple priority levels are desired, programmed polling is required. Most I/O devices have to interrupt because they do not have a program-controlled device interrupt-enable switch. For multiple devices, approximately three cycles (4.5 microseconds) are required to poll each interrupter.

REGISTER TRANSFER LEVEL

More detail is required than is provided by either the PMS or ISP levels to describe the internal structure and behavior of the processor and memory. Figure 4 shows the registers and controllers at a block diagram level, and Figure 6 gives a more detailed version using PMS notation. Table 1 gives the permissible register transfer operations that the processor's sequential control circuit can give to the PDP-8 registers.

Although electrical pulse voltages and polarities are not shown in Table 1, the operations are presented in considerably more detail than shown in Figure 4. As Figure 6 shows, the registers in the processor cannot be uniquely assigned to a single function. In a minimal machine such as the PDP-8, functional separation is not economical. Thus, there are not completely distinct registers and transfer paths for memory, arithmetic, program, and instruction flow. (This sharing complicates understanding of the machine.) However, Figure 6 clarifies the structure considerably by defining all the registers in the processor (including temporaries and controls). For example, the Memory Buffer (MB\Memory.Buffer<0:11>) is used to hold the word being read from or written to memory. The Memory Buffer also holds one of the operands for binary operations (for example, AC = AC And MB). The Memory Buffer is also used as an extension of the Instruction.Register during the instruction interpretation. The addi-

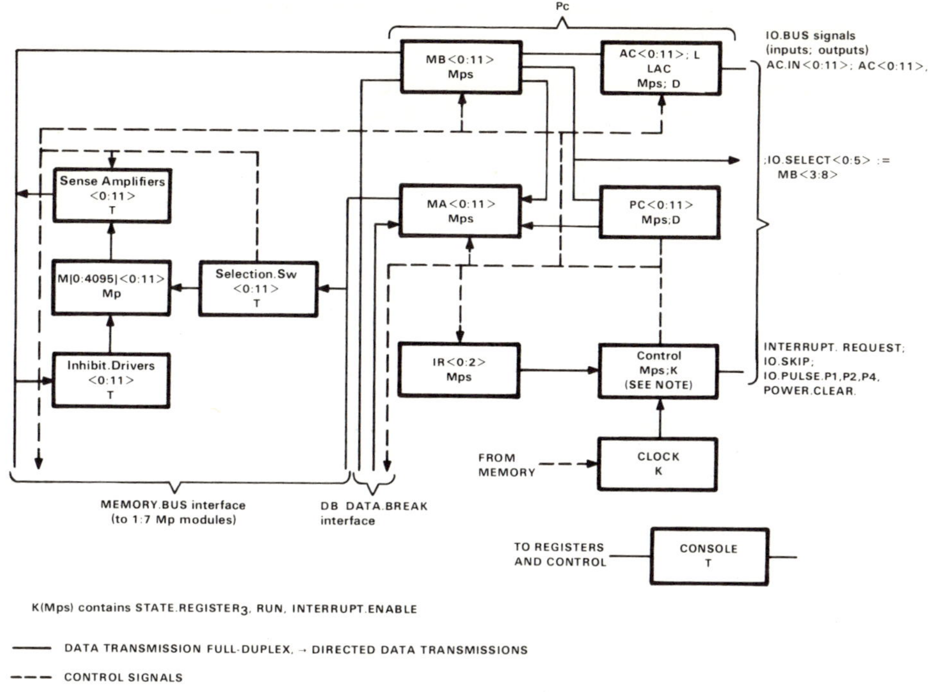

Figure 6. PDP-8 register transfer level PMS diagram.

tional physical registers, not part of the ISP, are:

MB\Memory.Buffer<0:11>
: Holds memory data, instruction, and operands.

MA\Memory.Address<0:11>
: Holds address of word in memory being accessed.

IR\Instruction.Register<0:2>
: Holds the value of current instruction being performed.

State.Register<0:1>
: A ternary state register holding the major state of memory cycle being performed - declared as 2 bits.

F\Fetch:=(If State.Register Eqv 0)
: Memory cycle to fetch instruction.

D\Deferred:=(If State.Register Eqv 1)
: Memory cycle to get address of operand.

E\Execute:=(If State.Register Eqv 2)
: Memory cycle to fetch (store) operand and execute the instruction.

The emphasis in Figure 6 is on the static definition (or declaration) of the information paths, the operations, and state. The ISP interpretation (Appendix 1) is the specification for the machine's behavior as seen by a program.

As the temporary hardware registers are added, a more detailed ISPS definition must be given in terms of time and in terms of temporary and control registers. Instead, a state diagram (Figure 7) is given to define the actual processor which is constrained by both the ISP registers, the temporary registers implied by the implementation, and time. The relationship among the state diagram, the ISP description, and the logic is shown in the hierarchy of Figure 1. In the relationships shown in the figures, one can observe that the ISPS definition does not have all the necessary detail for fully defining a

Table 1. PDP-8 Register Transfer Control Signals and Data Break Interface

AC\Accumulator, L\Link and combined L, AC LAC
AC = 0; AC = #7777; AC = Not AC; LAC = LAC + 1
L = 0; L = 1; L = Not L;
LAC = LAC Srr 1; LAC = LAC Srr 2; !rotates right
LAC = LAC Slr 1; LAC = LAC Slr 2; !rotates left
AC = AC Or SWITCHES; AC = AC And MB; AC = IO.BUS
AC = AC Xor MB; LAC = Carry (AC,MB);
(note that previous two commands form: LAC = AC + MB).

MB\Memory.Buffer
MB = 0; MB = MB + 1;
MB = PC; MB = AC; MB = M[MA]; MB = DB.DATA.

MA\Memory.Address
MA<0:4> = 0; MA = PC; MA = MB; MA<5:11> = MA<5:11>;
MA = DB.ADDRESS.

PC\Program.Counter
PC = 0; PC = PC + 1; PC<0:4> = 0;
PC = MB; PC<5:11> = MB<5:11>.

IR\Instruction.Register
IR = 0; IR = M[MA]<0:2>

M\Memory[0:4095]<0:11>
M[MA] = MB !write
MB = M[MA] !read

DB\DATA.BREAK interface

DB.DATA<0:11>	! Input to MB
DB.ADDRESS<0:11>	! Input to MA
MB<0:11>	
DB.REQUEST	! Control inputs to Pc
DB.DIRECTION	
DB.CYCLE.SELECT<0:11>	
ADDRESS.ACCEPTED	! Control outputs from Pc
WORD.COUNT.OK	
BREAK.STATE	

physical processor. The physical processor is constrained by actual hardware logic and lower level detals even at the circuit level. For example, a core memory is read by a destructive process and requires a temporary register (MB) to hold the value being rewritten. This is not represented within a single ISPS language statement because ISPS defines only the nondestructive transfer; however, it can be considered as the two parallel operations MB = M[MA]; M[MA] = 0. The explanation of the physical machine, including the rewriting of core using ISPS, is somewhat more tedious than the highest level description shown in Appendix 1. For this reason, the state diagram is used (Figure 7), and the description of the physical machine (in ISPS) is left as an exercise for the reader.

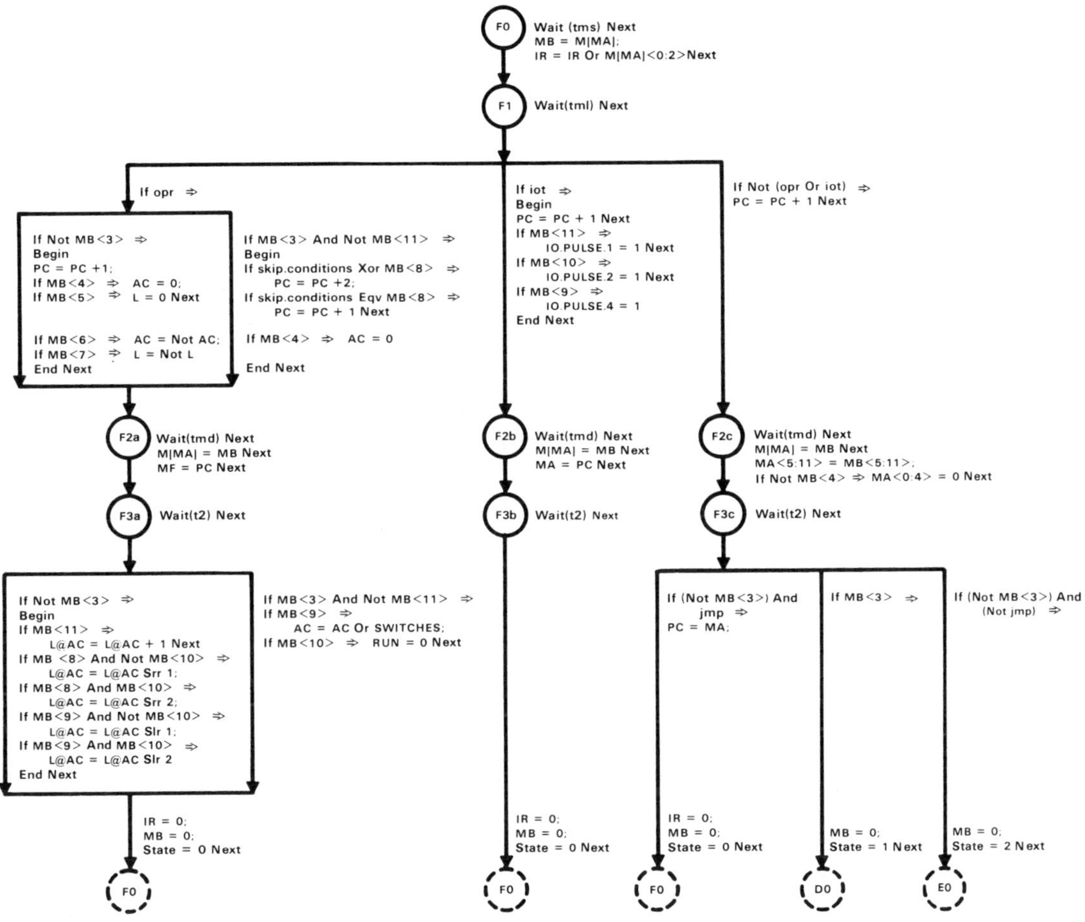

Figure 7. PDP-8 Pc state diagram (part 1 of 2).

The state diagram (Figure 7) is fundamentally driven by minor clock cycles as seen from both the state diagram and the times when the four clock signals are generated. Thus, there are 3 (State.Register Eqv #0,#1,#2) × 4 (clock) or 12 major states in the implementation. The Instruction Register is used to obtain two more states, F2b and F3b, for the description. The State.Register values 0, 1, and 2 correspond to fetching, deferred or indirect addressing (i.e., fetching an operand address), and executing. The state diagram does not describe the Extended Arithmetic Element operation, the interrupt state, or the data break states (which add 12 more states). The initialization procedure, including the console state diagram, is also not given. One should observe that, at the beginning of the memory cycle, a new State.Register

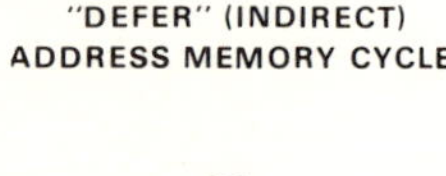

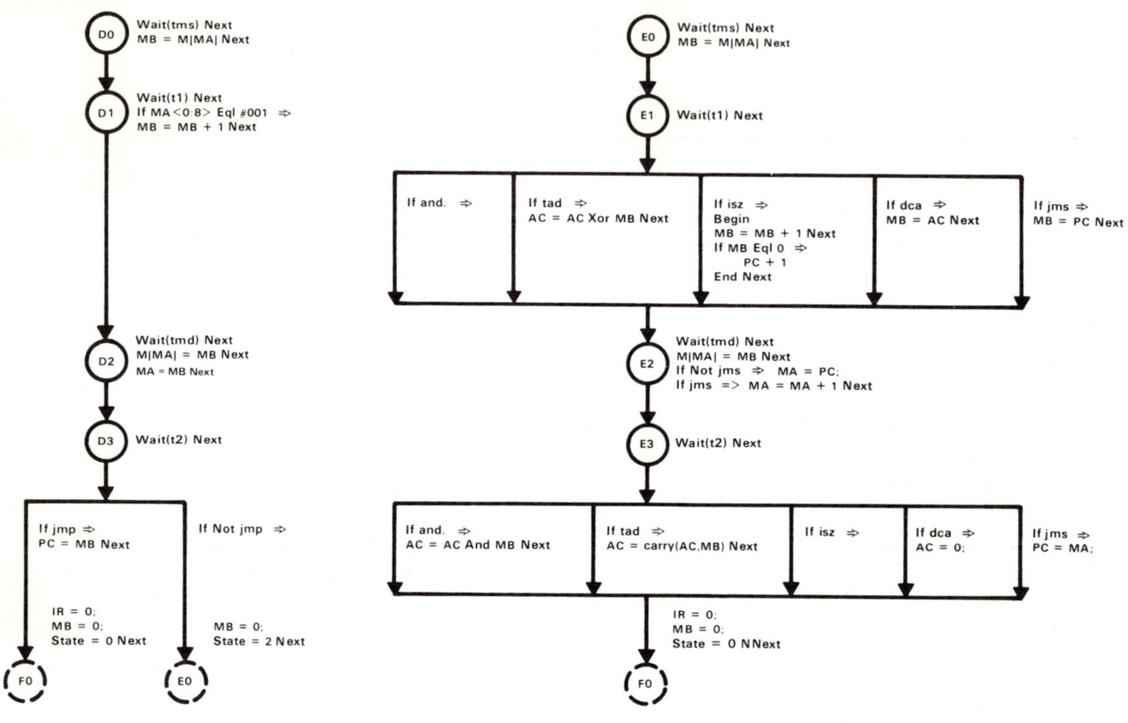

Figure 7. PDP-8 Pc state diagram (part 2 of 2).

value is selected. The State.Register value is always held for the remainder of the cycle; i.e., only the sequences F0, F1, F2, F3, or D0, D1, D2, D3, or E0, E1, E2, E3 are permitted.

LOGIC DESIGN LEVEL (REGISTERS AND DATA OPERATIONS)

Proceeding from the register transfer and ISP descriptions, the next level of detail is the logic module. Typical of the level is the 1-bit logic module for an accumulator bit, AC<j>, illustrated in Figure 8. The horizontal data inputs in the figure are to the logic module from AC<j>, MB<j>, AC<j> input from the IO.Bus.In, and SWITCHES<j>. The control signal inputs whose names are identified using the vertical bar (e.g., |AC = 0|) command the register operations (i.e., the transfers). They are labeled by their respective ISP operations (for example, AC = AC And MB, AC = AC Slr 1, for rotate once left). The sequential state machine, for the processor Pc(K), generates these control signal inputs using a combinational circuit such as the one shown in Figure 9.

LOGIC DESIGN LEVEL (PC CONTROL, PC(K) SEQUENTIAL STATE MACHINE NETWORK)

The output signals from the processor sequential machine (Figure 9) can be generated in

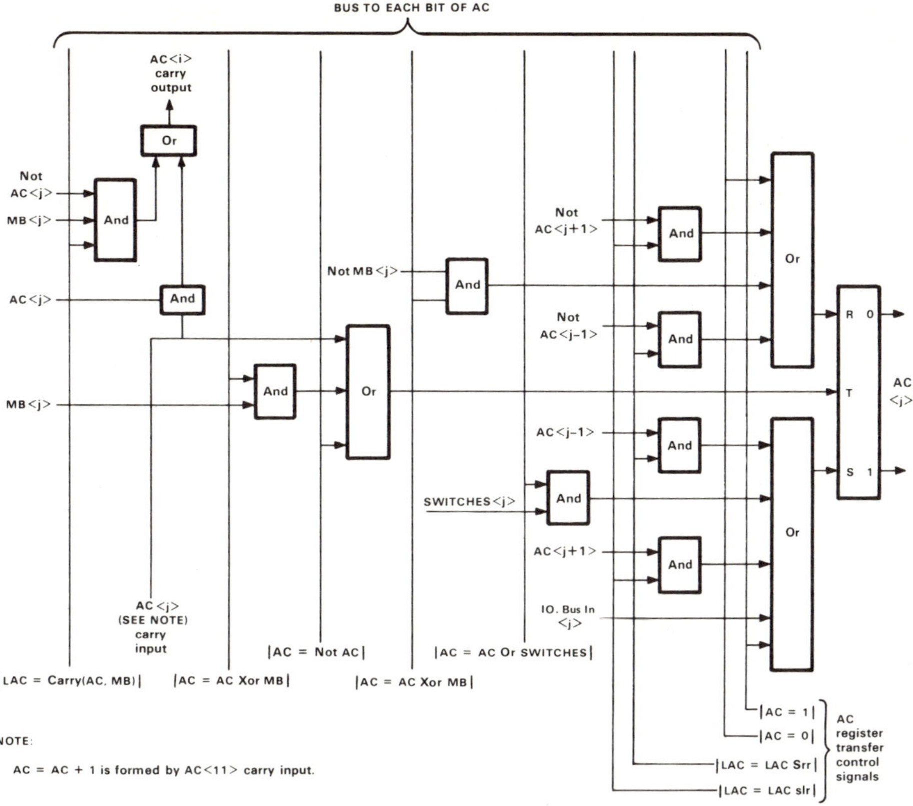

Figure 8. PDP-8 AC<j> bit logic diagram.

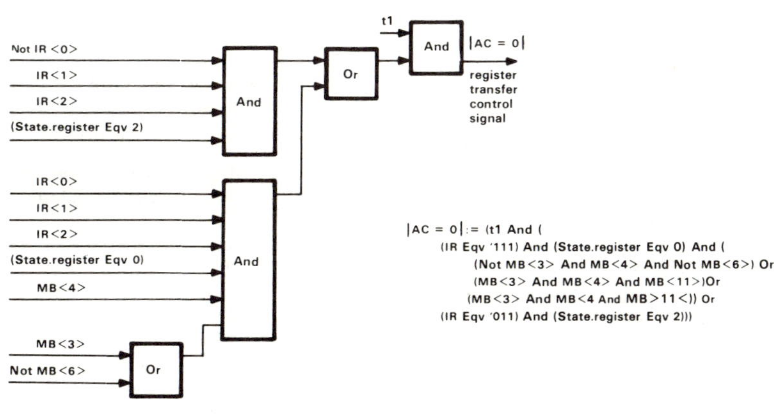

Figure 9. PDP-8 Pc(K) AC = 0 signal logic equation and diagram.

a straightforward fashion by formulating the Boolean expressions directly from the state diagram in Figure 7. For example, the AC = 0 control signal is expressed algebraically and with a combinational network in Figure 9. Obviously, these Boolean output control signals are functions which include the clock, the State.Register, and the states of the arithmetic registers (for example, AC = 0, L = 0, etc.). The expressions should be factored and minimized so as to reduce the hardware cost of the control for the interpreter. Although the sequential controller for the processor is mentioned here only briefly, it constitutes about half the logic within the processor.

CIRCUIT LEVEL

The final level of description is the circuits that form the logic functions of storage (flip-flops) and gating (NAND gates). Figures 10 and 11 illustrate some of these logic devices in detail. In Figure 10 a direct set/direct clear flip-flop (a sequential logic element) is described in

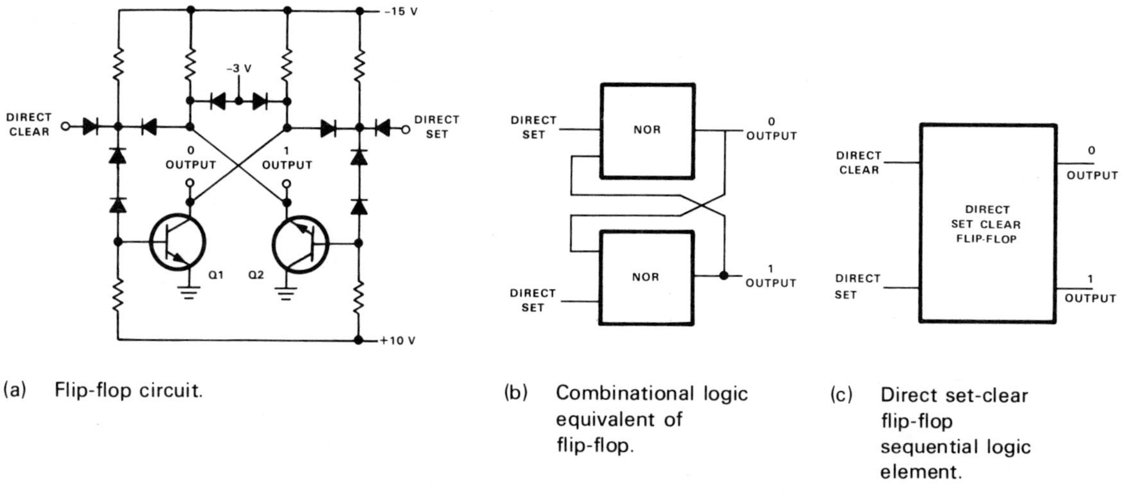

(a) Flip-flop circuit.

(b) Combinational logic equivalent of flip-flop.

(c) Direct set-clear flip-flop sequential logic element.

Table of Circuit Input-Output

Outputs (At t)		Inputs		Outputs (At t+) (See Note)	
1	0	Direct Set	Direct Clear	1	0
0	-3	-3	-3	0	-3
-3	0	-3	-3	-3	0
-3	0	-3	0	-3	0
0	-3	-3	0	-3	0
-3	0	0	-3	0	-3
0	-3	0	-3	0	-3

Table of Flip-Flop Input-Output

Outputs (At t)		Inputs		Outputs (at t+) (See Note)	
1	0	Direct Set	Direct Clear	1	0
1	0	0	0	1	0
0	1	0	0	0	1
0	1	0	1	0	1
1	0	0	1	0	1
0	1	1	0	1	0
1	0	1	0	1	0

Note this is not an "ideal" sequential circuit element because there is no delay in the output.

Figure 10. PDP-8 direct-coupled flip-flop and logic diagram.

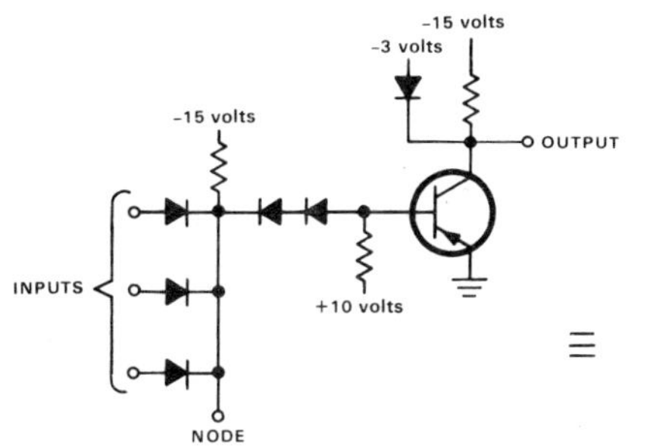

(a) Multiple input inverter circuit.

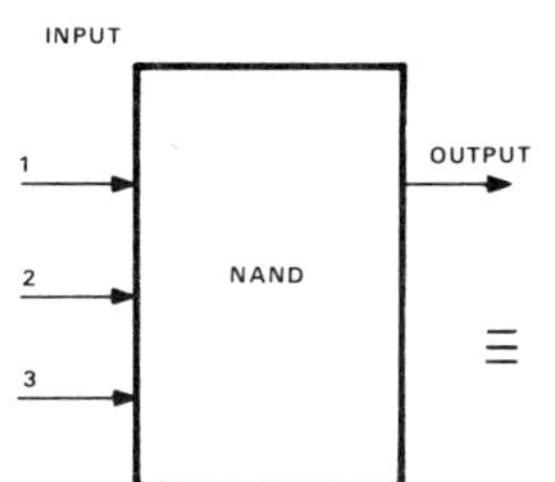

(b) NAND logic element.

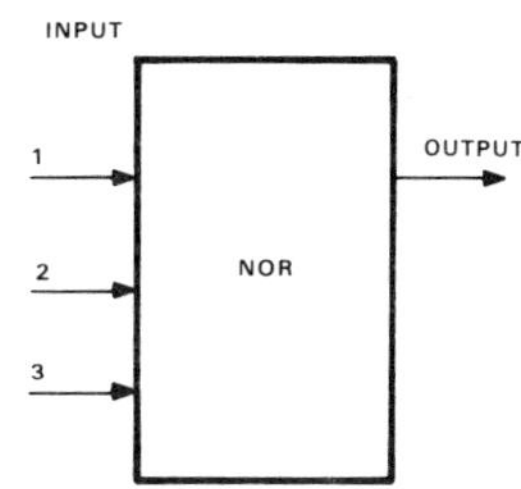

(c) NOR logic element.

Table of Circuit Behavior

Input 1	2	3	Output
0	0	0	-3
0	0	-3	-3
0	-3	0	-3
0	-3	-3	-3
-3	0	0	-3
-3	0	-3	-3
-3	-3	0	-3
-3	-3	-3	0

Table of NAND Behavior

Input 1	2	3	Output
0	0	0	1
0	0	1	1
0	1	0	1
0	1	1	1
1	0	0	1
1	0	1	1
1	1	0	1
1	1	1	0

Table of NOR Behavior

Input 1	2	3	Output
1	1	1	0
1	1	0	0
1	0	1	0
1	0	0	0
0	1	1	0
0	1	0	0
0	0	1	0
0	0	0	1

Figure 11. PDP-8 combinational circuit and logic diagram.

terms of circuit implementation, combinational logic equivalent, a state table, and its algebraic behavior. Note that this is not a conventional textbook circuit because it has no output delay and responds directly and immediately to an input. Some conventional sequential logic elements are used in the PDP-8, including RS (Reset-Set), T(Trigger), D(Delay), and JK. A delay in the flip-flops makes them behave in the same way as the "textbook" primitives in sequential circuit theory. The outputs require a series delay, Δt, such that, if the inputs change at time, t, the outputs will not change until $t + \Delta t$. In actuality, the PDP-8 uses capacitor-diode gates at the flip-flop inputs so that input changes will not be noticed until after the clock passes. This achieves the same effect.

Figure 11 illustrates the combinational logic elements used in the PDP-8. The circuit selection is limited to the inverter circuit with single or multiple inputs. These are more familiarly called NAND gates or NOR gates, depending on whether one uses positive and/or negative logic level definitions (described in Chapter 4).

The core memory structure is given in Figure 6. A more detailed block diagram showing the core stack with its twelve 64 × 64 1-bit core planes is needed. Such a diagram, though still a functional block diagram, takes on some of the aspects of a circuit diagram because a core memory is largely circuit level details. The memory (Figure 12) consists of the component units: the two address decoders (which select 1 each of 64 outputs in the X and Y axis directions of the coincident current memory); selection switches (which transform a coincident logic address into a high current path to switch the magnetic cores); the 12 inhibit drivers (which switch a high current or no current into a plane when either a 1 or 0 is rewritten); 12 sense amplifiers (which take the induced low sense voltage from a selected core from a plane being switched or not switched and transform it into a 1 or 0); and the core stack, an array M[#0:#7777]<0:11>. Figure 12 also includes the associated circuit level hardware needed in the core memory operation (e.g., power supplies, timing, and logic signal level conversion amplifiers).

The timing signals are generated within the control portion of the processor and are shown together with processor clock in Figure 13. The process of reading a word from memory is:

1. A 12-bit selection address is established on the MA<0:11> address lines, which is 1 of #10000 (or 4096) unique numbers. The upper 6 bits <0:5> select 1 of 64 groups of Y addresses, and the lower 6 bits <6:11> select 1 of 64 groups of X addresses.
2. The read logic signal is made a 1 at time t2.
3. A high current path flows via the X and Y selection switches. In each of the X and Y directions, 64 × 12 cores have selection current (Ix and Iy). Only one core in each plane is selected since Ix = Iy = Iswitching/2, and the current at the selected intersection = Ix + Iy = Iswitching.
4. If a core is switched to 0 (by having Iswitching amperes through it), then a 1 is present and is read at the output of the plane bit sense amplifiers. A sense amplifier receives an input from a winding that threads every core of every bit within a core plane [#0:#7777]. All 12 cores of the selected word are reset to 0. The time at which the sense amplifier is observed is tms (the memory strobe), which also causes the transfer MB = M[MA].
5. The read current is turned off by timing in the memory module.
6. The inhibit and write (slightly delayed) logic signals are turned on at time t1. The bit inhibit signal is present or not, depending on whether a 0 or 1, respectively, is written into a bit.

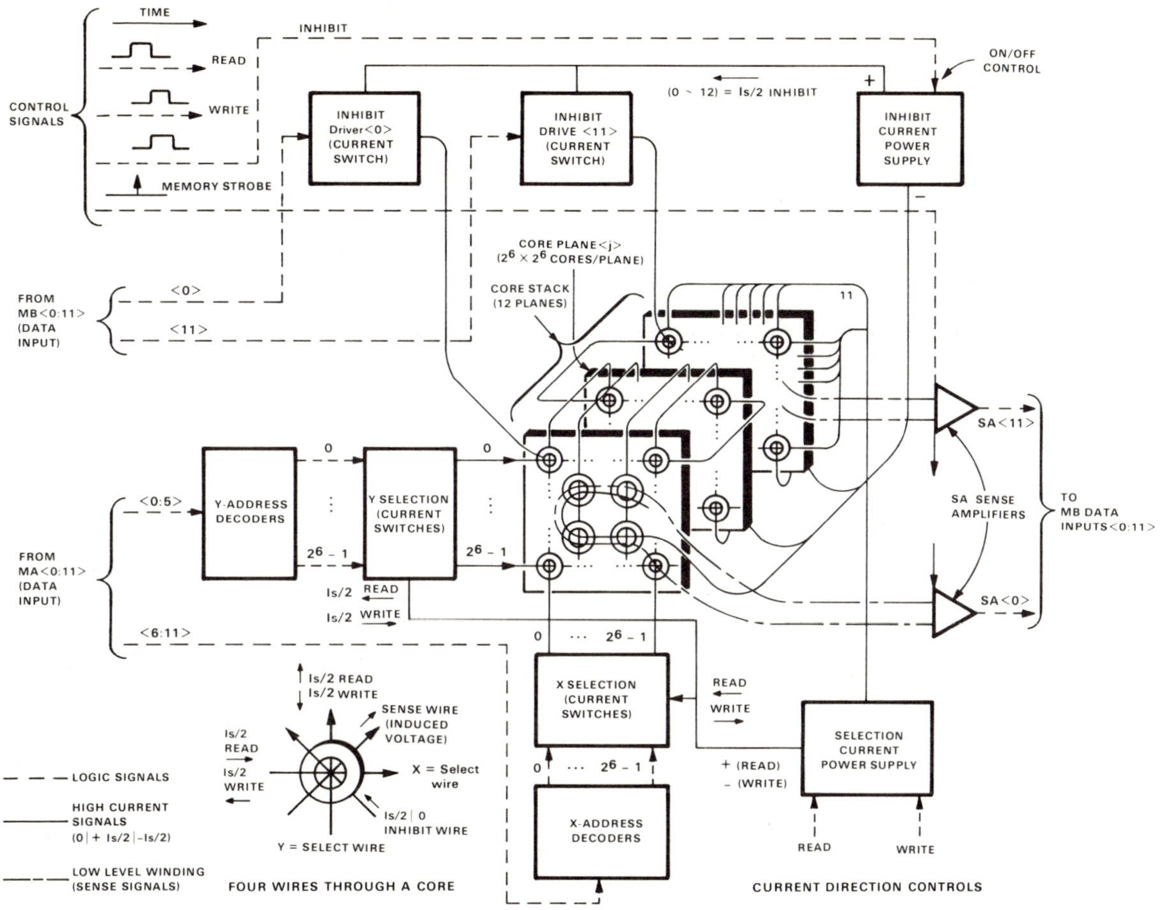

Figure 12. PDP-8 four-wire coincident current (three dimensions) core memory logic diagram.

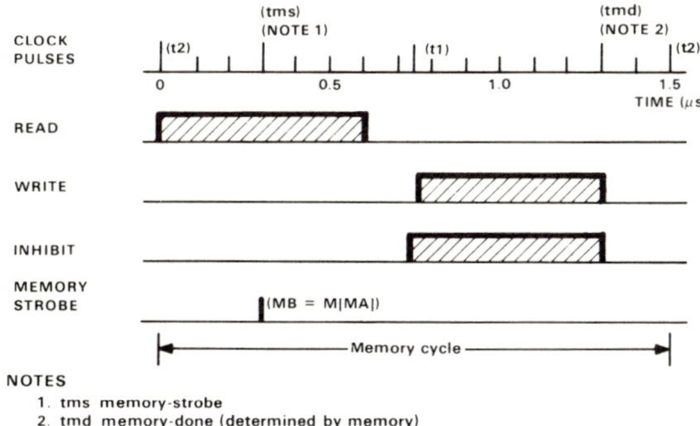

Figure 13. PDP-8 clock and memory timing diagram.

7. A high current path flows via the X and Y selection switches, but in an opposite direction to the read case (see item 2). If a 1 is written, no inhibit current is present and the net current in the selected core is −Iswitching. If a 0 is written, the current is −Iswitching +(Iswitching/2) and the core remains reset.
8. The inhibit and write logic signals are turned off at time tmd specified by timing in the memory module, and the memory cycle is completed.

Device Level

For a discussion of the behavior of the transistor as it is used in these switching circuit primitives, the reader should consult semiconductor electronics and physics textbooks. It is hoped that the reader has gained a sense of how to think about the hierarchical decomposition of computers into particular levels of analysis (and synthesis) and that the hierarchical approach will be of aid in the reading of Part III.

Opposite:

Top, left to right:
- PDT-11 programmable data terminal.
- VAX-11/780.

Bottom, left to right:
- Model 20 central processor.
- PDP-11 packaging showing cabinet level integration.

PART III

THE PDP-11 FAMILY

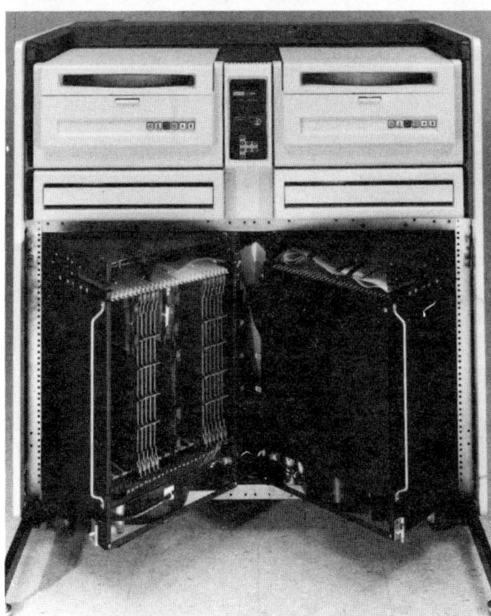

The PDP-11 Family

The PDP-11 has evolved quite differently from the other computers discussed in this book and, as a result, provides an independent and interesting story. Like the other computers, the factors that have created the various PDP-11 machines have been market and technology based, but they have generated a large number of implementations (ten) over a relatively short (eight-year) lifetime. Because there are multiple implementations spanning a performance range at the same time, the PDP-11 provides problems and insight which did not occur in the evolutions of the traditional mini (PDP-8 Family), the optimal price/performance machines (18-bit), and the high performance timesharing machines (the DECsystem 10). The PDP-11 designs cover a range of 500:1 in system price ($500 to $250,000) and 500:1 in memory size (4 Kwords to 2 Mwords).

Rather than attempt to summarize the goals of designers, sentiments of users, or the thoughts of researchers, the discussion of the PDP-11 is divided into chapters which, in most cases, consist of papers written contemporaneously with various important PDP-11 developments. The chapters are arranged in five categories: introduction to the PDP-11, conceptual basis for PDP-11 models, implementations of the PDP-11, evaluation of the PDP-11, and the virtual address extension of the PDP-11.

INTRODUCTION TO THE PDP-11

Chapter 9, first published when the PDP-11 was announced, introduces the PDP-11 architecture, gives its goals, and predicts how it might evolve. The concept of a family of machines is quite strong, but the actual development of that family has differed a good deal from the projections in this chapter. The major reasons (discussed in Chapter 16) for the disparity between the predicted and actual evolution are:

1. The notion of designing with improved technology, especially for a family of machines, was not understood in 1970. This understanding came later and was presented in a paper in 1972 [Bell *et al.*, 1972b].
2. The Unibus proved unacceptable for intercommunications at the very high and low-end designs. Although Chapter 9 suggests a multiprocessor and multiple Unibuses for high-end designs, such a structure did not evolve as a standard.
3. The address space for both physical and virtual memory was too small.

4. Several data-type extensions were not predicted. Although floating-point arithmetic was envisioned, the character string and decimal operations were not envisioned, or at least were not described. These data-types evolved in response to market needs that did not exist in 1970.

CONCEPTUAL BASIS FOR THE PDP-11 MODELS

Chapters 10 and 11 consist of two papers that form some of the conceptual basis for the various PDP-11 models. Chapter 10 by Strecker is an exposition of cache memory structure and its design parameters. The cache memory concept is the basis of three PDP-11 models, the PDP-11/34A, the PDP-11/60, and the PDP-11/70, in addition to the cache-8 (Chapter 7) and the KL10 processor for the PDP-10 (Chapter 21).

Strecker gives the performance evaluation in terms of cache miss ratios, whereas the reader is probably interested in performance or speedup. These two measures, shown in Figure 1, are related [Lee, 1969] in the following way (assuming an infinitely fast processor):

p = Total number of memory accesses by the processor Pc
m = Number of memory accesses that are missed by the cache and have to be referred to the primary memory Mp
$t.c$ = Cycle time of cache memory Mc
$t.p$ = Cycle time of primary memory Mp
R = $t.p/t.c$ (ratio of memory speeds), where R is typically 3 to 10

The relative execution speeds are:

$$t\ (no\ cache) = pR$$
$$t\ (to\ cache) = p + mR$$
$$speedup = pR/(p + mR) = R/(1 + (m/p)\ R)$$
$$a = miss\ ratio = m/p$$

Therefore:

$$speedup = R/(1 + aR) = 1/(a + 1/R)$$

Note that:

If a = 0 (100% hit), the speedup is R
If a = 1 (100% miss), the speedup is $R/(1 + R)$, i.e., the speedup is less than 1 (i.e., time to reference both memories)

Chapter 11 contains a unique discussion of buses – the communications link between two or more computer system components. Although buses are a standard of interconnection, they are the least understood element of computer design

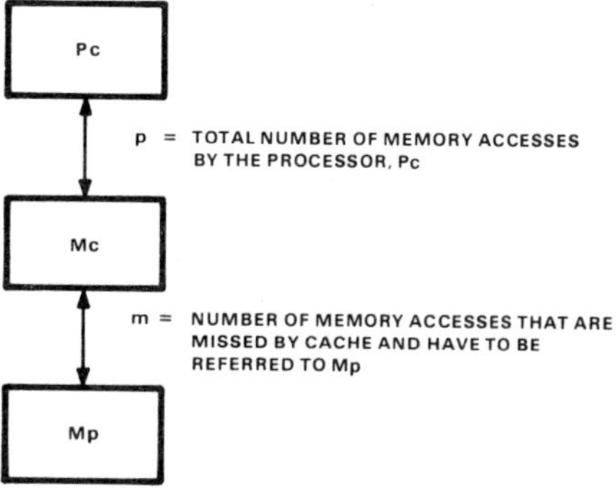

Figure 1. The structure of Pc, Mcache, and Mp of cached computer.

because their implementation is distributed in various components. Their behavior is difficult to express in a state diagram or other conventional representation (except a timing diagram) because the operation of buses is inherently pipelined; hence, design principles and understanding are minimal.

In Chapter 11, Levy first characterizes the intercommunication problem into the constituent dialogues that must take place between pairs of components. After giving a general model of interconnection, Levy provides examples of PDP-11 buses that characterize the general design space. Finally, he discusses the various intercommunications (model) aspects: arbitration (deciding which components can intercommunicate), data transmission, and error control.

IMPLEMENTATIONS OF THE PDP-11

Chapter 12 is a descriptive narrative about the design of the LSI-11 at the chip, board, and backplane levels. Since it was written from the viewpoint of a knowledgeable user, it lacks some of the detail that the designers at Western Digital (Roberts, Soha, Pohlman) or at DEC (Dickhut, Dickman, Olsen, Titelbaum) might have provided. A detailed account of the chip-level design is available, however [Soha and Pohlman, 1974].

Two design levels are described: the three chip set microprogrammed computer used to interpret the PDP-11 instruction set, and the particular PMS-level components that are integrated into a backplane to form a hardware system. Chapter 12 also provides a discussion of the microprogramming tradeoff that took place between the chip and module levels. This tradeoff was necessary to carry out the clock, console, refresh, and power-fail functions which are normally in hardware.

Since the time that the Sebern paper (Chapter 12) was written, packaging for LSI-11 systems has moved in two directions: toward the single board microcomputer and toward modularity. The single board microcomputer concept is exemplified by the bounded system shown in Figure 2. This integrated system contains an LSI-11 chip set, 32 Kwords of memory, connectors for six communication line interfaces, and a controller for two floppy disk drives. It uses 175 circuits (to implement the same functionality using standard LSI-11 modules would require 375 integrated circuits). The modularity direction is exemplified by the LSI-11/2, for which typical option modules are shown in Figure 3.

Unlike the reports from an architect's or reporter's viewpoint, Chapter 13 is a direct account of the design process from the project viewpoint. A mid-range machine is an inherently difficult design because it is neither the lowest cost nor

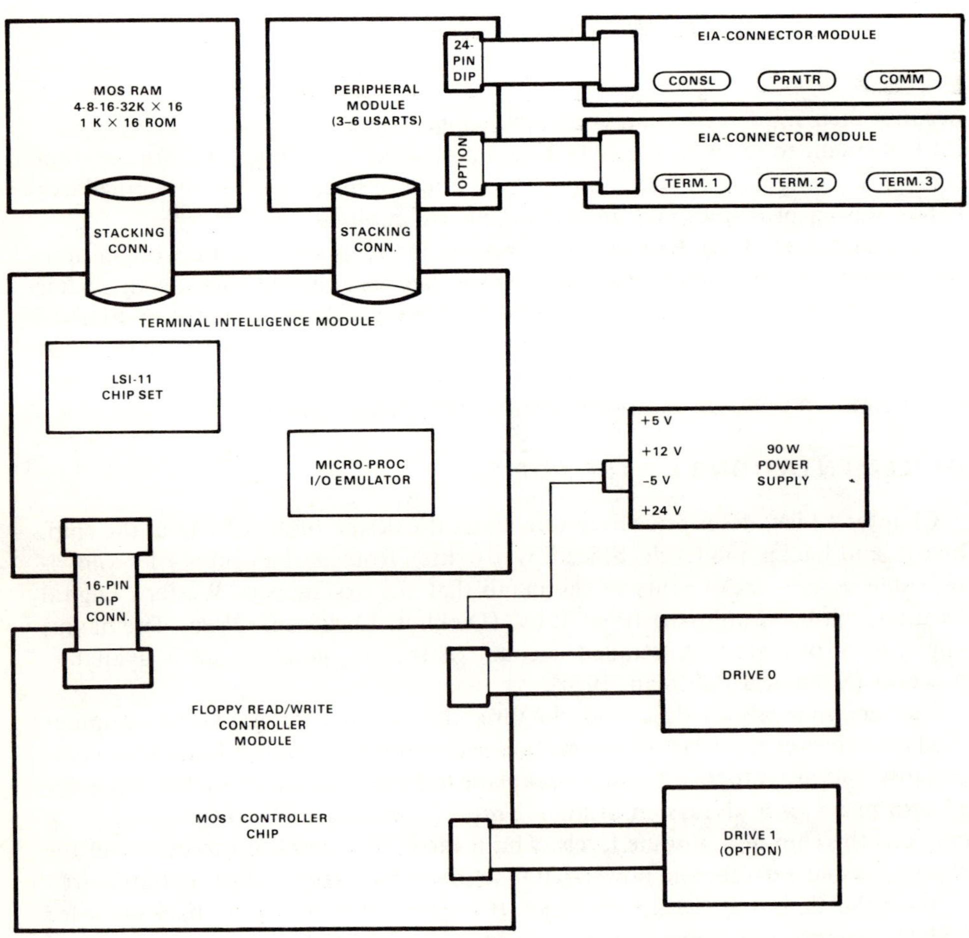

Figure 2. A bounded LSI-11 based system.

the highest performance machine of the family, and thus has to have the right balance of features, price, and performance against criteria that are usually vague.

Four interesting aspects of computer engineering are shown in the PDP-11/60: the cache to reduce Unibus traffic; trace-driven design of floating-point arithmetic processors; writable control store; and special features for reliability, availability, and maintainability.

The Unibus was found to be inadequate for handling all the data traffic in high performance systems, but by using a cache, most processor references do not use the Unibus and so leave it free for I/O traffic. In the PDP-11/60 work described in this chapter, Mudge uses Strecker's (Chapter 10) program traces and methodology. The cache design process is implicit in the way in which the work is carried out to determine the structure parameters. Sensitivity plots are used to determine the effects of varying each parameter of the design. The time between changes of context is an important parameter because all real-time and multiprogrammed systems have many context switches. The study leading to the determination of block size is also given.

Microprogramming is used to provide both increased user-level capability and increased reliability, availability, and maintainability. The writable control store option is described together with its novel use for data storage. This option has been recently used for emulating the PDP-8 at the OS/8 operating system level.

Chapter 14 presents a comprehensive comparison of the eight processor implementations used in the ten PDP-11 models. The work was carried out to investigate various design styles for a given problem, namely, the interpretation of the PDP-11 instruction set. The tables provide valuable insight into processor implementations, and the data is particularly useful because it comes from Snow and Siewiorek, non-DEC observers examining the PDP-11 machines.

The tables include:

1. A set of instruction frequencies, by Strecker, for a set of ten different applications. (The frequencies do not reflect all uses, e.g., there are no floating-point instructions, nor has operating system code been analyzed.)
2. Implementation cost (modules, integrated circuits, control store widths) and performance (micro- and macroinstruction times) for each model.
3. A canonical data path for all PDP-11 implementations against which each processor is compared.

With this background data, a top-down model is built which explains the performance (macroinstruction time) of the various implementations in terms of the microinstruction execution and primary memory cycle time. Because these two parameters do not fully explain (model) performance, a bottom-up approach is also used, including various design techniques and the degree of processor overlap. This analysis of a constrained problem should provide useful insight to both computer and general digital systems designers.

KD11-HA
LSI-11/2 microcomputer processor

MSV11-D
Dynamic MOS RAM memory

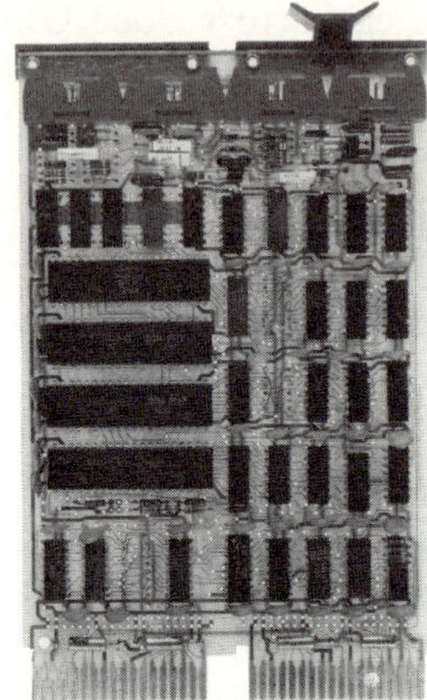

DLV11-J
Four-line serial interface

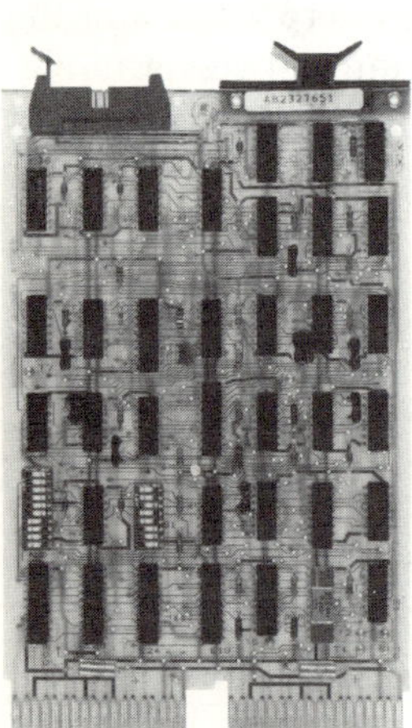

IBV11-A
IEEE instrument bus interface

MRV11-BA
4K UV PROM board with 256-word RAM

MRV11-AA
4K PROM board

Figure 3. The double-height modules forming the LSI-11/2 (part 1 of 2).

DRV11
16-bit parallel interface

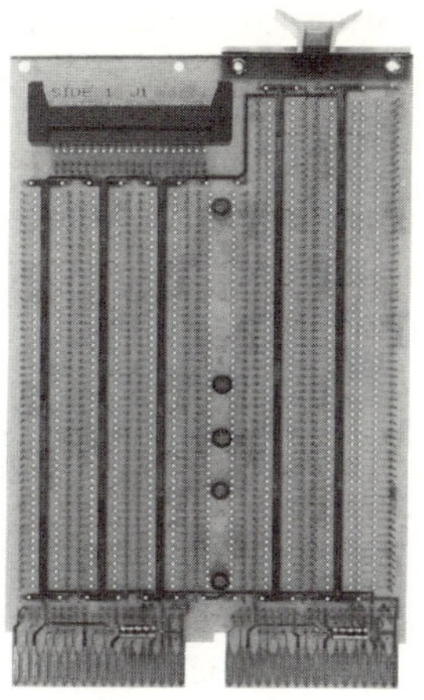

DCK11-AC
Interface foundation kit

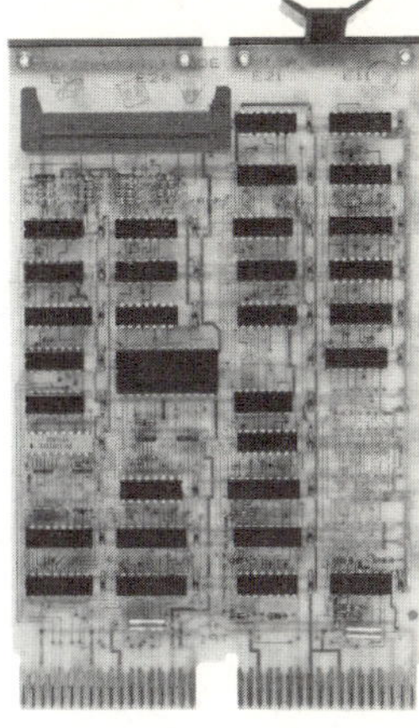

RXV11
Interface module for RX01 floppy disk

REV11-A
Refresh/ bootstrap/ diagnostic/ terminator module

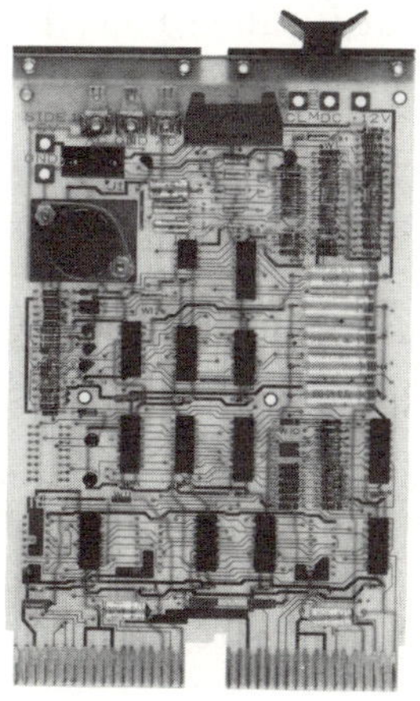

KPV11-A
Power sequencer/ line clock module

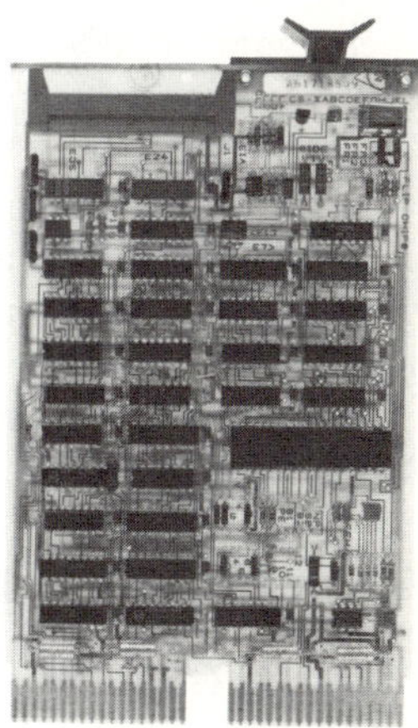

DLV11
Single-line serial interface

Figure 3. The double-height modules forming the LSI-11/2 (part 2 of 2).

EVALUATION OF THE PDP-11

Chapter 15 evaluates the PDP-11 as a machine for executing FORTRAN. Because FORTRAN is the most often executed language for the PDP-11, it is important to observe the PDP-11 architecture as seen by the language processor – its user. The first FORTRAN compiler and object (run) time system are described, together with the evolutionary extensions to improve performance. The FORTRAN IV-PLUS (optimizing) compiler is only briefly discussed because its improvements, largely due to compiler optimization technology, are less relevant to the PDP-11 architecture.

The chapter title, "Turning Cousins into Sisters," overstates the compatibility problem since the five variations of the PDP-11 instruction set for floating-point arithmetic are made compatible by essentially providing five separate object (run) time systems and a single compiler. This transparency is provided quite easily by "threaded code," a concept discussed in the chapter.

The first version of the FORTRAN machine was a simple stack machine. As such, the execution times turned out to be quite long. In the second version, the recognition of the special high-frequency-of-use cases (e.g., $A \leftarrow 0$, $A \leftarrow A + 1$) and the improved conventions for three-address operations (to and from the stack) allowed speedup factors of 1.3 and 2.0 for floating-point and integers.

It is interesting to compare Brender's idealized FORTRAN IV-PLUS machine with the Floating-Point Processors (on the PDP-11/34, 11/45, 11/55, 11/60, and 11/70). If the FORTRAN machine described in the paper is implemented in microcode and made to operate at Floating-Point Processor speeds, the resulting machines operate at roughly the same speed and programs occupy roughly the same program space.

The basis for Chapter 16, "What Have We Learned From the PDP-11?" [Bell and Strecker, 1976] was written to critique the original expository paper on the PDP-11 (Chapter 9) and to compare the actual with the predicted evolution. Four critical technological evolutions – bus bandwidth, PMS structure, address space, and data-type – are examined, along with various human organizational aspects of the design.

The first section of Chapter 16 compares the original goals of the PDP-11 (Chapter 9) with the goals of possible future models from the original design documents. Next, the ISP and PMS evolutions, including the VAX extension, are described. The Unibus characteristics are especially interesting as the bus turns out to be more cost-effective over a wider range than would be expected.

The section of the chapter which deals with multiprocessors and multicomputers gives the rationale behind the slow evolution of these structures. Because a number of these computer structures have been built (especially at Carnegie-Mellon University), they are described in detail.

The final section of the chapter interrelates technology with the various implementations (including VAX-11/780) that have occurred. Table 6 gives the performance characteristics for the various models with the relevant technology, contributions, and implementation techniques required to span the range.

VIRTUAL ADDRESS EXTENSION OF THE PDP-11

The latest member of the PDP-11 family, the Virtual Address Extension 11 or VAX-11, is described in Chapter 17. This paper, by the architect of VAX-11, discusses the new architecture and its first implementation, the VAX-11/780.

VAX-11 extends the PDP-11 to provide a large, 32-bit virtual address for each user process. The architecture includes a compatibility mode that allows PDP-11 programs written for the RSX-11M program environment to run unchanged. In this way, PDP-11 programs can be moved among VAX and PDP-11 computers, depending on the user's address size and computational and generality needs.

Chapter 17 provides a clean, somewhat terse, yet comprehensive description of the VAX-11 architecture. Because the VAX part of the architecture is so complete in terms of data-types, operators, addressing and memory management, it can also serve as a textbook model and case study for architecture in general. Goals, constraints, and various design choices are given, although explanations of what was traded away in the design choices are not detailed.

9

A New Architecture for Minicomputers —The DEC PDP-11

C. GORDON BELL, ROGER CADY, HAROLD McFARLAND,
BRUCE A. DELAGI, JAMES F. O'LOUGHLIN,
RONALD NOONAN, and WILLIAM A. WULF

INTRODUCTION

The minicomputer* has a wide variety of uses: communications controller, instrument controller, large-system preprocessor, real-time data acquisition systems, . . . desk calculator. Historically, Digital Equipment Corporation's (DEC) PDP-8 family, with 6000 installations has been the archetype of these minicomputers.

In some applications current minicomputers have limitations. These limitations show up when the scope of their initial task is increased (e.g., using a higher level language, or processing more variables). Increasing the scope of the task generally requires the use of more comprehensive executives and system control programs, hence larger memories and more processing. This larger system tends to be at the limit of current minicomputer capability, thus the user receives diminishing returns with respect to memory, speed efficiency, and program development time. This limitation is not surprising since the basic architectural concepts for current minicomputers were formed in the early 1960s. First, the design was constrained by cost, resulting in rather simple processor logic and

*The PDP-11 design is predicated on being a member of one (or more) of the micro, midi, mini, . . . maxi (computer name) markets. We will define these names as belonging to computers of the third generation (integrated circuit to medium-scale integrated circuit technology), having a core memory with cycle time of 0.5~2 μs, a clock rate of 5~10 MHz . . . a single processor with interrupts and usually applied to doing a particular task (e.g., controlling a memory or communications lines, preprocessing for a larger system, process control). The specialized names are defined as follows.

	Maximum Addressable Primary Memory (Words)	Processor and Memory Cost (1970 Kilodollars)	Word Length (Bits)	Processor State (Words)	Data-Types
Micro	8 K	~5	8~12	2	Integers, words, Boolean vectors
Mini	32 K	5~10	12~16	2–4	Vectors (i.e., indexing)
Midi	65 K ~ 128 K	10~20	16~24	4–16	Double length floating point (occasionally)

register configurations. Second, application experience was not available. For example, the early constraints often created computing designs with what we now consider weaknesses:

1. Limited addressing capability, particularly of larger core sizes.
2. Few registers, general registers, accumulators, index registers, base registers.
3. No hardware stack facilities.
4. Limited priority interrupt structures, and thus slow context switching among multiple programs (tasks).
5. No byte string handling.
6. No read-only memory (ROM) facilities.
7. Very elementary I/O processing.
8. No larger model computer, once a user outgrows a particular model.
9. High programming costs because users program in machine language.

In developing a new computer, the architecture should at least solve the above problems. Fortunately, in the late 1960s, integrated circuit semiconductor technology became available so that newer computers could be designed that solve these problems at low cost. Also, by 1970, application experience was available to influence the design. The new architecture should thus lower programming cost while maintaining the low hardware cost of minicomputers.

The DEC PDP-11 Model 20 is the first computer of a computer family designed to span a range of functions and performance. The Model 20 is specifically discussed, although design guidelines are presented for other members of the family. The Model 20 would nominally be classified as a third generation (integrated circuits), 16-bit word, one central processor with eight 16-bit general registers, using two's complement arithmetic and addressing up to 2^{16} 8-bit bytes of primary memory (core). Though classified as a general register processor, the operand accessing mechanism allows it to perform equally well as a 0- (stack), 1- (general register), and 2- (memory-to-memory) address computer. The computer's components (processor, memories, controls, terminals) are connected via a single switch, called the Unibus.

The machine is described using the processor-memory-switch (PMS) notation of Bell and Newell [1971] at different levels. The following descriptive sections correspond to the levels: external design constraints level; the PMS level – the way components are interconnected and allow information to flow; the program level – the abstract machine that interprets programs; and finally, the logical design level. (We omit a discussion of the circuit level, the PDP-11 being constructed from TTL integrated circuits.)

DESIGN CONSTRAINTS

The principal design objective is yet to be tested; namely, do users like the machine? This will be tested both in the marketplace and by the features that are emulated in newer machines; it will be tested indirectly by the life span of the PDP-11 and any offspring.

Word Length

The most critical constraint, word length (defined by IBM), was chosen to be a multiple of 8 bits. The memory word length for the Model 20 is 16 bits, although there are 32- and 48-bit instructions and 8- and 16-bit data. Other members of the family might have up to 80-bit instructions with 8-, 16-, 32- and 48-bit data. The internal, and preferred external character set, was chosen to be 8-bit ASCII.

Range and Performance

Performance and function range (extendability) were the main design constraints; in fact, they were the main reasons to build a new computer. DEC already has four computer families that span a range* but are incompatible. In addition to the range, the initial machine was constrained to fall within the small-computer product line, which means to have about the same performance as a PDP-8. The initial machine outperforms the PDP-5, LINC, and PDP-4 based families. Performance, of course, is both a function of the instruction set and the technology. Here, we are fundamentally only concerned with the instruction set performance because faster hardware will always increase performance for any family. Unlike the earlier DEC families, the PDP-11 had to be designed so that new models with significantly more performance can be added to the family.

A rather obvious goal is maximum performance for a given model. Designs were programmed using benchmarks, and the results were compared with both DEC and potentially competitive machines. Although the selling price was constrained to lie in the $5,000 to $10,000 range, it was realized that the decreasing cost of logic would allow a more complex organization than that of earlier DEC computers. A design that could take advantage of medium- and eventually large-scale integration was an important consideration. First, it could make the computer perform well; second, it would extend the computer family's life. For these reasons, a general register organization was chosen.

Interrupt Response. Since the PDP-11 will be used for real-time control applications, it is important that devices can communicate with one another quickly (i.e., the response time of a request should be short). A multiple priority level, nested interrupt mechanism was selected; additional priority levels are provided by the physical position of a device on the Unibus. Software polling is unnecessary because each device interrupt corresponds to a unique address.

Software

The total system including software is, of course, the main objective of the design. Two techniques were used to aid programmability. First, benchmarks gave a continuous indication as to how well the machine interpreted programs; second, systems programmers continually evaluated the design. Their evaluation considered: what code the compiler would produce; how would the loader work; ease of program relocatability; the use of a debugging program; how the compiler, assembler, and editor would be coded – in effect, other benchmarks; how real-time monitors would be written to use the various facilities and present a clean interface to the users; finally, the ease of coding a program.

Modularity

Structural flexibility (sometimes called modularity) for a particular model was desired. A flexible and straightforward method for interconnecting components had to be used because of varying user needs (among user classes and over time). Users should have the ability to configure an optimum system based on cost, performance, and reliability, both by interconnection and, when necessary, constructing new components. Since users build special hardware, a computer should be interfaced easily. As a by-product of modularity, computer components can be produced and stocked, rather than tailor-made on order. The physical structure is almost identical to the PMS structure discussed in the following section; thus,

* PDP-4, 7, 9, 15 family; PDP-5, 8, 8/S, 8/I, 8/L family; LINC, PDP-8/LINC, PDP-12 family; and PDP-6, 10 family. The initial PDP-1 did not achieve family status.

reasonably large building blocks are available to the user.

Microprogramming

A note on microprogramming is in order because of current interest in the "firmware" concept. We believe microprogramming, as we understand it [Wilkes and Stringer, 1953], can be a worthwhile technique as it applies to processor design. For example, microprogramming can probably be used in larger computers when floating-point data operators are needed. The IBM System 360 has made use of the technique for defining processors that interpret both the System 360 instruction set and earlier family instruction sets (e.g., 1401, 1620, 7090). In the PDP-11, the basic instruction set is quite straightforward and does not necessitate microprogrammed interpretation. The processor-memory connection is asynchronous; therefore, memory of any speed can be connected. The instruction set encourages the user to write reentrant programs. Thus, read-only memory can be used as part of primary memory to gain the permanency and performance normally attributed to microprogramming. In fact, the Model 10 computer, which will not be further discussed, has a 1024-word read-only memory, and a 128-word read-write memory.

Understandability

Understandability was perhaps the most fundamental constraint (or goal) although it is now somewhat less important to have a machine that can be understood quickly by a novice computer user than it was a few years ago. DEC's early success has been predicated on selling to an intelligent but inexperienced user. Understandability, though hard to measure, is an important goal because all (potential) users must understand the computer. A straightforward design should simplify the systems programming task; in the case of a compiler, it should make translation (particularly code generation) easier.

PDP-11 STRUCTURE AT THE PMS LEVEL*

Introduction

PDP-11 has the same organizational structure as nearly all present-day computers (Figure 1). The primitive PMS components are: the primary memory Mp which holds the programs while the central processor Pc interprets them; I/O controls Kio which manage data transfers between terminals T or secondary memories Ms to primary memory Mp; the components outside the computer at periphery X either humans H or some external process (e.g., another computer); the processor console (T.console) by which humans communicate with the computer and observe its behavior and affect changes in its state; and a switch S with its control K which allows all the other components to communicate with one another. In the case of PDP-11, the central logical switch structure is implemented using a bus or chained switch S called the Unibus, as shown in Figure 2. Each physical component has a switch for placing messages on the bus or taking messages off the bus. The central control decides the next component to use the bus for a message (call). The S (Unibus) differs from most switches because any component can communicate with any other component.

The types of messages in the PDP-11 are along the lines of the hierarchical structure common to present-day computers. The single

*A descriptive (block-diagram) level [Bell and Newell, 1970] to describe the relationship of the computer components: processors, memories, switches, controls, links, terminals, and data operators. PMS is described in Appendix 2.

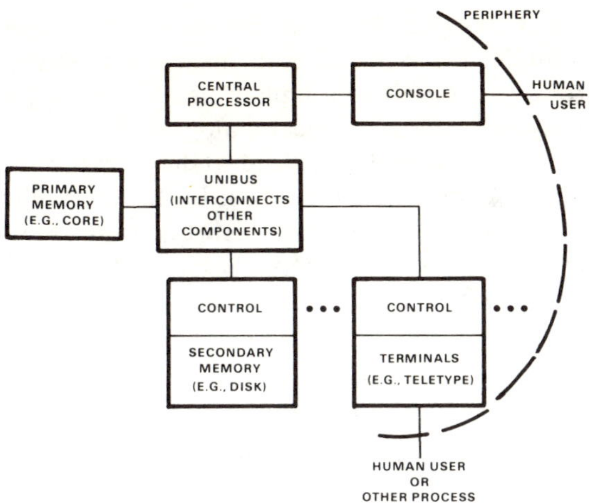

(a) Conventional block diagram.

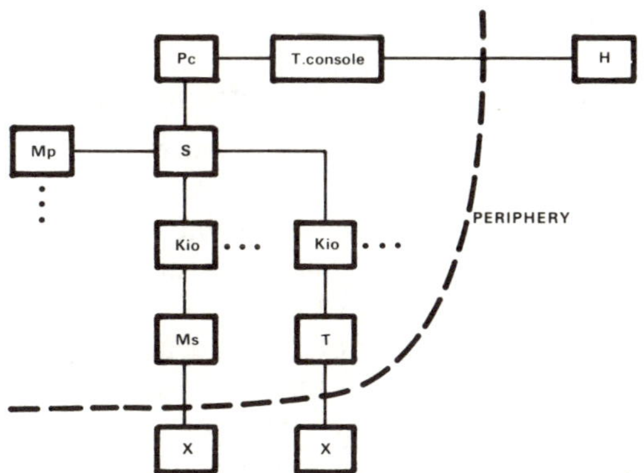

(b) PMS diagram (see Appendix 2).

Figure 1. Conventional block diagram and PMS diagram of PDP-11.

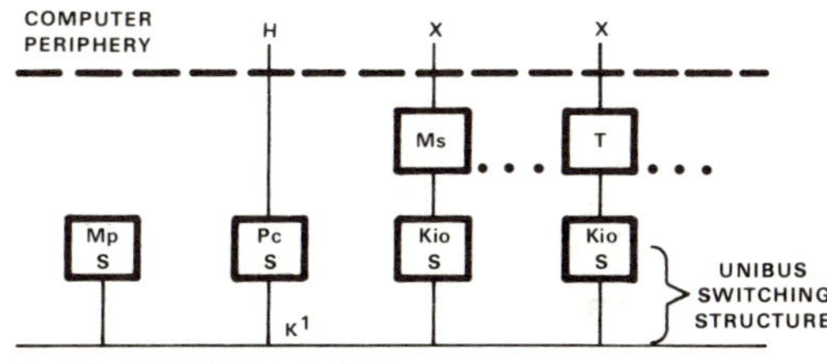

Figure 2. PDP-11 physical structure PMS diagram.

bus makes conventional and other structures possible. The message processes in the structure that utilize S (Unibus) are:

1. The central processor Pc requests that data be read or written from or to primary memory Mp for instructions and data. The processor calls a particular memory module by concurrently specifying the module's address, and the address within the modules. Depending on whether the processor requests reading or writing, data is transmitted either from the memory to the processor or vice versa.
2. The central processor Pc controls the initialization of secondary memory Ms and terminal T activity. The processor sets status bits in the control associated with a particular Ms or T, and the device proceeds with the specified action (e.g., reading a card or punching a character into paper tape). Since some devices transfer data vectors directly to primary memory, the vector control information (i.e., the memory location and length) is given as initialization information.
3. Controls request the processor's attention in the form of interrupts. An interrupt request to the processor has the effect of changing the state of the processor; thus, the processor begins executing a program associated with the interrupting process. Note that the interrupt process is only a signaling method, and when the processor interrupt occurs, the interrupter specifies a unique address value to the processor. The address is a starting address for a program.
4. The central processor can control the transmission of data between a control (for T or Ms) and either the processor or a primary memory for program controlled data transfers. The device signals for attention using the interrupt dialogue

and the central processor responds by managing the data transmission in a fashion similar to transmitting initialization information.

5. Some device controls (for T or Ms) transfer data directly to/from primary memory without central processor intervention. In this mode the device behaves similarly to a processor; a memory address is specified, and the data is transmitted between the device and primary memory.
6. The transfer of data between two controls, e.g., a secondary memory (disk) and say a terminal/T. display is not precluded, provided the two use compatible message formats.

As we show more detail in the structure there are, of course, more messages (and more simultaneous activity). The above does not describe the shared control and its associated switching which is typical of a magnetic tape and magnetic disk secondary memory systems. A control for a DECtape memory (Figure 3) has an S ('DECtape bus) for transmitting data between a single tape unit and the DECtape transport. The existence of this kind of structure is based on the relatively high cost of the control relative to the cost of the tape and the value of being able to run concurrently with other tapes. There is also a dialogue at the periphery between X-T and X-Ms that does not use the Unibus. (For example, the removal of a magnetic tape reel from a tape unit or a human user H striking a typewriter key are typical dialogues.)

All of these dialogues lead to the hierarchy of present computers (Figure 4). In this hierarchy we can see the paths by which the above messages are passed: Pc-Mp; Pc-K; K-Pc; Kio-T and Kio-Ms; and Kio-Mp; and, at the periphery, T-X and T-Ms; and T. console-H.

Model 20 Implementation

Figure 5 shows the detailed structure of a uniprocessor Model 20 PDP-11 with its various components (options). In Figure 5, the Unibus characteristics are suppressed. (The detailed properties of the switch are described in the logical design section.)

Extensions to Increase Performance

The reader should note (Figure 5) that the important limitations of the bus are: a concurrency of one, namely, only one dialogue can occur at a given time, and a maximum transfer rate of one 16-bit word per 0.75 microsecond, giving a transfer rate of 21.3 megabits/second. While the bus is not a limit for a uniprocessor structure, it is a limit for multiprocessor structures. The bus also imposes an artificial limit on the system performance when high-speed devices (e.g., TV cameras, disks) are transferring

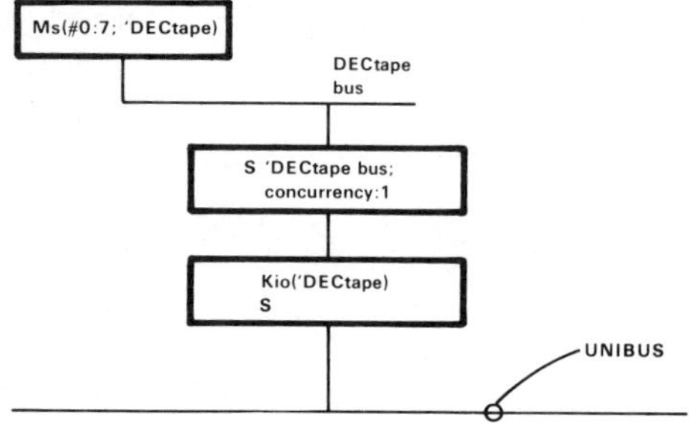

Figure 3. DECtape control switching PMS diagram.

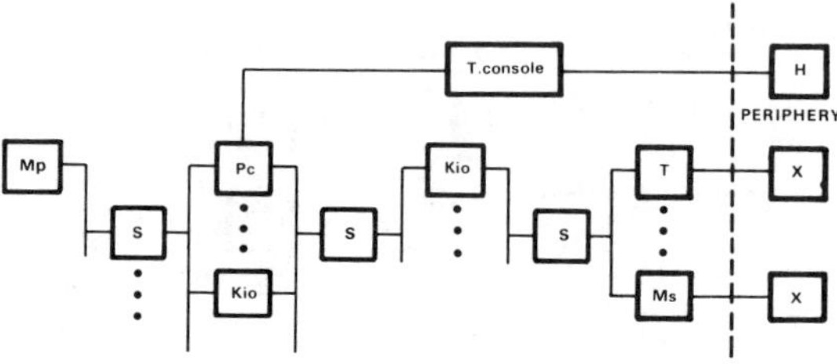

Figure 4. Conventional hierarchy computer structure.

data to multiple primary memories. On a larger system with multiple independent memories, the supply of memory cycles is 17 megabits/second times the number of modules. Since there is such a large supply of memory cycles per second and since the central processor can absorb only approximately 16 megabits/second, the simple one-Unibus structure must be modified to make the memory cycles available. Two changes are necessary. First, each of the memory modules has to be changed so that multiple units can access each module on an independent basis. Second, there must be independent control accessing mechanisms. Figure 6 shows how a single memory is modified to have more access ports (i.e., connect to four Unibuses).

Figure 7 shows a system with three independent memory modules that are accessed by two independent Unibuses. Note that two of the secondary memories and one of the transducers are connected to both Unibuses. It should be noted that devices that can potentially interfere with Pc-Mp accesses are constructed with two ports; for simple systems, both ports are connected to the same bus, but for systems with more buses, the second connection is to an independent bus.

Figure 8 shows a multiprocessor system with two central processors and three Unibuses. Two of the Unibus controls are included within the two processors, and the third bus is controlled by an independent control unit. The structure also has a second switch to allow either of two processors (Unibuses) to access common shared devices. The interrupt mechanism allows either

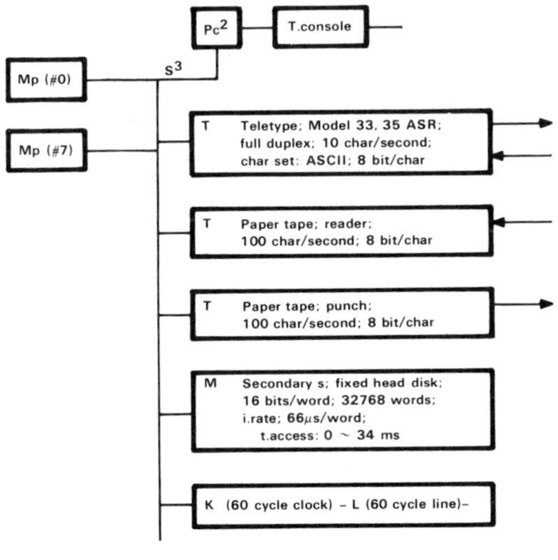

NOTES

1. Mp (technology: core; 4096 words; t.cycle: 1.2 μs; t.access: 0.6 μs; 16 bits/word)
2. P(central\c; Model 30; integrated circuit; general registers; 2 addresses/instruction; *addresses are: register, stack, Mp;* data-types: bits, bytes, words, word integers, byte integers, Boolean vectors; 8 bits/byte; 16 bits/word; operations: (+, −, / (optional), × (optional), /2, ×2, ¬, − (negate); (∨, ⊃); M(processor state; 'general registers; 8 + 1 word; integrated circuit))
3. S ('Unibus; non-hierarchy; bus; concurrency: 1; 1 word/0.75 μs)

Figure 5. PDP-11 structure and characteristics PMS diagram.

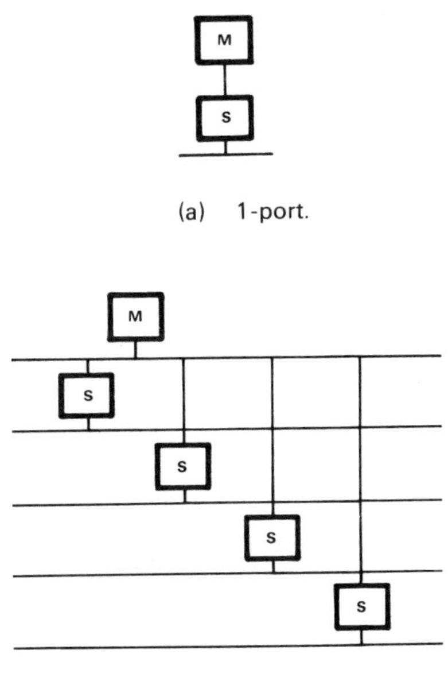

(b) 4-port.

Figure 6. 1- and 4-port memory modules PMS diagram.

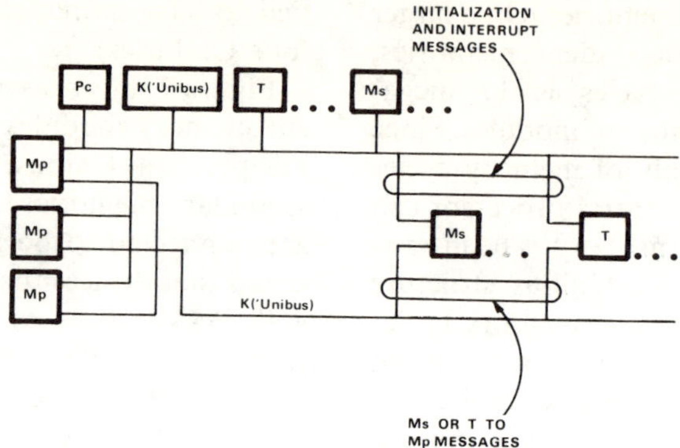

Figure 7. Three Mp, two S ('Unibus) structure PMS diagram.

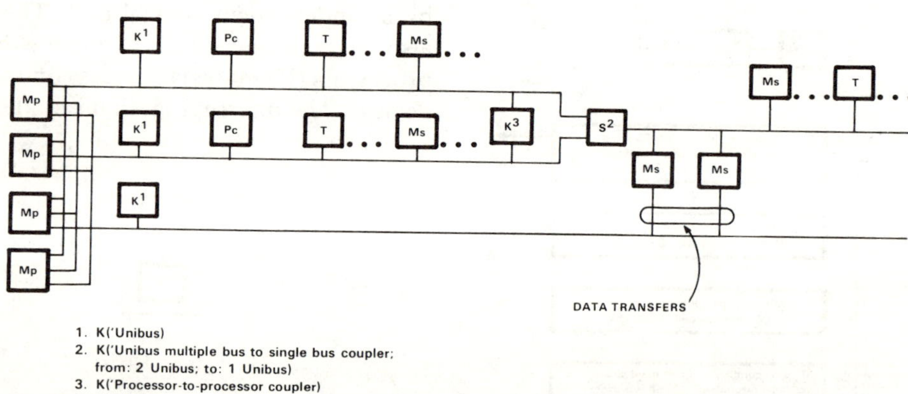

1. K('Unibus)
2. K('Unibus multiple bus to single bus coupler; from: 2 Unibus; to: 1 Unibus)
3. K('Processor-to-processor coupler)
4. Ms(duplex)

Figure 8. Dual Pc multiprocessor system PMS diagram.

processor to respond to an interrupt, and similarly either processor may issue initialization information on an anonymous basis. A control unit is needed so that two processors can communicate with one another; shared primary memory is normally used to carry the body of the message. A control connected to two Pc's (Figure 8) can be used for reliability; either processor or Unibus could fail, and the shared Ms would still be accessible.

Higher Performance Processors

Increasing the bus width has the greatest effect on performance. A single bus limits data transmission to 21.4 megabits/second, and though Model 20 memories are 16 megabits/second, faster (or wider) data path width modules will be limited by the bus. The Model 20 is not restricted, but for higher performance processors operating on double-word (fixed-point) or triple-word (floating-point) data, two or three accesses are required for a single data-type. The direct method to improve the performance is to double or triple the primary memory and central processor data path widths. Thus, the bus data rate is automatically doubled or tripled.

For 32- or 48-bit memories, a coupling control unit is needed so that devices of either width appear isomorphic to one another. The coupler maps a data request of a given width into a higher- or lower-width request for the bus being coupled to, as shown in Figure 9. (The bus is limited to a fixed number of devices for electrical reasons; thus, to extend the bus, a bus-repeating unit is needed. The bus-repeating control unit is almost identical to the bus coupler.) A computer with a 48-bit primary memory and processor and 16-bit secondary memory and terminals (transducers) is shown in Figure 9.

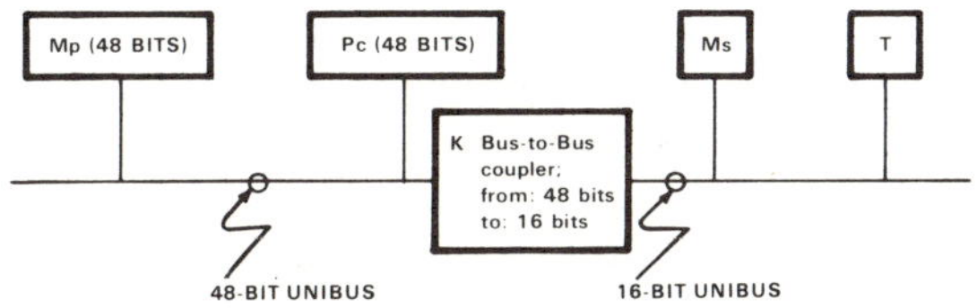

Figure 9. Computer with 48-bit Pc, Mp with 16-bit Ms, T.PMS diagram.

In summary, the design goal was to have a modular structure providing the final user with freedom and flexibility to match his needs. A secondary goal of the Unibus is open-endedness by providing multiple buses and defining wider path buses. Finally, and most important, the Unibus is straightforward.

THE INSTRUCTION SET PROCESSOR (ISP) LEVEL-ARCHITECTURE*

Introduction, Background, and Design Constraints

The Instruction Set Processor (ISP) is the machne defined by the hardware and/or software that interprets programs. As such, an ISP is independent of technology and specific implementations.

The instruction set is one of the least understood aspects of computer design; currently, it is an art. There is currently no theory of instruction sets, although there have been attempts to construct them [Maurer, 1966], and there has also been an attempt to have a computer program design an instruction set [Haney, 1968]. We have used the conventional approach in this design. First, a basic ISP was adopted and then incremental design modifications were made (based on the results of the benchmarks).†

Although the approach to the design was conventional, the resulting machine is not. A common classification of processors is as 0-, 1-, 2-, 3-, or 3-plus-1-address machines. This scheme has the form:

op *l*1, *l*2, *l*3, *l*4

*The word "architecture" has been operationally defined [Amdahl *et al.*, 1964] as "the attributes of a system as seen by a programmer, i.e., the conceptual structure and functional behavior, as distinct from the organization of the data flow and controls, the logical design, and the physical implementation."

†A predecessor multiregister computer was proposed that used a similar design process. Benchmark programs were coded on each of ten "competitive" machines, and the object of the design was to get a machine that gave the best score on the benchmarks. This approach had several fallacies: The machine had no basic character of its own; the machine was difficult to program since the multiple registers were assigned to specific functions and had inherent idiosyncrasies to score well on the benchmarks; the machine did not perform well for programs other than those used in the benchmark test; and finally, compilers that took advantage of the machine appeared to be difficult to write. Since all "competitive machines" had been hand-coded from a common flowchart rather than separate flowcharts for each machine, the apparent high performance may have been due to the flowchart organization.

where *l*1 specifies the location (address) in which to store the result of the binary operation (op) of the contents of operand locations *l*2 and *l*3, and *l*4 specifies the location of the next instruction.

The action of the instruction is of the form:

*l*1 ← *l*2 op *l*3; goto *l*4

The other addressing schemes assume specific values for one or more of these locations. Thus, the one-address von Neumann [Burks *et al.*, 1962] machines assume *l*1 = *l*2 = the accumulator and *l*4 is the location following that of the current instruction. The two-address machine assumes *l*1 = *l*2; *l*4 is the next address.

Historically, the trend in machine design has been to move from a 1- or 2-word accumulator structure as in the von Neumann machine toward a machine with accumulator and index register(s).* As the number of registers is increased, the assignment of the registers to specific functions becomes more undesirable and inflexible; thus, the general register concept has developed. The use of an array of general registers in the processor was apparently first used in the first generation, vacuum-tube machine, PEGASUS [Elliott *et al.*, 1956] and appears to be an outgrowth of both 1- and 2-address structures. (Two alternative structures – the early 2- and 3-address-per-instruction computers may be disregarded, since they tend to always access primary memory for results as well as temporary storage and thus are wasteful of time and memory cycles and require a long instruction.) The stack concept (0-address) provides the most efficient access method for specifying algorithms, since very little space, only the access addresses and the operators, needs to be given. In this scheme the operands of an operator are always assumed to be on the "top of the stack." The stack has the additional advantage that arithmetic expression evaluation and compiler statement parsing have been developed to use a stack effectively. The disadvantage of the stack is due, in part, to the nature of current memory technology. That is, stack memories have to be simulated with random-access memories; multiple stacks are usually required; and even though small stack memories exist, as the stack overflows, the primary memory (core) has to be used.

Even though the trend has been toward the general register concept (which, of course, is similar to a 2-address scheme in which one of the addresses is limited to small values), it is important to recognize that any design is a compromise. There are situations for which any of these schemes can be shown to be "best." The IBM System 360 series uses a general register structure, and their designers [Amdahl *et al.*, 1964] claim the following advantages for the scheme.

1. Registers can be assigned to various functions: base addressing, address calculation, fixed-point arithmetic, and indexing.
2. Availability of technology makes the general register structure attractive.

The System 360 designers also claim that a stack organized machine such as the English Electric KDF 9 [Allmark and Lucking, 1962] or the Burroughs B5000 [Lonergan and King, 1961] has the following disadvantages.

1. Performance is derived from fast registers, not the way they are used.
2. Stack organization is too limiting and requires many copy and swap operations.
3. The overall storage of general registers and stack machines are the same, considering point 2.

---

*Due, in part, to needs, but mainly to technology that dictates how large the structure can be.

4. The stack has a bottom, and when placed in slower memory, there is a performance loss.
5. Subroutine transparency is not easily realized with one stack.
6. Variable length data is awkward with a stack.

We generally concur with points 1, 2, and 4. Point 5 is an erroneous conclusion, and point 6 is irrelevant (that is, general register machines have the same problem). The general register scheme also allows processor implementations with a high degree of parallelism since all instructions of a local block can operate on several registers concurrently. A set of truly general purpose registers should also have additional uses. For example, in the DEC PDP-10, general registers are used for address integers, indexing, floating point, Boolean vectors (bits), or program flags and stack pointers. The general registers are also addressable as primary memory, and thus, short program loops can reside within them and be interpreted faster. It was observed in operation that PDP-10 stack operations were very powerful and often used (accounting for as many as 20 percent of the executed instructions in some programs, e.g., the compilers).

The basic design decision that sets the PDP-11 apart was based on the observation that by using *truly* general registers and by suitable addressing mechanisms, it was possible to consider the machine as a 0-address (stack), 1-address (general register), or 2-address (memory-to-memory) computer. Thus, it is possible to use whichever addressing scheme, or mixture of schemes, is most appropriate.

Another important design decision for the instruction set was to have only a few data-types in the basic machine, and to have a rather complete set of operations for each data-type. (Alternative designs might have more data-types with few operations, or few data-types with few operations.) In part, this was dictated by the machine size. The conversion between data-types must be accomplished easily either automatically or with one or two instructions. The data-types should also be sufficiently primitive to allow other data-types to be defined by software (and by hardware in more powerful versions of the machine). The basic data-type of the machine is the 16-bit integer which uses the two's complement convention for sign. This data-type is also identical to an address.

PDP-11 Model 20 Instruction Set (Basic Instruction Set)

A formal description of the basic instruction set is given in the original paper [Bell *et al.*, 1970] using the ISPL notation [Bell and Newell, 1970]. The remainder of this section will discuss the machine in a conventional manner.

Primary Memory. The primary memory (core) is addressed as either 2^{16} bytes or 2^{15} words using a 16-bit number. The linear address space is also used to access the input/output devices. The device state, data and control registers are read or written like normal memory locations.

General Register. The general registers are named: R[0:7]<15:0>; that is, there are eight registers each with 16 bits. The naming is done starting at the left with bit 15 (the sign bit) to the least significant bit 0. There are synonyms for R[6] and R[7]:

1. Stack Pointer\SP<15:0>
   := R[6]<@15:0>
   Used to access a special stack that is used to store the state of interrupts, traps, and subroutine calls.
2. Program Counter\PC<15:0>
   := R[7]<@15:0>
   Points to the current instruction being interpreted. It will be seen that the fact that PC is one of the general registers is crucial to the design.

Any general register, R[0:7], can be used as a stack pointer. The special Stack Pointer SP has additional properties that force it to be used for changing processor state interrupts, traps, and subroutine calls. (It also can be used to control dynamic temporary storage subroutines.)

In addition to the above registers there are 8 bits used (from a possible 16) for processor status, called PS<15:0> register. Four bits are the Condition Codes\CC associated with arithmetic results; the T-bit controls tracing; and 3 bits control the priority of running programs Priority <2:0>. Individual bits are mapped in PS as shown in the appendix.

Data-Types and Primitive Operations. There are two data lengths in the basic machine: bytes and words, which are 8 and 16 bits, respectively. The nontrivial data-types are word-length integers (w.i.); byte-length integers (by.i); word-length Boolean vectors (w.bv); i.e., 16 independent bits (Booleans) in a 1-dimensional array; and byte-length Boolean vectors (by.bv). The operations on byte and word Boolean vectors are identical. Since a common use of a byte is to hold several flag bits (Booleans), the operations can be combined to form the complete set of 16 operations. The logical operations are: "clear," "complement," "inclusive or," and "implication" ($x \supset y$ or $\neg x \vee y$).

There is a complete set of arithmetic operations for the word integers in the basic instruction set. The arithmetic operations are: "add," "subtract," "multiply" (optional), "divide" (optional), "compare," "add one," "subtract one," "clear," "negate," and "multiply and divide" by powers of two (shift). Since the address integer size is 16 bits, these data-types are most important. Byte-length integers are operated on as words by moving them to the general registers where they take on the value of word integers. Word-length-integer operations are carried out and the results are returned to memory (truncated).

The floating-point instructions defined by software (not part of the basic instruction set) require the definition of two additional data-types (of length two and three), i.e., double words (d.w.) and triple words (t.w.). Two additional data-types, double integer (d.i.) and triple floating-point (t.f. or f) are provided for arithmetic. These data-types imply certain additional operations and the conversion to the more primitive data-types.

Address (Operand) Calculation. The general methods provided for accessing operands are the most interesting (perhaps unique) part of the machine's structure. By defining several access methods to a set of general registers, to memory, or to a stack (controlled by a general register), the computer is able to be a 0-, 1-, and 2-address machine. The encoding of the instruction source (S) fields and destination (D) fields are given in Figure 10 together with a list of the various access modes that are possible. (The appendix gives a formal description of the effective address calculation process.)

It should be noted from Figure 10 that all the common access modes are included (direct, indirect, immediate, relative, indexed, and indexed indirect) plus several relatively uncommon ones. Relative (to PC) access is used to simplify program loading, while immediate mode speeds up execution. The relatively uncommon access modes, auto-increment and auto-decrement, are used for two purposes: access to a stack under control of the registers* and access to bytes or words organized as strings or vectors. The indirect access mode allows a stack to hold addresses of data (instead of data). This mode is desirable when manipulating longer and variable-length data-types (e.g., strings, double fixed, and triple floating

*Note that, by convention, a stack builds toward register 0, and when the stack crosses 400_8, a stack overflow occurs.

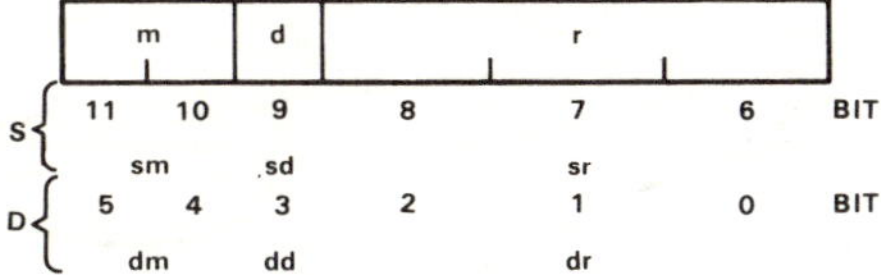

r = REGISTER SPECIFICATION R[r]
d = DEFER (INDIRECT) ADDRESS BIT
m = MODE (00 = R[r]; 01 = R[r]; NEXT R[r] + si; [1]
10 = R[r], R[r] -ai, NEXT R[2]
11 = INDEXED WITH NEXT WORD)

The following access modes can be specified:

0 Direct to a register R[r].

1 Indirect to a register, R[r] for address of data.

2 Auto increment via register (pop) – use register as address, then increment register.

3 Auto increment via register (pop) – defer.

4 Auto decrement via register (push) – decrement register, then use register as address.

5 Auto decrement indirect – decrement register, then use register as the address of the address of data.

2 Immediate data – next full word is the data (r = PC).

3 Direct data – next full word is the address of data (r = PC).

6 Direct indexed – use next full word indexed with R[r] as address of data.

7 Direct indexed – indirect – use next full word indexed with R[r] as the address of the address of data.

6 Relative access – next full word plus PC is the address (R = PC).

7 Relative indirect access – next full word plus PC is the address of the address of data (r = PC).

1. Address increment/ai value is 1 or 2.

Figure 10. Address calculation formats.

point). The register auto-increment mode may be used to access a byte string; thus, for example, after each access, the register can be made to point to the next data item. This is used for moving data blocks, searching for particular elements of a vector, and byte-string operations (e.g., movement, comparisons, editing).

This addressing structure provides flexibility while retaining the same, or better, coding efficiency than classical machines. As an example of the flexibility possible, consider the variations possible with the most trivial word instruction MOVE (Table 1). The MOVE instruction is coded in conventional 2-address, 1-address (general register) and 0-address (stack) computers. The 2-address format is particularly nice for MOVE, because it provides an efficient encoding for the common operation: A ← B (note that the stack and general registers are not involved). The vector moves A[I] ← B(I) is also efficiently encoded. For the general register (and 1-address format), there are about 13 MOVE operations that are commonly used. Six moves can be encoded for the stack (about the same number found in stack machines).

Instruction Formats. There are several instruction decoding formats depending on whether zero, one, or two operands have to be explicitly referenced. When two operands are required, they are identified as source S and destination D and the result is placed at destination D. For single operand instructions (unary operators), the instruction action is D ← u D; and for two operand instructions (binary operators), the action is D ← D b S (where u and b are unary and binary operators, e.g., ¬, – and +, –, ×, /, respectively. Instructions are specified by a 16-bit word. The most common binary operator format (that for operations requiring two addresses) uses bits 15:12 to specify the operation code, bits 11:6 to specify the destination D, and bits 5:0 to specify the source S. The other instruction formats are given in Figure 11.

Instruction Interpretation Process. The instruction interpretation process is given in Figure 12, and follows the common fetch-execute cycle. There are three major states: (1) interrupting – the PC and PS are placed on the stack accessed by the Stack Pointer/SP, and the new state is taken from an address specified by the source requesting the trap or interrupt; (2) trace (controlled by T-bit) – essentially one instruction at a time is executed as a trace trap occurs after each instruction, and (3) normal instruction interpretation. The five (lower) states in the diagram are concerned with instruction fetching, operand fetching, executing the operation specified by the instruction and storing the result. The nontrivial details for fetching and storing the operands are not shown in the diagram but can be constructed from the effective address calculation process (appendix). The

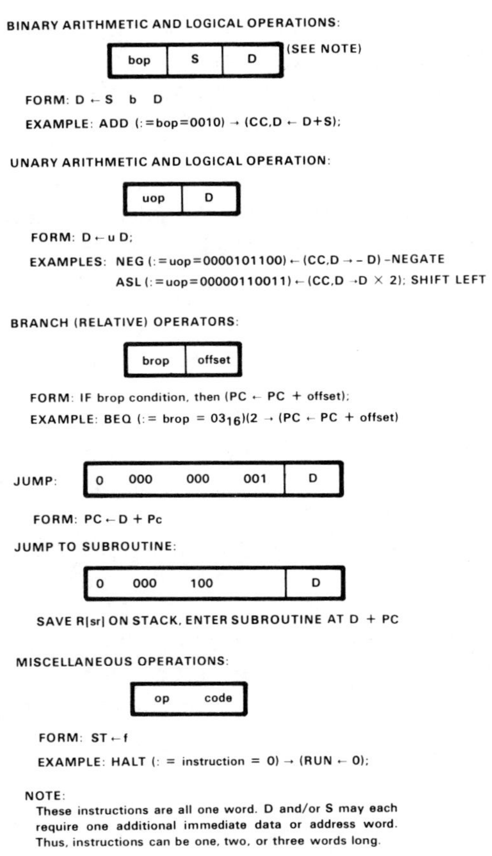

Figure 11. PDP-11 instruction formats (simplified).

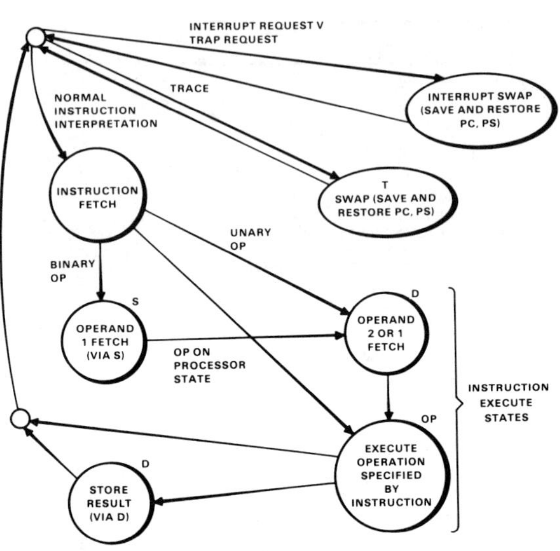

Figure 12. PDP-11 instruction interpretation process state diagram.

state diagram, though simplified, is similar to 2- and 3-address computers, but is distinctly different than a 1-address (1-accumulator) computer.

The ISP description (appendix) gives the operation of each of the instructions, and the more conventional diagram (Figure 11) shows the decoding of instruction classes. The ISP description is somewhat incomplete; for example, the add instruction is defined as:

$$\text{ADD } (:= \text{bop} = 0010_2) \Rightarrow (\text{CC,D} \leftarrow \text{D} + \text{S})$$

Addition does not exactly describe the changes to the Condition Codes CC (which means whenever a binary opcode [bop] of 0010_2 occurs the ADD instruction is executed with the above effect). In general, the CC are based on the result, that is, Z is set if the result is zero, N if negative, C if a carry occurs, and V if an overflow was detected as a result of the operation. Conditional branch instructions may thus follow the arithmetic instruction to test the results of the CC bits.

Examples of Addressing Schemes

Use as a Stack (Zero-Address) Machine. Table 2 lists typical 0-address machine instructions together with the PDP-11 instructions that perform the same function. It should be noted that translation (compilation) from normal infix expressions to reverse Polish is a comparatively trivial task. Thus, one of the primary reasons for using stacks is for the evaluation of expressions in reverse Polish form.

Consider an assignment statement of the form:

$$D \leftarrow A + B/C$$

Table 1. Coding for the MOVE Instruction To Compare with Conventional Machines

Assembler Format	Effect	Description
2-Address Machine Format		
MOVE B, A*	A ← B	Replace A with contents of B
MOVE #N, A	A ← N	Replace A with number B
MOVE B(RZ), A(RZ)	A[I] ← B[I]	Replace element of a connector
MOVE (R3)+, (R4)+	A[I] ← B[I]; I ← I + 1	Replace element of a vector, move to next element
General-Register Machine Format		
MOVE A, R1	R1 ← A	Load register
MOVE R1, A	A ← R1	Store register
MOVE @A, R1	R1 ← M[A]	Load or store indirect via element A
MOVE R1, R3	R1 ← R3	Register-to-register transfer
MOVE R1, A(R1)	A[I] ← R1	Store indexed (load indexed) (or store)
MOVE @A(R0), R1	R1 ← M[A[I]]	Load (or store) indexed indirect
MOVE (R1), R3	R1 ← M[R2]	Load indirect via register
MOVE (R1)+, R3	R3 ←M[I]	Load (or store) element indirect via register, move to next element
Stack Machine Format		
MOVE #N, –(R0)	S ← N	Load stack with literal
MOVE A, –(R0)	S ← A	Load stack with contents of A
MOVE @(R0)+, –(R0)	S ← M[S]	Load stack with memory specified by top of stack
MOVE (R0)+, A	A ← S	Store stack in A
MOVE (R0)+, @(R0)+	$M[S_2] \leftarrow S_1$	Store stack top in memory addressed by stack top –1
MOVE (R0), –(R0)	S ← S	Duplicate top of stack

*Assembler Format
( ) Denotes contents of memory addressed by
– Decrement register first
+ Increment register after
@ Indirect
# Literal

which has the reverse Polish form:

DABC/ + ←

and would normally be encoded on a stack machine as follows:

Load stack address of D
Load stack A
Load stack B
Load stack C
/
+
Store.

However, with the PDP-11, there is an address method for improving the program encoding and run time, while not losing the stack concept. An encoding improvement is made by doing an operation to the top of the stack from a direct-memory location (while loading). Thus, the previous example could be coded as:

Load stack B
Divide stack by C
Add A to stack
Store stack D

Use as a 1-Address (General Register) Machine. The PDP-11 is a general register computer and should be judged on that basis. Benchmarks have been coded to compare the

Table 2. Stack Computer Instructions and Equivalent PDP-11 Instructions

Common Stack Instruction	Equivalent PDP-11 Instruction
Place address value A on stack	MOVE M, –(R0)*
Load stack from memory address specified by stack	MOVE @(R0)+, –(R0)
Load stack from memory location A	MOVE A, –(R0)
Store stack at memory address specified by stack	MOVE (R0)+, @(R0)+
Store stack at memory location A	MOVE (R0)+, A
Duplicate top of stack	MOVE (R0), –(R0)
+, add two top data of stack to stack	ADD (R0)+, @R0
–, ×, /; subtract, multiply, divide	See add
–; negate top data of stack	NEG @R0
Clear top data of stack	CLR @R0
v; "inclusive or" two top data of stack "and" two top data of stack	BSET (R0)+, @R0
¬; complement of stack	COM @R0
Test top of stack (set branch indicators)	TST @R0
Branch on indicator	BR (–, ≠, <, ≥, >, ≤)
Jump unconditional	JUMP

Add addressed location A to top of stack (not common for stack machine) equivalent to: load stack, add swap top two stack data	ADD A, @R0
	MOVE (R0)+, R1
	MOVE (R0)+, R2
	MOVE R1, –(R0)
	MOVE R2, –(R0)

Reset stack location to N	MOVE N, R0 COM @R0
A, "and" two top stack data	BCLR (R0)+, @R0←

*Stack pointer has been arbitrarily used as register R0 for this example.

PDP-11 with the larger DEC PDP-10. A 16-bit processor performs better than the DEC PDP-10 in terms of bit efficiency, but not with time or memory cycles. A PDP-11 with a 32-bit-wide memory would, however, decrease time by nearly a factor of 2, making the times essentially comparable.

Use as a 2-Address Machine. Table 3 lists typical 2-address machine instructions together with the equivalent PDP-11 instructions for performing the same operations. The most useful instruction is probably the MOVE instruction because it does not use the stack or general registers. Unary instructions that operate on and test primary memory are also useful and efficient instructions.

Table 3. Two-Address Computer Instructions and Equivalent PDP-11 Instructions

Two-Address Computer	PDP-11
A ← B; transfer B to A	MOVE B, A
A ← A + B; add	ADD B, A
–, ×, /	See add
A ← – A; negate	NEG A
A ← A ∨ B; inclusive or	BSETB, A
A ← ¬A; not	COM
Jump unconditional	JUMP
Test A, and transfer to B	TST A BR (–, ≠, >, ≤, <, ≥) B

Extensions of the Instruction Set for Real (Floating-Point) Arithmetic

The most significant factor that affects performance is whether a machine has operators for manipulating data in a particular format. The inherent generality of a stored program computer allows any computer by subroutine to simulate another – given enough time and memory. The biggest and perhaps only factor that separates a small computer from a large computer is whether floating-point data is understood by the computer. For example, a small computer with a cycle time of 1.0 microsecond and 16-bit memory width might have the following characteristics for a floating-point add, excluding data accesses:

Programmed:	250 μs
Programmed (but special normalize and differencing of exponent instructions):	75μs
Microprogrammed hardware:	25 μs
Hardwired:	2 μs

It should be noted that the ratios between programmed and hardwired interpretation varies by roughly two orders of magnitude. The basic hardwiring scheme and the programmed scheme should allow binary program compatibility, assuming there is an interpretive program for the various operators in the Model 20. For example, consider one scheme that would add eight 48-bit registers that are addressable in the extended instruction set. The eight floating registers F would be mapped into eight double-length (32-bit) registers D. In order to access the various parts of F or D registers, registers F0 and F1 are mapped onto registers R0 to R2 and R3 to R5.

Since the instruction set operation code is almost completely encoded already for byte and word-length data, a new encoding scheme is necessary to specify the proposed additional instructions. This scheme adds two instructions: enter floating-point mode and execute one floating-point instruction. The instructions for floating-point and double-word data are shown in Table 4.

LOGICAL DESIGN OF S(UNIBUS) AND Pc

The logical design level is concerned with the physical implementation and the constituent combinational and sequential logic elements that form the various computer components (e.g., processors, memories, controls). Physically, these components are separate and connected to the Unibus following the lines of the PMS structure.

Unibus Organization

Figures 4 and 5 of Chapter 14 diagram the Pc and the entering signals from the Unibus. The control unit for the Unibus, housed in Pc for the Model 20, is not shown in the figure.

The PDP-11 Unibus has 56 bidirectional signals conventionally used for program-controlled data transfers (processor to control), direct memory data transfers (processor or control-to-memory) and control-to-processor interrupt. The Unibus is interlocked; thus,

Table 4. Floating-Point and Double-Word Data Instructions

Binary Ops			Op	Floating Point/f	Double Word/d
bop′	S	D	←	FMOVE	DMOVE
			+	FADD	DADD
			−	FSUB	DSUB
			×	FMUL	DMUL
			/	FDIV	DDIV
			compare	FCMP	DCMP
unary ops					
uop′	D		−	FNEG	DNEG

transactions operate independently of the bus length and response time of the master and slave. Since the bus is bidirectional and is used by all devices, any device can communicate with any other device. The controlling device is the master, and the device to which the master is communicating is the slave. For example, a data transfer from processor (master) to memory (always a slave) uses the Data Out dialogue facility for writing and a transfer from memory to processor uses the Data In dialogue facility for reading.

Bus Control. Most of the time the processor is bus master fetching instructions and operands from memory and storing results in memory. Bus mastership is determined by the current processor priority and the priority line upon which a bus request is made and the physical placement of a requesting device on the linked bus. The assignment of bus mastership is done concurrent with normal communication (dialogues).

Unibus Dialogues

Three types of dialogues use the Unibus. All the dialogues have a common protocol that first consists of obtaining the bus mastership (which is done concurrent with a previous transaction) followed by a data exchange with the requested device. The dialogues are: Interrupt; Data In and Data In Pause; and Data Out and Data Out Byte.

Interrupt. Interrupt can be initiated by a master immediately after receiving bus mastership. An address is transmitted from the master to the slave on Interrupt. Normally, subordinate control devices use this method to transmit an interrupt signal to the processor.

Data In and Data In Pause. These two bus operations transmit slave's data (whose address is specified by the master) to the master. For the Data In Pause operation, data is read into the master and the master responds with data which is to be rewritten in the slave.

Data Out and Data Out Byte. These two operations transfer data from the master to the slave at the address specified by the master. For Data Out, a word at the address specified by the address lines is transferred from master to slave. Data Out Byte allows a single data byte to be transmitted.

Processor Logical Design

The Pc is designed using TTL logical design components and occupies approximately eight 8 inch × 12 inch printed circuit boards. The Pc is physically connected to two other components, the console and the Unibus. The control for the Unibus is housed in the Pc and occupies one of the printed circuit boards. The most regular part of the Pc is the arithmetic and state section. The 16-word scratchpad memory and combinational logic data operators, D (shift) and D (adder, logical ops), form the most regular part of the processor's structure. The 16-word memory holds most of the 8-word processor state found in the ISP, and the 8 bits that form the Status word are stored in an 8-bit register. The input to the adder-shift network has two latches which are either memories or gates. The output of the adder-shift network can be read to either the data or address parts of the Unibus, or back to the scratchpad array.

The instruction decoding and arithmetic control are less regular than the above data and state and these are shown in the lower part of the figure. There are two major sections: the instruction fetching and decoding control and the instruction set interpreter (which, in effect, defines the ISP). The later control section operates on, hence controls, the arithmetic and state parts of the Pc. A final control is concerned with the interface to the Unibus (distinct from the Unibus control that is housed in the Pc).

CONCLUSIONS

In this paper we have endeavored to give a complete description of the PDP-11 Model 20 computer at four descriptive levels. These present an unambiguous specification at two levels (the PMS structure and the ISP), and, in addition, specify the constraints for the design at the top level, and give the reader some idea of the implementation at the bottom level logical design. We have also presented guidelines for forming additional models that would belong to the same family.

ACKNOWLEDGEMENTS

The authors are grateful to Mr. Nigberg of the technical publication department at DEC and to the reviewers for their helpful criticism. We are especially grateful to Mrs. Dorothy Josephson at Carnegie-Mellon University for typing the notation-laden manuscript.

APPENDIX. DEC PDP-11 INSTRUCTION SET PROCESSOR DESCRIPTION (IN ISPL)

The following description gives a cursory description of the instructions in the ISPL, the initial notation of Bell and Newell [1971]. Only the processor state and a brief description of the instructions are given.

Primary Memory State

M\Mb\Memory [0:2^{16} – 1]<7:0>	Byte memory
Mw[0:2^{15} – 1]<15:0> := M[0:2^{16} – 1]<7:0>	Word memory mapping

Processor State (9 words)

R\Registers [0:7]<15:0>	Word general registers
SP<15:0> := R[6]<15:0>	Stack pointer
PC<15:0> := R[7]<15:0>	Program counter
PS<15:0>	Processor state register
Priority\P<2:0> := PS<7:5>	Under program control; priority level of the process currently being interpreted; a higher level process may interrupt or trap this process.
CC\Condition-Codes<3:0> := PS<3:0>	
Carry\C := CC<0>	A result condition code indicating an arithmetic carry from bit 15 of the last operation.
Negative\N := CC<3>	A result condition code indicating last result was negative.
Zero\Z := CC<2>	A result condition code indicating last result was zero.

Overflow\V := CC<1>	A result condition code indicating an arithmetic overflow of the last operation.
Trace\T := ST<4>	Denotes whether instruction trace trap is to occur after each instruction is executed.
Undefined<7:0> := PS<15:8>	Unused
Run	Denotes normal execution.
Wait	Denotes waiting for an interrupt.

Instruction Set

The following instruction set will be defined briefly and is incomplete. It is intended to give the reader a simple understanding of the machine operation.

MOV (:= bop = 0001) → (CC,D ← S);	Move word
MOVB (:= bop = 1001) → (CC,Db ← Sb);	Move byte

Binary Arithmetic: D ← D b S;

ADD (:= bop = 0110) → (CC,D ← D + S);	Add
SUB (:= bop = 1110) → (CC,D ← D − S);	Subtract
CMP (:= bop = 0010) → (CC ← D − S);	Word compare
CMPB (:= bop = 1010) → (CC ← Db − Sb);	Byte compare
MUL (:= bop = 0111) → (CC, D ← D × S)	Multiply, if D is a register then a double length operator
DIV (:= bop = 1111) → (CC, D ← D/S);	Divide, if D is a register, then a remainder is saved

Unary Arithmetic: D ← uS;

CLR (:= uop = 050_8) → (CC,D ← 0);	Clear word
CLRB (:= uop = 1050_8) → (CC,Db ← 0);	Clear byte
COM (:= uop = 051_8) → (CC,D ← ¬D);	Complement word
COMB (:= uop = 1051_8) → (CC,Db ← ¬Db);	Complement byte
INC (:= uop = 052_8) → (CC,D ← D + 1);	Increment word
INCB (:= uop = 1052_8) → (CC,Db ← Db + 1);	Increment byte
DEC (:= uop = 053_8) → (CC,D ← D − 1);	Decrement word
DECB (:= uop = 1053_8) → (CC,Db ← Db − 1);	Decrement byte
NEG (:= uop = 054_8) → (CC,D ← − D);	Negate
NEGB (:= uop = 1054_8) → (CC,Db ← − Db)	Negate byte
ADC (:= uop = 055_8) → (CC,D ← D + C);	Add the carry
ADCB (:= uop = 1055_8) → (CC,Db ← Db + C);	Add to byte the carry
SBC (:= uop = 056_8) → (CC,D ← D − C);	Subtract the carry

SBCB (:= uop = 1056_8) → (CC,Db ← Db − C);	Subtract from byte the carry
TST (:= uop = 057_8) → (CC ← D);	Test
TST (:= uop = 1057_8) → (CC ← Db);	Test byte

Shift Operations: D ← D × 2^n;

ROR (:= sop = 060_8) → (C □ D ← C □ D/2{rotate});	Rotate right
RORB (:= sop = 1060_8) → (C □ Db ← C □ Db/2{rotate});	Byte rotate right
ROL (:= sop = 061_8) → (C □ D ← C □ D × 2 {rotate});	Rotate left
ROLB (:= sop = 1061_8) → (C □ Db ← C □ Db × 2 {rotate});	Byte rotate left
ASR (:= sop = 062_8) → (CC,D ← D × 2);	Arithmetic shift right
ASRB (:= sop = 1062_8) → (CC,Db ← Db/2);	Byte arithmetic shift right
ASL (:= sop = 063_8) → (CC,D ← D × 2);	Arithmetic shift left
ASLB (:= sop = 1063_8) → (CC,Db ← Db × 2);	Byte arithmetic shift left
ROT (:= sop = 064_8) → (C □ D ← D × 2^S);	Rotate
ROTB (:= sop = 1064_8) → (C □ Db ← D × 2^S);	Byte rotate
LSH (:= sop = 065_8) → (CC,D ← D × 2^S{logical});	Logical shift
LSHB (:= sop = 1065_8) → (CC,Db ← Db × 2^S{logical});	Byte logical shift
ASH (:= sop = 066_8) → (CC,D ← D × 2^S);	Arithmetic shift
ASHB (:= sop = 1066_8) → (CC,Db ← Db × 2^S);	Byte arithmetic shift
NOR (:= sop = 067_8 →(CC, D ← normalize (D)); (R[r'] → normalize␣exponent (D));	Normalize
NORD (:= sop = 1067_8 → (Db ←normalize (Dd)); (R[r'] ← normalize␣exponent (D));	Normalize double
SWAB (:= sop = 3) → (CC,D ← D<7:0, 15:8>)	Swap bytes

Logical Operations

BIC (:= bop = 0100) → (CC,D ← D ← D ∧ ¬S);	Bit clear
BICB (:= bop = 1100) → (CC,Db ← Db ∨ ¬Sb);	Byte bit clear
BIS (:= bop = 0101) → (CC,D ← D ∨ S);	Bit set
BISB (:= bop = 1101 → (CC,Db ← Db ∨ Sb);	Byte bit set
BIT (:= bop = 0011) → (CC ← D ∧ S);	Bit test under mask
BITB (:= bop = 1011) → (CC ← Db ∧ Sb);	Byte bit test under mask

Branches and Subroutines Calling: PC ← f;

JMP (:= sop = 0001_8) → (PC ← D');	Jump unconditional
BR (:= brop = 01_{16}) → (PC ← PC + offset);	Branch unconditional
BEQ (:= brop = 03_{16}) → (Z → (PC ← PC + offset));	Equal to zero
BNE (:= brop = 02_{16}) → (¬Z → (PC ← PC + offset));	Not equal to zero
BLT (:= brop = 05_{16}) → (N ⊕ V → (PC ← PC + offset));	Less than (zero)
BGE (:= brop = 04_{16}) → (N ≡ V → (PC ← PC + offset));	Greater than or equal (zero)
BLE (:= brop = 07_{16}) → (Z ∨ (N ⊕ V) → (PC ← PC + offset));	Less than or equal (zero)

BGT (:= brop = 06_{16}) → (¬(Z ∨ (N ⊕ V)) → (PC ← PC + offset));	Less greater than (zero)
BCS/BHIS (:= brop = 87_{16}) → (C → (PC ← PC + offset));	Carry set; higher or same (unsigned)
BCC/BLO (:= brop = 86_{16}) → (¬C → (PC ← PC + offset));	Carry clear; lower (unsigned)
BLOS (:= brop = 83_{16}) → (C ∧ Z → (PC ← PC + offset));	Lower or same (unsigned)
BHI (:= brop = 82_{16}) → ((¬C ∨ Z) → (PC ← PC + offset));	Higher than (unsigned)
BVS (:= brop = 85_{16}) → (V → (PC ← PC + offset));	Overflow
BVC (:= brop = 84_{16}) → (¬V → (PC ← PC + offset));	No overflow
BMT (:= brop = 81_{16}) → (N → (PC ← PC + offset));	Minus
BPL (:= brop = 80_{16}) → (¬N → (PC ← PC + offset));	Plus
JSR (:= sop = 0040_8) → (SP ← SP − 2; next M[SP] ← R[sr]; R[sr] ← PC; PC ← D);	Jump to subroutine by putting R[sr], PC on stack and loading R[sr] with PC, and going to subroutine at D)
RTS(: = i = 000200_8) → (PC ← R[dr]; R[dr] ← M[SP]; SP ← SP + 2);	Return from subroutine

Miscellaneous Processor State Modification:

RTI (: = i = 2_8) → (PC ← M[SP]; SP ← SP + 2; next PS ← M[SP]; SP ← SP + 2);	Return from interrupt
HALT (: = i = 0) → (Run ← 0);	
WAIT (: = i = 1) → (Wait ← 1);	
TRAP (: = i = 3) → (SP ← SP + 2; next M[SP] ← PS; SP ← SP + 2; next M[SP] ← PC; PC ← M[34_8]; PS ← M[12]);	Trap to M[34_8] store status and PC Enter new process
EMT (: = brop − 82_{16}) → (SP ← SP + 2; next M[SP] ← PS; SP ← SP + 2; next M[SP] ← PC; PC ← M[30_8]; PS ← M[32_8]);	Emulator trap
IOT (: = i = 4) → (see TRAP)	I/O trap to M[20_8]
RESET (: = i = 5) → (not described)	Reset to external devices
OPERATE(: = i<5:15> = 5) →	Condition code operate
(i<4> → (CC ← CC ∨ i<3:0>);	Set codes
¬i<4> → (CC ← CC ∧ ¬i<3:0>));	Clear codes

end Instruction␣execution

10

Cache Memories for PDP-11 Family Computers

WILLIAM D. STRECKER

INTRODUCTION

One of the most important concepts in computer systems is that of a memory hierarchy. A memory hierarchy is simply a memory system built of two (or more*) memory technologies. The first technology is selected for fast access time and necessarily has a high per-bit cost. Relatively little of the memory system consists of this technology. The second technology is selected for low per-bit cost and necessarily has a slow access time. The bulk of the memory system consists of this technology. The use of the hierarchy is coordinated by user software, system software, or hardware so that the overall characteristics of the memory system approximate the fast access of the fast technology, and the low per-bit cost of the low cost technology. An example of a user software managed hierarchy is core/disk overlaying; an example of a system software managed hierarchy is core/disk demand paging. The prime example of a hardware managed hierarchy is a bipolar cache/core memory system.

Until recently, the concept of cache memory appeared only in very large scale, performance-oriented computer systems such as the IBM 360/85 [Conti, 1969; Conti *et al.*, 1968] and 370 models 155 and larger. Recently a small cache was announced as an option for the DG Eclipse [Data General, 1974] computer system. A larger, internal cache memory is part of a recently announced Digital PDP-11 family computer system: the PDP-11/70 [DEC, 1975]. The content of this paper is a summary of the research done on the feasibility of using a bipolar cache/core hierarchy in PDP-11 family computer systems.

CACHE MEMORY

A cache memory is a small, fast, associative memory located between the central processor Pc and the primary memory Mp. Typically the cache is implemented in bipolar technology while Mp is implemented in MOS or magnetic

*Memory hierarchies can, of course, consist of three or more technologies. Discussion and analysis of these multilevel hierarchies is a fairly obvious generalization of the discussion and analysis given here.

core technology. Stored in the cache are address data AD pairs consisting of an Mp address and a copy of the contents of the Mp location corresponding to that address.

The operation of the cache is as follows. When the Pc addresses Mp, the address is first compared against the addresses stored in the cache. If there is a match, the access is performed on the data portion of the matched AD pair. This is called a hit and is performed at the fast access time of the cache. If there is no match – called a miss – Mp is accessed as usual. Generally, however, an AD pair corresponding to the latest access is stored in the cache, usually displacing some other AD pair. It is the latter procedure which tends to keep the contents of the cache corresponding to the Mp locations most commonly accessed by the Pc. Because programs typically have the property of locality (i.e., over short periods of time most accesses are to a small group of Mp locations), even relatively small caches have a majority of Pc accesses resulting in hits. The performance of a cache is described by its miss ratio – the fraction of all Pc references which result in misses.

CACHE ORGANIZATION

There are a number of possible cache organizational parameters. These include:

1. The size of the cache in terms of data storage.
2. The amount of data corresponding to each address in the AD pair.
3. The amount of data moved between Mp and the cache on a miss.
4. The form of address comparison used.
5. The replacement algorithm which decides which AD pair to replace after a miss.
6. The time at which Mp is updated on write accesses.

The most obvious form of cache organization is fully associative with the data portion of the AD pair corresponding to basic addressable unit of memory (typically a byte or word), as indicated by the system architecture. On a miss, this basic unit is brought into the cache from Mp. However, for several reasons, this is not always the most attractive organization. First, because procedures and data structures tend to be sequential, it is often desirable, on a miss, to bring a block of adjacent Mp words into the cache. This effectively gives instruction and data pre-fetching. Second, when associating a larger amount of data with an address, the relative amount of the cache storage which is used to store data is increased. The number of words moved between Mp and the cache is termed the block size. The block size is also typically the size of the data in the AD pair* and is assumed to be that for this discussion.

In a fully associative cache, any AD pair can be stored in any cache location. This implies that, for a single hardware address comparator, the Mp address must be compared serially against the address portions of the AD pairs – which is too slow. Alternatively there must be a hardware comparator for each cache location – which is too expensive. An alternative form of cache organization which allows for an intermediate number of comparators is termed set associative.

A set associative cache consists of a number of sets which are accessed by indexing rather than by association. Each of the sets contains one or more AD pairs (of which the data portion is a block). There are as many hardware comparators as there are AD pairs in a set. The

* In a few complex cache organizations such as that used in the IBM 360/85, the size of the D portion of the AD pair (called a sector in the 360/85) is larger than the block size. That potential will be ignored in this discussion.

understanding of the operation of a set associative cache is aided by Figure 1. The n bit Mp address is divided into three fields of l, i, and b bits. Assume that there are 2^i sets. The i-bit index field selects one of these sets. The A portion of each AD pair is compared against the l-bit label field* of the Mp address. If there is a match, the b-bit byte field selects the byte (or other sub-unit) in the D portion of the matched AD pair.

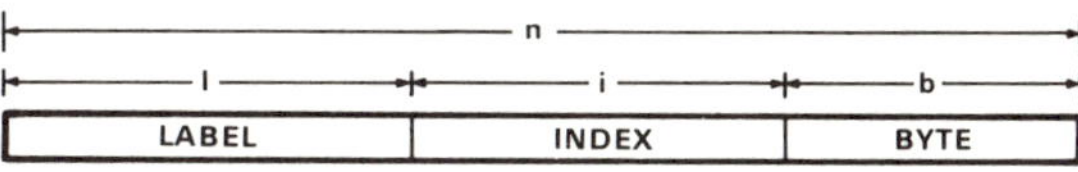

Figure 1. Address fields for a set associative cache.

If there is no match, Mp is accessed and (generally) a new AD pair is moved into the cache. Which of the AD pairs to be replaced in the set is selected by the replacement algorithm. Typical replacement algorithms are: first in, first out (FIFO); least recently used (LRU), or random (RAND).

There are two limiting cases of the set associative organization. When the number of sets is the cache size in blocks, only a single hardware comparator is needed. The resulting organization is called direct mapped. It is the simplest form of cache organization. When there is only one set, clearly a fully associative cache results.

So far in the discussion there has been no distinction made between read and write accesses. When the Pc makes a write access, ultimately Mp must be updated. There are two obvious times when this can be done. First is at the time the write access is made. Both Mp and the cache (if there is a hit) are updated simultaneously. This strategy is termed write-through. Alternatively, only the cache can be updated on a write hit, and only when the updated AD pair is replaced on some future miss is Mp updated. This strategy is termed write-back. The choice between these two strategies involves systems considerations which are beyond the scope of this paper.†

There are other possible asymmetries in the handling of reads and writes. One possibility is that after a write miss an AD pair corresponding to that access is not stored in the cache. This is termed no-write-allocate. The alternative is, of course, termed write-allocate.

CACHE MEMORY SIMULATION

The understanding of memory hierarchies (and programs) has not reached the point where cache performance can be predicted analytically as a function of cache organizational parameters. As a consequence, the studying of cache memory behavior is done through simulation. (Some cache simulation results for other computer architectures are reported in [Conti *et al.*, 1968; Meade, 1970; Bell *et al.*, 1974; Gibson, 1967].) For the purposes of this study, a two part simulator was constructed.

The first part was a PDP-11 simulator. This is a PDP-11 program which runs other PDP-11 programs interpretively. A variety of properties of the interpreted programs can be collected, including the sequence of generated Mp addresses. The latter is termed an address trace. The address trace is processed by the second part, the cache simulator. This is parameterized by cache organization and determines the miss ratio for a given address trace.

*Note that, in a set associative cache, only the label field must be stored in the cache AD pair – not the entire Mp address.

†For the PDP-11/70 system, write-through was chosen. The main impact of this is that each write access, as well as each read miss, results in an Mp access. Data suggests that, in PDP-11s, about 10 percent of Pc accesses are writes.

CACHE SIMULATION RESULTS

Since the performance of cache memory is a function not only of cache organization parameters but also of the program run, it is desirable to run cache simulations with a wide variety of programs. Multiplying these by a wide variety of a cache's organizational parameters to be simulated resulted in a considerable amount of simulation data of which only the highlights are reported here.

The first experiment was to determine the approximate overall size of the cache memory. Plots of the miss ratio against cache size for several programs* are given in Figure 2. (All sizes in both the figures and the discussion are 16-bit PDP-11 words.) A block size of two and a set size of one were held constant. In general, the miss ratio falls rapidly for caches up to 1024 words and falls less rapidly thereafter.

Figure 3 depicts the effect of set size (associativity) on cache performance. In order to clarify the results, Figures 3 through 6 only contain simulation data for a single program (the Macro assembler) which had the highest miss ratio in Figure 2. As expected, a larger set size reduces the miss ratio. The largest improvement occurs in going from set size one to set size two. Although not shown, even going to fully associative cache has little further effect on the miss ratio.

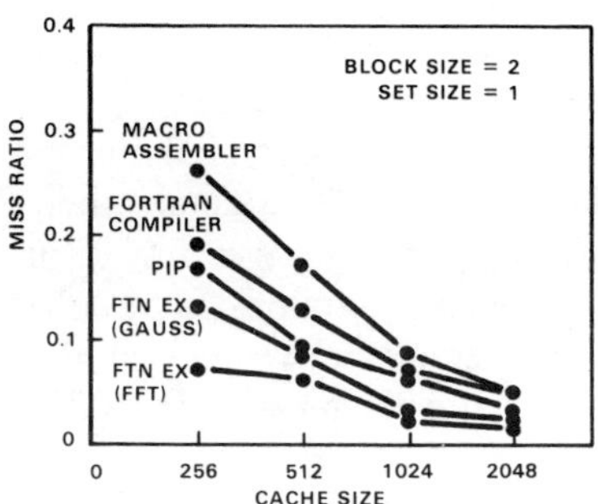

Figure 2. Effect of cache size on miss ratio.

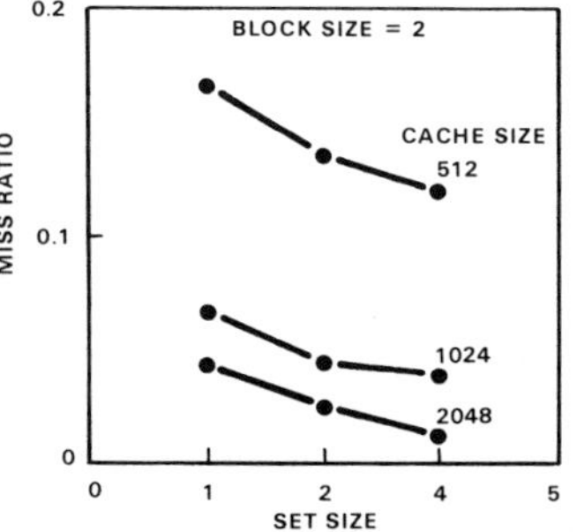

Figure 3. Effect of set size on miss ratio.

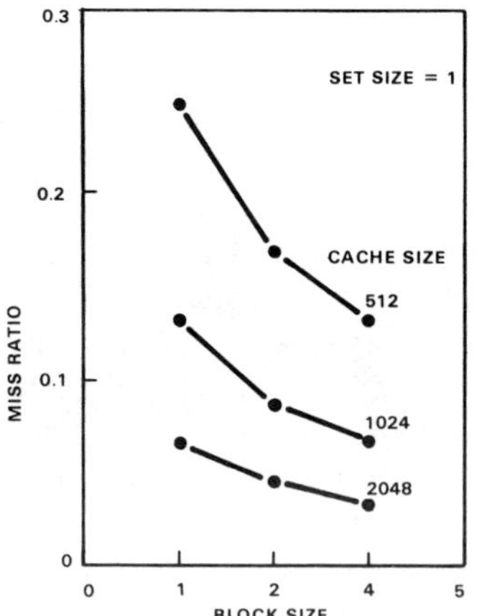

Figure 4. Effect of block size on miss ratio.

*These programs are system and user programs running under the PDP-11 DOS operating system. They include a Macro assembler, FORTRAN compiler, PIP (a file utility program), and FORTRAN executions of numerical applications. The range of miss ratios is typical for the much wider group of programs actually simulated. Indeed, the miss ratio for the Macro assembler for a given cache size was the *worst* of any program simulated.

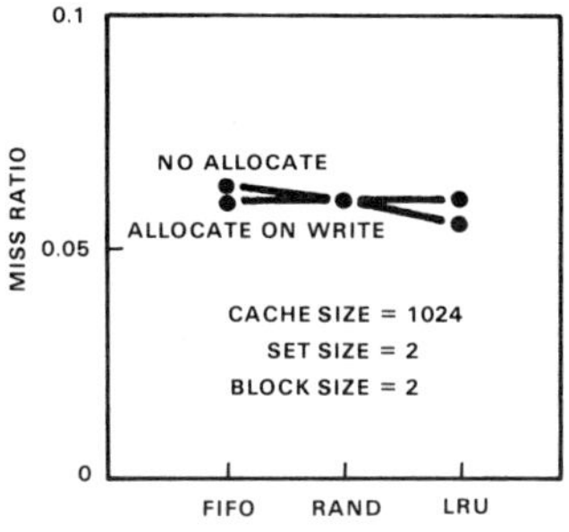

Figure 5. Effect of replacement algorithm and write allocation on miss ratio.

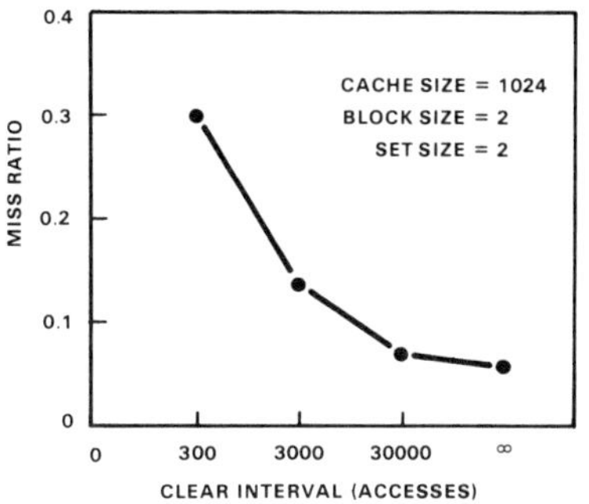

Figure 6. Effect of clear interval on miss ratio.

In Figure 4, the impact of block size is shown. Especially in smaller caches, going to a larger block significantly reduces the miss ratio. This is a result of a smaller cache depending more on the pre-fetching effect for its performance.

The effect of write allocation and replacement algorithm is given in Figure 5. For the program considered, there is a negligible performance difference across the different strategies.

In Figure 6, the effect of periodically clearing the cache is depicted. This approximates the effect on the cache of rapid context switching in that, when a new program is brought in, the cache appears "clear" to it. Even completely clearing the cache every 300 Pc accesses only degrades the miss ratio to 0.3. This represents a worst case condition that would be unrealized in practice. For example, the "new program" brought in every 300 Pc references might be an interrupt handler. Any program running that often would typically find that the cache always contained information relevant to it. Indeed, for the cache organization given, it is impossible in 300 accesses to significantly clear a 1024-word cache.

CONCLUSIONS

The performance goals of the PDP-11/70 computer system required the typical miss ratio to be 0.1 or less. Analysis of the preceding data, with emphasis on the breaks in the curves, suggested that the optimal organization was a cache size of 1024 words, block size of two words, and a set size of two. Because the data suggests that the replacement algorithm and write allocation strategies have negligible effect, a no-write-allocate strategy and a random replacement algorithm were selected.

11

Buses, The Skeleton of Computer Structures

JOHN V. LEVY

INTRODUCTION

A bus is a communication pathway connecting two or more electrical devices. In the context of minicomputer design, buses are the physical and electrical structures that determine how the building blocks are interconnected.

In every computer system, there are many buses: internal pathways connect the registers and arithmetic logic of a central processor; input/output pathways connect processors, memories, and peripheral devices; and external communication buses attach computer systems to the telephone and other data communication pathways. In this chapter, the discussion is restricted to buses that interconnect computer system components that are designed by different engineering groups.

This particular approach may sound out of place, but one of the most important functions of a bus is to provide a well specified interface between complex subsystems. We exclude from discussion internal processor register transfer buses, as well as external buses whose specifications are determined by engineers not involved in the minicomputer design process. Although none of the examples in this chapter is drawn from multiprocessor systems, most of the design experience presented is relevant to such systems.

What Does a Bus Do?

A bus is a communication medium. Each one exists in order to transfer information from place to place within a computer system. In this chapter, we attempt to illustrate the complexities of bus design by drawing on the real history of some PDP-11 Family designs.* In computer systems being manufactured and sold, the success of bus designs is measured by the following criteria:

1. Does the bus successfully establish the communication pathway required?

*All of the real buses presented as examples are proprietary products of Digital Equipment Corporation, protected by United States and foreign patents.

2. Is the bus well specified (and well documented), so that a series of interfaces designed either concurrently or over a period of time by different engineers will in fact be compatible?
3. Does the bus avoid imposing unnecessarily strict performance constraints on the system?
4. Is the cost of the bus and its connections commensurate with the computer system and the bus' role in it?
5. Does the bus design anticipate expansion of the system in the future (without excessive cost)?
6. Can the bus be manufactured and tested in high volume production without excessive hand-crafting or tuning?

Beyond the scope of this chapter are some additional functions of buses, such as providing a means to diagnose and repair the system components connected to it and to allow measurement of system loads and performance.

Why Buses Are Important

As the above list of criteria suggests, there are many ways in which poor bus design can spoil the performance or cost/performance ratio of an otherwise well designed computer system. Failure to anticipate future expansion of a computer system is a common problem in bus designs. The PDP-11 Unibus, a very successful bus, first became inadequate as the main interconnection pathway when processor and memory speeds surpassed the bandwidth capability of the Unibus. Later, the Unibus 18-bit memory address width became a limitation.

Computer design is driven by advances in semiconductor technology. Every time the cost of the components of a computer subsystem decreases by, say, 50 percent, the subsystem is redesigned to take advantage of the lower cost. At present, the performance/cost (or storage capacity/cost) ratio for logic and memory is increasing at a rate of up to 100 percent per year. But the bandwidth/cost and other performance ratios of interconnections are steady or decreasing slightly. As a result, bus designs tend to persist in time across several redesigns of the other computer system components. This justifies the extensive engineering effort required in the initial design of a bus.

How Buses Are Designed

To design a bus, the engineer must first find out what system components are to be interconnected. Then, studying the requirements of communications between these components, the engineer chooses a structure. Finally, the cost constraints and available technologies lead to a choice of implementation.

The five-function model given below is not a set of bus designs but a functional model that results from taking the commonly used minicomputer building blocks and asking: What communications need to occur between this component and each other component? The model shows the five types of communications which were the answers to that question. The five functional pathways are the maximum number of interconnections that would be useful in a conventional single-processor minicomputer. Real bus designs combine these functions in cost-effective implementations.

After choosing the structure and functions of buses, the engineer must write a specification. This is crucial to the success of bus design if it is to be interfaced by a number of different engineers. As an example of the detail that can go into a bus specification, Figures 1, 2, and 3 show how the Massbus Data Read operation has been specified in a DEC internal engineering document.

After writing a specification, the engineer builds a prototype and tests it. If other engineers concurrently build interfaces to the bus, discrepancies, errors, and misunderstandings will be uncovered sooner. Finally, it is important that the specification be maintained, updating it to conform to the latest known design constraints. A very useful appendix to a bus

DATA BUS READ SEQUENCE

1. A read command is loaded into the Control register of the drive. If the command is valid, the drive enables its data bus receivers and drivers and asserts OCC.
2. Not more than 100 microseconds after step 1, the controller asserts RUN.
3. After a cable delay, the drive receives the RUN assertion. Disk drives now begin searching for the desired sector. Tape drives begin tape motion.
4. When the drive has read the first data word, it generates parity for the word; the data and DPA are gated onto the data lines and SCLK is asserted.
5. After a cable delay, the controller receives the SCLK assertion.
6. The drive negates SCLK no less than T nanoseconds after asserting it, where T is either 225 nanoseconds or 30 percent of the nominal burst data period of the drive, whichever is greater. The Data lines should be maintained valid for no less than one half of the SCLK interval after SCLK is negated.
7. After a cable delay, the controller receives the SCLK negation. The controller strobes the D lines and DPA and checks parity.
8. If there is more data to be read in this block, then not less than T nanoseconds after step 6, the drive gates out the next data word onto the D lines, generates DPA, and asserts SCLK. Steps 5, 6, and 7 then follow.
9. After the negation of SCLK (step 6) on the last word of data in the block, the drive asserts EBL.
10. After a cable delay, the controller receives the EBL assertion. At this time, the controller must decide whether or not to have the drive read the next block of data without disconnecting from the data bus (the controller may already have negated the RUN line).
11. If the controller decides not to read the next block, it negates the RUN line not later than 500 nanoseconds after step 10.
12. After a cable delay, the drive receives the RUN negation (the RUN line may already have been negated).
13. Not less than 1500 nanoseconds after step 9, the drive negates EBL. At this time the drive strobes the RUN line. If RUN has been negated, the drive disconnects from the data bus (the DRY bit should be set and OCC negated at this time).
14. After a cable delay, the controller receives the EBL negation (the controller may now generate an end-of-transfer interrupt and start another data transfer).

Figure 1. The Massbus Data Read operation as described in the Massbus specification.

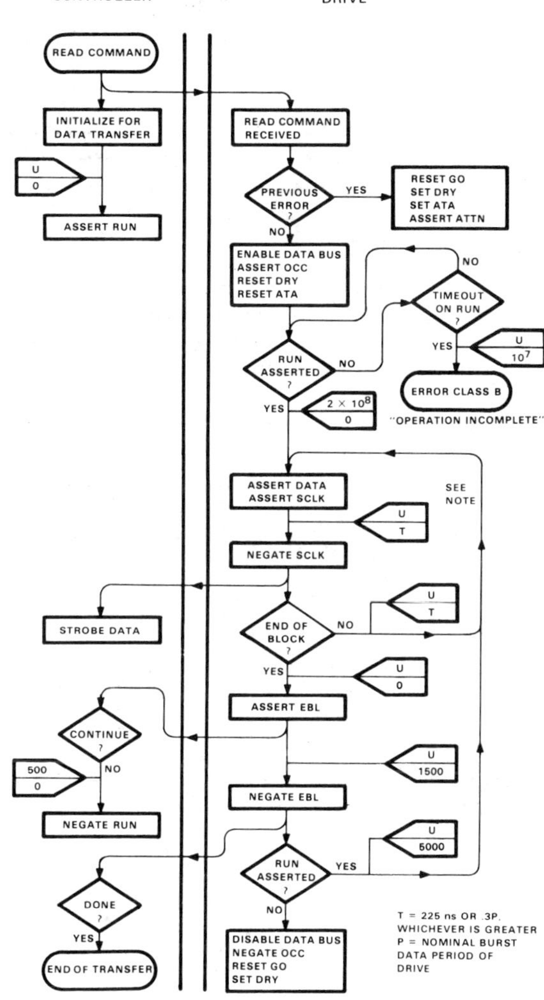

NOTE:
Minimum time from one assertion of SCLK to the next is either 500 ns or P, whichever is greater; maximum unspecified.

Figure 2. The Data Read flowchart in the Massbus specification.

specification is a list of the design problems that came up during the engineering of connections to it and the details of how they were resolved. This was done for the Massbus, in a section of the specification called "Design Notes."

FUNCTIONS OF BUSES IN COMPUTER SYSTEMS: A FIVE-FUNCTION MODEL

The functional building blocks of computers are central processing units, primary memory, input/output controllers, and peripheral units. Peripherals tend to be classed as either secondary memory or transducers (usually terminals).

Figure 4 shows these components in a traditional single-processor minicomputer system. Five different paths are shown interconnecting these components. These paths do not represent actual buses. Instead, we have considered each pair of components in the system and asked whether they need to communicate with each other. If so, a pathway between the pair has been inserted. This leads to a model which has more interconnection pathways than a typical computer has.

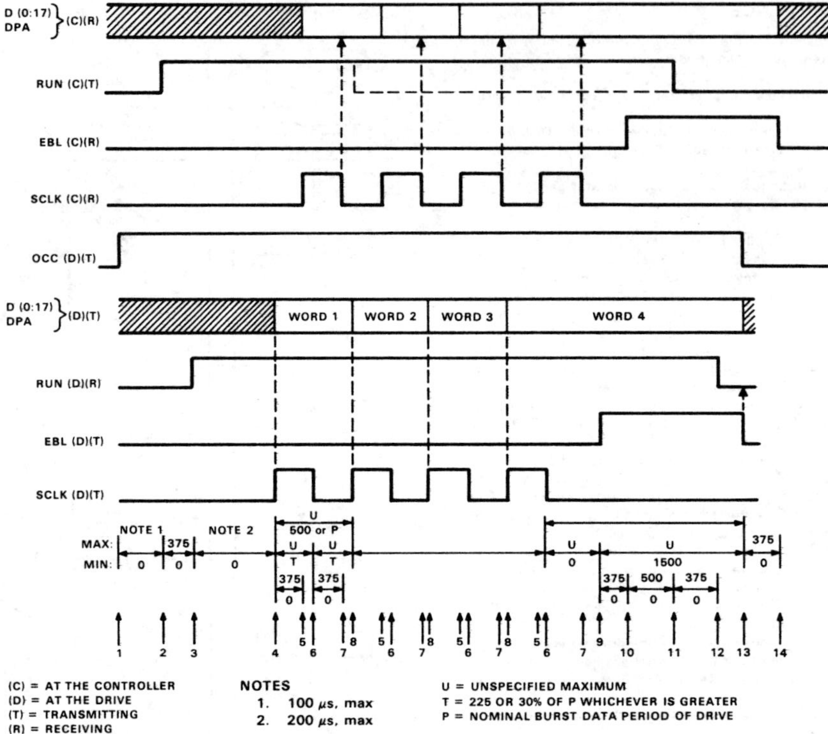

Figure 3. The timing diagram of a Data Read in the Massbus specification.

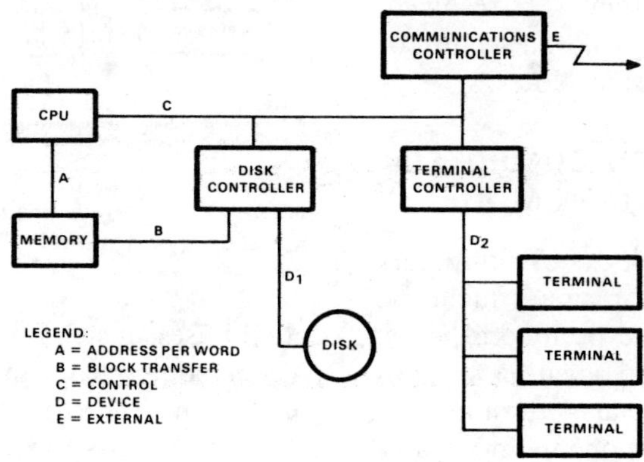

Figure 4. A five-function model of computer buses.

Table 1. Requirements for the Five Pathway Types

	Pathway Types				
	A	B	C	D	E
Requirement	**CPU–Memory**	**Controller–Memory**	**CPU–Controller**	**Controller–Peripheral**	**Controller–External**
Memory Address	Large: 2^{22} (one address per word)	Large: 2^{22} (one address per block)	None	None	None
Maximum Number of Connections	Small: 2^4	Small: 2^4	Medium: 2^6	Small-large: 2^8	Small-large: 2^8
Latency Tolerance	Low (0.5 μs)	High (50 μs)	Medium (5 μs)	Medium-high	Medium-high
Bandwidth	High (5 Mbytes/s)	Medium (1.2 Mbytes/s)	Low (0.1 Mbytes/s)	Low-high	Low-high
Length	Short (3 meters)	Medium (30 meters)	Long (30 meters)	Medium-long (to 300 meters)	Medium-long

In real computer systems, the functions of these pathways are combined into multifunction buses in order to get economical designs.

There are five types of interconnection shown in Figure 4, labeled *A, B, C, D,* and *E*. These labels have the mnemonic value given in the figure legend.

Pathway *A*, connecting the central processor (CPU) with the memory, is used to transfer instructions and data. This pathway is distinguished by requiring one address per word.

Pathway *B* connects one or more mass storage and communication controllers to the primary memory. It is distinguished by being a block transfer medium. Only one memory address per block transfer is needed because the data is stored in consecutive memory locations.

Pathway *C* is the control pathway. I/O commands are sent over this path from the CPU to the I/O controllers, and status information is returned from the controllers. I/O controllers can also cause an interruption to the CPU over this path. Small amounts of data are sometimes transferred over this path, for example, characters moved to and from a console terminal.

Pathways labeled *D* connect I/O controllers with their peripheral devices. In Figure 4, Pathway D_1 represents a disk connection and D_2 a multiple terminal connection path. The terminal interconnection does not normally transfer blocks of data. Both D_1 and D_2 carry control information as well as data.

Finally, pathway *E* represents a connection to external communication lines. Usually, the computer designer does not have control over the specification of such external pathways.

Five key parameters or requirements for these pathways affect cost and performance and are often traded against each other. Table 1 summarizes these requirements for the five types of pathways.

Memory addressing means selecting a word or block of words within the address space of the memory subsystem. Memory address bits are no different from data bits, from the standpoint of the bus designer. Both must be transmitted from one bus connection to another. However, type *A* pathways must transmit one address per word accessed, while type *B* pathways need only send one address per block of words. This difference can be exploited to gain lower cost buses in systems which implement separate buses for the *A* and *B* path functions.

The **maximum number of connections** to a bus tells us how many signals must be used to select a destination for a data transfer on the bus. Typically, a bus will carry some number, n, of "select" signals, and therefore be able to deliver data to as many as 2^n connections. On a type *A* pathway, a CPU accesses connections which contain memory. We do not typically need more than four "select" signals, allowing up to 16 memory connections. In the case of multiprocessor shared-memory systems, it may be necessary for some additional select codes to be available to identify the processor that is the destination for data from memory.

Latency tolerance refers to how long a delay (latency) a connection can tolerate, after it decides to make a data (word) transfer, until the transfer is complete. **Bandwidth** refers to how many data (word) transfers per second can be made.

Latency is different from bandwidth: latency refers to the interval, for any one data word transfer, from the time it is initiated until it is completed. Bandwidth is the repetition rate at which the initiation and completion of word transfers can be sustained over a given period of time. In particular, *peak bandwidth* – the maximum possible repetition rate – is a parameter which strongly affects the cost of a bus, and is the bandwidth we refer to here.

Type *A* pathways require both low latency and high bandwidth. The performance of a CPU-memory system depends heavily on the rate (bandwidth) at which words can be delivered to the central processor. Furthermore, the

Comments on Unibus Addressing

Transfers on the Unibus are not directed by the selection mechanism just described. Instead, there is the single concept of memory addresses. Each data transfer (type *A* or type *B*) on the Unibus is directed to or from a 1- or 2-byte section of memory. The memory address is broadcast to all connections. If one of the connections recognizes the address as being one of its own, then it participates in the data transfer. This anonymity allows a very large number of connections to be made to the Unibus, with each connection implementing a locally determined number of memory bytes.

For control transfers (type *C*), the Unibus has a concept called the "I/O page." A block of memory addresses (the I/O page) is reserved for use in accessing control and status registers in peripheral controllers and in the central processor. The uppermost 8,192 bytes of memory are never implemented in real memory. Instead, small segments are assigned (by administrative procedures) to each I/O controller type. Each controller responds to data transfers to and from addresses within its assigned segment.

No fixed amount of address space need be allocated to a given controller. If two controllers of the same type are connected to a Unibus, one of them is assigned to a "floating" address segment, an area reserved for such conflict resolution.

Unibus I/O controllers that perform Direct Memory Access (DMA) do so by making data transfers to memory at addresses below the I/O page. Block transfers are performed a word at a time to or from successive memory addresses, with the incrementing address being maintained by the I/O controller.

An I/O controller on the Unibus causes an interruption by doing a special control transfer whose destination is always the CPU. The interrupting controller transmits an "interrupt vector" as the data. The address lines of the Unibus are not used in this transfer.

CPU instruction execution and memory access times are typically closely matched. Therefore, the performance of the system is also very dependent on low latency in the CPU-memory pathway. In this type of pathway, effective bandwidth and latency are directly (inversely) related to each other.

On a type *B* pathway, high bandwidth is also typically required. Usually, this is the path by which disk and other mass storage data is moved to and from memory. In most cases, the rate at which data is transferred is determined by the disk subsystem. In minicomputer systems developed through 1977, the bandwidth required has not exceeded 1.2 megabytes per second for an individual disk controller-to-memory pathway.

Type *B* pathways, on the other hand, tolerate relatively long latencies. If there is sufficient buffering of data at the controller, system performance is relatively insensitive to delays of as much as 100 to 1000 microseconds in starting up a block transfer. The insensitivity is due to the dominance of relatively long delays already present in disk data accessing. (Mechanical positioning, both rotational and radial, may take tens of milliseconds in a typical disk access.)

Type *C* pathways – the control and interruption links – do not require high bandwidth compared with CPU instruction and DMA data activity. I/O control commands are issued relatively infrequently compared with the instruction execution rate in the CPU. Interruptions typically occur even less frequently. However, latency tolerance is not very high on the control pathway: it is important for interruptions to be delivered promptly, and CPU instructions that access I/O control and status registers usually are prevented from completing until the access has been completed. Therefore, Table 1 shows latency tolerance as "medium" (1 to 10 microseconds) for type *C* pathways: it is permissible to take a little longer to complete an I/O control instruction than other instructions, but not so long as initiating a block transfer from a disk.

Type *D* and *E* pathways handle interactions which are a mixture of type *B* and type *C*. Therefore, their requirements for latency and bandwidth vary over the range shown for types *B* and *C*.

Length refers to the maximum possible distance along the pathway from one connection to another. Maximum length is important because it affects both performance and cost of a bus. The CPU to memory pathway (type *A*) has been shrinking in length in recent computer designs because of the relationship between latency and length. The speed of light (or, more properly, of signals in a wire) sets the minimum delay between request and response. As a result, we see memories and central processors more frequently packaged together or in very close proximity. Fortunately, the continual size reduction of a given amount of CPU logic or memory has encouraged this trend. The current length range of a type *A* pathway for minicomputers is approximately 0.1 to 3 meters.

High speed block transfer I/O controllers also tend to be packaged closer to the memory in recent system designs. But since there may be many controllers, the length of the type *B* pathway may have to be two to ten times longer than the CPU-memory pathway (0.2 to 30 meters).

Design Tradeoffs

Control pathways connecting the central processor to all I/O controllers often have to be extended out of the CPU-memory package to reach peripheral subsystem packages. These tend to be the longest pathways in a system. Frequently, the design choice in connecting a peripheral to a minicomputer system is between: (1) extending the main types *B* and *C* buses out to reach the farthest peripherals and (2) designing type *D* buses that extend from a centrally packaged controller to a remote peripheral. Alternative (2) gives maximum flexibility and performance. But it costs more than

(1) and may lead to a proliferation of buses in the computer system. Figure 5 shows the two alternatives.

All parameters shown in Table 1 contribute to cost. The cost of a computer system could be allocated in a simple way to power, logic, memory, electromechanical parts, and package. As applied to the cost of buses, these become power, logic complexity, and cable/connector costs.

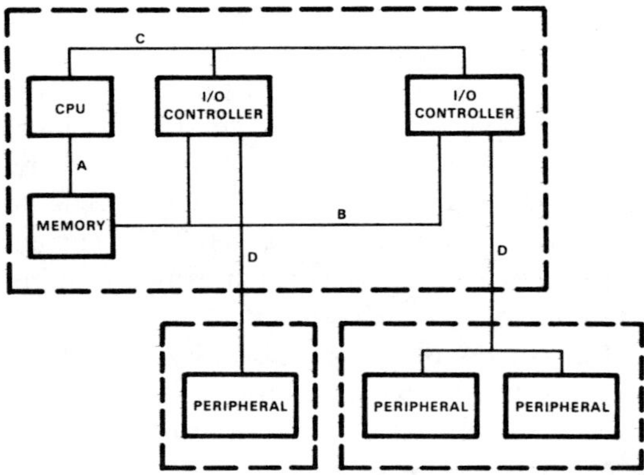

(a) Types *B* and *C* pathways contained within the "mainframe" package; longer type *D* paths.

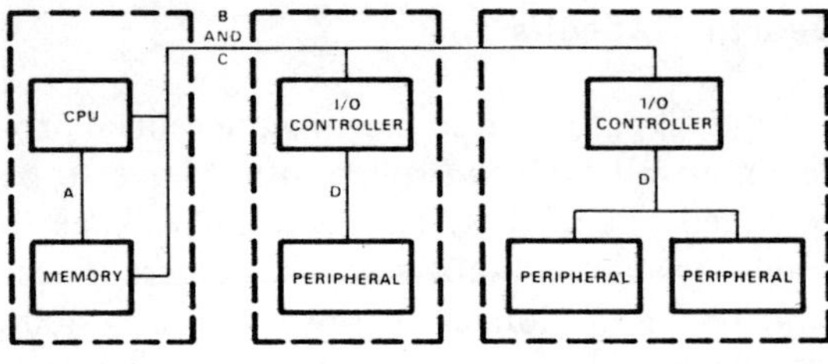

(b) Single types *B* and *C* pathways, extending out of the "mainframe" package; short type *D* paths.

Figure 5. A design tradeoff for types *B* and *C* pathways.

Increasing memory addressing requirements leads to more signals in the pathway. Each signal adds to power and cable costs. Lower bandwidth can be traded for wider memory addresses by time-multiplexing the addresses with data. Increasing the maximum number of connections adds to the electrical load and leads to increased power in the bus drivers or to lower bandwidth, as it takes longer for signals to settle. Also, more signals are required (logarithmically increasing with the number of connections) to select the destination of a transfer. Increasing maximum length also requires more bus drive power for a given signal level and increases the bus cost. Since longer buses have greater propagation delays, we can trade lower bandwidth and higher latency for increased length. Both length and load (connections) contribute to signal decay, and therefore these two are often traded against each other. For example, each section of a Unibus is rated for a maximum length of 50 feet or a maximum of 20 bus "loads." Exceeding either limit requires insertion of a "bus repeater" circuit. A Unibus with fewer loads could be operated at longer lengths than the maximum 50 feet, but configuration rules with fixed limits are easier to understand.

By accepting increased cost, some performance parameters can be enhanced as follows. Decreased latency and increased bandwidth can be achieved by using higher power driver and receiver circuits (such as ECL) which have lower propagation delays in their logic gates. Bandwidth can be increased by providing more buffering logic (complexity) at each connection. For a given level of reliability, the data clocking rate can be increased with either faster logic (higher power) or more logic parallelism (complexity). More data transmission parallelism would mean higher cable and connector costs. Lower latency can sometimes be achieved by distributing the task of arbitration among the connections. More logic is then required at each connection.

There are also considerations of physical and electrical environment that affect costs. To compensate for noisy environments, error detection and correction circuits may be added at each connection, adding to the complexity. Or shielded or twisted-pair cables may be included, adding to the cost of the interfaces. For physically stressful environments, cable costs may become dominant as the cables are armored, strengthened, or given noncorrosive wrapping. In general, we can trade reduced bandwidth for increased immunity to electrical noise, since most noise-induced errors can be overcome by repetition and redundant signaling. (At this tradeoff, bus design merges with applied communication theory.)

EVOLUTION OF THE HIGH PERFORMANCE PDP-11 SYSTEMS

The Unibus, introduced with the PDP-11 in 1970, is a novel bus structure because it is a single bus to which all system components are attached. It can be extended indefinitely; moreover, memory modules need not operate synchronously with the rest of the system.

In this section the evolution of the high performance descendants of the PDP-11/20 is traced, with emphasis on the development of buses in response to design goals for each model.

PDP-11/20

The Unibus design is integral to the PDP-11 architecture in the handling of interrupts (the priority level of the central processor affects arbitration) and in the I/O page concept (control registers appear as memory locations). But the important aspect of Unibus design, as a bus, is its support of modularity.

When the PDP-11/20 (Figure 6) was designed, it was natural to offer a bus that could be interfaced to many types of equipment, including users' laboratory devices. Digital offered Unibus interfacing modules (such as the DR11 series) which users of the PDP-11 could easily adapt to their own equipment.

The standardization of interfacing was also a deliberate attempt to prolong the service lives of Digital's peripheral equipment. As new members of the PDP-11 family were introduced, older peripherals could still be attached to the Unibus without electrical modifications.

The asynchronous data transfer of the Unibus has allowed DEC to introduce a series of memory subsystems with progressively increasing speeds without changing the Unibus timing or data transfer protocol. In a single system, various memory technologies can be intermixed.

PDP-11/45

The goal of the PDP-11/45 project (Figure 7) was to design a very fast central processor to match the speed of the 300-nanosecond semiconductor memory which was becoming available.

The PDP-11/45 design places the semiconductor memory in close proximity to the CPU and provides a private type *A* path, the Fastbus. This eliminates many of the access delays present when a Unibus was between the CPU and memory. For compatibility, however, it was necessary for the semiconductor memory to be accessible to DMA transfers from outside the CPU. Therefore, another Unibus was brought out of the CPU cabinet.

With higher CPU speed came the need for larger memory sizes. While the PDP-11/20 can have up to 64 Kbytes of memory (less 8 Kbytes reserved for the I/O page), the PDP-11/45 introduced a memory management unit (the

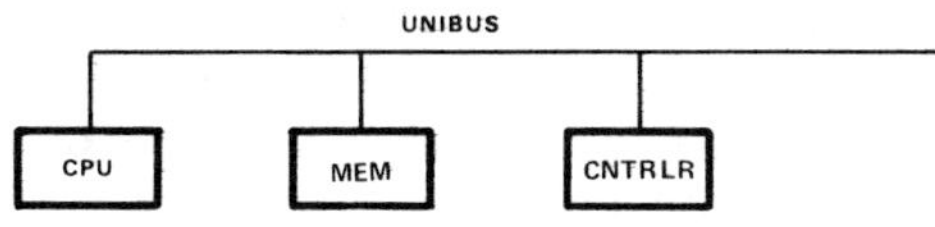

Figure 6. The PDP-11/20 Unibus configuration.

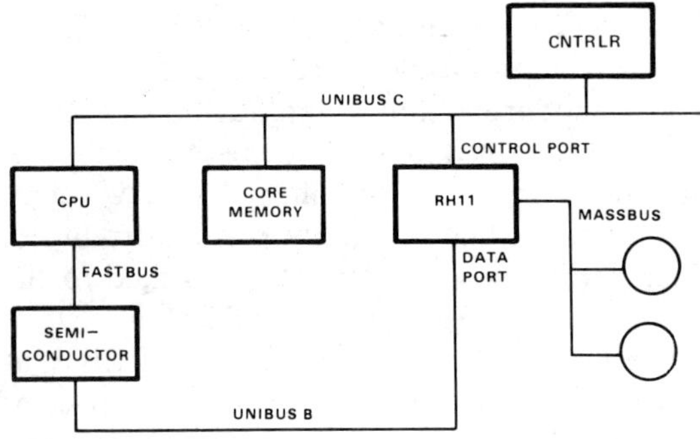

(a) Proposed configuration.

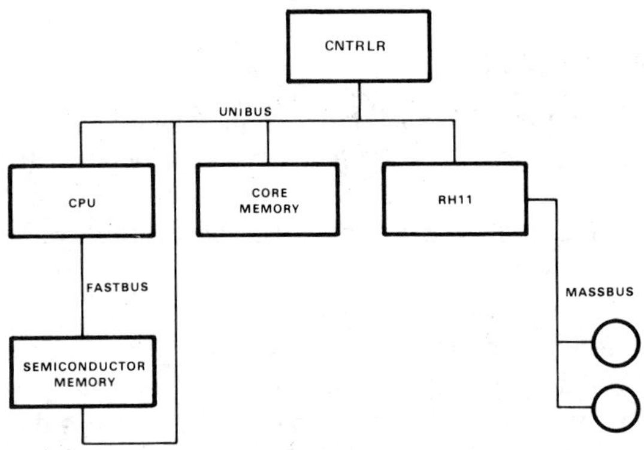

(b) Actual configuration.

Figure 7. PDP-11/45 configurations.

KT11) that allows addressing of up to 256 Kbytes. The Unibus design, with foresight, had been implemented with two spare address lines, allowing immediate use of the 18 bits of physical memory address from the PDP-11/45.

By 1973, the IBM 3330 disk technology (100 megabytes per spindle) had become available at a cost attractive to minicomputer system users. The Massbus was developed specifically to interface this and other high data rate devices which were being planned. The RH11 controller connects the Massbus to the two Unibuses of PDP-11/45 systems as shown in Figure 7*a*. The upper Unibus, Unibus C, was to carry the control and interruption (type *C*) transactions; the lower Unibus, Unibus B, was reserved exclusively for DMA (type *B*) data transfers. For this purpose, a special stand-alone Unibus Arbitrator module was developed because Unibus B has no processor present to perform Unibus arbitration. (Note, however, that the BR signals are not used on Unibus B, because there is no CPU to be interrupted).

Unfortunately, the configuration shown in Figure 7*a* could not be used for two reasons:

1. DMA transfers from the RH11 controller cannot reach memory modules attached to Unibus C if all block transfers are made on Unibus B. (The proposed solution of having the RH11 DMA port selected by program control was rejected because of the complexity of determining in software which memory is connected to which bus.)
2. DMA transfers from controllers on Unibus C cannot reach the semiconductor memory unit.

The second problem was fatal. The central processor is capable of dealing with only one I/O page, and that is on Unibus C. Therefore, old DMA controllers had to be attached to Unibus C. In fact, all controllers had to attach to Unibus C, because that is the only interruption path. Since compatible use of old peripherals was essential to success of the family, the PDP-11/45 was configured only as shown in Figure 7*b*. Unibus B, when connected to Unibus C (with the separate arbitrator module removed) becomes part of the single Unibus system.

PDP-11/70

By 1974, semiconductor memory costs had become much lower. Therefore, a cache memory became a feasible cost/performance enhancement to the PDP-11/45 (Chapter 10).

Without great modification to the CPU logic, a cache memory was added with a width of 32 bits – twice the word size of the PDP-11 (Figure 8). The cache effectively interfaced to the PDP-11/70 CPU over the same Fastbus that was present in the PDP-11/45.

In order to gain memory bandwidth for increases in both CPU and DMA performance, a new memory bus was added, with a 32-bit wide data path. Closely related to the memory bus was a backplane interconnection, which can carry 32 bits at a time to the RH70 controllers (up to four of them). In Figure 8 the RH70-to-memory path is shown going through the cache because of a look-aside feature of the cache memory.

The Massbus had been designed to provide very high block transfer bandwidth, while keeping the control registers accessible to the central processor at all times. The successful splitting of the type *C* path (the Unibus) from the type *B* path (the backplane data path) in the PDP-11/70 matched well with the Massbus design goals, and this match accounts in part for the relatively long life of the PDP-11/70 system in its marketplace.

The PDP-11/70 also required more memory addressing capacity to balance its increased speed. The KT11 memory management unit was easily expanded to address 4 megabytes of memory, and the RH70 controllers were designed to generate the required 22 bits of memory address directly.

Slower speed peripherals are still interfaced to the Unibus. In doing DMA transfers from them, it is necessary to transform the 18-bit address on the Unibus into a 22-bit main memory address. To do this, a Unibus Map module is inserted between the Unibus and the cache memory. This path carries 16 data bits at a time, and the bandwidth demands are relatively low.

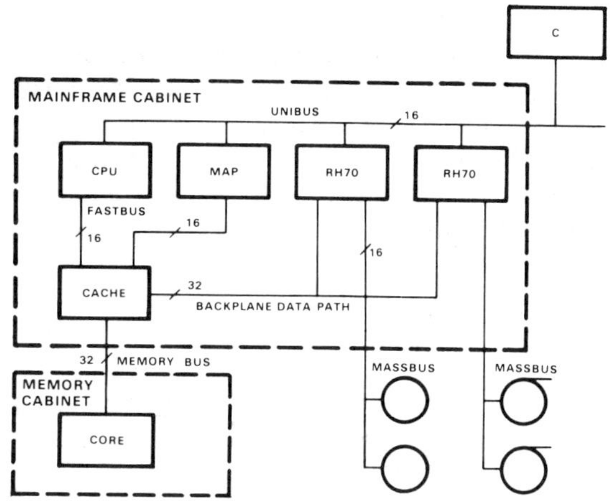

Figure 8. The PDP-11/70 configuration.

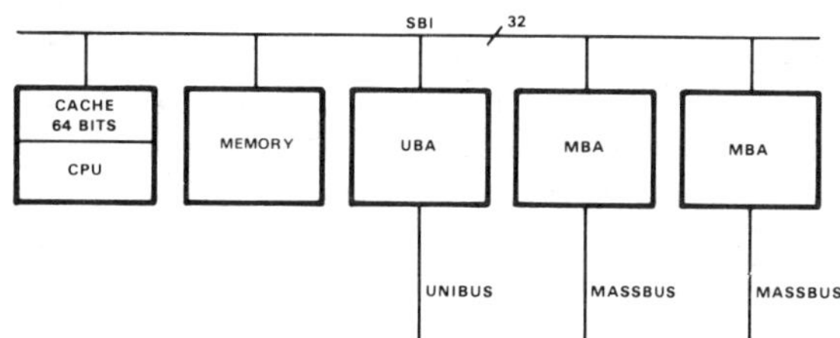

Figure 9. The VAX-11/780 organization, based on the SBI.

VAX-11/780

The VAX-11/780 (Figure 9) emerging in late 1977 returns to a single central bus organization, based on the Synchronous Backplane Interconnect (SBI).

The SBI was originally conceived in 1974 for use on a PDP-11 processor and was later planned for use on a PDP-10 processor. Those processors were not released, but the SBI was carried into the VAX-11/780 design and tailored for the 32-bit environment.*

*The VAX-11/780 SBI is the subject of a patent application filed by Digital Equipment Corporation.

High DMA bandwidth is obtained by the SBI short time-slot and by memory read operation splitting which releases the bus during the memory read-access delay. To help overcome the delay associated with having to do a full bus transaction to start a memory read cycle, the memory control logic is capable of receiving and storing a queue of up to 4 memory read and write requests while it is working on one of the requests.

Compatibility with existing PDP-11 peripherals is provided by controllers that adapt the SBI to a Unibus (the Unibus Adaptor (UBA) in Figure 9) and to several Massbuses (MBA).

On the SBI, the 1-gigabyte address space is divided in half with the Unibus I/O page concept extended to cover the upper half. Within this rather large address space are contained control registers for all peripherals, an 18-bit memory address space mapped onto the Unibus, and a number of internal status and control registers, such as those that contain error-reporting information.

Figure 10 shows an historical summary of the buses used in the PDP-11 computers.

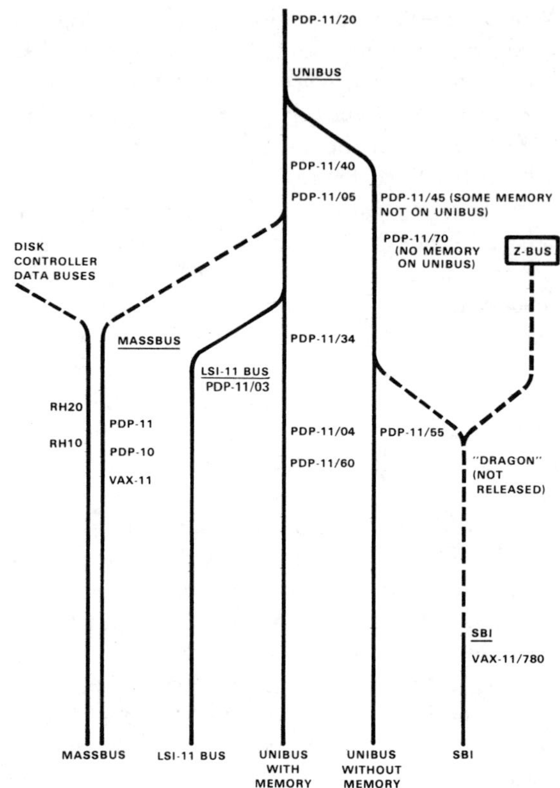

Figure 10. Genealogy of PDP-11 Family buses.

ARBITRATION METHODS

Since data transfer requests on a bus can originate from more than one source, there must be a means of deciding which source is to use the bus next. This process is called **arbitration**.

A connection follows a two-step procedure to transfer data on a bus:

1. **Arbitration.** Obtain the use of the bus.
2. **Data Transfer.** Transfer data on the bus.

To assist our examination of arbitration methods, we define twelve categories, using three discriminating criteria. The criteria are:

1. **Where?** Location of the arbitration logic (*Centralized* or *Distributed*).
2. **How?** Allocation rules (*Priority, Democratic,* or *Sequential*).
3. **When?** Timing relationship of arbitration to data transfer (*Fixed* or *Variable*).

Centralized arbitration means that a signal must pass from a requesting connection to a common arbitration point, and a response signal must return to the requesting connection before it may transfer data. In **distributed** arbitration there is no single common arbitration point. The Unibus, for example, has centralized arbitration (with the exception noted below). A contention-arbitrated serial bus, like the Ethernet [Metcalfe and Boggs, 1975], has distributed arbitration. The resolution of conflicting requests is accomplished in all arbitration methods by allocation rules. **Priority** arbitration means that in case of an apparent tie in the race to request use of the data transfer facilities, the rules always let one connection (or group) go ahead of another connection (or group). **Democratic** allocation means that there are no priority rules. An apparent tie is resolved arbitrarily or by some "fairness" rule which attempts to keep any one connection from monopolizing use of the data transfer facilities. **Sequential** allocation insures that there are never any apparent ties by giving request opportunities to only one connection at a time. (The sequence is not necessarily round-robin.)

The Unibus has priority allocation, by groups. Most contention-arbitrated serial buses have democratic allocation. Centralized, sequential (polled) buses are frequently used as type *D* pathways to connect character terminals to a concentrator (see Example 4, to follow).

Finally, there is the question of the timing relationship between the arbitration of a request and the data transfer that occurs as a result of the request. Arbitration **fixed** with respect to data transfer means that a connection must request the data transfer facilities at a fixed time relative to the data transfer. This category includes buses in which the same signal lines are used for data transfer and for arbitration.

Arbitration **variable** with respect to data transfer means that a connection may request use of the data transfer facilities at any time, independent of the current state of the data transfer facilities.

The Unibus has variable arbitration. Polled buses have fixed arbitration because data transfer always occurs in the time slot immediately after the arbitration logic has polled a requesting connection. Contention-arbitrated serial buses have fixed arbitration, too, in that the data transfer *is* the request for use of the bus.

Table 2 summarizes the categories of arbitration methods; description of five example buses follows.

Example 1: Unibus

Figure 11 shows a simplified diagram of the Unibus arbitration section with two controllers sharing a Bus Request (BR) line. When Controller 1 wants to use the bus for an interruption transaction, it asserts the shared BR signal line. When the processor is in a state capable of receiving an interruption, the arbitrator asserts the Bus Grant (BG) signal.

The arbitration logic of Controller 1 is shown in Figure 12. The timing of an arbitration sequence is shown in Figure 13. Controller 1 receives the assertion of BG and may make a data transfer as soon as the ongoing data transfer is complete. Controller 1 acknowledges its selection by asserting the Selection Acknowledge (SACK) signal. Controller 1 can use any BG assertion that arrives after the controller has asserted BR to perform an interruption transaction. The serial wiring of BG could be called a kind of priority arbitration, but it is preferable to think of it as a sequential type of allocation, in which the sequence begins on demand and always starts at the controller closest to the processor and arbitrator.

The Unibus actually has four groups of controllers, each group connected to a Bus Request line (called BR4, BR5, BR6, or BR7) and wired as shown in Figure 11. In addition, every controller capable of doing DMA data transactions is connected into a fifth group called Non-Processor Request (NPR) for data. All five groups share a common SACK line.

Memory modules do not participate in arbitration on the Unibus since they never initiate data transfers.

Table 2. The Twelve Categories of Arbitration Methods

Arbitration Category	Fixed with Respect to Data Transfer	Variable with Respect to Data Transfer
Central, Priority	Central, Priority, Fixed **SBI**	Central, Priority, Variable (plus some aspects of distributed, sequential below) **Unibus, LSI-11 Bus**
Central, Democratic	Central, Democratic, Fixed	Central, Democratic, Variable
Central, Sequential	Central, Sequential, Fixed **Polled Character-Input**	Central, Sequential, Variable
Distributed, Priority	Distributed, Priority, Fixed	Distributed, Priority, Variable
Distributed, Democratic	Distributed, Democratic, Fixed	Distributed, Democratic, Variable
Distributed, Sequential	Distributed, Sequential, Fixed	Distributed, Sequential, Variable

NOTE

The Massbus has no arbitration at all, because all control transfers originate from one point.

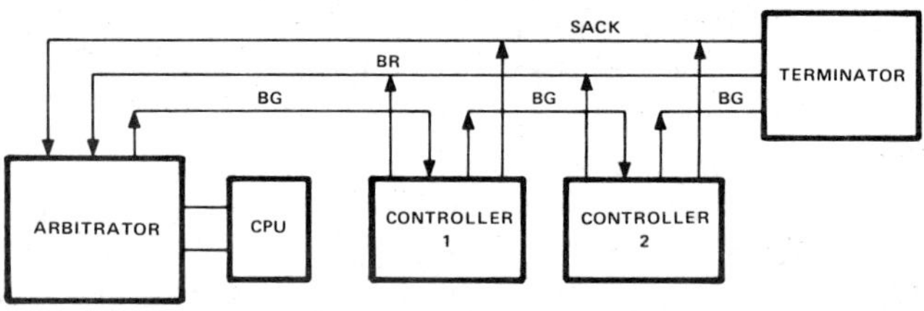

Figure 11. A simplified diagram of the Unibus arbitration section.

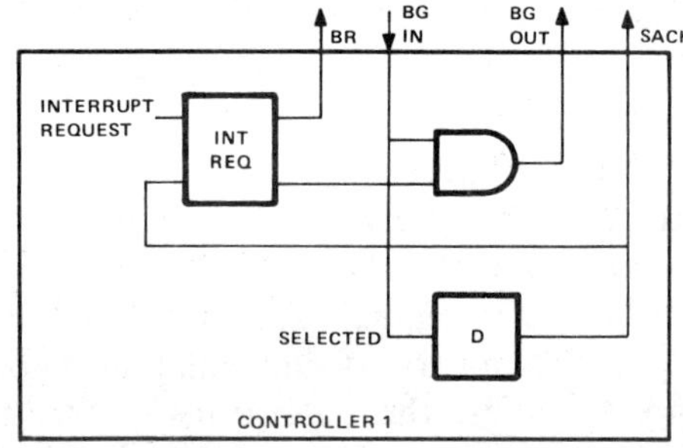

Figure 12. The arbitration logic of a controller attached to the Unibus.

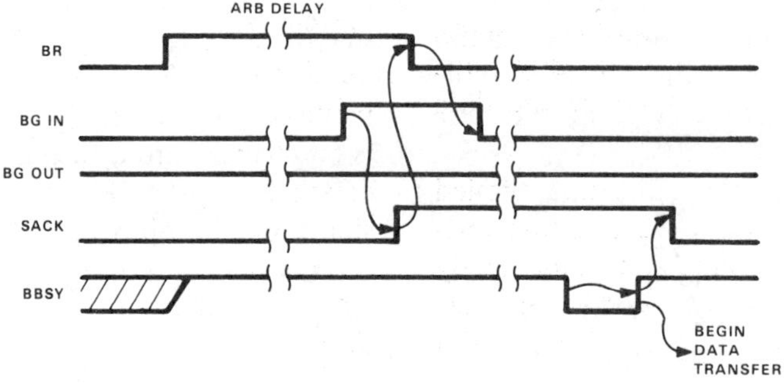

Figure 13. The timing of a Unibus arbitration sequence.

In the most general case, a single controller on a Unibus can participate in three types of transactions:

1. As the target of a control data transfer (type *C*), the controller behaves as if it were a memory. It receives commands (as data writes) into control registers and transmits status (as data reads) from status registers this way. The controller does not request the bus for these transactions: it is the "slave" of the processor which obtained the bus for this purpose.
2. As the originator of a DMA, type *B* data transfer, the controller moves data to or from memory. To obtain the bus for this purpose, it asserts the shared NPR line, and waits for a Non-Processor Grant (NPG) signal to be passed to it from the left.
3. As an interruption source (type *C*), the controller sends an interrupt vector to the processor. To obtain the bus for this purpose, the controller asserts one of the four BR lines (BR4, BR5, BR6, or BR7), and waits for the corresponding BG signal (BG4, BG5, BG6, or BG7) to be passed to it from the Arbitrator. Each controller is assigned a single BR level at the time of its installation in the system. Thereafter, it never blocks any of the other three BG signals.

Some controllers, such as simple terminal interfaces, do no DMA transfers, but perform an interruption transaction for each character of input or output.

The priority arbitration of the Unibus is affected directly by the priority state of the CPU. The CPU program execution priority (PRI) varies from 0 to 7. The Unibus Arbitrator grants use of the bus to non-CPU connections by the following rules:

1. At any time, when assertion of NPR is received, assert NPG. (Interpretation: a controller may do DMA data transfers at any time.)
2. Whenever the CPU is between instructions (i.e., is interruptable), then:
   a. If PRI <7 and BR7 is asserted, then assert BG7, else
   b. If PRI <6 and BR6 is asserted, then assert BG6, else
   c. If PRI <5 and BR5 is asserted, then assert BG5, else
   d. If PRI <4 and BR4 is asserted, then assert BR4.

   (Interpretation: when the CPU is interruptable, it will accept interruptions from a controller in a group whose priority is greater than the current program execution priority of the CPU.)

The priority arbitration rules of the Unibus involve both the processor priority and the relative priorities of the BR signals, among themselves. Assertion of a BR7, for example, blocks the grant signals BG6, BG5, and BG4 until all controllers asserting BR7 have accomplished their interruption transactions. Therefore, we classify the Unibus arbitration method as centralized and variable, with a mixture of priority and sequential allocation rules.

Example 2: The LSI-11 Bus

The LSI-11 Bus serves the same functions for the LSI-11 system that the Unibus serves for most of the other PDP-11 processors. The LSI-11 bus is constrained to use fewer conductors and, therefore, less power and logic than the Unibus. It achieves the reduction from 56 signals to 36 signals primarily by time-multiplexing memory addresses and data on the same conductors (accepting lower bandwidth in order to achieve lower cost).

Arbitration for DMA transfers is essentially identical to that of the Unibus (Figures 11 and 12). The corresponding signal names on the LSI-11 Bus are SACK (for Unibus SACK), DMR (for NPR), and DMG (for NPG).

Arbitration for the interruption transaction has only one priority-group for all interrupting controllers. When a controller wants to interrupt the processor, it asserts the Interrupt Request (IRQ) signal. This is similar to the BR signals on the Unibus. However, the LSI-11 Bus interruption transaction more closely resembles a data transfer, so it will be described in the section on data transfer synchronization. Arbitration on the LSI-11 Bus, like the Unibus, is classed as centralized and variable with a mixture of priority and sequential allocation rules. However, only one level of priority is used for interruption transactions.

Example 3: Synchronous Backplane Interconnect (SBI), the VAX-11/780 Memory Bus

This memory bus is distinguished by its limited length and its master clock which synchronizes all transactions on the bus. (The bus does not extend beyond the etched backplane of the computer cabinet.) The functions of the SBI are the same as those of the Unibus. However, the SBI differs in physical configuration because every controller must be directly connected to the backplane. Another difference between Unibus and SBI is that all transactions on the SBI are of fixed duration, which gives much higher bandwidth for data transfer. (The SBI is rated at 13.3 megabytes per second, while the Unibus is capable of approximately 1.7 megabytes per second when operating with equivalent speed memory.) To achieve this bandwidth, it was necessary to split the memory read operation into two bus transactions – one to transmit an address to the memory, another to transmit data back to, the requesting connection. In this way the SBI can accommodate memories of various cycle times, as can the Unibus, but the requesting connection does not occupy the bus facilities for the duration of the cycle.

Arbitration on the SBI is distributed, priority, and fixed. Figure 14 shows a simplified diagram of the signals involved in SBI arbitration.

A master clock, represented here by a single signal, defines a sequence of time-slots on the bus. Each slot (200 nanoseconds in the VAX-11/780) is of long enough duration to complete a transfer of data from one connection to any other connection, but not for a reply signal to be sent back.

There are four Transfer Request (TR) signals in this simplified example: TR0, TR1, TR2, and TR3. Each TR signal "belongs" to one connection; that is, only one connection is permitted to assert the signal.

Each TR signal has a priority associated with it: TR0 has highest priority. A connection requests the use of the SBI data transfer facilities by the following procedure:

1. At the beginning of the next time-slot (after deciding to transfer data), assert the TR signal that belongs to this connection.
2. At the end of the time-slot, sense the state of all of the higher priority TR lines.
3. If none of the higher priority TR lines is asserted, then at the beginning of the next slot negate "my own" TR signal and begin transmitting data.
   If any of the higher priority TR lines is asserted, then do not negate "my own" TR signal, and go back to step 2.

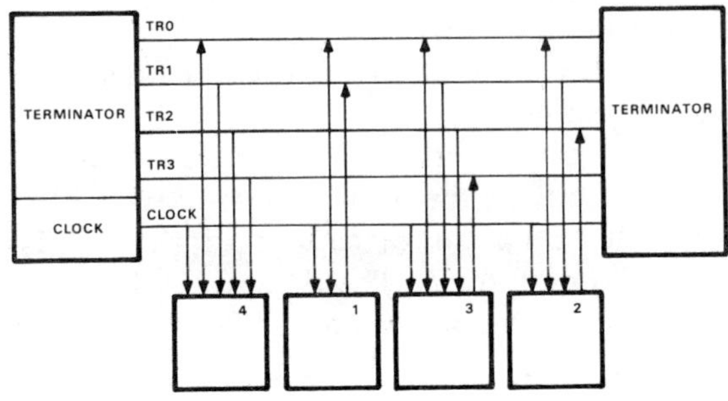

Figure 14. A simplified diagram of SBI arbitration signals.

Figure 15 shows a timing diagram for a sample set of data transfers on the simplified SBI of Figure 14. In this example, connection number 3 (corresponding to TR3) requests the bus during slot 1, and connection numbers 1 and 2 (corresponding to TR1 and TR2) request the bus during slot 2.

At the end of slot 1, connection 3 detects no higher priority TR signals, so it negates TR3 and transmits data during slot 2.

At the end of slot 2, connection 2 senses that TR1 is asserted, and therefore waits, leaving TR2 asserted. At the same time, connection 1 senses no higher priority TR signals, so it negates TR1 and transmits data during slot 3.

Some transactions on the SBI require that a connection transmit on two or more consecutive slots. A connection that requires a slot beyond its first one asserts TR0 at the beginning of its first data transfer slot. TR0, the highest priority TR signal, is not assigned to any one connection.

The example in Figure 15 shows connection 2 doing a two-slot data transfer. After waiting for connection 1 to transfer, connection 2 "holds" the bus for slot 5 by asserting TR0 (hold signal) at the beginning of slot 4. In the SBI of the VAX-11/780, connections are limited to transmitting in no more than three consecutive slots.

We have shown four connections in this example, although only three TR signals are assigned. The lowest priority connection, number 4, does not have a TR signal assigned to it because there is no need to sense a TR signal from this lowest priority connection. Connection 4 transmits only when no other connection is requesting the next slot. Connection 4 gains an advantage by being lowest priority: it may transmit in any slot not used by the other SBI connections without asserting a TR signal of its own in the preceding slot. This gives it a shorter memory-access latency. For this reason, the CPU is usually given lowest priority on the SBI.

The master clock is crucial to the operation of the SBI. In the VAX-11/780, the slots are defined by combining three clocks into four equal-interval phase markers. All transmitted TR signals are asserted at the beginning of phase 1, and all received TR signals are sensed at the beginning of phase 4, three-fourths of the way through the nominal slot period. This guarantees that signals from nearby connections are not sensed too early and that distant TR signals are sensed early enough.

Example 4: A Polled Character-Input Bus (Type D)

Figure 16 shows a diagram of a hypothetical simple character-input bus. The controller at the left end accepts all input from the keyboards. It "asks" each keyboard in turn whether it has a character to send, and if so, the controller accepts the character during the next

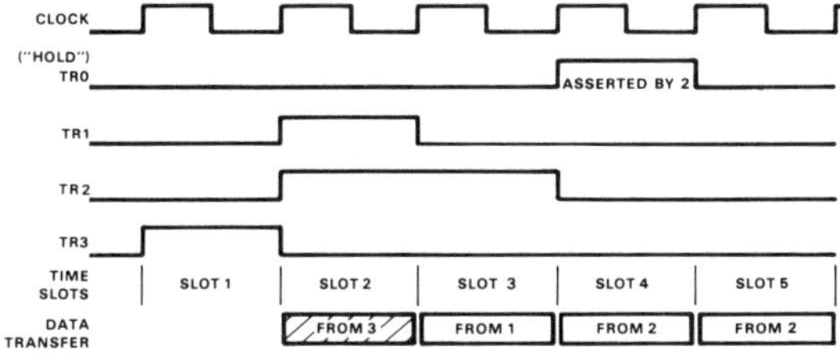

Figure 15. Timing diagram of arbitration for an example set of data transfers on a simplified SBI.

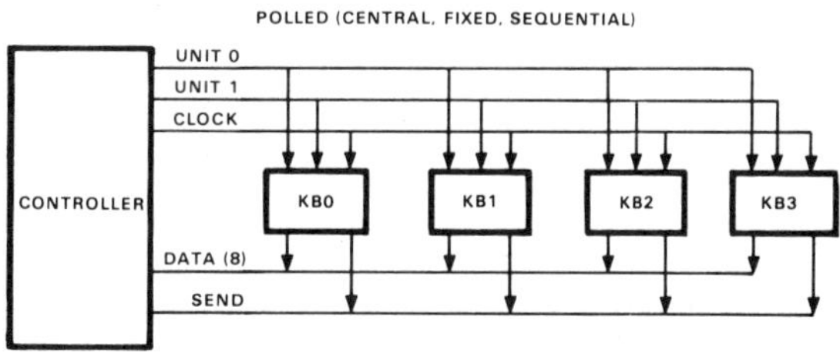

Figure 16. A hypothetical polled character-input bus.

time slot. This arbitration scheme is centralized, sequential, and fixed with respect to data transfer.

Three signals are broadcast from the controller to all terminals. One is the Clock, which defines the time-slots. The other two signals, called Unit 0 and Unit 1, send out a two-bit code which selects one of the four keyboards during each slot. The coding is binary.

The controller changes the Unit Select signals at the beginning of each slot. The keyboard selected, if it contains a character to be transmitted, asserts the Send signal, and transmits the character at the beginning of the next slot.

In the timing diagram shown in Figure 17, keyboard 1 transmits two characters and keyboard 2 transmits one character. In this type of

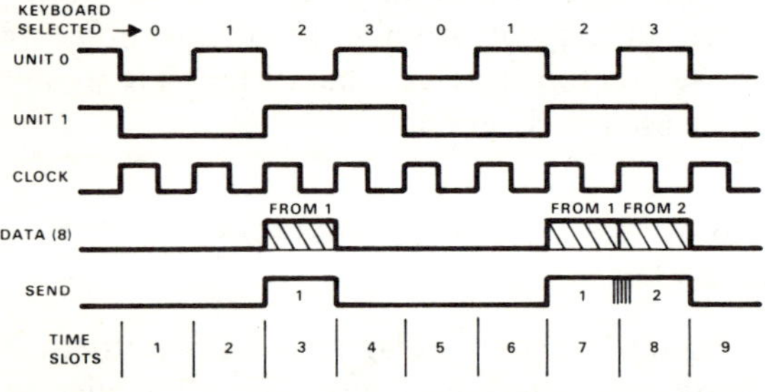

Figure 17. Timing diagram of a polled character-input bus.

arbitration scheme, the polling (sequential sampling) of possible sources of data (the keyboards) eliminates the need for contention or priority rules. The logic of each connection is simple, but the scheme in this example limits each connection (keyboard) to using a maximum of 25 percent of the data transfer bandwidth.

Example 5: Massbus

The Massbus is a peripheral-to-controller (type *D*) bus that has no arbitration at all. As in the previous example, a single controller at one end of the bus receives or sends on each data transfer. Control information is transferred as on the Unibus, but the "master" of the transfer is always the controller. Data blocks are transferred using a peripheral-generated clock, and the transfers are always initiated by writing a control word into a register in the peripheral.

Interruptions to the CPU are generated by the controller on demand from any peripheral. For this purpose an Attention signal exists in the control section of the Massbus. Each peripheral is capable of asserting this signal.

SYNCHRONIZATION OF DATA TRANSFERS

Synchronization of a data transfer is coordinating the timing between two bus connections which are involved in a data transfer. The method by which data transfer is coordinated can be very different from the arbitration method.

To classify the methods of data transfer synchronization, we use two criteria:

1. **Source**. The location of the source of the synchronizing signals (*centralized*, *one* of the sending or receiving connections, or *both* connections).
2. **Periodicity**. The type of synchronizing signals (*periodic* or *aperiodic*).

Table 3 shows the six resulting categories and how the examples fit into them.

The location of the synchronizing signal or signals may be at one of the connections sending or receiving data (*one*), at both of the connections (*both*), or at neither (*centralized*).The Unibus data transfer is synchronized by signals from both the sending and receiving connections.

The synchronizing signal may be a clock (*periodic*), or it may be something else (*aperiodic*). The Unibus uses an aperiodic "handshake."

Table 3. Data Transfer Synchronization Methods

Location of Signal Source	Periodicity	
	Periodic	Aperiodic
Centralized	SBI polled character-input	No examples
One connection	Massbus Data	No examples
Both connections	No examples	Unibus, LSI-11 Bus, Massbus Control

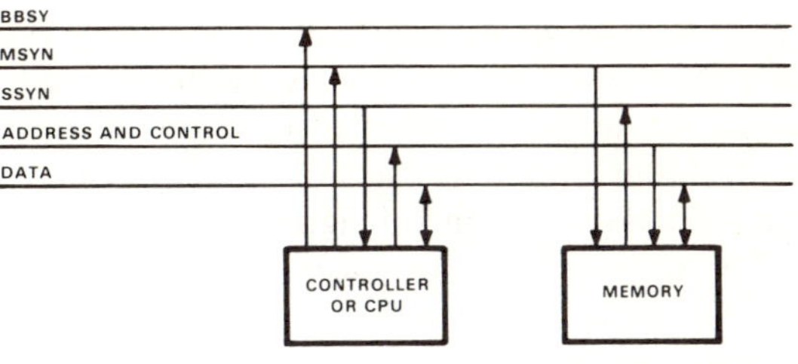

Figure 18. Unibus data transfer section.

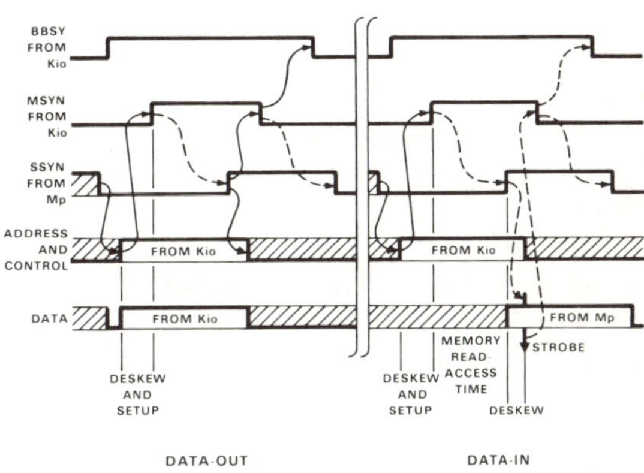

Figure 19. Timing diagram of transfers on Unibus.

Example 1: Unibus

DMA (type *B*) and CPU-memory (type *A*) data transfers on the Unibus are accomplished with the same data timing. The interrupt-vector transaction timing is similar and thus is omitted from this discussion.

Figure 18 shows the data transfer section of a Unibus with two connections: a controller or CPU (the "master" in a data transfer), and a memory (the "slave"). (For control and status register transfers (type *C*), a controller plays the role of memory or slave.) The timing of transfers on a Unibus is shown in Figure 19. Bus Busy (BBSY) indicates that the data transfer facilities are in use. Control and Address signals are a group that specify the kind of transfer and the memory address. Master Sync (MSYN) is asserted by the master (the CPU or controller) to indicate that Control and Address signals are present.

Slave Sync (SSYN) is asserted by the slave connection (memory) to indicate that data is present on the Data lines.

Unibus Data-Out moves data from the requesting connection into memory.

Having received permission from the arbitrator and acknowledged it by asserting Select Acknowledge (SACK), the connection waits for Bus Busy (BBSY) to be negated. It then asserts BBSY and negates SACK. This connection now "owns" the data transfer section of the Unibus.

Next, it must wait for SSYN to be negated to prevent its own logic from mistakenly sensing SSYN in the asserted state too early.

Next, the master connection transmits the Address and Control signals and the Data. It then waits for an interval, the deskew time, before asserting MSYN, to compensate for the variable delay in transmission of different signals from one connection to another. An additional set-up time is inserted to allow all slave connections time to sense and compare against the Address and Control signals.

The slave connection senses the Address and Control signals at all times. In this example, the address being transmitted by the controller matches one of the memory addresses "owned" by this memory connection. Therefore, this slave responds to the assertion of MSYN by sensing and storing the signals on the Data lines.

Having captured the data, the slave asserts the SSYN signal. When the master receives the assertion of SSYN it knows that the data transfer has been completed.

The master then stops transmitting the Address and Control, Data signals, MSYN, and BBSY.

Unibus Data-In is a read from memory. The timing is similar to Unibus Data-Out, except that data is transmitted on the data lines by memory. The second part of Figure 19 shows the Data-In timing.

Data transfer on the Unibus is aperiodic – there is no clock. Synchronization occurs by a "handshake" interaction between the MSYN and SSYN signals. In fact, two round-trips of signaling occur. We could look at this signaling in tabular form (Table 4).

Table 4. Synchronization of Unibus Data Transfer

	Data-Out	Data-In
MSYN assertion	Address and Control and Data present	Address and Control present
SSYN assertion	Data captured (by slave)	Data present
MSYN negation	Stop transmitting Data and BBSY	Data captured (by master); stop transmitting BBSY
SSYN negation	–	Stop transmitting Data

The sequence of four events insures a fully "interlocked" data transfer. The timing of a transfer is variable, depending on the speed of the slave's memory (for Data-In) and on the speed of the logic at both connections. On the Unibus, 75 nanoseconds are allowed for deskew time and an additional 75 nanoseconds for set-up, where noted.

Example 2: LSI-11 Bus

Data transfers on the LSI-11 Bus also serve the functions of pathway types *A* and *B*. Synchronization is from both sender and receiver and is aperiodic. Below the CPU-memory (type *A*) transfers are described.

The signals involved in data transfers between the central processor and memory are DAL, SYNC, DIN, DOUT, and RPLY. These are similar to the Unibus signals shown in Figure 18. The processor initiates all data transfers of this type. Type *C* (control and status) transfers are also made using the synchronization described next, with a controller playing the part of memory in the transfer.

Figures 20 and 21 show the timing of data transfers. The 16 DAL signals are used to transmit address and then data, one after the other. SYNC is the signal which tells all memory devices on the bus to examine the DAL lines and to test for a matching address. DIN and DOUT initiate the memory read and memory write cycles, for Data-In and Data-Out transfers, respectively. RPLY, which is similar to the Unibus SSYN signal, indicates the presence of a response from the memory.

Before proceeding with a transfer, the CPU must wait until both SYNC and RPLY have been negated, to be sure that no other transfer is in progress on the bus.

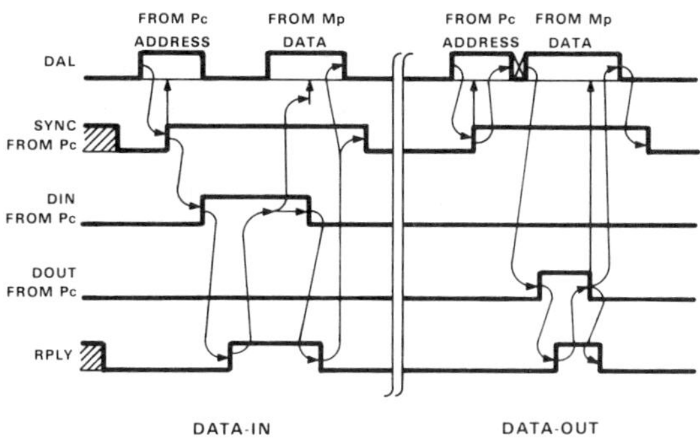

Figure 20. LSI-11 Bus Data-In and Data-Out synchronization.

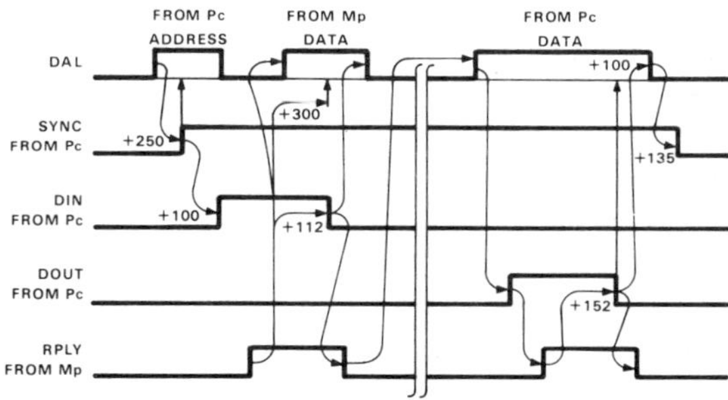

Figure 21. LSI-11 Bus Data-In-Out synchronization.

The CPU transmits the memory address on the DAL lines. After waiting for a fixed interval, to allow for deskew and set-up time at the memory, the processor asserts SYNC.

The memory senses the DAL lines when it receives the assertion of SYNC. The memory matches the address received and decides that the data word being addressed is in this memory module.

After another fixed delay, to guarantee that the SYNC assertion always arrives at the memory first, the processor asserts DIN and stops transmitting the address on the DAL lines.

As soon as the memory receives the DIN assertion, it knows that a read cycle is desired. It retrieves the data word and transmits it on the DAL lines. Meanwhile, it may assert the RPLY signal as much as 125 nanoseconds before transmitting the data.

When the processor receives the RPLY assertion, it waits at least 200 nanoseconds to be sure that the data has arrived, and then senses and stores the data. Then the processor negates DIN.

As soon as the memory receives the DIN negation, it stops asserting RPLY. Not more than 100 nanoseconds later, the memory stops transmitting the data on the DAL lines.

When the processor receives the negation of RPLY, it negates SYNC. The bus is now available for the next data transfer.

The second part of Figure 20 shows the timing of a Data-Out (write to memory) transfer.

Figure 21 shows the timing of another type of LSI-11 Bus data transfer, the Data-In-Out operation. In this transfer, a data word is read from memory, sent to the CPU, and then a word is sent back to the same memory location. This operation is useful for certain PDP-11 instructions such as "increment memory" (INC), which modifies a single word in memory, and ADD, which stores a result at the address of the second operand. Bus transmission time is saved by not requiring the address to be sent a second time for the Data-Out portion of the cycle. On the other hand, the CPU may delay the operation by an arbitrary amount of time, while the word to be written is generated.

Figure 22 shows the timing of the interruption transaction on the LSI-11 Bus. This transaction includes both arbitration and the transfer of a data word (an interrupt vector) from a controller to the CPU.

All controllers share the single Interruption Request (IRQ) line. It is similar to the Unibus BR signals, causing an interruption when asserted.

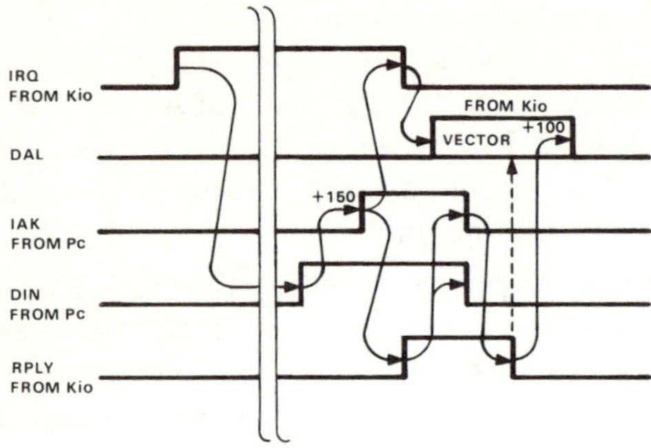

Figure 22. LSI-11 Bus interruption transaction synchronization.

The Interruption Acknowledge (IAK) signal is similar to the Unibus BG signals. IAK is wired from the processor (arbitrator) serially through all controllers, just like a Unibus priority group.

A controller may assert IRQ at any time. When the processor is ready to receive an interrupt vector, it begins a sequence which resembles a Data-In transfer. However, the SYNC signal is not used and no address is sent out on the DAL lines.

Example 3: Synchronous Backplane Interconnect (SBI)

The SBI synchronization method is centralized and periodic. There is only one sequence of events which causes information transfers on the SBI, and that sequence is quite simple. However, the information transferred from one connection to another has two possible interpretations: Command and Address, or Data. A memory read or write operation always consists of two sequences: one to transfer a command to the memory connection, the other to transfer data. The read operation is split, allowing other transactions to take place while a memory is accessing data.

There are four groups of signals used to effect data transfer: ID, DATA, FLAG, and CLOCK. The ID signals are used to identify the destination of the transfer when the information transferred is data. The other use of the ID signals is explained below.

The Data lines carry 32 bits of information. This information is either: (1) 32 bits of data, or (2) 28 bits of address and 4 bits of command code. The Flag signal is asserted to indicate case (2). In this case, the destination of the transfer is determined by the 28 address bits, in a way similar to Unibus addressing. For these transfers, the ID lines carry the identity of the *source* of the transfer. The connection receiving a Read command saves this source ID value, so it can use it as a destination ID on a later data transfer.

Figure 23 shows the timing of the two SBI transfers which make up a read operation from memory. Remember that there is a master clock which defines a series of time-slots. The Transfer Request (TR) signals are shown again to illustrate the fixed time relationship of arbitration before a transfer.

In Figure 23, the controller (connection 1) decides at the beginning of slot 1 to initiate a

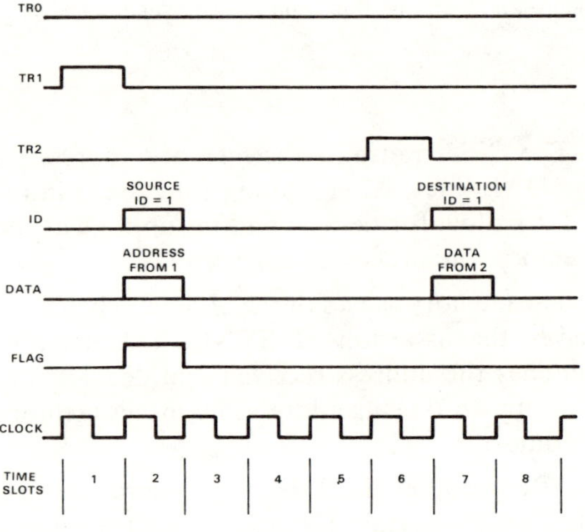

Figure 23. The timing of two SBI transfers which make up a read operation.

memory read operation. In slot 2 it transmits the following bits:

ID = 1, the identity of the source connection.
DATA = Read command code, plus 28 bits of memory address.
FLAG = asserted, indicating that DATA contains command and address.

At the end of slot 2, the memory connection senses all of these bits and captures them in a buffer register. In fact, every connection on the SBI captures all of these bits on every slot. Subsequently, each connection matches the ID bits to determine if it should respond.

In this case, the memory connection detects that the address refers to memory contained in itself, and it therefore begins a read cycle.

The memory connection asserts its TR signal (TR2) one slot before it is ready to transmit data. The memory transmits its data to the requesting controller in the next slot. (slot 7):

ID = 1, the identity of the destination connection.
DATA = 32 bits of data from memory.
FLAG = negated, indicating that DATA carries data.

At the end of slot 7, all connections to the SBI capture this information, and controller 1 recognizes the match between the ID bits and its own identity. A memory read has now been finished.

On the SBI, a memory may wait a variable number of slots before replying to a Read command. Clearly there is a performance penalty for memories that require slightly more than an integral number of slot-times to access a word. Therefore, the SBI clock is "tuned" to be an integral submultiple of the access time of the memory subsystem we intend to use. However, we could attach a variety of memory subsystems with different access times to one SBI, without serious performance degradation, as long as the memory access times are sufficiently large multiples of the slot-time.

The VAX-11/780 system uses a slot-time of 200 nanoseconds and has a memory subsystem access time of just under 800 nanoseconds (including error detection). The four-slot access time shown in Figure 23 is typical of this system.

Figure 24 shows the timing of a memory write operation on the SBI. The controller, connection 1, transmits in the two consecutive slots following arbitration. In the first slot (slot 10), FLAG is asserted to indicate that the Write command and address information is present. In slot 11, the data is transmitted. The memory connection must be prepared to accept and capture the sequence of two transmissions.

During slots 10 and 11, the ID lines contain the identification of the controller, allowing the memory to verify that both transmissions came from the same source.

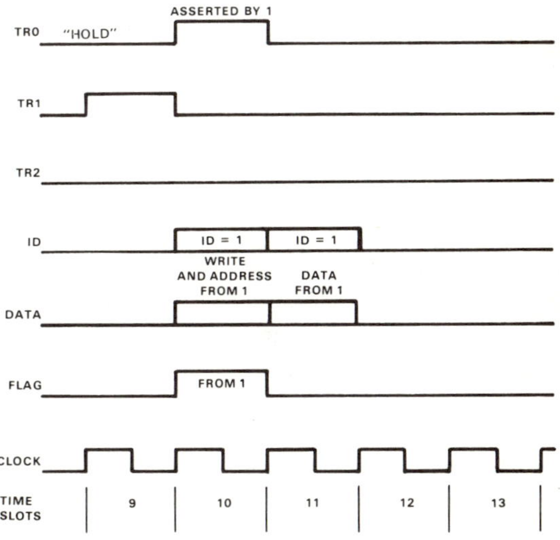

Figure 24. The timing of a memory write operation on the SBI.

The two-slot write operation is kept contiguous by using the highest priority TR0 "hold" signal to obtain use of the second slot. The SBI minimizes the slot interval and maximizes bandwidth by eliminating all round-trip delays.

Example 4: Polled Character-Input Bus

Data transfer on this bus was described in the section on arbitration methods. The synchronization method is centralized and periodic.

Data transfer occurs in time-slots just as on the SBI. The time-slots are defined by a master clock, and the receiver (always the controller) must accept the data at the end of the time-slot. In contrast to the SBI, this bus preallocates one of every four slots to each keyboard connection. The controller must keep internally an indication of which character is received from which keyboard.

Example 5 (a): Massbus Control Section

The Massbus actually consists of two sections: a Control Section for reading and writing the contents of registers in the peripherals, and a Data Section for moving blocks of data. All transfers are between the controller and one of the (up to eight) peripherals. The two sections operate independently, except that a Control Section write into a control register of a peripheral is required to initiate a block transfer on the Data Section.

The Control Section of the Massbus is a miniature Unibus. However, the controller is always the master, and one of the peripherals is always the slave in the transfer. Figure 25 shows the Control Section signals involved in data (i.e., control and status register) transfers. The Demand (DEM) signal takes the place of MSYN, and Transfer (TRA) takes the place of SSYN. Instead of Address and Control lines, there is an eight-bit address on the Massbus Control Section: three bits of Drive Select (DS),

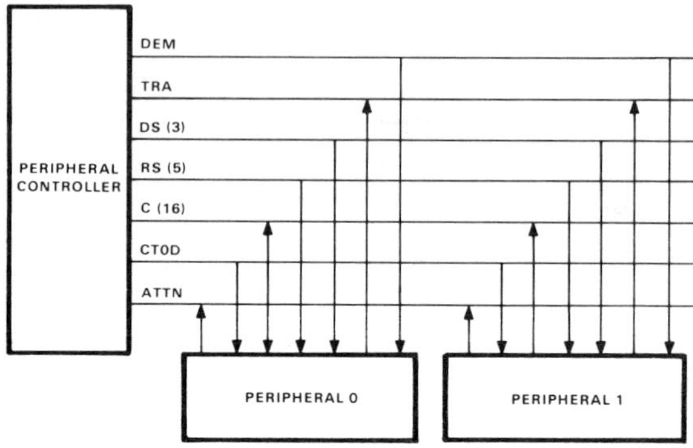

Figure 25. The Control Section signals of the Massbus.

and five bits of Register Select (RS). Thus, each of eight peripherals (drives) may contain up to 32 two-byte registers. The Controller to Drive (CTOD) signal, when asserted, indicates that the transfer is a write into a peripheral register.

Control information is transferred 16 bits at a time on the C lines. Timing of these transfers is equivalent to that shown for the Unibus in Figure 19.

There is also a shared Attention (ATTN) signal in the Control Section that may be asserted at any time by a peripheral which requires CPU intervention. The controller normally creates an interruption to the CPU soon after ATTN is asserted.

Timing of normal Read transfers is shown in Figure 26. It is equivalent to a Unibus Data-In transfer (compare with Figure 19, second part).

There is one special case which uses different timing on the Massbus Control Section. In order to determine which of the peripherals has caused an Attention interruption, the CPU reads the Attention Summary pseudo-register via the controller. This is a special "register" which is composed of one bit stored in each peripheral. Figure 27 shows the timing for reading this register. When the RS lines carry a code of 04, and the direction of transfer is drive to controller (CTOD negated), each peripheral (drive)

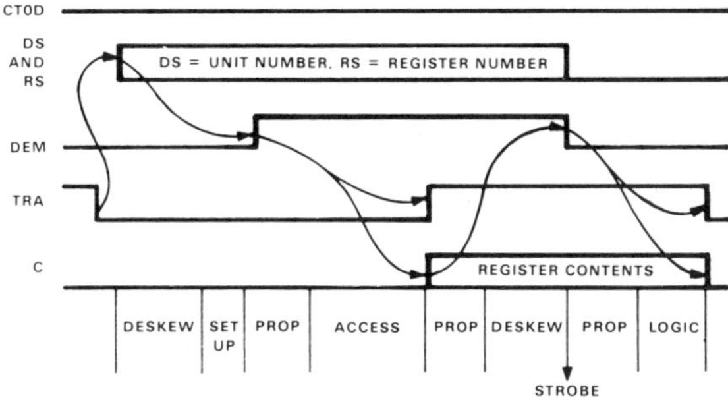

Figure 26. Timing of a control read in the control section of the Massbus.

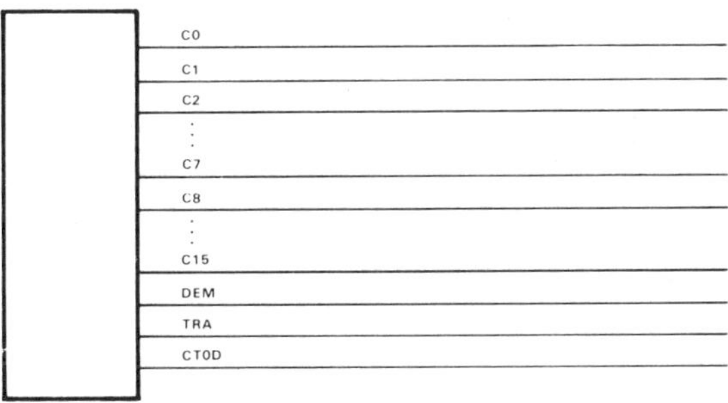

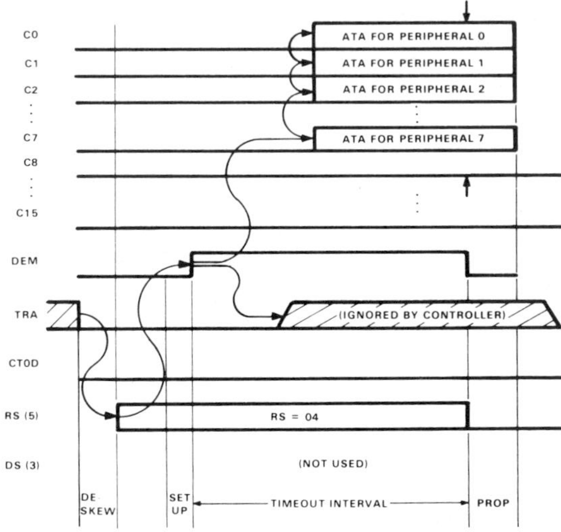

Figure 27. Timing of a control read from Attention Summary pseudo-register.

transmits its Attention Active (ATA) bit onto one of the Control (C) lines. Peripheral number 0 transmits its ATA on C0, peripheral 1 on C1, and so on.

The timing of this transfer is different because the TRA signal is driven by more than one peripheral. There is no way of knowing when all peripherals have asserted their ATA bits, so the controller must wait the maximum possible access time. This maximum delay "time-out" is present in the controller logic for normal reads and writes, to guard against possible nonresponse from an addressed peripheral or register. The Attention Summary read operation makes use of this time-out interval to terminate its wait for the ATA bits.

Example 5 (b): Massbus Data Section

The Massbus Data Section is shown in Figure 28. It contains 18 Data (D) lines, which carry data in both directions. Two clock signal lines, Synchronizing Clock (SCLK) and Write Clock (WCLK), carry a clock from and back to the peripheral, respectively. The RUN and End-of-Block (EBL) signals control the termination of a block data transfer. The Exception (EXC) signal is used to indicate error conditions.

Data in the Massbus Data Section is always transferred in multiple-word blocks. The data read from or written to a mass storage device, such as a disk drive, must be synchronized with the mechanical motion of the recording medium. Therefore, the clock (SCLK) originates in the peripheral.

A Massbus Data Read begins when a control register in the selected peripheral is written with a Read command code. Figure 29 shows the timing of a Massbus Data Read. The controller asserts the RUN signal as soon as it is ready to receive data.

When the peripheral has received the RUN assertion, it begins reading data from its storage medium. The peripheral asserts SCLK when a

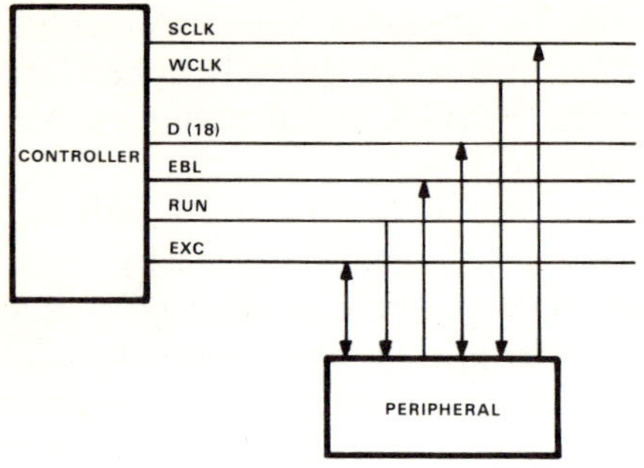

Figure 28. Massbus Data Section.

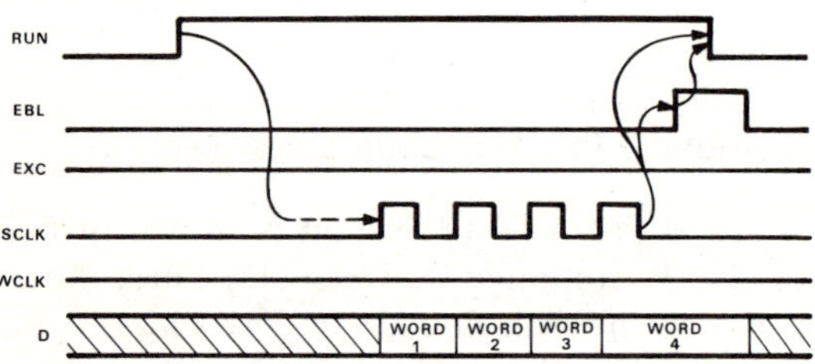

Figure 29. Timing of a Massbus Data Read.

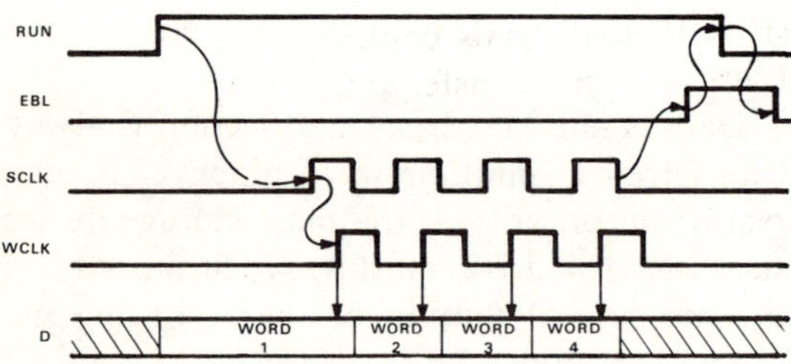

Figure 30. Timing of a Massbus Data Write.

new data word is present on the D lines. The peripheral continues to assert and negate the SCLK signal at the characteristic data rate.

Each time the controller receives the negation of SCLK, the controller captures and stores the data word from the D lines.

Note that the peripheral does not receive any positive indication that the data word was received by the controller: the data transfer is "open loop."

At the end of the block of data words, the peripheral asserts EBL to indicate that it has reached the end of a data block.

When the controller receives the EBL assertion, it decides whether to continue (usually by inspecting a word count register). Within slightly over one microsecond, the controller must negate RUN or else accept another block of data.

As the peripheral negates EBL, it senses the RUN signal. If it is negated (as shown in Figure 29), the peripheral disconnects itself from the Massbus Data Section. Otherwise, the peripheral would transmit the next block of data.

If the number of words desired by the controller is less than an integral number of data blocks, the controller may negate RUN before EBL is asserted. The controller then simply ignores the remaining data words being transmitted.

Figure 30 shows the timing of a Massbus Data Write. As for a data read, the peripheral controls the rate at which data is transmitted. However, this time the data is coming from the controller, which asserts the WCLK signal whenever it puts data onto the D lines.

The controller must have a data word ready each time it receives the negation of SCLK. Otherwise a "data overrun" condition occurs, which causes abnormal termination of the transfer.

ERROR CONTROL STRATEGIES

Unfortunately, buses do not always succeed in delivering to the receiving connection what was transmitted from the sending connection. Some of the causes of errors are logic failures, electromagnetic interference, broken conductors, shorted conductors, and power failures. In this section, we examine the following

Table 5. Error Control Methods Used By Example Buses

Bus	Check Bits (Parity)	ACK	Time-Out	Retry	Log
1. Unibus	No	Yes (SSYN)	Yes	a	b
2. LSI-11 Bus	No	Yes (RPLY)	Yes	b	b
3. SBI	Yes	Yes (CNF)	Yes	Yes	b
4. Polled Character-Input	–	–	–	–	–
5a. Massbus Control	Yes	Yes (TRA)	Yes	a	b
5b. Massbus Data	Yes	Yes (EXC)	Yes	a	b

a. Retry is implemented by software in some PDP-11 operating systems.
b. Logging is implemented at various levels by operating system software.

five categories of countermeasures to these errors:

1. **Check bits**. Extra information is sent which allows the receiver to detect and sometimes to correct errors in the data.
2. **Acknowledgement**. A reply from the receiver to the sender tells whether the data appeared "good."
3. **Time-out**. Failure of an expected acknowledgement to be received by the sender within a time limit indicates unsuccessful data transmission.
4. **Retry.** A transfer which was unsuccessful is attempted one or more additional times.
5. **Error reporting and logging.** Failures of all categories are recorded and reported to higher level (usually software) logic. Logging means recording the errors in a file which can be read later by a service engineer.

Depending on the cost and service objectives, a real bus should have a data transfer procedure with all of the following steps:

1. **Arbitration.** Obtain the use of the bus.
2. **Data transfer.** Transfer data (and check bits) on the bus.
3. **Check.** Check for error-free transfer, and transfer an acknowledgement.
4. **Retry.** If the check or acknowledgement fails, repeat steps 1 through 3.
5. **Log**. If all retries fail, enter a failure report in the log file, and send a message to higher level logic (software routines).

Table 5 summarizes the error-control methods used in the five example buses.

Example 1: Unibus

Data transfer on the Unibus is not checked. However, two lines are used by memory connections to signal whether a parity error has been detected while reading a word from memory.

A controller or CPU on the Unibus times out 20 microseconds after MSYN has been asserted, if assertion of SSYN has not been received. Time-out occurs whenever an invalid or nonexistent memory address is given as the target of a Unibus transfer.

Example 2: LSI-11 Bus

This bus does not have check bits for data transfers. However, it has two lines (DAL 17 and 16) that can be used for transmitting the results of memory parity error checking.

The LSI-11 Bus also has time-outs specified for responses to the assertion of DIN and DOUT. If a memory does not respond within 10 microseconds, the CPU or controller assumes that the address is invalid.

Example 3: SBI

Data transfers on the SBI carry several parity check bits. Parity is generated at the sending connection and is checked at the receiving connection.

The SBI also does acknowledgement on every data transfer. A code is returned to the sending connection two time-slots after the data was sent. Separate Confirm (CNF) lines are used to carry this code. The code indicates one of four possible events:

1. **No Response**. There is no connection responding to this address or ID value.
2. **Parity Error**. The parity check shows an error in transmission; transfer is rejected by the receiving connection.
3. **Busy**. (For commands only.) The receiving connection (memory) addressed cannot accept another command now.
4. **Accepted**. Parity checks "good" and the command or data is accepted.

The Confirm code itself is error-protected. The No Response code is with all CNF signals negated. The other codes differ from each other and from the No Response code in at least two bit positions. Therefore, an error in one CNF bit results in an invalid code.

Figure 31 shows the timing of SBI data transfer acknowledgements. The example in this figure is a data word transfer from memory (the second half of a read operation). The CNF lines are always reserved for a reply from a receiving connection exactly two slots after a data transfer.

The error-control philosophy on the SBI says that if any connection detects bad parity on a data transfer, then the validity of the data transfer is suspect. Therefore, any connection may assert a Parity Error Confirm code at the beginning of slot 4 in Figure 31.

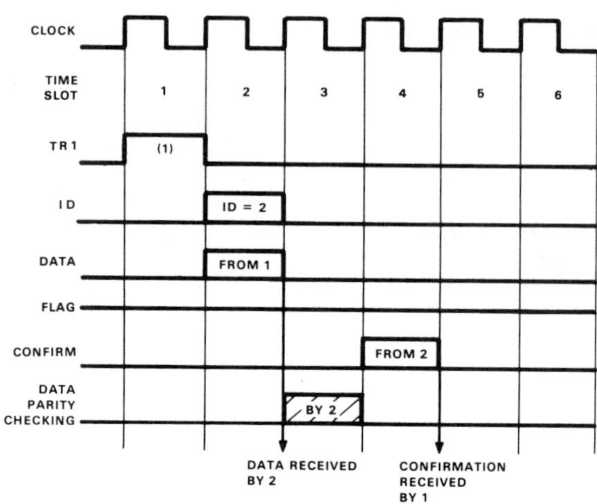

Figure 31. Timing of SBI data transfer acknowledgements, including parity check.

As implemented in the VAX-11/780, the SBI also uses time-outs, in case the memory does not respond within a fixed number of slots. The CPU or controller causes an interruption, possibly leading to software-driven retry or logging of the event. The VAX-11/780 CPU also does microprogram-controlled retry of transfer requests that receive the Busy confirmation code.

Example 4: Polled Character-Input Bus

Since this example is hypothetical, we cannot claim to explain its actual error-control methods. It is reasonable, however, to add one data signal to carry a parity check bit for each character. A time-out is not relevant here, but an acknowledgement could be implemented by having the controller send a Confirm signal back to the keyboard during the slot following

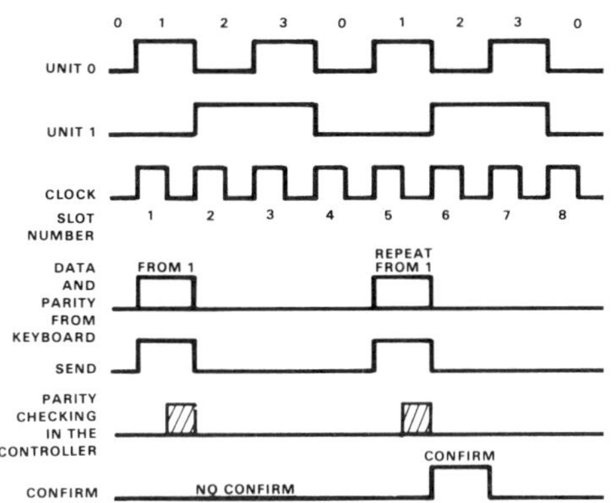

Figure 32. Timing of a plausible error-checking scheme with acknowledgement and retry for polled character-input bus.

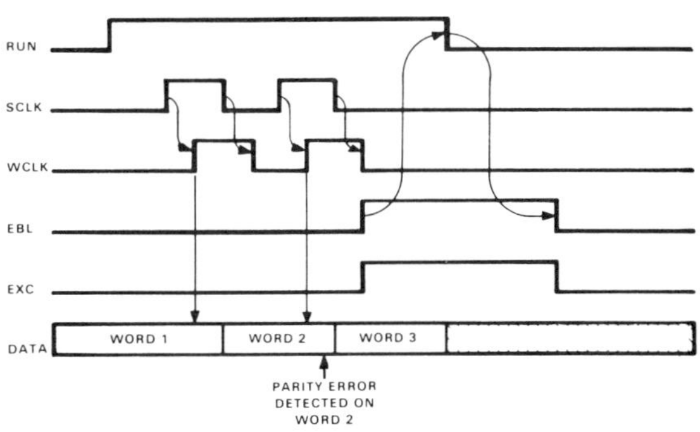

Figure 33. Timing of Exception signal in Massbus Data Write operation.

the data transfer (Figure 32). If the Confirm signal does not indicate "good transfer," the keyboard can send the character again 4 slots later (when its turn comes around again).

Example 5a: Massbus Control Section

The Massbus Control Section closely resembles the Unibus in timing, but it does carry one data parity check signal. If an error occurs on reading a control register, the controller passes the "bad parity" indication on to the CPU, with consequences the same as a memory parity error.

If an error occurs on writing a control register, the peripheral ignores the data word and asserts the Attention signal. "Control Bus Parity Error" is displayed in the Peripheral Error Status Register.

The Massbus Control Section also has the same acknowledgement and time-out properties as the Unibus, with the exception of reading the Attention Summary pseudo-register, which always uses the time-out to terminate the read cycle.

Example 5b: Massbus Data Section

The Massbus Data Section carries a parity check bit with each 18-bit word of data. A signal called Exception (EXC) can be asserted from either end to indicate a bad data transfer or other exceptional conditions. Figure 33 shows an example of a Massbus Data Write operation that suffers a parity error during the transmission of the second word. The peripheral asserts the EXC signal as soon as the error is detected. Although this is too late to stop the next word from being transmitted, the peripheral stops accepting data words, and it terminates the block transfer early. The entire block has to be retransmitted. In this example, the controller displays a "Transfer Error" when it interrupts the CPU for "end-of-transfer" service.

Two time-outs are used on the Massbus Data Section, both in the controller. One starts timing at the assertion of RUN and waits up to seven seconds for the SCLK signal to make a transition. This long time is required for ANSI standard magnetic tapes which may have up to of 25 feet of inter-record gap.

A shorter time-out, approximately 100 microseconds, is used to detect a failure in a peripheral after at least one SCLK signal transition has been received. If this limit is reached, the controller asserts EXC to tell the peripheral to disconnect.

ACKNOWLEDGEMENTS

The chapter author wishes to acknowledge the patience of J. Craig Mudge, the editor who provided the impetus to produce this chapter, and of Heidi Baldus, who spent a great many hours overseeing the production of this work, many of them on the telephone at a distance of 3000 miles from the author.

Robert Chen and Alice Parker contributed greatly by their detailed reviews of the first draft. Others who helped were Sas Durvasula, Robert E. Stewart, Harold Stone, Mike Riggle and Don Vonada. George Herbster, patent attorney and friend to many engineers, provided reference materials on short notice.

APPENDIX: A GLOSSARY OF TERMS

The definitions below are offered as an aid to understanding the technical meaning of some words used in this chapter.

Assert (*transitive verb*) – to cause a signal to take the "true" or asserted state.
Asserted (*nominal*) – to be in the "true" state.
Assertion (*noun*) – the transition from negated to asserted.
Bandwidth (*noun*) – data transfer rate measured in information units (e.g., bits, bytes, or words) per unit time.
Connection (*noun*) – an attachment to a bus and the logic and functions of the attached subsystem. Synonyms: *node, interface.*
Interval (*noun*) – an extent in time. Synonym: *period.*
Negate (*transitive verb*) – to cause a signal to take the "false" or negated state.
Negated (*nominal*) – to be in the "false" state.
Negation (*noun*) – the transition from asserted to negated.
Read (*transitive verb*) – to move data from a register, memory, or secondary storage.
Sense (*transitive verb*) – to capture data from bus signal lines. Synonyms: *receive, gate in, strobe.*
Slot (*noun*) – a particular interval.
Time-out (*intransitive verb*) – to wait for the end of an interval and to take an action associated with the failure of some event to occur within the interval.
Transfer (*transitive verb*) – to move data (a data word).
Transmit (*transitive verb*) – to place data on bus signal lines. Synonyms: *drive, gate out.*
When (*adverb*) – at the instant that.
Whenever (*adverb*) – every time that.
While (*adverb*) – throughout the interval that.
Write (*transitive verb*) – to move data into a register, memory, or secondary storage.

ANNOTATED BIBLIOGRAPHY

For further reading on bus design in general, the following references will provide an entry into some of the published literature.

Blaauw, Gerrit A., *Digital System Implementation*, Chapter 9, "Communication," pp 286–316; Prentice-Hall (1976). [*I/O channel architecture, data synchronization*]

Chen, Robert C.H., "Bus Communications Systems," Ph.D. thesis, Department of Computer Science, Carnegie-Mellon University (January 1974). [*synchronization, arbitration, and deadlock*]

Enslow, Philip H., Jr. (ed.), *Multiprocessors and Parallel Processing*, Chapter 2, "Systems Hardware," pp. 26–80; Wiley (1974). [*Multiprocessor bus organization; Unibus; tradeoffs in bus design; I/O topology*]

Ornstein, S.M., W.R. Crowther, M.F. Kraley, R.D. Bressler, A. Michel, and F.E. Heart, "Pluribus – a reliable multiprocessor," *AFIPS Conference Proceedings*, Vol. 44 (1975), National Computer Conference, pp. 551–559. [*Multiprocessor IMP for ARPANET*]

Thurber, Kenneth J., E. Douglas Jensen, Larry A. Jack, Larry L. Kinney, Peter C. Patton, and Lynn C. Anderson, "A systematic approach to the design of digital bussing structures," *AFIPS Conference Proceedings* (1972), Vol. 41, Part II, Fall Joint Computer Conference. [*polling, arbitration methods, data synchronization; annotated bibliography with 93 entries*]

The following four references cover the Unibus and some bus related aspects of the PDP-11 architecture.

Bartee, T., *Digital Computer Fundamentals (Fourth Edition)*, Chapter 10, section 10.6, "Interconnecting System Components," and section 10.7, "Interfacing - Buses," pp. 455–470, McGraw-Hill (1977). [*bus structures, including Unibus*]

Cohen, J., Janson, P., McFarland, H., and Young, J. Jr., Data Processing System, U.S. patent 3,710,324 (9 Jan 1973). [*PDP-11 system and Unibus*]

Sutherland, Ivan E., and Carver A. Mead, "Microelectronics and Computer Science," *Scientific American*, Vol. 237, no. 3 (September 1977), pp. 210–228. [*interconnections, Unibus*]

Tanenbaum, Andrew S., *Structured Computer Organization*, Chapter 4, section 4.12, "The PDP-11/40 Microprogramming Level," pp. 196–204, Prentice-Hall (1976). [*PDP-11/40 internal organization and Unibus operation*]

Cohen, J., Janson, P., McFarland, H., and Young, J. Jr., Data Processing System, U.S. patent 3,815,099 (4 Jun 1974). [*PDP-11 memory and peripherals*]

The following references are the patents covering the Massbus design.

Jenkins S., Secondary Storage Facility for Data Processing System, U.S. patent 4,047,157 (6 Sept 1977). [*Dual-Unibus RH11 Massbus controller*]

Levy, J., Jenkins, S., Ku, V., McLean, P., and Hastings, T., Drive Condition Detecting Circuit for Secondary Storage Facilities in Data Processing Systems, U.S. patent 3,911,400 (7 Oct 1975). [*Massbus Attention Summary register*]

Levy, J., Jenkins, S., and McLean, P., Secondary Storage Facility for Data Processing Systems, U.S. patent 3,999,163 (21 Dec 1976). [*Massbus*]

McLean, P., Jenkins, S., and Ku, V., Diagnostic Circuit for Data Processing System, U.S. patent 3,911,402 (7 Oct 1975). [*Massbus peripheral maintenance register*]

Sergeant, O., Levy, J., Lignos, D., and Griggs, K., Drive for Connection to Multiple Controllers in a Digital Data Secondary Storage Facility, U.S. patent 4,007,448 (8 Feb 1977). [*Dual-Massbus disk drive*]

The Honeywell Megabus, described in the first reference below, was an independent development that has some ideas similar to the SBI and the Unibus. The second reference has a short description of the SBI. The third reference contains an intellectual precursor to the SBI, the "z-bus", which was implemented only in a simulation.

Conway, J.W., "Approach to Unified Bus Architecture Sidestepping Inherent Drawbacks," *Computer Design* (Jan 1977). [*Honeywell Megabus*]

Digital Equipment Corporation, *VAX-11/780 Architecture Handbook*, (1977), Chapter 2, section 2.2, "The Synchronous Backplane Interconnect," p. 23. [*SBI*]

Levy, John V., "Computing with Multiple Microprocessors," Report SLAC-161, Stanford Linear Accelerator Center, (Apr 1973); (Ph.D. thesis, Computer Science Department, Stanford University). [*Z-machine and z-bus*]

The next three references relate to a relatively new development, the contention-arbitrated serial bus. These are distributed-arbitration buses which have a single signal used for both arbitration and for data transfer. Further references can be found in these publications.

MacLaren, Don, Contention-arbitrated serial buses, Digital Equipment Corporation R&D Group internal memo (13 Sep 1977). [*with 8 references*]

Metcalfe, Robert M., Packet Communication, Report MAC TR-114, Massachusetts Institute of Technology Project MAC, (December 1973).

Metcalfe, Robert M. and David R. Boggs, "Ethernet: Distributed packet switching for local computer networks," report CSL 75-7, Xerox Palo Alto Research Center (November 1975).

12

A Minicomputer-Compatible Microcomputer System: The DEC LSI-11

MARK J. SEBERN

INTRODUCTION

In recent years, minicomputers have found application in a wide range of areas. In so doing, they have displaced larger computer systems in many traditional maxicomputer markets. At the same time, they have opened up many new markets, primarily because of their low cost, small size, and general ease of use. Still, in spite of this remarkable success, minicomputers are not without competition. In cost-sensitive areas, the minicomputer is being eased out of its dominant position by a new generation of LSI microcomputers; the new "processors on a chip" have found a warm reception from designers seeking inexpensive computing power. That warm reception sometimes cools, however, when the user finds himself with a collection of components, instead of a complete computing system. The discovery that he is largely on his own when it comes to software and debugging support has a similarly chilling effect. The entry into the world of programming PROMs, using FORTRAN cross-assemblers and simulators, and writing even simple software routines from scratch can be a traumatic experience indeed. Still, the advantages of LSI microcomputers are very real, and many users have found the difficulties well worthwhile. Even so, some cannot help but wonder why they cannot simply have the best of both worlds: the cost and size of the microcomputer, and the ease of use and performance of the minicomputer systems with which they are familiar.

Therefore, the appearance of a new LSI microcomputer system that is fully compatible with a line of 16-bit minicomputers is an event of some significance. This new microcomputer, the DEC LSI-11 (see Figure 1), is a complete 4 K PDP-11 on a 21.6 cm × 26.7 cm (8.5 inch × 10.5 inch) board; priced to compete with other LSI microcomputers, it offers true minicomputer performance and maxicomputer support. The LSI-11, while not meant to be yet another low-end minicomputer, does bring many minicomputer strengths to the new microcomputer applications for which it is intended.

To provide minicomputer performance at a microcomputer price, the LSI-11 was designed to optimize system costs, rather than component costs. A one-chip central processor, then, was not necessarily superior to a four-chip

Figure 1. On one 21.6 cm × 26.7 cm board, the LSI-11 provides a complete PDP-11 processor, 4 Kwords of 16-bit memory, an ASCII console, a real-time clock, an automatic dynamic memory refresh, and interface bus control.

one; the choice was made on the basis of total system cost and performance. On this basis, a microprogrammed processor was selected, permitting the inclusion of features like a "zero cost" real-time clock and automatic dynamic memory refresh. The built-in ASCII programmer's console was also made feasible by the LSI-11's microprogrammed nature.

Awareness of system costs and performance, then, was a primary motivation in the LSI-11 design. System issues include cost and ease of interconnection, the customer's investment in training and software, and the availability of design support for both hardware and software. The impact of these system concerns should become apparent in the following sections which detail the LSI-11 design. Two viewpoints are taken in this description: the first section treats the internals of the LSI-11 from the computer designer's point of view, while the second considers the system from the user's perspective. The former examines the architecture, organization, and implementation of the LSI-11, while the latter discusses interfacing, special features, and PDP-11 compatibility. Together, these two viewpoints will provide the reader with an introduction to the DEC LSI-11, the first microprogrammed minicomputer-compatible LSI microcomputer, which provides minicomputer performance at a microcomputer price.

THE COMPUTER DESIGNER'S VIEW

For the purpose of this discussion, the design of the LSI-11 will be studied at the following three levels: (1) architecture – the machine as seen by the programmer, (2) organization – the block diagram view of subsystems and their interconnection, and (3) implementation – the actual fabrication and physical arrangement of the various pieces at the component level.

Architecture

Instruction Set. The architectural level of a computer system includes its instruction set, address space, and interrupt structure. The basic LSI-11 instruction set is that of the PDP-11/40, without memory mapping. These instructions include several operations not found in other small PDP-11 processors, such as Exclusive-Or (XOR), Sign-Extend (SXT), Subtract One and Branch (SOB), etc. Full integer multiply/divide (Extended Instruction Set or EIS) and floating-point arithmetic (Floating Instruction Set or FIS) may be provided by the addition of a single control read-only memory chip (to be discussed later). Unlike other PDP-11s, there are two special operation codes which facilitate access to the processor's program status word (PSW). The instruction set is, then, more comprehensive than that of the PDP-11/05, while the execution times (see Table 1) are a little slower.

To take advantage of the microprogrammed nature of the LSI-11, it may at times be desirable to invoke a user-written microroutine. This

Table 1. LSI-11 Instruction Timing

Instruction	Execution Time (μs)	Comments
ADD R1, R2	3.5	Register-register
MOV R1, R2	3.5	
MOV A (PC), B (R2)	11.55	PC-relative, indexed
TSTB (R1)+	5.25	Auto-indexed
JMP (R1)	4.2	Indirect
JSR PC, A (R1)	8.05	Subroutine call
Bxx L	3.5	Conditional branch
RT1	8.75–9.45	Rtn from interrupt
MUL*	24–64	
FADD*	42.1	
EMUL*	52.2–93.7	
FDIV*	151–232	

NOTES
R1, R2 = Registers
A, B = Index constants
Bxx = Any conditional branch
L = 8-bit offset

*Third MICROM installed for EIS/FIS.

is made possible by a set of reserved instructions which cause branching to a fixed microaddress. These reserved instructions cause an illegal instruction trap to occur if user microcode is not present.

Address Space. Like other microcomputers without memory mapping facilities, the LSI-11 virtual and physical address spaces are the same, both being 16 bits, or 64 Kbytes. (Since two 8-bit bytes make one 16-bit word, this is equivalent to 32 Kwords.) As in other members of the PDP-11 family, the top 4 Kwords of the address space are normally reserved for peripheral device control and data registers. Thus the nominal maximum main memory size is 28 K 16-bit words.

Interrupt Structure. The LSI-11 interrupt structure is a subset of the full PDP-11 interrupt system. Like other PDP-11 processors, the LSI-11 features arbitration between multiple peripheral devices and automatic-service routine "vectoring." It differs, however, in having only a single interrupt level. Interrupts on the LSI-11 are either enabled or masked, these states being equivalent to PDP-11 processor levels 0 and 4. With this exception, however, interrupt operation follows the same familiar sequence. Upon acknowledging an interrupt request, the processor stores the current processor status word (PSW) and program counter (PC) on the stack and picks up a new PSW and PC from a memory location (vector) specified by the interrupting device.

Organization

PMS Level Description. The "organization" of a computer system denotes the collection of building blocks that comprise it, and the logical and physical links that connect them. A block diagram of the LSI-11 organization is shown in Figure 2. The LSI-11 CPU, being a microprogrammed processor, is partitioned logically and physically into three main sections – data path, control logic, and micromemory. Each of these units is, in fact, a separate LSI chip. Interconnection of these chips is through the microinstruction bus (MIB).

The Data Chip. The data chip contains an 8-bit register file and arithmetic logic unit (ALU). The chip also provides a 16-bit interface to the data/address lines (DAL) upon which the external LSI-11 bus is built.

The register file consists of 26 8-bit registers; of these registers, 10 may be addressed directly by the microinstruction, 4 may be addressed either directly or indirectly, and the remaining 12 may be addressed only indirectly. Indirect addressing is accomplished by means of a special 3-bit register known as the G register, which may be easily loaded from the register address field of the PDP-11 instruction. Addressing of the register file is illustrated in Table 2.

The 12 indirectly addressed 8-bit registers are used to realize the 6 PDP-11 general purpose registers, R0 through R5. The 4 registers which may be addressed either directly or indirectly

Table 2. Micromachine Register File Addressing

File Registers	Directly Addressed	Indirectly Addressed	PDP-11 Equivalent
0–1		x	R0
2–3		x	R1
4–5		x	R2
6–7		x	R3
10–11		x	R4
12–13		x	R5
14–15	x	x	R6(SP)
16–17	x	x	R7(PC)
20–21	x		IR
22–23	x		BA
24–25	x		SRC
26–27	x		DST
30–31	x		PSW

NOTES

SP = Stack Pointer
PC = Program Counter
IR = Instruction Register
BA = Bus Address
SRC = Source Operand
DST = Destination Operand
PSW = Processor Status Word

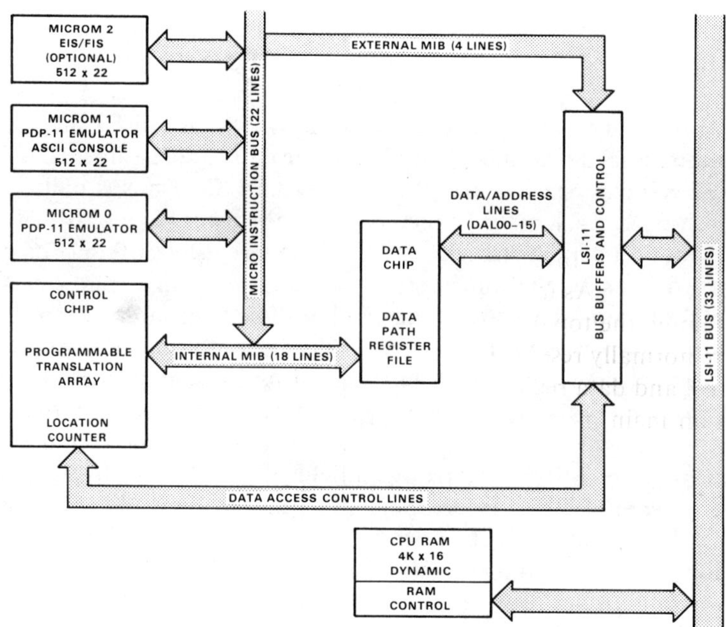

Figure 2. Organization of the LSI-11 CPU.

contain the PDP-11 program counter (PC) and stack pointer (SP), since they provide special processor functions and are accessed very frequently. The 5 remaining pairs of directly addressed registers are used for microprogram workspace, and normally contain the following: (1) the PDP-11 macroinstruction, (2) the bus address, (3) the source operand, (4) the destination operand, and (5) the macro PSW and other status information.

The 8-bit ALU operates on two operands addressed by the microinstruction. When a full-word operation is specified, the data path is cycled twice, with the low order bit of each register address complemented during the second cycle. Thus a 16-bit macrolevel register is realized by two consecutive 8-bit registers in the register file. An 8-bit operand may also be sign-extended and used in a 16-bit operation, or an 8-bit literal value from the microinstruction may be used as one of the operands.

In addition to the register file and ALU, the data chip contains storage for several condition codes. These include flags for zero or negative results, as well as for carry or overflow; 4- or 8-bit carry flags are also provided for use in decimal arithmetic. Special flag-testing circuitry is also provided for efficiency in executing PDP-11 conditional branch instructions.

The Control Chip. The control chip generates MICROM addresses and control signals for external I/O operations. It contains an 11-bit location counter (LC), which is normally incremented after each MICROM access. The LC may also be loaded by "jump" instructions, or by the output of the programmable translation array. A one level subroutine capability is also provided by an 11-bit return register (RR), which may be used to save or restore the LC contents.

The programmable translation array (PTA), the heart of the control chip, consists of two programmable logic arrays (PLAs); the PTA generates new LC addresses which are a function of the microprocessor state and of external signals. Included in the microprocessor state is the 16-bit macroinstruction currently being interpreted; in this way, much of the macromachine emulation may be done with the high efficiency provided by the PTA. The combinational logic of the two PLAs allows the PTA to arbitrate interrupt priorities, translate macroinstructions, and, in general, to replace the conventional "branch-on-microtest" microprimitive. Since the microlocation counter is one of the PTA inputs, it is normally unnecessary to specify explicitly the desired translation or multiway branch; this information is implicit in the address of the microinstruction which invokes the PTA. External condition handling is made possible by four microlevel interrupt lines which are input to the PTA. Also feeding the PTA are three internal status flags which are set and reset under microprogram control.

The MICROM Chip. The micro read-only memory, or MICROM, serves as the control store for the microprocessor. The microinstruction width is 22 bits. Sixteen of these bits comprise the traditional microinstruction; one is used to latch a subroutine return address, and one to invoke programmed translations; the remaining four bits (which drive TTL-compatible outputs) perform special system-defined functions.

Each MICROM chip contains 512 words, or one-fourth of the 2 K microaddress space. Proper "chip-select" decode is accomplished by masking a 2-bit select code (along with the microcode) into each MICROM at the time of manufacture; no external selection logic is required.

The Microinstruction Bus. As seen in Figure 2, microinstructions and microaddresses share the microinstruction bus lines (MIB 00:21). Instructions thus fetched are executed by the data chip while the next microaddress is computed by the control chip. The bus design, then, allows fully pipelined microinstruction execution, with data and control operations overlapped.

Microinstruction Repertoire. Using the accepted distinction between horizontal (unencoded) and vertical (highly encoded) micro-order codes, the LSI-11 may be classified as an extremely vertical machine. In fact, the microinstruction set strongly resembles the PDP-11 code it emulates; the two differ largely in addressing modes, not in primitive operations. (Microinstruction formats are depicted in Figure 3, while a number of operation codes are tabulated in Table 3.) This similarity of instruction sets is not accidental; while general-purpose emulation machines have a place, a micromachine designed with the macro order code in mind usually offers better performance. Thus while many operations are general purpose, like Add, Subtract, Compare, Decrement, And, Test, Or, Exclusive-Or, etc., others serve primarily in the emulation of the macrolevel PDP-11 instruction set, such as Read and Increment Word By 2 and so on. I/O primitives allow for Read, Write, and Read-Modify-Write operations, as well as special polling transactions.

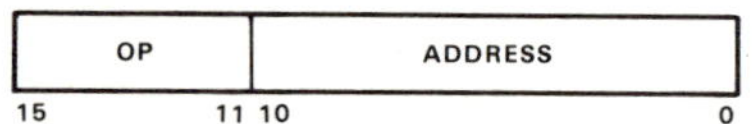

(a) Jump format.

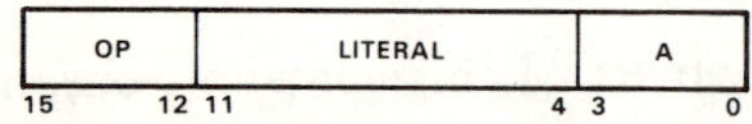

(b) Literal format.

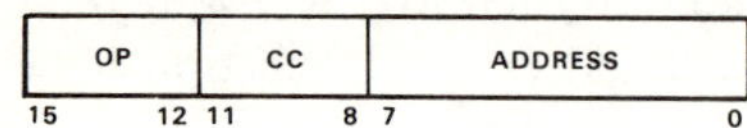

(c) Conditional jump format.

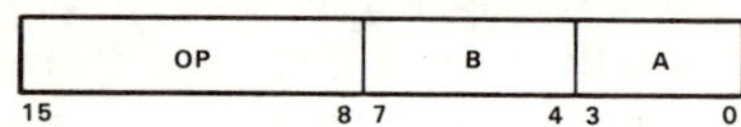

(d) Register format.

Figure 3. Microinstruction formats.

Implementation

LSI Technology. The "implementation" of the LSI-11, or how it is actually put together, is a combination of both custom large-scale integration (LSI) and medium- and small-scale transistor-transistor logic (TTL) integration. The control, data, and MICROM chips are fabricated in n-channel silicon-gate four-phase MOS. This technology was chosen as a reasonable compromise between performance expectations and development risks. Existing n-channel components exhibited the desired performance range, while other technologies (such as CMOS silicon-on-sapphire) were perceived as too risky for production during 1975 and 1976.

The micromachine operates with a nominal cycle time of 350 nanoseconds. A simple primitive operation such as a register-to-register 8-bit addition requires only one cycle, a marked speed advantage over other available MOS "processors on a chip." A comparable 16-bit operation takes only two cycles. This intrinsic performance of the LSI-11 "inner machine" means extra flexibility when an application suggests the use of a user-written microcode.

The CPU Module. The LSI-11 CPU, a quad-height (21.6 cm × 26.7 cm) module, consists of the microprogrammed processor and a 4 Kword memory, together with bus transceivers and control logic. The processor itself consists of four 40-pin LSI parts – one control chip, one data chip, and two MICROM chips. These two MICROMs handle emulation of the basic PDP-11 instruction set. In addition, one extra 40-pin socket is provided to allow the installation of a third MICROM, implementing the extended-arithmetic and floating-point instructions. Optionally, a custom MICROM containing user microcode may be installed in its place.

The 4 Kword memory on board the CPU module consists of sixteen 4 K dynamic n-channel random-access memories (RAMs). This memory is implemented so as to logically appear on the external LSI-11 bus, while being physically resident on the CPU module. Accessibility to the bus allows external Direct Memory Access (DMA) transfers to take place to and from the basic 4-Kword memory. Furthermore, an optional jumper allows the CPU module memory to occupy either the first or second 4 K block of the bus address space. That is, it may respond to address 000000–017776 or 020000–037776 as desired.

Table 3. Some LSI-11 Microinstructions

Arithmetic Operations
- Add Word (byte, literal)
- Test word (byte, literal)
- Increment word (byte) by 1
- Increment word (byte) by 2
- Negate word (byte)
- Conditionally increment (decrement) byte
- Contitionally add word (byte)
- Add word (byte) with carry
- Conditionally add digits
- Subtract word (byte)
- Compare word (byte, literal)
- Subtract word (byte) with carry
- Decrement word (byte) by 1

Logical Operations
- And word (byte, literal)
- Test word (byte)
- Or word (byte)
- Exclusive-Or word (byte)
- Bit clear word (byte)
- Shift word (byte) right (left) with (without) carry
- Complement word (byte)

General Operations
- MOV word (byte)
- Jump
- Return
- Conditional jump
- Set (reset) flags
- Copy (load) condition flags
- Load G low
- Conditionally MOV word (byte)

Input/Output Operations
- Input word (byte)
- Input status word (byte)
- Read
- Write
- Read (write) and increment word (byte) by 1
- Read (write) and increment word (byte) by 2
- Read (write) acknowledge
- Output word (byte, status)

Available Memory Options. The LSI-11 macromemory is available in several forms; these include semiconductor random-access memories (RAM), ROM (or PROM), and magnetic core.

Both static and dynamic semiconductor memories are available. The MSV11-A is a 1024-word static RAM, packaged on a double-height (21.6 cm × 12.7 cm) module. It may be used when dynamic memory is not desired. The MSV11-B is a 4-Kword dynamic memory, again packaged on one double-height module. The availability of automatic memory refresh (discussed in a later section) will in many cases make the dynamic memory a more attractive alternative than core or static semiconductor RAM.

The use of a ROM for program storage is often desirable; not only is the program safe from unintentional modification, but no external device is needed to load the system each time it is started. The LSI-11 instruction set is well suited to ROM program storage, since program and data are easily separable. To take advantage of this, the LSI-11 series includes a ROM module (designated the MRV11-AA); either a masked ROM or a programmable ROM (PROM) may be used. This memory uses standard 256 × 4 or 512 × 4 ROM or PROM chips, to a maximum of 2 Kwords or 4 Kwords depending on the chips employed. Programmable ROMs may be used for program development, and less expensive masked ROMs substituted for production use.

For applications that require nonvolatile READ/WRITE memory, a 4-Kword core memory (the MMV11-A) is available. This memory occupies two quad-height modules, and must overhang the last slot in a backplane unit.

THE USER'S OUTLOOK

Interfacing to the LSI-11

The LSI-11 Bus. The LSI-11 bus (Table 4) serves as the link between the processor, memory, and peripheral devices. Narrower (in terms of the number of signal lines) than some other minicomputer buses, it was designed to allow low cost peripheral interfaces for microcomputer applications, rather than to support the wide range of peripheral configurations common in large minicomputer systems. The wider PDP-11 Unibus, for example, is better suited to larger systems in which CPU and interconnection comprise a smaller part of the total system cost.

To reduce the number of bus signals, sixteen bidirectional lines (BDAL 00:15) are time-multiplexed between data and address. Transfers on these lines are sequenced by several control lines. BSYNC signals that a bus transaction is in progress and clocks address decoding logic; BDIN and BDOUT request input and output transfers, respectively; BWTBT is used to distinguish word and byte output transfers; BRPLY is returned by the bus slave when data is ready or has been accepted. A special address line, BBS7, indicates that the bus address is in the range of 28 K–32 K; this simplifies peripheral device design by indicating that the "I/O page" is being addressed.

Two bus signals, BIRQ and BIAK, are used to control processor interrupts. An interrupting device asserts BIRQ and waits for an interrupt transaction from the CPU. When the proper

Table 4. The LSI-11 Bus

Bus Signal	Signal Function
BDAL 00:15 L	Buffered data/address lines (time-multiplexed)
BDIN L	Data input transfer control line
BDOUT L	Data output transfer control line
BSYNC L	Synchronizing control signal; asserted by bus master (normally CPU)
BRPLY L	Reply control signal; returned by bus slave (memory or peripheral device)
BWTBT L	Write/Byte control: At address time, specifies a write At data time, a byte output
BBS7 L	Marks an address in the range 28 K – 32 K, the "I/O page"
BREF L	Signals a refresh transaction; overrides normal memory addressing for dynamic memories
BIRQ L	Interrupt request from device
BIAK I L	Interrupt grant in
BIAK O L	Interrupt grant out; used with BIAK I to arbitrate interrupt priority
BDMR L	Direct Memory Access (DMA) request line
BDMG I L	DMA grant in
BDMG O L	DMA grant out; like BIAK
BSACK L	Bus DMA acknowledge
BHALT L	Forces entry to ASCII console microcode
BEVNT L	External event line; used with real-time clock
BINIT L	Bus initialize signal
BPOK H	Power OK line from supply
BDCOK H	DC power OK, from supply

conditions have been met, the CPU, which remains bus master, strobes the interrupting devices by asserting BIAK. During this bus cycle, BIAK is "daisy-chained" through all peripherals, allowing priority arbitration to take place. The selected device then places an interrupt vector address on the bus and returns BRPLY, terminating the transaction. In a similar manner, BDMR, BDMG, and BSACK are used to control requests for direct memory access transactions by other peripherals desiring to become bus master. The lines BINIT, BPOK, and BDCOK are used for system reset and power-fail/restart.

Three other bus lines perform additional system functions; these are BREF, BHALT, and BEVNT. BHALT is used to stop PDP-11 emulation and enter console mode; BREF and BEVNT are used for microcode refresh of dynamic memories and real-time clock operation, to be discussed in a later section.

Standard Modules. To assist the system designer, the LSI-11 series includes several standard interface modules. Currently available are both serial and parallel I/O interfaces. The DLV-11 handles a single asynchronous serial line at speeds of 50–9600 baud, while the DRV-11 provides a full 16-bit parallel interface complete with two interrupt control units. The DRV-11 is completely compatible with the DR-11C interface used with other PDP-11s. In order to facilitate program loading when volatile memory is used, a flexible disk drive and interface is also available. This unit, the RXV-11, employs industry-standard media and formatting.

An Interfacing Example. The design of a simple interface to the LSI-11 system is pictured in Figure 4. Here, the problem is to interface an analog-to-digital (A/D) converter and a four-digit light-emitting-diode (LED) display. The A/D converter is presumed to have a resolution of 8–16 bits, and the LED display is driven as four binary-coded-decimal (BCD) digits of four

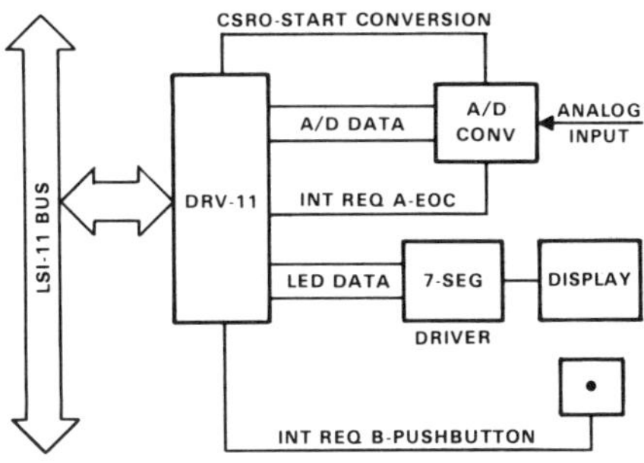

Figure 4. An interfacing example.

bits each. To simplify the design further, the standard DRV-11 parallel interface module is employed.

On the input side, the data lines from the A/D converter are connected to the input lines (IN00:15) of the DRV-11, and the End-of-Conversion signal (EOC) from the A/D is fed to one of the interface's interrupt request lines (INT REQ A). If the processor enables the interrupt control in the interface, the EOC signal will now cause an interrupt, and the CPU may read in the data. To initiate sampling of the analog input signal, a control line (Start Conversion) is needed; this is controlled by an output line (CSR0) from the DRV-11.

On the output side, the data lines (OUT 00:15) from the DRV-11 are fed directly to the seven-segment decoder drivers which control the LED displays. The processor may then write out a single 16-bit word containing four BCD digits, and the data will appear in the display. Since a second interrupt input (INT REQ B) is available, an operator pushbutton is connected to this line; by interrupting the processor, the user may request a new sample from the A/D converter or perform some other function.

To aid the designer in applying the LSI-11, detailed interfacing information is available [DEC, 1975a; DEC, 1975b]; these manuals cover both the standard interface modules and the methods used to interface directly to the LSI-11 Bus (Figure 5). In most cases, peripheral interface design is a little simpler than in the case of the traditional PDP-11 Unibus.

Special Features

Several special features of value in low cost systems have been implemented in the LSI-11 microcode. These include an ASCII console, a real-time clock, an automatic dynamic memory refresh, flexible power-up options, and internal maintenance features.

ASCII Console. The LSI-11 ASCII console serves to replace the conventional "lights and switches" front panel often associated with minicomputer operation. The ASCII console functions with a standard terminal device which communicates over a serial or parallel link at any desired rate. The available functions are very similar to those of PDP-11 octal debugging technique (ODT), which is familiar to users of other PDP-11 systems. These include examination and alteration of the contents of memory and processor registers, calculation of effective addresses for PC-relative and indirect addressing, and the control functions of Halt, Single-Step, Continue, and Restart. Internal processor registers are also accessible, making possible a determination of the type of entry to the console routines (Halt instruction, etc.).

The advantages of the ASCII console include low cost, remote diagnostic capability, and high-level operator interface. The user retains all the direct hardware control of a conventional front panel, while being freed from tedious switch register operation. This use of the terminal device in no way conflicts with its

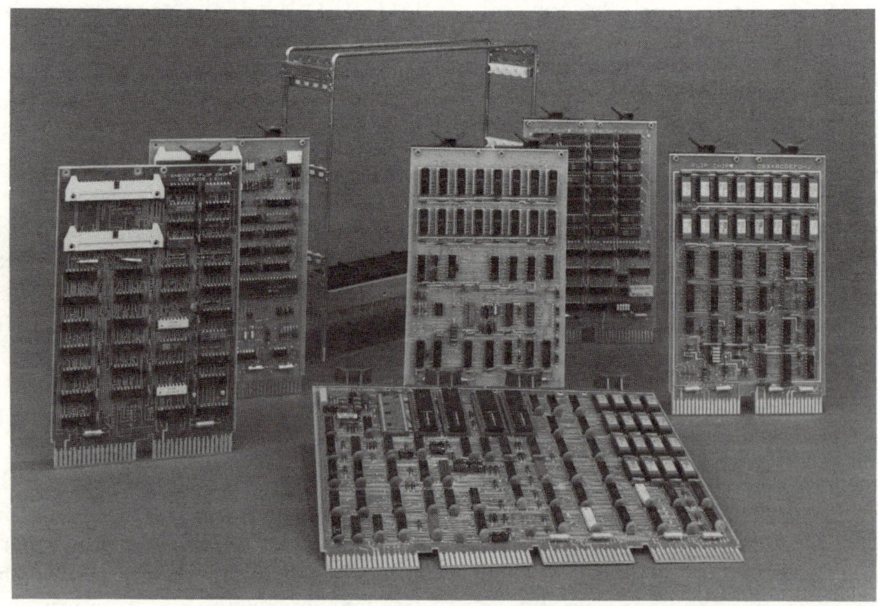

Figure 5. The LSI-11 series contains the LSI-11 CPU (center), together with parallel and serial interfaces, and RAM and ROM memory modules. These modules may be housed in a backplane assembly, connected by the LSI-11 bus.

normal use by the program being debugged. The ASCII console routines also allow the user to boot load from a specified device in a byte transfer mode. All together, the ASCII console routines occupy about 340 words of microcode; since this space is available in the second MICROM, the console functions are made possible at no extra cost.

Real-Time Clock. Many low-end configurations require a real-time clock, driven by the power-line frequency or other timing signal, which is normally implemented with external control logic. To save this expense, such a device has been programmed into the LSI-11 processor microcode. To use this clock, the user need only connect the timing signal to the processor through the bus line BEVNT. Once connected, this clock is identical to the KW-11L line clock when used in an interrupt mode, except that it may not be turned on and off. An optional jumper disables the real-time clock if its operation is not desired.

Automatic Dynamic Memory Refresh. One disadvantage of using dynamic MOS memories is the necessity of refreshing their contents at appropriate intervals. This refresh operation is needed to replace the stored charge in each memory cell which has been lost through leakage current. In typical dynamic MOS memories, each cell must be refreshed every 2 milliseconds. Most dynamic memories are implemented in such a way that any normal memory access refreshes a group of cells (or "row") on all selected memory chips. One access must then be made to each row of every memory chip; the 4 K memories used in the LSI-11 system require that 64 accesses be made. Normally, the logic to control the refresh operation would include a 6-bit counter, a clock, and memory access arbitration circuitry.

In order to minimize this control circuitry, the LSI-11 CPU microcode features automatic refresh control. When enabled by an optional jumper, the CPU takes a refresh trap approximately every 1.6 ms. At this time, it performs 64 memory references while asserting a special bus signal, BREF. This signals all dynamic memories to cycle at the same time. Direct Memory Access (DMA) requests are arbitrated between bus refresh cycles to reduce DMA latency. External interrupts, however, are locked out during the burst refresh time, temporarily increasing interrupt latency. (When this latency can not be tolerated, external refresh circuitry can drive the bus and assert BREF, allowing use of either refresh method with the same memory modules.) The automatic refresh feature is not needed, of course, in systems without dynamic memories.

Power-Fail/Restart Options. The flexibility of the LSI-11 system is further enhanced by the availability of several power-fail/restart options. The power-fail sequence, which is normally of use only with nonvolatile main memory, is compatible with other members of the PDP-11 family. Upon sensing a warning signal from the power supply, the power-fail trap is taken. The current PSW and PC are pushed on the processor stack, and a new PC and PSW are taken from a vector at octal location 24. Normally, the routine thus invoked would save processor registers, set up a restart routine, and HALT. When volatile memory is used, the register may not be saved; in this case, the power-fail trap allows an orderly system shut-down to occur.

Four power-up options are selected by two jumpers on the LSI-11 CPU module. The first of these is to load a previously set-up PSW and PC from the vector at location 24. Normally used with nonvolatile memory to continue execution from the power-fail point, this option is compatible with the normal PDP-11 power-up sequence. If ROM program storage is employed, this option allows the program to be started at an arbitrary address. If the BHALT line on the bus (the HALT switch) is asserted during this power-up sequence, the console microcode will be entered immediately after loading the PSW and PC.

The second power-up option causes an unconditional entry to the ASCII console routines. This allows remote system startup without the necessity of controlling the bus Halt line. The processor may then be started, as usual, by an ASCII console command.

The last two options allow program execution to begin at a specified address in either macrocode or microcode. Option three sets the macro PC to 173 000 octal and starts normal execution. Option four causes a jump to microcode location 3002 octal, in the fourth MICROM page. Here, the CPU expects to find a user-written microcode routine to perform a special power-up sequence. The state of the BHALT line is not checked in this last case until the execution of the first macrocode instruction is completed.

The Maintenance Instruction. For ease in hardware checkout, a special maintenance instruction is included in the LSI-11 repertoire. This instruction stores the contents of five internal registers in a specified block in the main memory. The information may then be used by a diagnostic program to probe the internal operation of the microlevel processor.

The LSI-11 as a Member of the PDP-11 Family

Upward Compatibility. Because the basic instruction set of the LSI-11 processor is that of the entire PDP-11 family, the user has an extremely large range of compatible processing systems at his disposal. This range extends from the LSI-11 on the low end to the PDP-11/70 on the high end. The consistency of the instruction set provides economies in training and documentation costs, as well as the ability to carry specific application programs, or even complete operating systems, from one family member to another. Thus, a user currently employing a small PDP-11, like the PDP-11/05, can easily convert to the low cost LSI-11 without losing a past investment in software development. This compatibility also eases the program development problems often associated with microcomputer systems; assembly, compilation, and initial debugging may be done on any PDP-11 system, with the generated code loaded into an LSI-11 system for testing and final debug. Through the use of the LSI-11 ASCII console, a central PDP-11 system may initialize, load, and start up a remote LSI-11 system over an asynchronous serial line or other link.

Software Support. Other members of the PDP-11 family, beginning with the Model 20 (Chapter 9), have been in service for some time. Thus the system designer has at immediate hand a large number of language processors, utility routines, and application programs. Many of these programs will run with little or no modification on an LSI-11 system. This existing library of software provides the user with a head start in the application of microcomputers, at little or no development cost.

Network Capability. Since the LSI-11 shares a common set of data-types and file structures with other PDP-11 systems, many communication problems disappear. When linked through line protocols such as DDCMP (digital data communications message protocol [DEC, 1974; DEC, 1974a]), LSI-11s may exchange programs and files with other PDP-11s without adjustments for differing word sizes, operating systems, file structures, etc. This fact makes the LSI-11 the ideal choice for a network node processor. Used with distributed programming systems such as RSX-11, RSTS, or RT-11, the individual LSI-11 processors may not even require their own mass storage devices, but rather share those of other network nodes. A monitoring network might then consist of a large central PDP-11 with disks, magnetic tape units, and other peripherals, together with several remote LSI-11s which would directly control transducers and communication lines. Yet, even in such a functionally differentiated system, all processors would be homogeneous in instruction set; the distributed nature of the network need not even be visible to the user.

SUMMARY

The LSI-11, then, is the first of a new class of microcomputers and offers the user most of the advantages of a full-blown minicomputer at a significantly lower cost. It is, in fact, the first member of the PDP-11 family ever offered as a single-board component to original equipment manufacturers and others. Gaining power and flexibility from its microprogrammed design, the LSI-11 provides a number of important system features not yet found in other LSI microcomputers. With its minicomputer-compatible instruction set, the LSI-11 offers a new level of microcomputer accessibility and ease of use. Whether seen as low-end minicomputers or high-end microcomputers, machines like the LSI-11 serve to bridge the gap which has separated minicomputer performance and convenience from microcomputer economy and flexibility.

And so, the computer revolution continues; from the maxi to the mini to the micro, the number and breadth of computer applications continue to grow. The DEC LSI-11, a microprogrammed minicomputer-compatible microcomputer system, contributes to this growth. The LSI-11 is an important step in this continuing evolution; it will certainly not be the last. For both designers and users of this new generation of computer systems, there remain many interesting days ahead.

ACKNOWLEDGEMENTS

The author wishes to express his gratitude to the many people who helped in the peparation and review of this paper, especially S. Teicher, M. Titelbaum. D. Dickhut, R. Olsen, and R. Eckhouse.

13

Design Decisions for the PDP-11/60 Mid-Range Minicomputer

J. CRAIG MUDGE

INTRODUCTION

Design evolution of a minicomputer family usually proceeds along three basic dimensions: cost, functionality, and size. That is, the minicomputer becomes cheaper, more powerful, and smaller with time. The underlying hardware technology is the dominant factor in determining the evolution. In contrast to the evolution of large computers, market factors have less influence on the growth pattern of minicomputers. However, minicomputer software characteristics are affected by the market. These requirements rapidly feed down to modify the hardware, given that the technology will support user needs.

The DEC PDP-11/60 serves to demonstrate minicomputer designing with improved technologies. Being a mid-range machine, i.e., neither the lowest in cost nor the highest in performance, its design is a rich source of tradeoff examples. Its cache design illustrates a price/performance trade; the decreasing cost of read-only memories (ROMs) show how hardware-microcode tradeoffs change over time, and its integral floating-point arithmetic unit exemplifies a software-hardware tradeoff.

DESIGN STYLES

Equipment history reveals that a member is added to a minicomputer family whenever technology advances by a factor of 2; for example, doubling of bit density on a memory chip. Over the past 15 years, such an improvement has occurred about every two years.

These advances in technology can be translated into either of two fundamentally different design styles. One provides essentially constant functionality at a minimal price (which decreases over time); the second keeps cost constant and increases functionality. (Here, and in the discussion to follow, the definition of functionality has been broadened from its conventional single component, speed, to include components such as extended instructions and self-checking.) Both design approaches coordinate with the basic marketing philosophy of the minicomputer industry: more computation for more users at less cost. There have been ten models, or implementations, of the PDP-11 architecture since the unit was introduced in 1970 (Chapter 9). Figure 1 illustrates how the two design styles affected successive implementations within this minicomputer family.

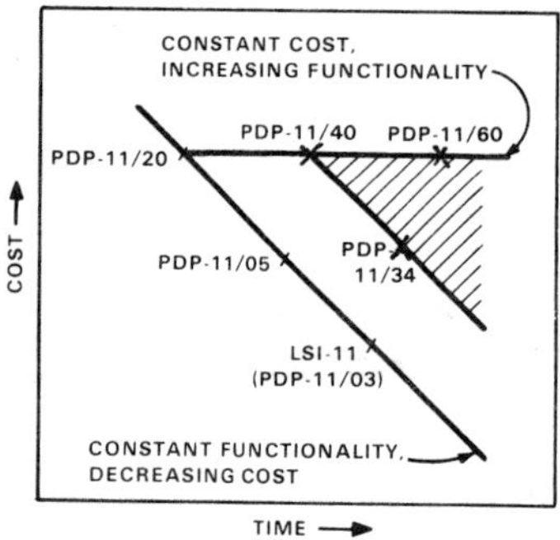

Figure 1. Minicomputer family evolution. Advances in technology translate into two design styles: constant cost/increasing functionality and constant functionality/decreasing cost. The PDP-11/60 represents former design style. Functionality added to PDP-11/40 is depicted by shaded area. Tradeoffs discussed occur within this area.

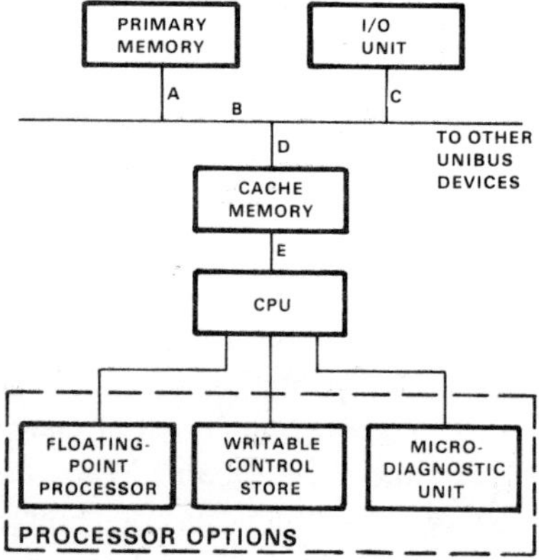

Figure 2. Internal structure. Cache placement between Unibus and CPU permits faster execution and allows use of standard memories. However, DMA monitoring mechanism is needed for traffic on path CBA. Module count is six for CPU and cache, one for writable control store, one for microdiagnostics unit, and four for floating-point processor. This processor operates in parallel with CPU execution of nonfloating-point instructions; instruction times are 1.02 μs for double-precision add and 1.53 μs for single-precision multiply. Writable control store uses 1024 control words that are reloadable and that control 170 ns inner machine. Machine is design optimized for user environment characterized by real-time operating system and FORTRAN.

Lower cost members trace the decreasing cost/constant functionality curve. (This is the 11/20, 11/05, and LSI-11 or 11/03 line.) The horizontal line in Figure 1 connects the constant cost/increasing functionality designs. (Not shown are "growth-path" members that provide greater performance at slightly increased costs; 11/45, 11/55, and 11/70 machines trace an upward growth-path curve.) Shaded area in the figure represents the added functionality possible through technology advances. Mid-range minicomputers attempt to optimize price/functionality and, hence, offer an excellent vantage point for discussing design tradeoffs made under the constant-cost design style.

In addition to the capabilities provided by technological advances, a mature family architecture and user base allows the minicomputer designer to include those capabilities that were not considered feasible in the original architecture. These features may not have been included because they were too costly to implement, not sufficiently general purpose to justify their inclusion, or not perceived as being essential to users. Reliability, maintainability, the integral floating-point unit, and the writable control store (WCS) option represent such capabilities.

Internal structure of the 11/60 (Figure 2) incorporates a 2048-byte cache, memory management unit (for virtual-to-physical address translation), and an integral floating-point unit as standard components. The unit can perform a register-to-register add instruction in an average time of 530 ns; internal cycle time is 170 ns. Available as options are a floating-point processor, which implements at higher speed the same 46 instructions as the integral unit, a writable control store, and a microdiagnostic unit.

ADVANCES IN MEMORY TECHNOLOGY

Improvements in memory technology have been the principal forces in minicomputer developments. Memory is the most basic component of a computer, and it is utilized throughout the design. In addition to obvious uses as main program and data memory, and as file storage devices (disks and tapes), memory is also located within the central processor in the form of registers, state indicators, control, and buffer storage between the central processor and main (primary) memory. In input/output (I/O) devices, there are buffers and staging areas. Memory can be substituted for nearly all logic by substituting table lookup for computation.

The constantly increasing bit density mentioned previously has been the most dramatic development in memories. For example, bipolar read-write or random-access memory (RAM) chips have advanced as follows.

Year When First Widely Available	Number of Bits
1969–70	16
1971–72	64
1973	256
1975	1024
1977	4096

Cost reductions have paralleled bit density increases. A consequence of high density RAM technology is that cache memories are now extensively used in mid- and upper-range minicomputers. Bipolar ROM densities have led RAM densities by about a year. Thus, the 2048-bit ROM, organized as 512×4, was available in 1975.

These factors have made microprogrammed control increasingly attractive to the minicomputer designer. While large-scale computers utilized extensive microprogramming during the 1960s, it was not a cost-effective choice for the minicomputer designer because of the prohibitive cost of the read-only storage technology then available.

Both hardwired control devices and microprogrammed control devices have curves that trace increases in cost as they implement increasing functionality (Figure 3). However, the rate of cost increase is less for microprogrammed controls than for hardwired controls. Davidow [1972] demonstrates that a factor of 4 difference exists between the two slopes.

At some point, the two related hardwired and microprogrammed curves cross. Beyond that intersection, microprogrammed controls are

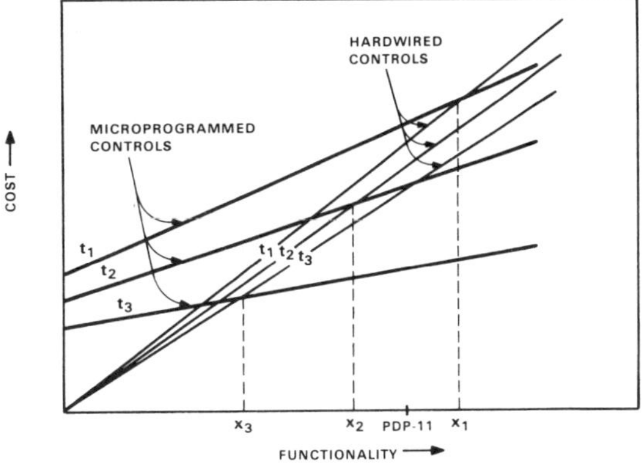

Figure 3. Semiconductor technology trends in control implementations. Cost comparisons, at three different points in time, of conventional hardwired control and advanced microprogrammed control show two important trends. First, at fixed point in time in 1970s (e.g., time $t3$), microprogrammed control is less expensive above certain level of complexity ($x3$). For simplest type of machine, random logic gives most economical design. Microprogrammed design has base cost associated with address sequencing and memory selection circuitry. Microprogrammed control cost increases slowly with number of sequencing cycles, which are added as complexity increases, because each additional cycle requires one additional word of control store. Second, because rate of cost-decrease for memories is greater than the rate for random logic, crossover points move with time, gradually shifting in favor of microprogrammed control. When 11/20 was designed (time $t1$) hardwired controls were cheaper. Its successor, the 11/40, was designed at time $t2$ and used microprogramming. The 11/60, at time $t3$, used increased microprogramming.

more economical to use in a design. Both of these curves are moving downward in cost with time, but the curve for microprogrammed controls is moving downward at a faster rate. Thus, the intersection point of the two curves is gradually shifting in favor of microprogrammed controls because the two technologies are moving at different rates. The PDP-11 family offers an example of this trend. At the time the 11/20 was designed, the crossover point was to the right of the PDP-11 instruction set on the abscissa. Hence, the 11/20 used hardwired controls. However, all subsequent implementations have used a ROM-controlled microprogrammed processor. O'Loughlin [1975] contrasts the control implementations of four members of the family.

Instruction decode on the 11/60 provides an example of a different use of ROMs. For the secondary decode (the primary is done by combinational logic), part of the instruction register addresses a ROM in which control-store-address offsets are stored. This data-table approach offers both a component saving and a more systematic design. Another example is a ROM-stored table that inspects memory addresses to detect those that refer to locations internal to the processor.

Other advances in semiconductor technology that have affected the minicomputer designer's task include the development of 3-state logic devices and greater levels of gate integration in logic chips. Widely available in 1975, 3-state logic encourages bus-oriented designs. Six 3-state buses are implemented in the 11/60. Examples are the 48-bit-wide control signal bus in the CPU and the 60-bit-wide fraction data and 10-bit-wide exponent data buses in the floating-point processor.

Increased gate integration in logic chips had its major impact on constant-cost minicomputers when the design evolution moved from the 11/20 to the 11/40. The latter machine made heavy use of medium-scale integration (MSI). The MSI available to 11/60 designers had negligible density gains over that available to the 11/40 designers. However, after the basic technology decision for the 11/60 was made, a significant step in gate integration occurred. The bit-slice technology, as typified by the 4-bit-wide bipolar AM2901 microprocessor slice, became widely available. A 1977 technology decision for a mid-range minicomputer would clearly choose bit-slice components. For the 11/60, however, improvements came from the introduction of 3-state logic and from availability of a wider range of Schottky logic components.

Three semiconductor technology advances contributed to the 11/60 price/performance design in differing degrees. Most important was the cost reduction in ROMs, next was the density improvement in RAMs, and third was the (minor) increase in random logic density.

PRICE/PERFORMANCE BALANCE

Two components, the cache memory and the medium-bandwidth I/O structure, demonstrate the price/performance balance characteristic of the 11/60 mid-range minicomputer.

Cache is now a well-proven technique in computer memory implementation. Its purpose is to achieve the effect of an all-high-speed memory by using two memories – one slow (primary) and one fast (cache) – and by taking advantage of the fact that, most of the time, data being used is in the fast or cache memory. Programs typically have the property of locality; that is, over short periods of time, most accesses are to a small number of memory locations. The hardware algorithm managing the cache attempts to keep copies of these locations in the cache. The term "hit ratio" is used to describe the proportion of requests for data or instructions that are satisfied by reference only to the cache. Alternatively, "miss ratio" is the complement of hit ratio. Performance is determined by the hit ratio, which is a function of several cache organizational parameters, including: (1) cache size, (2) block size (amount of data moved between the slow or primary memory and the cache), and (3) form of address comparison used.

Strecker (Chapter 10) describes the research that led to the use of a cache memory in the 11/70. His simulation models were also used in the 11/60 design. By comparing the designs of these machines, several tradeoffs made to obtain a lower cost memory system appropriate to the mid-range 11/60 can be noted.

The first parameter to be determined was the amount of data to be moved between primary memory and cache. This decision was closely related to the width of the internal memory bus connecting I/O devices to primary memory. Since the 11/70 was planned to support several high speed Direct Memory Access (DMA) devices, (e.g., swapping disks operating concurrently), its designers provided a 32-bit bus to memory to supplement the 16-bit-wide Unibus. Because the target 11/60 users do not require such a large I/O bandwidth, the Unibus is used for DMA traffic. The 11/70 cache has a block size of two 16-bit words and transfers 32 bits from memory to cache across its dedicated memory bus. Since the 11/60 uses the 16-bit Unibus as its memory bus, the simplest block size – one 16-bit word – was chosen. Note that a 2-word block size can be achieved with a 16-bit bus; the bus is cycled twice to effect a 2-word transfer. Cache simulations showed that this bus cycling would raise the hit ratio of the 11/60 from 87 to 92 percent. However, the associated performance gain was judged not to be worth the significant added cost of the extra control logic needed to cycle the bus twice.

The next decision concerned the size of the cache. Simulation results showed that the miss ratio decreases rapidly for cache sizes up to 1024 words and less rapidly for larger sizes. But how should the 1024 words be partitioned? Because a full-associative cache requires an expensive content-addressed memory, the partitioning choice for minicomputers is for a set-associative cache. Since a complete discussion of associativity and replacement is beyond the scope of this article, the reader is referred to the papers by Meade [1971] and Strecker (Chapter 10).

Degree of associativity and total cache size was dominated by the form factors of two candidate RAM chips (256 × 1 and 1024 × 1). These factors are illustrated in Figure 4. The following list shows the clear price/performance advantage of the chosen 1024-word, set-size-of-one cache.

RAM Chip Capacity	Set Size	Cache Size	RAM Chip Count	Hit Ratio
256 × 1	1	256	n	0.70
256 × 1	1	512	2n	0.75
256 × 1	2	512	2n	0.82
1024 × 1	1	1024	n	0.87
256 × 1	2	1024	4n	0.93
1024 × 1	2	2048	2n	0.93

The resulting structure is shown in Figure 5. This simple, direct-mapped organization should dominate minicomputer cache designs in the near-term future. By using the design evolution model shown in Figure 1, it is projected that the two candidate RAM chips for the successor to the 11/60 cache will be the 1024 × 1 and 4096 × 1 chips. Obviously, the design choice for that new class of machine will be a 4096-word direct-mapped cache.

Since simulation data show negligible performance difference between various write-allocation strategies, the lowest cost strategy, that of allocate-on-write, was implemented. Because the 11/60 utilized a set-size-of-one cache, there was no need to decide upon a replacement algorithm. The 11/70 uses a random-replacement algorithm.

The next decision to be made concerned placement of cache. Two choices were evaluated. The cache could be placed between the Unibus and the primary memory or between

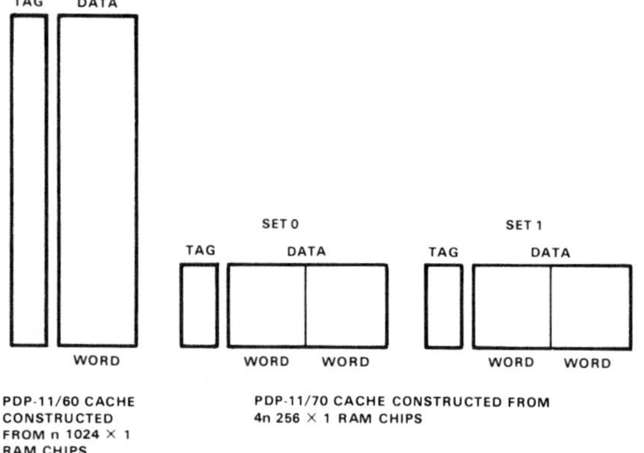

Figure 4. Cache comparison. Simple direct mapped cache of the 11/60 contrasted with the 11/70 cache illustrates a price-performance tradeoff. The 11/70 cache has a block size of two (two words are transferred from primary memory) and a set size of two (a word may be placed in either set). Component savings of the simpler organization are clear; only one address comparator is needed, no multiplexer is required to select the output of the data store, and only one set of parity checkers is needed. Hit ratio of the simpler 11/60 cache is 0.87 as compared with 0.93 for the 11/70 cache, which required five times the component count.

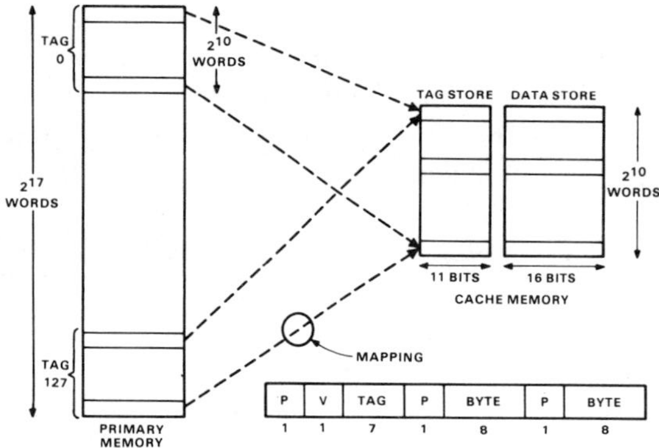

Figure 5. Direct-mapped cache. Mapping occurs from 128 Kwords of primary memory to 1024-word cache. High-order seven bits of an 18-bit address are stored in tag store to ensure uniqueness in mapping. Tag store also holds a valid bit and parity bits. Cache word format (27 bits in total) is as shown in the bit map.

the Unibus and the central processor. The latter was chosen because of the following advantages.

1. Machine execution is faster since the high speed cache is local to the central processor. Time delays associated with synchronization and transmission on the Unibus are avoided.
2. Instead of designing specific 11/60 memory modules, existing memory subsystems that interface to the Unibus could be used. Moreover, as faster Unibus-interfaced memories become available, they can be installed on the machine without change.
3. DMA traffic interferes with processor activity to a lesser extent. DMA activity takes place over the path labeled ABC in Figure 2. Processor speed is degraded by interference with I/O operations only when the cache needs to reference the primary memory, using path ABD in Figure 2. This happens only in the event of a read miss, typically less than 13 percent of the time, and on write operations (10 percent of memory references).

The disadvantage of this placement is that a mechanism to monitor DMA traffic must be added to the cache to avoid the "stale data" problem. (When the processor reads a location that has been written by DMA, it must receive the information from primary memory.) The alternative placement avoids this extra mechanism by handling both DMA and processor requests with the same mechanism. However, there is more interference between the processor and I/O activity.

Increased memory chip density and the cache performance tradeoff resulted in a significant component reduction. The 11/70 cache occupies four printed circuit boards (approximately 440 chips); the 11/60 occupies less than one board (approximately 85 chips). This factor of 5 component reduction is due to: (1) absence of the 32-bit bus, (2) simpler cache organization, and (3) semiconductor technology advances. These three factors contributed in approximately equal proportions.

FREQUENCY-DRIVEN DESIGN

Because the 11/60 implemented a stable, mature instruction set, several years of programming experience were incorporated into the system design. A simulator program was used to gather execution statistics on a range of programs. Frequency distributions of operation codes and addressing modes drove the design of the base 11/60 and the floating-point processor option.

Functions implemented in hardware, as opposed to microcode, require less time to execute. However, microprogrammed implementations are less expensive, as shown in Figure 3. Frequency distributions of operation codes guided the tradeoff. A balanced mixture of hardwired and microprogrammed implementation of functions produced a central processor that approached the speed of a computer with completely hardwired control functions, but at a lower cost.

Frequency distributions of floating-point operands were also used. Sweeney [1965] analyzed the execution of more than one million floating-point additions and tabulated the behavior of preshift alignment and postshift normalization. Both distributions are highly skewed toward low numbers of shifts. By exploiting these data, the floating-point processor performs a double-precision add in 1.02 microseconds as compared with 1.68 microseconds on a comparable unit that uses a conventional algorithm.

To measure the price/performance advantage claimed for the frequency-driven design approach in the base 11/60, a similar machine was needed for comparison. Obviously, such a machine, realized in the same semiconductor technology and designed so that the hardware resources were divided equally among all instructions, was not available. However, data was available on floating-point implementations. The floating-point processor design was a four printed circuit board unit that exploited the frequency distributions of operation codes, addressing modes, and shift amounts. A theoretical comparison was made with another four board design that did not use a frequency-driven approach. The 11/60 floating-point processor was estimated to exhibit a performance gain of 30 to 40 percent on the standard set of benchmark programs used throughout the design process.

INTEGRAL FLOATING-POINT ARITHMETIC UNIT

Addition of an integral floating-point arithmetic unit to the 11/60 was a direct consequence of market feedback. In particular, it was determined that the majority of the machine's users would use FORTRAN IV as a source language. In addition, among those using that language, many were not interested in heavy floating-point computation because integer arithmetic dominated their applications.

The FORTRAN IV-PLUS compiler has been optimized for execution speed (as opposed to compile speed) – typically a factor of three over other available FORTRAN IV compilers. This compiler, however, employs the instruction set and auxiliary registers of the PDP-11 floating-point processors. Thus, to take advantage of the compiler's efficiency without burdening the user with the cost of a fast floating-point processor, the central processor must provide those floating-point instructions. This is done by emulating the 46 instructions, including the 64-bit data operations, of the full floating-point instruction set using the 16-bit-wide data path of the base 11/60. For users who require FORTRAN IV but have low floating-point content in their programs, the integral floating-point unit is all that is necessary.

Additional microcode and register space added a few percent to the CPU cost. However, for that small cost increase, FORTRAN IV performance on integer programs was increased by 300 percent – a dramatic increase.

CABINET-LEVEL INTEGRATION

Physical packaging of minicomputer systems involves another set of tradeoffs. Several levels of size integration are available, ranging from the chip level (LSI-11), through the board level (11/04) and the box level (11/34), to the cabinet level (11/60).

At the cabinet level, packaging techniques are generally traditional. System fabrication is frequently the result of determining methods to install subassemblies into standard racks. At this configuration level, generalized subassemblies are usually chosen for certain functions.

This generally evokes a cost. For instance, there may be a great deal of unused space in conventional industrial racks; in most cases this excess space is simply covered with blank paneling. The cooling system, however, must be designed as if all the racks within the cabinet were occupied with subassemblies.

It was projected that the majority of the configurations sold would be system oriented; thus, design optimization at the cabinet level would be worthwhile. Therefore, the standard 11/60 is cabinet packaged. Figure 6 shows how the CPU, memory, disk units, power supplies, and expansion backplane are packaged to gain the advantages that stem from cabinet level integration. This integration also yielded added volume, allowing a more powerful blower system to be installed. Acoustic sound power emittance is very low, considering that the rated operating environment is DEC Standard 102 Class C (122° F) for the processor. Improved power efficiency, appearance for the office environment, and subassembly accessibility are also provided.

USER MICROPROGRAMMING OPTION

User microprogramming was incorporated in the system to meet growing market demands. The option allows the user to create instructions that tailor the central processor, particularly the data flow, to his particular application.

Many potential applications of microprogramming were considered during the design of the data path and control sections of the 11/60. They ranged from instruction set extensions, e.g., translation, string, and decimal arithmetic operations, to application kernels, such as node manipulation in list processing and fast Fourier transform in signal processing. Merely substituting RAM for ROM control

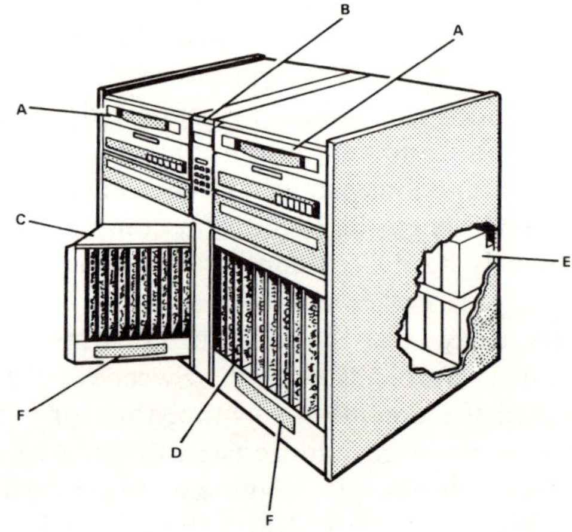

Figure 6. Cabinet packaging. Primary design goals were reliability and maintainability. System logic is mounted on swing-out card cages C and D for easy access. Rear access power supplies E are modular. Cable routing reduces electrical noise and crosstalk. Blower system F keeps all devices cool. Keypad B with numerical display facilitates machine control and maintenance. Disks A are top- or front-loading units.

does not result in a microprogrammable computer. A microprogrammable computer system should have the following:

1. Extra address space in the control store.
2. Generality in the data path's processing elements.
3. A means to load the writable control store (WCS).
4. User-oriented hardware documentation.
5. Software to support writing and debugging microprograms.
6. Integration of hardware and software protocols.

All these capabilities were designed into the 11/60 WCS option.

A previously reserved operation code, 0767XX in the PDP-11 instruction set, has been allocated for users. Its designation is XFC, extended function code. When this code is recognized, the CPU transfers control to the upper 1024-word block of the 4096-word microprogram address space. User-written microcode may take over from there.

A second (asynchronous) type of entry to user's microcode is also provided. This occurs when a WCS-serviced interrupt is recognized by the base machine. Thus, a user can write interrupt service routines in microcode and invoke them without the usual inerrupt overhead. Such routines may even be complete I/O channel emulations.

Implementation of the basic 11/60 demonstrated flexibility of microprogramming. The techniques were used in such diverse functions as console service, error logging, floating-point arithmetic, and cache initialization.

Microprogramming does not always result in significant performance gains. Well-suited applications can gain by a factor of 5; poorly suited ones may give only minimal improvement. This is supported by measurements on digital signal processing software reported by Morris and Mudge [1977]. Prospective users must carefully analyze the execution behavior of the application to determine which parts are "hot spots," i.e., most frequently executed. For the average application, an overall factor of 2 improvement should be expected. This average, found to be a useful rule of thumb, is derived by assuming that all hot spots are microprogrammed and the remainder of the program is left unchanged.

Two user-microprogramming options are available. The first is composed of the writable control store module, software tools, and associated manuals. The second is a board containing control logic and sockets ready for the insertion of custom-programmable ROMs (PROMs) containing microprograms developed with the writable control store. This extended control store (ECS) option is designed for situations where microcode integrity and/or multiple installations are required.

A novel structuring of the writable control store allows it to be used to store data. Availability of data storage local to a processor, i.e., not accessed through a main, general purpose memory bus, can increase system speed. Such local store is usually implemented in some special technology that has low capacity but high performance. Writable control store has been structured so that the 48-bit microinstruction storage words can be read and written as 16-bit data words. In addition to conventional writable control store hardware, logic is available to realize a local store address register (LSAR) and a local store data register (LSDR).

Thus, the microprogrammer has fast local store available. This storage is block-oriented. A three-cycle overhead is needed to start a block read (or block write); then, words are read (or written) at the rate of one per microcycle. The microprogram can be logically partitioned into two sections: control store – 48-bit control words; and local store – 16-bit data words (three per microword). A common partitioning would be 512 words of control store and 1536 words of local store.

RELIABILITY AND MAINTAINABILITY

Design decisions to allocate a portion of the cost of the 11/60 to reliability and maintainability, rather than to further improving performance, were motivated by user and market needs. Prime considerations were the increasing labor cost associated with maintenance and the growing use of minicomputers in applications demanding more reliability.

The first goal was to increase the mean time between failures (MTBF) by: (1) reducing the occurrence and impact of normally fatal hardware malfunctions, (2) providing error statistics, and (3) providing operating alternatives to keep the system running after failures occur, albeit at a lower performance.

The second goal was to reduce the mean time to repair (MTTR) when hardware malfunctions occur by: (1) hardware design and packaging that facilitate error diagnosis and repair during scheduled and nonscheduled maintenance, (2) continuous logging of hardware errors during system operation, and (3) provision of software and microdiagnostic tools for problem isolation.

MTBF

Reducing the incidence of fatal hardware malfunctions was a joint effort by engineering and manufacturing. The Schottky transistor-transistor logic (TTL) used in the machine, having been in widespread use for over five years, is a well proven family of devices. Moreover, conservative electrical design practices were followed.

Plotted against time, chip failure rate tends to follow a bathtub-shaped curve, high at either end of the life cycle. The 11/60 production pro cess includes extensive thermal cycling to ensure that "infant mortality" cases are discovered early during manufacturing.

The cabinet is designed to minimize buildup of hot air over the processor boards. Power supplies are mounted at the rear of the cabinet, away from the logic, so that radiant heating effects are minimized. A blower system cools the logic card cage by drawing fresh, filtered air down over the printed circuit boards such that no board receives exhaust air from another.

Other physical packaging to reduce hardware problems include cable troughs, impact-absorbing casters, and special cabinet grounding. A filter is attached to the maintenance console to reduce electrostatic noise interference.

Console microcode double checks every entry to verify data received from the keypad. A significant proportion of the 11/60 microcode (Table 1) is devoted to logging microlevel state upon the occurrence of a detected error. This logged state can be accessed via a maintenance examine and deposit (MED) instruction. Logged information is used by an operating system to compile error records, which aid in tracking down intermittent errors.

To reduce the impact of hardware malfunctions on the user environment, a number of fail-soft capabilities have been implemented.

1. If the cache fails, it is turned off and the still-functioning primary memory is used to keep the system running.
2. If a parity error occurs in WCS, the processor disables that control store. Then the operating system is notified, and program execution can continue using the basic PDP-11 instructions.
3. Systems can be programmed to fall back onto the integral floating-point unit if an error is detected in the floating-point processor.
4. The bootstrap loader permits system loading from an alternative device if the primary bootstrapping device is disabled.

MTTR

Error diagnosis is the most time-consuming problem facing the field service engineer. Special diagnostic tools, both hardware and software, have been designed to reduce the time spent in error isolation.

Table 1. Control Store Usage by Category

Category		Number of Microwords		Percentage of Total
A	PDP-11 Instruction Set			
	Initialization	95		4
	Operand fetch, execution, and operand store	515		20
	Infrequent intraprocessor transfers	230	840	9
B	Integral Floating-Point Instruction Set	1010		40
C	Reliability and Maintainability			
	Error logging, MED, and cache fail-soft	190		7
	Console, boot, and initial diagnostic	230		9
D	Support of Options			
	Writable control store	60		2
	Floating-point processor	80		3
E	Reserved for Future Changes and Additions	150		6
		2560		100

Total address space for microprograms is 4096 words, of which the 2560 categorized in the table are implemented in ROM.

Note the increased utilization of microprogramming in the 11/60, as compared to the 11/40. Category A, totaling 840 words, was implemented in 256 words for the 11/40. The two machines have comparable microword widths.

The third subcategory in Category A illustrates the use of microprogramming in the frequency-driven design approach. Examples of infrequent intraprocessor transfers are error handling and data transfer to and from internal addresses, e.g., memory management relocation registers.

One of the benefits of a microprogrammed implementation of control is the ease with which engineering change orders (ECO) can be implemented. Space in Category E is reserved for such use and for the further correction of undetected errors in the microcode itself.

Focal point of the hardware maintainability effort is the microdiagnostic unit. This single board tests the logic on five of the six processor boards. When faults are detected, an error code is displayed on light-emitting diodes (LEDs). A fault directory can then be used to determine which boards are to be replaced. The unit requires only a small portion of the internal machine (the microword sequencing) to be operational.

In addition, a number of on-board diagnostic aids are included in the CPU design. These include LEDs to display the contents of the next microaddress register, a single-step mode, and a microbreak function.

Software diagnostic programs are used to diagnose errors in system peripherals as well as in all CPU subsystems, such as memory management unit and cache. User mode diagnostic programs allow peripheral diagnosis to occur while the system is available for other users. Conventional standalone diagnostic programs can also be used.

Physical packaging facilitates quick repair. Hinged card cages and modular power supplies allow easy access and module change.

SUMMARY

The design of a mid-range minicomputer has been used as a concrete illustration of tradeoffs made to effect a price/performance balance. Designers use technology advances, e.g., doubling of density on a memory chip, to produce new designs in one of two design styles: constant cost/increasing functionality or constant functionality/decreasing cost. Increased use of microprogramming, a factor of 3 in this case study, is a trend that was observed.

By choosing a less powerful cache organization, the 11/60 design obtained a factor of 5 component reduction. Cache design also illustrates how some design parameters are highly interdependent. The frequency-driven design approach used on the floating-point processor can lead to a 40 percent performance gain.

Examples of added functionality in the constant-cost style of design include greater reliability and maintainability, and user microprogramming.

14

Impact of Implementation Design Tradeoffs on Performance: The PDP-11, A Case Study

EDWARD A. SNOW and DANIEL P. SIEWIOREK

INTRODUCTION

As semiconductor technology has evolved, the digital systems designer has been presented with an ever increasing set of primitive components from which to construct systems: standard SSI, MSI, and LSI as well as custom LSI components. This expanding choice makes it more difficult to arrive at a near-optimal cost/performance ratio in a design. In the case of highly complex systems, the situation is even worse since different primitives may be cost-effective in different subareas of such systems.

Historically, digital system design has been more an art than a science. Good designs evolved from a mixture of experience, intuition, and trial and error. Only rarely have design methodologies been developed (e.g., two level combinational logic minimization, wire-wrap routing schemes, etc.). Effective design methodologies are essential for the cost-effective design of more complex systems. In addition, if the methodologies are sufficiently detailed, they can be applied in high level design automation systems [Siewiorek and Barbacci, 1976].

Design methodologies may be developed by studying the results of the human design process. There are at least two ways to study this process. The first involves a controlled design experiment where several designers perform the same task. By contrasting the results, the range of design variation and technique can be established [Thomas and Siewiorek, 1977]. However, this approach is limited to a fairly small number of design situations due to the redundant use of the human designers.

The second approach examines a series of existing designs that meet the same functional specification while spanning a wide range of design constraints in terms of cost, performance, etc. This paper considers the second approach and uses the DEC PDP-11 minicomputer line as a basis of study. The PDP-11 was selected due to the large number of implementations (eight are considered here) with designs spanning a wide range in performance (roughly 7:1) and component technology (bipolar SSI, MSI, MOS custom LSI). The designs are relatively complex and seem to embody good design tradeoffs as ultimately reflected by their price/performance and commercial success.

The design tradeoffs considered fall into three categories: circuit technology, control unit implementation, and data path topology. All three have had considerable impact on performance. Attention here is focused mainly upon the CPU. Memory performance enhancements such as caching are considered only in so far as they affect CPU performance.

This paper is divided into two major parts. The first part presents an archetypal implementation followed by the model-specific variations from the archetype. These variations represent the design tradeoffs. The second part presents methodologies for determining the impact of various design parameters on system performance. The magnitude of the impact is quantified for several parameters and the use of the results in design situations is discussed.

The PDP-11 Family is a set of small- to medium-scale stored program central processors with compatible instruction sets. The 11 Family evolution in terms of increased performance, constant cost, and constant performance successors is traced in Figure 1. Since the 11/45, 11/55 and 11/70 use the same processor, the KB11, only the 11/45 is treated in this study.

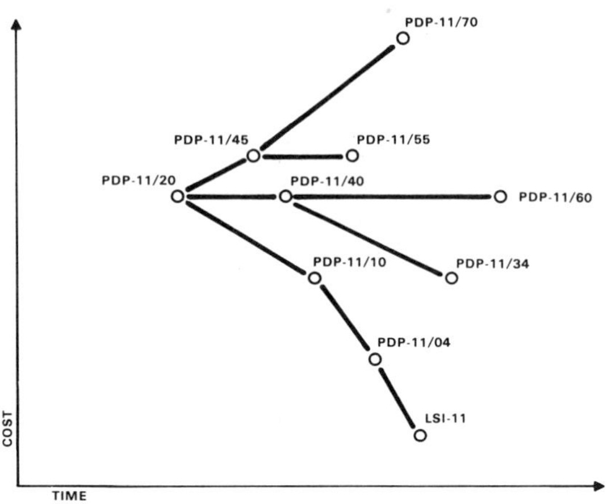

Figure 1. PDP-11 Family tree.

IMPLEMENTATION OF MEDIUM PERFORMANCE PDP-11s

The broad middle range of PDP-11s have comparable implementations yet their performances vary by a factor of 2. The processors making up this group are the PDP-11/04, 11/10,* 11/20, 11/34, 11/40, and 11/60. This section discusses the features common to these implementations and the variations found between machines which provide the dimensions along which they may be characterized.

Common Implementation Features

All PDP-11 implementations, be they low, medium, or high performance, can be decomposed into a set of data paths and a control unit. The data paths store and operate upon byte and word data and interface to the Unibus, permitting them to read from and write to memory and peripheral devices. The control unit provides all the signals necessary to evoke the appropriate operations in the data paths and Unibus interface. Mid-range PDP-11s have comparable data path and control unit implementations allowing them to be contrasted in a uniform way. In this section, a basis for comparing these machines is established and used to characterize them.

Data Paths. An archetype may be constructed from which the data paths of all mid-range PDP-11s differ but minimally. This archetype is diagrammed in Figure 2. All major registers and processing elements as well as the links and switches which interconnect them are indicated. The data path illustrations for individual implementations are grouped with Figure 2 at the end of the chapter. These figures are laid out in a common format to encourage comparison. Note that with very few exceptions, all data paths are 16 bits wide (PDP-11 word size).

The heart of the data paths is the arithmetic logic unit or ALU through which all data circulates and where most of the processing actually takes place. Among the operations performed by the ALU are addition, subtraction, one's

*The 11/05 and the 11/10 are identical machines sold to different markets. This chapter refers to the machine as the 11/10.

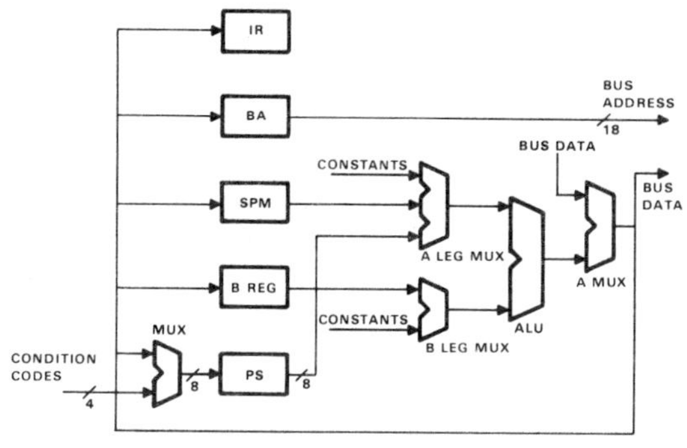

Figure 2. Archetypal medium-range PDP-11 data paths.

and two's complementation, and logical ANDing and ORing.

The inputs to the ALU are the A leg and the B leg. The A leg is normally fed from a multiplexer (A leg MUX) which may select from an operand supplied to it from the Scratchpad Memory (SPM) and possibly from a small set of constants and/or the Processor Status register (PS). The B leg also is typically fed from its own MUX (B leg MUX), its selections being from the B Register and certain constants. In addition, the B leg MUX may be configured so that byte selection, sign extension, and other functions may be performed on the operand which it supplies to the ALU.

Following the ALU is a multiplexer (the A MUX) typically used to select between the output of the ALU, the data lines of the Unibus, and certain constants. The output of the A MUX provides the only feedback path in all mid-range PDP-11 implementations except the 11/60 and acts as an input to all major processor registers.

The internal registers lie at the beginning of the data paths. The Instruction Register (IR) contains the current instruction. The Bus Address register (BA) holds the address placed on the Unibus by the processor. The Program Status register (PS) contains the processor priority, memory management unit modes, condition code flags, and instruction trace trap enable bit. The Scratchpad Memory (SPM) is an array of 16 individually addressable registers which include the general registers (R0–R7) plus a number of internal registers not accessible to the programmer. The B Register (B Reg) is used to hold the B leg operand supplied to the ALU.

The variations from this archetype are minor as discussed in the section entitled "Characterization of Individual Implementations." Variations encountered include routings for Bus Address and Processor Status register, the point of generation for certain constants, the positioning of the byte swapper, sign extender, and rotate/shift logic, and the use of certain auxiliary registers present in some designs and not others. In general, these variations are all peripheral to the major elements and interconnections of the data paths.

Control Unit. The control unit for all PDP-11 processors (with the exception of the PDP-11/20) is microprogrammed [Wilkes and Stringer, 1953]. The considerations leading to the use of this style of control implementation in the PDP-11 are discussed in [O'Loughlin, 1975]. The major advantage of microprogramming is flexibility in the derivation of control signals to gate register transfers, synchronization with Unibus logic, control of microcycle timing, and evocation of changes in control flow. The way in which a microprogrammed control unit accomplishes all of these actions impacts performance.

Figure 3 represents the archetypal PDP-11 microprogrammed control unit. The contents of the Microaddress Register determine the current control unit state and are used to access the next microinstruction word from the control store. Pulses from the clock generator strobe the Microword and Microaddress Registers loading them with the next microword and next microaddress respectively. Repeated clock pulses thus cause the control unit to sequence through a series of states. The period spent by the control unit in one state is called a microcycle (or simply cycle when this does not lead to

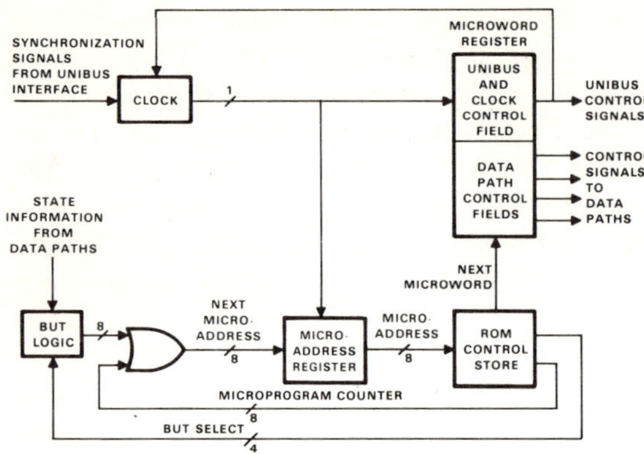

Figure 3. Archetypal microprogrammed PDP-11 control unit.

confusion with memory or instruction cycles), and the duration of the state as determined by the clock is known as the cycle time. The Microword Register shortens cycle time by allowing the next microword to be fetched from the control store while the current microword is being used.

Most of the fields of the microword supply signals for conditioning and clocking the data paths. Many of the fields act directly or with a small amount of decoding, supplying their signals to multiplexers and registers to select routings for data and to enable registers to shift, increment, or load on the master clock. Other fields are decoded based upon the state of the data paths. An instance of this is the use of auxiliary ALU control logic to generate function select signals for the ALU as a function of the instruction contained in the IR. Performance as determined by microcycle count is in large measure established by the connectivity of the data paths and the degree to which their functionality can be evoked by the data path control fields of the microprogram word.

The complexity of the clock logic varies with each implementation. Typically, the clock is fixed at a single period and duty cycle; however, processors such as the 11/34 and 11/40 can select from two or three different clock periods for a given cycle depending upon a field in the Microword Register. This can significantly improve performance in machines where the longer cycles are necessary only infrequently. The clock logic must provide some means for synchronizing processor and Unibus operation since the two operate asynchronously with respect to one another. Two alternate approaches are employed in mid-range implementations. Interlocked operation, the simpler approach, shuts off the processor clock when a Unibus operation is initiated and turns it back on when the operation is complete. This effectively keeps microprogram flow and Unibus operation in lockstep with no overlap. Overlapped operation is a somewhat more involved approach which continues processor clocking after a DATI or DATIP is initiated. The microinstruction requiring the result of the operation has a function bit set which turns off the processor clock until the result is available. This approach makes it possible for the processor to continue running for several microcycles while a data transfer is being performed, improving performance.

The sequence of states through which the control unit passes would be fixed if not for the branch on microtest (BUT) logic. This logic generates a modifier based upon the current state of the data paths and Unibus interface (contents of the Instruction Register, current bus requests, etc.) and a BUT field in the microword currently being accessed from the control store which selects the condition on which the branch is to be based. The modifier (which will be zero in the case that no branch is selected or that the condition is false) is ORed in with the next microinstruction address so that the next control unit state is not only a function of the current state but also a function of the state of the data paths as well. Instruction decoding and addressing mode decoding are two prime examples of the application of BUTs. Certain code points in the BUT field do not select branch conditions, but rather provide control signals to the data paths, Unibus interface, or the control unit itself. These are known as active or working BUTs.

The JAM logic is a part of the microprogram flow-altering mechanism. This logic forces the Microaddress Register to a known state in the event of an exceptional condition such as a memory access error (bus timeout, stack overflow, parity error, etc.) or power up by ORing all one's into the next microaddress through the BUT logic. A microroutine beginning at the all-one's address handles these trapped conditions. The old microaddress is not saved (an exception to this occurs in the case of the PDP-11/60); consequently, the interrupted microprogram sequence is lost and the microtrap ends by restarting the instruction interpretation cycle with the fetch phase.

The structure of the microprogram is determined largely by the BUTs available to implement it and by the degree to which special cases in the instruction set are exploited by these BUTs. This may have a measurable influence on performance as in the case of instruction decoding. The fetch phase of the instruction cycle is concluded by a BUT that branches to the appropriate point in the microcode based upon the contents of the Instruction Register. This branch can be quite complex since it is based upon source mode for double operand instructions, destination mode for single operand instructions, and operation code for all other types of instructions. Some processors can perform the execute phase of certain instructions like set/clear condition code during the last cycle of the fetch phase meaning that the fetch or service phases for the next instruction might also be entered from BUT IRDECODE. Complicating the situation is the large number of possibilities for each phase. For instance, there are not only eight different destination addressing modes, but also subcases for each that vary for byte and word and for memory modifying, memory nonmodifying, MOV, and JMP/JSR instructions.

Some PDP-11 implementations such as the 11/10 make as much use of common microcode as possible to reduce the number of control states. This allows much of the IR decoding to be deferred until some time into a microroutine which might handle a number of different cases. For instance, byte and word operand addressing is done by the same microroutine in a number of PDP-11s. With the cost of control states dropping with the cost of control store ROM, there has been a trend toward providing separate microroutines optimized for each special case as in the 11/60. Thus, more special cases must be broken out at the BUT IRDECODE, making the logic to implement this BUT increasingly involved. There is a payoff, though, because there is a smaller number of control states for IR decoding and fewer BUTs. Performance is boosted as well since frequently occurring special cases such as MOV register to destination can be optimized.

Typical Instruction Interpretation Cycle. To get a feel for the PDP-11 data paths and control unit in operation, consider the interpretation of a representative instruction by the archetypal PDP-11. The instruction to be followed is a word bit set (BIS), an instruction which takes its source operand, logically ORs it with the destination operand, and returns the result to the destination. Register addressing with register 2 is used for the source; indexed addressing with register 7 is used for the destination.

What follows is the sequence of microinstructions evoked during the execution of the macroinstruction described in Table 1. Each microinstruction is numbered and consists of the register transfers and any Unibus operation or branch on microtest initiated by the microword.

Table 1. Microinstructions Evoked During Execution of Macroinstruction

Phase	Cycle	Operation	Explanation
FETCH	1	BA ← PC; DATI; CLKOFF	A read operation is initiated to fetch the instruction addressed by the Program Counter.
	2	IR ← BUSDATA	The instruction is placed in the Instruction Register.
	3	PC ← PC + 2; BUT IRDECODE	The Program Counter is incremented to address the next location in the instruction stream (in this case the location containing the index for the destination). The instruction (held in the IR) is decoded by the BUT and found to be a double operand instruction causing a branch to the microcode for source mode 0.
		BUT IRDECODE double operand word source mode zero • • •	
SOURCE	4	SRCOPR ← RS; BUT DESTINATION	The contents of the register addressed by the source field of the instruction (register 2) are copied into the Scratchpad Register reserved for source operands. The next state is determined by the destination addressing mode and the fact that BIS is a word instruction which modifies its destination.
		BUT DESTINATION modifying word; destination mode b • • •	
DESTINATION	5	BA ← PC; DATI	A read operation is initiated to get the index word (pointed to currently by the Program Counter) for the effective address of the destination operand.
	6	PC ← PC + 2; CLKOFF	The Program Counter is incremented to point to the next instruction. Note that this cycle is overlapped with the DATI started in cycle 5.
	7	B ← BUSDATA	The index is stored for use in the next cycle.
	8	BA ← RD + B; DATIP; CLKOFF	The index is added to the contents of the destination register to form the effective address of the destination operand. A DATIP is performed to read the operand since the operand is to be modified and then restored to its original location in memory.
	9	B ← BUSDATA	The destination operand is stored so it is available to the B leg of the ALU.

Table 1. Microinstructions Evoked During Execution of Macroinstruction (Cont)

Phase	Cycle	Operation	Explanation
EXECUTE	10	BUSDATA ← SRCOPR OP B; DATO; CLKOFF; BUT SERVICE	The source and destination operands are logically ORed together and put out on the Unibus to be written into the memory location from which the destination operand was read. (Note that the destination address is still in BA.) Upon completion of the DATO, the control unit branches into the service phase if a serviceable condition is pending; otherwise, it branches back to repeat the fetch phase for the next instruction. Although it performs an execute phase function, this microinstruction is part of the same destination mode microroutine that generated cycles 5 through 9.
		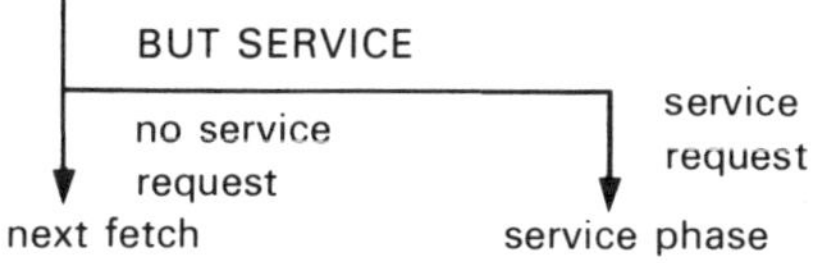 BUT SERVICE: no service request → next fetch; service request → service phase	

Notation used in microinstructions for Table 1:

B = B Register
BA = Bus Address register
BUSDATA = Unibus data lines
CLKOFF = Stop the processor clock until a Unibus transaction is completed; used for processor/Unibus overlap
IR = Instruction Register
PC = Program Counter (Scratchpad Register 7)
RD = Scratchpad Register addressed by macroinstruction destination field (IR<2:0>)
RS = Scratchpad Register addressed by macroinstruction source field (IR<8:6>)
SRCOPR = Scratchpad Register 10 (not accessible to programmer); used as a temporary for source operands
a OP b = Operand a (on the A leg of the ALU) and operand b (on the B leg of the ALU) are combined according to the operation specified by the macroinstruction. The ALU function is selected by the auxiliary ALU logic as described in the subsection "Control Unit."
a ← b = Register a is loaded with operand b

At a detailed level, the instruction interpretation process of each PDP-11 implementation varies significantly from that outlined in

Table 1; however, the scenario is still highly representative of the operation of the control unit and data paths in the designs to be considered.

Characterization of Individual Implementations

A set of common implementation features may be used to characterize each mid-range PDP-11 to provide the raw data upon which comparisons may be based. A summary of these characteristics is given in Tables 2 and 3.

PDP-11/20. The 11/20 was the first of the PDP-11 family. The 11/20 is atypical in a number of important aspects. Because the semiconductor read-only memory technology which makes microprogramming economically attractive was unavailable when the PDP-11/20 was designed, control was implemented in random logic in contrast to the microprogrammed control used in all the succeeding members of the PDP-11 family. This causes control to be forced into a very stylized form so as to minimize the number of control unit states. Finally, the Unibus control generates a number of signals controlling the operation of the data paths. This makes it necessary for the Unibus and processor control unit to operate in tight lockstep with each other with no possibility of asynchronous data transfer.

The absence of MSI also has significant impact on the implementation of the data paths (Figures 4 and 5). The extensive use of SSI logic has several ramifications beyond increased cost and complexity. The A leg and B leg MUXs are set up to act as latches in addition to acting as data selectors (Figure 5). One may think of a B leg being placed between the B leg MUX and the ALU. The ALU is a simple adder in contrast to the multifunctioned TTL MSI 74181 ALUs used in every other medium performance PDP-11. Logical operations are carried out in the A leg MUX/latch. The MUX can select either the true or complemented form of operands to support logical NOT. Logical OR is accomplished by gating the two operands into the MUX simultaneously (one operand may have been latched beforehand). Logical AND is performed by making use of DeMorgan's Rule ($A \sim B \equiv \sim[\sim A V \sim B]$). Since there is no logic for complementing the output of the A leg MUX/latch, two cycles are necessary: the first to form $\sim A V \sim B$, the second to run it through the A leg MUX again to form the complement. The rotate/shift/byte swap logic is built into the MUX following the adder. A final peculiarity of the 11/20 is the separate paths provided from the Unibus for the IR and PS. Interestingly enough, even with all of these rather striking differences in implementation, the PDP-11/20 still shows a strong kinship to its successors.

PDP-11/40. The PDP-11/40 was designed to improve upon the performance of the PDP-11/20 without an increase in price by taking advantage of the TTL MSI technology arising after the introduction of the 11/20. With the exception of the PDP-11/60 (and the 11/20 which exceeds the 11/40 in cost), the 11/40 is both the fastest and most expensive mid-range PDP-11 processor.

The data paths of the 11/40 (Figure 6) correspond closely to those of the archetype except in the immediate vicinity of the ALU. What has been indicated as the A leg MUX is really the negative-logic wired OR of a number of signals. Options such as the Floating-Point Processor are added by simply tying them into the D MUX output and A leg. Two paths exist out of the PS: one running to the A leg MUX as in the archetype and a second running directly to the Unibus as in the 11/20. A path from the A leg MUX directly to the D MUX (equivalent to the A MUX of other models) exists allowing the ALU (and thus the propagation delay incurred by passing through it) to be bypassed in those cases where the contents of the SPM or PS are to be routed directly back to the B Register of SPM. Single-bit shifts and rotates right are handled in the D MUX in a fashion similar to the

Table 2. PDP-11 Circuit Technology and Data Paths

		Circuit Technology		Data Paths					
Model	Performance Relative to LSI-11	Logic Family	Level of Integration	Scratchpad Memory	ALU	Sign Extension	Rotate/ Shift	Byte Swap	Other Features
LSI-11	1.000	N-channel MOS	LSI	• Organized 26 registers × 8 bits • 1 write/2 read ports	8-bit nMOS ALU	Not needed; done in microcode	In ALU	Not needed; done in microcode	• 8-bit-wide data paths, 16-bit operands require two cycles • Non-Unibus, data/ address lines MUXed
11/04	1.455	TTL	MSI	16 × 16 with SP Reg for write after read	74181s with 74182 carry lookahead	In B leg MUX	B Reg is bidirectional shift register	Before SPM	• Complementor at ALU A leg for subtract instruction
11/10	1.436	TTL	MSI	16 × 16 read and write may not take place within same cycle	74181s with 74182 carry lookahead	In B leg MUX	B Reg is bidirectional shift register	None performed as 8 shifts	—
11/20	1.667	TTL	SSI	16 × 16 with input latches for write after read	7482 adders, ripple carry plus combinational logic	In B leg MUX/ latch	Following adder	Following adder	• Bus data has own path to IR and PS • PS has own path out to bus data, no other outgoing paths
11/34	1.942	TTL TTL/S	MSI	16 × 16 write while read	74S181s with 74S182 carry lookahead	Following AMUX	B Reg is bidirectional shift register	Following AMUX, speeds odd-byte accesses	• B extension register (BX Reg) for EIS instructions

Table 2. PDP-11 Circuit Technology and Data Paths (Cont)

	Circuit Technology					Data Paths			
Model	Performance Relative to LSI-11	Logic Family	Level of Integration	Scratchpad Memory	ALU	Sign Extension	Rotate/ Shift	Byte Swap	Other Features
11/40	2.819	TTL	MSI	16 × 16 D Reg and multiphase cycle allow write after read	74181s with 74182 carry lookahead	In B leg MUX	To left in ALU to right in DMUX	In B leg MUX	• Bypass from A leg MUX around ALU and D Reg • Two paths into BA
11/45	6.820 (with bipolar memory)	TTL/S	MSI	• Two banks of 16 × 16 for 1 write/2 read parts • Read and write may not occupy same cycle	74S181s with 74182 carry lookahead	In ALU	To left in ALU To right in SHFMUX	In SHFMUX	• PC broken out separately from scratchpads • Multiple paths into ALU • Fastbus supports semiconductor memory
11/60	3.727 (87% cache hit ratio)	TTL/S	MSI	• Two banks of 32 registers × 16 bits • Only R0–R7 and user R6 duplicated • Write after read	74S181s with 74182 carry lookahead	In shift tree	In shift tree	In shift tree	• Shift tree allows multibit shifts • Scratchpad C for constants, bus input, and status logging • 3-state logic used extensively

Table 3. PDP-11 Control Unit and Physical Assembly

	Controller						Physical Assembly		
Model	Control Derivation	Cycle Time(s) (ns)	Processor/ Unibus Synchronization	Control Store Size (bits × words)	Control Store Words Used	Other Features	Circuit Boards	Integrated Circuit Packages	Integrated Circuit Types
LSI-11	Vertical microcode	400	Interlocked	22 × 1024 (expandable to 2048)	994	• No next microaddress in microword; microwords are selected sequentially until a branch, jump, or translate is encountered	1 quad (4 positions)	48	24
11/04	Horizontal microcode	260	Interlocked	40 × 256	249	—	1 hex (6 positions)	138	40
11/10	Horizontal microcode	300 (150 for fast shift)	Overlapped	40 × 256	249	• Microword is not buffered	2 hex (12 positions)	203	60
11/20	Random logic	280	Interlocked	—	—	• Control states are encoded in major and minor state shift registers	6 quad, 6 double, 2 single (38 positions)	523	27
11/34	Horizontal microcode	180 240	Interlocked	48 × 512	488	—	2 hex (12 positions)	231	54
11/40	Horizontal microcode	140 200 300	Overlapped	56 × 256	251	• BUT field is buffered, BUT must be placed one micro-instruction ahead of where it is to take place	4 hex, 1 quad (28 positions)	417	53
11/45	Horizontal microcode	150	Overlapped	64 × 256	256	• Forks and microbranches may be enabled together, microbranches taking precedence	7 hex, 1 quad (46 positions)	696	78
11/60	Horizontal microcode	170	Interlocked	48 × 2560 (excluding user control store space)	2410 (including integral floating point)	• Multilevel microsubroutines • Page-addressed microstore • Extensive use of residual control • Control store available to user through WCS	6 hex (36 positions)	648	74

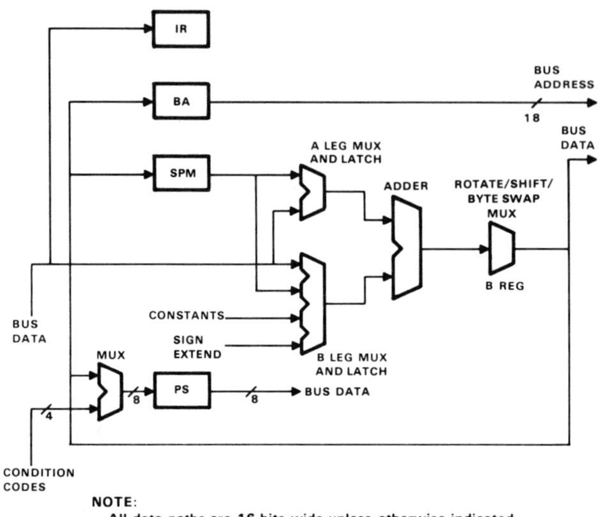

Figure 4. PDP-11/20 data paths.

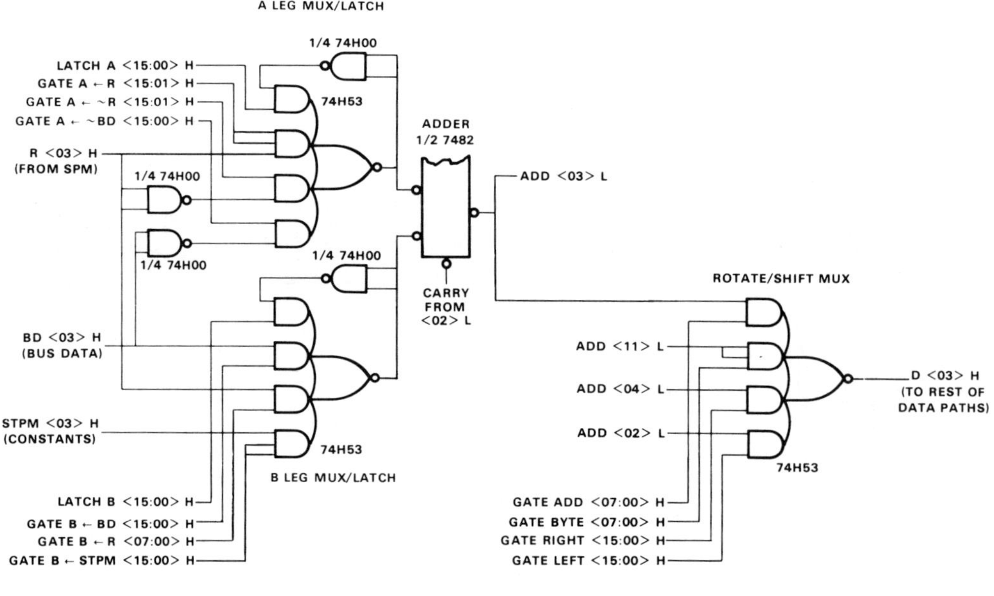

Figure 5. Detail of central part of PDP-11/20 data paths. One-bit (03) slice (adapted from *KC11 Processor Manual).*

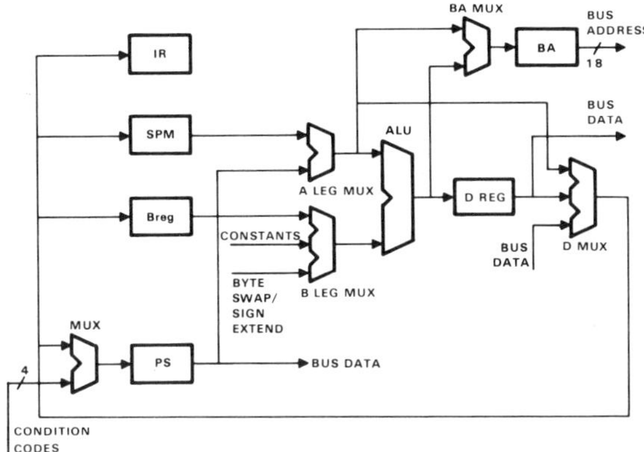

Figure 6. PDP-11/40 data paths.

11/20. Rotate/shifts to the left, however, are performed in the ALU. Sign extension and byte swapping are performed in the B leg MUX. Since the Scratchpad Register may not be both simultaneously read and written, the D Register (D Reg) is used to hold results generated while the SPM is being read in one processor clock phase so that during a later phase they may be written back into the Scratchpad. In this way the D Register permits read-write access of the SPM within a single cycle. A final feature is the presence of two paths into the Bus Address register, one from the A leg MUX and one from the ALU. This is of benefit in such operations as autoincrement and autodecrement addressing modes in which the contents of a register can be modifed and either the premodification (autoincrement) or postmodification (autodecrement) value of the register can be put into the Bus Address register in a single cycle.

The 11/40 microprogrammed control unit is quite elaborate to gain full benefit of the potential of the data paths. Among its features are overlapped processor/Unibus operation and three selectable microcycle clock periods. The latter feature increases performance immensely since the maximum cycle time of 300 nanoseconds is needed only when a full circle from Scratchpad through ALU and back to Scratchpad is made. In cycles which do not write into the Scratchpad, a 200-nanosecond cycle may be selected. When the data paths are unused and only microbranching is involved, an even shorter cycle time of 140 nanoseconds is possible. A final unique feature of the 11/40 is a variation in the branch on microtest logic from that of the archetypal control unit. To increase microbranch speed, the microword BUT select field is buffered in the Microword Register rather than being routed directly from the control store to the BUT logic. This causes a one-cycle delay in processing the branch and forces all BUTs to be placed one microinstruction ahead of where they are to take effect. In some cases, dummy steps are required to provide sufficient lead time for BUT action to occur, somewhat offsetting the speedup of this arrangement.

One way in which the 11/40 uses its processor/Unibus overlap feature to advantage is by prefetching words from memory whenever possible. At the end of the fetch phase, a check is made to see if the next memory reference fetches an instruction or operand index. If it does, the read access is begun immediately using the contents of the PC as the address. Exceptions to this are when the PC is used as a destination or when a service request is pending, both of which mean that the current value of the PC will not be the address of the next instruction. Starting the access early allows it to proceed in parallel with the execution of the current instruction. This reduces the time the processor idles waiting for the accessed word. Updating of the PC is deferred until the proper point in the instruction interpretation process is reached. This guarantees that references to the PC will result in the proper value being used.

PDP-11/10. The PDP-11/10 was designed as a minimal cost processor. The implementation is again TTL MSI but stripped to the bare essentials without the elaboration of the 11/40.

The data paths of the 11/10 (Figure 7) follow the conventions of the archetype closely. A constant zero may be selected onto the A MUX in addition to ALU or Unibus data. The ALU A leg multiplexer allows selection of the PS, some constants, and some internal addresses as well as the Scratchpad memory. The B Register is implemented as a universal bidirectional shift register so that single-bit shifts and rotates may be performed without additional logic. The ALU B leg multiplexer includes the constants one and zero and permits sign extension of the low order byte of the B Register. The Scratchpad Memory may not be both read and written in the same cycle; thus, operations such as incrementing the PC, which takes only a single microcycle on other processors, takes two microcycles to complete on the 11/10. A byte swapping path is absent in the 11/10. As a consequence, odd-byte addressing and swapping must be accomplished by a series of eight shifts or rotates.

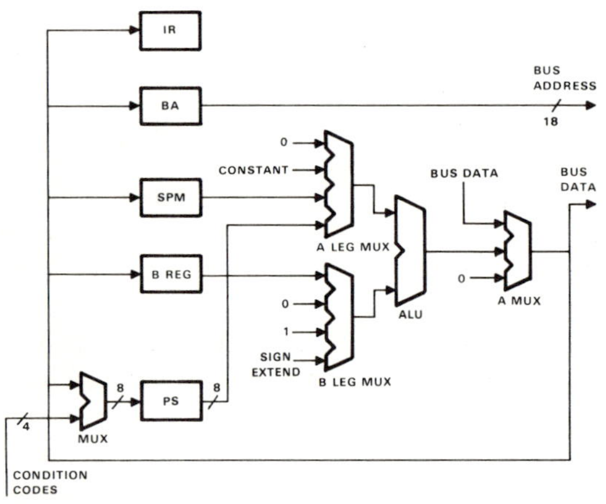

Figure 7. PDP-11/10 data paths.

The 11/10 control unit has a relatively austere implementation. There is no Microword Register in the control unit although there is necessarily a Microaddress Register. As a consequence, the output of the control store is used directly to condition the data paths. This precludes the overlap of current microinstruction execution with next microinstruction fetch. Hence, the propagation delay of the control store must be added to that of the data paths in setting the microcycle time, causing it to be a relatively long 300 nanoseconds. The simplicity of the data paths allows the use of a microword only 40 bits wide. The microcode contains very few frills and gains very little in performance from special cases. A notable example of this is the jump address calculation for JMP and JSR instructions. The 11/10 uses the same section of microcode for JMP and JSR destination modes as it uses to fetch conventional destination operands. This costs an extra memory reference over the separate microroutines used in other PDP-11 processors because, in addition to the effective address of the jump being calculated, its contents are also fetched (the microprogram logic precludes using this operand as a prefetched instruction even though this is effectively what it is). Overlapped processor/Unibus operation allows some of the extra microcycles necessitated by the data paths to be effectively hidden by putting them in parallel with Unibus accesses. The other concession to performance is clock speed doubling during shift operations to partially compensate for the performance lost in the absence of a byte swapper.

PDP-11/04. The PDP-11/04 is the simplest PDP-11 except for the LSI-11. Although simple, the 11/04 embodies a very good set of design tradeoffs. Figure 8 diagrams the 11/04 data paths. The Scratchpad Memory has a register (SP Reg, part of the SPM shown in Figure 8) sitting between it and the A MUX. This register allows the Scratchpad to support read-modify-write accesses, saving a microcycle in each such access over the 11/10. A multiplexer sitting before the SPM implements the swap byte operation, allowing the halves of a word to be interchanged. This improves byte operation performance considerably over the 11/10 and obviates the need for the 11/10's fast shift logic. Also eliminated is overlapped processor/Unibus operation because the savings from it are reduced with the overall reduction in number of microcycles.

The A MUX (the major data bus and the multiplexer which drives it) can select the PS and a number of constants in addition to ALU output and Unibus data. Between the SPM and ALU is a one's complementor so that the 74181 ALU may be used to perform the B leg minus A leg operation used in the "subtract" instruction, in addition to the A leg minus B leg operation used in the "compare" instruction. The A leg MUX also directly drives the Unibus address lines without a Bus Address register (if processor/Unibus overlap had been used, a BA register would have been necessary). Between the B Register and ALU is a multiplexer which allows the B Register, sign-extended low order byte of the B Register, or the constants zero or one to be selected into the B leg of the ALU in a manner identical to that of the B leg MUX of the 11/10. The B Register is also identical to that of the 11/10 in that it is a bidirectional shift register implementing rotate/shifts.

The final contributor to increased performance of the 11/04 is the decrease in cycle time from 300 nanoseconds in the 11/10 to 260 nanoseconds, made possible in part by pipelining the microword fetch. On the whole, the 11/04 is superior in performance to the 11/10 in all cases except the fetch phase and certain addressing modes where the use of its processor/Unibus overlap capability is sufficient to put the 11/10 ahead.

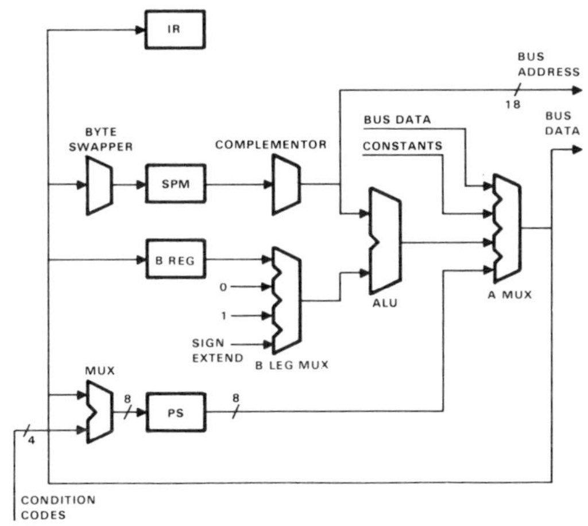

Figure 8. PDP-11/04 data paths.

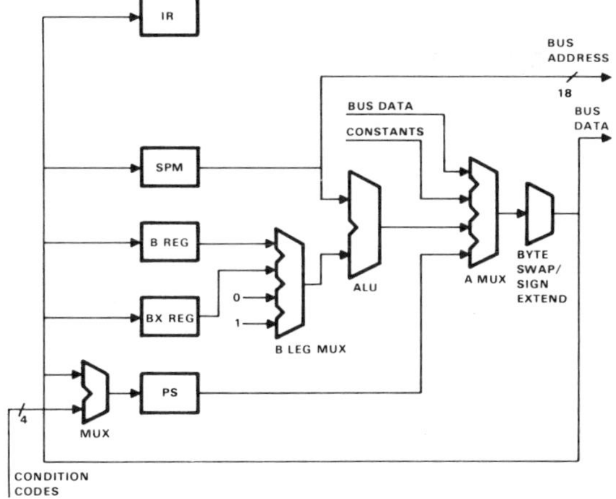

Figure 9. PDP-11/34 data paths.

PDP-11/34. The PDP-11/34 is an elaboration of the 11/04. The 11/34 data paths (Figure 9) bear close resemblance to those of the 11/04. The 11/04 complementor has been replaced in the 11/34 by additional microcode which reverses the placement of source and destination operands on the A and B legs of the ALU during the subtract instruction from that of the other double operand instructions. This frees the 11/34 from performing the adjustments that must be made in the data paths of the PDP-11 processors to make the subtract instruction operate correctly under the restrictions of the 74181 ALU. Added is a B Extension register (BX register) which, when concatenated with the B Register, forms a 32-bit register for double-width operand and results manipulated by extended instruction set operations such as multiply and divide. Also notable is the relocation of the byte swapper to the tail of the A MUX allowing odd-byte accessing to occur as data is entered from or placed upon the Unibus without the customary extra microcycle needed in other implementations to right adjust the byte. Included with the byte swapper is the sign extension logic. Schottky TTL is used in critical places in the data paths, notably the ALU, to speed up microcycle time from the 260 nanoseconds of the 11/04 to 180 nanoseconds. Additional hardware for memory management (not shown in Figure 9) and extended instruction set microcode are standard features.

The 11/34 microprogrammed control unit makes some concessions to the improved performance of the data paths. In addition to the normal 180-nanosecond cycle, there is a 240-nanosecond cycle used primarily for Unibus operations. Again, there is no processor/Unibus overlap feature because considerations of simplicity (i.e., cost) outweighed the incremental improvement in performance that would be netted. Because of its additional logic, the PDP-11/34 has a wider microword than the 11/04 (48 bits versus 40 bits). Also, since many more cases are broken out by the BUT IRDECODE in the 11/34 than in the machines preceding it, the size of the control store has been increased to 512 words, double that of earlier horizontally microprogrammed implementations.

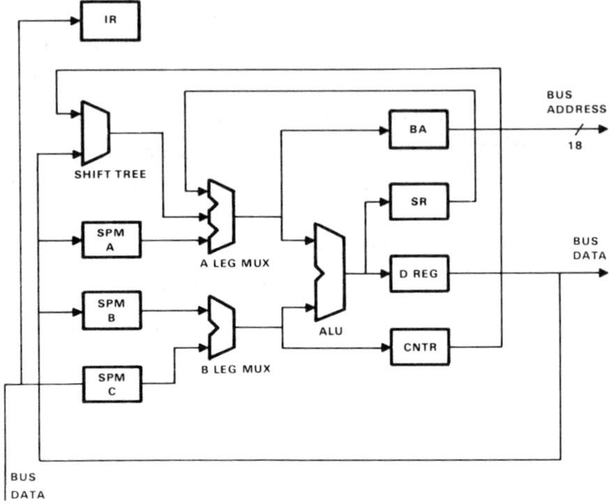

Figure 10. PDP-11/60 data paths.

PDP-11/60. The PDP-11/60 is the latest implementation covered in this paper and in many ways the most unique. Its design exploits advances in circuit technology occurring since the introduction of the earlier models giving it a number of features which set it apart from other PDP-11 family members. Two major enhancements are a larger microcode addressing space, making an integral floating-point instruction set and a writable control store option feasible, and a cache memory.* Both are possible due to increases in the density and decreases in the cost of bipolar ROM and RAM (see Chapter 13).

As illustrated in Figure 10, the 11/60 data paths show significant differences from those of other midrange implementations. A major difference is the presence of three Scratchpad Memories feeding the ALU. Scratchpads A and B are 32-word × 16-bit register arrays, each having twice the number of registers of the

*The PDP-11/70 also uses a cache.

single Scratchpad found in other mid-range designs. As with the 11/45 (see the section entitled "Implementation of a High-Performance PDP-11"), the contents of the general registers are kept in both Scratchpads allowing different registers to be read onto the A and B legs of the ALU simultaneously within the same cycle. This speeds register-to-register operations. The additional registers in the A and B Scratchpads are used as floating-point registers by the integral floating-point microcode, working storage by user microprograms, and console, maintenance, and status registers by the processor. Scratchpad C is a 16-word × 16-bit array which holds bus data and constants used by the processor and takes the place of the constants ROM on the B leg of other midrange implementations. During exceptional situations these constants may be overwritten with other information but must be restored before execution of the base machine microcode may be resumed.

The 11/60 is the first PDP-11 implementation to make use of three-state devices to eliminate many of the multiplexers used in other designs (the 11/40 uses open-collector logic on the A leg bus to the same effect). For instance, instead of actual A leg and B leg MUXs, the 11/60 uses registers and combinational elements with three-state outputs that can be independently enabled onto a common bus for each ALU leg. The ALU itself is the conventional 181 type used in all of the other MSI implementations. As in the 11/40, the D Register (D Reg) latches the ALU output so that results may be rewritten to the Scratchpads during a later clock phase of the microcycle in which they are generated. The output of the D Register is the major, but not sole, feedback route in the data paths.

The Bus Address register (BA) is loaded from the A leg bus as in the 11/04 and 11/34. The Address Out bus is driven by the BA and supplies addresses to the memory subsystem (cache, relocation hardware, and Unibus interface). The Data In (DIN) bus routes data into the processor from the memory subsystem, internal registers accessed via Unibus addresses such as the PS, and constants emitted by the microinstruction word. Scratchpad C and the Instruction Register are loaded directly from DIN in a manner reminiscent of the 11/20. A register in SPM C is set aside specifically for transfers from memory to the data paths. Results are routed from the data paths back to the memory subsystem and internal registers via a separate bus data out (DOUT) bus.

As compared to the other mid-range machines, several data path elements are unique to the 11/60. The counter (CNTR) is an iteration counter used by the Extended Instruction Set and floating-point microcode. The Shift Register and Shift Register guard (shown together as the SR in Figure 10) can be loaded in parallel with D Reg and shifted one position right or left. Either all or the low order seven bits of the SR may be gated onto the A leg bus through the X MUX (not shown). The shift tree is a network of multiplexers used for byte swapping, sign extension, and field isolation and positioning. It is unusual in that it allows right shifts of from 1 to 14 bit positions combinationally in a single microcycle.

The PDP-11/60 control unit is horizontally microprogrammed in much the same manner as the other midrange implementations. Extensive use of Schottky logic throughout the processor allows a fixed 170-nanosecond microcycle time. Processor/Unibus communication is interlocked unlike either the 11/40 or 11/45. There are several significant differences from the more conventional implementations. Many of these differences are generalizations of the microprogram flow control mechanism to allow more functions of the base machine to be performed by microcode rather than hardwired logic and to create a user microprogramming environment which can be put to uses beyond executing the PDP-11 instruction set. The 11/60 has a larger and more generalized set of BUTs than earlier machines. Also included for the first time in a horizontally microprogrammed machine is a multilevel microsubroutine call/return capability.

Increased reliance on microcode has expanded the control store to 4,096 words by 48 bits. Of this, 2,560 words are used to implement the basic machine. The remaining 1,536 words are available to the user through a ROM control store option; 1,024 are available through a writable control store option. Since addressing the microstore requires 12 bits, a page-addressing scheme has been adopted to avoid widening the microword. Page size is 512 words reducing microaddresses to 9 bits within a page. Microbranches across a page boundary require that an additional 3-bit page field be specified.

Another concept used extensively in the 11/60 to reduce microword size is residual control. In this technique relatively static control information is kept in set-up registers separate from the microword. The microprogram must load these registers to affect the data path elements which they control. Set-up registers are used in the 11/60 to gate registers onto DIN bus, enable data into registers from the DOUT bus, select SR functions, and control certain actions of the shift tree.

The overlapping of a number of different control fields by bit steering is a final means of keeping the microword relatively narrow. Certain bits in the microword control the interpretation of corresponding microword fields. This allows a single field to control several different functions. The one drawback of this technique is that these functions become mutually exclusive within a single microword since their simultaneous use would involve two different interpretations of the same microfield.

Hardwired logic in the memory subsystem detects internal addresses in a manner similar to other PDP-11 processors. However, the actual access to these registers is accomplished through microcode instead of additional control logic. Internal address access has been added to the exceptional conditions detected by the JAM logic of the 11/60. If the JAM microroutine finds that a microtrap has been caused by an internal address access, an intraprocessor transfer to or from the addressed register is performed. Unlike other JAM sequences, such transfers are terminated by resuming the interrupted microprogram. Microcoded register access requires much more time than the corresponding hardwired access. Reading the PS, for instance, takes 33 microcycles or 5.610 microseconds using microcode where a single microcycle suffices for the hardwired approach. This is justified, however, by the decreased cost of microcode versus hardwired logic and by the infrequent access made to these registers.

Like the 11/40, the 11/60 prefetches instructions and operand indices whenever possible. Unlike the 11/40, the PC is incremented at the time the prefetch is performed. Because of this, prefetching cannot be done when the current instruction uses the PC as either a source or destination register. A second difference is that service requests are not polled until the end of the current instruction, when the next instruction may already be prefetched and the PC updated. When this occurs, two microcycles must be spent to decrement the PC to restore its old value before proceeding with the service phase.

IMPLEMENTATION OF A MINIMAL COST PDP-11

The LSI-11 (Chapter 12) is designed for the low-end market where there is more concern for low cost than high performance. Integrated circuit package count and printed circuit board area, the main determinants of manufacturing cost, are kept low through an n-channel MOS LSI technology implementation of the CPU. The result is a PDP-11 processor with four kilowords of semiconductor memory on a single 8.5 × 10.5-inch (standard DEC quad height) printed circuit board which can execute the entire PDP-11/40 instruction set.

The constraints imposed by current semiconductor technology dictate much of the implementation of the LSI-11. The entire CPU consists of four LSI packages plus a number of standard TTL SSI and MSI packages for clock generation and bus interfacing. A system control chip provides microinstruction addressing logic plus an interface to external signals used in bus control. A data paths chip contains the registers and arithmetic logic unit of the machine. Two chips are microcode ROMs (MICROMs). Each contains 512 microinstruction words with a width of 22 bits. An optional third MICROM adds the Extended Instruction Set/floating-point instruction set option of the PDP-11/40. To decrease the complexity of the machine, the traditional Unibus was abandoned in favor of a scheme requiring fewer bus lines. Most notable is the multiplexing of both data and addresses onto a single set of 18 data/address lines, DAL<17:00>. A significant savings over the 34 lines dedicated to data and address in the Unibus results at the expense of bus cycle speed.

The 22-bit microinstruction word of the LSI-11 is quite narrow compared to the microwords of the horizontally microprogrammed PDP-11s which range from 40 to 64 bits wide. Four bits are not decoded and provide direct TTL-compatible signals which are used by logic external to the CPU chips. Another two bits are used within the CPU chips to control next microinstruction addressing. The remaining 16 bits are decoded as a microinstruction by the CPU chips. LSI-11 microinstructions differ little in form from conventional minicomputer instructions with their operation code and operand (which may be register, microcode address, or literal) fields. These require a great deal more decoding than the horizontal microinstructions of other designs.

The LSI-11 microstore is larger than the control store of any other PDP-11 except the 11/60. Since LSI-11 microinstructions lack the possibilities for parallelism inherent in the horizontal microinstructions, more LSI-11 microinstructions are needed to code a given operation. In addition, certain functions which are handled with combinational logic in other PDP-11 control units and data paths are microcoded in the LSI-11. Finally, the LSI-11 has more elaborate console microcode than the other implementations. As a result, the LSI-11 has 22,528 bits of microstore versus 14,336 bits for the PDP-11/40, 16,384 bits for the PDP-11/45, and 122,880 bits for the PDP-11/60. The narrow microword is used in spite of its attendant problems due to the limitation imposed by the packaging of the MOS CPU chips. Only 40 pins are available to carry power and signals to and from each chip, limiting the number of lines available for transmitting the microword from the MICROMs to the control and data path chips.

Technology also imposes a serious constraint on instruction decoding. The equivalent of a branch on microtest allows only eight bits to be decoded at a time. This is sufficient for decoding the majority of instructions; however, the remainder require additional decoding which may consume as many as eight microcycles. This is in marked contrast with all other PDP-11s which require only a single microcycle to do the initial instruction decode at the end of the fetch phase (BUT IRDECODE).* The effect that this has on the average duration of the LSI-11 fetch phase is evident from Table 4.

Figure 11 details the data paths around which the operands of the macroinstruction level machine circulate. As with the medium-performance implementations, the ALU is the hub of activity, operating upon quantities supplied from the Scratchpad memory. The A MUX selects from the output of the ALU, the high or

*The 11/60 requires two microcycles to decode certain instructions.

Table 4. Average PDP-11 Instruction Execution Times in Microseconds

	Fetch	Source	Dest.	Execute	Total	Speed Relative to LSI-11
LSI-11	2.514	0.689	1.360	1.320	5.883	1.000
PDP-11/04	1.940	0.610	0.811	0.682	4.043	1.455
PDP-11/10	1.500	0.573	0.929	1.094	4.096	1.436
PDP-11/20	1.490	0.468	0.802	0.768	3.529	1.667
PDP-11/34	1.630	0.397	0.538	0.464	3.029	1.942
PDP-11/40	0.958	0.260	0.294	0.575	2.087	2.819
PDP-11/45 (bipolar memory)	0.363	0.101	0.213	0.185	0.863	6.820
PDP-11/60 (87 percent cache hit ratio)	0.541	0.185	0.218	0.635	1.578	3.727

low byte of the data/address lines, and the processor flags. The selected quantity is fed back to be rewritten into the Scratchpad. Constants supplied as literals from the microinstruction word may be gated into the data paths through the B leg MUX to the ALU. Additional paths exist for transmitting information in and out on the data/address lines.

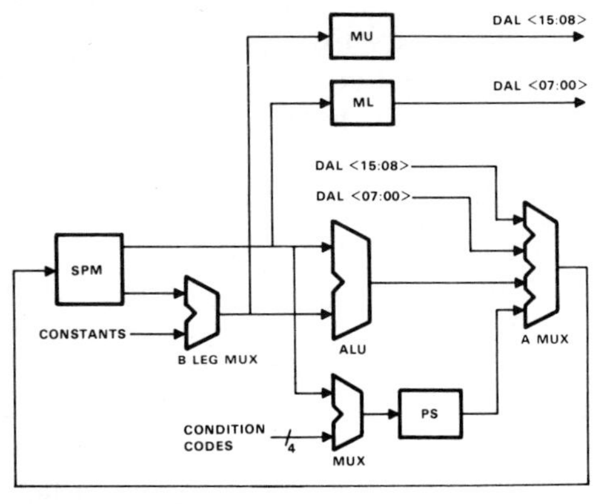

Figure 11. LSI-11 data paths.

Significant differences exist between the data paths of the LSI-11 and the mid-range machines. One major difference is in the width of the data paths. The LSI-11 is the only member of the PDP-11 family with data paths 8 bits rather than 16 bits wide. This is necessitated by limitations in current semiconductor chip density. Bus paths in particular occupy large amounts of chip real estate dictating their reduction in width. Since only 8 bits of data can be processed at a time, 2 microcycles are required to accomplish any 16-bit operation. A second effect is the elimination of logic that would otherwise be necessary to configure the data paths for both byte and word operations. A last unique characteristic is the absence of a B Register for feeding the B leg of the ALU. Instead, the B leg is fed from a second read port into the Scratchpad Memory. In this, the LSI-11 bears a curious resemblance to the PDP-11/45 and 11/60. The difference is that while the LSI-11 uses this feature to eliminate cycles that would be needed to load a B Register, there is not sufficient logic to allow source and destination registers to be accessed simultaneously. Consequently, multiple cycles are still required to set up register/register operations on the LSI-11.

The final important performance factor is again a direct result of the circuit technology employed. NMOS logic is not as fast as the bipolar logic found in every other PDP-11 implementation so that the microcycle time of the LSI-11 is 400 nanoseconds or one-third slower than the next slowest PDP-11. Coupled with the larger number of microcycles necessary to execute a given macroinstruction, this causes the LSI-11 to lag in performance.

IMPLEMENTATION OF A HIGH PERFORMANCE PDP-11

The PDP-11/45 was designed for maximum performance and followed the 11/20 to become the second member of the PDP-11 family. Maximum performance is achieved with a complex set of data paths allowing highly parallel operation and an optional high-speed semiconductor memory (bipolar or MOS) with its own path into the processor called the Fastbus. The extensive use of Schottky TTL in the processor makes possible a 150-nanosecond cycle time, half as long as that in some mid-range designs.

The complexity of the PDP-11/45 data paths is evident from Figure 12 even with several of the special purpose registers and buses omitted for clarity. The overall organization still bears some resemblance to the mid-range PDP-11 data paths, however. The ALU remains the hub of data path activity with its output the primary feedback path to the processor registers, although not the only one as in other implementations. The ALU is based upon the Schottky equivalent of the 74181 chip used in most other PDP-11 designs. The difference begins with the multiplexers driving the A and B legs of the ALU. These MUXs allow operands to be routed directly to the proper leg without using additional cycles to move operands from register to register. K0 MUX and K1 MUX (combined in Figure 12) are multiplexers used in conjunction with the B MUX to gate constants, trap vector addresses, and branch offsets into the B leg of the ALU.

Among the registers supplying the A MUX and B MUX are the source and destination operand registers (S Reg and D Reg, respectively). These, in turn, are supplied by the SR MUX and DR MUX which select data from individual Scratchpad Registers or the Program Counter. Besides holding operands from the general registers, the S Reg and D Reg act as working registers. In particular, D Reg is a shift

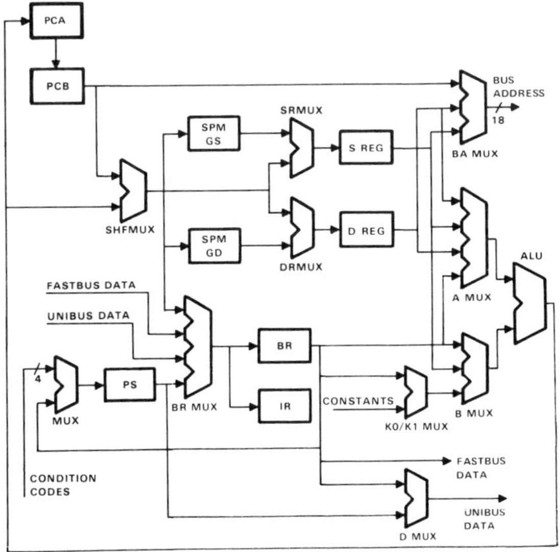

Figure 12. PDP-11/45 data paths.

register used to accumulate the less significant half of results during multiply and divide.

Separate Scratchpads are maintained so that source and destination general registers may be read simultaneously and independently. This necessitates both Scratchpads being written together to keep their contents identical. Each Scratchpad is organized as 16 words of 16 bits each. Fifteen words in each Scratchpad are actually used: two sets of general registers (R0 through R5) and three sets of stack pointers (R6). Register set selection is controlled by status bits in the PS.

The Program Counter is not maintained in the Scratchpad Registers as in other PDP-11s. Rather, it is held separately so that it may be routed directly to the BA MUX while the S Reg and D Reg are occupied with other operations. Moreover, two Program Counters are implemented. PCB holds the current value of the Program Counter and is used as a general register or bus address. PCA holds the new value of the Program Counter allowing the PC to be updated while the old PC value is still in use, after which PCB is clocked to load it with the new value contained in PCA.

The SHF MUX can right shift or byte swap data from the ALU before it is clocked into the Scratchpads. It also provides a route from PCB to the S Reg and/or D Reg when the PC is used as a general register. This arrangement precludes the shifting or byte swapping of data being loaded into the PC that is possible with data destined for one of the other general registers residing in the Scratchpads. As a consequence, arithmetic shift left and byte swap operations on the PC do not cause the PC to be modified, although the condition codes are updated as though it were.

Processor access to the Unibus, Fastbus, and internal registers is via the Bus Register MUX (BR MUX), the bus register (BR and BRA), and the Data Out MUX (D MUX). The BR and BRA (the duplication is due to electrical loading considerations) are logically a single register as shown in Figure 12. They receive all incoming data and transmit almost all outgoing data in addition to accumulating the more significant half of results during multiply and divide. The BR MUX selects the input to the BR (and BRA) from among the two external buses and internal input bus for input to the processor and from the SHF MUX for output from the processor via the BR and D MUX to the external buses and internal output bus. The internal buses connect a number of special registers and an optional Floating-Point Processor to the data paths. Of these, only the PS is indicated in Figure 12. The Instruction Register (duplicated as IR and AF IR, again for electrical loading reasons) are also loaded from the BR MUX but are clocked only when an instruction is fetched.

Bus addresses are applied directly to the Unibus or to an optional memory mapping unit by the Bus Address multiplexer (BA MUX). No Bus Address register is needed since memory access and processor clocking are fully interlocked except during an overlapped fetch in which case the PCB is held selected while operations continue in other parts of the data paths.

The PDP-11/45 control unit is horizontally microprogrammed and is for the most part quite similar to the archetype described for mid-range PDP-11 implementations. The control store is 256 words × 64 bits. The relatively wide microword is necessary for generating the large number of control signals used in conditioning and clocking the complicated data paths. An additional source of complexity is the timing logic needed to produce and use the five processor clock phases.

There are two classes of microsequence-altering functions corresponding to the BUTs of other PDP-11s. The first class consists of simple branches having four or fewer possible branch addresses. These operate in the same fashion as BUTs. The second class of branches consists of three complex instruction decoding functions called forks. The first, fork A, does the initial instruction decode and corresponds to the BUT

IRDECODE of other implementations. Fork B dispatches to an execute phase microroutine following a destination operand fetch. Fork C dispatches to a destination phase microroutine following a source operand fetch. A fork enable field in the microword is used to enable one fork at most during a cycle. When a fork and branch are combined in the same cycle, the fork is disabled if the branch is taken. This permits the implementation of certain functions without the use of additional cycles.

The 11/45 microcode is structured to take full advantage of the data paths and processor/Unibus overlap. Besides intensively exploiting special cases in the addressing modes and instruction set, the microprogram implements operand and instruction fetch overlap in much the same way as the 11/40. The one difference between the two prefetch mechanisms is that the 11/45 updates the PC value in PCB and stores it in PCA at the time the prefetch is started. References to the PC work correctly because PCB holds the old PC value until it is updated at the appropriate time.

All the design decisions described above are directed toward implementing the fastest system possible. Tradeoffs involving circuit technology and control unit and data path organization have all been made with this end in mind.

MEASURING THE EFFECT OF DESIGN TRADEOFFS ON PERFORMANCE

There are two alternative approaches to the problem of determining just how the particular binding of different design decisions affects the performance of each machine:

1. **Top-down approach**. Attempt to isolate the effect of a particular design tradeoff over the entire space of implementations by fitting the individual performance figures for the whole family of machines to a mathematical model which treats the design parameters as independent variables and performance as the dependent variable.
2. **Bottom-up approach**. Make a detailed sensitivity analysis of a particular tradeoff within a particular machine by comparing the performance of the machine both with and without the design feature while leaving all other design features the same.

Each approach has its assets and liabilities for assessing design tradeoffs. The first method requires no information about the implementation of a machine, but does require a sufficiently large collection of different implementations, a sufficiently small number of independent variables, and an adequate mathematical model in order to explain the variance in the dependent variable to some reasonable level of statistical confidence. The second method, on the other hand, requires a great deal of knowledge about the implementation of the given system and a correspondingly great amount of analysis to isolate the effect of the single design decision on the performance of the complete system. The information that is yielded is quite exact, but applies only to the single point chosen in the design space and may not be generalized to other points in the space unless the assumptions concerning the machine's implementation are similarly generalizable. In the following subsections the first method is used to determine the dominant tradeoffs, and the second method is used to estimate the impact of individual implementation tradeoffs.

Quantifying Performance

Measuring the change in performance of a particular PDP-11 processor model due to design changes presupposes the existence of some performance metric. Average instruction execution time was chosen because of its obvious relationship to instruction stream throughput.

Neglected are such overhead factors as Direct Memory Access, interrupt servicing, and, on the LSI-11, dynamic memory refresh. Average instruction execution times may be obtained by benchmarking or by calculation from instruction frequency and timing data. The latter method was chosen due to its freedom from the extraneous factors noted above and from the normal clock rate variations found from machine to machine of a given model. This method also allows the designer to calculate the change in average instruction execution time that would result from some change in the implementation. Such frequency-driven design has already been applied in practice to the PDP-11/60 (Chapter 13).

The instruction frequencies are tabulated in Appendix A and include the frequencies of the various addressing modes. These figures were calculated from measurements made by Strecker [1976a] on 7.6 million instruction executions traced in ten different PDP-11 instruction streams encountered in various applications. While there is a reasonable amount of variation of frequencies from one stream to the next, the figures in Appendix A should be representative.

Instruction times are tabulated in Appendix B. These times were calculated from the engineering documents for each machine. The times vary from those published in the PDP-11 processor handbooks for two reasons. First, in the handbooks, times have been redistributed among phases to ease the process of calculating instruction times. In the appendix an attempt has been to accurately characterize each phase. Second, there are inaccuracies in the handbooks arising from conservative timing estimates and engineering revisions. The figures included here may be considered more accurate.

A performance figure is derived for each machine by weighting its instruction times by frequency. The results, given in Table 4, form the basis of the analyses to follow.

Analysis of Variance of PDP-11 Performance Top-Down Approach

The first method of analysis described is employed in an attempt to explain most of the variance in PDP-11 performance in terms of two parameters:

1. **Microcycle time**. The microcycle time is used as a measure of processor performance which excludes the effect of the memory subsystem.
2. **Memory read pause time**. The memory read pause time is defined as the period of time during which the processor clock is suspended during a memory read. For machines with processor/Unibus overlap, the clock is assumed to be turned off by the same microinstruction that initiates the memory access. Memory read pause time is used as a measure of the memory subsystem's impact on processor performance. Note that this time is less than the memory access time since all PDP-11 processor clocks will continue to run at least partially concurrently with a memory access.

The choice of these two factors is motivated by their dominant contribution to, and (approximately) linear relationship with, performance. Keeping the number of independent variables low is also important due to the small number of data points being fit to the model.

The model itself is of the form:

$$t_i = k_1 c_{1i} + k_2 c_{2i}$$

where t_i is the average instruction execution time of machine i from Table 3. The microcycle time of machine i is c_{1i} (for machine with selectable microcycle times, the predominant time is used). c_{2i} is the memory read pause time of machine i.

This model is only an approximation since it assumes k_1 and k_2 will be constant over all machines. In general this will not be the case. k_1 is the number of microcycles expected in a canonical instruction. This number will be a function mainly of data path connectivity, and strictly speaking, another factor should be included to take that variability into account; however, since the data path organization of all PDP-11 implementations considered here (excepting the 11/03, 11/45, and 11/60) are comparable, the simplifying assumption of calling them all identical at the price of explaining somewhat less of the variance is made. The number of memory accesses expected in a canonical instruction is k_2; it also exhibits some variability from machine to machine. A small part of this is due to the fact that some PDP-11s actually take more memory cycles to perform a given instruction than do others (this is really only a factor in certain 11/10 instructions, notably JMP and JSR, and the 11/20 MOV instruction). A more important source of variability is the Unibus/processor overlap logic incorporated into some PDP-11 implementations which effectively reduces the actual contribution of the $k_2 c_{2i}$ term by overlapping more memory access-time with processor operation than is excluded from the memory read pause time.

Given the model and the dependent and independent data for each machine (Table 5), a linear regression is applied to determine the coefficients k_1 and k_2 and to find out how much of the variance is explained by the model.

Applying the regression over all eight processors: $k_1 = 11.580$, $k_2 = 1.162$, $R^2 = 0.904$. R^2 is the amount of variance accounted for by the model or 90.4 percent. If the regression is applied to just the six mid-range processors, $k_1 = 10.896$, $k_2 = 1.194$, $R^2 = 0.962$. R^2 increases to 96.2 percent partly because the LSI-11 and 11/45 can be expected to have a different k coefficients than the mid-range machines and do not fit the model as well. Note that if two mid-range machines, the 11/04 and the 11/40, are eliminated instead of the LSI-11 and 11/45, R^2 decreases to 89.3 percent rather than increasing. The k coefficients are close to what should be expected for average microcycle and memory cycle counts. Since k_1 is much larger than k_2, average instruction time is more sensitive to microcycle time than to memory read pause time by a factor of k_1/k_2 or approximately 10. The implication for the designer is that much more performance can be gained or lost by perturbing the microcycle time than memory read pause time.

Although this method lacks statistical rigor, it is reasonably safe to say that memory and microcycle speed do have by far the largest impact on performance and that the dependency is quantifiable to some degree.

Table 5. Top-Down Model Parameters in Microseconds

	Independent Variables		Dependent Variable
	Micro-Cycle Time	Memory Read Pause Time	Average Instruction Execution Time
LSI-11	0.400	0.400	5.883
PDP-11/04	0.260	0.940	4.043
PDP-11/10	0.300	0.600	4.096
PDP-11/20	0.280	0.370	3.529
PDP-11/34	0.180	0.940	3.029
PDP-11/40	0.140	0.500	2.087
PDP-11/45 (bipolar memory)	0.150	0.000	0.863
PDP-11/60 (87 percent cache hit ratio)	0.170	0.140	1.578

Measuring Second Order Effects: Bottom-Up Approach

It is much harder to measure the effect of other design tradeoffs on performance. The approximate methods employed in the previous section cannot be used because the effects being measured tend to be swamped out by first order effects and often either cancel or reinforce one another making linear models useless. For these reasons, such tradeoffs must be evaluated on a design-by-design basis as explained above. This subsection evaluates several design tradeoffs in this way.

Effect of Adding a Byte Swapper to the 11/10. It is evident that the lack of a byte swapper on the PDP-11/10 has a negative effect on performance. In this subsection, the performance gained by the addition of a byte swapper either before the B Register or as part of the B leg multiplexer is calculated. Adding a byte swapper would change five different parts of the instruction interpretation process: the source and destination phases where an odd-byte operand is read from memory, the execute phase where a swap byte instruction is executed in destination mode 0 and in destination modes 1 through 7, and the execute phase where an odd-byte address is modified. In each of these cases, seven fast shift cycles would be eliminated and the remaining normal speed shift cycle could be replaced by a byte swap cycle resulting in a savings of seven fast shift cycles or 1.050 microseconds. None of this time is overlapped with Unibus operations; hence, all would be saved. This savings is effected, however, only when a byte swap or odd-byte access is actually performed. The frequency with which this occurs is just the sum of the frequencies of the individual cases noted above or 0.0640. Multiplied by the time saved per occurrence gives a savings of 0.0672 microsecond or 1.64 percent of the average instruction execution time. The insignificance of this savings could well be used to support the decision for leaving the byte swapper out of the PDP-11/10.

Effect of Adding Processor/Unibus Overlap to the 11/04. Processor/Unibus overlap is not a feature of the 11/04 control unit. Adding this feature involves altering the control unit/Unibus synchronization logic so that the processor clock continues to run until a microcycle requiring the Unibus data from a DATI or DATIP is detected. A Bus Address register must also be added to drive the Unibus lines after the microcycle initiating the DATIP is completed. This alteration allows time to be saved in two ways. First, processor cycles may be overlapped with memory read cycles as explained in the subsection on control units. Second, since Unibus data is not read into the data paths during the cycle in which the DATIP occurs, the path from the ALU through the A MUX and back to the registers is freed. This permits certain operations to be performed in the same cycle as the DATIP. For example, the microword BA ← PC; DATI; PC ← PC + 2 could be used to start fetching the word pointed to by the PC while simultaneously incrementing the PC to address the next word. The cycle following could then load the Unibus data directly into a Scratchpad register rather than loading the data into the B Register and then into the Scratchpad on the following cycle as is necessary without overlap logic. A savings of two microcycle times would result.

DATI and DATIP operations are scattered liberally throughout the 11/04 microcode; however, only those cycles in which an overlap would produce a time savings need be considered. An average of 0.730 cycles can be saved or overlapped during each instruction. If all of the overlapped time is actually saved, 0.190 microsecond or 4.70 percent will be pared from the average instruction execution time. This amounts to a 4.93 percent increase in performance.

Effect of Caching on the 11/60. The PDP-11/60 uses a cache to decrease its effective memory read pause time. The degree to which this time is reduced depends upon three factors:

the cache read hit pause time, the cache read miss pause time, and the ratio of cache read hits to total memory read accesses. A write-through cache is assumed; therefore, the timing of memory write accesses is not affected by caching and only read accesses need be considered. The performance of the 11/60 as measured by average instruction execution time is modeled exactly as a function of the above three parameters by the equation:

$$t = k_1 + k_2(k_3 a + k_4[1 - a])$$

where t is the average instruction execution time, a is the cache hit ratio, k_1 is the average execution time of a PDP-11/60 instruction excluding memory read pause time but including memory write pause time (1.339 microseconds); k_2 is the number of memory reads per average instruction (1.713); k_3 is the memory read pause time for a cache hit (0.000 microseconds); and k_4 is the memory read pause time for a cache miss (1.075 microseconds).

The above equation can be rearranged to yield:

$$t = (k_1 + k_2 k_4) - k_2(k_4 - k_3)a$$

The first term and the coefficient of the second term in the equation above evaluate to 3.181 microseconds and 1.842 microseconds, respectively, with the given k parameter values. This reduces the average instruction time to a function of the cache hit ratio making it possible to compare the effect of various caching schemes on 11/60 performance in terms of this one parameter.

The effect of various cache organizations on the hit ratio is described for the PDP-11 Family in general (Chapter 10) and for the PDP-11/60 in particular in Mudge (Chapter 13). If no cache is provided, the hit ratio is effectively zero and the average instruction execution time reduces to the first term in the model or 3.181 microseconds. A set associative cache with a set size of 1 word and a cache size of 1,024 words has been found through simulation to give a 0.87 hit ratio. An average instruction time of 1.578 microseconds results in a 101.52 percent improvement in performance over that without the cache.

The cache organization described above is that actually employed in the 11/60. It has the virtue of being relatively simple to implement and therefore reasonably inexpensive. Set size or cache size can be increased to attain a higher hit ratio at a correspondingly higher cost. One alternative cache organization is a set size of 2 words and a cache size of 2,048 words. This organization boosts the hit ratio to 0.93 resulting in an instruction time of 1.468 microseconds, an increase in performance of 7.53 percent. This increased performance must be paid for, however, since twice as many memory chips are needed. Because the performance increment derived from the second cache organization is much smaller than that of the first while the cost increment is approximately the same, the first organization is more cost-effective.

Design Tradeoffs Affecting the Fetch Phase. The fetch phase holds much potential for performance improvement since it consists of a single short sequence of micro-operations that, as Table 4 clearly shows, involves a sizable fraction of the average instruction time due to the inevitable memory access and possible service operations. In this subsection, two approaches to cutting this time are evaluated for four different processors.

The Unibus interface logic of the PDP-11/04 and 11/34 are very similar. Both insert a delay into the initial microcycle of the fetch phase to allow time for Bus Grant arbitration circuitry to settle so that a microbranch can be taken if a serviceable condition exists. If the arbitration logic were redesigned to eliminate this delay, the average instruction execution time would drop by 0.220 microsecond for the 11/04 and

0.150 microsecond for the 11/34.* The resulting increases in performance would be 5.75 percent and 5.21 percent, respectively.

Another example of a design feature affecting the fetch phase is the operand/instruction fetch overlap mechanism of the 11/40, 11/45, and 11/60. From the normal fetch times in Appendix B and the actual average fetch times given in Table 4, the savings in fetch phase time alone can be calculated to be 0.162 microsecond for the 11/40, 0.087 microsecond for the 11/45, and 0.118 microsecond for the 11/60 or an increase of 7.77 percent, 10.07 percent, and 8.11 percent over what their respective performances would be if fetch phase time were not overlapped.

These examples demonstrate the practicality of optimizing sequences of control states that have a high frequency of occurrence rather than just those which have long durations. The 11/10 byte swap logic is quite slow, but is utilized infrequently causing its impact upon performance to be small while the bus arbitration logic of the 11/34 exacts only a small time penalty, but does so each time an instruction is executed and results in a larger performance impact. The usefulness of frequency data should thus be apparent since the bottlenecks in a design are often not where intuition says they should be.

SUMMARY AND USE OF THE METHODOLOGIES

The PDP-11 offers an interesting opportunity to examine an architecture with numerous implementations spanning a wide range of price and performance. The implementations appear to fall into three distinct categories: the mid-range machines (PDP-11/04, 11/10, 11/20, 11/34, 11/40, 11/60); an inexpensive, relatively low performance machine (LSI-11); and a comparatively expensive, but high performance machine (PDP-11/45). The mid-range machines are all minor variations on a common theme with each implementation introducing much less variability than might be expected. Their differences reside in the presence or absence of certain embellishments rather than in any major structural differences. This common design scheme is still quite recognizable in the LSI-11 and even in the PDP-11/45. The deviations of the LSI-11 arise from limitations imposed by semiconductor technology rather than directly from cost or performance considerations although the technology decision derives from cost. In the PDP-11/45, on the other hand, the quantum jump in complexity is motivated purely by the desire to squeeze the maximum performance out of the architecture.

From the overall performance model presented in the section on top-down performance analysis, it is evident that instruction stream processing can be sped up either by improving the performance of the memory subsystem or the performance of the processor. Memory subsystem performance depends upon number of memory accesses in a canonical instruction and the effective memory read pause time. There is not much that can be done about the first number since it is a function of the architecture and thus largely fixed. The second number may be improved, however, by the use of faster memory components or techniques such as caching.

Performance of the PDP-11 processor itself can be enhanced in two ways: by cutting the number of processor cycles to perform a given function or by cutting the time used per microcycle. Several approaches to decreasing the effective microcycle count have been demonstrated:

1. **Structure the data paths for maximum parallelism**. The PDP-11/45 can perform much more in a given microcycle than any of the mid-range PDP-11s and, thus, needs fewer microcycles to complete an instruction. To obtain this increased

*These figures are typical. Since the delay is set by an RC circuit and Schmitt trigger, the delay may vary considerably from machine to machine of a given model.

functionality, however, a much more elaborate set of data paths is required in addition to a highly developed control unit to exercise them to maximum potential. Such a change is not an incremental one and involves rethinking the entire implementation.

2. **Structure the microcode to take best advantage of instruction features**. All processors except the 11/10 handle JMP/JSR addressing modes as a special case in the microcode. Most do the same for the destination modes of the MOV instruction because of its high frequency. Varying degrees of sophistication in instruction dispatching from the BUT IR-DECODE at the end of every fetch is evident in different machines resulting in various performance improvements.
3. **Cut effective microcycle count by overlapping processor and Unibus operation**. The PDP-11/10 demonstrates that a large microcycle count can be effectively reduced by placing cycles in parallel with memory access operations whenever possible.

Increasing microcycle speed is perhaps more generally useful since it can often be applied without making substantial changes to an entire implementation. Several of the mid-range PDP-11s achieve most of their performance improvement by increasing microcycle speed in the following ways:

1. **Make the data paths faster**. The PDP-11/34 demonstrates the improvement in microcycle time that can result from the judicious use of Schottky TTL in such heavily travelled points as the ALU. Replacing the ALU and carry-lookahead logic alone with Schottky equivalents saves approximately 35 nanoseconds in propagation delay. With cycle times running 300 nanoseconds and less, this amounts to better than a 10 percent increase in speed.
2. **Make each microcycle take only as long as necessary**. The 11/34 and 11/40 both use selectable microcycle times to speed up cycles which do not entail long data path propagation delays.

Circuit technology is perhaps the single most important factor in performance. It is only stating the obvious to say that doubling circuit speed doubles total performance. Aside from raw speed, circuit technology dictates what it is economically feasible to build as witnessed by the SSI PDP-11/20, the MSI PDP-11/40, and the LSI-11. Just the limitation of a particular circuit technology at a given point in time may dictate much about the design tradeoffs that can be made – as in the case of the LSI-11.

Turning to the methodologies, the two presented in the previous section can be used at various times during the design cycle. The top-down approach can be used to estimate the performance of a proposed implementation or to plan a family of implementations, given only the characteristics of the selected technology and a general estimate of data path and memory cycle utilization. The bottom-up approach can be used to perturb an existing or planned design to determine the performance payoff of a particular design tradeoff. The relative frequencies of each function (e.g., addressing modes, instructions, etc.), while required for an accurate prediction, may not be available. There are, however, alternative ways to estimate relative frequencies. Consider the three following situations:

1. **At least one implementation exists**. An analysis of the implementation in typical usage (i.e., benchmark programs for a stored program computer) can provide the relative frequencies.
2. **No implementation exists, but similar systems exist**. The frequency data may be extrapolated from measurements made on a machine with a similar architecture. For example, the Gibson Mix [Bell and

Newell, 1971] provided the relative frequencies of IBM 7090 functions from which the relative frequencies of IBM 360 functions were estimated.

3. **No implementation exists, and there are no prior similar systems**. From knowledge of the specifications, a set of most-used functions can be estimated (e.g., instruction fetch, register and relative addressing, move and add instructions for a stored program computer). The design is then optimized for these functions.

Of course, the relative frequency data should always be updated to take into account new data.

Our purpose in writing this paper has been twofold: to provide data about design tradeoffs and to suggest design methodologies based on this data. It is hoped that the design data will stimulate the study of other methodologies while the results of the design methodologies presented here have demonstrated their usefulness to designers.

APPENDIX A: INSTRUCTION TIME COMPONENT FREQUENCIES

	Frequency
Fetch	1.0000
Source Mode	0.4069
0 R	0.1377
1 @R or (R)	0.0338
2 (R)+	0.1587
3 @(R)+	0.0122
4 -(R)	0.0352
5 @-(R)	0.0000
6 X(R)	0.0271
7 @X(R)	0.0022
No Source	0.5931
NOTE: Frequency of odd-byte addressing (SM1-7) = 0.0252.	
Destination	0.6872
Data Manipulation Mode	0.6355
0 R	0.3146
1 @R or (R)	0.0599
2 (R)+	0.0854
3 @(R)+	0.0307
4 -(R)	0.0823
5 @-(R)	0.0000
6 X(R)	0.0547
7 @X(R)	0.0080
NOTE: Frequency of odd-byte addressing (DM1-7) = 0.0213.	

	Frequency
Jump (JMP/JSR) Mode	0.0517
0 R	0.0000 (ILLEGAL)
1 @R or (R)	0.0000
2 (R)+	0.0000
3 @(R)+	0.0079
4 -(R)	0.0000
5 @-(R)	0.0000
6 X(R)	0.0438
7 @X(R)	0.0000
Execute Instruction	1.0000
Double Operand	0.4069
ADD	0.0524
SUB	0.0274
BIC	0.0309
BICB	0.
BIS	0.0012
BISB	0.0013
CMP	0.0626
CMPB	0.0212
BIT	0.0041
BITB	0.0014
MOV	0.1517
MOVB	0.0524
XOR	0.

	Frequency
Single Operand	0.2286
CLR	0.0186
CLRB	0.0018
COM	0.
COMB	0.
INC	0.0224
INCB	0.
DEC	0.0809
DECB	0.
NEG	0.0038
NEGB	0.
ADC	0.0070
ADCB	0.
SBC	0.
SBCB	0.
ROR	0.0036
RORB	0.
ROL	0.0059
ROLB	0.
ASR	0.0069
ASRB	0.
ASL	0.0298
ASLB	0.
TST	0.0329
TSTB	0.0079
SWAB	0.0038
SXT	0.

	Frequency
No Destination	0.3128
Branch	0.2853
All Branches (true)	0.1744
All Branches (false)	0.1109
SOB (true)	0.
SOB (false)	0.
Jump	0.0517
JMP	0.0272
JSR	0.0245
Control, Trap, and Miscellaneous	0.0270
Set/Clear Condition Codes	0.0017
MARK	0.
RTS	0.0236
RTI	0.
RTT	0.
IOT	0.
EMT	0.0017
TRAP	0.
BPT	0.

NOTES:
Frequency of destination odd-byte addressing (DM1–7) = 0.0213
Execution frequencies indicated as 0. have an aggregate frequency <0.0050.

Appendix B: Instruction Execution Times for PDP-11 Models

Microcycle (μs)	LSI-11 0.40	PDP-11/04 0.26	PDP-11/10 0.30	PDP-11/20 0.28	PDP-11/34 .18/.34	PDP-11/40 .14/.20/.30	PDP-11/45 0.15	PDP-11/60 0.17
Fetch	1/5 2.40	1/3 1.94	1/5 1.50	1/4 1.49	1/3 1.63	1/4 1.12	1/3 0.45	1/3 0.51
Source*								
0 R	0/1 0.40	0/2 0.52	0/2 0.60	0/0 0.0	0/1 0.18 1	0/0 0.0	0/0 0.0	0/0 0.0
1 @ R or (R)	1/3 1.60 1	1/2 1.46	1/3 1.50	1/4 1.49	1/1 1.12	1/3 0.78	1/2 0.30	1/2 0.34
2 (R) +	1/4 2.00 3	1/3 1.72	1/5 1.50	1/4 1.49	1/2 1.30	1/3 0.84	1/2 0.30	1/2 0.34
3 @ (R) +	2/7 3.60 1	2/5 3.18	2/7 2.70	2/7 2.70	2/3 2.42	2/5 1.72	2/5 0.75	2/5 0.85
4 – (R)	1/5 2.40 2	1/3 1.72	1/4 1.50	1/4 1.49	1/2 1.30	1/3 0.84	1/3 0.45	1/3 0.51
5 @ – (R)	2/8 4.00 1	2/5 3.18	2/6 2.70	2/7 2.70	2/3 2.42	2/5 1.72	2/6 0.90	2/6 1.02
6 X (R)	2/9 4.40 1	2/6 3.44	2/7 2.70	2/7 2.70	2/4 2.60	2/5 1.34	2/4 0.60	2/4 0.68
7 @ X (R)	3/12 6.00 1	3/8 4.9	3/9 3.90	3/10 3.91	3/5 3.72	3/7 2.12	3/7 1.05	3/7 1.19
Destination								
0 R	0/1 0.40	0/1 0.26	0/2 0.60 1	0/1 0.28	0/1 0.18 1,2	/0 0.0	0/0 0.0	0/0 0.0
1 @ R or (R)	1/4 2.00	1/1 1.20	1/3 1.50	1/4 1.39	1/1 1.12	1/3 0.78	1/2 0.3	1/2 0.34
2 (R) +	1/5 2.40 1	1/2 1.46	1/5 1.50	1/4 1.39	1/2 1.30 1	1/3 0.84	1/2 0.3	1/2 0.34
3 @ (R) +	2/8 4.00	2/4 2.92	2/7 2.70	2/7 2.60	2/3 2.42	2/5 1.70	2/5 0.15	2/5 0.85
4 – (R)	1/6 2.80 1	1/2 1.46	1/4 1.50	1/4 1.39	1/2 1.30	1/3 0.84	1/3 0.45	1/3 0.51
5 @ – (R)	2/9 4.40	2/4 2.92	2/6 2.70	2/7 2.60	2/3 2.42	2/5 1.70	2/6 0.9	2/6 1.02
6 X (R)	2/10 4.80	2/5 3.18	2/7 2.70	2/7 2.60	2/4 2.60	2/5 1.78 1	2/5 0.75 1	2/5 0.85 1
7 @ X (R)	3/13 6.40	3/7 4.64	3/9 3.90	3/10 3.81	3/5 3.72	3/7 2.56 1	3/8 1.2 1	3/8 1.36 1
Jump (JMP/JSR)								
1 @ R or (R)	0/3 1.20	0/2 0.52	1/1 0.90	0/4 1.12	0/0 0.0 1	0/2 0.34	0/2 0.3	0/1 0.17
2 (R) +	0/5 2.00	0/3 0.78	1/3 0.90	0/4 1.12	0/2 0.36	0/3 0.64	0/2 0.3	0/2 0.34
3 @ (R) +	1/5 2.40	1/3 1.72	2/5 2.10	1/7 2.33	1/2 1.30	1/2 0.94	1/4 0.6	1/2 0.34
4 – (R)	0/5 2.00	0/3 0.78	1/2 0.90	0/4 1.12	0/1 0.18	0/2 0.44	0/2 0.3	0/1 0.17
5 @ – (R)	1/6 2.80	1/3 1.72	2/4 2.10	1/7 2.33	1/2 1.30	1/2 0.94	1/5 0.75	1/3 0.51
6 X (R)	1/7 3.20	1/4 1.98	2/5 2.10	1/7 2.33	1/2 1.30 1	1/4 0.84	1/3 0.45	1/2 0.34
7 @ X (R)	2/10 4.80	2/6 3.44	3/7 3.30	2/10 3.54	2/4 2.60	2/4 1.34	2/6 0.90	2/5 0.85
MOV	1/3 1.60 2	1/2 1.06 1,2	1/4 1.80 1	1/3 0.80 1	1/1 0.78 1	1/3 0.64 4	1/0 0.0 1,3	1/2 1.17 1,6
MOVB	1/2 1.20 1	1/2 1.06 1,2	1/4 1.80 1	1/3 0.80 1	1/1 0.78 1	1/3 0.64 4	1/2 0.3 1	1/2 1.17 4
ADD	1/3 1.60 3	1/2 1.06 1	1/4 1.80 1	1/3 0.80 1	1/1 0.78 1	1/3 0.54 1,2	1/2 0.3 1	1/2 1.17 1,6
SUB	1/3 1.60 3	1/2 1.06 1	1/4 1.80 1	1/3 0.80 1	1/1 0.78 1	1/4 0.68 1	1/2 0.3 1	1/3 1.34 1,7
BIC	1/3 1.60 3	1/2 1.06 1	1/4 1.80 1	1/5 1.40 1	1/1 0.78 1	1/3 0.54 1,2	1/2 0.3 1	1/2 1.17 1,6,C
BICB	1/2 1.20 3	1/2 1.06 1	1/4 1.80 1	1/5 1.40 1	1/1 0.78 1	1/3 0.54 1,2	1/2 0.3 1	1/2 1.17 1,6,C
BIS	1/3 1.60 3	1/2 1.06 1	1/4 1.80 1	1/3 0.80 1	1/1 0.78 1	1/3 0.54 1,2	1/2 0.3 1	1/2 1.17 1,6,C
BISB	1/2 1.20 3	1/2 1.06 1	1/4 1.80 1	1/3 1.80 1	1/1 0.78 1	1/3 0.54 1,2	1/2 0.3 1	1/2 1.17 1,6,C
BIT	0/2 0.80	0/1 0.26	0/2 0.60	0/4 1.12	0/1 0.18	0/3 0.48 3	0/1 0.15 1,2	0/1 0.17 1
BITB	0/1 0.40	0/1 0.26	0/2 0.60	0/4 1.12	0/1 0.18	0/3 0.48 3	0/1 0.15 1,2	0/1 0.17 1
CMP	0/2 0.80	0/1 0.26	0/2 0.60	0/2 0.56 1	0/1 0.18	0/3 0.48 3	0/1 0.15 1,2	0/1 0.17 1,B

*Format: r/m t.tt n (r = number of memory reads or writes, m = number of microcycles; t.tt = time in μs; n = footnotes number).

Microcycle (μs)	LSI-11 0.40	PDP-11/04 0.26	PDP-11/10 0.30	PDP-11/20 0.28	PDP-11/34 .18/.34	PDP-11/40 .14/.20/.30	PDP-11/45 0.15	PDP-11/60 0.17	
CMPB	0/1 0.40	0/1 0.26	0/2 0.60	0/2 0.56	0/1 0.18	0/3 0.48 3	0/1 0.15 1,2	0/1 0.17	1,B
XOR	1/3 1.60 3				1/1 0.78 1		1/2 0.3 1	1/3 1.34	7
CLR (B), COMB	1/3 1.60 2	1/2 1.06 1	1/5 2.10 1	1/3 0.84 1	1/1 0.78 1	1/4 0.62 1,2	1/2 0.3 1	1/3 1.34	2,7
COM	1/4 2.00 2	1/2 1.06 1	1/5 2.10 1	1/3 0.84 1	1/1 0.78 1	1/4 0.62 1,2	1/2 0.3 1	1/3 1.34	2,7
INC, DEC	1/5 2.40 3	1/2 1.06 1	1/5 2.10 1	1/3 0.84 1	1/1 0.78 1	1/4 0.62 1,2	1/2 0.3 1	1/3 1.34	2,7,8
INCB, DECB	1/4 2.00 3	1/2 1.06 1	1/5 2.10 1	1/3 0.84 1	1/1 0.78 1	1/4 0.62 1,2	1/2 0.3 1	1/3 1.34	2,7,8
ADC	1/5 2.40 3	1/2 1.06 1	1/5 2.10 1	1/3 0.84 1	1/1 0.78 1	1/4 0.62 1,2	1/2 0.3 1	1/3 1.34	2,7,8
ADCB	1/4 2.00 3	1/2 1.06 1	1/5 2.10 1	1/3 0.84 1	1/1 0.78 1	1/4 0.62 1,2	1/2 0.3 1	1/3 1.34	2,7,8
SBC	1/5 2.40 3	1/2 1.06 1	1/5 2.10 1	1/3 0.84 1	1/1 0.78 1	1/4 0.62 1,2	1/2 0.3 1	1/4 1.51	6,8
SBCB	1/4 2.00 3	1/2 1.06 1	1/5 2.10 1	1/3 0.84 1	1/1 0.78 1	1/4 0.62 1,2	1/2 0.3 1	1/4 1.51	6,8
ROL, ASL	1/4 2.00 3	1/3 1.32 1	1/5 2.10 1	1/3 0.84 1,2	1/2 0.96 2	1/4 0.62 1,2	1/2 0.3 1	1/3 1.34	2,7,8
ROLB, ASLB	1/3 1.60 3	1/3 1.32 1	1/5 2.10 1	1/3 0.84 1,2	1/2 0.96 2	1/4 0.62 1,2	1/2 0.3 1	1/3 1.34	2,7,8
ROR	1/8 3.60 3	1/3 1.32 1	1/5 2.10 1	1/3 0.84 1,2	1/2 0.96 2	1/4 0.84 5	1/2 0.3 1,5	1/4 1.51	6
RORB	1/5 2.40 3	1/3 1.32 1	1/5 2.10 1	1/3 0.84 1,2	1/2 0.96 2	1/4 0.84 5	1/2 0.3 1,5	1/4 1.51	6
ASR	1/9 4.00 3	1/3 1.32 1	1/5 2.10 1	1/3 0.84 1,2	1/2 0.96 2	1/4 0.84 5	1/2 0.3 1,5	1/5 1.68	7,9
ASRB	1/8 3.60 4	1/3 1.32 1	1/5 2.10 1	1/3 0.84 1,2	1/2 0.96 2	1/4 0.84 5	1/2 0.3 1,5	1/5 1.68	7,9
TST	0/4 1.60	0/1 0.26	0/3 0.90	0/2 0.56	0/1 0.18	0/4 0.62 1,2	0/1 0.15 1,2	0/2 0.34	2,5
TSTB	0/3 1.20	0/1 0.26	0/3 0.90	0/2 0.56	0/1 0.18	0/4 0.62 1,2	0/1 0.15 1,2	0/2 0.34	2,5
NEG	1/4 2.00 2	1/2 1.06 1	1/5 2.10 1		1/2 0.96 1	1/3 0.54 1,2	1/4 0.6 4	1/4 1.51	7,8
NEGB	1/3 1.60 2	1/2 1.06 1	1/5 2.10 1		1/2 0.96 1	1/3 0.54 1,2	1/4 0.6 4	1/4 1.51	7,8
SWAB	1/3 1.60 2	1/3 1.32 1	1/12 3.15 1,2	1/3 0.84 1	1/1 0.78 2	1/3 0.54 1	1/2 0.3 1	1/5 1.68	7
SXT	1/6 2.80 3				1/1 0.78 1	1/4 0.62 1,2	1/2 0.3 1	1/6 1.85	7
BRANCH									
BRANCH (TRUE)	0/4 1.66	0/3 0.78	0/3 0.90	0/4 1.12	0/3 0.54	0/3 0.64	0/1 0.15	0/4 0.68	3
BRANCH (FALSE)	0/4 1.60	0.0	0/3 0.30	0/0 0.0	0/0 0.0	0/2 0.28	0/0 0.0 6	0/2 0.34	
SOB (TRUE)	0/8 3.20	–			0/4 0.78	0/5 1.24	0/3 0.45 6	0/10 1.70	3
SOB (FALSE)	0/6 2.40	–			0/2 0.42	0/5 .92	0/2 0.3 6	0/7 1.19	
JUMP									
JMP	0/2 0.80	0.0	0/2 0.60	0/0 0.0	0/1 0.18	0/2 0.34	0/1 0.15	0/1 0.17	
JSR	10/6 2.80 9	1/7 2.36	1/9 3.30	1/10 2.80	1/5 1.50	1/6 1.48	1/5 0.75	1/6 1.85	3,A
SET/CLEAR CC	0/3 1.20	0/2 0.52	0/3 0.90	0/0 0.0	0/2 0.36	0/2 0.6	0/2 0.15	0/8 1.19	
MARK	1/16 6.80				1/8 2.38	1/6 1.54	1/4 0.6 6	1/9 1.53	
RTS	1/6 2.80	1/5 2.24	1/7 2.10	1/6 2.05	1/4 1.66	1/4 1.28	1/4 0.6	1/4 .68	
RTI	2/15 6.80 5,6	2/6 3.44	2/9 2.70	2/9 3.26	2/6 2.96	2/6 2.32	2/7 1.05	2/10 1.70	
RTT	2/15 6.80 5,7				2/6 2.96	2/6 2.32	2/7 1.05	2/19 3.23	
IOT, EMT, TRAP, E BPT	2/33 14.80 5,8	2/12 6.08	2/13 6.3	2/21 6.62	2/13 5.42	2/14 4.18	2/11 1.65 7	2/22 5.40	

* Format: r/m t.tt n (r = number of memory reads or writes, m = number of microcycles; t.tt = time in μs; n = footnotes number).

LSI-11 NOTES

Fetch:

All single-operand instructions except SWAB, SXT, MFPS, and MTPS add 1 μcycle (+0.400 μs).
XOR, JMP, RTS, RTI, RTT, set/clear condition codes add 1 μcycle (+0.400 μs).
SWAB adds 2 μcycles (+0.800 μs).
SXT adds 5 μscycles (+2.000 μs).
BPT, IOT add 6 μcycles (+2.400 μs).
MARK adds 8 μcycles (+3.200 μs).

Source:

(1) Byte addressing subtracts 1 μcycle (–0.400 μs).
(2) Byte addressing adds 1 μcycle (+0.400 μs).
(3) If register ≠ R6 or R7, byte addressing adds 1 μcycle (+0.400 μs).

Destination:

For MOV: DMO subtracts 1 μcycle (–0.400 μs). DM1-7 subtracts 2 μcycles and memory read (–1.200 μs).
Byte addressing (DM1-7) subtracts 1 μcycle (–0.400 μs).
(1) If register = R6 or R7, byte addressing adds 2 μcycles (+0.800 μs) additive to the time noted directly above.

Execute:

(1) DMO adds 1 μcycle and subtracts memory write (+0.000 μs).
(2) DMO subtracts memory write (–0.400 μs).
(3) DMO subtracts 1 μcycle and memory write (–0.800 μs).
(4) DMO subtracts 3 μcycles and memory write (–1.600 μs).
(5) If new PS has bit 7 clear, add 1 μcycle (+0.400 μs).
(6) If new PS has bit 4 set, add 9 μcycles (+3.600 μs).
(7) If new PS has bit 4 set, add 10 μcycles (+4.000 μs).
(8) If new PS has bit 4 set, add 1 μcycle (+0.400 μs).
(9) If register not 7, then 1/15 (6.40 μs).

Times Assumed for All Calculations:

(1) Microcycle time is 0.400 μs.
(2) Microcycle time is extended by 0.400 μs during DATI/DATIP/DATO/DATOB. (Note: 1 extra wait μcycle is actually generated for each memory access; however, these μcycles have not been tallied in the microcycle counts above.)

PDP-11/04 NOTES

Source:

Odd-byte addressing (SM1-7) adds 2 μcycles (+0.520 μs).

Destination:

Odd-byte addressing (DM1-7) adds 2 μcycles (+0.520 μs).

Execute:

(1) Destination odd-byte addressing (DM1-7) adds 2 μcycles (+0.520 μs). DMO subtracts memory write (–0.540 μs).
(2) DMO subtracts 1 additional μcycle (–0.260 μs).

Times Assumed for All Calculations:

(1) Microcycle time is 0.260 μs.
(2) Microcycle time is extended by 0.220 μs by bus priority arbitration delay during BUT SERVICE.
(3) Microcycle time is extended by 0.940 μs during DATI/DATIP (MOS memory).
(4) Microcycle time is extended by 0.540 μs during DATO/DATOB (MOS memory).

PDP-11/10 NOTES

Source:

Odd-byte addressing (SM1-7) adds 7 fast shift (0.150 μs/μcycle) and 1 regular μcycle for a total of +1.350 μs.

Destination:

Odd-byte addressing (DM1-7) adds 7 fast shift (0.150 μs/μcycle) and 1 regular μcycle for a total of +1.350 μs.

(1) MOV subtracts 1 μcycle (–0.300 μs).

Execute:

(1) Destination odd-byte addressing (DM1-7) adds 7 fast shift μcycles (0.150 μs/μcycle) for a total of +1.050 μs. DMO subtracts 2 μcycles and memory write (–1.200 μs).
(2) Byte swap consists of 7 fast shift (0.150 μs/μcycle) and 1 regular μcycle for a total of +1.350 μs.

Times Assumed for All Calculations:

(1) Microcycle time is 0.300 μs.
(2) A CKOFF following a DATI/DATIP/DATO/DATOB extends μcycle time by 0.600 μs minus 0.300 μs for each μcycle that the CKOFF is removed from the cycle initiating the bus transaction.

PDP-11/20 NOTES

Source:

Odd-byte addressing (SM1-7) adds 2 lcycles (+0.560 μs).

Destination:

Odd-byte addressing (DM1-7) adds 2 μcycles (+0.560 μs).
Non-modifying instruction (CMP(B), BIT(B), TST(B)) adds 0 μcycles (+0.100 μs for DATI in place of DATIP).

Execute:

(1) DMO subtracts 1 μcycle and memory write (–0.280 μs). PS as destination adds 1 μcycle (+0.280 μs).
(2) Odd-byte addressing (DM1-7) adds 2 μcycles (+0.560 μs).

Times Assumed for All Calculations:

(1) Microcycle time is 0.280 μs
(2) Microcycle time is extended by 0.370 μs during DATI.
(3) Microcycle time is extended by 0.270 μs during DATIP.
(4) Microcycle time is extended by 0.000 μs during DATO/DATOB.

PDP-11/34 NOTES

Source:

(1) DMO subtracts 1 μcycle (–0.180 μs).

Destination:

MOV(B) and DM1-7 changes long to short μcycle and subtracts memory read (–1.000 μs).

(1) MOV(B) subtracts an additional μcycle (–0.180 μs)
(2) Single-operand instruction except NEG(B) subtracts 1 μcycle (–0.180 μs).

Execute:

(1) DMO subtracts memory write and changes long to short μcycle (–0.600 μs).
(2) DMO subtracts memory write, changes long to short μcycle, and adds 1 μcycle (–0.420 μs).

Times Assumed for All Calculations:

(1) Microcycle times are 0.180 and 0.240 μs.
(2) Microcycle time is extended by 0.150 μs by bus priority arbitration delay during BUT SERVICE.

(3) Microcycle time is extended by 0.940 μs during DATI/DATIP (MOS memory).
(4) Microcycle time is extended by 0.540 μs during DATO/DATOB (MOS memory).
(5) Memory management unit delay is not included (+0.120 μs/memory cycle when enabled).

PDP-11/40 NOTES

Source:

Odd-byte addressing (SM1-7) adds 2 μcycles (+0.340 μs).

Destination:

Odd-byte addressing (DM1-7) adds 2 μcycles (+0.340 μs).
(1) Single-operand instruction or SMO subtracts 0 μcycles (–0.440 μs).

Execute:

If (single-operand instruction or SMO and double-operand instruction except MOVB), DMO, destination ≠ register 7, and no service request pending, then next fetch is overlapped (–1 μcycle/–0.640 μs from next fetch).
(1) If DMO, phase takes 3 μcycles and memory write is not done (0.480 μs).
(2) If odd-byte addressing (DM1-7), phase takes 5 μcycles (1.020 μs).
(3) If odd-byte addressing (DM1-7), phase takes 5 μcycles (0.820 μs).
(4) If byte instruction and DM1-7, phase takes 4 μcycles (0.880 μs). For DMO: If word instruction, phase takes 2 μcycles (0.340 μs). If byte instruction, phase takes 4 μcycles (0.680 μs).
(5) For DMO: If word instruction, phase takes 3 μcycles (0.740 μs). If byte instruction, phase takes 4 μcycles (0.880 μs). In neither case is memory write done.

Times Assumed for All Calculations:

(1) Microcycle times are 0.140, 0.200, and 0.300 μs.
(2) A CLKOFF following a DATI/DATIP extends μcycle time by 0.500 μs minus sum of cycle times between DATI/DATIP (exclusive) and CLKOFF (inclusive).
(3) A CLKOFF following a DATO/DATOB extends μcycle time by 0.200 μs minus sum of cycle times between DATO/DATOB (exclusive) and CLKOFF (inclusive).
(4) Memory management unit delay is not included (+0.150 μs/memory cycle when enabled).

PDP-11/45 NOTES

Fetch:

Execute phase of previous instruction may be overlapped with fetch. Consult execute phase note for effect on timing.

Destination:

MOV and DM1-7 subtracts memory read (–0.000 μs). Odd-byte addressing (DM1-7) adds 1 μcycle (+0.150 μs).
(1) Single-operand instruction or SMO subtracts 1 μcycle (+0.150 μs).

Execute:

(1) For DMO:
If double-operand instruction, destination ≠ register 7, and SM1–7:
If odd-byte addressing, then phase takes 2 μcycles (0.300 μs), else phase takes 1 μcycle (0.150 μs). If no service request is pending, then next fetch is overlapped (–1 μcycle/–0.150 μs from next fetch).

If double-operand instruction, destination = register 7, and SMI1–7:

Phase takes 2 μcycles (0.300 μs).

Otherwise (single-operand instruction or SMO):

Phase takes 1 μcycle (0.150 μs). If destination ≠ register 7 and no service request is pending, then next fetch is overlapped (–2 μcycles/–0.300 μs from next fetch).

No memory write is done.

(2) For DM1-7, if destination fetch is via Fastbus and no service request is pending, then next instruction fetch is overlapped (–1 μcycle/–0.150 μs from next fetch).
(3) DM1-2 adds 1 μcycle (+0.150 μs). If no service request is pending, then next fetch is overlapped (–1 μcycle/–0.150 μs from next fetch).
(4) DMO subtracts 2 μcycles and memory write (–0.300 μs).
(5) Odd-byte addressing adds 1 μcycle (+0.150 μs).
(6) If no service request is pending, then next fetch is overlapped (–1 μcycle/–0.150 μs from next fetch).
(7) IOT 1.65 μs, BPT 1.8 μs.

Times Assumed for All Calculations:

(1) Microcycle time is 0.150 μs.
(2) Memory access time does not influence microcycle times (bipolar memory).
(3) Memory management unit delay is not included (+0.090 μs/memory cycle when enabled).

PDP-11/60 NOTES

Fetch:

The following instructions take 1 additional μcycle (+0.170μs) to decode: XOR, SWAB, SXT, JSR, set/clear condition codes, MARK, SOB, RTS, RTI, RTT, IOT, EMT, TRAP, BPT, MFPI(D), MTPI(D).

Fetch or execute phase of previous instruction may be overlapped with fetch. Consult execute phase notes for effect on timing.

Source:

For SM1-7: Word instruction except MOV and DM1-7 adds 1 μcycle (+0.170 μs). Byte instruction adds 2 μcycles (+0.340 μs).

Destination:

Byte addressing (DM1-7) adds 2 μcycles (0.340 μs).

(1) Single-operand instruction except SWAB or SXT or SMO and double-operand instruction except XOR subtracts 1 μcycle (–0.170 μs).

Execute:

(1) If SMO, DMO, source ≠ register 7, and destination ≠ register 7, then fetch overlap is attempted. If no service request is pending at conclusion of instruction, then next fetch is overlapped (–2 μcycles/–0.340 μs from next fetch); otherwise, add 2 μcycles (+0.340 μs) to service phase following instruction for PC rollback, add 1 memory read (+0.000 μs) to next fetch for instruction refetch.
(2) If DMO and destination ≠ register 7, then fetch overlap is attempted. If no service request is pending at conclusion of instruction, then next fetch is overlapped (–2 μcycles/–0.340 μs from next fetch); otherwise, add 2 μcycles (+0.340 μs) to service phase following instruction for PC rollback, add 1 memory read (+0.000 μs) to next fetch for instruction refetch.

(3) If no service request is pending, then next fetch is overlapped (–2 μcycles/–0.340 μs from next fetch); otherwise, subtract 1 μcycle (–0.170 μs) from execute.
(4) For DMO: SMO subtracts memory write (–0.830 μs). SM1-7 subtracts 1 μcycle and memory write (–1.000 μs).
(5) DMO subtracts 1 μcycle (–0.170 μs).
(6) DMO subtracts 1 μcycle and memory write (–1.000 μs).
(7) DMO subtracts 2 μcycles and memory write (–1.170 μs).
(8) DM1-7 and byte addressing adds 1 μcycle (+0.170 μs).
(9) DM1-7 and byte addressing adds 3 μcycles (+0.510 μs).
(A) DM3, 5–7 adds 1 μcycle (+0.170 μs).
(B) SM1-7, DMO, and word addressing adds 1 μcycle (+0.170 μs).
(C) SMO, DM1-7, and byte addressing adds 1 μcycle (+0.170 μs).
(D) SMO adds 1 μcycle (+0.170 μs).
(E) If new PC odd: Microcontrol transfers to writable control store if present and instruction timing does not apply; otherwise, trap sequence continues normally with 3 extra μcycles (+0.510 μs).

Accessing the following internal addresses invokes microcode which adds additional microcycles in all phases:

772300-16	Kernel Page Descriptor Registers
772340-56	Kernel Page Address Registers
777540	Writable Control Store Status Register
777542	Writable Control Store Address Register
777544	Writable Control Store Data Register
777570	Console Switch and Display Register
777572	Memory Management Status Register 0
777574	Memory Management Status Register 1
777576	Memory Management Status Register 2
777600-16	User Page Descriptor Registers
777640-56	User Page Address Registers
777744	Memory System Error Register
777746	Cache Control Register
777752	Cache Hit/Miss Register
777766	CPU Error Register
777770	Microprogram Break Register
777774	Stack Limit Register
777776	Processor Status Word

Times Assumed for All Calculations:

(1) Microcycle time is 0.170 μs.
(2) Microcycle time is extended by 0.000 μs during DATI/DATIP with cache hit (all tabulated times assume cache hit on read).
(3) Microcycle time is extended by 1.075 μs during DATI/DATIP with cache miss.
(4) Microcycle time is extended by 0.830 μs during DATO/DATOB.
(5) Memory Management unit adds no delay when enabled.

15

Turning Cousins into Sisters: An Example of Software Smoothing of Hardware Differences

RONALD F. BRENDER

INTRODUCTION

In 1970, the PDP-11 was Digital Equipment Corporation's newly announced minicomputer and its first offering in the 16-bit world. Among the many software components needed to complement the hardware, a FORTRAN system was high on the list. A FORTRAN project was begun in 1970 and the first release of the resulting product took place in mid-1971. In the succeeding years, the number of PDP-11 CPUs and related options increased dramatically to provide a wide range of price/performance alternatives. What makes the original FORTRAN interesting, even today, is the extent to which the basic implementation approach was able to be extended gracefully to span the entire family with modest incremental effort.

This paper describes the design concepts, threaded code and a FORTRAN virtual machine, used to implement the original PDP-11 FORTRAN product. As the PDP-11 family of processors expanded with new models and options, these original design concepts proved both stable enough and flexible enough to be employed successfully across the entire family.

When this FORTRAN was finally superseded in early 1975, it had two successors. One, called FORTRAN IV, continued the threaded code and virtual machine concepts of the earlier product with similar execution performance across the PDP-11 family, but offered much faster compilation rates in smaller memory. The other successor, called FORTRAN IV-PLUS, produced direct PDP-11 code and obtained significantly improved execution performance for the PDP-11/45, PDP-11/70, and PDP-11/60 with FP11 floating-point hardware relative to both of the other FORTRANs.

In the Beginning

The PDP-11/20 was a significant advance over other minicomputers of its time, but was a bare machine architecture by today's standards. There was no floating-point hardware of any kind (even as an option) and integer multiply and divide operations were available only by means of an I/O bus option, the Extended Arithmetic Element (EAE). (The EAE also provided multiple-bit arithmetic shift operations;

the PDP-11/20 instructions provided only single-bit shifts.)

The first disk-based operating system, DOS, was designed for a minimum standard system that included 8 Kwords (16 Kbytes) of memory. After allowing typically 2 Kwords for the resident parts of the monitor, only 5 K to 6 K remained for other use. Consequently, size constraints played a major role in the FORTRAN system design and implementation.

There were not many competitors at the time, but at least one, the IBM 1130, offered a disk-based operating system and FORTRAN system. To meet this competition, an important goal was to deliver the PDP-11 FORTRAN system to the market as quickly as possible, even at the cost of performance, if necessary.

Neither Compiler nor Interpreter, but Threaded Code

The fundamental design strategy to be determined was the structure of the executing code, the "run-time environment" [DEC, 1974b; DEC, 1974c].

We were leery of a compiler that generated direct machine code primarily because of the size of compiled code. Much of the compiled code would necessarily consist of calls to floating-point and other support routines, and on the PDP-11, each subroutine call required two words of memory, not counting argument transmission.

An interpreter would easily solve the space problem, but this had its own disadvantages. The basic interpreter loop overhead was a concern, but not crucial at that stage in our deliberations. However, a disadvantage of interpreters is that they must be "always present" even though not all of the capabilities are being used. For example, routines for complex arithmetic are part of the interpreter even though the particular program in use does not perform complex arithmetic. Further, we wanted to maintain the traditional FORTRAN features of independent compilation and linking of routines, and easy writing of routines in assembler for inclusion in the program.

The solution was threaded code [Bell, J., 1973]. Threaded code is a kind of combination of an interpreter and compiled code with most of the best features of each. On the PDP-11 it works in the following way.

The "compiled code" consists simply of a sequence of service routine addresses. A single register (we used R4) is chosen to contain a pointer to the next address in the sequence to be invoked. Each service routine completes by transferring control to the next routine in the sequence and simultaneously advancing the pointer.

To illustrate, consider a service routine whose purpose is to perform floating-point addition of two real values found in a stack (we used R6, the hardware stack pointer, for the value stack) and leave the result on the top of the stack in place of the parameters. The service routine would look like the following.*

```
$ADR: <<code for floating point add>>
      JMP @(R4)+
```

The JMP instruction with deferred auto-increment addressing mode provides just the

*The brackets << and >> are used in examples in place of code to indicate the purpose of code that is too bulky and/or not relevant for the example.

In the PDP-11 MACRO assembler language [DEC, 1976], identifiers may consist of up to six characters from among the letters, numerals, "." and "$". Identifiers created by the FORTRAN compiler include either a period or dollar sign to assure that they are distinct from FORTRAN language identifiers.

In the PDP-11 MACRO assembler language, a colon follows a label and separates the label from assembler instructions.

combination needed to sequence through the table of addresses. It is a single one-word instruction.

The instruction corresponds to the basic loop of an interpreter. Consequently, there is no centralized interpreter: the interpreter is distributed throughout every one of the service routines.

Arguments to a service routine can also be placed in-line following the routine address. The routine picks up the arguments using the pointer register, each time advancing the pointer for the next use. For this, both the auto-increment and deferred auto-increment addressing modes are ideal.

For example, the following service routine copies onto the stack the value of an integer variable whose address follows the call:

```
$PUSHV: MOV @(R4)+,-(SP)
        JMP @(R4)+
```

Similarly, the following routine pops a value from the stack and stores it in the variable whose address follows the call:

```
$POPV:  MOV (SP)+,@(R4)+
        JMP @(R4)+
```

Using the two primitives $PUSHV and $POPV, the FORTRAN assignment statement:

```
I = J
```

can be implemented by "compiling" code as follows:*

```
$PUSHV  ; Address of $PUSHV routine
J       ; Address of storage for J
$POPV   ; Address of $POPV routine
I       ; Address of storage for I
```

The principal disadvantage of a normal interpreter is avoided by representing the address of a service routine in symbolic fashion as the name of a module to be obtained from a library of routines. Only those routines that are actually referred to are included in the program when it is linked for execution.

We complete this introduction by briefly illustrating how flow of control and changing modes is accomplished.

A simple transfer of control, e.g., the FORTRAN statement:

```
GOTO 100
```

can be compiled to:

```
$GOTO,.100
```

using the service routine:

```
$GOTO:  MOV  (R4),R4
        JMP  @(R4)+
```

The implementation of the FORTRAN-computed GOTO statement is illustrated in Figure 1. Notice that the count of the number of labels is included in the arguments to the service routine. The service routine checks that the index value is in the correct range; if it is not, an error is reported and control continues in-line (no transfer takes place). In this example, register 1 (R1) is used as a temporary location within the service routine.

To enter threaded code mode when executing normal code, the following call is executed:

```
JSR R4,$POLSH
```

*In subsequent examples, the arguments of a service routine will be written on the same line as the routine address. Thus, the above would appear as:

```
$PUSHV,J
$POPV,I
```

This is more compact and suggestive of conventional assembler notations; the effect is identical to the previous example.

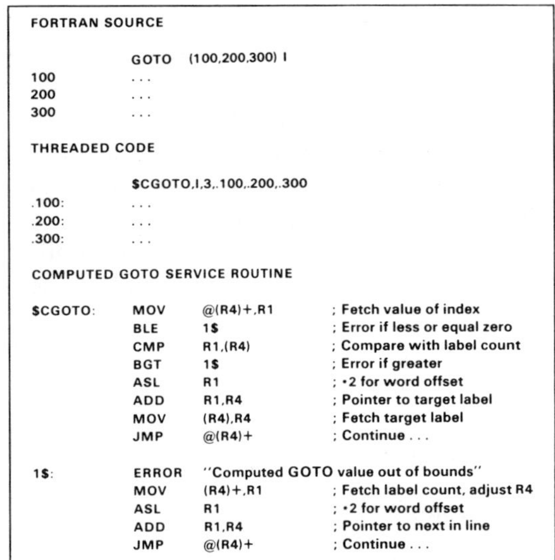

```
FORTRAN SOURCE

              GOTO    (100,200,300) I
100           . . .
200           . . .
300           . . .

THREADED CODE

              $CGOTO,I,3,.100,.200,.300
.100:         . . .
.200:         . . .
.300:         . . .

COMPUTED GOTO SERVICE ROUTINE

$CGOTO:       MOV     @(R4)+,R1        ; Fetch value of index
              BLE     1$               ; Error if less or equal zero
              CMP     R1,(R4)          ; Compare with label count
              BGT     1$               ; Error if greater
              ASL     R1               ; •2 for word offset
              ADD     R1,R4            ; Pointer to target label
              MOV     (R4),R4          ; Fetch target label
              JMP     @(R4)+           ; Continue . . .

1$:           ERROR   "Computed GOTO value out of bounds"
              MOV     (R4)+,R1         ; Fetch label count, adjust R4
              ASL     R1               ; •2 for word offset
              ADD     R1,R4            ; Pointer to next in line
              JMP     @(R4)+           ; Continue . . .
```

Figure 1. Threaded code for FORTRAN-computed GOTO statement.

Threaded mode begins immediately following this call. The service routine is:

```
$POLSH: MOV (SP)+,R4
        JMP @(R4)+
```

Leaving threaded mode requires no service routine at all; the operator is simply the address of the immediately following word of memory.

A Virtual Machine

By now it should be apparent that we have the beginning of a FORTRAN *virtual machine.* Instructions in this machine language are encoded as the addresses of the service routines. The PDP-11 instruction set provides the pseudo-microinstruction set used to emulate the FORTRAN machine. Register 4 (R4) is the virtual program counter.

For a complete characterization of a virtual machine, it is necessary to identify the complete state of the machine, that is, all of the values that must be preserved in order to interrupt the execution of the machine, apply the machine to another purpose, and later resume the original execution as though the interruption had not occurred. In this sense, the state clearly includes the stack pointer (SP) register and the program counter (R4) register as well as the memory regions occupied by the program, variables, and values on the stack. In the actual implementation, some virtual machine instructions also left values in general register 0 (R0) or in the processor condition codes for use by the subsequent virtual machine instruction. Thus, these values must also be considered part of the virtual machine state. However, the remaining general registers of the PDP-11 are not part of the state even though they are used freely by individual instructions to hold temporary values during the execution of a single virtual instruction, as illustrated in Figure 1.

This FORTRAN machine went through two phases of development. In the first phase, the virtual machine specification did not change; rather, the implementation was broadened to take advantage of newer models of the PDP-11 family. Increased performance was achieved through improved performance of the new CPU and the floating-point hardware options. In the second phase, the virtual machine specification itself was extended to achieve greater performance across all of the PDP-11 family processors.

FORTRAN MACHINE – PHASE 1

The introduction described the basic technique, threaded code, by which it was possible to produce a FORTRAN processor for the first PDP-11 processor, the PDP-11/20. This section focuses on the design of the FORTRAN virtual machine proper and how it was implemented across the range of PDP-11 CPUs.

The major part of the FORTRAN virtual machine was relatively *ad hoc* in form, more or less closely following the form of the FORTRAN language. The previous example of the computed GOTO statement is representative of the approaches taken. This correspondence between the language and the virtual machine greatly simplified the compiler. Variations in the order of arguments and/or the introduction of extra arguments (such as the label list count) were made to aid the speed and/or the error checking capability of the supporting service routines.

One part of the machine had a more regular structure – assignment statements and expression evaluation. We will focus our attention on this part of the machine because this is where the majority of FORTRAN execution time is spent.

Many details of the machine are easily sketched. It was a stack-oriented machine – values were pushed onto the stack, and operators took their operands from the stack and replaced them with the result. The hardware stack pointer (SP) was used to control the value stack. Consideration was given to using the PDP-11 general registers as fast top-of-stack locations. However, this was rejected because it violated the inherent simplicity of the pure stack model and because analysis showed that the extra overhead of managing these locations substantially eliminated any benefits.

Naming conventions were adopted for the operators as a mnemonic convenience. The arithmetic operators were named as illustrated in Figure 2. For example, $ADR designated the routine to add two single-precision (real) operands, while $ADC designated the routine to add two complex operands, and so on.

Throughout this design process the size of the generated code continued to be the most important factor. This led to the most unusual aspect of the machine design.

To push a value onto the stack required two words: one for the push instruction and one for the address of the variable. To reduce this to a single word, the compiler produced a service routine for each variable that would push the value of the variable onto the stack. Such a routine was called a push routine. In this way, the compiler reduced the size of the compiled code by producing specialized service routines that complemented the general service routines obtained from the FORTRAN library.

```
FORM:  $sot

WHERE o  =  AD   For addition
         =  SB   For subtraction
         =  ML   For multiplication
         =  DV   For division
         =  PW   For exponentiation (raising to a power)

      t  =  B    For byte data
         =  L    For logical data
         =  I    For integer data
         =  R    For real data
         =  D    For double-precision data
         =  C    For complex data
```

NOTE:
"$PW" has a 2-letter suffix. The first indicates the base data-type, the second the exponent data-type.

Figure 2. FORTRAN Phase 1 arithmetic instructions.

For example, the push routine for an integer variable, *I*, would be:

```
$P.I:     MOV   I,-(SP)
          JMP   @(R4)+
```

The push routine for a complex variable, *C*, would be:*

```
$P.C:     MOV   #C+8,R0
          MOV   -(R0),-(SP)
          MOV   -(R0),-(SP)
          MOV   -(R0),-(SP)
          MOV   -(R0),-(SP)
          JMP   @(R$)+
```

Of course, each push routine itself took space: three words for an integer variable and five words for a real variable. Consequently, the

*Note that since the stack of the PDP-11 grows downward in memory, values must be copied from high address toward low address to obtain a correct copy on the stack.

breakeven point was three uses for an integer variable and five uses for a real variable.

Three uses of an integer variable were deemed likely to be achieved in most programs, especially in larger and more complex programs where space would be most critical. The five uses for a real variable were reduced by some complex merging of code for multiple push routines for real, complex, and double-precision variables. The compiler also maintained a bit in the symbol table entry for each variable indicating that a push routine was actually needed. (It is fairly common for a particular subroutine to reference only a few variables out of a large COMMON block.)

Pop routines for each variable were also considered, but rejected. There are typically more uses of a variable's value than assignments of new values. Consequently, the breakeven point is less likely to be consistently achieved. Instead, general pop routines for each data-type (actually, each size of data value – 1, 2, 4, or 8 bytes) were used.

Figure 3 presents a complete example of the compiled code produced by the compiler for two sample assignment statements. The figure includes push routines automatically generated by the compiler, as well as the allocation of storage for the variables of the program. All service routines not shown are obtained from the FORTRAN library when the program is linked for execution.

It should be apparent from this figure that the compiled code corresponds to the well-known Polish postfix notation, which is a rearrangement of expression information suitable for stack evaluation disciplines.

The Virtual Machine Across the PDP-11 Family

Even as the FORTRAN system was in its early development phase, new models of the PDP-11 family were under development by the hardware groups. The next in line was the PDP-11/45 with a floating-point hardware option. How could the software development group that had just produced a FORTRAN tailored for an 8 K PDP-11/20 without even integer multiply/divide instructions respond with another FORTRAN for the high-performance

```
FORTRAN SOURCE

      K = K + 1
      X2 = (A - (B**2-4.*A*C))/(2.*A)
      END

THREADED CODE

$START:    JSR R4,$POLSH
           $P.K                          ; Push K
           $P.1                          ; Push 1
           $ADI                          ; Add integer giving K + 1
           $POPI,K                       ; Pop to K

           $P.A                          ; Push A
           $P.B                          ; Push B
           $P.2                          ; Push 2
           $PWRI                         ; B**2
           $P.4.                         ; Push 4.
           $P.A                          ; Push A
           $MLR                          ; 4.*A
           $P.C                          ; Push C
           $MLR                          ; 4.*A*C
           $SBR                          ; B**2-4.*A*C
           $SBR                          ; (A-(B**2-4.*A*C))
           $P.2.                         ; Push 2.
           $P.A                          ; Push A
           $MLR                          ; 2.*A
           $DVR                          ; ( . . . )/(2.*A)
           $POP2,X2                      ; Pop to X2

; PUSH ROUTINES

$P.K:      MOV      K,-(SP)
           JMP      @(R4)+
$P.1:      MOV      #1,-(SP)
           JMP      @(R4)+
$P.A:      MOV      #A+4,R0
           BR       $F
$P.B:      MOV      #B+4,R0
           BR       $F
$P.2:      MOV      #2,-(SP)
           JMP      @(R4)+
$P.4.:     MOV      #$R.4.,R0
           BR       $F
$P.C:      MOV      #C+4,R0
           BR       $F
$P.2.:     MOV      #$R.2+4,R0
$F:        MOV      -(R0),-(SP)          ; Shared code for pushing
           MOV      -(R0),-(SP)          ; the values of A, B, C and
           JMP      @(R4)+               ; the constants 2. and 4.

; STORAGE ALLOCATION

K:         .BLKW    1
A:         .BLKW    2
B:         .BLKW    2
$R.4.:     .FLT2    4.
C:         .BLKW    2
$R.2.:     .FLT2    2.

           .END     $START
```

Figure 3. Example of code generation.

PDP-11/45 with optional hardware floating point? Fortunately, the virtual FORTRAN machine approach made it relatively easy. All that was needed was to re-implement the virtual machine using the new and more extensive "microcode." The compiler did not even have to be changed at all! How this was accomplished is discussed below.

The PDP-11/20, with its EAE option, required two implementations of the virtual machine. The PDP-11/45 added two more: one for the floating-point option and another because it added instructions for integer multiply/divide and multiple bit shifting as part of the standard instruction set.*

Later the PDP-11/40 added a fifth variation for its Floating Instruction Set (FIS) option.†

By the time we were done, there were five versions of the FORTRAN machine which corresponded to the family processors as follows:

1. Basic PDP-11/20, PDP-11/40

2. EAE PDP-11/20 with EAE, PDP-11/40 with EAE

   Integer multiply/divide

3. EIS PDP-11/40 with EIS, PDP-11/45

   Integer multiply/divide

4. FIS PDP-11/40 with EIS and FIS

   Integer multiply/divide and single-precision floating point

5. FP11 PDP-11/45 with FP11

   Integer multiply/divide and single/double precision floating point

Later processors (PDP-11/70, 11/60, 11/34, 11/05, 11/04, and LSI-11) have all matched one of these five categories.

Figure 4 illustrates the general logical structure of a typical floating-point service routine. As presented in this logically extreme form, it consisted of *five* completely independent implementations. They were combined in a single source file to help manage and minimize the proliferation of files. (This also significantly

```
$ADR:   .IF NDF EAE!EIS!FIS!FPP
        <<no option basic implementation>>
        .ENDC

        .IF DF EAE
        <<EAE version>>
        .ENDC

        .IF DF EIS
        <<EIS version>>
        .ENDC

        .IF DF FIS
        <<FIS version>>
        .ENDC

        .IF DF FPP
        <<FPP version>>
        .ENDC

        .END
```

NOTE:
In the PDP-11 MACRO assembler language, ."IF" introduces a sequence of statements (instructions) that are included in a given assembly only if a specified condition is satisfied. The statement, ".ENDC" terminates the sequence. Also, conditional sequences can be tested within other conditional sequences, as illustrated in other figures. In this figure, the condition, "DF EAE" is satisfied if the name EAE has a defined value. "DF EIS" is satisfied if EIS is defined, and so on. The condition, "NDF EAE!EIS!..." is satisfied if none of the given names has a defined value.

Figure 4. General logical structure of conditionalized FORTRAN operator routine.

*These Extended Instruction Set (EIS) operations were similar in function to the capability of the EAE, but were an integral part of the instruction set instead of an I/O bus add-on. This was more efficient since the initialization necessary to begin execution of these functions was less.

†On the PDP-11/40, the EIS instructions were an option also.

aided maintenance.) This one file would be assembled five times, each time with a different conditional assembly parameter, to produce the five different object files that implemented the same operation on the different systems.

In practice, the separation of implementations was not as complete as shown. Some instructions, such as the computed GOTO, remained independent of the hardware configuration. Generally, the EIS and EAE versions were localized variations of the basic (no option) implementation, while the FP11 and FIS versions tended to be totally distinct.

A more representative illustration of the kind of conditionalization used is shown in Figure 5. Notice that the conditional use of EIS or EAE operations is nested within an outer conditionalization for neither FIS nor FP11. The FIS and FP11 versions are distinct.

```
$ADR:   .IF NDF FIS!FPP
        <<basic implementation>>

                .IF DF EAE
                <<EAE variation>>
                .ENDC

                .IF DF EIS
                <<EIS variation>>
                .ENDC

                .IF NDF EIS!EAE
                <<no option variation>>
                .ENDC

        <<basic implementation>>
        .ENDC ;NDF FIS!FPP

        .IF DF FIS
        FADD SP
        JMP @(R4)+
        .ENDC ;DF FIS

        .IF DF FPP
        SETF
        LDF     (SP)+,F0
        ADDF    (SP)+,F0
        STF     F0,-(SP)
        JMP     @(R4)+
        .ENDC   ;DF FPP

        .END
```

Figure 5. Partial detail of implementation of $ADR.

The FORTRAN Machine and the PDP-11/40 EIS

Because of the incompatibility in operand addressing capability between the FP11 and FIS, the FIS option of the PDP-11/40 seems at best an architectural curiosity and at worst an unfathomable aberration. In a broader perspective, however, it was an excellent compromise between goals and constraints for the combined hardware and software system at the time it was introduced.

The marketing requirement was simple. There must be at least a single-precision floating-point option for the PDP-11/40 to maintain competitive FORTRAN performance and it must sell for no more than a given (relatively low) price. The cost constraint, combined with other engineering factors, precluded the implementation of even a simple subset of the FP11 instruction set.

Consultation between the hardware and software engineers led to the resulting Floating Instruction Set. The FIS provided four single-precision floating-point instructions (add, subtract, multiply, and divide) which corresponded exactly with the FORTRAN virtual machine requirements. As seen in Figure 5, the FIS version of the FORTRAN $ADR service routine consists of just two single-word instructions (compared to the FP11 variant that occupies five words).

The FIS option for the PDP-11/40 accomplished everything that it was supposed to accomplish.

FORTRAN MACHINE – PHASE 2

While the FORTRAN product successfully "supported" the full range of the PDP-11 family, the design tradeoffs made for the original and low end of the family were not valid at the high end. Benchmark competition of FORTRAN on the PDP-11/45 with FP11 became significant even though the underlying hardware was the fastest available by clear margins. The reason is easy to understand. The FORTRAN virtual machine and its implementation did not fully exploit the hardware capability.

To illustrate, consider the execution of the statement, $I = I + 1$, as shown in Figure 3. This statement compiled to five words of threaded code (not counting the overhead of service or push routines), and required 18 memory cycles to execute. In conrast, the single PDP-11 instruction, INC I, would obtain the same effect with only two words of code and three memory cycles to execute. Similar overheads existed for floating-point operations. As shown in Figure 5, the basic arithmetic operators had to copy their operands from the stack into the FP11 registers to do the operation, and then immediately return the result to the stack.

On the PDP-11/20, integer execution times of 20 microseconds instead of 4 microseconds did not matter much when floating-point times where typically 300 to 1000 microseconds. However, with FP11 times under 10 microseconds for these operations, the tradeoffs are much different.

Since the existing compiler was based totally on the threaded code implementation, a complete new compiler that generated direct PDP-11 code would be needed to fully exploit the hardware potential. In the meantime, something was needed to immediately improve performance and relieve the competitive pressure.

That something was provided, not by discarding threaded code, but by extending the FORTRAN virtual machine architecture. The extension devised was based on a combination of systematic and *ad hoc* pragmatic considerations.

The primary considerations were to:

1. Focus attention on operations for integer, real, and double-precision data-types. Logical and complex data-types do not occur frequently enough to merit much concern [Knuth, 1971].

2. Limit the impact on the compiler to as small a portion as possible to limit the programming effort. Fortunately, expression handling and assignment statements were well modularized in the implementation.

Addressing Modes

The principal concept that formed the basis of the extended machine was the recognition that operands could be in any of a number of locations and that arithmetic operators should be able to take operands from any of them and deliver the result to any of them, instead of just the stack. The principal locations identified were:

- The stack.
- In memory at an address given as a parameter.
- In memory at an address given in R0 as a result of an array subscripting operation.

Other "locations" were formalized for particular groups of operators as will be seen later.

Conceptually, these locations became addressing modes associated with each operator. However, any kind of decoding of addressing modes during execution would destroy the performance objective. Consequently, each combination of operator and addressing modes was implemented by a unique threaded service routine.

At this point, a new consideration came into play. Not only would each routine take some memory, but the number of global symbols that must be handled by the linking loader would rise dramatically. (The system linking loader maintained its global symbol table in free main memory; hence, the number of symbols that could be handled was limited by main memory size. Fortunately, the minimum system main memory requirement had independently increased from 8 Kwords to 12 Kwords; otherwise, the approach would not have been acceptable.) The above three modes for each of three operand locations for each of the four basic operations for each of the three important data-types required 3 * 3 * 3 * 4 * 3 or 324 new service routines. Care would be needed to keep this explosive cross-product in bounds.

The memory size increase was offset by the fact that in many cases the push routines of a variable were no longer needed. This can be appreciated better by looking at some examples.

The Extended Machine

Figures 6 through 11 detail most of the extended machine and give numerous sample code sequences.

There were three principal groups of extended operations dealing with one-dimensional array subscript calculation, arithmetic operations, and general data movement. Once again, naming conventions were used for mnemonic aids. Generally, the first two or three letters (after the "$") designated an addressing mode, the next letter designated the kind of operation and the final letter designated the data-type. For example, the $ADR routine used in previous figures acquired the name $SSSAR in this new scheme.

As an example, consider the FORTRAN statement:

I = J + K + L

This would be compiled to:

```
$CCSAI,J,K      ; Add J,K and
                ; put result on stack
$SCCAI,L,I      ; Add stack,L and
                ; put result in I
```

The PDP-11 code for these service routines is:

```
$CCSAI:    MOV   @(R4)+,-(SP)
           ADD   @(R4)+,@SP
           JMP   @(R4)+

$SCCAI:    ADD   @(R4)+,@SP
           MOV   (SP)+,@(R4)+
           JMP   @(R4)+
```

FORM: $sbXz, sarg, barg

WHERE			
	s	= C	If subscript is in memory (core) and directly addressable (i.e., not a parameter or array element)
		= R	If subscript is pointed at by R0 at execution time
		= S	If subscript on execution stack
		= P	If subscript is a parameter
		= G	If subscript is contents of R0 (i.e., results of function call)
	b	= C	If array is not a parameter
		= A	If array is a parameter
	z	= 1,2,4,8	The array element size in bytes
	sarg	=	Argument address if s = C
		=	Argument list offset if s = P
		=	Not present otherwise
	barg	=	Array address minus element size if b = C
		=	Address of array descriptor block (ADB) if b = A

SPECIAL CASES

$CCXO, address

Is generated when the subscript is a constant and the array is not a FORTRAN dummy argument. The final address is computed at compile time and is the argument.

$KAXO, scaled-constant, adb-address

is generated when the subscript is a constant and the array is a FORTRAN dummy argument; the constant subscript is converted to a byte offset at compile time.

Figure 6. One-dimensional array subscripting instructions.

ASSUME

```
SUBROUTINE SUB(A,I)
DIMENSION A(10), B(10), M(10)
```

FORTRAN SOURCE	COMPILED CODE
B(J)	$CCX4,J,B-4
B(I)	$PCX4,4,B-4
B(5)	$CCXO,B+20
A(5)	$KAXO,20,$A.A
B(M(2))	$CCXO,M+2 $RCX4,B-4

NOTE:
$A.A is the address of an array descriptor block for A.

Figure 7. Example of subscripting operations.

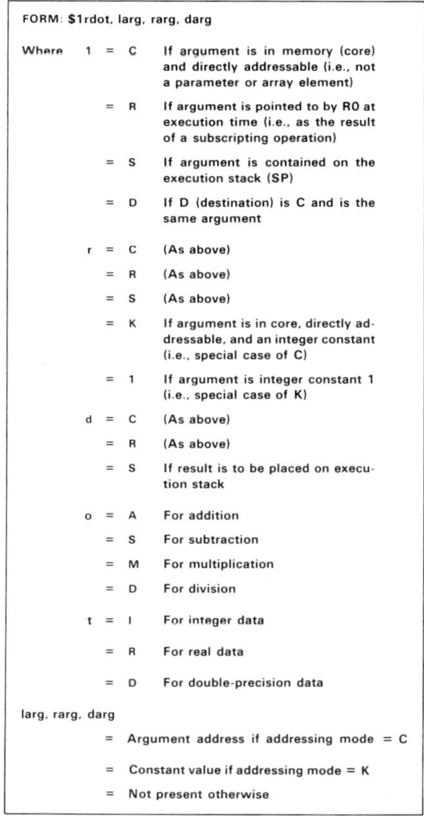

FORM: $1rdot, larg, rarg, darg

Where			
1	=	C	If argument is in memory (core) and directly addressable (i.e., not a parameter or array element)
	=	R	If argument is pointed to by R0 at execution time (i.e., as the result of a subscripting operation)
	=	S	If argument is contained on the execution stack (SP)
	=	D	If D (destination) is C and is the same argument
r	=	C	(As above)
	=	R	(As above)
	=	S	(As above)
	=	K	If argument is in core, directly addressable, and an integer constant (i.e., special case of C)
	=	1	If argument is integer constant 1 (i.e., special case of K)
d	=	C	(As above)
	=	R	(As above)
	=	S	If result is to be placed on execution stack
o	=	A	For addition
	=	S	For subtraction
	=	M	For multiplication
	=	D	For division
t	=	I	For integer data
	=	R	For real data
	=	D	For double-precision data

larg, rarg, darg

= Argument address if addressing mode = C

= Constant value if addressing mode = K

= Not present otherwise

Figure 8. Arithmetic instructions.

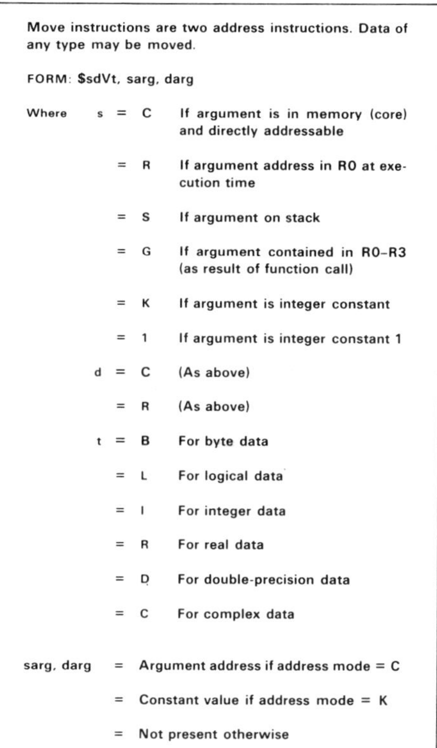

Move instructions are two address instructions. Data of any type may be moved.

FORM: $sdVt, sarg, darg

Where			
s	=	C	If argument is in memory (core) and directly addressable
	=	R	If argument address in R0 at execution time
	=	S	If argument on stack
	=	G	If argument contained in R0–R3 (as result of function call)
	=	K	If argument is integer constant
	=	1	If argument is integer constant 1
d	=	C	(As above)
	=	R	(As above)
t	=	B	For byte data
	=	L	For logical data
	=	I	For integer data
	=	R	For real data
	=	D	For double-precision data
	=	C	For complex data

sarg, darg = Argument address if address mode = C

= Constant value if address mode = K

= Not present otherwise

Figure 10 Move instructions.

ASSUME

DIMENSION L(10)

FORTRAN SOURCE	COMPILED CODE
A = B + C	$CCCAR,B,C,A
A = B + C*D	$CCSMR,C,D $CSCAR,B,A
I = J + 5	$CKCAI,J,5,I
I = I - 5	$DKCSI,5,I
J = J + 1	$D1CAI,J
L(J + 1) = J + 2	$C1SAI,J $SCX2,L-2 $CKRAI,J,2
I = L(I) + 2	$CCX2,I,L-2 $RKCAI,2,I

Figure 9. Example of arithmetic operations.

ASSUME

DIMENSION ARRAY (10)

FORTRAN SOURCE	COMPILED CODE
A = B	$CCVR,B,A
I = 1	$1CVI,I
B = ARRAY(J)	$CCX4,J,ARRAY-4 $RCVR,B
ARRAY(1) = ARRAY(I+1)	$C1SAI,I $SCX4,ARRAY-4 $GET3 $CCX0,ARRAY+0 $SRVR

Figure 11. Example of move instructions.

Notice that no push routines are needed for any of the variables.

All subscripting operations resulted in the address of the array element being left in R0 at execution time. Only one-dimensional arrays were handled. Two- and three-dimensional arrays continued to be handled as in the more general Phase 1 implementation.

These forms can occur on both left- and right-handed sides of assignment statements.

The arithmetic instructions are three address instructions, taking two arguments and putting the result in a designated place. These instructions are limited to +, –, *, / on integer, real, and double-precision data.

Ad Hoc Special Cases

Within this general framework, a number of additional *ad hoc* addressing modes were incorporated.

For each of the arithmetic operators and each of the three data-types, the first operand addressing mode could be given as D to designate that it was the same as the destination core address and the destination parameter was eliminated. This was not done for the second operand based on the simple observation that programmers will almost always write assignments as:

```
A = A + . . .
```

instead of:

```
A = . . . + A
```

This added 12 more service routines.

For the integer operators only, the second operand could be given as K to designate that it was a constant given as the parameter instead of the address of the value. This was not done for the first operand for reasons similar to the case above.

For integer add and subtract operators only, the second operand could be given as 1 to designate that it is the constant value 1 and no parameter is present. This is simply a frequent special case of the previous use of K.

By combining the above, the FORTRAN statement:

```
K = K + 1
```

is compiled to:

```
$D1CAI,K
```

where the service routine is simply:

```
$D1CAI:     INC    @(R4)+
            JMP    @(R4)+
```

This code occupies two words and requires five memory cycles to execute. This is not quite as good as the two words and three cycles needed for direct PDP-11 code, but far better than the five words and 18 cycles required by the earlier implementation.

General Results

Execution improvement varied, of course, with the particular programs used. Over a large set of programs, the following guidelines were obtained.

- Programs that were floating-point intensive increased in speed by factors of 1.1 to 1.6, with 1.3 being representative.
- Programs that were integer intensive increased in speed by factors of 1.4 to 2.4, with 2.0 being representative. (One particularly simple benchmark increased in speed by a factor of 4!)

Moreover, because of the reduced need for push routines, most programs increased in size by less than 10 percent.

The improvement for integer operations was better than for floating-point operations for several reasons. Integer operations were more easily "optimized" because they took place in the basic CPU general registers. The FP11 has a separate set of floating-point registers, and floating-point computations must be performed only in those registers. Also, the FP11 operates in either single-precision or double-precision mode depending on a status bit; the compiler implementation was not suitable for tracking the state of this bit and, hence, each floating-point operation continued to bear the overhead of reestablishing the state as needed by that operation. (This is the purpose of the SETF instruction shown in Figure 5.)

The performance improvements of the Phase 2 system with its extended virtual machine were obtained with a design, development, and testing effort of about three man-months. For that effort, PDP-11 FORTRAN regained a strong competitive position that held reasonably well until FORTRAN IV-PLUS, an optimizing PDP-11 code-generating system, replaced it 18 months later (in early 1975).

REAL MICROCODE AND THE FORTRAN MACHINE

Clearly, the FORTRAN virtual machine described above could be implemented in "real" microcode instead of the PDP-11 instruction set. This was considered during the design planning for the PDP-11/60 which features a writable control store microprogramming option [DEC, 1977a]. But, while the analysis showed that a significant improvement could be obtained, the result, at best, would be comparable to the performance already achieved by the FORTRAN IV-PLUS product. Consequently, it was not done.

The analysis proceeded along the following lines. Execution time was considered in three categories: instruction fetch and decode, operand fetch and/or store, and execution time proper. Since the analysis is a comparison of different FORTRAN implementations for a given machine, the basic execution times are assumed to be the same and neglected. The resulting comparison, thus, shows the number of words of memory and the number of memory cycles for each implementation.

For this presentation we shall consider the following two FORTRAN statements as reasonably representative of FORTRAN as a whole.

```
   I = J * K + L
A(I) = B(J) + 4
```

For these statements, the size and memory cycles are easily determined by examination of the code generated by FORTRAN and FORTRAN IV-PLUS, respectively. These values are shown in Table 1.

For the hypothesized micro-thread implementation, the code size is unchanged from FORTRAN, while the memory cycle count is

Table 1. Comparison of Size and Time Requirements of Sample Statements with Different Implementation Techniques

	I = J * K + L		A(I) = B(J) + 4	
Technique	**Size**	**Time**	**Size**	**Time**
PDP-11 threads	6 words	20 cycles	9 words	38 cycles
FORTRAN IV-PLUS	8 words	12 cycles	14 words	20 cycles
Micro-threads	6 words	12 cycles	9 words	22 cycles
Model	7 words	11 cycles	9 words	17 cycles

reduced by eliminating the instruction fetches that occur in the service routines. These results are also shown in the table. Comparison of the results shows that the micro-thread implementation is faster (as expected), but also that its speed is no better than that of FORTRAN IV-PLUS. Could this be coincidence or is there reason to believe these results should be obtained?

To answer this, we formulated a simple intuitive model for the expected size and speed of code on an idealized FORTRAN machine. To estimate the code size:

- Count one unit for each variable that is referenced (e.g., A(I) counts as two).
- Count one unit for each operation performed (e.g., assignment or subscripting are unit operations).

To estimate the memory cycles for execution:

- Count one unit for each variable that is referenced.
- Count one unit for each operation performed.
- Count one, two, or four units for each value fetch or store operation depending on the size of the data.

This very simple model is appropriate only for compilers that produce code based only on isolated source information, which is true of the original FORTRAN. Optimizing compilers, such as FORTRAN IV-PLUS, do better than suggested by this model by eliminating or simplifying operations (for example, by constant expression elimination or moving invariant computations out of loops, and/or by keeping values in registers instead of main memory, especially across loops). Consequently, the model serves primarily as a relatively implementation-independent frame of reference for comparing alternative implementations.

The sizes and cycle counts from this model for the sample statements are also shown in Table 1. These values are quite similar to values for both the micro-thread and FORTRAN IV-PLUS implementations.

We interpreted these results as a clear demonstration that a micro-threaded implementation could not significantly outperform the existing FORTRAN IV-PLUS implementation. Further, effort expended for greater performance would be better directed toward improved optimization in FORTRAN IV-PLUS (which would benefit existing hardware products) or toward faster hardware *per se.**

There is also a broader interpretation of the results that is worth reflection. The threaded implementation was designed to be a good FORTRAN architecture. Yet, when implemented in microcode in a manner comparable with the host PDP-11 architecture, the performance is close to that achieved by the FORTRAN IV-PLUS compiler and also close to that of an "ideal" model. One is led to speculate that the PDP-11 with FP11 is also a good FORTRAN architecture.

ACKNOWLEDGEMENTS

Many individuals contributed to the design, implementation, and evolution of the PDP-11 FORTRAN product. The following were particularly involved in those aspects described in this paper. Jim Bell, Dave Knight, and the author participated in the initial design evaluation that led to the basic virtual machine. Dave was project leader for the first versions of the product. Rich Grove participated in the support of the FP11 and FIS options. The extended virtual machine design and implementation, and the microcode feasibility analysis were done by the author. Finally, Craig Mudge assisted in the preparation of this paper with valuable discussion and criticism, and by not accepting "no" for an answer.

---

*Note that Digital did both. FORTRAN IV-PLUS V2 and the FP11-C were both released in early 1976 with each offering significant performance improvements.

16

The Evolution of the PDP-11

C. GORDON BELL and J. CRAIG MUDGE

A computer is not solely determined by its architecture; it reflects the technological, economic, and organizational aspects of the environment in which it was designed and built. In the introductory chapters the nonarchitectural design factors were discussed: the availability and price of the basic electronic technology, the various government and industry rules and standards, the current and future market conditions, and the manufacturing process.

In this chapter one can see the result of the interaction of these various forces in the evolution of the PDP-11. Twelve distinct models (LSI-11, PDP-11/04, 11/05, 11/20, 11/34, 11/34C, 11/40, 11/45, 11/55, 11/60, 11/70, and VAX-11/780) exist in 1978.

The PDP-11 has been successful in the marketplace: over 50,000 were sold in the first eight years that it was on the market (1970–1977). It is not clear how rigorous a test (aside from the marketplace) the design has been given, since a large and aggressive marketing organization, armed with software to correct architectural inconsistencies and omissions, can save almost any design.

Many ideas from the PDP-11 have migrated to other computers with newer designs. Although some of the features of the PDP-11 are patented, machines have been made with similar bus and instruction set processor structures. Many computer designers have adopted a unified data and address bus similar to the Unibus as their fundamental architectural component. Many microprocessor designs incorporate the PDP-11 Unibus notion of mapping I/O and control registers into the memory address space, eliminating the need for I/O instructions without complicating the I/O control logic.

It is the nature of computer engineering to be goal-oriented, with pressure to produce deliverable products. It is therefore difficult to plan for an extensive lifetime. Nevertheless, the PDP-11 evolved rapidly over a much wider range than expected. An outline of a family plan was set forth in a memo on April 3, 1969, by Roger Cady, head of the PDP-11 engineering group at the time (Table 1). The actual evolution is shown in tree form in Figure 1 and is mapped onto a cost/performance representation in Figure 2.

Table 1. PDP-11 Family Projection as of April 3, 1969

Model	Processor	Logic Power	Arithmetic Power	Speed (μs)	Price ($K)	Configuration	Software Paper Tape	Disk
11/10	—	0.7	0.7	2-3	4	Technologically cost reduced 11/20 with Mos		
11/20	KA11	1	1	2.2	5.2	Pc, 1-Kbyte ROM, 128 byte R/W turnkey console		
11/30	KA11	1	1	2.2	9.3	Pc, 8-Kbyte core, console, TTY	Assembler, editor, math utility FOCAL, BASIC, ASA BASIC ‡ FORTRAN)	8-like monitor (system builder w/ODT, DDT, PIP)†
11/40	KB11	2*	10-20	1.2	13	Adds * , / , normal-ize, etc. possible microprogrammed processor, no EAE saves $1,000	Possible 16-Kbyte FORTRAN IV improved assembler	FORTRAN IV
11/45	KB11	2*	10-20	1.2	15 + disk	11/45 with memory protect/relocate maximum core 262 Kbyte, maximum physical memory (using disk) 2^{22} bytes	—	Super monitor** 65-Kbyte virtual memory/user for either small or large disk
11/50	KC11	2*	50-100	1.2	25	Adds hardware floating point 32-bit processor, 16-bit memory (16 Kbyte)	—	—
11/55	KC11	2*	50-100	1.2	27 + disk	With memory protect/relocate		
11/65	KD11	4	100-200	1.2 32-bit	45 + disk	32-bit separate memory bus, 32-bit processor		

NOTES:

*If microprogrammed, then logical power could be tailored to user and go to 20-50, 40-100 for 11/65.

†Business language system under consideration.

‡Possible by-product of FOCAL.

**Super monitor for 11/45, 11/55, 11/65 is priority multi-user real-time system.

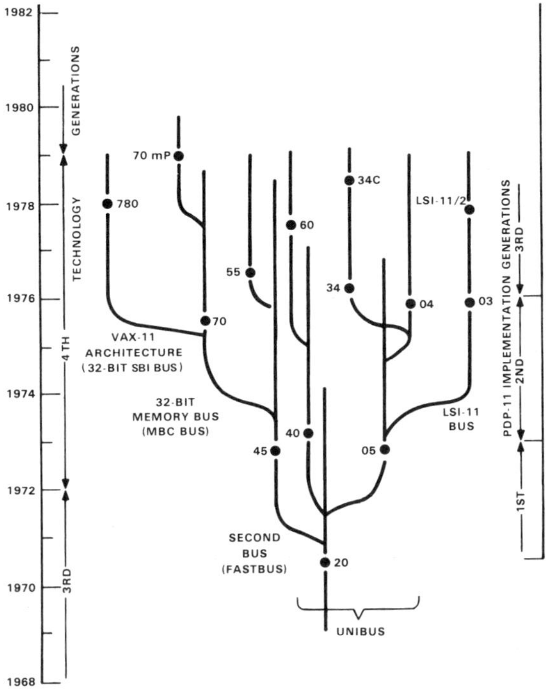

Figure 1. The PDP-11 Family tree.

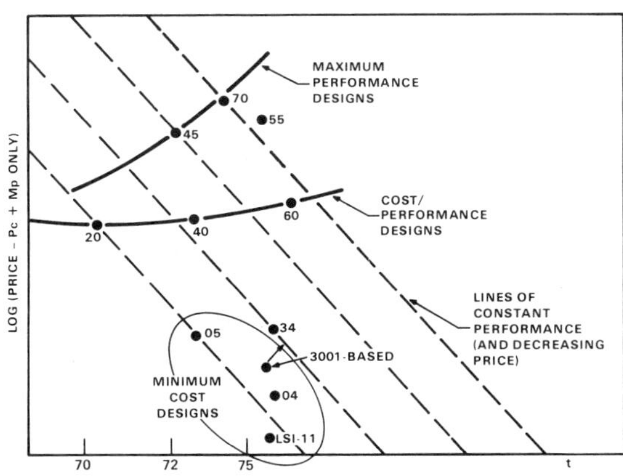

Figure 2. PDP-11 models price versus time with lines of constant performance.

EVALUATION AGAINST THE ORIGINAL GOALS

In the original 1970 PDP-11 paper (Chapter 9), a set of design goals and constraints were given, beginning with a discussion of the weaknesses frequently found in minicomputers. The designers of the PDP-11 faced each of these known minicomputer weaknesses, and their goals included a solution to each one. This section reviews the original goals, commenting on the success or failure of the PDP-11 in meeting each of them.

The weaknesses of prior designs that were noted were limited addressability, a small number of registers, absence of hardware stack facilities, limited interrupt structures, absence of byte string handling and read-only memory facilities, elementary I/O processing, absence of growth-path family members, and high programming costs.

The first weakness of minicomputers was their limited addressing capability. The biggest (and most common) mistake that can be made in a computer design is that of not providing enough address bits for memory addressing and management. The PDP-11 followed this hallowed tradition of skimping on address bits, but it was saved by the principle that a good design can evolve through at least one major change.

For the PDP-11, the limited address problem was solved for the short run, but not with enough finesse to support a large family of minicomputers. That was indeed a costly oversight, resulting in both redundant development and lost sales. It is extremely embarassing that the PDP-11 had to be redesigned with memory management* only two years after writing the paper that outlined the goal of providing increased address space. All earlier DEC designs suffered from the same problem, and only the

*The memory management served two other functions besides expanding the 16-bit processor-generated addresses into 18-bit Unibus addresses: program relocation and protection.

PDP-10 evolved over a long period (15 years) before a change occurred to increase its address space. In retrospect, it is clear that another address bit is required every two or three years, since memory prices decline about 30 percent yearly, and users tend to buy constant price successor systems.

A second weakness of minicomputers was their tendency to skimp on registers. This was corrected for the PDP-11 by providing eight 16-bit registers. Later, six 64-bit registers were added as the accumulators for floating-point arithmetic. This number seems to be adequate: there are enough registers to allocate two or three registers (beyond those already dedicated to program counter and stack pointer) for program global purposes and still have registers for local statement computation.* More registers would increase the context switch time and worsen the register allocation problem for the user.

A third weakness of minicomputers was their lack of hardware stack capability. In the PDP-11, this was solved with the autoincrement/autodecrement addressing mechanism. This solution is unique to the PDP-11, has proved to be exceptionally useful, and has been copied by other designers. The stack limit check, however, has not been widely used by DEC operating systems.

A fourth weakness, limited interrupt capability and slow context switching, was essentially solved by the Unibus interrupt vector design. The basic mechanism is very fast, requiring only four memory cycles from the time an interrupt request is issued until the first instruction of the interrupt routine begins execution. Implementations could go further and save the general registers, for example, in memory or in special registers. This was not specified in the architecture and has not been done in any of the implementations to date. VAX-11 provides explicit load and save process context instructions.

A fifth weakness of earlier minicomputers, inadequate character handling capability, was met in the PDP-11 by providing direct byte addressing capability. String instructions were not provided in the hardware, but the common string operations (move, compare, concatenate) could be programmed with very short loops. Early benchmarks showed that this mechanism was adequate. However, as COBOL compilers have improved and as more understanding of operating systems string handling has been obtained, a need for a string instruction set was felt, and in 1977 such a set was added.

A sixth weakness, the inability to use read-only memories as primary memory, was avoided in the PDP-11. Most code written for the PDP-11 tends to be reentrant without special effort by the programmer, allowing a read-only memory (ROM) to be used directly. Read-only memories are used extensively for bootstrap loaders, program debuggers, and for simple functions. Because large read-only memories were not available at the time of the original design, there are no architectural components designed specifically with large ROMs in mind.

A seventh weakness, one common to many minicomputers, was primitive I/O capabilities. The PDP-11 answers this to a certain extent with its improved interrupt structure, but the completely general solution of I/O computers has not yet been implemented. The I/O processor concept is used extensively in display processors, in communication processors, and in signal processing. Having a single machine instruction that transmits a block of data at the interrupt level would decrease the central processor overhead per character by a factor of 3; it

* Since dedicated registers are used for each Commercial Instruction Set (CIS) instruction, this was no longer true when CIS was added.

should have been added to the PDP-11 instruction set for implementation on all machines. Provision was made in the 11/60 for invocation of a micro-level interrupt service routine in writable control store (WCS), but the family architecture is yet to be extended in this direction.

Another common minicomputer weakness was the lack of system range. If a user had a system running on a minicomputer and wanted to expand it or produce a cheaper turnkey version, he frequently had no recourse, since there were often no larger and smaller models with the same architecture. The PDP-11 has been very successful in meeting this goal.

A ninth weakness of minicomputers was the high cost of programming caused by programming in lower level languages. Many users programmed in assembly language, without the comfortable environment of high-level languages, editors, file systems, and debuggers available on bigger systems. The PDP-11 does not seem to have overcome this weakness, although it appears that more complex systems are being successfully built with the PDP-11 than with its predecessors, the PDP-8 and the PDP-15. Some systems programming is done using higher level languages; however, the optimizing compiler for BLISS-11 at first ran only on the PDP-10. The use of BLISS has been slowly gaining acceptance. It was first used in implementing the FORTRAN-IV PLUS (optimizing) compiler. Its use in PDP-10 and VAX-11 systems programming has been more widespread.

One design constraint that turned out to be expensive, but worth it in the long run, was the necessity for the word length to be a multiple of eight bits. Previous DEC designs were oriented toward 6-bit characters, and DEC had a large investment in 12-, 18-, and 36-bit systems, as described in Parts II and V.

Microprogrammability was not an explicit design goal, partially because fast, large, and inexpensive read-only memories were not available at the time of the first implementation. All subsequent machines have been microprogrammed, but with some difficulty because some parts of the instruction set processor, such as condition code setting and instruction register decoding, are not ideally matched to microprogrammed control.

The design goal of understandability seems to have received little attention. The PDP-11 was initially a hard machine to understand and was marketable only to those with extensive computer experience. The first programmers' handbook was not very helpful. It is still unclear whether a user without programming experience can learn the machine solely from the handbook. Fortunately, several computer science textbooks [Gear, 1974; Eckhouse, 1975; Stone and Siewiorek, 1975] and other training books have been written based on the PDP-11.

Structural flexibility (modularity) for hardware configurations was an important goal. This succeeded beyond expectations and is discussed extensively in the Unibus Cost and Performance section.

EVOLUTION OF THE INSTRUCTION SET PROCESSOR

Designing the instruction set processor level of a machine – that collection of characteristics such as the set of data operators, addressing modes, trap and interrupt sequences, register organization, and other features visible to a programmer of the bare machine – is an extremely difficult problem. One has to consider the performance (and price) ranges of the machine family as well as the intended applications, and difficult tradeoffs must be made. For example, a wide performance range argues for different encodings over the range; for small systems a byte-oriented approach with small addresses is optimal, whereas larger systems require more operation codes, more registers, and larger addresses. Thus, for larger machines, instruction coding efficiency can be traded for performance.

The PDP-11 was originally conceived as a small machine, but over time its range was gradually extended so that there is now a factor of 500 in price ($500 to $250,000) and memory size (8 Kbytes to 4 Mbytes*) between the smallest and largest models. This range compares favorably with the range of the IBM System 360 family (16 Kbytes to 4 Mbytes). Needless to say, a number of problems have arisen as the basic design was extended.

Chronology of the Extensions

A chronology of the extensions is given in Table 2. Two major extensions, the memory management and the floating point, occurred with the 11/45. The most recent extension is the Commercial Instruction Set, which was defined to enhance performance for the character string and decimal arithmetic data-types of the commercial languages (e.g., COBOL). It introduced the following to the PDP-11 architecture:

1. Data-types representing character sets, character strings, packed decimal strings, and zoned decimal strings.
2. Strings of variable length up to 65 Kcharacters.
3. Instructions for processing character strings in each data-type (move, add, subtract, multiply, divide).
4. Instructions for converting among binary integers, packed decimal strings, and zoned decimal strings.
5. Instructions to move the descriptors for the variable length strings.

The initial design did not have enough operation code space to accommodate instructions for new data-types. Ideally, the complete set of operation codes should have been specified at initial design time so that extensions would fit. With this approach, the uninterpreted operation codes could have been used to call the various operation functions, such as a floating-point addition. This would have avoided the proliferation of run-time support systems for the various hardware/software floating-point arithmetic methods (Extended Arithmetic Element, Extended Instruction Set, Floating Instruction Set, Floating-Point Processor). The extracode technique was used in the Atlas and Scientific Data Systems (SDS) designs, but these techniques are overlooked by most computer designers. Because the complete instruction set processor (or at least an extension framework) was unspecified in the initial design, completeness and orthogonality have been sacrificed.

At the time the PDP-11/45 was designed, several operation code extension schemes were examined: an escape mode to add the floating-point operations, bringing the PDP-11 back to being a more conventional general register machine by reducing the number of addressing modes, and finally, typing the data by adding a global mode that could be switched to select floating point instead of byte operations for the same operation codes. The floating-point instruction set, introduced with the 11/45, is a version of the second alternative.

It also became necessary to do something about the small address space of the processor. The Unibus limits the physical memory to the 262,144 bytes addressable by 18-bits. In the PDP-11/70, the physical address was extended to 4 Mbytes by providing a Unibus map so that devices in a 256 Kbyte Unibus space could transfer into the 4-Mbyte space via mapping registers. While the physical address limits are acceptable for both the Unibus and larger systems, the address for a single program is still confined to an instantaneous space of 16 bits, the user virtual address. The main method of

*Although 22 bits are used, only 2 megabytes can be utilized in the 11/70.

Table 2. Chronology of PDP-11 Instruction Set Processor (ISP) Evolution

Model(s)	Evolution
11/20	Base ISP (16-bit virtual address) and PMS (16-bit processor physical memory address) Unibus with 18-bit addressing
11/20	Extended Arithmetic Element (hardware multiply/divide)
11/45 (11/55,11/70, 11/60,11/34)	Floating-point instruction set with 6 additional registers (46 instructions) in the Floating-Point Processor
11/45 (11/55,11/70)	Memory management (KT11C), 3 modes of protection (Kernel, Supervisor, User); 18-bit processor physical addressing; 16-bit virtual addressing in 8 segments for both instruction and data spaces
11/45 (11/55,11/70)	Extensions for second set of general registers and program interrupt request
11/40 (11/03)	Extended Instruction Set for multiply/divide; floating-point instruction set (4 instructions)
11/40 (11/34,11/60)	Memory Management (KT11D), 2 modes of protection (Kernel, User); 18-bit processor physical addressing; 16-bit virtual addressing in 8 segments
11/70	22-bit processor physical addressing; Unibus map for peripheral controller 22-bit addressing
11/70 (11/60)	Error register accessibility for on-line diagnosis and retry (e.g., cache parity error)
11/03 (11/04,11/34)	Program access to processor status register via explicit instruction (versus Unibus address)
11/03	One level program interrupt
11/60	Extended Function Code for invocation of user-written microcode
VAX-11/780	VAX architectural extensions for 32-bit virtual addressing; VAX ISP
11/03	Commercial Instruction Set (CIS)
11/70mP	Interprocessor Interrupt and System Timers for multiprocessor

dealing with relatively small addresses is via process-oriented operating systems that handle many small tasks. This is a trend in operating systems, especially for process control and transaction processing. It does, however, enforce a structuring discipline in (user) program organization. The RSX-11 series of operating systems for the PDP-11 are organized this way, and the need for large addresses is lessened.

The initial memory management proposal to extend the virtual memory was predicated on dynamic, rather than static, assignment of memory segment registers. In the current memory management scheme, the address registers are usually considered to be static for a task (although some operating systems provide functions to get additional segments dynamically).

With dynamic assignment, a user can address a number of segment names, via a table, and directly load the appropriate segment registers. The segment registers act to concatenate additional address bits in a base address fashion. There have been other schemes proposed that extend the addresses by extending the length of the general registers – of course, extended addresses propagate throughout the design and include double length address variables. In effect, the extended part is loaded with a base address.

With larger machines and process-oriented operating systems, the context switching time becomes an important performance factor. By providing additional registers for more processes, the time (overhead) to switch context from one process (task) to another can be reduced. This option has not been used in the operating system implementations of the PDP-11s to date, although the 11/45 extensions included a second set of general registers. Various alternatives have been suggested, and to accomplish this effectively requires additional operators to handle the many aspects of process scheduling. This extension appears to be relatively unimportant since the range of computers coupled with networks tends to alleviate the need by increasing the real parallelism (as opposed to the apparent parallelism) by having various independent processors work on the separate processes in parallel. The extensions of the PDP-11 for better control of I/O devices is clearly more important in terms of improved performance.

Architecture Management

In retrospect, many of the problems associated with PDP-11 evolution were due to the lack of an ongoing architecture management function. As can be seen from Table 1, the notion of planned evolution was very strong at the beginning. However, a formal architecture control function was not set up until early in 1974. In some sense this was already too late – the four PDP-11 models designed by that date (11/20, 11/05, 11/40, 11/45) had incompatibilities between them. The architecture control function since then has ensured that no further divergence (except in the LSI-11) took place in subsequent models, and in fact resulted in some convergence. At the time the Commercial Instruction Set was added, an architecture extension framework was adopted. Insufficient encodings existed to provide a large number of additional instructions using the same encoding style (in the same space) as the basic PDP-11, i.e., the operation code and operand specifier addressing mode specifiers within a single 16-bit word. An instruction extension framework was adopted which utilized a full word as the opcode, with operand addressing mode specifiers in succeeding instruction stream words along the lines of VAX-11. This architectural extension permits 512 additional opcodes, and instructions may have an unlimited number of operand addressing mode specifiers. The architecture control function also had to deal with the Unibus address space problem.

With VAX-11, architecture management has been in place since the beginning. A definition of the architecture was placed under formal change control well before the VAX-11/780 was built, and both hardware and software engineering groups worked with the same document. Another significant difference is that an extension framework was defined in the original architecture.

An Evaluation

The criteria used to decide whether or not to include a particular capability in an instruction set are highly variable and border on the artistic.* Critics ask that the machine appear elegant, where elegance is a combined quality of instruction formats relating to mnemonic significance, operator/data-type completeness and orthogonality, and addressing consistency. Having completely general facilities (e.g., registers) which are not context dependent assists in minimizing the number of instruction types and in increasing understandability (and usefulness). The authors feel that the PDP-11 has provided this.

At the time the Unibus was designed, it was felt that allowing 4 Kbytes of the address space for I/O control registers was more than enough. However, so many different devices have been interfaced to the bus over the years that it is no longer possible to assign unique addresses to every device. The architectural group has thus been saddled with the chore of device address bookkeeping. Many solutions have been proposed, but none was soon enough; as a result, they are all so costly that it is cheaper just to live with the problem and the attendant inconvenience.

Techniques for generating code by the human and compiler vary widely and thus affect instruction set processor design. The PDP-11 provides more addressing modes than nearly any other computer. The eight modes for source

*Today one would use the *S*, *M*, and *R* measures and methodology defined in Appendix 3.

and destination with dyadic operators provide what amounts to 64 possible ADD instructions. By associating the Program Counter and Stack Pointer registers with the modes, even more data accessing methods are provided. For example, 18 varieties of the MOVE instruction can be distinguished as the machine is used in two-address, general register, and stack machine program forms. (There is a price for this generality – namely, fewer bits could have been used to encode the address modes that are actually used most of the time.)

How the PDP-11 Is Used

In general, the PDP-11 has been used mostly as a general register (i.e., memory to registers) machine. This can be seen by observing the use frequency from Strecker's data (Chapter 14). In one case, it was observed that a user who previously used a one-accumulator computer (e.g., PDP-8), continued to do so. A general register machine provides the greatest performance, and the cost (in terms of bits) is the same as when used as a stack machine. Some compilers, particularly the early ones, are stack oriented since the code production is easier. In principle, and with much care, a fast stack machine could be constructed. However, since most stack machines use primary memory for the stack, there is a loss of performance even if the top of the stack is cached. While a stack is the natural (and necessary) structure to interpret the nested block structure languages, it does not necessarily follow that the interpretation of all statements should occur in the context of the stack. In particular, the predominance of register transfer statements are of the simple 2- and 3-address forms:

$$D \leftarrow S$$

and

$$D1(\text{index } 1) \leftarrow f(S2(\text{index } 2), S3(\text{index } 3)).$$

These do not require the stack organization. In effect, appropriate assignment allows a general register machine to be used as a stack machine for most cases of expression evaluation. This has the advantage of providing temporary, random access to common subexpressions, a capability that is usually hard to exploit in stack architectures.

THE EVOLUTION OF THE PMS (MODULAR) STRUCTURE

The end product of the PDP-11 design is the computer itself, and in the evolution of the architecture one can see images of the evolution of ideas. In this section, the architectural evolution is outlined, with a special emphasis on the Unibus.

The Unibus is the architectural component that connects together all of the other major components. It is the vehicle over which data flow between pairs of components takes place. Its structure is described in Chapter 11.

In general, the Unibus has met all expectations. Several hundred types of memories and peripherals have been interfaced to it; it has become a standard architectural component of systems in the \$3K to \$100K price range (1975). The Unibus does limit the performance of the fastest machines and penalizes the lower performance machines with a higher cost. Recently it has become clear that the Unibus is adequate for large, high performance systems when a cache structure is used because the cache reduces the traffic between primary memory and the central processor since about one-tenth of the memory references are outside the cache. For still larger systems, supplementary buses were added for central processor to primary memory and primary memory to secondary memory traffic. For very small systems like the LSI-11, a narrower bus was designed.

The Unibus, as a standard, has provided an architectural component for easily configuring systems. Any company, not just DEC, can easily build components that interface to the bus. Good buses make good engineering neighbors, since people can concentrate on structured design. Indeed, the Unibus has created a secondary industry providing alternative sources of supply for memories and peripherals. With the exception of the IBM 360 Multiplexer/Selector Bus, the Unibus is the most widely used computer interconnection standard.

The Unibus has also turned out to be invaluable as an "umbilical cord" for factory diagnostic and checkout procedures. Although such a capability was not part of the original design, the Unibus is almost capable of controlling the system components (e.g., processor and memory) during factory checkout. Ideally, the scheme would let all registers be accessed during full operation. This is possible for all devices except the processor. By having all central processor registers available for reading and writing in the same way that they are available from the console switches, a second system can fully monitor the computer under test.

In most recent PDP-11 models, a serial communications line, called the ASCII Console, is connected to the console, so that a program may remotely examine or change any information that a human operator could examine or change from the front panel, even when the system is not running. In this way computers can be diagnosed from a remote site.

Difficulties with the Design

The Unibus design is not without problems. Although two of the bus bits were set aside in the original design as parity bits, they have not been widely used as such. Memory parity was implemented directly in the memory; this phenomenon is a good example of the sorts of problems encountered in engineering optimization. The trading of bus parity for memory parity exchanged higher hardware cost and decreased performance for decreased service cost and better data integrity. Because engineers are usually judged on how well they achieve production cost goals, parity transmission is an obvious choice to pare from a design, since it increases the cost and decreases the performance. As logic costs decrease and pressure to include warranty costs as part of the product design cost increases, the decision to transmit parity may be reconsidered.

Early attempts to build tightly coupled multiprocessor or multicomputer structures (by mapping the address space of one Unibus onto the memory of another), called Unibus windows, were beset with a logic deadlock problem. The Unibus design does not allow more than one master at a time. Successful multiprocessors required much more sophisticated sharing mechanisms such as shared primary memory.

Unibus Cost and Performance

Although performance is always a design goal, so is low cost; the two goals conflict directly. The Unibus has turned out to be nearly optimum over a wide range of products. It served as an adequate memory-processor interconnect for six of the ten models. However, in the smallest system, DEC introduced the LSI-11 Bus, which uses about half the number of conductors. For the largest systems, a separate 32-bit data path is used between processor and memory, although the Unibus is still used for communication with the majority of the I/O controllers (the slower ones). Figure 1 summarizes the evolution of memory-processor interconnections in the LSI-11 Family. Levy (Chapter 11) discusses the evolution in more detail.

The bandwidth of the Unibus is approximately 1.7 megabytes per second or 850 K transfers/second. Only for the largest configurations, using many I/O devices with very high data rates, is this capacity exceeded. For most configurations, the demand put on an I/O bus is limited by the rotational delay and head positioning of disks and the rate at which programs (user and system) issue I/O requests.

An experiment to further the understanding of Unibus capacity and the demand placed against it was carried out. The experiment used a synthetic workload; like all synthetic workloads, it can be challenged as not being representative. However, it was generally agreed that it was a heavy I/O load. The load simulated transaction processing, swapping, and background computing in the configuration shown in Figure 3. The load was run on five systems, each placing a different demand on the Unibus.

Each run produced two numbers: (1) the time to complete 2,000 transactions, and (2) the number of iterations of a program called HANOI that were completed.

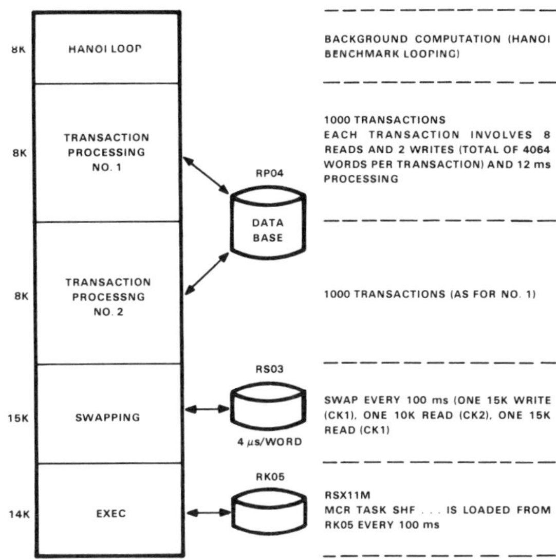

Figure 3. The synthetic workload used to measure Unibus capacity.

System	Benchmark Time (minutes)*	Number of HANOI Iterations
11/60 cache on	15	12
11/60 cache off	15	2
11/40	15	3
11/70 MBCBUS	15	23
11/70 Unibus	26	38

*2,000 transactions plus swapping plus HANOI.

The results were interpreted as follows:

1. **I/O throughput**. For this workload the Unibus bandwidth was adequate. For systems 1 through 4 the I/O activity took the same amount of time.
2. **11/70 Unibus.** The run on this system (no use was made of the 32-bit wide processor/memory bus) took longer because of the retries caused by data lates (approximately 19,000) on the moving head disk (RP04). The extra time taken for the benchmark allowed more iterations of HANOI to occur. The PDP-11/70 Unibus had a bandwidth of about 1 megabyte. It was less than the usual Unibus (about 1.7 megabyte) because of the map delay (100 nanoseconds), the cache cycle (240 nanoseconds), and the main memory bus redriving and synchronization.
3. **11/60 Cache**. Systems 1 and 2 clearly show the effectiveness of a cache. Most memory references for HANOI were to the cache and did not involve the Unibus, which was the PDP-11/60s I/O Bus. Systems 2 and 3 were essentially equivalent, as expected. There are two reasons for the 11/40 having slightly more compute bandwidth than an 11/60 with its cache off. First, the 11/40 memory is faster than the 11/60 backing store, and second, the 11/40 processor relinquishes the Unibus for a direct memory access cycle; the 11/60 processor must request the Unibus for a processor cycle.

There are several attributes of a bus that affect its cost and performance. One factor affecting performance is simply the data rate of a single conductor. There is a direct tradeoff involving cost, performance, and reliability. Shannon [1948] gives a relationship between the fundamental signal bandwidth of a link and the error rate (signal-to-noise ratio) and data rate. The performance and cost of a bus are also affected by its length. Longer cables cost proportionately more, since they require more complex circuitry to drive the bus.

Since a single-conductor link has a fixed data rate, the number of conductors affects the net speed of a bus. However, the cost of a bus is directly proportional to the number of conductors. For a given number of wires, time domain multiplexing and data encoding can be used to trade performance and logic complexity. Since logic technology is advancing faster than wiring technology, it seems likely that fewer conductors will be used in all future systems, except where the performance penalty of time domain multiplexing is unacceptably great.

If, during the original design of the Unibus, DEC designers could have foreseen the wide range of applications to which it would be applied, its design would have been different. Individual controllers might have been reduced in complexity by more central control. For the largest and smallest systems, it would have been useful to have a bus that could be contracted or expanded by multiplexing or expanding the number of conductors.

The cost-effectiveness of the Unibus is due in large part to the high correlation between memory size, number of address bits, I/O traffic, and processor speed. Gene Amdahl's rule of thumb for IBM computers is that 1 byte of memory and 1 byte/sec of I/O are required for each instruction/sec. For traditional DEC applications, with emphasis in the scientific and control applications, there is more computation required per memory word. Further, the PDP-11 instruction sets do not contain the extensive commercial instructions (character strings) typical of IBM computers, so a larger number of instructions must be executed to accomplish the same task. Hence, for DEC computers, it is better to assume 1 byte of memory for each 2 instructions/sec, and that 1 byte/sec of I/O occurs for each instruction/sec.

In the PDP-11, an average instruction accesses 3–5 bytes of memory, so assuming 1 byte of I/O for each instruction/sec, there are 4–6 bytes of memory accessed on the average for each instruction/sec. Therefore, a bus that can support 2 megabytes/sec of traffic permits instruction execution rates of 0.33–0.5 mega-instructions/sec. This implies memory sizes of 0.16–0.25 megabytes, which matches well with the maximum allowable memory of 0.064–0.256 megabytes. By using a cache memory on the processor, the effective memory processor rate can be increased to balance the system further. If fast floating-point instructions were added to the instruction set, the balance might approach that used by IBM and thereby require more memory (an effect seen in the PDP-11/70).

The task of I/O is to provide for the transfer of data from peripheral to primary memory where it can be operated on by a program in a processor. The peripherals are generally slow, inherently asynchronous, and more error-prone than the processors to which they are attached.

Historically, I/O transfer mechanisms have evolved through the following four stages:

1. **Direct sequential I/O under central processor control.** An instruction in the processor causes a data transfer to take place with a device. The processor does not resume operation until the transfer is complete. Typically, the device control may share the logic of the processor. The first input/output transfer (IOT) instruction in the PDP-1 is an example; the IOT effects transfer between the Accumulator and a selected device. Direct I/O simplifies programming because every operation is sequential.

2. **Fixed buffer, 1-instruction controllers.** An instruction in the central processor causes a data transfer (of a word or vector), but in this case, it is to a buffer of the simple controller and thus at a speed matching that of the processor. After the high speed transfer has occurred, the processor continues while an asynchronous, slower transfer occurs between the buffer and the device. Communication back to the processor is via the program interrupt mechanism. A single instruction to a simple controller can also cause a complete block (vector) of data to be transmitted between memory and the peripheral. In this case, the transfer takes place via the direct memory access (DMA) link.
3. **Separate I/O processors – the channel.** An independent I/O processor with a unique ISP controls the flow of data between primary memory and the peripheral. The structure is that of the multiprocessor, and the I/O control program for the device is held in primary memory. The central processor informs the I/O processor about the I/O program location.
4. **I/O computer.** This mechanism is also asynchronous with the central processor, but the I/O computer has a private memory which holds the I/O program. Recently, DEC communications options have been built with embedded control programs. The first example of an I/O computer was in the CDC 6600 (1964).

The authors believe that the single-instruction controller is superior to the I/O processor as embodied in the IBM Channel mainly because the latter concept has not gone far enough. Channels are costly to implement, sufficiently complex to require their own programming environment, and yet not quite powerful enough to assume the processing, such as file management, that one would like to offload from the processor. Although the I/O traffic does require central processor resources, the addition of a second, general purpose central processor is more cost-effective than using a central processor-I/O processor or central processor-multiple I/O processor structure. Future I/O systems will be message-oriented, and the various I/O control functions (including diagnostics and file management) will migrate to the subsystem. When the I/O computer is an exact duplicate of the central processor, not only is there an economy from the reduced number of part types but also the same programming environment can be used for I/O software development and main program development. Notice that the I/O computer must implement precisely the same set of functions as the processor doing direct I/O.*

MULTIPROCESSORS

It is not surprising that multiprocessors are used only in highly specialized applications such as those requiring high reliability or high availability. One way to extend the range of a family and also provide more performance alternatives with fewer basic components is to build multiprocessors. In this section some factors affecting the design and implementation of multiprocessors, and their effect on the PDP-11, are examined.

It is the nature of engineering to be conservative. Given that there are already a number of risks involved in bringing a product to the market, it is not clear why one should build a higher risk structure that may require a new way of programming. What has resulted is a sort of deadlock situation: people cannot learn how to program multiprocessors and employ them in a

*The I/O computer is yet another example of the wheel of reincarnation of display processors (see Chapter 7).

single task until such machines exist, but manufacturers will not build the machine until they are sure that there will be a demand for it, i.e., that the programs will be ready.

There is little or no market for multiprocessors even though there is a need for increased reliability and availability of machines. IBM has not promoted multiprocessors in the marketplace, and hence the market has lagged.

One reason that there is so little demand for multiprocessors is the widespread acceptance of the philosophy that a better single-processor system can always be built. This approach achieves performance at the considerable expense of spare parts, training, reliability, and flexibility. Although a multiprocessor architecture provides a measure of reliability, backup, and system tunability unreachable on a conventional system, the biggest and fastest machines are uniprocessors – except in the case of the Bell Laboratories Safeguard Computer [Bell Laboratories, 1975].

Multiprocessor systems have been built out of PDP-11s. Figure 4 summarizes the design and performance of some of these machines. The topmost structure was built using 11/05 processors, but because of inadequate arbitration techniques in the processor, the expected performance did not materialize. Table 3 shows the expected results for multiple 11/05 processors sharing a single Unibus and compares them with the PDP-11/40.

From the results of Table 3 one would expect to use as many as three 11/05 processors to achieve the performance of a model 11/40. More than three processors will increase the performance at the expense of the cost-effectiveness. This basic structure has been applied on a production basis in the GT40 series of graphics processors for the PDP-11. In this scheme, a second display processor is added to the Unibus for display picture maintenance. A similar structure is used for connecting special signal-processing computers to the Unibus although these structures are technically coupled computers rather than multiprocessors.

As an independent check on the validity of this approach, a multiprocessor system has

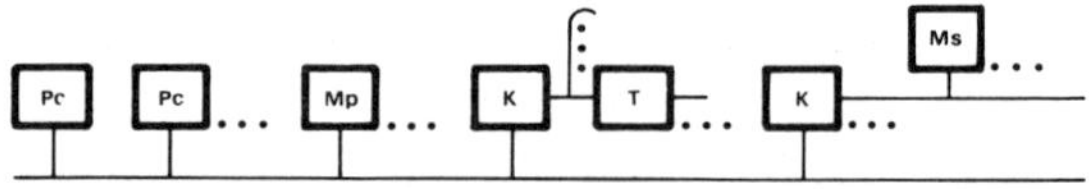

(a) Multi-Pc structure using a single Unibus.

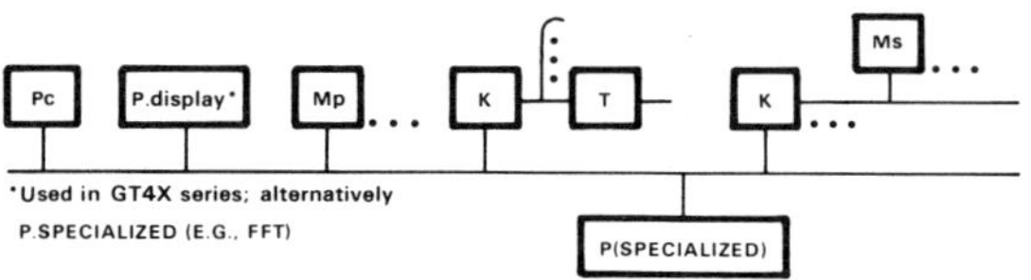

(b) Pc with P.display using a single Unibus.

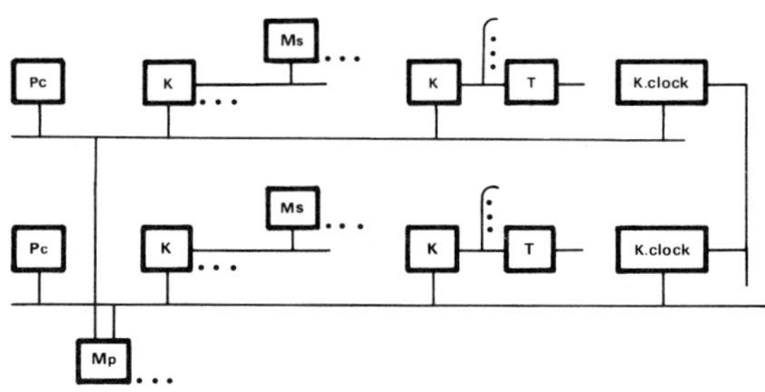

(c) Multiprocessor using multiport Mp.

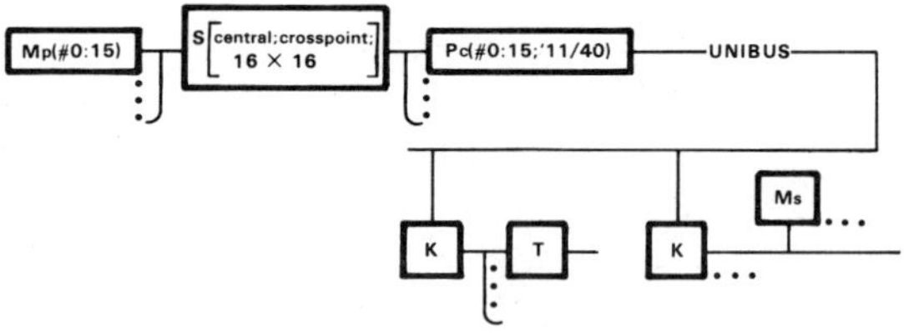

(d) C.mmp CMU multi-miniprocessor computer structure.

Figure 4. PDP-11 multiprocessor PMS structures.

Table 3. Multiple PDP-11/05 Processors Sharing a Single Unibus

Number and Processor Model	Processor Performance (Relative)	Processor Price	Price*/Performance	System Price	Price†/Performance
1–11/05	1.00	1.00	1.00	3.00	1.00
2–11/05	1.85	1.23	0.66	3.23	0.58
3–11/05	2.4	1.47	0.61	3.47	0.48
1–11/40	2.25	1.35	0.60	3.35	0.49

*Processor cost only.
†Total system cost assuming one-third of system is processor cost.

been built, based on the Lockheed SUE [Ornstein *et al.*, 1972]. This machine, used as a high speed communications processor, is a hybrid design: it has seven dual-processor computers with each pair sharing a common bus as outlined above. The seven pairs share two multiport memories.

The second type of structure given in Figure 4 is a conventional, tightly coupled multiprocessor using multiple-port memories. A number of these systems have been installed, and they operate quite effectively. However, they have only been used for specialized applications because there has been no operating system support for the structure.

PDP-11 Based Multiprocessor: Carnegie-Mellon University Research Computers

The PDP-11 architecture has been employed to pioneer new ideas in the area of multiprocessors. The three multiprocessors built at Carnegie-Mellon University (CMU) are discussed: C.mmp [Wulf and Bell, 1972], a 16-processor multiprocessor; C.vmp [Siewiorek *et al.*, 1976], a triplicated, voting multiprocessor computer for high reliability; and Cm* (Chapter 20), a set of computer modules based on LSI-11.

The three CMU multiprocessors are good examples of multiprocessor development directions because it is quite likely that technology will force the evolution of computing structures to converge into three styles of multiprocessor computers: (1) C.mmp style, for high performance, incremental performance, and availability (maintainability); (2) C.vmp style for very high availability motivated by increasing maintenance costs, and (3) loosely coupled computers like Cm* to handle specialized processing, e.g., front end, file, and signal processing. This argument is based on history, present technology, and resulting price extrapolations:

1. MOS technology appears to be increasing in both speed and density faster than the technology (such as ECL) from which high performance machines are usually built.
2. Standards in the semiconductor industry tend to form more quickly for high volume products. For example, in the 8-bit microcomputer market, one type supplies about 50 percent of the market and three types supply over 90 percent.
3. The price per chip of the single MOS chip processors decreases at a substantially greater rate than for the low volume, high performance special designs. Chips in both designs have high design costs, but the single-MOS-chip processors have a much higher volume.

4. Several 16-bit processor-on-a-chip processors, with an address space matching and appropriate data-types matching the performance, exist in 1978. Such a commodity can form the basis for nearly all future computer designs.
5. The performance (instructions per second) per chip, which is already greater for MOS processor chips than for any other kind, is improving more rapidly than for large scale computers. This will pull usage more rapidly into large arrays of processors because of the essentially "free cost" of processors (especially relative to large, low volume custom-built machines).

Therefore, most subsequent computers will be based on standard, high volume parts. For high performance machines, since processing power is available at essentially zero cost from processor-on-a-chip-based processors, large scale computing will come from arrays of processors, just as memory subsystems are built from arrays of 64 Kbit integrated circuits.

The multiprocessor research projects at CMU have emphasized synthesis and measurement. Operating systems have been built for them, and the executions of user programs have been carefully analyzed. All the multiprocessor interferences, overheads, and synchronization problems have been faced for several applications; the resultant performance helps to put their actual costs in perspective. Figure 5 shows the HARPY speech recognition program and compares the performance of C.mmp and Cm* with three DEC uniprocessors (PDP-10 with KA10 processor, PDP-10 with KL10 processor, and PDP-11/40).

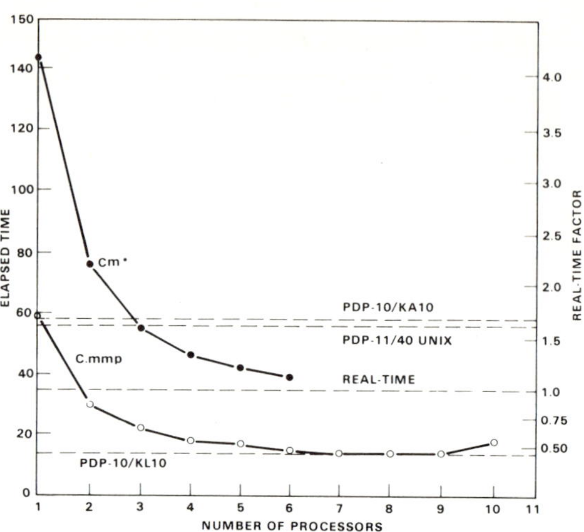

Figure 5. A performance comparison of two multiprocessors, C.mmp and Cm*, with three uniprocessors at Carnegie-Mellon University. The application used is HARPY, a speech recognition program. This graph is based on work done by Peter Oleinick [1978] and Peter Feiler at CMU.

C.mmp

C.mmp (Figure 6) a 16 processor (11/40s and 11/20s) system has 2.5 million words of shared primary memory. It was built to investigate the programming (and resulting performance) questions associated with having a large number of processors. Since the time that the first paper [Wulf and Bell, 1972] was written, C.mmp has been the object of some interesting studies, the results of which are summarized below.

C.mmp was motivated by the need for more computing power to solve speech recognition and signal processing problems and to understand the multiprocessor software problem. Until C.mmp, only one large, tightly coupled multiprocessor had been built – the Bell Laboratories Safeguard Computer [Bell Laboratories, 1975].

The original paper [Wulf and Bell, 1972] describes the economic and technical factors influencing multiprocessor feasibility and argues for the timeliness of the research. Various problems to be researched and a discussion of particular design aspects are given. For example, since C.mmp is predicated on a common operating systems, there are two sources of degradation: memory contention and lock contention.

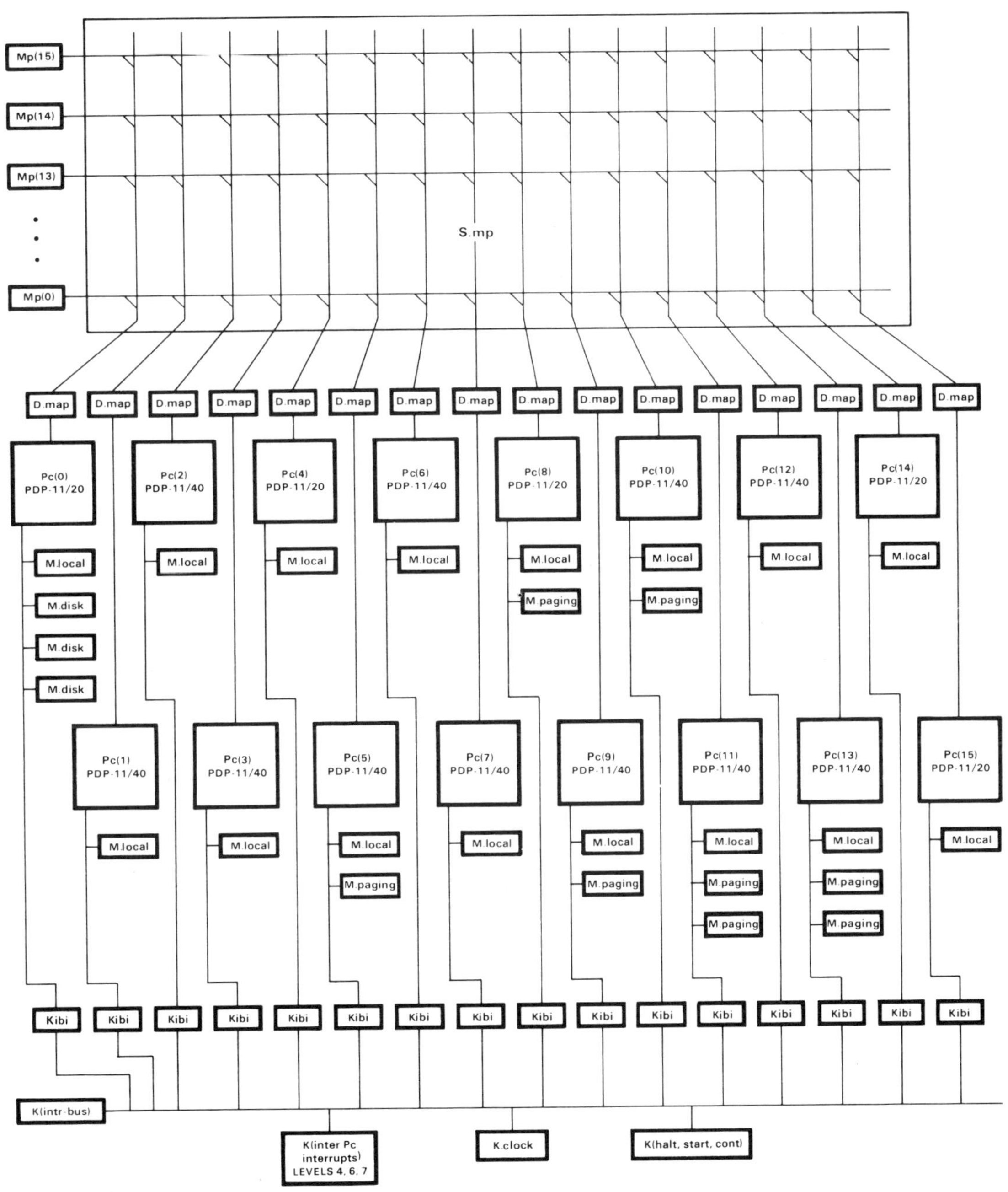

NOTE:
Kibi stands for K(inter-bus-interface).

Figure 6. A PMS diagram of C.mmp (from |Oleinick,1978|).

The machine's theoretical performance as a function of memory-processor interference is based on Strecker's [1970] work. In practice, because the memory was not built with low-order address interleaving, memory interference was greater than expected. This problem was solved by having several copies of the program segments.

As the number of memory modules and processors becomes very large, the theoretical performance (as measured by the number of accesses to the memory by the processors) approaches half the memory bandwidth (i.e., the number of memory modules memory cycle time) [Baskett and Smith, 1976]. Thus, with infinite processors, there is no maximum limit on performance, provided all processors are not contending for the same memory.

Although there is a discussion in the original paper outlining the design direction of the operating system, HYDRA, later descriptions should be read [Wulf *et al.,* 1975]. Since the small address of the PDP-11 necessitated frequent map changes, PDP-11/40s with writable control stores were used to implement the operating systems calls which change the segment base registers.

There are three basic approaches to the effective application of multiprocessors:

1. System level workload decomposition. If a workload contains a lot of inherently independent activities, e.g., compilation, editing, file processing, and numerical computation, it will naturally decompose.
2. Program decomposition by a programmer. Intimate knowledge of the application is required for this time-consuming approach.
3. Program decomposition by the compiler. This is the ideal approach. However, results to date have not been especially noteworthy.

C.mmp was predicated on the first two approaches. ALGOL 68, a language with facilities for expressing parallelism in programs, has since been implemented. It has assisted greatly with program decomposition and looks like a promising general approach. It is imperative, however, to extend the standard languages to handle vectors and arrays.

The contention for shared resources in a multiprocessor system occurs at several levels. At the lowest level, processors contend at the cross-point switch level for memory. On a higher level there is contention for shared data in the operating system kernel; processes contend for I/O devices and for software processes, e.g., for memory management. At the user level shared data implies further contention. Table 4 points to models on experimental data at these different levels.

Marathe's data show that the shared data of HYDRA is organized into enough separate objects so that a very small degradation (less than 1 percent) results from contention for these objects. He also built a queueing model which projected that the contention level would be about 5 percent in a 48 processor system.

Oleinick [1978] has used C.mmp to conduct an experimental, as opposed to theoretical, study of the implementation of parallel algorithms on a multiprocessor. He studied the operation of Rootfinder, a program that is an

Table 4. References for Experimental Data on Contention at Each of Three Levels in the C.mmp System

Contention Level	Reference
User-program	Oleinick [1978] Fuller and Oleinick [1976]
HYDRA kernel objects	Marathe and Fuller [1977]
Cross-point switch	Baskett and Smith [1976] Fuller [1976] Strecker [1970] Wulf and Bell [1972]

extension of the bisection method for finding the roots of an equation.

A natural decomposition of the binary search for a root into n parallel processes is to evaluate the function simultaneously at n points. Under ideal conditions, all processes would finish the function evaluation (required at each step) at the same time, and then some brief bookkeeping would take place to determine the next subinterval for the n processes to work on. However, because the time to evaluate the function is data dependent, some processes are completed before others. Moreover, if the bookkeeping task is time consuming relative to the time to evaluate the function, the speedup ratio will suffer. Oleinick systematically studied each source of fluctuation in performance and found the dominant one to be the mechanism used for process synchronization.

Four different locks for process synchronization, called: (1) spin lock, (2) kernel semaphore, (3) PM0, and (4) PM1, are available to the C.mmp user. The spin lock, the most rudimentary, does not cause an entry to the HYDRA operating system. It is a short sequence of instructions which continually test a semaphore until it can be set successfully. The process of testing for the availability of a resource, and seizing the resource if available, could be called TEST-AND-LOCK. When the resource is no longer needed, it is released by an UNLOCK process. These two processes are called the *P* operation and the *V* operation respectively, as originally named by Edgar Dijkstra. The *P* and *V* operations in the C.mmp spin lock are in fact the following PDP-11 code sequences:

```
P:  CMP SEMAPHORE,
    #1                  ;SEMAPHORE=1?
    BNE P               ;loop until it is 1
    DEC SEMAPHORE       ;Decrement SEMAPHORE
    BNE P               ;If not equal 0 go to P

V:  MOV #1, SEMAPHORE ;Reset SEMAPHORE to 1
```

Although this repeating polling is extremely fast, it has two major drawbacks: first, the processor is not free to do useful work; second, the polling process consumes memory cycles of the memory bank that contains the semaphore.

The kernel semaphore, implemented in HYDRA, is the low level synchronization mechanism intended to be used by system processes. When a process blocks or wakes up, a state change for that process is made inside the kernel of HYDRA. If a process blocks (fails to obtain a needed resource) while trying to P (test and lock) a semaphore, the kernel swaps the process from the processor, and the pages belonging to that process are kept in primary memory. The other semaphore mechanisms (PM0 and PM1) take proportionately more time (>1 millisecond).

C.vmp

C.vmp, is a triplicated, voting multiprocessor designed to understand the difficulty (or ease) of using standard, off-the-shelf LSI-11s to provide greatly increased reliability. There is concern for increased reliability because systems are becoming more complex, are used for more critical applications, and because maintenance costs for all systems are increasing. Because the designers themselves carry out and analyze the work, this section provides first-hand insight into high reliability designs and the design process – especially its evaluation.

Several design goals were set and the work has been carried out. The C.vmp system has operated since late 1977, when the first phase of work was completed.

The goal of software and hardware transparency turned out to be easier to attain than expected, because of an idiosyncrasy of the floppy disk controller. Because the controller effects a word-at-a-time bus transfer from a one-sector buffer, voting can be carried out at a very low level. It is unclear how the system would have been designed without this type of controller; at a minimum, some part of the software transparency goal would not have been met, and a significant controller modification would have been necessary.

A number of models are given by which the design is evaluated. From the discussion of component reliabilities the reader should get some insight into the factors contributing to reliability. It should be noted that a custom-designed LSI voter is needed to get a sufficiently low cost for a marketable C.vmp. While the intent of C.vmp development was not a product, it does provide much of the insight for such a product.

Cm*

Cm* is described in Chapter 20; however, because it is one of the three CMU machines pointing to future technology-driven trends in multiprocessor use of LSI-11 architecture, it is given some mention here. The Cm* work, sponsored by the National Science Foundation (NSF) and the Advanced Research Projects Agency (ARPA), is an extension of earlier NSF-sponsored research [Bell *et al.*, 1973] on register transfer level modules. As large-scale integration and very large-scale integration enable construction of the processor-on-a-chip, it is apparent that low level register transfer modules are obsolete for the construction of all but low volume computers. Although the research is predicated on structures employing a hundred or so processors, Chapter 20 describes the culmination of the first (10-processor) phase.

In Chapter 20 the authors base their work on diseconomy-of-scale arguments. To provide additional context for their research, computer modules (Cm*), multiprocessors (C.mmp), and computer networks are described in terms of performance and problem suitability. They give a description of the modules structure, together with its associated limitations and potential research problems.

The grouping of processor and memory into modules and the hierarchy of bus structures – LSI-11 Bus, Map Bus, and Intercluster bus, radical departures from conventional computer systems – is given. The final, most important part of the chapter evaluates the performance of Cm* for five different problems.

Since the time that Chapter 20 was written, construction of a 50 computer modules Cm* has begun and will be operational by the end of 1978 for evaluation in 1979. The extension of Cm* is known as Cm*/50 and is shown in Figure 7. It will be used to test parallel processing methods, fault tolerance, modularity, and the extensibility of the Cm* structure.

The PDP-11/70mP Experimental Multiprocessor Computer

The PDP-11/70mP aims to extend the reliability, availability, maintainability and performance range of the PDP-11 Family. It uses 11/70 processor hardware and the RSX-11M software as basic building blocks.

The systems can have up to four processors which have access to common central memories as shown in Figure 8. Each MOS primary memory contains 256 Kbyte to 1 Mbyte and a port (switch) by which up to four processors may access it. A failed memory may be isolated for repair. Usually two processors share (have access to) each of the I/O devices through a Unibus switch or dual ported disk memories.

Failure of a high speed mass storage bus controller, a processor, or one port of a device will not preclude use of that device through the other port. These devices can also be isolated from their respective buses so that failure of a device will not preclude access to other devices.

Each of the processor units has a write-through cache memory. Through normal system operation, data within these local caches may become inconsistent with data elsewhere in the system. To eliminate this problem, the operating system and the hardware components have been modified. The RSX-11M system either clears the cache of inconsistent data or avoids using the cache for specific situations.

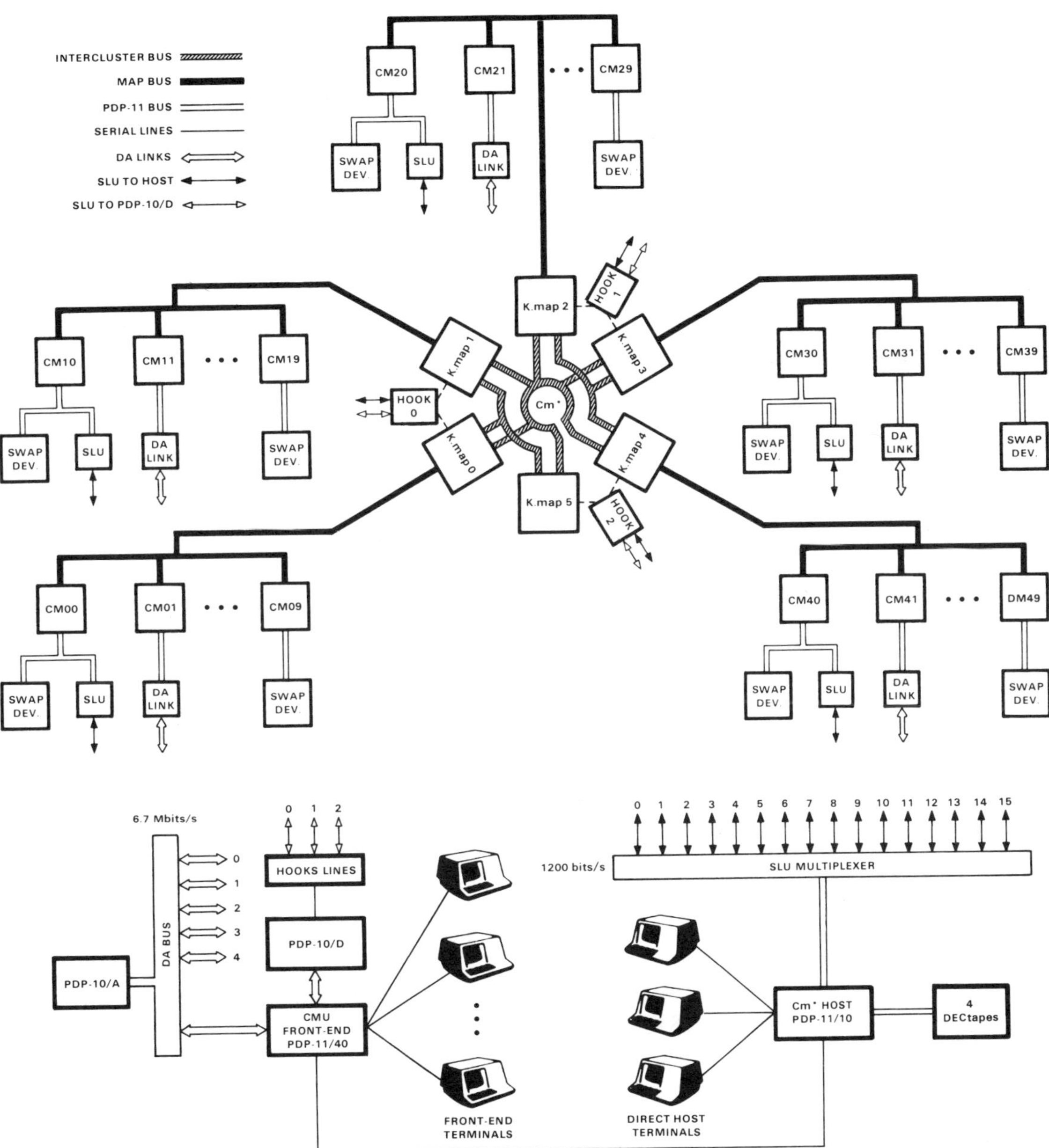

Figure 7. Details of the Cm*/50 system.

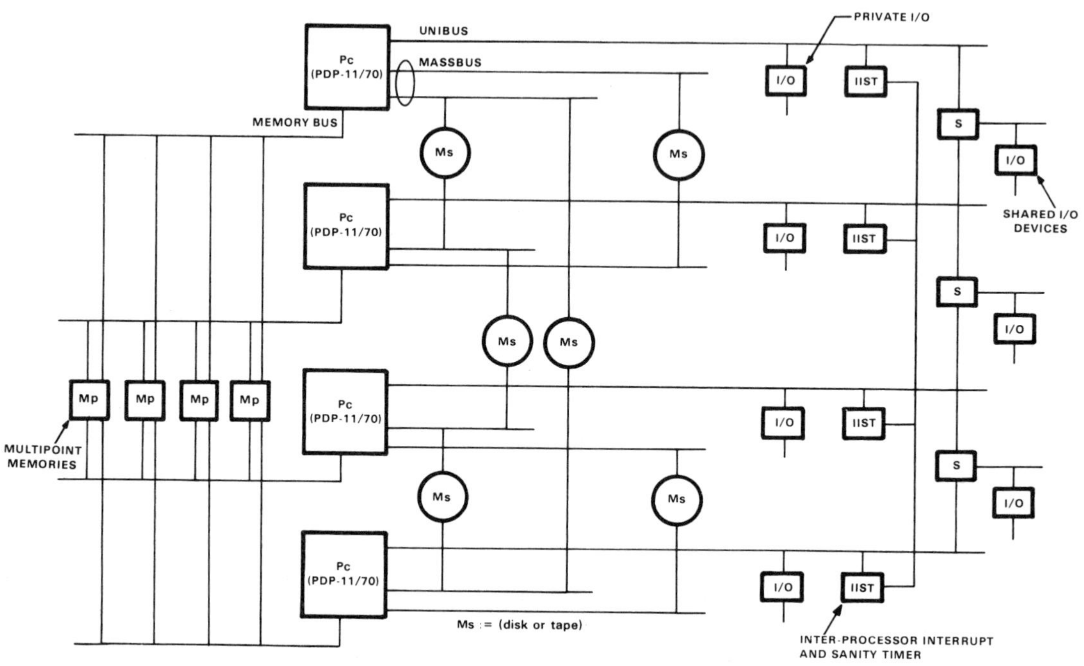

Figure 8. Four-processor multiprocessor based on PDP-11/70 processors.

The software to manipulate the cache is contained in the executive and is transparent to user programs.

An Interprocessor Interrupt and Sanity Timer (IIST) provides the executive software with a mechanism to interrupt processors for rescheduling. The IIST includes a timer for each processor which is periodically refreshed by software after execution of diagnostic check routines. If the refresh commands do not occur within a prescribed interval, the IIST will issue an interprocessor interrupt to inform the other processors of faulty operation. The IIST also contains a mechanism for initially loading the multiprocessor system.

The system design results in an extension to the PDP-11 that is transparent to user programs and yields increases in performance over a single processor 11/70 system. This performance increase is due to the symmetry, such that nearly any resource can be accessed by any process with minimum overhead. Also, unlike multiple computer systems that communicate via high speed links, the large primary memory can be combined and used by a single process. Moreover, dynamic assignment of processes to specific computer systems (Figure 9) can be made.

The system has been designed to increase the availability by reducing the impact of failures on system performance through the use of multiple redundant components. In this way, failed elements can be isolated for repair. The design is such that the system may be easily reconfigured so that system operation can be resumed and the failed component repaired off-line.

Extensions to the diagnostic software and hardware error detection mechanisms facilitate quick location of faults. User-mode diagnostics are run concurrently with the application software; this permits maintenance of the disk and tape units to be done on-line.

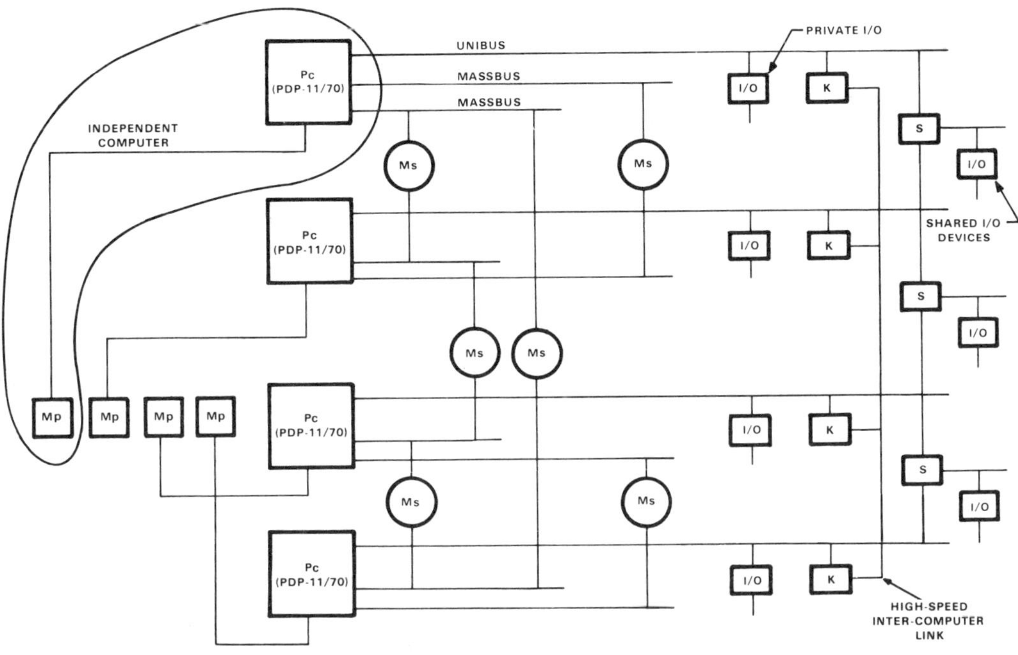

Figure 9. Four-processor multicomputer system based on PDP-11/70 processors.

Now that the 11/70mP has implemented its IIST and defined an architectural extension for multiprocessing, another roadblock to the use of multiprocessors has been passed; namely, an extension for interprocessor signaling has been defined. This might have been defined much earlier in the life of the PDP-11. In the IBM computers the SIGP instruction was not available on 360s until the 370 extensions.

PULSAR: A Performance Range mP System

PULSAR is a 16 LSI-11 multiprocessor computer for investigating the cost-effectiveness of multiple microprocessors. It covers a performance range of approximately a single LSI-11 to better than a PDP-11/70 for simple instructions.

The breadboard system (Figure 10) is based on the PDP-11/70 processor-memory-switch structure, including multiple interrupt levels and 22-bit physical addressing. However, it does not implement instruction (I) and data (D) space or Supervisor mode, and it lacks the Floating-Point Processors.

The processors (P-Boards) communicate with each other, the Unibus Interface (UBI), and a Common Cache and Control via a high-bandwidth, synchronous bus.

The Common Cache and Control contains a large (8 Kword), direct-mapping, shared cache with a 2-word block size, interfacing to the 2- or 4-way interleaved 11/70 Memory Bus. This prevents the memory subsystem from becoming a bottleneck, in spite of the large reduction in bandwidth demand provided by the cache. The control provides all the mapping functions for both Unibus and processor accesses to memory. The Unibus map registers and the process map registers for each processor are held in a single bipolar memory.

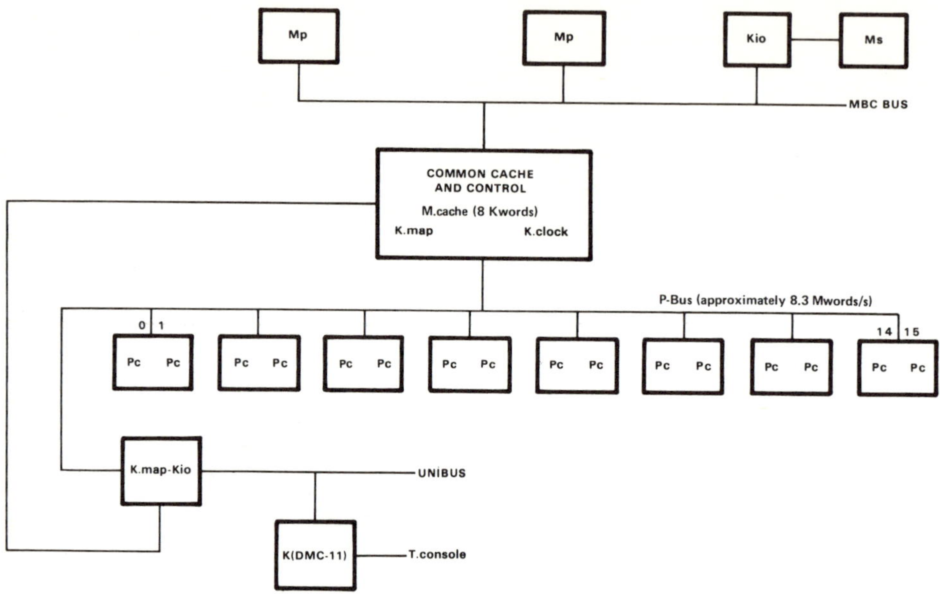

Figure 10. PMS diagram of the breadboard version of the DEC PULSAR.

The Unibus Interface provides the Unibus control functions of a conventional PDP-11. Interrupts are fielded by the first enabled processor with preferential treatment for any processor in WAIT state.

Each processor board contains two independent microprocessor chip sets with modified microcode. Internal contention for the adapter is eliminated by running the two processors out of phase with each other. Such contention as does exist is resolved by the mechanism for arbitration of the processor bus itself. The PULSAR has a serial line (ASCII) console interfacing via a microcode driven communications controller, equipped with modified microcode. In addition, a debugging panel has displays for every stage of the processor bus and controller pipeline.

Console operations are effected by the Unibus Interface interrogating or changing a save area for each processor, physically held in the mapping array, in response to ASCII console messages over the Unibus. Each processor places all appropriate status in the save area on every HALT, and restores from the save area prior to acting upon every CONTINUE or START.

The PULSAR system is pipeline oriented with specific time slots for each processor. This permits a single simple arbitration mechanism, rather than separate complex ones for each resource.

Once the pipeline is assigned to a transaction, the successive intervals of time are assigned to the following resources in order:

1. The mapping array.
2. The address translation logic.
3. The cache.
4. The address validation logic.
5. The data lines of the P-Bus.

The memory subsystem, which is not a part of this resource pipeline, has an independent arbitration mechanism. Interfacing between these independent mechanisms is by means of queues.

There are some operations that require more than one access to the same resource in the pipeline. These operations are effectively handled as two transactions. Examples of such operations are memory writes and internal I/O page (memory-management register) accesses. A memory write may need a second access to the cache for update, while the Internal I/O Page may need another access to the map array.

There are other operations in which the timing does not permit the use of a particular resource in the specific interval that is allocated to that transaction. This happens, for instance, when a read operation results in a cache miss. The data is not available in time. In this case a second transaction takes place, initiated when backing store data becomes available.

Cost projections indicate that a multiprocessor will have an increase in parts count over each possible equivalent performance uniprocessor in the range. This will range from a 20 percent increase for a two-processor, multiprocessor system to 0 percent at the top of the range. The 20 percent premium can be reduced if no provision is made for expansibility over the entire range. Clearly, a separate single processor structure can be cost-effective (since this is the LSI-11). The premium is based on parts count only and excludes considerations of cost benefits due to production learning, common spares and manuals, lower engineering costs, etc.

A number of computer systems have been built based on multiple processors in systems ranging from independent computers (with no interconnection) through tightly coupled computer networks which communicate by passing messages, to multiprocessor computers with shared memory. Table 5 gives a comparison of the various computers. Although n independent computers is a highly reliable structure, it is hard to give an example where there is no interconnection among the computers. The standard computer network interconnected via standard communications links is not given.

It is interesting to compare the multiprocessor and the tightly coupled multicomputer configurations (Figure 8 and 9) where the configurations are drawn in exactly the same way and with the same peripherals. In this way, columns 2 and 6 of Table 5 can be more easily compared. The tradeoff between the two structures is between lower cost and potentially higher performance for the multiprocessor (unless tasks can be statically assigned to the various computers in the network) versus somewhat higher reliability, availability, and maintainability for the network computer (because there is more independence among software and hardware). Varying the degree of coupling in the processors through the amount of shared memory determines which structure will result. The cost and the resultant reliability differentials for the two systems are determined by the size and the reliability of the software.

TECHNOLOGY: COMPONENTS OF THE DESIGN

In Chapter 2, it was noted that computers are strongly influenced by the basic electronic technology of their components. The PDP-11 Family provides an extensive example of designing with improved technologies. Because design resources have been available to do concurrent implementations spanning a cost/performance range, PDP-11s offer a rich source of examples of the three different design styles: constant cost with increasing functionality, constant functionality with decreasing cost, and growth path.

Memory technology has had a much greater impact on PDP-11 evolution than logic technology. Except for the LSI-11, the one logic family (7400 series TTL) has dominated PDP-11 implementations since the beginning. Except for a small increase after the PDP-11/20, gate density has not improved markedly. Speed improvement has taken place in the Schottky

Table 5. Characteristics of Various PDP-11 Based Multiprocessor and Multicomputers

	C.mmp	11/70mP	Pulsar	Cm*	C.vmp	11/70mC	n Computers
Coupling	Multiprocessor	Multiprocessor	Multiprocessor	Tightly coupled network	Triple modular redundant voting computer	Tightly coupled computer network	Independent
Page/figure	395/6	400/8	402/10	399/7	Not shown	401/9	Not shown
Processor type	20, 40	70	LSI-11	LSI-11	LSI-11	70	70
Reliability, Availability, Maintainability	Medium Medium Medium	High High High	Medium Low Low	Medium Medium Low	Very high Very high Very high	High High High	High High High
Performance range (times base processor)	1 - 16	1 - 4	2 - 16	1 - 100	1	1 - 4	1 - 12
Advantages	All resources can operate on any task(s); large processes occupying all Mp can be run			Range	Very high R, A, M	Backup of tasks to alt. computer; fast inter-C transfers	Complete Independence
Disadvantage	Single switch		Single memory and peripherals	Static assignment of tasks	1 Pc performance	Static assignment of tasks to computers	

TTL, and a speed/power improvement has occurred in the low power Schottky (LS) series. Departures from medium-scale integrated transistor-transistor logic, in terms of gate density, have been few, but effective. Examples are the bit-slice in the PDP-11/34 Floating-Point Processor, the use of programmable logic arrays in the PDP-11/04 and PDP-11/34 control units, and the use of emitter-coupled logic in some clock circuitry.

Memory densities and costs have improved rapidly since 1969 and have thus had the most impact. Read-write memory chips have gone from 16 bits to 4,096 bits in density and read-only memories from 16 bits to the 8 or 16 Kbits widely available in 1978. Various semiconductor memory size availabilities are given in Chapter 2 using the model of semiconductor density doubling each year since 1962.

The memory technology of 1969 imposed several constraints. First, core memory was cost-effective for the primary (program) memory, but a clear trend toward semiconductor primary memory was visible. Second, since the largest high speed read-write memories available were just 16 words, the number of processor registers had to be kept small. Third, there were no large high speed read-only memories that would have permitted a microprogrammed approach to the processor design.

These constraints established four design attitudes toward the PDP-11's architecture. First, it should be asynchronous, and thereby capable of accepting different configurations of memory that operate at different speeds. Second, it should be expandable to take eventual advantage of a larger number of registers, both user registers for new data-types and internal registers for improved context switching, memory mapping, and protected multiprogramming. Third, it could be relatively complex, so that a microcode approach could eventually be used to advantage: new data-types could be added to the instruction set to increase performance, even though they might add complexity. Fourth, the Unibus width should be relatively large, to get as much performance as possible, since the amount of computation possible per memory cycle was relatively small.

As semiconductor memory of varying price and performance became available, it was used to trade cost for performance across a reasonably wide range of PDP-11 models. Different techniques were used on different models to provide the range. These techniques include: microprogramming for all models except the 11/20 to lower cost and enhance performance with more data-types (for example, faster floating point); use of faster program memories for brute-force speed improvements (e.g., 11/45 with MOS primary memory, 11/55 with bipolar primary memory, and the 11/60 with a large writable control store); use of caches (11/70, 11/60, and 11/34C); and expanded use of fast registers inside the processor (the 11/45 and above). The use of semiconductors versus cores for primary memory is a purely economic consideration, as discussed in Chapter 2.

Table 6 shows characteristics of each of the PDP-11 models along with the techniques used to span a cost and performance range. Snow and Siewiorek (Chapter 14) give a detailed comparison of the processors.

VAX-11

Enlarging the virtual address space of an architecture has far more implications than enlarging the physical address space. The simple device of relocating program-generated addresses can solve the latter problem. The physical address space, the amount of physical memory that can be addressed, has been increased in two steps in the PDP-11 Family (Table 2).

The virtual address space, or name space, is a much more fundamental part of an architecture. Such addresses are programmer generated: to name data objects, their aggregates (whether they be vectors, matrices, lists, or

Table 6. Characteristics of PDP-11 Models with Techniques Used to Span Cost and Performance Range

Model	First Shipment	Performance: Basic Instructions Per Second (relative to PDP-11/03)	Performance: Floating-Point Arithmetic (whetstone instructions per second)	Memory Range (Kbytes)	Range-Spanning Techniques: For High Performance	Range-Spanning Techniques: For Low Cost	Notable Attributes
11/03 (LSI-11)	6/75	1	26	8–56		8 bit wide datapath; LSI-11 Bus; tailored PLA control	LSI–4 chips; ODT; Floating-Point (FIS), CIS, WCS mid-life kickers
11/04	9/75	2.8	18	8–56		Standard package; ROM; PLA	Backplane compatible with 11/34 for field upgrade; built-in ASCII console; self-diagnosis
11/05	6/72	2.5	13	8–56		Microprogrammed; ROM	Minimal 11 (2 boards)
11/20	6/70	3.1	20	8–56			ISP; Unibus
11/34	3/76	3.5	204	16–256		Shared use of ALU; PLA; ROM; microprogrammed	Cost-performance balance; 11/34C mid-life kicker; bit-slice FPP
11/34C	5/78	7.3	262	32–256			Classic use of cache
11/40	1/73	3.6	57	16–256	Variable cycle length	Microprogrammed	FIS extension
11/60	6/77	27	592	32–256	Fetch overlap; dual scratch-pads; TTL/S	Heavily microprogrammed	Integral floating-point; WCS for local storage; RAMP
11/45	6/72	Core: 13 MOS: 23 Bipolar: 41	~260 ~335 ~362	8–256	Instruction prefetch; dual scratchpads; Fastbus; autonomous FPP; TTL/S		Pc speed to match 300 ns bipolar; high speed minicomputer FPP; memory management
11/55	6/76	41	725	16–64 (0–192 core)	All bipolar memory		
11/70	3/75	36	671	64-2048	32-bit-wide DMA bus; large memory		Cache; multiple buses, RAMP, FP11-C mid-life kicker; remote diagnosis
70mP							Multiprocessor architectural extensions; on-line maintainability; performance; availability
		range: 41–1	range: 56–1	range: 256–1			

shared data segments) and instructions (subroutine addresses, for example). Names seen by an individual program are part of a larger name space – that managed by an operating system and its associated language translators and object-time systems. An operating system provides program sharing and protection among programs using the name space of the architecture.

As the PDP-11/70 design progressed, it was realized that for some large applications there would soon be a bad mismatch between the 64-Kbyte name space and 4-Mbyte memory space. Two trends could be clearly seen: (1) minicomputer users would be processing large arrays of data, particularly in FORTRAN programs (only 8,096 double precision floating-point numbers are needed to fill a 16-bit name space), and (2) applications programs were growing rapidly in size, particularly large COBOL programs. Moreover, anticipated memory price declines made the problem worse. The need for a 32-bit integer data-type was felt, but this was far less important than the need for 32-bit addressing of a name space.

Thus, in 1974, architectural work began on extending the virtual address space of the PDP-11. Several proposals were made. The principal goal was compatibility with the PDP-11. In the final proposed architecture each of the eight general registers was extended to 32 bits. The addressing modes (hence, address arithmetic) inherent in the PDP-11 allowed this to be a natural, easy extension.

The design of the structure to be placed on a 32-bit virtual address presented the most difficulty. The most PDP-11 compatible structure would view a 32-bit address as 2^{16} 16-bit PDP-11 segments, each having the substructure of the memory management architecture presently being used. This segmented address space, although PDP-11 compatible, was ill-suited to FORTRAN and most other languages, which expect a linear address space.

A severe design constraint was that existing PDP-11 subroutines must be callable from programs which ran in the Extended Address mode. The main problem areas were in establishing a protocol for communicating addresses (between programs between the operating systems and programs on the occurrence of interrupts). Saving state (the program counter and its extension) on the stack was straightforward. However, the accessing of linkage addresses on the stack after a subroutine call instruction or interrupt event was not straightforward. Complicated sequences were necessary to ensure that the correct number of bytes (representing a 32-bit or 16-bit address) were popped from the stack.

The solution was hampered by the fact that DEC customers programmed the PDP-11 at all levels – there was no clear user level, below which DEC had complete control, as is the case with the IBM System 360 or the PDP-10 using the TOPS-10 or TOPS-20 monitors.

The proposed architecture was the result of work by engineers, architects, operating system designers and compiler designers. Moreover, it was subjected to close scrutiny by a wider group of engineers and programmers. Much was learned about the consequences of strict PDP-11 compatibility, the notions of degree of compatibility, and the software costs which would be incurred by an extended PDP-11 architecture.

Fortunately, the project was discontinued. There were many reservations about its viability. It was felt that the PDP-11 compatibility constraint caused too much compromise. Any new architecture would require a large software investment; a quantum jump over the PDP-11 was needed to justify the effort.

In April 1975, work on a 32-bit architecture was started on VAX-11, with the goal of building a machine which was culturally compatible with PDP-11. The initial group, called VAXA, consisted of Gordon Bell, Peter Conklin, Dave Cutler, Bill Demmer, Tom Hastings, Richy Lary, Dave Rodgers, Steve Rothman, and Bill Strecker as the principal architect. As a result of the experience with the extended PDP-11 designs, it was decided to drop the constraint of the PDP-11 instruction format in designing the extended virtual address space, or Native mode, of the VAX-11 architecture. However, in order to run existing PDP-11 programs, VAX-11 includes PDP-11 Compatibility mode. This mode provides the basic PDP-11 instruction set without privileged instructions (as defined by the RSX-11M operating system) and floating-point instructions. Nor is the former memory management architecture (KT-11) preserved in this mode.

Preserving the existing PDP-11 instruction formats with VAX-11 would have required too high a price in dynamic bit efficiency. Whereas the PDP-11 has a high level of efficiency in this area, adding the new operation codes for the anticipated data-types, access modes, and different length addresses would have lowered the instruction stream bit efficiency. An operation code extension field would have been required. It was also felt that data stream bit efficiency could be improved. For example, measurements showed that 98 percent of all literals were 6 bits or less in length.

Besides the desire to add the data-types for string, 32- and 64-bit integers, and decimal arithmetic, there were many other extensions proposed. These included a common procedure CALL instruction, demand paging, true indexing, context-sensitive indexing, and more I/O addressing.

Along the way, some major perturbations to the PDP-11 style were considered and rejected, often because they violated the notion of compatibility with PDP-11. Typed data and descriptor addressing were rejected on the grounds of dynamic bit efficiency. Although system software costs may be lower with such architectures, it was not possible to quantify the gain convincingly. Also, such an architecture destroyed any compatibility, cultural or otherwise, with PDP-11.

The experience with PDP-11 (floating point, in particular) led the VAX designers to reject a soft-machine architecture, i.e., one with an instruction set (and highly microprogrammed implementations) for general purpose emulation. Their PDP-11 experience showed that embedding a data-type (once it is understood) in the architecture gives a higher performance gain than embedding the higher level language control constructs. There was also a general objection to soft machines: the problem of controlling a proliferation of instruction sets invented by many small software groups was felt to be unmanageable. Moreover, higher level instruction sets jeopardize the ability to communicate between programs that are written in different languages. This compatibility is a major goal of VAX.

A capabilities-based architecture was rejected because it was not fully understood and because there was no performance or reliability data available from the few experimental machines which had been built.

ACKNOWLEDGEMENTS

We gratefully acknowledge the suggestions of Roger Cady, Dick Clayton, and Bruce Delagi who were eminently qualified and intimately involved in the PDP-11's evolution.

17

VAX-11/780: A Virtual Address Extension to the DEC PDP-11 Family

WILLIAM D. STRECKER

INTRODUCTION

Large Virtual Address Space Minicomputers

Perhaps the most useful definition of a minicomputer system is based on price: Depending on one's perspective, such systems are typically found in the \$20 K to \$200 K range. The twin forces of market pull – as customers build increasingly complex systems on minicomputers – and technology push – as the semiconductor industry provides increasingly lower cost logic and memory elements – have induced minicomputer manufacturers to produce systems of considerable performance and memory capacity. Such systems are typified by the DEC PDP-11/70. From an architectural point of view, the characteristic that most distinguishes many of these systems from larger mainframe computers is the size of the virtual address space: the immediately available address space seen by an individual process. For many purposes, the 65-Kbyte virtual address space typically provided on minicomputers (such as the PDP-11) has not been and probably will not continue to be a severe limitation. However, there are some applications whose programming is impractical in a 65-Kbyte virtual address space and, perhaps most importantly, others whose programming is appreciably simplified by having a large virtual address space. Given the relative trends in hardware and software costs, the latter point alone will ensure that large virtual address space minicomputers play an increasingly important role in minicomputer product offerings.

In principle, there is no great challenge in designing a large virtual address minicomputer system. For example, many of the large mainframe computers could serve as architectural models for such a system. The real challenge lies in two areas: compatibility – very tangible and important; and simplicity – intangible but nonetheless important.

The first area is preserving the customer's and the computer manufacturer's investment in existing systems. This investment exists at many levels: basic hardware (principally buses and peripherals); systems and applications software;

files and data bases; and personnel familiar with the programming, use, and operation of the systems. For example, to preserve this investment a major computer manufacturer just recently abandoned a major effort for new computer architectures in favor of evolving its current architectures [McLean, 1977].

The second, less tangible area is the preservation of those attributes (other than price) that make minicomputer systems attractive. These include approachability, understandability, and ease of use. Preservation of these attributes suggests that simply modeling an extended virtual address minicomputer after a large mainframe computer is not wholly appropriate. It also suggests that during architectural design, tradeoffs must be made between more than just performance, functionality, and cost. Performance or functionality features which are so complex that they appreciably compromise understanding or ease of use must be rejected as inappropriate for minicomputer systems.

VAX-11 Overview

VAX-11 is the **v**irtual **a**ddress e**x**tension of PDP-11 architecture (Chapter 9) [Bell and Strecker, 1976]. The most distinctive feature of VAX-11 is the extension of the virtual address from 16 bits as provided on the PDP-11 to 32 bits. With the 8-bit byte as the basic addressable unit, the extension provides a virtual address space of about 4.3 gigabytes which, even given rapid improvement in memory technology, should be adequate far into the future.

Since maximal PDP-11 compatibility was a primary goal, early VAX-11 design efforts focused on literally extending the PDP-11: preserving the existing instruction formats and instruction set and fitting the virtual address extension around them. The objective was to permit, to the extent possible, the running of existing programs in the extended virtual address environment. While realizing this objective was possible (there were three distinct designs), it was felt that the extended architecture designs were overly compromised in the areas of efficiency, functionality, and programming ease.

Consequently, it was decided to drop the constraint of the PDP-11 instruction format in designing the extended virtual address space or native mode of the VAX-11 architecture. However, in order to run existing PDP-11 programs, VAX-11 includes a PDP-11 compatibility mode. Compatibility mode provides the basic PDP-11 instruction set without privileged instructions (such as HALT) and floating-point instructions (which are optional on most PDP-11 processors and not required by most PDP-11 software).

In addition to compatibility mode, a number of other features to preserve PDP-11 investment have been provided in the VAX-11 architecture, the VAX-11 operating system VAX/VMS, and the VAX-11/780 implementation of the VAX-11 architecture. These features include the following.

1. The native mode data-types and formats are identical to those on the PDP-11. Also, while extended, the VAX-11 native mode instruction set and addressing modes are very close to those on the PDP-11. As a consequence, VAX-11 native mode assembly language programming is quite similar to PDP-11 assembly language programming.
2. The VAX-11/780 uses the same peripheral buses (Unibus and Massbus) and the same peripherals as the PDP-11.
3. The VAX/VMS operating system is an evolution of the PDP-11 RSX-11M and IAS operating systems. It offers a similar although extended set of system services and uses the same command languages. Additionally, VAX/VMS supports most of the RSX-11M/IAS system service requests issued by programs executing in compatibility mode.

4. The VAX/VMS file system is the same as that used on the RSX-11M/IAS operating systems, permitting interchange of files and volumes. The file access methods as implemented by the RMS record manager are also the same.
5. VAX-11 high level language compilers accept the same source languages as the equivalent PDP-11 compilers, and execution of compiled programs gives the same results.

The coverage of all these aspects of VAX-11 is well beyond the scope of any single paper. The remainder of this paper discusses the design of the VAX-11 native mode architecture and gives an overview of the VAX-11/780 system.

VAX-11 NATIVE ARCHITECTURE

Processor State

Like the PDP-11, VAX-11 is organized around a general register processor state. This organization was favored because access to operands stored in general registers is fast (because the registers are internal to the processor and register accesses do not need to pass through a memory management mechanism). Also, only a small number of bits in an instruction are needed to designate a register. Perhaps most importantly, the registers are used (as on the PDP-11) in conjunction with a large set of addressing modes which permit unusually flexible operand addressing methods.

Some consideration was given to a pure stack-based architecture. However, it was rejected because real program data suggests the superiority of two or three operand instruction formats [Myers, 1977]. Actually VAX-11 is very stack-oriented, and although not optimally encoded for the purpose, it can easily be used as a pure stack architecture if desired.

VAX-11 has 16 32-bit general registers (denoted R0 through R15) which are used for both fixed and floating-point operands. This is in contrast to the PDP-11 which has eight 16-bit general registers and six 64-bit floating-point registers. The merged set of fixed and floating registers was preferred because programming is simplified and a more effective allocation of the registers is permitted.

Four of the registers are assigned special meaning in the VAX-11 architecture.

1. R15 is the **program counter** (PC) which contains the address of the next byte to be interpreted in the instruction stream.
2. R14 is the **stack pointer** (SP) which contains the address of the top of the processor defined stack used for procedure and interrupt linkage.
3. R13 is the **frame pointer** (FP). The VAX-11 procedure calling convention builds a data structure on the stack called a stack frame. FP contains the address of this structure.
4. R12 is the **argument pointer** (AP). The VAX-11 procedure calling convention uses a data structure called an argument list. AP contains the address of this structure.

The remaining element of the user-visible processor state (additional processor state seen mainly by privileged procedures is discussed later) is the 16-bit processor status word (PSW). The PSW contains the N, Z, V, and C condition codes which indicate, respectively, whether a previous instruction had a negative result, a zero result, a result that overflowed, or a result that produced a carry (or borrow). Also in the PSW are the IV, DV, and FU bits which enable processor trapping on integer overflow, decimal overflow, and floating underflow conditions, respectively. (The trap on conditions of "floating overflow" and "divide by zero" for any data-type is always enabled.)

Finally, the PSW contains the T bit which, when set, forces a trap at the end of each instruction. This trap is useful for program debugging and analysis purposes.

Data-Types and Formats

The VAX-11 data-types are a superset of the PDP-11 data-types. Where the PDP-11 and VAX-11 have equivalent data-types, the formats (representation in memory) are identical. Data-type and data-format identity is one of the most compelling forms of compatibility. It permits free interchange of binary data between PDP-11 and VAX-11 programs. It facilitates source level compatibility between equivalent PDP-11 and VAX-11 languages. It also greatly facilitates hardware implementation and software support of the PDP-11 compatibility mode in the VAX-11 architecture.

The VAX-11 data-types divide into five classes.

1. Integer data-types are the 8-bit **byte,** the 16-bit **word,** the 32-bit **longword,** and the 64-bit **quadword.** Usually these data-types are considered signed with negative values represented in two's complement form. However, for most purposes they can be interpreted as unsigned, and the VAX-11 instruction set provides support for this interpretation.

2. Floating data-types are the 32-bit **floating** and the 64-bit **double** floating. These data-types are binary normalized, have an 8-bit signed exponent, and have a 25- or 57-bit signed fraction with the redundant most significant fraction bit not represented.

3. The **variable bit field** data-type is 0 to 32 bits located arbitrarily with respect to addressable byte boundaries. A bit field is specified by three operands: the address of a byte, the starting bit position (P) with respect to bit 0 of that byte, and the size (S) of the field. The VAX-11 instruction set provides for interpreting the field as signed or unsigned.

4. The **character string** data-type is 0 to 65535 contiguous bytes. It is specified by two operands: the length and starting address of the string. Although the data-type is named "character string," no special interpretation is placed on the values of the bytes in the character string.

5. The **decimal string** data-types are 0 to 31 digits. They are specified by two operands: a length (in digits) and a starting address. The primary data-type is **packed decimal** with two digits stored in each byte (except the byte containing the least significant digit contains a single digit and the sign). Two ASCII character decimal types are supported: **leading separate** sign and **trailing embedded** sign. The leading separate type is a "+", "–", or "<blank>" (equivalent to "+") ASCII character followed by 0 to 31 ASCII decimal digit characters. A trailing embedded sign decimal string is 0 to 31 bytes which are ASCII decimal digit characters (except for the character containing least significant digit which is an arbitrary encoding of the digit and sign).

All of the data-types except field may be stored on arbitrary byte boundaries – there are no alignment constraints. The field data-type, of course, can start on an arbitrary bit boundary.

Attributes of and symbolic representations for most of the data-types are given in Table 1 and Figure 1.

Instruction Format and Address Modes

Most architectures provide a small number of relatively fixed instruction formats. Two problems often result. First, not all operands of an instruction have the same specification generality. For example, one operand must come from memory and another from a register, or one

Table 1. Data-Types

Data-Type	Size	Range (decimal)	
Integer		**Signed**	**Unsigned**
Byte	8 bits	−128 to +127	0 to 255
Word	16 bits	−32768 to +32767	0 to 65535
Longword	32 bits	-2^{31} to $+2^{31}-1$	0 to $2^{32}-1$
Quadword	64 bits	-2^{63} to $+2^{63}-1$	0 to $2^{64}-1$
Floating Point	$\pm 2.9 \times 10^{-37}$ to 1.7×10^{38}		
Floating	32 bits	Approximately seven decimal digits precision	
Double Floating	64 bits	Approximately 16 decimal digits precision	
Packed Decimal String	0 to 16 bytes (31 digits)	Numeric, two digits per byte Sign in low half of last byte	
Character String	0 to 65535 bytes	One character per byte	
Variable-Length Bit Field	0 to 32 bits	Dependent on intrepretation	

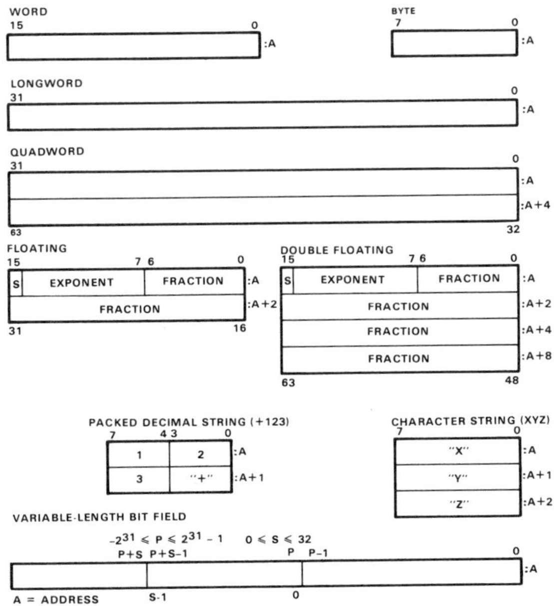

Figure 1. Data formats.

must come from the stack and another from memory. Second, only a limited number of operands can be accommodated: typically, one or two. For instructions that inherently require more operands (such as field or string instructions), the additional operands are specified in *ad hoc* ways: small literal fields in instructions, specific registers or stack positions, or packed in fields of a single operand. Both these problems lead to increased programming complexity: they require superfluous move-type instructions to get operands to places where they can be used and increase competition for potentially scarce resources such as registers.

To avoid these problems, two criteria were followed in the design of the VAX-11 instruction format: (1) all instructions should have the "natural" number of operands, and (2) all operands should have the same generality in specification. These criteria led to a highly variable instruction format. An instruction consists of a one- or two-byte* opcode followed by the specifications for *n* operands ($n \geqslant 0$) where *n* is an implicit property of the opcode. An operand specification is one to ten bytes in length and consists of a one- or two-byte operand specifier followed by (as required) zero to eight bytes of specifier extension. The operand specifier includes the address mode and designation of any registers needed to locate the operand. A specifier extension consists of a displacement, an address, or immediate data.

The VAX-11 address modes are, with one exception, a superset of the PDP-11 address modes. The PDP-11 address mode autodecrement deferred was omitted from VAX-11 because it was rarely used.

Most operand specifiers are one byte long and contain two 4-bit fields: The high-order field (bits 7:4) contains the address mode designator, and the lower field (bits 3:0) contains a general register designator. The address modes include:

1. **Register mode,** in which the designated register contains the operand.
2. **Register deferred mode,** in which the designated register contains the address of the operand.
3. **Autodecrement mode,** in which the contents of the designated register are first decremented by the size (in bytes) of the operand and are then used as the address of the operand.
4. **Autoincrement mode,** in which the contents of the designated register are first used as the address of the operand and are then incremented by the size of the operand. Note that if the designated register is PC, the operand is located in the instruction stream. This use of autoincrement mode is called immediate mode. In immediate mode, the one to eight bytes of data are the specifier extention.

   Autoincrement mode can be used sequentially to process a vector in one direction, and autodecrement mode can be used to process a vector in the opposite direction. Autoincrement, register deferred, and autodecrement modes can be applied to a single register to implement a stack data structure: autodecrement to "push," autoincrement to "pop," and register deferred to access the top of the stack.
5. **Autoincrement deferred mode,** in which the contents of the designated register are used as the address of a longword in memory which contains the address of the operand. After this use, the contents of the register are incremented by four (the size in bytes of the longword address). Note that if PC is the designated register, the absolute address of the operand is located in the instruction stream. This use of autoincrement deferred mode is termed absolute mode. In absolute mode, the 4-byte address is the specifier extension.
6. **Displacement mode,** in which a displacement is added to the contents of the designated register to form the operand address. There are three displacement modes depending on whether a signed byte, word, or longword displacement is the specifier extension. These modes are termed byte, word, and longword displacement, respectively. Note that if PC is the designated register, the operand is located relative to PC. For this use, the modes are termed byte, word, and longword relative mode, respectively.
7. **Displacement deferred mode,** in which a displacement is added to the designated register to form the address of a longword containing the address of the operand. There are three displacement

*No currently defined instructions use two-byte opcodes.

deferred modes depending on whether a signed byte, word, or longword displacement is the specifier extension. These modes are termed byte, word, and longword displacement, respectively. Note that if PC is the designated register, the operand address is located relative to PC. For this use the modes are termed byte, word, and longword relative deferred mode, respectively.

8. **Literal mode,** in which the operand specifier itself contains a 6-bit literal which is the operand. For integer data-types, the literal encodes the values 0 through 63; for floating data-types, the literal includes three exponent and three fraction bits to give 64 common values.

9. **Index mode,** which is not really a mode but rather a one-byte prefix operator for any other mode which evaluates a memory address (i.e., all modes except register and literal). The index mode prefix is cascaded with the operand specifier for that mode (called the base operand specifier) to form an aggregate two-byte operand specifier. The base operand specifier is used in the normal way to evaluate a base address. A copy of the contents of the register designated in the index prefix is multiplied by the size (in bytes) of the operand and added to the base address. The sum is the final operand address. There are three advantages to the VAX-11 form of indexing: (1) the index is scaled by the data size, and thus the index register maintains a logical rather than a byte offset into an indexed data structure; (2) indexing can be applied to any of the address modes that generate memory addresses, and this results in a comprehensive set of indexed addressing methods; and (3) the space required to specify indexing and the index register is paid only when indexing is used.

The VAX-11 assembler syntax for the address modes is given in Figure 2. The bracketed ({ }) notation is optional, and the programmer rarely needs to be concerned with displacement sizes or whether to choose literal or immediate mode. The programmer writes the simple form; the assembler chooses the address mode which produces the shortest instruction length.

In order to give a better feeling for the instruction format and assembler notation, several examples are given in Figures 3 through 5. Figure 3 shows an instruction that moves a word from an address that is 56 plus the contents of R5 to an address that is 270 plus the

Mode	Syntax	
LITERAL (IMMEDIATE)	{S↑ / I↑} # CONSTANT	
REGISTER	Rn	
REGISTER DEFERRED	(Rn)	INDEXED [Rx]
AUTODECREMENT	- (Rn)	
AUTOINCREMENT	(Rn) +	
AUTOINCREMENT DEFERRED	@ (Rn) +	
(ABSOLUTE)	@ # ADDRESS	
DISPLACEMENT (RELATIVE)	{B↑ / W↑ / L↑} DISPLACEMENT (Rn) / ADDRESS	
DISPLACEMENT DEFERRED (RELATIVE DEFERRED)	@{B↑ / W↑ / L↑} DISPLACEMENT (Rn) / ADDRESS	

n = 0 THROUGH 15
x = 0 THROUGH 14

Figure 2. Assembler syntax.

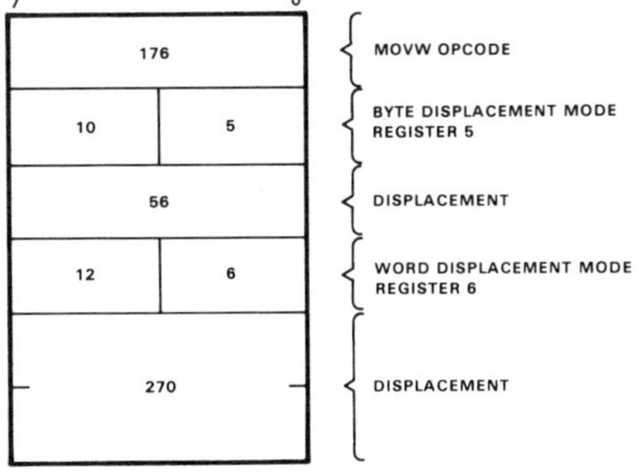

Figure 3. MOVW 56(R5), 270(R6).

contents of R4. Note that the displacement 56 can be represented in a byte while the displacement 270 requires a word. The instruction occupies six bytes. Figure 4 shows an instruction that adds 1 to a longword in R0 and stores the result at a memory address which is the sum of *A* and four times the contents of R2. This instruction occupies nine bytes. Finally, a "return from subroutine" instruction is shown in Figure 5. It has no explicit operands and occupies a single byte.

The only significant instance where there is nongeneral specification of operands is in the specification of targets for branch instructions. Since invariably the target of a branch instruction is a small displacement from the current PC, most branch instructions simply take a one-byte PC relative displacement. This is exactly as if byte displacement mode were used with the PC used as the register, except that the operand specifier byte is not needed. Because of the pervasiveness of branch instructions in code, this one-byte saving results in a nontrivial reduction in code size. An example of the branch instruction branch on equal is given in Figure 6.

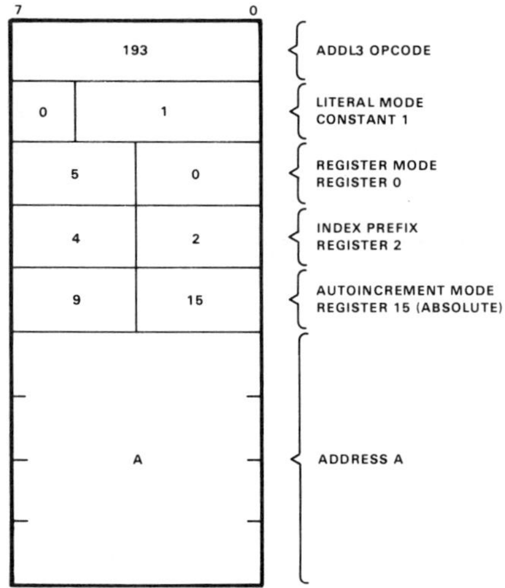

Figure 4. ADDL3 #1, R0, @#A(R2).

Instruction Set

A major goal of the VAX-11 instruction set design was to provide for effective compiler-generated code. Four decisions helped to realize this goal.

1. A very regular and consistent treatment of operators. Thus, for example, because there is a divide longword instruction, there are also divide word and divide byte instructions.
2. An avoidance of instructions unlikely to be generated by a compiler.
3. Inclusion of several forms of common operators. For example, the integer add instructions are included in three forms: (1) one operand where the value one is added to a operand, (2) two operand where one operand is added to a second, and (3) three operand where one operand is added to a second and the result stored in a third. Because the VAX-11 instruction format allows general specifications of the operands, VAX-11 programs often have the structure (though not the encoding) of the canonic program form proposed in [Flynn, 1977].

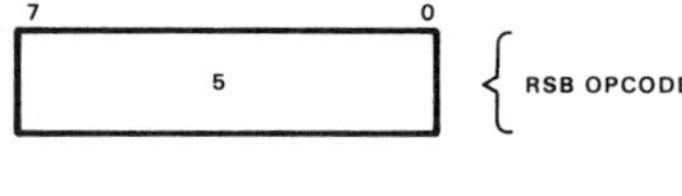

Figure 5. RSB.

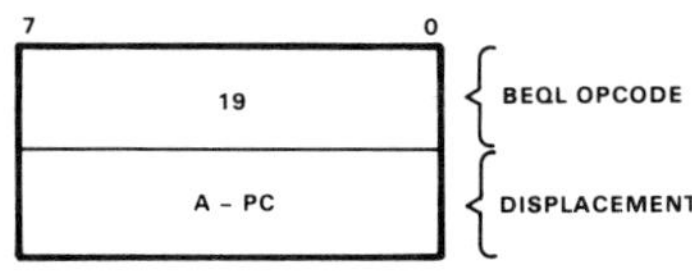

Figure 6. BEQL A.

4. Replacement of common instruction sequences with single instructions. Examples of this include procedure calling, multiway branching, loop control, and array subscript calculation.

The effect of these decisions is reflected through several observations. First, despite the larger virtual address and instruction set support for more data-types, compiler (and hand) generated code for VAX-11 is typically smaller than the equivalent PDP-11 code for algorithms operating on data-types supported by the PDP-11. Second, of the 243 instructions in the instruction set, about 75 percent are generated by the VAX-11 FORTRAN compiler. Of the instructions not generated, most operate on data-types not part of the FORTRAN language.

A complete list of the VAX-11 instructions is given in the appendix. The following is an overview of the instruction set.

1. **Integer logic and arithmetic.** Byte, word, and longword are the primary data-types. A fairly conventional group of arithmetic and logical instructions is provided. The result-generating dyadic arithmetic and logical instructions are provided in two and three operand forms. A number of optimizations are included: "clear," which is a move of zero; "test," which is a compare against zero; and "increment" and "decrement," which are optimizations of add one and subtract one, respectively. A complete set of converts is provided which covers both the integer and the floating data-types. In contrast to other architectures, only a few shift-type instructions are provided; it was felt that shifts are mostly used for field isolation which is much more conveniently done with the field instructions described later. In order to support greater-than-longword precision integer operations, a few special instructions are provided: "extended multiply," "divide," "add with carry," and "subtract with carry."
2. **Floating-point instructions.** Again a conventional group of instructions are included with result-producing dyadic operators in two and three operand forms. Several specialized floating-point instructions are included. The "extended modulus" instruction multiplies two floating operands together and stores the integer and fraction parts of the product in separate result operands. The "polynomial" instruction computes a polynomial from a table of coefficients in memory. Both these instructions employ greater than normal precision and are useful in high accuracy mathematical routines. A "convert rounded" instruction is provided which implements ALGOL rather than FORTRAN conventions for converting from floating-point to integer.
3. **Address instructions.** The "move address" instructions store in the result operand the effective address of the source operand. The "push address" optimizations push on the stack (defined by SP) the effective address of the source operand. The latter are used extensively in subroutine calling.
4. **Field instructions.** The "extract field" instructions extract a 0- to 32-bit field, sign- or zero-extend it if it is less than 32 bits, and store it in a longword operand. The "compare field" instructions compare a (sign- or zero-extended if necessary) field against a longword operand. The "find first" instructions find the first occurrence of a set or clear bit in a field.
5. **Control instructions.** There is a complete set of conditional branches supporting both a signed and, where appropriate, an unsigned interpretation of the various

data-types. These branches test the condition codes and take a one-byte PC relative branch displacement. There are three unconditional branch instructions: the first taking a one-byte PC relative displacement, the second taking a word PC relative displacement, and the third – called "jump" – taking a general operand specification. Paralleling these three instructions are three "branch to subroutine" instructions. These push the curent PC on the stack before transferring control. The single-byte "return from subroutine" instruction returns from subroutines called by these instructions. There is a set of "branch on bit" instructions which branch on the state of a single bit and, depending on the instruction, set, clear, or leave unchanged that bit.

The "add compare and branch" instructions are used for loop control. A step operand is added to the loop control operand and the sum is compared to a limit operand. Optimizations of loop control include the "add one and branch" instructions which assume a step of one, and the "subtract one and branch" instructions which assume a step of minus one and a limit of zero.

The "case" instructions implement the computed goto in FORTRAN and case statements in other languages. A selector operand is checked to see that it lies in range and is then used to select one of a table of PC relative branch displacements following the instruction.

6. **Queue instructions.** The queue representation is a double-linked circular list. Instructions are provided to insert an item into a queue or to remove an item from a queue.
7. **Character string instructions.** The general move character instruction takes five operands specifying the lengths and starting addresses of the source and destination strings and a fill character to be used if the source string is shorter than the destination string. The instruction functions correctly regardless of string overlap. An optimized move character instruction assumes the string lengths are equal and takes three operands. Paralleling the move instructions are two "compare character" instructions. The "move translated characters" instruction is similar to the general move character instruction except that the source string bytes are translated by a translation table specified by the instruction before being moved to destination string. The "move translated until escape" instruction stops if the result of a translation matches the escape character specified by one of its operands. The "locate character" and "skip character" instructions find, respectively, the first occurrence or non-occurrence of a character in a string. The "scan" and "span" instructions find, respectively, the first occurrence or non-occurrence of a character within a specified character set in a string. The "match characters" instruction finds the first occurrence of a substring within a string which matches a specified pattern string.
8. **Packed decimal instructions.** A conventional set of arithmetic instructions is provided. The "arithmetic shift and round" instruction provides decimal-point scaling and rounding. Converts are provided to and from longword integers, leading separate decimal strings, and trailing embedded decimal strings. A comprehensive "edit" instruction is included.

VAX-11 Procedure Instructions

A major goal of the VAX-11 design was to have a single system-wide procedure calling convention that would apply to all intermodule calls in the various languages, calls for operating system services, and calls to the common run-time system. Three VAX-11 instructions support this convention: two "call" instructions (which are indistinguishable as far as the called procedure is concerned) and a "return" instruction.

The call instructions assume that the first word of a procedure is an entry mask which specifies which registers are to be used by the procedure and thus need to be saved. (Actually only R0 through R11 are controlled by the entry mask and bits 15:12 of the mask are reserved for other purposes.) After pushing the registers to be saved on the stack, the call instruction pushes AP, FP, PC, a longword containing the PSW and the entry mask, and a zero-valued longword which is the initial value of a condition-handler address. The call instruction then loads FP with the contents of SP and AP with the argument list address. The appearance of the stack frame after the call is shown in the upper part of Figure 7.

The form of the argument list is shown in the lower part of Figure 7. It consists of an argument count and list of longword arguments which are typically addresses. The CALLG instruction takes two operands: one specifying the procedure address and the other specifying the address of the argument list assumed arbitrarily located in memory. The CALLS instruction also takes two operands: one the procedure address and the other an argument count. CALLS assumes that the arguments have been pushed on the stack and pushes the argument count immediately prior to saving the registers controlled by the entry mask. It also sets bit 13 of the saved entry mask to indicate that a CALLS instruction is used to make the call.

The return instruction uses FP to locate the stack frame. It loads SP with the contents of FP and restores PSW through PC by popping the stack. The saved entry mask controls the popping and restoring of R11 through R0. Finally, if the bit indicating CALLS is set, the argument list is removed from the stack.

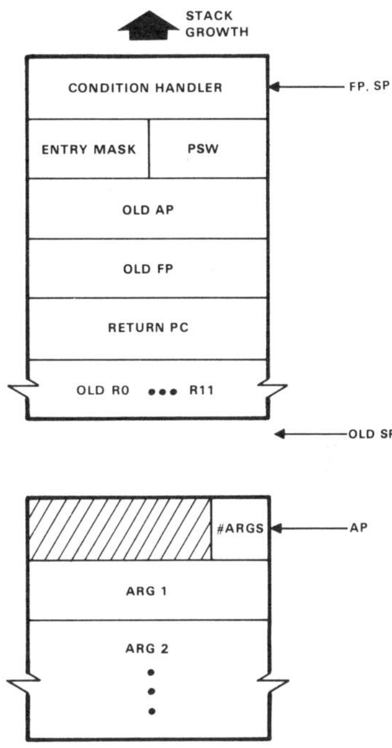

Figure 7. Stack frame.

Memory Management Design Alternatives

Memory management is comprised of the mechanisms used: (1) to map the virtual addresses generated by processes to physical memory addresses; (2) to control access to memory (i.e., to control whether a process has read, write, or no access to various areas of memory); and (3) to allow a process to execute even if all of its virtual address space is not simultaneously mapped to physical memory (i.e., to provide so-called virtual memory facilities). The memory management was the most difficult part of the architecture to design. Three alternatives were pursued, and full designs were completed for the first two alternatives and nearly completed for the third. The three alternatives were:*

1. A paged form of memory management with access control at the page level and a small number (four) of hierarchical access modes whose use would be dedicated to specific purposes. This represented an evolution of the PDP-11/70 memory management.
2. A paged and segmented form with access control at the segment level and a larger number (eight) of hierarchical access modes which would be used quite generally. Although it differed in a number of ways, the design was motivated by the Multics [Organick, 1972; Schroeder and Saltzer, 1971] architecture and the Honeywell 6180 implementation.
3. A capabilities [Needham, 1972; Needham and Walker, 1977] form with access control provided by the capabilities and the ability to page larger objects described by the capabilities.

The first alternative was finally selected. The second alternative was rejected because it was felt that the real increase in functionality inadequately offset the increased architectural complexity. The third alternative appeared to offer functionality advantages that could be useful over the long term. However, it was unlikely that these advantages could be exploited in the near term. Further, it appeared that the complexity of the capabilities design was inappropriate for a minicomputer system.

Memory Mapping

The 4.3-gigabyte virtual address space is divided into four regions as shown in Figure 8.

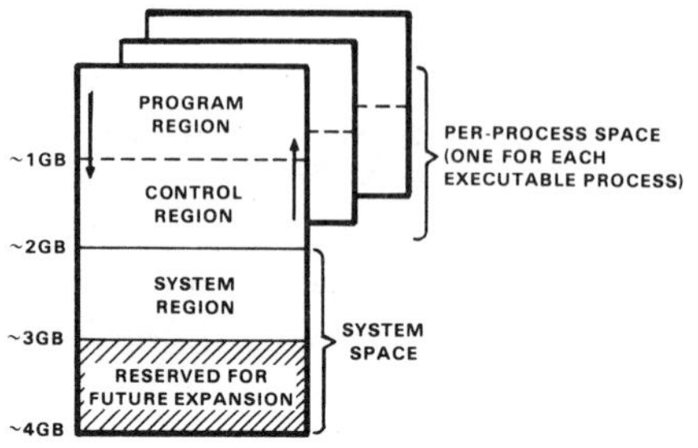

Figure 8. Virtual address space.

The first two regions – the program and control regions – comprise the per-process virtual address space which is uniquely mapped for each process. The second two regions – the system region and a region reserved for future use – comprise the system virtual address space which is singly mapped for all processes.

Each of the regions serves different purposes. The program region contains user programs and data, and the top of the region is a dynamic memory allocation point. The control region contains operating system data structures specific to the process and the user stack. The system region contains procedures that are common to all processes (such as those that comprise the operating system and RMS) and (as will be seen later) page tables.

A virtual address has the structure shown in the upper part of Figure 9. Bits 8:0 specify a byte within a 512-byte page which is the basic unit of mapping. Bits 29:9 specify a virtual page number (VPN). Bits 31:30 select the virtual address region. The mechanism of mapping consists of using the region select bits to select a page table which consists of page table entries (PTEs). After a check to see that it is not too large, the VPN is used to index into the page

*It should not be construed that memory management is independent of the rest of the architecture. The various memory management alternatives required different definitions of the addressing modes and different instruction level support for addressing.

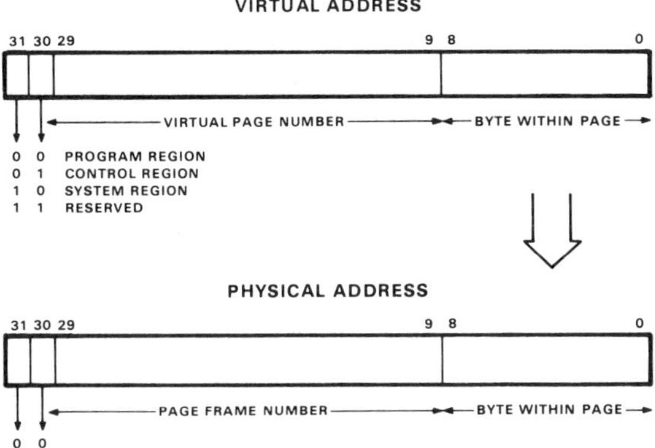

Figure 9. Virtual and physical addresses.

table to select a PTE. The PTE contains either: (1) 21-bit physical page frame number which is concatenated with the nine low order bytes in page bits to form a 30-bit physical address as shown in the lower part of Figure 9, or (2) an indication that the virtual page accessed is not in physical memory. The latter case is called a page fault. Instruction execution in the current procedure is suspended and control is transferred to an operating system procedure which causes the missing virtual page to be brought into physical memory. At this point, instruction execution in the suspended procedure can resume transparently.

The page table for the system region is defined by the system base register which contains the physical address of the start of the system region page table and the system length register which contains the length of the table. Thus, the system region page table is contiguous in physical memory.

The per-process space page tables are defined similarly by the program and control region base registers and length registers. However, the base registers do not contain physical addresses; rather, they contain system region virtual addresses. Thus, the per-process page tables are contiguous in the system region virtual address space and are not necessarily contiguous in physical memory. This placement of the per-process page tables permits them to be paged and avoids what would otherwise be a serious physical memory allocation problem.

Access Control

At a given point in time, a process executes in one of four access modes. The modes from most to least privileged are called Kernel, Executive, Supervisor and User. The use of these modes by VAX/VMS is as follows.

1. **Kernel.** Interrupt and exception handling, scheduling, paging, physical I/O, etc.
2. **Executive.** Logical I/O as provided by RMS.
3. **Supervisor.** The command interpreter.
4. **User.** User procedures and data.

The accessability of each page (read, write, or no access) from each access mode is specified in the PTE for that page. Any attempt to improperly access a page is suppressed and control is transferred to an operating system procedure. The accessibility is assumed hierarchically ordered: If a page is writable from any given mode, it is also readable; and if a page is accessible from a less-privileged mode, it is accessible from a more privileged mode. Thus, for example, a page can be readable and writable from Kernel mode, only readable from Executive mode, and inaccessible from Supervisor and User modes.

A procedure executing in a less-privileged mode often needs to call a procedure that executes in a more privileged mode; e.g., a user program needs an operating system service performed. The access mode is changed to a more privileged mode by executing a "change mode" instruction that transfers control to a routine executing at the new access mode. A return is made to original access mode by executing a "return from exception or interrupt" instruction (REI).

The current access mode is stored in the processor status longword (PSL) whose low-order 16 bits comprise the PSW. Also stored in the PSL is the previous access mode, i.e., the access mode from which the current access mode was called. The previous mode information is used by the special "probe" instructions which validate arguments passed in cross-access mode calls.

Procedures running at each of the access modes require separate stacks with appropriate accessibility. To facilitate this, each process has four copies of SP which are selected according to the current access mode field in the PSL. A procedure always accesses the correct stack by using R14.

In an earlier section it was stated that the VAX-11 standard CALL instruction is used for all calls including those for operating system services. Indeed, procedures do call the operating system using the CALL instruction. The target of the CALL instruction is the minimal procedure consisting of an entry mask, a change mode instruction and a return instruction. Thus, access mode changing is transparent to the calling procedure.

Interrupts and Exceptions

Interrupts and exceptions are forced changes in control flow other than those explicitly indicated by the executing program. The distinction between them is that interrupts are normally unrelated to the currently executing program while exceptions are a direct consequence of program execution. Examples of interrupt conditions are status changes in I/O devices; examples of exception conditions are arithmetic overflow or a memory management access control violation.

VAX-11 provides a 31-priority-level interrupt system. Sixteen levels (16 through 31) are provided for hardware while 15 levels (1 through 15) are provided for software. (Level 0 is used for normal program execution.) The current interrupt priority level (IPL) is stored in a field in the PSL. When an interrupt request is made at a level higher than IPL, the current PC and PSL are pushed on the stack and new PC is obtained from a vector selected by the interrupt requester (a new PSL is generated by the CPU). Interrupts are serviced by routines executing with Kernel mode access control. Since interrupts are appropriately serviced in a system-wide context rather than a specific process context, the stack used for interrupts is defined by another stack pointer called the interrupt stack pointer. (Just as for the multiple stack pointers used in process context, an interrupt routine accesses the interrupt stack using R14.) An interrupt service is terminated by execution of an REI instruction which loads PC and PSL from the top two longwords on the stack.

Exceptions are handled like interrupts except for the following: (1) because exceptions arise in a specific process context, the Kernel mode stack for that process is used to store PC and PSL, and (2) additional parameters (such as the virtual address causing a page fault) may be pushed on the stack.

Process Context Switching

From the standpoint of the VAX-11 architecture, the process state or context consists of:

1. The 15 general registers R0 through R13 and R15.
2. Four copies of R14 (SP): one for each of Kernel, Executive, Supervisor, and User access modes.
3. The PSL.
4. Two base and two limit registers for the program and control region page tables.

This context is gathered together in a data structure called a process control block (PCB) which normally resides in memory. While a process is executing, the process context can be considered to reside in processor registers. To switch from one process to another, it is necessary that the process context from the previously executing process be saved in its PCB in memory, and that the process context for the process about to be executed be loaded from its PCB in memory. Two VAX-11 instructions support context switching. The "save process context" instruction saves the complete process context in memory while the "load process context" instruction loads the complete process context from memory.

I/O

Much like the PDP-11, VAX-11 has no specific I/O instructions. Rather, I/O devices and device controllers are implemented with a set of registers that have addresses in the physical memory address space. The CPU controls I/O devices by writing these registers, the devices return status by writing these registers, and the CPU subsequently reading them. The normal memory management mechanism controls access to I/O device registers, and a process having a particular device's registers mapped into its address space can control that device using the regular instruction set.

Compatibility Mode

As mentioned in the VAX-11 overview, compatibility mode in the VAX-11 architecture provides the basic PDP-11 instruction set less-privileged and floating-point instructions. Compatibility mode is intended to support a user as opposed to an operating system environment. Normally a Compatibility mode program is combined with a set of Native mode procedures whose purpose it is to map service requests from some particular PDP-11 operating system environment into VAX/VMS services.

In Compatibility mode, the 16-bit PDP-11 addresses are zero-extended to 32 bits where standard native mode mapping and access control apply. The eight 16-bit PDP-11 general registers overmap the Native mode general registers R0 through R6 and R15; thus, the PDP-11 processor state is contained wholly within the native mode processor state.

Compatibility mode is entered by setting the compatibility mode bit in the PSL. Compatibility mode is left by executing a PDP-11 "trap" instruction (such as that used to make operating system service requests), and on interrupts and exceptions.

VAX-11/780 IMPLEMENTATION

VAX-11/780

The VAX-11/780 computer system is the first implementation of the VAX-11 architecture. For instructions executed in Compatibility mode, the VAX-11/780 has a performance comparable to that of the PDP-11/70. For instructions executed in Native mode, the VAX-11/780 has a performance in excess of that of the PDP-11/70 and, thus, represents the new high end of the 11 family (LSI-11, PDP-11, VAX-11).

A block diagram of the VAX-11/780 system is given in Figure 10. The system consists of a central processing unit (CPU), the console subsystem, the memory subsystem, and the I/O subsystem. The CPU and the memory and I/O subsystems are joined by a high-speed synchronous bus called the synchronous backplane interconnect (SBI).

CPU

The CPU is a microprogrammed processor that implements the Native and Compatibility mode instruction sets, the memory management, and the interrupt and exception mechanisms. The CPU has 32-bit main data paths and is built almost entirely of conventional Shottky TTL components.

To reduce effective memory access time, the CPU includes an 8-Kbyte write-through cache

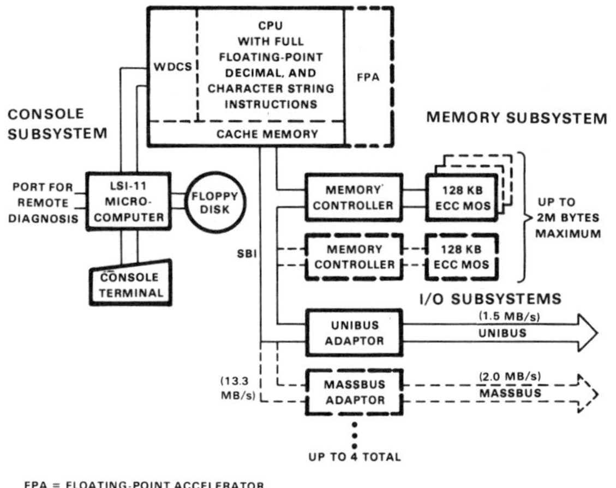

Figure 10. VAX-11/780 system.

or buffer memory. The cache organization is two-way associative with an eight-byte block size. To reduce delays due to writes, the CPU includes a write buffer. The CPU issues the write to the buffer and the actual memory write takes place in parallel with other CPU activity.

The CPU contains a 128-entry address translation buffer which is a cache of recent virtual-to-physical translations. The buffer is divided into two 64-entry sections: one for the per-process regions and one for the system region. This division permits the system region translations to remain unaffected by a process context switch.

A fourth buffer in the CPU is the eight-byte instruction buffer. It serves two purposes. First, it decomposes the highly variable instruction format into its basic components and, second, it constantly fetches ahead to reduce delays in obtaining the instruction components.

The CPU includes two standard clocks. The programmable real-time clock is used by the operating system for local timing purposes. The time-of-year clock with its own battery backup is the long-term reference for the operating system. It is automatically read on system startup to eliminate the need for manual entry of date and time.

The CPU includes 12 Kbytes of writable diagnostic control store (WDCS) which is used for diagnostic purposes, implementation of certain instructions, and for future microcode changes. As an option for very sophisticated users, another 12 Kbytes of writable control store is available.

A second option is the Floating-Point Accelerator (FPA). Although the basic CPU implements the full floating-point instruction set, the FPA provides high speed floating-point hardware. It is logically invisible to programs and affects only their running time.

Console Subsystem

The console subsystem is centered around an LSI-11 computer with 16 Kbytes of RAM and 8 Kbytes of ROM (used to store the LSI-11 bootstrap, LSI-11 diagnostics, and console routines). Also included are a floppy disk, an interface to the console terminal, and a port for remote diagnostic purposes.

The floppy disk in the console subsystem serves multiple purposes. It stores the main system bootstrap and diagnostics and serves as a medium for distribution of software updates.

SBI

The SBI is the primary control and data transfer path in the VAX-11/780 system. Because the cache and write buffer largely decouple the CPU performance from the memory access time, the SBI design was optimized for bandwidth and reliability rather than the lowest possible access time.

The SBI is a synchronous bus with a cycle time of 200 nanoseconds. The data path width of the SBI is 32 bits. During each 200-nanosecond cycle, either 32 bits of data or a 30-bit physical address can be transferred. Because each 32-bit read or write requires transmission of both address and data, two SBI cycles are used for a complete transaction. The SBI protocol permits 64-bit reads or writes using one address cycle and two data transfer cycles; the CPU and I/O subsystem use this mode whenever possible. For read transactions the bus is reacquired by the memory in order to send the data; thus, the bus is not held during the memory access time.

Arbitration of the SBI is distributed: each interface to the SBI has a specific priority and its own bus request line. When an interface wishes to use the bus, it asserts its bus request line. If, at the end of a 200-nanosecond cycle, there are no interfaces of higher priority requesting the bus, the interface takes control of the bus.

Extensive checking is done on the SBI. Each transfer is parity-checked and confirmed by the receiver. The arbitration process and general observance of the SBI protocol are checked by each SBI interface during each SBI cycle. The processor maintains a running 16-cycle history of the SBI; any SBI error condition causes this history to be locked and preserved for diagnostic purposes.

Memory Subsystem

The memory subsystem consists of one or two memory controllers with up to 1 Mbytes of memory on each. The memory is organized in 64-bit quadwords with an 8-bit ECC which provides single-bit error correction and double-bit error detection. The memory is built of 4 Kbit MOS RAM components.

The memory controllers have buffers that hold up to four memory requests. These buffers substantially increase the utilization of the SBI and memory by permitting the pipelining of multiple memory requests. If desired, quadword physical addresses can be interleaved across the memory controllers.

As an option, battery backup is available which preserves the contents of memory across short-term power failures.

I/O Subsystem

The I/O subsystem consists of buffered interfaces or adapters between the SBI and the two types of peripheral buses used on PDP-11 systems: the Unibus and the Massbus. One Unibus adapter and up to four Massbus adapters can be configured on a VAX-11/780 system.

The Unibus is a medium speed multiplexer bus that is used as a primary memory as well as peripheral bus in many PDP-11 systems. It has an 18-bit physical address space and supports byte and word transfers. In addition to implementing the Unibus protocol and transmitting interrupts to the CPU, the Unibus adapter provides two other functions. The first is mapping 18-bit Unibus addresses to 30-bit SBI physical addresses. This is accomplished in a manner substantially identical to the virtual-to-physical mapping implemented by the CPU. The Unibus address space is divided into 512 512-byte pages. Each Unibus page has a page table entry (residing in the Unibus adapter) which maps addresses in that page to physical memory addresses. In addition to providing address translation, the mapping permits contiguous transfers on the Unibus which cross page boundaries to be mapped to discontiguous physical memory page frames.

The second function performed by the Unibus adapter is assembling 16-bit Unibus transfers (both reads and writes) into 64-bit SBI transfers. This operation (which is applicable only to block transfers such as from disks) appreciably reduces SBI traffic due to Unibus operations. There are 15 8-byte buffers in the Unibus adapter permitting 15 simultaneous buffered transactions. Additionally, there is an unbuffered path through the Unibus adapter permitting an arbitrary number of simultaneous unbuffered transfers.

The Massbus is a high speed block transfer bus used primarily for disks and tapes. The Massbus adapter provides much the same functionality as the Unibus adapter. The physical addresses into which transfers are made are defined by a page table; again, this permits contiguous device transfers into discontiguous physical memory.

Buffering is provided in the Massbus adapter which minimizes the probability of device over-runs and assembles data into 64-bit units for transfer over the SBI.

ACKNOWLEDGEMENTS

Although the final architecture is the result of several design iterations involving many hardware and software engineers, the author would like to acknowledge the other members of the initial architectual group: Gordon Bell, Peter Conklin, Dave Cutler, Bill Demmer, Tom Hastings, Richy Lary, Dave Rodgers, and Steve Rothman. Mary Jane Forbes and Louise Principe deserve special thanks for typing this manuscript.

APPENDIX – VAX-11 INSTRUCTION SET

Integer and Floating-Point Logical Instructions

MOV-	Move (B, W, L, F, D, Q)*
MNEG-	Move Negated (B, W, L, F, D)
MCOM-	Move Complemented (B, W, L)
MOVZ-	Move Zero-Extended (BW, BL, WL)
CLR-	Clear (B, W, L = F, Q = D)
CVT-	Convert (B, W, L, F, D) (B, W, L, F, D)
CVTR-L	Convert Rounded (F, D) to Longword
CMP-	Compare (B, W, L, F, D)
TST-	Test (B, W, L, F, D)
BIS-2	Bit Set (B, W, L) 2-Operand
BIS-3	Bit Set (B, W, L) 3-Operand
BIC-2	Bit Clear (B, W, L) 2-Operand
BIC-3	Bit Clear (B, W, L) 3-Operand
BIT-	Bit Test (B, W, L)
XOR-2	Exclusive OR (B, W, L) 2-Operand
XOR-3	Exclusive OR (B, W, L) 3-Operand
ROTL	Rotate Longword
PUSHL	Push Longword

Integer and Floating-Point Arithmetic Instructions

INC-	Increment (B, W, L)
DEC-	Decrement (B, W, L)
ASH-	Arithmetic Shift (L, Q)
ADD-2	Add (B, W, L, F, D) 2-Operand
ADD-3	Add (B, W, L, F, D) 3-Operand
ADWC	Add with Carry
ADAWI	Add Aligned Word Interlocked
SUB-2	Subtract (B, W, L, F, D) 2-Operand
SUB-3	Subtract (B, W, L, F, D) 3-Operand
SBWC	Subtract with Carry
MUL-2	Multiply (B, W, L, F, D) 2-Operand
MUL-3	Multiply (B, W, L, F, D) 3-Operand
EMUL	Extended Multiply
DIV-2	Divide (B, W, L, F, D) 2-Operand
DIV-3	Divide (B, W, L, F, D) 3-Operand
EDIV	Extended Divide
EMOD-	Extended Modulus (F, D)
POLY-	Polynomial Evaluation (F, D)

* B = byte, W = word, L = longword, F = floating, D = double floating, Q = quadword, S = set, C = clear.

Packed Decimal Instructions

MOVP	Move Packed
CMPP3	Compare Packed 3-Operand
CMPP4	Compare Packed 4-Operand
ASHP	Arithmetic Shift and Round Packed
ADDP4	Add Packed 4-Operand
ADDP6	Add Packed 6-Operand
SUBP4	Subtract Packed 4-Operand
SUBP6	Subtract Packed 6-Operand
MULP	Multiply Packed
DIVP	Divide Packed
CVTLP	Convert Long to Packed
CVTPL	Convert Packed to Long
CVTPT	Convert Packed to Trailing
CVTTP	Convert Trailing to Packed
CVTPS	Convert Packed to Separate
CVTSP	Convert Separate to Packed
EDITPC	Edit Packed to Character String

Character String Instructions

MOVC3	Move Character 3-Operand
MOVC5	Move Character 5-Operand
MOVTC	Move Translated Characters
MOVTUC	Move Translated Until Character
CMPC3	Compare Characters 3-Operand
CMPC5	Compare Characters 5-Operand
LOCC	Locate Character
SKPC	Skip Character
SCANC	Scan Characters
SPANC	Span Characters
MATCHC	Match Characters

Variable-Length Bit Field Instructions

EXTV	Extract Field
EXTZV	Extract Zero-Extended Field
INSV	Insert Field
CMPV	Compare Field
CMPZV	Compare Zero-Extended Field
FFS	Find First Set
FFC	Find First Clear

Index Instruction

INDEX	Compute Index

Queue Instructions

INSQUE	Insert Entry in Queue
REMQUE	Remove Entry from Queue

Address Manipulation Instructions

MOVA-	Move Address (B, W, L = F, Q = D)
PUSHA-	Push Address (B, W, L = F, Q = D) on Stack

Processor State Instructions

PUSHR	Push Registers on Stack
POPR	Pop Registers from Stack
MOVPSL	Move from Processor Status Longword
BISPSW	Bit Set Processor Status Word
BICPSW	Bit Clear Processor Status Word

Unconditional Branch and Jump Instructions

BR-	Branch with (B, W) Displacement
JMP	Jump

Branch on Bit Instructions

BLB-	Branch on Low Bit (S, C)
BB-	Branch on Bit (S, C)
BBS-	Branch on Bit Set and (S, C) Bit
BBC-	Branch on Bit Clear and (S, C) Bit
BBSSI	Branch on Bit Set and Set Bit Interlocked
BBCCI	Branch on Bit Clear and Clear Bit Interlocked

Loop and Case Branch

ACB-	Add, Compare and Branch (B, W, L, F, D)
AOBLEQ	Add One and Branch Less Than or Equal
AOBLSS	Add One and Branch Less Than
SOBGEQ	Subtract One and Branch Greater Than or Equal
SOBGTR	Subtract One and Branch Greater Than
CASE-	Case on (B, W, L)

Subroutine Call and Return Instructions

BSB-	Branch to Subroutine with (B, W) Displacement
JSB	Jump to Subroutine
RSB	Return from Subroutine

Procedure Call and Return Instructions

CALLG	Call Procedure with General Argument List
CALLS	Call Procedure with Stack Argument List
RET	Return from Procedure

Access Mode Instructions

CHM-	Change Mode to (Kernel, Executive, Supervisor, User)
REI	Return from Exception or Interrupt
PROBER	Probe Read
PROBEW	Probe Write

Branch on Condition Code

BLSS	Less Than
BLSSU	Less Than Unsigned
(BCS)	(Carry Set)
BLEQ	Less Than or Equal
BLEQU	Less Than or Equal Unsigned
BEQL	Equal
(BEQLU)	(Equal Unsigned)
BNEQ	Not Equal
(BNEQU)	(Not Equal Unsigned)
BGTR	Greater Than
BGTRU	Greater Than Unsigned
BGEQ	Greater Than or Equal
BGEQU	Greater Than or Equal Unsigned
(BCC)	(Carry Clear)
BVS	Overflow Set
BVC	Overflow Clear

Privileged Processor Register Control Instructions

SVPCTX	Save Process Context
LDPCTX	Load Process Context
MTPR	Move to Process Register
MFPR	Move from Processor Register

Special Function Instructions

CRC	Cyclic Redundancy Check
BPT	Breakpoint Fault
XFC	Extended Function Call
NOP	No Operation
HALT	Halt

Opposite:

- A small Register Transfer Module (RTM) system.

PART IV

EVOLUTION OF COMPUTER BUILDING BLOCKS

Evolution of Computer Building Blocks

As discussed in Chapter 1, a computer system can be viewed as a hierarchy of structural levels, each level consisting of a set of elements that are aggregates of those at the next lower level. From that point of view, the PDP-1 was constructed from elements or building blocks that were DEC Systems Modules, each containing elements from the switching circuit level of the structural hierarchy (AND gates, OR gates, etc.). When the integrated circuit was introduced, the number of components in one indivisible package became an order of magnitude larger than it had been with discrete components. The functionality contained in a single DEC module increased accordingly, and it was not long before computers were constructed using building blocks from the next higher level in the structural hierarchy. At that level, the register transfer (RT) level, modules each contained register files, multiplexers, arithmetic logic units, and so on. The functions available in a single integrated circuit, and the functionality available in a single module, have been dictated by the search for universal functions discussed in the section "LSI dilemma," in Chapter 2.

While Chapters 4 and 5 are devoted to the history of DEC modules and the circuit and logic level characteristics that developed in the various module families as a result of the advances in semiconductor technology, the chapters in Part IV emphasize the role of modules as digital systems and computer building blocks. Thus, the emphasis is on the use of modules at the register transfer and processor-memory-switch (PMS) levels of the structural hierarchy.

Two types of building block are discussed:

1. Module sets are building blocks used to construct digital systems, often specialized computers, where short design time is the primary goal. For example, they are used in constructing low volume special purpose equipment, or in teaching.
2. Computer elements are mainstream building blocks used to construct computers when the primary goal is cost/performance of the design and design time is secondary.

REGISTER TRANSFER MODULES (RTMs)

The most complete examples of the module set building blocks are the Register Transfer Modules (RTMs) produced by DEC in the late 1960s and the Macromodules proposed by Wes Clark in 1967 [Clark, 1967; Ornstein *et al.*, 1967]. The Register Transfer Modules are of interest because they were building blocks of a

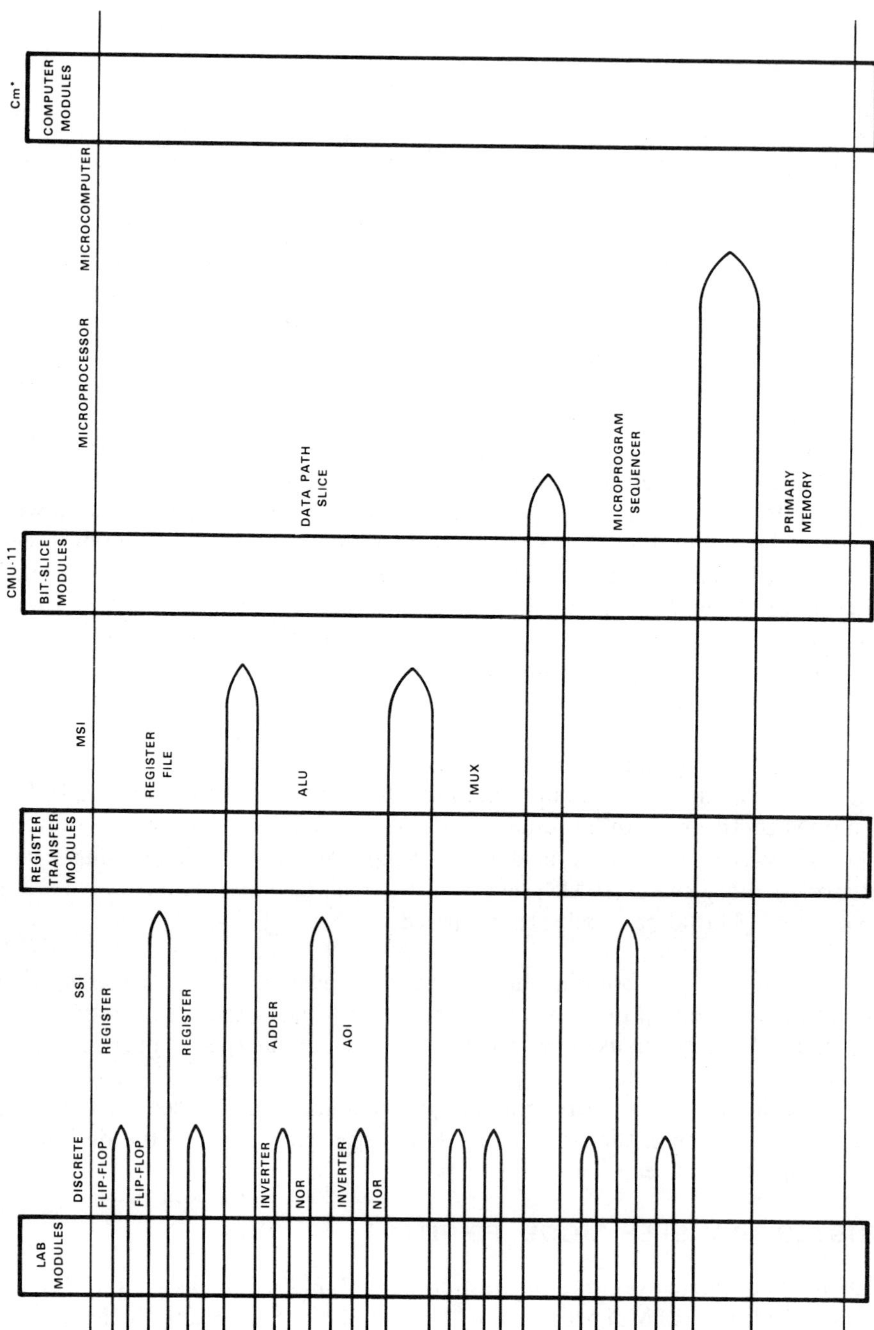

Figure 1 Progression of packaging of computer elements showing four levels treated in Part IV.

high level of functionality which were produced and marketed commercially. Moreover, they offer an opportunity to assess design at the register transfer level and to assess the use of design languages. The Macromodules are of interest because they preceded the Register Transfer Modules and differed from RTMs in several important ways. Macromodules were five times as expensive as RTMs but twice as fast. Macromodule systems were less permanent when constructed than RTMs but were easier to wire. The two building block types also differed in design style. The data memory system with general purpose arithmetic capability available in Register Transfer Modules led to a central accumulator style of design, whereas Macromodules used a distributed data and memory style.

Table 1. Register Transfer Module Types

K Type	Data Operator	Memory
2-way Branch	2-input AND, OR	Byte
8-way Branch	4-input AND, OR	Word Transfer
Bus Sense and Termination	4-input Decoder	4-word Constants
	2-input EXCLUSIVE-OR	24-word Constants
Clock	NOT	16-word Scratchpad
Delay	Flags (Boolean)	256-word Array
Integrating Delay	General Purpose Aritmetic	1,024-word Array
Diverge (null)		1,024-word Read-only
Evoke		
No Operation	**Transducers**	
Parallel Merge		
2-way Serial Merge	Analog-to-Digital	
4-way Serial Merge	Digital-to-Analog	
Subroutine Call	General Purpose Interface	
Program Controlled	Input Interface	
Sequencer	Lights and Switches	
	Output Interface	
	Serial Interface	

The RTM paper (Chapter 18) describes the module set and the design decisions leading to it. Two design examples are given, the second being a small stored program computer, a nontrivial test of the completeness of the set. The module set consisted of 36 modules, of which 10 came from the standard DEC catalog. Table 1 gives a list of the modules available.

Additional studies on Register Transfer Modules documented user experience with RTMs. A 1973 workshop on the architecture and application of digital modules is reported by Fuller and Siewiorek [1973], who compare the cost, performance, and design time of the modular systems to standard small- and medium-scale integration systems. They note that modular systems were more expensive because a substantial portion of their cost was a result of those features that made them modular. These included features to establish module protocol, to allow word extendability, and to ensure electrical compatibility. It was estimated that this cost was 50–70 percent of the total cost of Macromodules and 30 percent of the total cost of RTMs. Systems built with modules cost between two and ten times that of comparable systems built from small- and medium-scale integrated circuits. Performance comparisons were also reported and included:

1. A PDP-8 designed with Register Transfer Modules performed at 40 percent of the speed of the DEC-built PDP-8 and cost twice as much.
2. Matrix multiply programmed on a small machine built with RTMs took 400 microseconds, 5 microseconds on a CDC 7600, and 35 microseconds in Macromodules.
3. The Fast Fourier Transform butterfly multiply implemented in Macromodules was comparable in execution time to one programmed on a CDC 6600.
4. A program for the major path of an electrocardiogram preprocessor executed in 7 microseconds on a CDC 6600 and 37 microseconds on a PDP-9. A Macromodule system took 3 microseconds and a TTL design took a projected 1.5 microseconds.

Register Transfer Modules clearly met their educational goal. Their use in Carnegie-Mellon's Digital Systems Laboratory is reported in [Grason and Siewiorek, 1975]. Four student projects are described: a system to simulate the soft landing of a rocket under computer control, real-time monitoring of an instrument flight trainer, a computer-controlled transit system, and a computer-guided vehicle with ultrasonic obstacle detection.

Module sets have been used in research on design automation at the register transfer level. The work with the Carnegie-Mellon RT-CAD system, reported in [Siewiorek and Barbacci, 1976], attempted to go beyond the conventional work (register transfer level simulation and synthesis of designs from register transfer level descriptions) into the realm of automated design space exploration.

While Register Transfer Modules were used in educational projects and in research projects, the DEC-built computer using Register Transfer Modules, the PDP-16, was not as commercially successful as had been hoped. Until 1965, the DEC Modules sector of DEC's business had been as profitable as any other and had been growing as fast. However, once integrated circuits became widely used in 1966, the revenues from DEC Modules ceased to grow. Register Transfer Modules were an attempt to revive growth in modules by offering building blocks at the right level, i.e., the one suggested by the underlying circuit technology. There appear to have been two reasons for their lack of success. The first, as described in [Grason, *et al.,* 1973], was designer resistance to designing at the higher level; the second was that Register Transfer Modules were introduced too late. The availability of complex functions in a single chip, particularly microprocessors such as the Intel 8008 introduced in the early 1970s, cut short the life of the RTM.

History might have been different if the module for microprogrammed control had been available at the outset, but because low cost semiconductor read-only memories were not available, it was not. A second reason for not using microprogramming at the outset was that the parallelism inherent in the data-memory part of a system could not be fully exploited unless an arbitrarily wide control store could be built. Indeed, this limitation is experienced in the use of today's bit-slice sequencers.

Perhaps the highest payoff from Register Transfer Modules, both an indirect and intangible benefit, has been their influence on the bit-slice and other building blocks such as the Fairchild MACROLOGIC and AMD 2900-series devices. RTMs have provided experience in thinking about the process of design and have stimulated thinking about the choices of primitives, notations, and levels. They have influenced the choice of data-memory and processor elements and the use of microprogrammed controls.

BIT-SLICES (FRACTIONAL REGISTER TRANSFER LEVEL MODULES) AS BUILDING BLOCKS

Chapter 19 on the CMU-11 is important because it documents the experience of testing a set of building blocks in a real design. Only by carrying out a complete design (whether on paper or to the breadboard stage) can the suitability be measured. The paper is a strong case study; it provides good engineering data, such as the breakdown of the package count for each of the three major parts of the design: data, control, and Unibus.

The CMU-11 was built using Intel 3000-series bit-slices. Since the time that the CMU-11 project was started, newer series of bit-slice components have become available, most notably the AMD 2900-series. Today, these components are the dominant mainstream building blocks and have been used in a variety of applications. For example, the 4 bit wide AM2901 slice was used in 1976 to implement the 64 bit wide data path of the Floating-Point Processor for the PDP-11/34, and bit-slices are now the technology of choice for mid-range PDP-11 processors (Chapter 13).

The building blocks available in 1978 are reasonably represented by the following:

1. **Datapath slice**. A 4-bit-wide slice containing an arithmetic and logic unit, 16 registers in a two-port file, data buses, shifter, and multiplexers (the AM2901).
2. **Microprogram control unit**. A circuit which generates control store addresses; it contains the micro-level program counter, incrementer, a stack, and the circuitry to select the machine state inputs (AM2909: 4 bits wide, or AM2911: 12 bits wide).
3. **Interrupt processing unit**. (AM2914).
4. **Interface circuits**. The AM2917 is a typical circuit and contains bus transceivers for 4 lines, a data register, latch, and parity tree.

Design aids include a microprogram assembler, an evaluation kit, and a microprogram debugging and editing facility.

In late 1977, two new circuits with higher functionality were introduced. The AM2903, a successor to the AM2901, has added multiplication and division primitives, extended shifting, and an expandable register file [Coleman *et al.*, 1977]; and the AM2904 to control shift register linkages, a micro-level status register, and carry control. Given this wider range for the designer to choose from, the proportion of a processor that can cost-effectively use bit-slices should be higher than the 20 percent in CMU-11. However, it probably would not exceed 40 percent. For example, 29 percent of the CMU-11 cost (board area) is due to the circuits for a Unibus interface which could not be implemented with acceptable performance by the bit-slice components; even the newly available bit-slices would not impact this area. Moreover, as more PDP-11 specific functions are added, the area would decrease.

The bit-slices discussed above use Schottky TTL logic and result in a microinstruction cycle time of between 100 and 300 nanoseconds (200 is average). Bit-slices in other logic families exist, for example, the Motorola 10800, an ECL slice, which has a microinstruction cycle time of 55 nanoseconds.

COMPUTER MODULES

As the underlying circuit technology moves to higher and higher levels of complexity per chip, competition from modules at the next higher level of design becomes viable. An example is the substitution of PMS level modules for RT level modules (RTMs). Register transfer level module sets are then either abandoned or applied in a different application area – the higher speed area.

The proposal for a set of PMS level system-building modules of about minicomputer complexity was first made in [Bell *et al.*, 1973], where they were called "Computer Modules" (CMs). A CM consists of a processor and memory, together with several carefully designed ports, as shown in Figure 2. Given that the

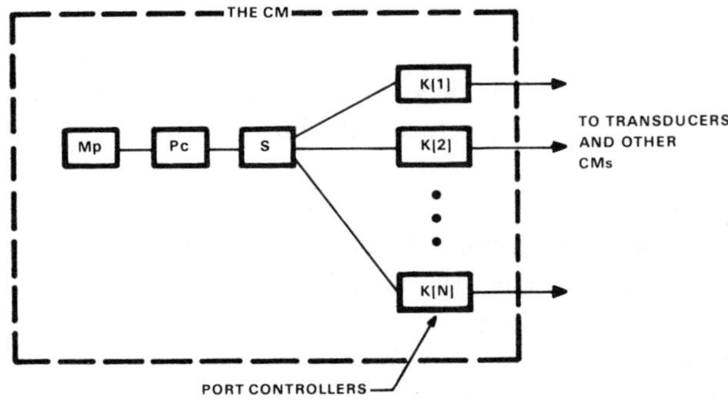

Figure 2. PMS diagram of Computer Module.

I/O and interrupt structure of conventional computers makes it difficult to construct closely coupled networks, the port architecture was proposed. It was designed to handle operations such as handshaking and buffering, executing concurrently with the processor of the CM. The port was intended to allow construction of CM systems covering a wide range of cost and performance.

The paper argued strongly, based on the increasing complexity and decreasing cost of large-scale integrated circuits, for the investigation of large digital modules. The then current microprocessors of Intel, National Semiconductor, and AMD were seen as precursors of computer modules. The Computer Module was also viewed as part of the evolution of centralized computer structures into highly distributed, intelligent networks.

The set of applications investigated included array processing (Fast Fourier Transform processing, generalized array processing, and radar signal processing), sorting, language processing (compilation and machine language interpretations), and process control. In each case, the intermodule communications requirements were emphasized, as was the range of performance that could be achieved by varying the CM system structure. The following table gives some of the expected characteristics of CM systems together with the actual values Cm*, the CMU multiprocessor that is the subject of Chapter 20.

Attribute	**1973 Paper**	**Cm* (1977)**
Processors	1	1
Memory Size	1 Kwords and over	28 Kwords
Word Size	8 to 16 bits	16
Ports	2 to 5	2
CMs per system	A few to several thousand	10

By late 1973, much of the design of CMs had been solidified. Bus structures were postulated, and the inter-CM communication was to be based on mappings between address spaces. A system of four CMs is shown in Figure 3.

In 1975, a second design was started. It used an LSI-11 as the basic CM. A 10 processor, 512-Kbyte primary memory prototype was completed and made available for experimentation in the spring of 1977. The detailed design and implementation of Cm* are discussed in a set of papers [Jones *et al.*, 1977; Swan *et al.*, 1977; and Swan *et al.*, 1977a]. Chapter 20 postdates these papers and is included because of the real performance data it contains.

The Chapter 20 Cm* work, sponsored by the National Science Foundation and the Advanced Research Projects Agency (ARPA) of the Department of Defense is an extension of earlier NSF-sponsored research [Bell *et al.*, 1973] on register transfer level modules. As large- and very large-scale integration enable construction of the processor-on-a-chip, it is apparent that low level Register Transfer

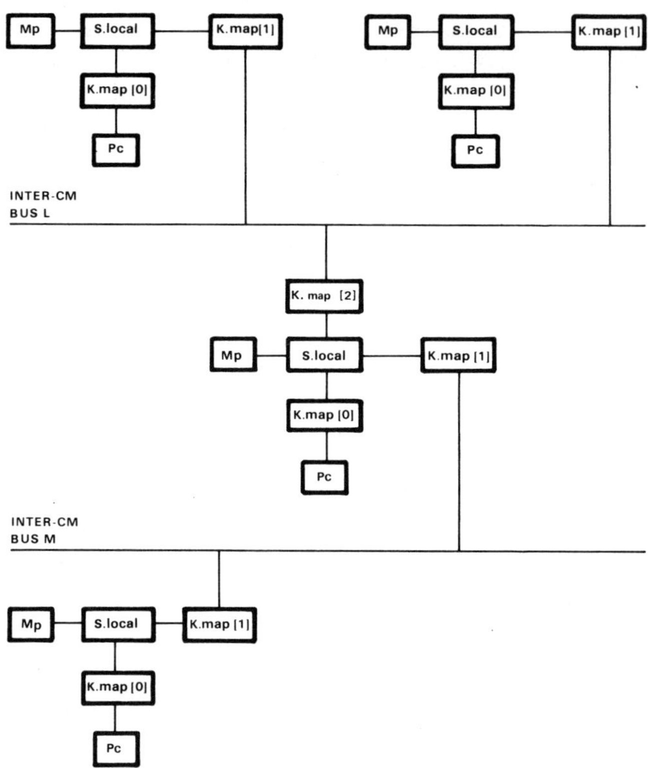

Figure 3. PMS diagram of four Computer Modules.

Modules are obsolete for the construction of all but low volume computers. Although the research is predicated on structures employing a hundred or so processors, this chapter describes the culmination of the first (10 processor) phase.

The authors motivate their work by appealing to diseconomy-of-scale arguments. To provide additional context for their research, computer modules (Cm*), multiprocessors (C.mmp), and computer networks are described in terms of performance and problem suitability. The chapter gives a description of the modules structure, together with associated limitations and potential research problems. The final, most important part of the chapter evaluates the performance of Cm* for five different problems.

It is interesting to note how the major focus has shifted from computer modules *per se* to multiprocessors. Three separate efforts in the Cm* project can be identified:

1. Multiprocessor architecture research.
2. Solving the 16-bit addressing limitation of the PDP-11.
3. Operating systems primitives – capabilities.

Table 2. Comparison of Computer Building Blocks

	DEC Modules 1000 Series	RTMs	Bit-Slices	CMs
Design level	Combinational and sequential circuit level	Register transfer level	Algorithm for interpreting ISP	PMS level (algorithm of application)
Number of module types	35	35	22 plus standard logic	2 (CM, port controller) plus LSI-11 options
Package	Plug-in	Plug-in	40-pin DIP	Plug-in
Number of pins	22	72	40	144
Dimensions (inches)	1/2×4-1/2×7	1/2×8-1/2×5	1/2×2×1/2	1/2×8-1/2×10
Volume (in^3)	16	21	5	42
Number of transistors	10	200	500	2,000 + 64 Kbits
Delay cycle time	200 ns	500 ns	200 ns	2–4 μs
Logical interconnect between modules	Data	Anything	Data bus	Several data buses; map bus and intercluster buses
Control	Anything	Sequence of K.evoke activate and timing interlock (later K(PCS))	Microprogram generated module control signals and clock ticks	Control messages via map bus intercluster bus
Design tools		Chartware; book ("how to")	Microprogramming tools	Languages and ISP notation operating system
Computer example	PDP-1	PDP-8/RTM	CMU-11	Cm*
Speed	100 Kips	120 Kips	240 Kips	640 Kips (Descal)

A companion paper to the chapter on Cm* discusses the programming issues raised by a computer module structure [Jones *et al.*, 1978]. An operating system, called "Star OS," manages a single Cm* cluster. It provides capability addressing, memory allocation, software module declaration, process management, message transmission, processor multiplexing, and trap and interrupt handling. Star OS is distributed in such a fashion that any kernel function can be executed in any CM. To decrease average memory reference time, 8 Kbytes of what the designers believe to be the most frequently executed Star OS software (interrupt handling, process switching, and message communication) is duplicated in each CM.

Since the time that the article was written, construction of a 50 computer modules Cm* has begun and is planned to be operational by the end of 1978 for evaluation in 1979. The extension of Cm* is known as "Cm*/50" and is described in Chapter 16. It will be used to test ideas on parallel processing methods, fault tolerance, modularity, and the extendability of the Cm* structure.

CONCLUSIONS

The four design methods presented in this part are compared in Table 2. As stated in Chapter 2, the predominant design level in the future will be the PMS level, using fifth generation components (microcomputers) as building blocks. The challenge to designers and researchers is therefore to understand what communication structures are needed to interconnect these building blocks.

18

The Description and Use of Register Transfer Modules (RTMs)

C. GORDON BELL, JOHN EGGERT,
JOHN GRASON, and PETER WILLIAMS

INTRODUCTION

In the design of digital systems (e.g., computers) the problem formulation and the design solution are most likely carried out at a register transfer concept level. Early and recent texts on logical and computer design discuss the register transfers as primitive components [Bartee *et al.*, 1962; Chu, 1970]. Logical design simulators that use a register transfer language have been written, and there have been several attempts to carry out detailed sequential and combinational logic designs from register transfer descriptions [Friedman and Yang, 1969]. Despite the acknowledgment that there are primitives based on register transfers, there is yet to emerge a common set of modules that are taken as primitive in the same way we think of various flip-flop types and NAND and NOR gates. However, Clark at Washington University, St. Louis, Mo. [Clark, 1967], has been developing and evaluating such a basic set of modules, called Macromodules.

Register Transfer Modules are our first attempt at providing a basic set of modules for high level digital systems design. These modules have been implemented by the Digital Equipment Corporation (DEC). The design of RTMs has been influenced by many of the above approaches and disciplines, and by programming methods. This note presents the general problem RTMs are trying to solve, the factors constraining their design, a brief description of the more important modules from a user's point of view, and two examples of their use.

Several aspects of the RTM system are important.

1. Digital system design is carried out entirely in terms of the modules; combinational and sequential switching circuit design are not used. (The process is akin to programming a sequential computer.) Design time is significantly less than with conventional logical design.
2. The most abstract representation, and usually the only representation of a given design, has enough information for constructing the system. This representation is a standard flowchart to specify the control flow, coupled to a data part that holds the data and carries out data operations.

3. The Register Transfer Modules make extensive use of MSI circuitry and can use LSI circuitry to provide even lower cost modules.

MODULE DESIGN CONSIDERATIONS

The three problem classes for which the modules were designed are: special purpose, computer-related, and educational digital systems. Although the initial motivation for the modules was for education, they were not designed solely for this purpose. The goals for educational use place too many constraints on the design. The main influence of the educational market has been to clarify the pedagogical nature; hence, the description of systems is made easy. The special purpose digital systems are larger than 20 MSI circuits, but smaller than a stored program computer (a typical RTM system would have 4~100 control states, 1~4 arithmetic units, and a small memory of 16~1000 words). Computer-related applications range from computer peripherals to the emulation of computers.

We make no attempt to show that the modules are an optimum set, according to an objective function. Because of the elementary nature of the control and data operations, the set is sufficient to construct digital systems. Table 1 shows the important design variables for RTMs, together with many of the constraints. Their design is described in Bell and Grason, [1971].

THE RTM SYSTEM

The RTM system consists of about 20 different modules and a method of interconnecting modules via a common bus that carries data and timing interlock signals for the register transfers. Some of the modules (DM, T, and M types) connect to the bus in order to transfer data, and the remaining modules (K type) "control" when data are to be transferred. The module name types are based on the structure primitive types of Bell and Newell [1966; 1971].

A register transfer language, ISP (instruction set processor) [Bell, Newell, 1966; Bell, Newell, 1971], is used to define the register transfer operations of the RTMs. Here we use only the parts of ISP that are commonly known by the digital systems engineer and are similar to a programming language (e.g., FORTRAN). The four main module types are as follows.

DM-Type (Data Operation Combined with Memory)

These modules are what we commonly think of as being a digital system (or at least the arithmetic unit). They are the register transfer gating paths and combinational circuits for the simple arithmetic and logical functions – hence the D part (for data operations). The D part carries out the evaluation of the right-hand side of an arithmetic expression as in a programming language in which an integer value is computed prior to storing, e.g., ←A+B, ←A–B, ←A⊕B, ←A+1. Thus, an expression "left-hand-side←right-hand side" (e.g., H←C+D) is used to indicate the integer value of the right-hand side being read and placed in the register on the left-hand side.

M-Type (Memory)

The memory (M) part is just the registers (e.g., A, B) that hold data between statements; these essentially correspond to the variables that are declared in a program. The operations on memory are usually reading (←M) and writing (M←). Types of DM and M modules are the general purpose arithmetic unit, a single-transfer register, Boolean flags (1-bit registers), read-write memories, and read-only memories. The memories hold two's complement 8-, 12-, or 16-bit integers.

K-Type (Control)

The K modules are responsible for controlling the transfer of data among the various registers by appropriately evoking operations

Table 1. Basic RT Design Decisions

1. Logic: TTL (acceptable for speed and noise immunity; low cost).
2. Packaging: Printed circuit boards of 5 × 8-1/2 inches or 2-1/2 × 8-1/2 inches with 72 or 36 pins (DEC compatible).
3. Intermediate connection: Pre-wired buses; wirewrap and push-on connections over wire-wrap pins.
4. Logic interconnection rules: One kind of control signal and data bus. Very small number of rules compared to IC use.
5. Problem size: 4~100 control steps; 1~4 arithmetic registers; 16~100 variables; possibly read-only memory.
6. Word length: 8-, 12-, and 16-bit (present *de facto* standard – can be extended).
7. Universality and extendability: The modules are not a panacea. There are provisions for escape to regular integrated circuits, standard DEC modules, and DEC computers (and their components).
8. Selection of primitives: Basic register, bus interconnection structure, and data representation were first determined. The operations that formed a complete set for the data representation were then specified. With this basic module set, designs were carried out for benchmark problems and design iteration occurred.
9. Notations: PMS and ISP of Bell and Newell [1971].
10. Automatic (algorithmic) mapping of algorithm into hardware: The basic RT design archetype representation is a flowchart. The register transfer operations are expressed in the ISP language.
11. Parallelism and speed: Provision for multiple buses; the modules are asynchronous. (The application classes put relatively low weight on speed.) For teaching purposes parallelism is an important principle. (A decision to use a bus, and thereby limit parallelism to the number of buses, was made for both cost and simplicity reasons.)

by DM and M types. The K modules are analogous to the control structure of a program. The K modules called K.evoke control the times when the various operations of the DMs and Ms are evoked (executed). The K.branch modules are used to make decisions about which operations are to be evoked next. The K.subroutine modules are used to connect a sequence of operations together as a subroutine. K.serial-merge allows control flow to merge into a single control flow when any flow input is present. K.parallel-branch and K.parallel-merge modules synchronize control where there is more than one operation taking place at a time. Other control modules include clocks, delays, and manual start keys.

T-Type (Transducers)

These modules provide an interface to the environment outside RTM. These include the Teletype interface, analog/digital converters, lights, switches, and interfaces to computers. These modules also connect to the common data bus.

The details of the modules will be introduced by giving the four modules that are necessary for nontrivial digital systems: K.evoke, DM.gpa, K.branch, and K.bus.

K (Evoke)

K.evoke (Ke) is the basic module that evokes a function consisting of a data operation and a register transfer – in essence an arithmetic expression. When a Ke is evoked, it in turn evokes the function, consisting of the data operation followed by a register transfer, and when the function is complete, Ke evokes the next K in the control sequence. The diagram for Ke with its two inputs and two outputs is shown in Figure 1. In terms of a finite state machine, Ke is a state with the ability to evoke an output action and then make a transition to another state. K.evoke is as follows.

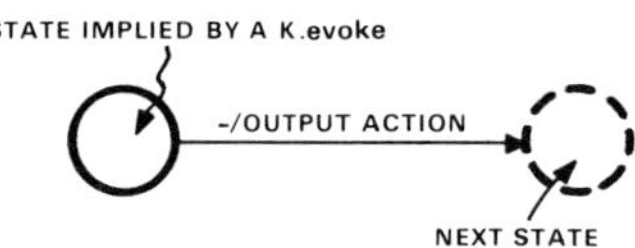

K (Branch)

K.branch (Kb) provides for the routing of control flow based on the condition of a Boolean input. The diagram for Kb with its two inputs and two outputs is shown in Figure 2. Each time a branch control is evoked, it in turn evokes either of the controls following it, depending on whether the Boolean input is true (a 1) or false (a 0). In terms of a finite state machine, Kb is a state with the capability of going to either of two next states, depending on a Boolean input. K.branch is as follows.

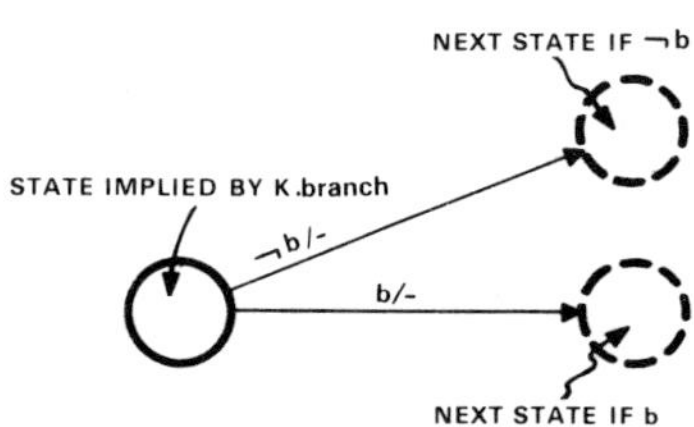

DM (General Purpose Arithmetic/gpa)

The DM.gpa allows arithmetic function results (data operations) that have been performed on its two registers A and B to be written into other registers (using the bus). Results can also be transferred (written) into A and B (A←; B←). The data operations are: ←A, ←B, ←¬A, ←¬B, ←A+B, ←A–B, ←A–1, ←A+1, ←A×2, ←A∧B, ←A∨B, and ←A⊕B. An input that evokes the function ←(Result)/2 can be combined with the previous function outputs to give ←A/2, ←B/2, ←(A+B)/2, etc. Two Boolean inputs, shift in <16, -1>, allow data to be shifted into the left- and right-hand bits on /2 and ×2 operations, respectively. Bits of registers A and B are available as Boolean outputs.

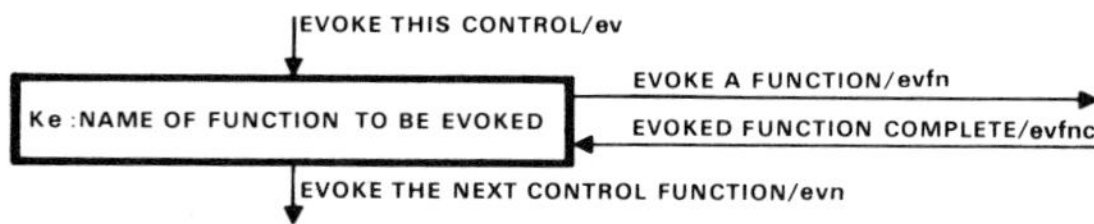

Figure 1. Diagram for the control module K.evoke.

K (Bus Sense and Control Module/Bus)

Each independent data bus in the system requires a centralized control module. It has a register, Bus, that always contains the result of the last register transfer that took place via the bus. K.bus carries out of several functions: monitoring register transfer operations; providing for single-step manual control for algorithm

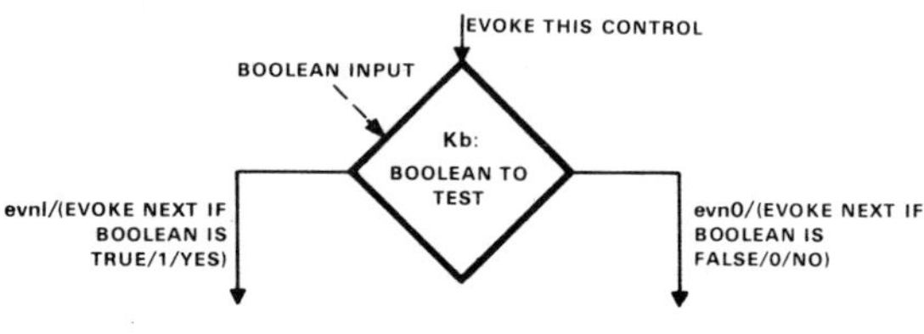

Figure 2. Diagram for the control module K.branch.

flow checkout by the user; providing for sense lights (indicators); providing for a word source of zero, i.e., ←0; forming Boolean functions of the Bus register; power-on initialization; manual startup; and bus termination.

DESIGN WITH RTMs

Digital systems engineers are concerned with formulating algorithms that, when executed by hardware, behave according to the solution of the original design problem. The solutions of digital systems design problems using programming, conventional logical design, and RTM design are all similar. The three design and implementation processes have the same goal: to construct a program for a machine, or a hard-wired machine to execute the algorithm stated (or implied) in the problem. Thus, programming and digital systems engineering are concerned with interconnecting basic components or building blocks for executing algorithms; the building blocks are machine operations and logical design components, respectively. RTMs are a basic set of components for constructing hardware algorithms. That is, they are the components for digital systems design.

The design protocol using RTMs is very much akin to that of designing a program. The designer takes a natural language statement of the problem and carries out the conversion to a process description that acts on a set of data variables (and any temporary data variables). An RTM design has two parts: (1) the explicitly declared data variables and the implied data operations that are attached to these variables; and (2) the control part, a finite state machine, that accepts inputs and evokes the various operations on the data part. The control part is shown as a combined flowchart-wiring diagram.

Two examples show how this design is carried out. The schematic for the first example, an algorithm to sum integers, shows all wires and modules and the schematic for the second example, a small stored program computer, shows the control flow and the data part but excludes the connections between the control and data parts.

Example: Sum of Integers to N

A small system to sum the integers to N (S←0+1+2+ . . . +N) can be built that uses the four aforementioned modules: DM.gpa, K.bus, K.evoke, and K.branch together with a switch register to enter N and a manual start control module to start the system. The data and control parts together are given in the RTM wiring diagram (Figure 3); the data part is shown on the right and the control part on the left. The final result S and the variable N are held in a general purpose arithmetic module DM.gpa. N is held in the switch register T initially. The control sequence is initiated by a K.manual-start (a human presses a key). Instead of counting to N, we start with N and count down to zero while tallying the sum S.

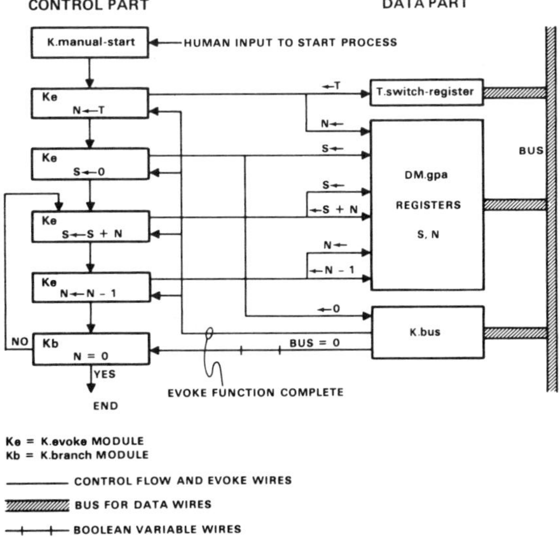

Figure 3. RTM digital system to take a value from a switch register input and to sum the integers to the input value.

The first control step reads T to register N (N←T). The second step initializes the sum S (S←0). The inner loop consists of the three functions: S←S+N; N←N–1; and a test for N=0.

Example: A Small Stored Program Computer Design Using RTMs

Figure 4 shows an RTM diagram for a small stored program computer that was initially constructed as an application experiment to demonstrate the feasibility of the modules and to investigate systems problems. The process of specifying the machine took approximately two hours (with three people). The computer was wired and, aside from minor system/circuit problems (for which the experiment was designed), the computer operated essentially when power was applied because there were no logic

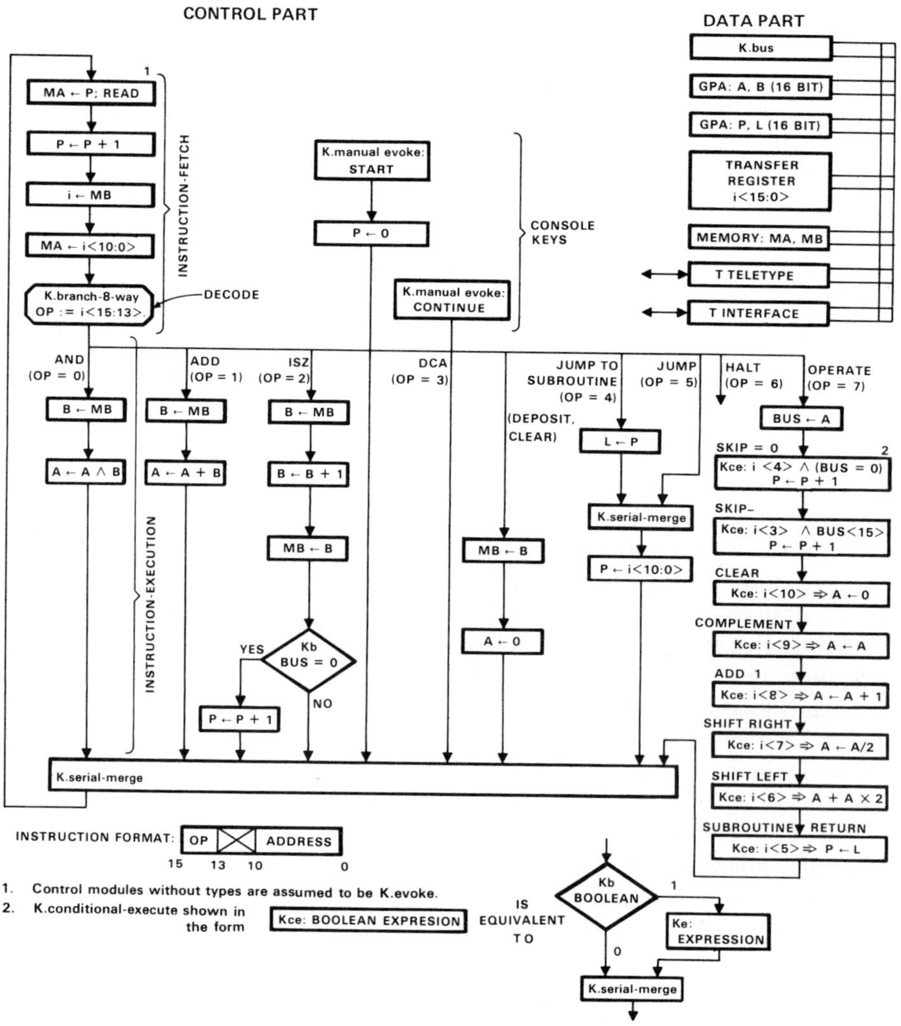

Figure 4. RTM design of a small stored program digital computer.

errors. The computer was designed for an actual application that had about 300 constants, 600 control steps, and about 16 variables. (An alternative approach would have been to hardwire the 600 control steps directly, thereby operating faster, but being more expensive and less flexible.) The computer has only 24 evoke and 16 branch controls. (By way of comparison, RTM interpreters to emulate the PDP-8 and the Data General NOVA computers require about 90 evoke and branch control modules, 2 DM.gpa's, and core memory.) Since the price ratio of a single hardwired control to a single read-only memory control word is approximately 10:1, and since the overhead price of a 1000-word read-only memory is about 100 controls, it was cheaper in the above application to use RTMs to first build an interpreter, commonly called a stored program digital computer, and then let the computer program execute the control steps.

The data part of the machine is shown in the upper right of Figure 4. Three DM-type RTMs hold the processor state and temporary registers. The processor state, that part of memory accessible and controlled by the program, includes: A, the accumulator; P, the program counter; and L, a register used to hold subroutine return addresses (links). The temporary registers needed in the interpretation of the instructions are: i, instruction holding register; and B, used for binary operations on A (e.g., Add, And). Also connected to the RTM bus are the read-only and read-write memories and the Teletype, as well as a special input/output register interface to the remainder of the system.

The method of defining the interpreter can be seen from the RTM diagram (Figure 4). The control part consists of three subparts: the Start and Continue keys that are used to initialize the processor to start at location 0 and to restart the processor, the instruction fetch, and the instruction execution. The instruction fetch consists of picking up the instruction from the memory word addressed by the program counter P and incrementing P to point to the next instruction. The instruction is placed in the i register, which has been specially wired to allow decoding of the three most significant bits. Individual bits of i can be tested for the Operate (OPR) instruction, and the address field i<10:0> can be read.

After the instruction is fetched and placed in i, Ke(MA←i<10:0>) is evoked to address data referenced by the instruction. Immediately following this evoke operation, an eight-way K.branch allows control to move to the one path corresponding to the operation code of the instruction being interpreted; that is, the instruction is decoded, and control is transferred to execute it. After the execution of the appropriate instruction, control returns to fetch the next instruction. For example, executing the Add (two's complement add) instruction consists of loading the data from memory into the temporary register B (i.e., B←MB) and then adding B to the accumulator A (i.e., A←A+B).

For the Operate instruction, which does not reference memory, each bit of the address part of the instruction specifies an operation to be carried out on the accumulator ("test for – or 0," "clear," "complement," "add one," "shift right or left," or "return from the subroutine"). Each bit is tested in sequence, and if a one, the corresponding operation is carried out. If the instruction code with OP=6 is given, the computer halts; pressing Continue restarts it.

The instruction set is shown to be straightforward and simple. Subroutine return addresses are stored in a link register L. Thus to call subroutines at a depth of more than one level requires the called subroutine to save the link register in a temporary location. But there is no way of storing this register; thus it is difficult to call a subroutine and pass parameter information (e.g., the location of tables). Since the computer requires a few minor changes to allow nested subroutines and parameter passing, the reader is invited to make the appropriate incremental changes.

CONCLUSIONS

The concept of using high level building blocks is not new, but we think this particular implementation of a set of simple blocks is quite useful to many digital systems engineers. The design time using this approach is significantly less than with conventional logical design. The modules are especially useful for teaching digital system design. We have solved many benchmark designs with reasonably consistent results. The modules can be applied quickly and economically where there are between 4 and 100 control steps, a small read-write memory (100 words), and perhaps some read-only memory. Larger system problems are usually solved better with a stored program computer, although such a computer can be designed using RTMs. The user need only be familiar with the concept of registers and register operations on data, and have a fundamental understanding of a flowchart.

ACKNOWLEDGEMENT

These modules were formally proposed in March 1970 in a form essentially described herein by one of the authors, C. G. Bell. In June 1970 the project was seriously started by constructing the computer of the previous example using them. The authors gratefully acknowledge the organization and management contributions of F. Gould, A. Devault, and S. Olsen (Digital Equipment Corporation) without whose goal-oriented commitment the RTMs could not have been built. The authors are also indebted to Mrs. D. Josephson of Carnegie-Mellon University for typing the manuscript.

19

Using LSI Processor Bit-Slices to Build a PDP-11 – A Case Study in Microcomputer Design

THOMAS M. McWILLIAMS, SAMUEL H. FULLER, and WILLIAM H. SHERWOOD

INTRODUCTION

Several semiconductor manufacturers have recently developed high speed LSI circuits that are designed to simplify the construction of microprogrammed processors and device controllers. These integrated circuits are called "bit-slices" because they implement 2 or 4 bits of the registers, arithmetic units, and primary data paths of a processor. This article presents the design and evaluation of the processor built at Carnegie-Mellon University [Fuller *et al.*, 1976] that uses the Intel 3000 bit-slices [Intel, 1975; Signetics, 1975] and that is microprogrammed to emulate the PDP-11 computer architecture [DEC, 1973].* The purpose of this project was to investigate the assertions of semiconductor manufacturers that their LSI bit-slices would in fact simplify the design and construction of processors.

Rather than specify a new architecture (i.e., instruction set) for this experiment in processor design, we decided to reimplement an established computer architecture: the PDP-11. We chose the PDP-11 architecture for several reasons. Using an existing and well-known architecture allowed others to more easily evaluate the results of our experiment and kept us from consciously or unconsciously tailoring the processor architecture to fit the capabilities and idiosyncrasies of the LSI bit-slices. PDP-11s are in extensive use at Carnegie-Mellon University in a wide variety of applications and, if our experiment was successful, the processor could be put to work on any one of several practical tasks. It was this second reason that helped establish a criterion that proved to be critical: we demanded that the processor we constructed support the standard DEC Unibus [DEC, 1973] that is common to all PDP-11s except the LSI-11 [DEC, 1975]. Finally, the PDP-11 architecture is an unusually good test of the capabilities of a bit-slice circuit family because it is a relatively complete architecture with numerous addressing modes and instruction formats.

*We gratefully acknowledge the donation of 3000 microcomputer sets by both Intel and Signetics Corporations.

In the next section we begin with a description of the design of the CMU-11 processor. We then discuss the performance, cost, and implementation difficulties uncovered during the design and testing of the machine. In addition to the evalution of the LSI bit-slice circuits for general purpose processors, we are interested in the problems of computer design in general. For this reason, a fairly complete set of digital design automation aids are available at Carnegie-Mellon University: an interactive drawing package that generates engineering drawings, wire-lists, and aids in engineering changes; a digital simulation system that is interfaced to the drawing system; and microprogram assemblers. Later sections review our experiences with these design aids and we draw some conclusions concerning the process of designing and debugging prototypes of digital systems built with LSI circuits.

ORGANIZATION OF THE CMU-11

Figure 1 is a register transfer level diagram of the CMU-11 microprogrammable processor.

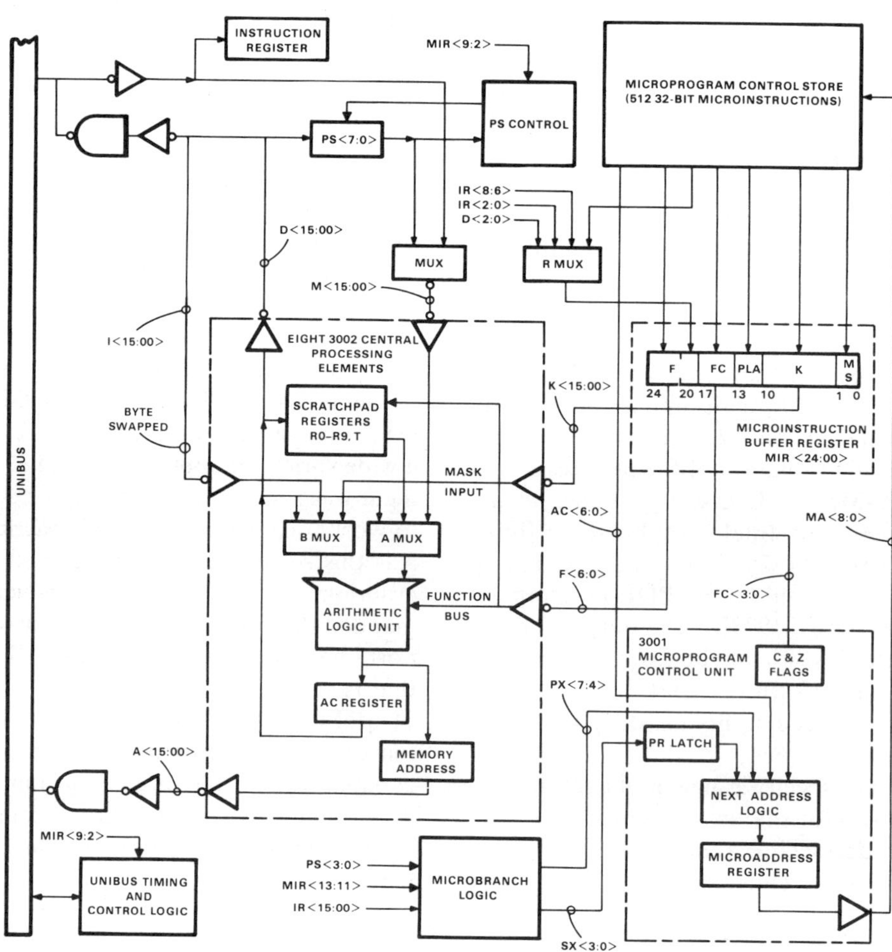

Figure 1. Register transfer level diagram.

The processor's components are arranged in the diagram into three sections: the *data part, control part,* and *Unibus interface.* We were able to build the entire processor on a single board and Figure 2 is a top view of the CMU-11.

The Data Paths and Working Registers

The data part of the processor is designed around the 3002 (central processing element) bit-slice. A single 3002 circuit implements a 2-bit slice of the data paths and, hence, eight 3002s have been used in the CMU-11. Although not explicitly shown in Figure 1, the 3003 carry-lookahead circuit is also used. With the 3003, the 3002 array is capable of cycling through operations every 150 nanoseconds. However, other delays in the clock and control part dictate that the CMU-11 has a 200-nanosecond microcycle time. The eight general purpose working registers of the PDP-11 architecture can be kept in the register scratchpad on the 3002s, and the three remaining internal registers, R8, R9, and T are sufficient for source and destination operand computations as well as other intermediate results. It was not possible to locate the program status (PS) and instruction register (IR) within the 3002s without a severe loss in performance.

The relatively generous number of input and output lines of the 3002s are used to good advantage. The D<15:0> and A<15:0> buses feed the Unibus data and address lines respectively. In addition, the D bus allows access to the extra data paths necessary to include the PS register and to facilitate the byte swap operation needed by many of the PDP-11's instructions. The M<15:0> bus is used as the principal data input bus. The function bus, F<6:0>, specifies both the operation to be performed by the arithmetic/logic unit as well as the selection of the register in the scratchpad to be involved in the operation. The K<15:0> bus is used to input masks or constants from the microinstruction. The 3000 circuit set makes frequent use of the K lines to specify masks (usually all zeros or all ones) that effectively extend the operation code on the function bus.

Figure 2. CMU-11 processor board.

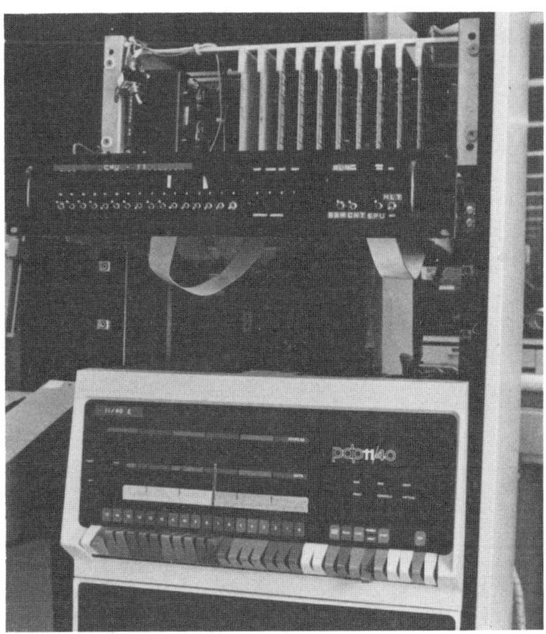

Figure 3. CMU-11 system with associated PDP-11.

Control Part

The control part of the CMU-11 uses the Microprogram Control Unit and a 512-word control store* with 32-bit microinstructions. Figure 4 shows the format of the microinstruction and Table 1 briefly describes the function of each of the fields. A microinstruction buffer register was included in the design to allow the overlap of the fetch of the next microinstruction with the execution of the current microinstruction, which is a common technique to improve the performance of microprogrammed processors.

The "next-address logic" of the 3001 has been augmented by additional microbranch control logic external to the 3001. This external logic uses the contents of the instruction register, the condition codes in the PS, and the PLA field from the microinstruction register to determine the AC<6:0> lines to input to the 3001.

The other major section of control logic that had to be added to the design was the processor status logic to control the setting of the 4-bit condition code in the PS register and control access to the PS. In fact, the PS register is defined as primary memory location 177776 in the PDP-11 architecture and requires special logic to load and store the PS.

Interface to the Unibus

A significant fraction of the components of the CMU-11 are devoted to the support of the Unibus. Given the demanding electrical requirements of the Unibus, the tri-state A, D, and M lines of the 3002 array could not be directly attached to the Unibus. Instead, separate transceiver packages had to be used to provide this buffering.

Due to the asynchronous operation of the Unibus and interrupt and nonprocessor

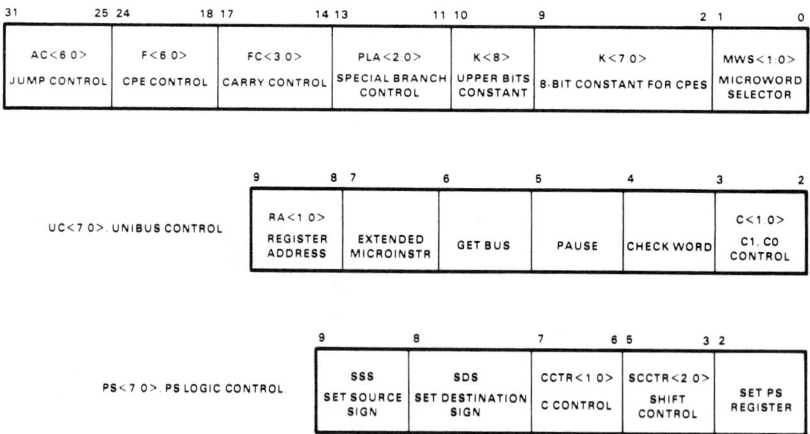

Figure 4. Microinstruction format.

*In order to expedite the debugging of the microprogram for the CMU-11, we built a fast, simple writable control store for the CMU. We used 45-nanosecond access time, 1024-bit random-access memory (RAM) packages to ensure a writable control store as fast as the final read-only memory (ROM) control store. The writable control store is interfaced to a Unibus (of a PDP-11 other than the CMU-11) for initial loading of microprograms. Figure 3 shows the CMU-11 interfaced to the supporting PDP-11 and writable control store.

requests (i.e., Direct Memory Access request via the Unibus), it was not practical to drive the Unibus directly from fields in the micro-instruction. Instead, a bus control and timing section was added to the processor. The rest of the processor interfaces to this control unit via the UC<7:0> field in the microinstruction. See Table 1 for a description of the functions of the subfields within UC<7:0>.

Console Functions

In place of a standard front panel, the CMU-11 has front panel functions accessible from a

Table 1. Description of Microinstruction Fields

Field	Description
MWS<1:0> : = MI<1:0>	**Microinstruction Selector.** Specifies if MI<9:2> should define a constant, Unibus control, or PS control.
K<8:0> : = MI< 10:2>	**Literal.** K<7:0> is a byte constant used by the least-significant byte of the K input lines of the 3002 array. K<8> is extended to feed the most significant byte of the K input lines.
UC<7:0> : = MI<9:2>	**Unibus Control.**
UC<1:0>	**C1, CO Control.** Specified the C1 and CO lines on the Unibus.
UC<2>	**Check Word.** Tests whether a word address is specified in Unibus operation.
UC<3>	**Pause.** Halt processor clock until completion of Unibus operation.
UC<4>	**Get Bus.** Request access of Unibus for a data transfer.
UC<5>	**Extended Microinstruction Code.** If set, defines alternate meaning for PLA<2:0>.
UC<7:6>	**Register Address.** Specifies which input register address multiplexer should be used.
PS<7:0> : = MI<9:2>	**Processor Status Control.**
PS<0>	**Set PS Register.** Controls loading of PS.
PS<3:1>	**Shift Control.**
PS<5:4>	**Carry Control.**
PS<6>	**Set Destination Sign.** Controls latching of sign of destination operand in flag external to 3002s.
PS<7>	**Set Source Sign.** Analogous to PS<6>.
PLA<2:0> : = MI<13:11>	**Special Branch Control.** Used by microbranch logic to tell which fields of IR and PS to examine for branch conditions.
FC<3:0> : = MI<17:14>	**MCU Flag Control.** Controls testing and setting of flags in 3001 (MCU).
F<6:0> : = MI<24:18>	**CPE Control.** Drives function bus of 3002 (CPE) array.
AC<6:0> : = MI<31:25>	**Address Control.** Connected directly to the AC<6:0> bus of the 3001 (MCU). This is the one field of the microinstruction not buffered in the microinstruction register. (The microprogram address register internal to the MCU performs the buffering function.)

standard Teletype attached to the Unibus. Memory locations can be examined and loaded by typing the octal address followed by a slash. The current value is displayed and a new value may be entered, if desired, followed by a carriage return. The processor may also be started and continued from the Teletype, and there is a halt switch on the front panel that causes the machine to return to the console microprogram.

This use of a Teletype for a console is similar to the console Teletype used by the LSI-11 [DEC, 1975c]. In order to make it easier to maintain the processor, we have added a microprocessor console that displays the microprogram address and allows the microprocessor to be single-stepped. The microconsole proved invaluable for debugging the prototype processor.

EVALUATION OF CMU-11 DESIGN

The critical questions to be asked about this design concern cost and performance. It has been fairly easy to evaluate the performance of the CMU-11 by looking at several representative instruction times and by running a set of benchmarks on the machine. Evaluating the cost of the CMU-11 has been more difficult. Rather than try to compare the price of existing PDP-11 implementations with the cost of the CMU-11, we chose instead to compare it with other PDP-11s with respect to circuit complexity. The other significant costs, i.e., development costs, are discussed in a later section.

Performance of the CMU-11

The CMU-11 runs at a microinstruction cycle time of 200 nanoseconds. The specifications for the Intel 3000 microcomputer family state that it is possible to build a 16-bit minicomputer with a 150-nanosecond cycle time. However, given our objective to design as cost-effective an implementation as possible, we avoided the sensitive and complex timing circuits that would be required to approach a 150-nanosecond cycle time.

If we had used clocks with sufficient buffering and pulse shaping, a worst-case analysis shows that with the particular IC packages used in the CMU-11, we could approach a 149-nanosecond cycle time with Intel 3000 packages and a 126-nanoseond cycle time with Signetics' version of the 3000 set. We have, in fact, replaced the Intel 3000 circuits with the Signetics circuits and although the CMU-11 continues to run reliably at 200 nanoseconds, we cannot reduce the cycle time below 200 nanoseonds. The critical path is in the control part and not the 3002 array.

Tables 2 and 3 show the execution time for six of the most frequently executed instructions and the eight addressing modes of the PDP-11. The instructions in Table 2 assume a register-to-register operation (i.e., a source and destination mode of 0). Table 3 shows the additional time that is added to the instruction execution time for the various source addressing modes.* The

Table 2. Execution Times of Common Instructions

	Basic Execution Time (in μs)		
Instruction	LSI-11	CMU-11	PDP-11/40
MOV	3.50	2.06	0.90
CMP	3.50	2.19	0.99
ASL	3.85	2.46	0.99
ADD	2.46	3.85	0.99
BRx (branch)	3.50	2.82	1.76
(no branch)	3.50	1.48	1.40
JSR	6.40	4.39	2.94

*In particular, the times in Table 3 are the source addressing mode times for the CMU-11 as measured on the BIS instruction. Addressing times on the other instructions are similar to the BIS times.

destination mode times are about the same as the given source mode times.

In order to measure the performance of the CMU-11 for various instruction mixes, several benchmarks were collected and run on the CMU-11, an LSI-11, and a PDP-11/40. Four benchmarks were collected that attempt to span a reasonable range of applications common to minicomputers.

1. **Quicksort.** This is a program that uses Hoare's quicksort procedure to sort a set of 16-bit integers. The benchmark also includes a pseudo-random number generator to provide the initial data.
2. **Trigonometric functions.** This is a set of trigonometric, floating-point routines. We do not assume the existence of a floating-point option on any of the processors and hence this benchmark heavily exercises software floating-point emulation routines.

Table 3. Execution Times for the Source Addressing Modes

Addressing Mode	LSI-11 (μs)	CMU-11 (μs)	PDP-11/40 (μs)
0: Register	0.00	0.00	0.00
1: Register Deferred	1.40	1.21	0.78
2: Autoincrement	1.40	0.64	0.84
3: Autoincrement Deferred	3.50	1.91	1.74
4: Autodecrement	2.10	1.00	0.84
5: Autodecrement Deferred	4.20	2.28	1.74
6: Indexed	4.20	1.78	1.46
7: Indexed Deferred	6.30	2.99	2.36

3. **Partial differential equations.** This program uses a straightforward iterative relaxation technique to solve a partial differential equation over a two-dimensional space. Fixed-point values are used.
4. **Text searching.** This searches an input string for names in a symbol table. This benchmark makes extensive use of the byte and compare features in the instruction set.

Table 4 shows the execution times on the LSI-11, CMU-11, and PDP-11/40 for each of the four benchmarks. From these results we see that the CMU-11 is approximately twice as fast as the LSI-11 and 63 percent of the speed of the PDP-11/40. As expected, there is a moderate amount of variation in the relative performance of the three machines for the different benchmarks. The two dominant effects that can be seen in Table 4 are that the PDP-11/40 design has optimized register-to-register operations more than either the LSI-11 or the CMU-11 (as demonstrated in the partial differential equation benchmark). Byte operations are more efficiently performed in the CMU-11 because of its byte-swap data path provided by the D and I buses. The last line in Table 4 is the data published by O'Loughlin [1975] in an article comparing the different DEC PDP-11 implementations.

It is mildly disappointing that the CMU-11, built with Schottky TTL bit-slices, could not equal the performance of the PDP-11/40, built with standard TTL circuits. The next two sections will examine in detail where performance was lost (and gained) in the CMU-11 design. Before continuing with this review of the design, we turn to a brief discussion of the cost of the CMU-11.

A principal objective of the 3000 microcomputer bit-slice packages is to simplify the design of processors like the CMU-11. Table 5

Table 4. Performance of CMU-11 Relative to Other PDP-11s

	Execution Times Relative to PDP-11/40*					
Benchmarks	**LSI-11**	**11/10**	**11/20**	**CMU-11**	**11/40**	**11/45**
Quicksort	2.88 (366)			1.48 (188)	1.0 (127)	
Partial differential equation	3.48 (268)			1.75 (135)	1.0 (77)	
Trigonometric functions	3.36 (111)			1.57 (52)	1.0 (33)	
Text searching	2.76 (204)			1.45 (107)	1.0 (74)	
Average	3.1	–	–	1.6	1.0	–
O'Loughlin's Data	–	2.32	1.85	–	1.0	0.91

*Numbers in parentheses are the absolute run times in seconds for the benchmarks.

Table 5. Integrated Circuit Statistics

Processor Component	No. IC Packages	No. 16 Pin Equivalent Packages	
Data Part			
3002 (CPE) Array	8	20	
PS and Instruction Registers	6	6	
Miscellaneous	4	5	
Subtotal	18	31	(19%)
Control Part			
Control Store ROMs	8	8	
Microinstruction Register	10	10	
3001 (MCU)	1	3	
Microbranch Logic	26	27	
PS Control	16	16	
Miscellaneous	18	18	
Subtotal	79	82	(52%)
Unibus Interface			
Bus Transceivers and Inverters	19	19	
Unibus Control	28	28	
Subtotal	47	47	(29%)
Total	144	160	

is a summary of the complexity (measured in integrated circuits) of the CMU-11. There are two columns in Table 5: a simple count of the number of integrated circuit packages used in the CMU-11, and a column that converts the design to "16-pin equivalent" packages (a measure of the size of the design in a standard unit). Table 6 gives a breakdown of the actual cost of the CMU-11 at January 1976 prices.

It is surprising that less than 20 percent of the design is now in the data part of the processor: the part of the processor largely implemented with the LSI bit-slices. A larger part of the design, 29 percent, is needed just to interface to the PDP-11 Unibus.

In order to put the 144-package complexity of the CMU-11 in perspective, the IC package counts for other PDP-11s are: PDP-11/10 – 203 packages; PDP-11/40 – 417 packages; and PDP-11/45 – 696 packages. The LSI-11 is able to implement the basic processor in 42 packages but does not interface to a Unibus. It is clear that the bit-slices do not approach the economy of the Western Digital NMOS microcomputer circuits which were specifically designed to emulate the PDP-11.

Another measure of the degree to which the CMU-11 processor can efficiently emulate the PDP-11 architecture is given by the size of the microprograms. Table 7 gives the size of microprograms for several PDP-11 processors. It is somewhat surprising that the CMU-11 uses fewer bits in its control store than any of the other processors except the LSI-11. This is in

Table 6. Cost Breakdown for CMU-11

Components	Prices*	
	Single Units	Quantities of 100+
LSI Microcomputer Parts	$207	$125
(Intel 3001, 3002s, 3003)	(184)	
PROMs		
(3601, 3602, 3604, 745168)	204	136
SSI/MSI Parts	179	158
Integrated Circuit Subtotal	$590	$419
Augat Wire-Wrap Board	379	(Use printed circuit)
Wire-Wrapping	107	–
Total	$1076	–

*Signetics prices.

Table 7. PDP-11 Control Store Sizes

LSI-11	PDP-11/10*	CMU-11	PDP-11/40*	PDP-11/45*
22 bits × 512 words (includes console)	40 bits × 239 words	32 bits × 287 words (without console) 414 words (with console)	56 bits × 251 words	64 bits × 256 words

*[O'Loughlin, 1975].

large part due to the fact the 11/10, 11/40, and 11/45 use MSI arithmetic/logic packages that did not have as useful a set of primitive operations as the 3002 arithmetic logic unit (ALU).

SOME PITFALLS FOUND IN IMPLEMENTING THE PDP-11 WITH THE 3000 BIT-SLICES

Since the CMU-11 project was started, a number of different bit-slice chips have become available whose organizations are significantly different from the 3000 circuits and which provide an interesting contrast. Two of the more interesting bit-slice chips are the Advanced Micro Devices AM2901 [AMD, 1975] and the Monolithic Memories Inc. MM16701. These bit-slice chips have a very similar data path organization with only minor differences, the AM2901 being the faster device. Because of the similarity of these devices, we will limit the discussion here to the AM2901, but all of the microinstruction sequences discussed will work on both bit-slice sets.

The basic data path of the AM2901 is shown in Figure 5. The chip contains a register file of 16 4-bit accumulators and an accumulator extension register, the Q register. In one microinstruction, two operands can be read out of the register file, passed through the ALU, the result can be written shifted left or right, and written back into the register file. In parallel with this, there is an addressing mode which controls the RAM and Q shifters, allowing the output of the ALU and the Q register to be right shifted simultaneously, which is well suited for the inner loop of multiply or divide instructions.

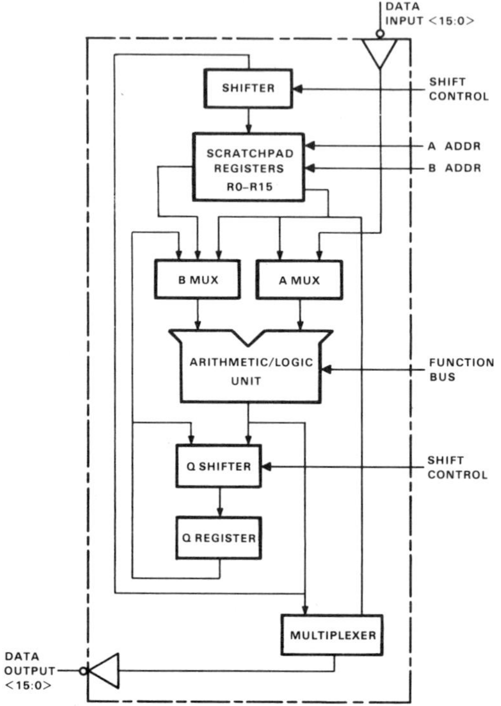

Figure 5. The AM2901 – a 4-bit bipolar microprocessor slice.

I/O Buses

The main advantage of the 3000 bit-slice over the AM2901 is its five fully parallel data buses for transferring data in and out of the chip. It has two tri-state output buses (the A and D buses) and three input buses (M, I, and K). If the minicomputer to be emulated has fairly short I/O and memory buses, the 3000 buses can directly drive them, resulting in a substantial savings in bus driver packages. In the CMU-11, we needed to drive a DEC Unibus, so we had to use separate bus drivers and receivers. Once external bus drivers are added, the advantage of the two output buses for the address and data is minimal, because an equivalent external address register can be loaded as fast as the existing internal address register and combination bus drivers/latches are available (e.g., AM2905). The savings realized by having three input buses is the cost of adding eight dual 4-to-1 line multiplexer chips at the input to the bit-slice chips. The savings achieved with the five buses in the 3000 bit-slices over the

AM2901's single-input and single-output bus is twelve 16-pin circuits, plus 3 bits in the control store (2 for the select lines on the input multiplexer, and 1 to control loading of the address register).

Arithmetic Overflow with the 3000

One of the biggest problems encountered with the PDP-11 implementation using the 3000 bit-slice was detection of arithmetic overflow. The 3000 bit-slice has no overflow output, and the signals needed to directly detect overflow are not available at the external pin connections. This results in considerable overhead in emulating instructions that must detect overflow (e.g., instructions that set the V bit in the PS register of the PDP-11). The CMU-11 overflow handling was implemented with two external flip-flops that contain the signs of the source and destination operands. After an instruction is fetched, its operands are first fetched either from memory or the register stack and are put in the source and destination registers within the 3002. As the operands are fetched, the source and destination flip-flops are set to the signs of the operands. When an instruction is executed, the overflow logic can use the signs of the operands and result to detect overflow. This technique works well when the operands are from memory, but really slows down the register-to-register operations because the operands have to be moved to the AC so their signs can be latched in the external source and destination sign flip-flops.

The sequence of instructions needed to emulate a register-to-register ADD is shown in Figure 6. The first instruction in the sequence loads the source operand into register AC, in order to get its sign out of the chip. The next instruction specifies for the source sign flip-flop to be set to the sign of the AC, and to store the AC into the *T* register. The following two instructions load the destination operand into the AC and set the destination sign flip-flop. The last two instructions do the add and store the result back in the destination register. Because of the multiple use of fields in the microinstruction, it is not possible to specify that a register address comes from the instruction register in the same microinstruction that sets the source sign, the destination sign flip-flops, or the condition codes. If the microprocessor were to be redesigned to allow this, the register-to-register add could be done in three rather than six microinstructions with the 3000 chips. However, we would pay for this performance improvement by having to use a wider microinstruction. The AM2901 provides external access to the overflow detect output on the chip and the register-to-register add can be done with only one microinstruction, resulting in a considerable speed increase over the 3000 chips.

```
ILR     SR              ;AC←Source Register
SDR     T, 1, SETSS     ;T←AC and SET Source Sign
ILR     DR              ;AC←Destination Register
NOR     SETDS           ;SET Destination Sign
ALR     T, SETCC        ;AC←AC+T
                        ;And Set Condition Codes
SDR     DR, 1           ;Destination Register←AC
```

Figure 6. Microsequence example: register-to-register ADD with overflow detect.

Example of a Multiply Instruction

The inner loop of a 16-bit integer multiply instruction on the 3000 chips requires either three or six microinstructions, depending on whether that cycle is a double register shift and add, or just a shift. The high order word of the product is stored in the AC register, and the low order word is stored in the *T* register. Initially, AC is zero, and *T* holds the multiplicand. For each iteration of the multiply, the loop count is decremented and if the low order bit of the *T* register is a 1, then the multiplier is added into the AC, and the AC and *T* registers are shifted right. Because the 3000 cannot add a register to the AC without also putting the result in the register, it takes three microinstructions to perform the inner loop addition.

For the AM2901, the inner loop of the multiply can be done in two microinstructions with no external loop counter, and in one with an external counter. This is possible because the AM2901 in one microinstruction can add two general registers together, shifting the result and the accumulator extension register right 1 bit. A similar speedup also occurs for division.

ADDITIONAL COMMENTS ON THE CMU-11 DESIGN

The 3000 microcomputer circuits are not the only area in which to look for improvements in the CMU-11 design. A major source of complexity was the Unibus interface (29 percent of processor's packages). The 3002 bit-slices provide tri-state drivers for their A and D lines and if Unibus compatibility is not essential, the outputs from the 3002 circuits could directly drive a memory and I/O bus of moderate size. If synchronous operation of the memory bus is adequate, further simplification of the bus interface section of the processor is possible.

A number of integrated circuit packages are now available that could help simplify the design of the control part of the processor. Most significantly, 4 Kbit programmable read-only memories (PROMs) appropriate for use in the control store are now available with internal latches for use as a microinstruction buffer. This would eliminate the need for the separate latches used in the CMU-11's microinstruction register. A related optimization to the CMU-11 would be to move from the partly encoded microinstruction format of the CMU-11 to a wider, fully horizontal format. The random logic needed to decode an encoded microinstruction is simply more expensive than the extra bits in the control store needed for the horizontal format.

We attempted to use programmable logic arrays (PLAs) in our initial design, but converted to ROMs when the PLAs we were designing with were discontinued. By now, however, several useful PLAs are readily available. For example, the Signetics FPLA, with its 16 inputs, is well suited to the decoding of PDP-11 instructions.

The cumulative reduction in package counts that might be expected in a second iteration of the CMU-11 design are as follows:

CMU-11	160 IC packages
Non-Unibus Design	128
Integrated ROM/MIR and horizontal microinstruction format	113
Convert to AM2900 circuits	95

COMPUTER-AIDED DESIGN TOOLS

Aside from freeing the designer of bookkeeping and clerical tasks, the main advantage of any design automation system is its inherent ability to maintain correct and consistent documentation (schematic prints and wire-lists) and the reduced turnaround time for design iterations. The fact that the total prototype development time for the CMU-11 was 39 (40-hour) man-weeks is an example of the savings possible with even modest design automation aids.

Description of Facilities Used at CMU

The Stanford University Drawing System (SUDS) was used to enter the schematic print set with a graphics display terminal. The drawing package includes a set of satellite programs to extract information for wire-lists and cross-reference tables from its data base. Incorporated in the system are libraries of integrated circuit definitions which contain not only the pictorial representation of the gates but also pin section information and some loading data. Hard copy prints were conveniently generated by a digitally controlled Xerox Graphic Printer (XGP). The wire-list program can search the data base interactively for specific information or produce complete tables of run lists, stuff lists, error reports (wire-ANDing violations, etc.), and loading analyses, which all proved extremely helpful.

The logic simulator used was Simulation of Asynchronous Gate Elements (SAGE), which is a 4-state (0, 1, high impedance for tri-state buses, and undefined for initialization and uncertainty in delay parameters) gate-level simulator. It reads the data base directly from the output of the SUDS for utmost convenience, since it allowed a turnaround time in the order of five minutes for print set corrections. SAGE has models in its libraries for the TTL and Schottky families, and special routines were written by us to emulate the 3000 microcomputer set. This allowed improvements in the efficiency of the simulation execution. Macro facilities are also available for quickly defining MSI circuits from more basic logic gates. The results of the simulations are in the form of register and signal reports and timing/trace diagrams.

Debugging with the Simulator

About 95 percent of the original design errors were eliminated through the use of the simulation program. Naturally, not all combinations and sequences of instructions can be simulated, but a standard PDP-11 diagnostic program was run in addition to a number of other programs. A total of about 100 milliseconds of CMU-11 compute time was simulated before debugging on the actual hardware began.

The limitation here was that the SAGE simulation of the CMU-11 required about 10^6 seconds of CPU time on a PDP-10 to simulate 1 second of CMU-11 execution. We simply could not afford to consume more than about 30 hours of CPU time for this project.

Whatever amount of time is spent on simulation, the simulations cannot be exhaustive and the final set of errors must be tracked down with more extensive tests on the real machine. We discovered eight to ten errors in the actual CMU-11. However, when an error was found in the physical machine, the simulations were again run to help track down the bug through the use of timing traces and other results. The correction was then entered into the machine print set and the simulator was rerun before implementing the change on the processor wire-wrap board or in the microprogram.

An example of the worth of the computer-aided design system came to light when a major implementation change was made; several ROMs were incorporated into the design to replace a discontinued programmable logic array (PLA). Our design aids were essential in effecting this change within four man-days. In order to recover so quickly from such a massive wiring change, an engineering change order (ECO) wrap/unwrap program was run to compare the old and new wire-lists produced by the drawing package. Thus, at all times during development, the processor reflected the exact connectivity of the print set.

Several of the errors discovered on the real machine were timing errors that were not revealed in the simulation debugging. These errors were not detected because the simulation models did not consider the effects of loading on the propagation delays and only maximum delays in all gates were used as an approximation to worst case conditions. In fact, if time had permitted, minimum and "typical" (Gaussian-distributed) parameters should also have been tested. However, we again face a fundamental problem with simulation in that the computation time becomes excessive as different sets of delays are simulated to find worst-case conditions.

CONCLUDING COMMENTS

The CMU-11 project was initiated as an experiment in constructing general purpose (mini) processors with LSI bit-slice components. Table 8 is a summary of the results. As the table

Table 8. Summary of Comparison between CMU-11 and Other PDP-11 Implementations

Parameter	LSI-11	PDP-11/10	CMU-11	PDP-11/40
Microcycle time (ns)	400		200	140,200,300
Relative Execution Times	3.2	2.32	1.6	1.0
IC Packages	42	203	144	417
Control Store Size (bits)	11,264	9,960	9,184	14,056

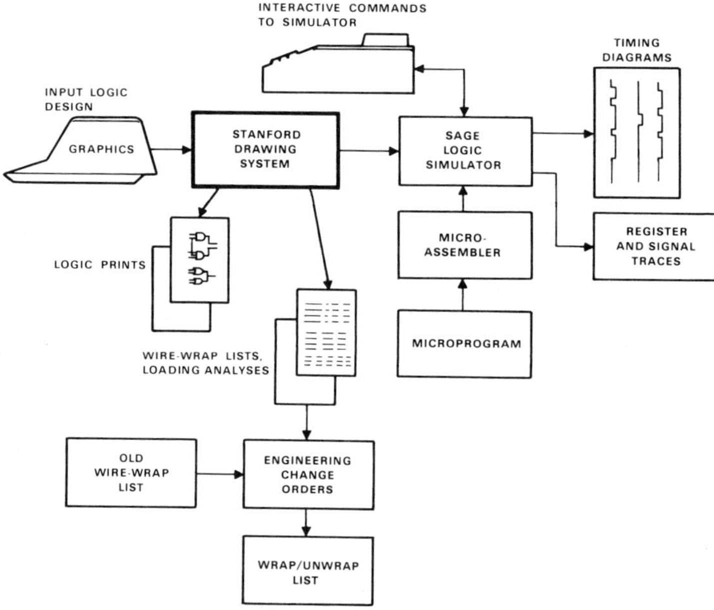

Figure 7. CAD system at CMU.

shows, the CMU-11 was implemented with significantly less components (IC packages) than either the PDP-11/10 or the PDP-11/40, which are processors built with MSI components, and the performance of the CMU-11 falls between these two MSI processors. However, the economy of implementation is not nearly as significant as was realized with the LSI-11 although the CMU-11 is able to perform at twice the speed of the LSI-11. The LSI-11 is a processor implemented with NMOS LSI microcomputer packages in which the entire data path (with 8-bit data paths) was put in a single package and both the control and data packages for the LSI-11 have been specialized to efficiently emulate the PDP-11 architecture.

Earlier we discussed improvements that are possible in the CMU-11 design and argued that a second iteration on the design could boost the performance to that of the PDP-11/40 and could be implemented in about 95 rather than 144 packages. To achieve a more cost-effective design than this will require either the development of some LSI control circuits specific to the processor's instruction set or the specification of a new computer architecture tailored to make the most efficient use of the functions provided in the LSI circuits.

20

Multi-Microprocessors: An Overview and Working Example

SAMUEL H. FULLER, JOHN K. OUSTERHOUT, LEVY RASKIN, PAUL I. RUBINFELD, PRADEEP S. SINDHU, and RICHARD J. SWAN

INTRODUCTION

An interesting phenomenon over the past several years has been the spontaneous growth of interest in multiple-microprocessor computer systems in many universities and research laboratories. This interest is not hard to understand given the inexpensive computational power offered by microprocessors today and the cost-performance improvements promised by those to be delivered in the near future. Microprocessors have had a dramatic impact on applications that require a small amount of computing. They have been used in instruments, industrial controllers, intelligent terminals, communications systems as special function processors in large computers, and, more recently, in consumer goods and games.

The question naturally arises as to whether the microprocessor, which has proved so successful in these diverse applications, can be used as a building block for large general purpose computer systems. In other words, can a suitably interconnected set of microprocessors be used for tasks that currently require large uniprocessors capable of executing millions of instructions per second? At present, there is no definitive answer to this question, but there are several reasons to believe that multiple-microprocessor systems might indeed be viable.

A strong argument for a microprocessor-based system is its potential cost-effectiveness. This point is graphically demonstrated in Figure 1 which shows cost/performance as a function of computer system size.* Each point in this figure represents a (uniprocessor) system currently available and introduced between 1975 and 1977 [GML Corp., 1977]. For example, the computer represented by the point labelled A has a purchase price of about $10,000. It is capable of transferring data between memory and the central processor at about 200 Mbits/second, yielding a figure of merit of 2×10^4 bits/second/dollar. The figure shows that with conventional methods of organizing computers, the cost/performance of a

*The measure of system size used here is its purchase price.

system degrades as its size increases. If systems were, instead, configured using microprocessors, and if there was no additional cost in interconnecting the microprocessors, then the points would fall along an ideal multiprocessors line such as shown in the figure. In reality, both costs associated with the physical interconnect and performance degradation due to synchronization overhead will cause the price/performance curve to have a negative slope (the realistic multiprocessors line in the figure). In terms of Figure 1, the critical question facing multiprocessors is whether the realistic multiprocessors price/performance line falls above or below the line for conventional uniprocessor systems.

Another important attribute of a multiple-processor computer system is its potential for reliability. Computers are being applied increasingly in situations where a failure might have serious economic and even life-endangering consequences. Since the basic ingredient in the design of a reliable system using real components is redundancy in one form or another, a structure consisting of large numbers of identical processors represents the natural framework in which to design reliable computers. Prior to the advent of the microprocessor, it was unrealistic to consider multiprocessor structures involving more than a few processors because the cost of building the individual processors themselves was high.

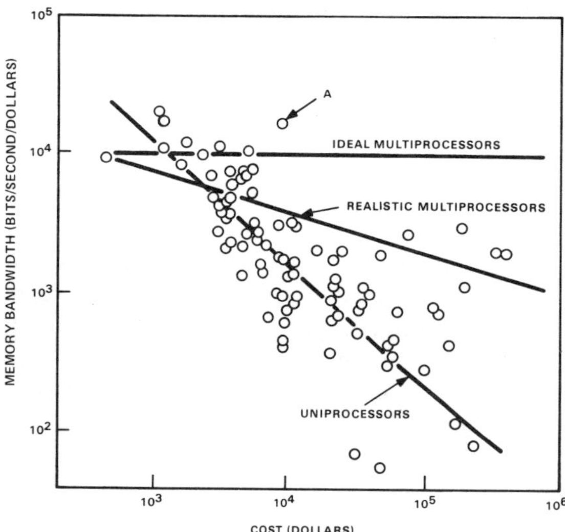

Figure 1. Cost performance as a function of system cost.

Yet another factor that favors the use of multiple processors is the resulting modularity of the system. There has always been a motivation for making computer systems modular for reasons of incremental expandability, ease of maintenance, and enhanced production. A computer system that is built using identical processors, and a small set of interconnection elements that have clean, well-defined interfaces would benefit fully from a modularity in processing power that is currently seen only in memory units of computer systems.

In spite of the advantages offered by multiprocessor organizations, there have been few commercially viable systems constructed to date.* The reason for this is that a number of problems and open issues remain to be resolved before such systems are a practical alternative to more conventional organizations. The major problems currently facing such systems are as follows.

1. **Task decomposition.** How should tasks now executed on uniprocessors be decomposed so that they can be run on a set of smaller processors? Can compilers

*While the authors know of no commercially available multi-microprocessor systems, Pluribus [Heart *et al.*, 1973] and Tandem [1977] are two multiple-processor systems based on a processor of minicomputer size that are commercially available.

or specialized run-time systems be developed to do this decomposition automatically or must the programmer do the decomposition explicitly?

2. **Interconnection structures.** What are the most effective types of processor/memory and processor/processor interconnection structures, and what are the related communication protocols?
3. **Address mapping mechanisms.** What mechanisms are appropriate for performing the virtual-to-physical address translation? These mechanisms should allow processors to share code and data while ensuring adequate levels of protection and performance.
4. **Software system structure.** What software structures are suitable for large systems containing hundreds of processors? Among the important problems in this area are resource management, software distribution, protection, and reliability.
5. **Interprocessor interference.** Even after tasks have been decomposed to run on multiple processors, how should interprocessor interference and contention for memory and I/O resources be minimized?
6. **Deadlock avoidance.** With multiple processors contending for resources, the potential exists for a situation where each of a group of processors is waiting for resources assigned to other processors in the group, and none of the processors in the group is able to proceed until its demands are satisfied. This situation, known as deadlock, effectively disables all the processors involved, and special care must be taken in the design to avoid it.
7. **Fault tolerance.** What hardware and software structures will allow a multiprocessor system to realize its potential for surviving the failure of components in the system?
8. **Input/output.** How should input/output devices in general, and secondary storage devices in particular, be integrated into a multi-microprocessor system?

The next section in this article surveys the spectrum of multiple-processor systems that are under active consideration and that hold some promise for becoming viable organizations for future computer systems. Given the relatively ill-defined nature of many of the unresolved questions listed above, the real potential and limitations of a multi-microprocessor architecture can only be understood by considering a specific system in depth. The section summarizing the architecture of the Cm* system, which has recently been developed at Carnegie-Mellon University (CMU), is presented to highlight some of the important considerations in implementing and programming a real multiprocessor system. The detailed design and implementation of Cm* are discussed in a recent set of papers [Jones *et al.,* 1977; Swan *et al.,* 1977; Swan *et al.,* 1977a[. The principal conclusions of the performance studies of Cm* are presented in the fourth section of this paper. The structure of the virtual addressing mechanism and the kernel operating system now running on Cm* are the subject of a paper by [Jones *et al.,* 1978].

OVERVIEW OF MULTIPLE PROCESSOR STRUCTURES

There is currently no established methodology for interconnecting sets of processors for the purpose of building large, general purpose or even special purpose computer systems. However, there does exist an interesting range of possibilities and Figures 2 through 4 show three generic organizations that span this range: computer networks, multiprocessors, and multiple arithmetic unit processors. Other taxonomies of multiple-processor systems have been proposed [Flynn, 1966; Jensen and Anderson, 1977], but this relatively straightforward grouping into three organizations is most suitable for the following discussion.

All of these organizations existed prior to the advent of the microprocessor. The economics of the microprocessor, however, open up the possibilities of using these structures in many new application areas. In our review of these alternative computer organizations, we will reference some older computer systems built with conventional components to help make the discussion more concrete.

Computer Networks

Figure 2 shows a computer network. In this type of multiple-processor organization, each processor is embedded in a conventional computer system, and the computers are then interconnected via communication links. The intercomputer communication links are often serial, but in some cases, such as the channel-to-channel adapter of multicomputer IBM S/370 systems, high-bandwidth parallel buses are used.

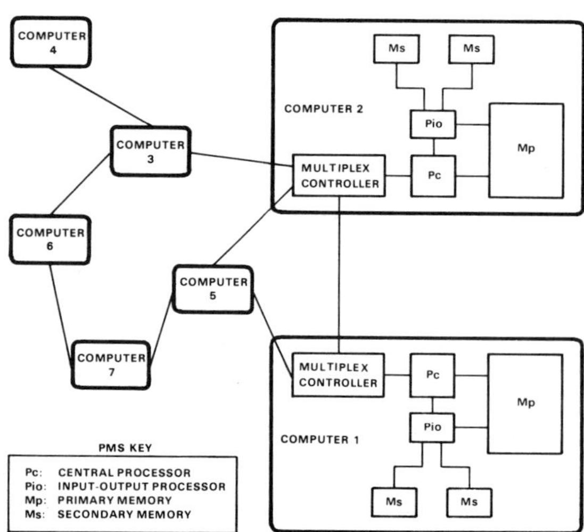

Figure 2. A network of computers.

Perhaps the most widely known computer network is the ARPA network [Kahn, 1972], but other computer networks have also been implemented and are now in use. These include the Ethernet [Metcalfe and Boggs, 1976], DCS [Farber, 1975], and the Spider network [Fraser, 1975]. Furthermore, most large computer installations are really computer networks. Computer manufacturers are establishing standard network protocols, for example, IBM's system network architecture (SNA) and Digital Equipment Corporation's DECnet protocol, to facilitate the construction of computer networks tailored to individual user needs.

An important attribute of a computer network is the data transmission bandwidth between computers. This bandwidth ranges from a few thousand bits per second up to about 10 Mbits/second. The other important attribute of the inter-computer links is the access or latency time for each unit of information sent between computers. In describing interprocessor communication capability it is common to refer to the degree of coupling between processors in the system. The ARPA network is an example of a loosely coupled (and geographically distributed) computer network because of the 50 Kbit/second links between computers in the network and the 100–250 ms latency times associated with cross-network transmissions of packets of information. A more tightly coupled (and geographically centralized) network is the Ethernet with 3 Mbit/second inter-computer bandwidth and latency times of the order of a small number of milliseconds. As more and more closely coupled computer networks are considered, however, another type of multiple processor structure, the multiprocessor, becomes an increasingly competitive alternative. Multiprocessors will be discussed shortly.

As microprocessors are incorporated into computer terminals, point-of-sale terminals, data acquisition transducers, and other such applications, the natural form of organization will be a loosely coupled computer network. Closely coupled microcomputer networks might provide an attractive organization for reliable systems,* systems that must manage a large data base on many disks or other secondary storage, or even as a computational structure tailored to the data flow of a specialized application. It is questionable, however, whether a multiple microprocessor organized in the form of a network could replace a large conventional uniprocessor.

Multiprocessor System

Figure 3 shows the basic structure of a multiprocessor. Its distinguishing characteristic is that, unlike the processors in computer networks, the processors in a multiprocessor share primary memory. Note that in the computer network of Figure 2, each processor has its own, private primary memory. Data is shared in a computer network by passing interprocessor messages, whereas in a multiprocessor, the central processors can directly share data in primary memory. The concept of a multiprocessor is not new; the Burroughs D825 (1962), Bendix G-21 (1963), GE 645 (1969), and IBM 360/65 (1969) provide early examples. In these multiprocessors, conventional, relatively expensive central processors were used, making it uneconomical to have more than a few processors. With small numbers of processors, it is not mandatory to decompose a single job into a set of concurrent, cooperating processes to use all the central processors at once; enough independent programs are usually resident in the primary memory of a conventional multiprogramming system to keep a few processors busy. More recently, multiprocessors using minicomputers have been implemented, and configurations now exist with as many as 14 to 16 processors in a single computer system [Wulf and Bell, 1972; Heart *et al.*, 1973]. To effectively utilize the processors in such a system, a task must be explicitly decomposed to run concurrently on different processors.

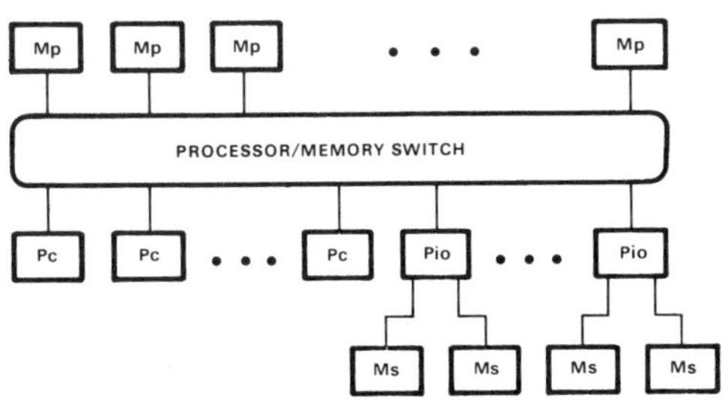

Figure 3. The basic structure of a multiprocessor.

One of the most challenging problems in designing and implementing the hardware of multiprocessor systems, especially for large number of processors, is the processor/memory switching structure. Many techniques have been tried and used successfully in particular systems: multiple ports per memory unit, electronic crossbar switches, time-multiplexed common buses, and combinations and hierarchies of simpler switches.

Multiple Arithmetic Unit Processors

The third form of computer organization that incorporates multiple processing elements is the multi-arithmetic logic unit (ALU) processor. The fundamental difference between this type

*Examples of closely coupled computer networks built with minicomputers and designed for ultra-reliable applications include the Tandem computer [1977] and the five processor system for NASA's space shuttle [Sklaroff, 1976; Cooper, Chow, 1976].

of structure and multiprocessors is that all the ALUs in the multi-ALU processor support a single instruction stream, as shown in Figure 4, while each of the processors in the multiprocessor supports its own instruction stream.

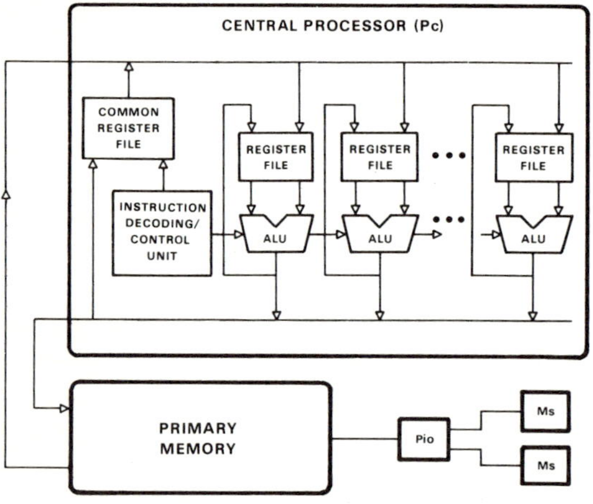

Figure 4. Multi-ALU processor.

If we define a processor to be a unit capable of both decoding and executing instructions, then the multi-ALU processor is not really a multiple processor system. However, multi-ALU organizations are often considered as alternatives to multiprocessors and derive the same benefits from advances in LSI technology as multiprocessors.

A number of well-known computer systems fall into the multi-ALU category. Classical examples include the CDC 6600, with its ten functional units (specialized ALUs), the IBM 360/91 with independent and pipelined floating-point add/subtract and multiply/divide units. Array or vector processors such as ILLIAC IV and CRAY I also fall into this category, but use a specialized vector instruction stream to direct the execution of an array of arithmetic units or a highly pipelined arithmetic unit.

Comparing Alternative Multiple Processor Structures

Networks, multiprocessors, and multi-ALU computers have been presented as three generic methods of organizing processors to build highly parallel computer systems. The three classes can be thought of as varying along a single dimension – the degree of coupling between processors in the system. This term is often used in a general way, but let us define it to be the worst case processor's minimum access time to a global data structure in the system. For example, in the computer network of Figure 3, the minimum data access time for a processor is the access time to local memory. Assuming that the global data structure in this particular network resides in the primary memory of computer 1, an access to global data by computer 1 would take a single memory fetch (on the order of 1 microsecond), while computer 5 will have to send a message to computer 1 requesting the necessary information (on the order of 50 milliseconds). However, the worst case access time is seen by computer 4, which must access the data in computer 1 via a three-hop sequence involving computers 3 and 2, and this might take more than 100 milliseconds.

In a multiprocessor, each processor has direct access to global data stored in primary memory. Since interprocessor communication occurs by sharing primary memory, the interaction times are on the order of 1 to 50 microseconds. In a multi-ALU computer, the analog of interprocessor communication is the transfer of control information that occurs between the control unit and its associated processing elements. Typically, this information is transferred over direct control lines and does not involve memory fetches, making it considerably faster than interprocessor communication in a multiprocessor.

Figure 5 illustrates the range of the degree of coupling for the three types of multiple processor organizations considered here. The position of an organization in this range has a strong influence on its suitability to a particular application. An application consisting of a set of

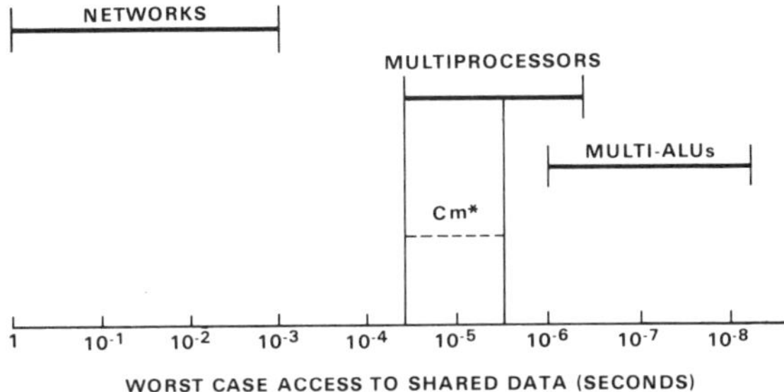

Figure 5. Degree of coupling of multiple-processor organizations.

parallel processes that need to interact or share data only every 10 to 100 seconds can clearly run on a loosely coupled computer network. At the other extreme, algorithms that require the parallel execution of arithmetic operations within single expressions force the interaction times between processing elements to occur almost every instruction cycle. The large interprocessor communication times in a computer network, and probably even in a multiprocessor, make these organizations impractical for such applications. Hence, the average time between interprocess interaction becomes a critical "time constant" of an application and provides a good indication of the type of multiple processor organization that will be most suitable.

The Cm* multiple microprocessor computer system described in the remainder of this article supports time constants in the range of 5 to 50 microseconds. A motivating factor in the construction of Cm* was to have an experimental multiple processor structure that could be used as a vehicle to investigate a range of multiprocessor and closely coupled network organizations. Microprogrammed interprocessor communication controllers provide the flexibility needed for this experimentation.

THE ARCHITECTURE OF Cm*

The structure of the Cm* system grew from a consideration of system organizations like those mentioned in the previous section, and from several other notions. First, we wanted a system that potentially could contain several hundreds of processing elements since we wished to explore greater degrees of parallelism than had previously been available. This required a dramatic change in the processor/memory interconnection structure. Tightly coupled multiprocessors, with uniform access by all processing elements to all of main memory, have a switching structure whose cost grows as the product of the number of processors and the number of memory units. Thus, the processor/memory interconnect becomes prohibitively expensive as the number of processing elements and memory modules grows beyond 10 or 20.

A requirement, set early in the design, was that each processor be able to address directly all of main memory, rather than require a message transmission for access to remote units as in a network. We considered this important in order to allow for experimentation with a variety of interprocess communication mechanisms, both message-based and shared-memory-based.

Uniformly fast access to all of memory by each processor was not, however, considered necessary, either for system performance or for generality of experimentation. The success of cache memories has shown that a processor's memory references tend to cluster in a small portion of its address space [Gibson, 1974; Liptay, 1978]. Results presented later in this article indicate that for the processors used in Cm*, instructions and temporary data usually account for between 90 and 99 percent of the memory references. When a task is subdivided so that several processors may perform different parts of it in parallel, the shared global data accessed by many or all of the processors often accounts for most of the total main memory required by the task. However, our results indicate that these global locations are accessed so infrequently that it makes little difference if their access times are substantially longer than those for code and temporary data.

The structure of Cm* is depicted in Figure 6 and has been described in detail in [Swan *et al.*, 1977; Swan *et al.*, 1977a]. The fundamental unit of Cm* is a computer module (CM). Each CM consists of a processing element, local memory, input/output devices, and a local switch (S.local) which provides a simple interface between the CM and the rest of the system. The primary memory of the system consists exclusively of the local memory of the CMs.

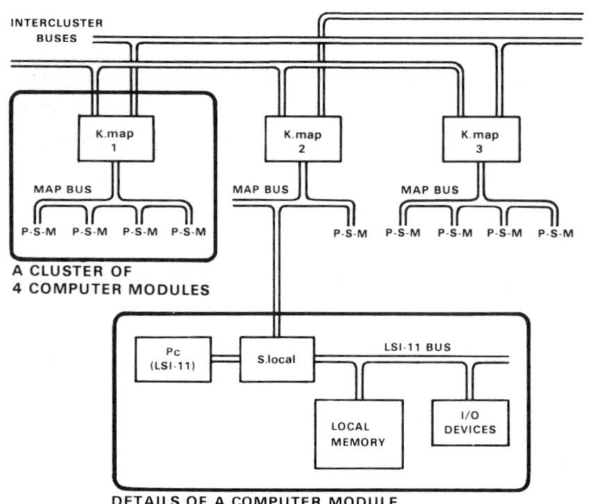

Figure 6. The basic structure of Cm*

A processor may directly reference any location in main memory. The S.local uses simple mapping tables to decide on a reference-by-reference basis whether the physical address being referred to is in the local memory. If it is, the S.local performs a simple mapping function and the reference proceeds very quickly. If it is not, the S.local passes the reference to a mapping controller (K.map). The K.maps, which comprise a distributed processor/memory switch, communicate with each other and the S.locals of the system to perform non-local references for processors. The fact that a memory reference is nonlocal is completely transparent to the processor. While the reference is being performed by the K.maps and S.locals, the processor waits just as if the reference were local. The duration of this wait varies strongly with the "distance" the reference must travel to reach the addressed memory, but it is fundamental to Cm* that the addressing mechanism at the processor level be exactly the same no matter where the physical memory being addressed is located.

Two levels of locality are present in Cm*, the first being the computer module level discussed previously. A second level of locality, that of a cluster, is also present. With the expectation that most references fall into local memory (and thus do not require use of the global switching mechanism) came the assumption that a given processor would not, by itself, make heavy use of the intermodule communication paths. It was decided to share a communication path, consisting of a K.map and a parallel Map Bus, between several CMs. However, a single Map Bus would not have sufficient bandwidth to service 100 or more CMs; furthermore, the presence of a single intercommunication channel would pose a reliability hazard. Thus, the CMs are grouped in clusters containing 1 to 14 modules. References between a processor in a cluster and a nonlocal memory in the same cluster involve only the K.map and Map Bus of the cluster; performance of a large system is dependent on most nonlocal references being cluster-local in order to avoid saturation of the intercluster buses.

An Example Program

The structure of Cm* suggests a complexity in the processor/memory interconnection not seen in more conventional machines. Although we believe this type of switching structure is justified based on economic, performance, reliability, and modularity considerations, it is important that Cm* also be programmable. Given the cost and difficulty of writing good software systems for even the simplest of architectures, a structure that adds to the programmer's problems is highly suspect. Numerous proposals have been made in recent years for various multiple processor structures, and there is no doubt that many of them could be constructed. However, a critical question is whether they could be programmed in any practical sense. Much of the effort on Cm* has been directed toward evaluating how effectively it can be programmed. This issue is dealt with in depth by Jones *et al.*, [1978], in which the operating system for Cm* and a large application program are described. Here, we use an example to point out that although the memory is physically nonhomogeneous, it appears completely uniform to a programmer.

Figure 7 shows an example of how a programmer might organize a program and its associated data structures in his virtual address space; Figure 8 indicates how these program segments might be mapped into the physical

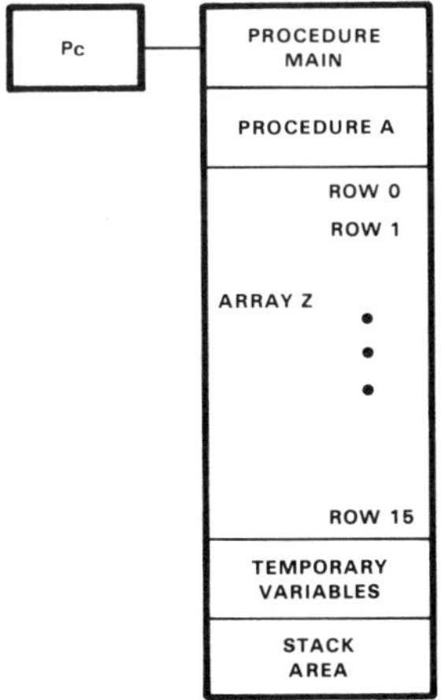

Figure 7. Example organization of a user program.

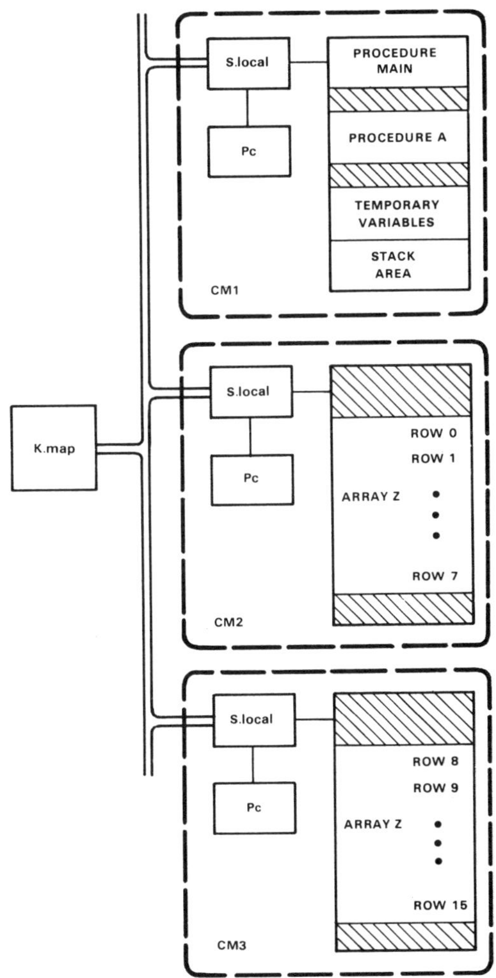

Figure 8. Physical layout of the program in memory.

memory of a Cm* system. When writing programs, the programmer thinks of a process' address space as a large uniform piece of memory exactly as if he were working on a conventional uniprocessor. When the program is loaded onto the Cm* machine, its component segments may be placed anywhere in the physical memory of the system; the relocation tables associated with the processor that will execute the program are then initialized to make these segments addressable.

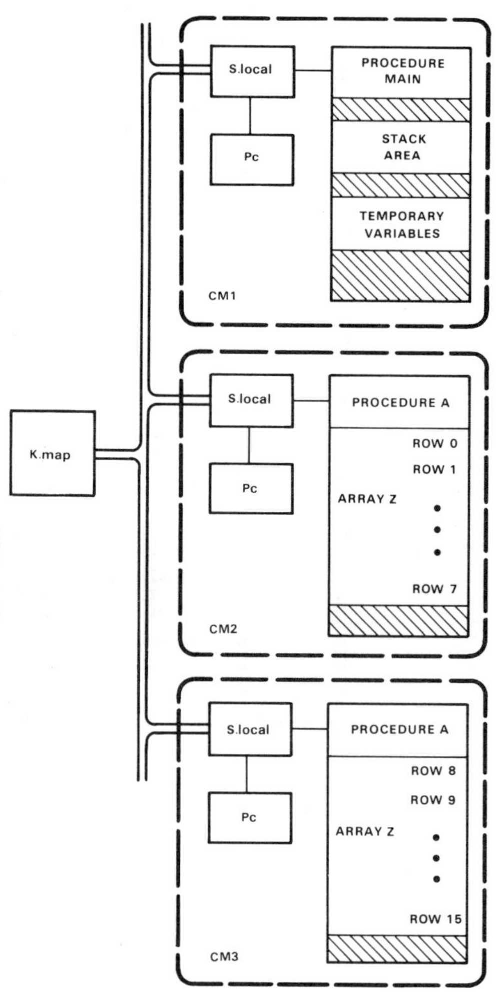

Figure 9. Physical layout of program showing duplication of code.

Figure 8 shows the case where the segments of the example program have been distributed in the memory modules of several different CMs, and the relocation tables in the S.local and K.map set up to make the segments appear in Pc1's virtual address space as in Figure 7. The S.local will recognize that instruction fetches by Pc1 map to procedure MAIN which is in local memory; these references will proceed at full speed without involving the K.map or Map Bus. As the process needs to pop and push words from its working stack, the S.local again will direct the reads and writes to local memory. However, procedure MAIN will eventually call procedure A which will need to access words in the array Z. When such an access is made, the S.local will recognize it as an external reference and pass the virtual address to the K.map; the K.map will translate it to the correct physical address and initiate a memory request to the S.local of either CM2 or CM3, depending on which row of array Z is being accessed. The programmer, and in fact Pc1, are unaware that reading a word of array Z has resulted in a nonlocal reference. The only difference that Pc1 sees is that it takes about 9 microseconds (rather than 3 microseconds for local references) to access the array. During this time, Pc2 and Pc3 are unaffected and may be executing other programs.

There is no reason that Pc1 must execute procedure MAIN. Pc2 or Pc3 could also execute this procedure out of CM1's memory if the appropriate relocation tables were initialized properly. Pc2 would run this program about three times as slowly as Pc1 since each instruction fetch would now be handled as an inter-CM read from Pc2 to CM1. Because of this performance degradation, current Cm* programs are almost always executed on the processor for which the code is local.

Figure 9 shows how several additional processors can be used to advantage. Now when

MAIN calls procedure A, it sends interprocessor messages to Pc2 and Pc3 to initiate concurrent execution of copies of procedure A on both of these processors. By passing the appropriate parameters to Pc2 and Pc3, they can each concentrate on a different part of array Z. In this way, operations being repeated on the whole array may be completed in substantially less time than if a single processor were involved. If array Z is sufficiently large, it may make sense to initiate many more than two other processors in parallel to operate on array Z.

Although the identity of the processor that is dispatched to execute a process and the physical location of segments of memory can be made transparent to the programmer, the decomposition of the program into parallel cooperating tasks cannot. In fact, the whole problem of how to decompose application programs into sets of parallel cooperating processes is an active and interesting area of research. Programming languages such as CONCURRENT PASCAL and MODULA support constructs to express algorithms with explicit parallelism [Hansen, 1975; Wirth, 1977]. In addition, there are some efforts on Cm* [Hibbard, *et al.*, 1978] and elsewhere [Kuck *et al.*, 1972] concerning ideas related to automatically decomposing algorithms slated in higher level languages such as ALGOL and FORTRAN.

Cm* Implementation Overview

The implementation of Cm* has been presented in detail in [Swan *et al.*, 1977a] and will only be summarized here. Figure 10 depicts a computer module. The processing element is Digital Equipment Corporation's LSI-11; both it and the memory and I/O devices on its local bus are standard commercial components. However, the processor has been modified to allow the logical insertion of an S.local, which was designed and built at CMU, between the processor and its LSI-11 bus. The S.local uses information in its relocation tables to direct memory references from the processor either to the local bus, providing simple address relocation while doing so, or out to the K.map for external references. This address translation performed by the S.local is illustrated in Figure 11. In addition, the S.local is capable of accessing the module's memory on behalf of the K.map without intervention from the local processor. Figure 12 is a photograph of one of the CMs in the current system.

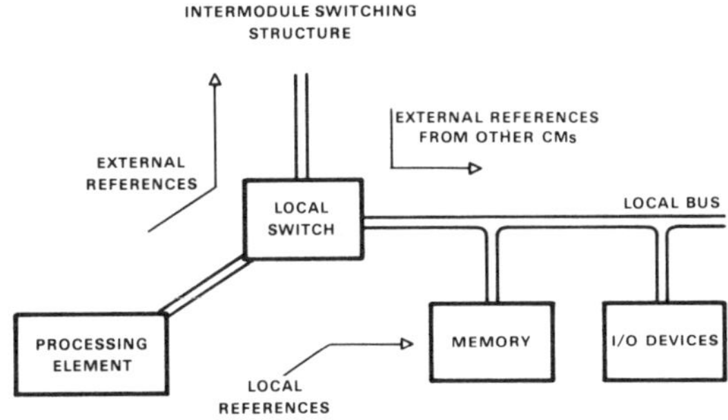

Figure 10. Structure of a computer module.

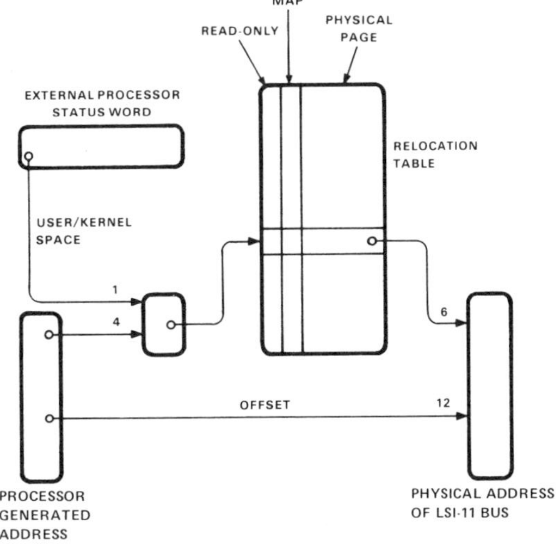

Figure 11. Virtual-to-physical address translation for a local memory reference.

Figure 12. A computer module with its S.local mounted on an extender.

We feel that this notion of a computer module building block is appropriate for LSI implementation. Considering either the processor S.local combination as a single chip (possible using 1977 technology) or the processor, its S.local, and the local memory as a single chip (likely to be possible in 1980) is reasonable because of the small number of external connections required. Although more than 100 wires are currently required in the LSI-11 Bus and Map Bus combined, this number could be reduced enough to allow integration on a single chip.

This new kind of building block requires a minor change in perspective among integrated circuit manufacturers. Current microprocessors are being built with some memory on the microprocessor chip and the capability to access off-chip memory and I/O devices. However, apart from a few notable exceptions [Forbes, 1977; Intel Corp., 1977], it is either difficult or impossible for off-chip units to access the on-chip memory without direct processor intervention, introducing unnecessary complications in the design of the switching structure. Given complete freedom, there are other characteristics of the LSI-11 microprocessor that we would like to change.* However, the purpose of the Cm* project has been to investigate alternate multiple microprocessor structures, not to design a better microprocessor *per se.* The LSI-11 was chosen since it had an adequate architecture,† and had no problems that could not be circumvented via logic in the S.local. Thus, we avoided what may have been a two-year delay had we decided to design and implement our own microprocessor.

The K.maps of Cm* are microprogrammed processors built at CMU which together form a distributed and intelligent processor/memory switching structure. Each K.map presides over a single cluster and has complete control over the processors and memory of that cluster. A K.map's primary function is to process the external memory references of the modules in its cluster, and in so doing to communicate with the S.locals of the cluster and the K.maps of other clusters.

Because the K.maps are responsible for the mapping of external processor addresses to physical memory, their microprograms define the address translation mechanism and thus the virtual memory architecture of the Cm* system. The use of 2048-word writable control stores

The principal deficiency in the LSI-11's architecture from the standpoint of Cm is the limited processor address space of 64 Kbytes. However, in 1975 there were no other microprocessors that had a larger address space.

†In 1973, during discussions of initiating a Cm*-like project at CMU, it was decided that none of the existing microprocessors, e.g., the Intel 8080, had an architecture that could support a programmable multiple processor system.

within the K.maps has allowed us to implement and measure two different architectures. We expect to experiment with several others in the near future.

Figure 13 shows the sequence of transactions that occur on the Map Bus during the processing of an external memory reference. The first transaction on the Map Bus is initiated by the S.local of the source CM when it recognizes that the processor has made an external memory reference. The K.map accepts the processor address from the S.local, performs the virtual-to-physical address translation, and sends the physical address, which includes the number of the destination CM, out on the Map Bus. Assuming that the reference is a simple read, the destination CM accepts the address, reads the indicated word from its local memory, and then, in the third and final Map Bus transaction, returns the data directly to the source CM.

In addition to the concurrency afforded in the mapping mechanism by having multiple clusters, the K.map is partitioned into three units that allow pipelining of the communication mechanism within a cluster. Figure 14 shows the components of the K.map: a mapping processor (P.map) is responsible for address translation and directs the actions of the other two components; a Map Bus controller (K.bus) is master of all transactions on the synchronous Map Bus and schedules activities for execution in the P.map; the third component (Linc) is responsible for shipping and receiving intercluster messages on the two intercluster buses to which each K.map may connect. The three components are relatively independent and communicate via shared memory and a set of hardware queues. The K.map contains a total of about 750 MSI integrated circuit packages on six cards.*

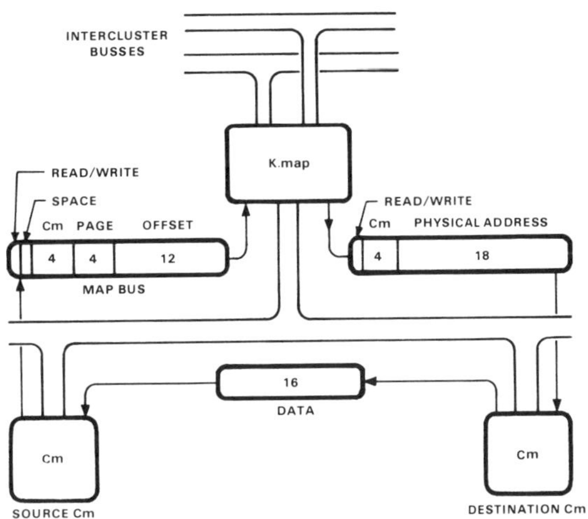

Figure 13. The mechanism for external references.

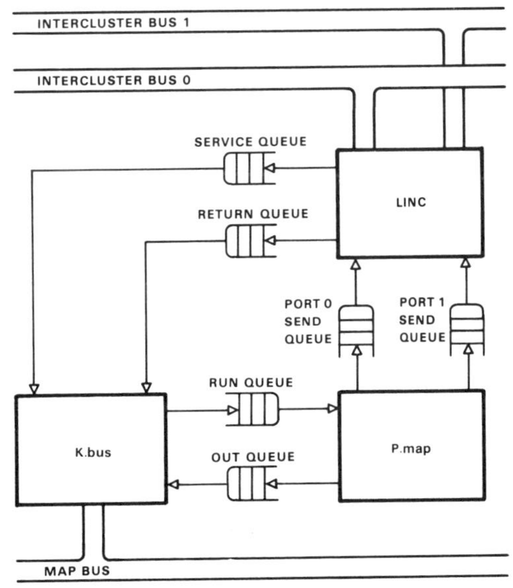

Figure 14. The components of a K.map.

*Much of the complexity of the K.map is a direct result of our desire to ensure that the K.map was a flexible microprogrammable unit that would allow maximum opportunity for experimentation. Over one third of the K.map is devoted to the writable control store.

Current Configuration

The current operating configuration of Cm* is depicted in Figure 15. Ten LSI-11s, with 28 Kwords of memory each, are configured into three clusters of sizes 4, 2, and 4. Figure 16 shows one of the four-CM clusters, with the four CMs visible in the top rack and the K.map and Hooks processor visible in the bottom rack. For several of the benchmark programs, the system was reconfigured into clusters of different sizes. Two more LSI-11s, called Hooks Processors, have special control over the K.maps and are used for microprogram loading and debugging and hardware diagnosis; they are not part of the Cm* system, but rather provide support processing. Each LSI-11 is connected to a PDP-11/10 Host via a serial line; the Host runs a simple operating system built at CMU [Scelza, 1977] to allow users at remote terminals to load programs into LSI-11's from the Host's DECtape drives, to start and stop processors, and to communicate directly with the processors via their serial lines. A front-end terminal processor permits terminals anywhere within the CMU computing environment to access the

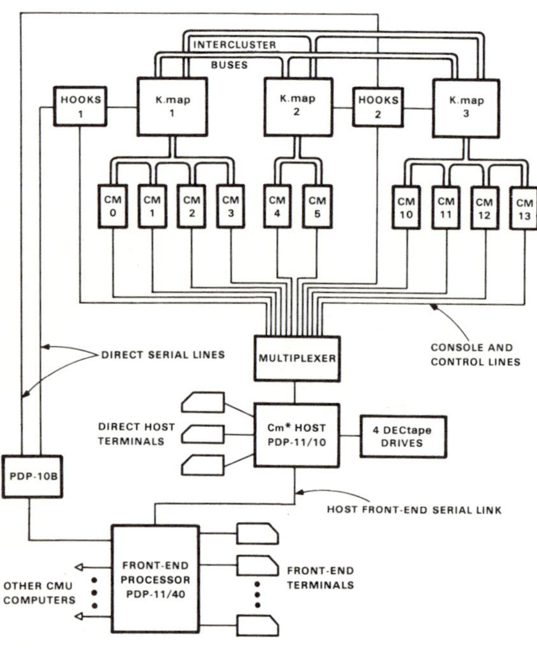

Figure 15. The current configuration of Cm*.

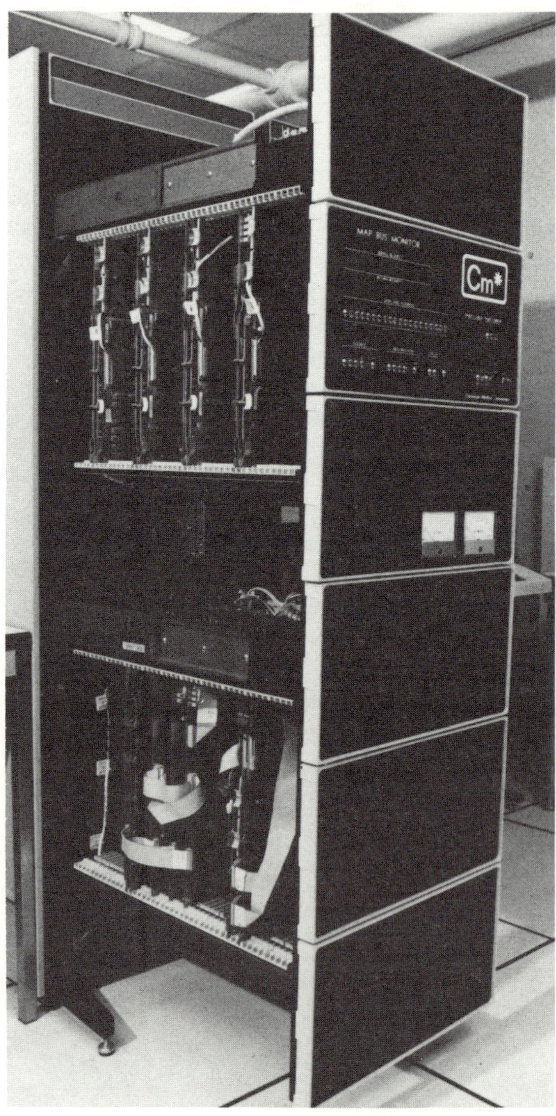

Figure 16. A four-CM cluster.

Host, and thus Cm*, as well as the other CMU computers.

Two versions of K.map microcode have been written and evaluated to date. The first is a simple version written to provide the bare minimum facilities needed for interprocessor communication and memory sharing. Although primarily written to enable system diagnostics to be run, this version was also used for the benchmarks described in the next section as it was available eight months before the more powerful second version. The second version of K.map microcode provides a complete virtual addressing system including protected execution environments and capability-based addressing. The facilities provided by this version are presented in detail in Jones *et al.*, [1978] and Swan *et al.*, [1977].

Under the simple microcode, each processor is permitted to map any of its 16 virtual pages onto any 2048-word physical page in the multicluster system. A processor may specify whether pages residing in its local memory are to be referenced locally or externally (for test and measurement purposes it was convenient to be able to force references to local memory to pass through the K.maps and then come back to the local memory rather than being made directly). Since control operations, e.g., interprocessor interrupts, are invoked by referencing special physical memory locations, this microcode provides completely general intercommunication, although it does not implement any protection. The total size of the simple microcode is 505 80-bit microinstructions.

MEASUREMENT AND EVALUATION OF Cm*

Multi-microprocessor computer structures are sufficiently unconventional that standard metrics of computer system performance are hard to apply effectively. For example, a common measure of the performance of a computer is the number of instructions per second that the processor can execute. A single LSI-11 processor in Cm* is capable of executing about 170K instructions/second; a 10-CM configuration will, therefore, have the potential of 1700K instructions/second and a 100-processor configuration a potential of 17M instructions/second. However, such linear scale-up in performance is difficult to achieve when processors have to cooperate in performing a given task. Overheads associated with ensuring cooperation usually cause the increase in performance to be less than linear.

Measurements on other multiprocessors show that these overheads can become large enough so that the performance of the system actually degrades as more processors are added. Anyone who has suffered through the deliberations of a committee of more than two or three people trying to make a decision should have an intuitive appreciation for the fact that coordination can be expensive.

Initial performance measurements were made on Cm* to quantify this overhead and to determine how it varies with the number of active processors for various configurations. The evaluation was done using what is perhaps the only practical method at the present time: writing a set of benchmark programs and running them on the bare machine. The programs used in the evaluation are outlined below, and are discussed in greater detail in the appendix.

1. **Partial differential equations – a numerical application.** This program solves Laplace's partial differential equation over a rectangular grid. The method of finite differences is used and is relatively easily decomposed with each available processor iterating over a separate region of the grid.
2. **Sorting.** This benchmark program is a decomposition of the well known Quicksort algorithm into a set of asynchronous parallel processes. Each sorting

pass consists of dividing the current list of elements into two and placing the smaller sublist in a stack. Whenever a processor is free, it removes a sublist from the top of the stack and executes a sorting pass over this sublist.

3. **Integer programming – the set partitioning problem.** Set partitioning is typically solved by an enumeration algorithm that searches a large, relatively sparse binary matrix for a feasible solution. While it is easy to initiate parallel searches in paths, it is critical to retain the effectiveness of pruning rules to limit the extent of the search.
4. **The HARPY speech recognition system.** This is a relatively large program that searches a Markovian network to find the most probable utterance given the digitized input of a speech signal. The HARPY algorithm has been studied extensively on uniprocessors [Lowerre, 1976] and is discussed in depth in the paper by Jones *et al.,* [1978].
5. **ALGOL 68 run-time system.** Another large programming system that now exists on Cm* is the run-time system for a useful subset of ALGOL 68 [Hibbard, *et al.,* 1978]. It allows low level activity such as calls to standard functions, array manipulations, and copying of large values to be performed automatically in parallel without requiring the programmer to specify the parallel activity explicitly.

Measurement Techniques

Measurements on the stand-alone Cm* system were made using both specially designed hardware and standard measuring equipment. Each K.map in the system was provided with a hardware device called a Map Bus Monitor (Figure 17), which allowed signals on the Map Bus to be displayed selectively and counted. Particular data or address values passing to and from a given CM in the cluster could thus be monitored. For example, the hit ratio to local memory for a given processor was determined by comparing the overall memory reference rate of the processor to the nonlocal memory reference rate indicated by the Map Bus Monitor.

A standard logic analyzer was used to determine what fraction of the K.map's time was being spent in each of its different operations. This was done by connecting the logic analyzer to the microinstruction address lines in the K.map, and counting the rates at which the microroutines corresponding to the K.map's operations were being invoked.

Memory Reference Times and Hit Ratios

To determine the cost of various types of references, benchmark programs have been measured running in three configurations: (1) with all references local, (2) with all references nonlocal but within the same cluster, and (3) with all references proceeding across cluster boundaries. The times between successive memory references measured under these conditions were

Figure 17. The Map Bus Monitor.

3.5 microseconds for the local case (this was determined by the LSI-11 used as processing element and was in no way affected by the Cm* switching structure), 9.3 microseconds for the intracluster case, and 26 microseconds for the intercluster case.

Table 1 shows the results of our measurements of memory reference patterns for three of the five programs measured on Cm*. *Code* refers to all the primary memory access resulting from fetching instructions from memory. *Stack* refers to all the accesses related to the pushing and popping of operands from the processor's primary stack. This stack is commonly used for temporary variables as well as subroutine call and return information. *Local variables* are operands referenced only by a single copy of a procedure and *global variables* are the basic, shared data structures related to the problem or flags and semaphores used by cooperating processes to coordinate their activities.

Table 1. Memory Reference Distribution for Several Programs

Program	Code	Stack	Local Variables	Global Variables
PDE	82%	11.5%	4%	2.5%
Sorting	71%	12.5%	6.5%	9.5%
Set Partitioning	71.5%	23.5%	4%	1%

For the remaining two programs, HARPY and ALGOL 68, the fraction of references to global data were 14 and 18 percent, respectively. The somewhat surprising fact that can be seen is that even if *all* accesses to the shared, global variables are nonlocal memory accesses, we can still achieve between 82 and 99 percent references to local memory. Ignoring, for the moment, interference on the Map Bus, and contention for the local memory of the CMs, a hit ratio of 90 percent to local memory yields an average access time of 4.1 microseconds. These hit ratios illustrate the value of developing memory management and processor scheduling strategies that attempt to keep code (and the stack) local to the processor executing the program.

Execution Speedup and Bus Contention

Figure 18 shows the average measured execution speedup as a function of the number of processors allocated to the task for the five application programs just discussed. For these measurements the code, stack, and local variable segments were local to each processor, and only the access to global data structures required external references. The nearly linear speedup experience by the PDE and Integer Programming programs is very encouraging.

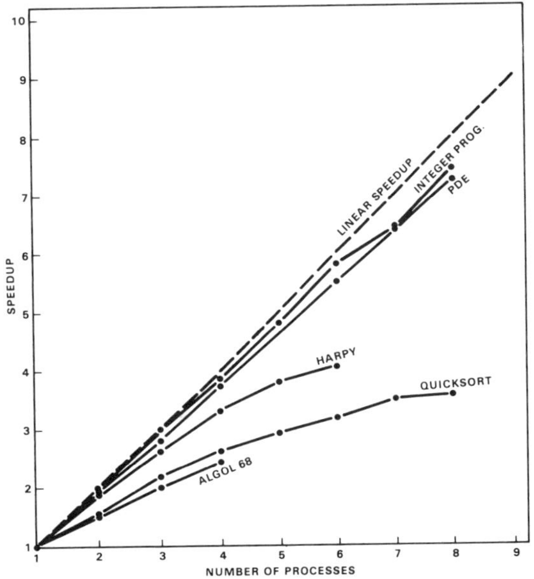

Figure 18. Average speedup of five algorithms of Cm*

The curves for HARPY, ALGOL 68, and QUICKSORT, however, do not show a linear speedup. The reason for this, in each case, is that the problem does not have enough inherent parallelism to keep more than a few processors busy all the time, so that adding more processors does not result in proportionally large speedups. To understand how many processors might effectively be used in larger systems, a number of experiments were conducted. These experiments, which are summarized in the graphs of Figures 19 and 20 were done for the following memory reference patterns.

1. All processors share code, stack, and all data from the memory in a single CM. In other words, the memory bandwidth of an individual CM is the performance bottleneck. This curve indicates that performance cannot be improved by using more than three or four processors. The saturation reference rate of a single CM's memory was measured to be 270K references/second. Now consider more practical cases in which most of the code and local variables are in the local memory of each CM, and only the global data structures are shared. Even if 10 percent of all memory references of the active processors were to global data in the memory of a single CM, the system would saturate between 30 and 40 CMs. To date, we have had no difficulty in distributing shared data structures over the memory of several CMs so that the memory bandwidth of a CM is not a serious constraint.
2. All processors make external references that are mapped back to their own local memory. This case was used to study saturation of the Map Bus and K.map. The curve indicates that the K.map (and Map Bus) saturated when six or seven processors were simultaneously active in this mode; the saturation rate of the

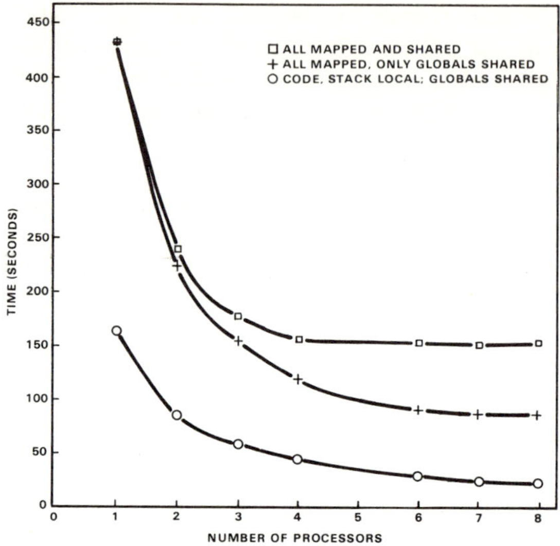

Figure 19. PDE execution time.

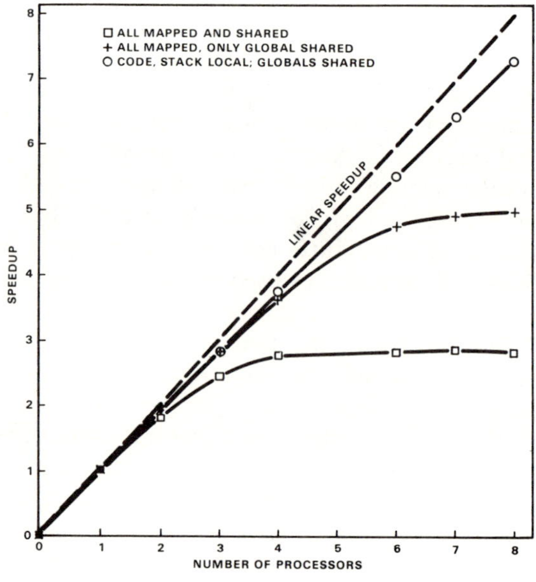

Figure 20. PDE speedup.

Map Bus is about 550K references/second. Assuming that the measured benchmarks represent typical situations, and that a 90 percent hit ratio to local memory can be achieved, we see that a Map Bus and K.map can support a cluster of about 60 CMs. The bandwidth of the Map Bus is an important limiting factor that constrains the number of CMs in a cluster, so that there is a need to consider multicluster configurations independent of reliability or availability considerations.

3. All processors access their local memory for the code, stack, and local variables, and use the K.map only for mapping to shared global data. This is the case already considered, and for up to eight processors, negligible contention is experienced (Figure 18).

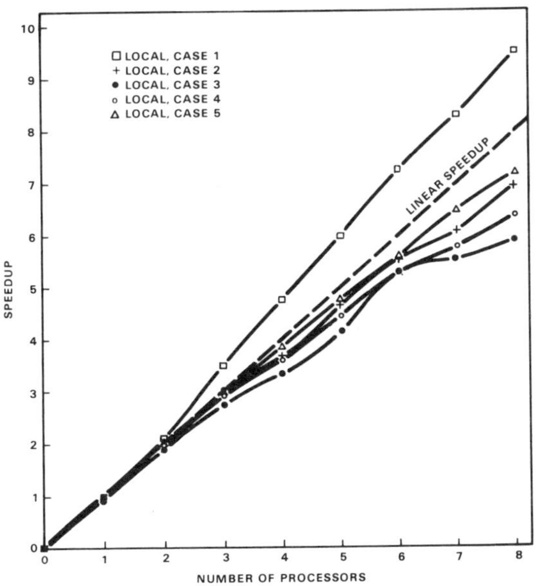

Figure 21. Integer programming speedup.

From additional measurements, we estimate the intercluster saturation rate to be about 287K references/second, with the source K.map being the bottleneck component in the system.

Figure 21 shows another interesting measurement on Cm*. Here, a number of different cases of the Integer Programming program are shown as a plot of execution speedup versus the number of available processors. Most of the time, almost linear speedups were observed. This is a consequence not of a breakthrough in algorithmic design, but rather of the fact that the time to find the optimal solution in a search tree is dependent on the order in which the tree is searched. In other words, some search orders allow quicker, more radical prunes of the tree than other search orders. Therefore, the chance will always exist that one of the parallel paths initiated will fortuitously find a good solution and allow early pruning of the search tree.

Fundamentally, the multiprocessor cannot expect speedups greater than linear in the number of available processors. If, for example, the speedup of the Integer Programming problem was observed to increase as the square of the number of processors, then a new program could be written for a uniprocessor that, in effect, emulated the operation of a set of parallel processors by round-robin sharing of the uniprocessor among the parallel processes. In special instances, parallel processes may allow the elimination of some overhead, but linear speedup in the number of available processors is the ideal situation.

Performance of Multiple Cluster Configurations

The results of Figure 18 imply that many more than ten CMs could be managed in a single cluster before the Map Bus becomes a performance bottleneck. However, since we are interested in the potential of the Cm* structure for much larger systems, we also examined the performance of multi-cluster Cm* configurations to predict the performance degradations associated with intercluster references. Figure 22 shows the performance of Cm* on two different versions of the PDE program for both single-cluster and multi-cluster configurations. Note that nearly negligible degradation was achievable, particularly in method 4, which is an asynchronous version of the PDE specifically designed to cope with processors of

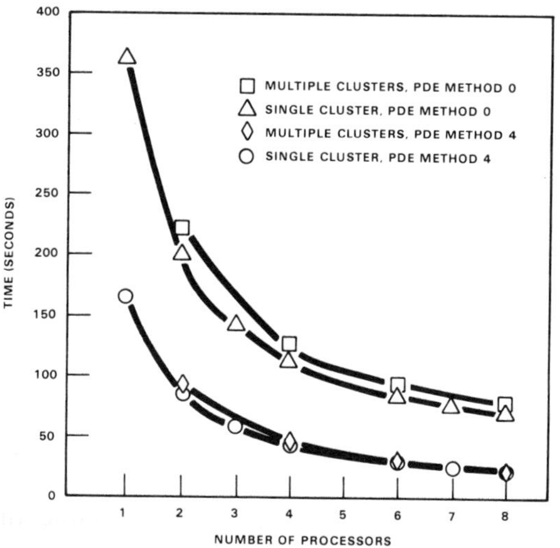

Figure 22. Single- and multiple-cluster execution time.

varying run times. The small degradation in going from the one cluster configuration to the multi-cluster configuration gives considerable hope that hierarchical switching structures like the one used in Cm* can provide very nearly the performance of much more expensive switching structures that give uniformly fast access to all of physical memory.

CONCLUDING REMARKS

The major accomplishment of the Cm* project has been to bring an experimental multi-microprocessor system to an operational state, and to demonstrate that almost-linear speedup can be achieved with several applications. Moreover, there have been no serious bottlenecks or deficiencies in the processor/memory bus structure that preclude configurations with 100 or more processors.

Many aspects of Cm*, and multi-microprocessors in general, require further investigation. Our own plans call for considering alternative memory mapping and interprocess control architectures, developing a large application system on Cm* to test larger configurations, and integrating a practical I/O system into the Cm* structure.

As other multi-microprocessors become operational and competing solutions are found to some of the problems currently facing multiprocessors, the relative merit of the Cm* organization will be put into much better perspective. A comparison of alternate multiprocessor organizations is especially important in the initial stages when most investigations are necessarily empirical, and no one solution may claim optimality.

APPENDIX: DESCRIPTION OF THE BENCHMARK PROGRAMS

Five programs from different application areas were used in the initial performance evaluation of the Cm* system. Four of these programs are described here, and the HARPY speech recognition program is described in Jones *et al.*, [1978]. More detailed descriptions of these programs may be found in Fuller *et al.*, [1977].

Partial Differential Equations, a Numerical Application

This is the solution to Dirichlet's problem of Laplace's partial differential equation (PDE) by the method of finite difference. This program solves the PDE:

$$\frac{\partial^2 u\,(x,\,y)}{\partial x^2} + \frac{\partial^2\,(x_2\,y)}{\partial y^2} = 0$$

on a rectangular grid of size $M \times N$, where only the values at the outer edges of the grid are given.

A finite difference method [Baudet, 1976] that transforms the problem into a set of linear equations $Ax = b$ is used. Here, x is an MN vector of all the points in the grid, A is an $MN \times MN$ sparse matrix, and b is an MN vector derived from the boundary conditions. This set of linear equations is derived from the new approximate values of the points (in each iteration) by averaging the values of the four adjacent neighbors of each point. The solution of this PDE is required in many application areas (e.g., in electromagnetic fields, hydrodynamics). Other PDE problems can be similarly solved using this method.

The computation is initially decomposed into P processes, where P is equal to the number of processors available. Each process (and processor) iterates on a fixed subset of MN/P components out of the total MN components. One processor, the "master" processor, initializes and starts the other "slave" processors, and prints the results when all have finished. Note that the master participates in the computation just like the slave processors.

Sorting

This problem concerns the decomposition of the well-known QUICKSORT algorithm [Singleton, 1969] into asynchronous parallel processes. The median for each sort pass was chosen as the median of the first, middle, and last elements in the sublist. During a sorting pass, a processor partitions its list of elements into two sublists: elements larger than the median of the original set and elements smaller than the median. The processor then pushes the address and size of the smaller of the two subsets onto a stack shared by all the processors. Making the smaller subset available to the other processors tends to put more work onto the shared stack in order to keep as many processors as possible busy. The processor proceeds to further partition the remaining (larger) subset. When the remaining subset cannot be partitioned further, the processor selects the next available subset from the shared stack.

Simple assumptions about the algorithm give a theoretical sorting time of:

$$cN\ [(K - M)/P + 2\ (1 - (1/2)^M\ )]$$

where N is the number of elements tc sort, K is $\text{Log}_2\ N$, c is constant, P is the number of processors, and M is $\text{Log}_2\ P$.

When the number of processors is much smaller than the number of items to be sorted, almost linear speedup can be achieved. The performance degrades considerably when the number of processors is large and asymptotically approaches a speed of $T = c\ \text{Log}\ N/2$. See Stone [1971] for a description of sorting methods that speed up as $N/\text{Log}\ N$ for large numbers of processors.

Integer Programming – The Set Partitioning Problem

The particular integer programming considered here is one of the most practical and applicable methods. It is used, for example, in airline crew scheduling [Bales and Padberg, 1976].

The set-partitioning problem is to solve:

$$\min \{c.x \mid Ax = 0,\ x_j = 0 \text{ or } 1 \text{ for } 0 < j \leqslant N\}$$

where A is an $M \times N$ binary matrix, c is an N vector, and $c = (1 \ldots 1)\ M$ vector.

This problem typically is solved by performing an N-ary tree search on a large relatively sparse binary matrix. As an example of this method, consider the airline crew scheduling problem. The rows of the A matrix correspond to a set of flight legs from city A to city B, in time T to be covered during a specified period, and the columns of A correspond to a possible sequence of tours of flight legs done by one crew; c is the vector of the associated cost of each tour. A possible solution includes a set of tours that satisfies all the flight legs (one and only one crew makes a flight leg). We are looking for the solution with the lowest cost.

As in the previous applications, the master processor initializes the computation, creates the array according to user's specification, and puts enough initial possible search-path solutions in a global stack from which all the processors pick their work. We arbitrarily choose to put more than $10 \times P$ path solutions into the stack where P equals the number of processors so the work is more evenly distributed between the processors, and all are occupied for a large percentage of the time.

To enhance pruning in the search, a global variable contains the cost of the best solution found so far by any of the processors, and all compare their current cost value to it and begin to backtrack in the search when that global cost is lower.

ALGOL 68 System

A semantically rich subset of the programming language ALGOL 68 was implemented on Cm* [Hibbard, *et al.*, 1978]. In order to take advantage of the parallel architecture of Cm*, the language has been extended by including several methods of specifying concurrent execution and synchronization of subtasks.

The run-time system measured runs upon a small, special purpose kernel which provides basic support for interrupt and I/O handling, segment allocation and swapping, bootstrapping, and the collection of performance statistics. To facilitate locality of memory references, the run-time system is loaded into the local memory of each processor.

Modifications are being studied to provide automatic decomposition of tasks into small-grain subtasks. These modifications comprise a software implementation of multiple parallel-instruction pipelines, in which the instructions are the primitive actions of the ALGOL 68 run-time system, e.g., floating-point operations, array indexing and other vector operations, and assignments of large values. These actions are executed by slave processors on behalf of the master processors which are placing the actions in the pipelines.

ACKNOWLEDGEMENTS

The Cm* project has greatly benefited from interaction with other research projects and individuals at the Computer Science Department at CMU; experiences gained from the C.mmp project [Harbison and Wulf, 1977] have been particularly useful. Among those who have made direct contributions to the design and implementation of Cm* are Andy Bechtolsheim, Paolo Coraluppi, Kwok-Woon Lai, Pradeep Reddy, and Daniel Siewiorek.

Opposite:

Top:
- KI10-based DECsystem-10.

Bottom, left to right:
- KL10-based DECSYSTEM-20.
- PDP-6.
- KA10.

PART V

THE PDP-10 FAMILY

The PDP-10 Family

This final part of *Computer Engineering* contains only a single chapter, "The Evolution of the DECsystem 10." It is a fitting conclusion because it summarizes many of the aspects of computer engineering discussed in the rest of this book. The introduction and historical setting with which the chapter begins are condensations of the historical information included in Parts I and II of this book; the goals, constraints, and design decisions elaborated on in the remainder of the chapter are specific examples of the concepts discussed throughout the book. The paragraph headings, such as "logic," "fabrication," "packaging," and "price/performance," have counterparts in earlier chapters.

The authors of this chapter, which first appeared as a paper in the January 1978 issue of *Communications of the ACM*, have been key figures in the evolution that they describe. Thus, when they talk about design decisions and tradeoffs, they are talking from first-hand experience.

The 36-bit Family has been important to DEC for a number of reasons. The designers of these machines have realized that software development is very costly, and have put a great deal of emphasis on making their systems easy to program, even if additional hardware expense is involved. Furthermore, their hardware has been very conservatively designed, with rigid design rules to assure that the vast number of circuits required to implement each function operate correctly under all conditions. Although the chapter conclusion suggests that the PDP-10 engineers have transferred hardware technology to minicomputer engineering, the technology transfer has been principally in the area of automated design aids, as it has only been with the ECL logic of the KL10 that PDP-10 designs have used logic families or module technology not previously used in the minicomputer segment of DEC. The paragraphs on "logic" and "packaging" within the main body of the chapter elaborate on this.

The role of the PDP-6 in PDP-10 history is described in detail in the chapter, but it has interesting aspects in addition to those mentioned. Because the PDP-6 was the first computer to offer elegant, powerful capabilities at a low price, a great many of the PDP-6s built found their way into university and scientific environments, giving DEC a strong foothold in that market and providing both educated customer input for future models and a source of bright young future employees to assist in the hardware and software development for those future models. The impact of the PDP-6 was particularly noteworthy because fewer PDP-6s were built than any other DEC machine: only 23. The sales were sufficiently disappointing to management, in fact, that a decision was made (but fortunately reversed) not to build any more 36-bit machines. Since then, however, with the possible exception of the KI10 processor, each processor has been more successful than the last, and the contributions of "large computer thinking" (design rules, strict program compatibility, etc.) to the company as a whole have been extremely useful. This final chapter is an excellent summary of computer engineering.

21

The Evolution of the DECsystem-10

C. GORDON BELL, ALAN KOTOK,
THOMAS N. HASTINGS, and RICHARD HILL

INTRODUCTION

The project from which the PDP-6, DECsystem-10, and DECSYSTEM-20 series of scientific, timeshared computers evolved began in the spring of 1963 and continued with the delivery of a PDP-6 in the summer of 1964. Initially, the PDP-6 was designed to extend DEC's line of 18-bit computers by providing more performance at increased price. Although the PDP-6 was not designed to be a member in a family of compatible computers, the series evolved into five basic designs (PDP-6, KA10, KI10, KL10, and KL20) with over 700 systems installed by January 1978. During the initial design period, we neither understood the notions and need for compatibility nor did we have adequate technology to undertake such a task. Each successive implementation in the series has generally offered increased performance for only slightly increased cost. The KL10 and KL20 systems span a five to one price range.

TOPS-10, the major user software interface, developed from a 6-Kword monitor for the PDP-6. A second user interface, TOPS-20, introduced in 1976 with upgraded facilities, is based on multiprocess operating systems advances.

This paper is divided into seven sections. Section 2 provides a brief historical setting followed by a discussion of the initial project goals, constraints, and basic design decisions. The instruction set and system organization are given in Sections 4 and 5, respectively. Section 6 discusses the operating system, while Section 7 presents the technological influences on the designs. Sections 4 through 7 begin with a presentation of the goals and constraints, proceed to the basic PDP-6 design, and conclude with the evolution (and current state). We try to answer the often-asked questions, "Why did you do . . .?", by giving the contextual environment. Figure 1 helps summarize this context in the form of a timeline that depicts the various hardware/software technologies (above line) and when they were applied (below line) to the DECsystem-10.

HISTORICAL SETTING

The PDP-6 was designed for both a timeshared computational environment and realtime laboratory use with straightforward interfacing capability. At the initiation of the project, three timeshared computers were

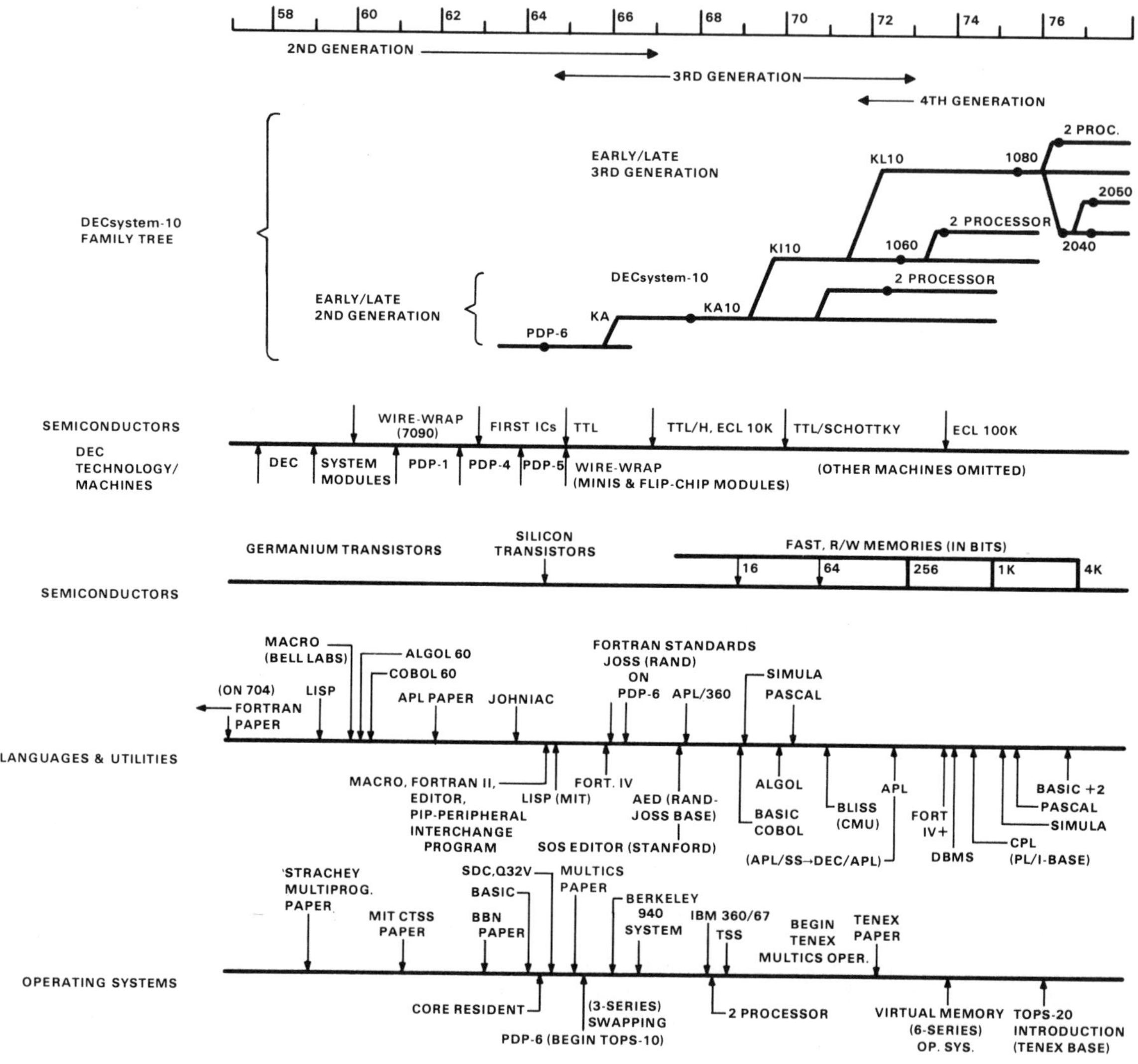

Figure 1. Timeline of DECsystem-10 evolution.

operational: a PDP-1 at Bolt, Beranek, and Newman (BBN) which used a high-speed drum that could swap a 4 Kword core image in one 34 ms revolution; an IBM 7090 system at MIT called CTSS, which provided each of 32 users a 32 Kword environment; and an AN/FSQ-32V at SDC, which could serve 40 simultaneous users.

The Bell Laboratory's IBM 7094 Operating System was a model operating system for batch users. Burroughs had implemented a multiprogrammed system on the B5000. Dartmouth was considering the design of a single language, timesharing system which subsequently became BASIC. The MIT Multics system, the Berkeley SDS 940, the Stanford PDP-1 based timeshared system for computer-aided instruction, and the BBN Tenex system all contributed concepts to the DECsystem-10 evolution in the 1960s.

In architecture, the Manchester Atlas [Bell, Newell, 1971:Ch. 23] was exemplary, not because it was a large machine that we would build, but because it illustrated a number of good design principles. Atlas was multiprogrammed with a well defined interface between the user and operating system, had a very large address space, and introduced the notion of extra codes to extend the functionality of its instruction set. Paging was a concept we just could not afford to implement without a fast, small memory. The IBM Channel concept was in use on their 7094; it was one we wanted to avoid since our minicomputers (e.g., PDP-1) were generally smaller than a single channel and could outperform the 7094 in terms of I/O concurrency and I/O programmability by a clean, simple interrupt mechanism.

The DEC product line in 1964 is summarized in Table 1. Sales totaled $11 million then, and it was felt that computers had to be offered in the $20,000 to $300,000 range. We were sensitive to the problems encountered by not having enough address bits, having watched DEC and IBM machines exceed their addressing capacities.

On the software side, most programmers at DEC had been large-machine (16 Kword to 32 Kword) users, although they had most recently programmed minicomputers where program size of 4 Kwords to 8 Kwords was the main constraint. There was not a good understanding of operating systems structure and design in either academia or industry. MIT's Multics project was just being formed and IBM's 360/TSS project did not start until 1965. Generally, there were no people who directly represented the users within the company, although all the designers were computer users. A number of users in the Cambridge (Mass.) community advised on the design (especially John McCarthy, Marvin Minsky, and Peter Sampson at the MIT Artificial Intelligence Laboratory).

Table 1. DEC's 1964 Computer Products

Name	Year Introduced	Word Size (Bits)	Price ($K)	Status
PDP-1	1960	18	120	Marketed
PDP-2	1960	24	–	Reserved for future implementation
PDP-3	1961	36	–	Paper machine
PDP-4	1962	18	60	Marketed
PDP-5	1964	12	27	Introduced
PDP-6	1964	36	300	Introduced

Although there was little consensus that FORTRAN would be so important, it was clear that our machine would be used extensively to execute FORTRAN. The macroassemblers, basically unchanged even today, were used in various laboratories; our first one for the PDP-1 was done by MIT in 1961. We also felt that the list languages, especially LISP for symbolic processing, were important. There was virtually no interest in business data processing although we had all looked at COBOL.

We did not understand the concept of technology evolution very well, even though integrated circuits were both forecast and in development. Germanium transistors were available, and silicon transistors were just on the market. IBM was using machine wirewrap technology, while DEC back panels were hand-wired and soldered. The basic DEC logic circuits were saturating transistors as distinct from the more expensive current mode used by IBM in the 7094 and Stretch computers. Production core memories of 2 microseconds were beginning to appear, and their speed was improving. The PDP-1 used a 5 microseconds core. Hence, it was unclear what memory speed a processor should support.

The notions of compatibility and family range were not appreciated even though SDS (which eventually became XDS and is now nonexistent) had built a range of 24-bit computers. We adhered to the then-imposed convention of the word length being a multiple of six bits (the number of bits in the standard character code), but designed the machine to handle arbitrary length characters.

OVERALL GOALS, CONSTRAINTS, AND BASIC DESIGN DECISIONS

Table 2 lists the initial goals, constraints, and some basic design decisions. Presenting this list separately from the design is difficult because the goals and constraints were not formally recorded as such and have to be extracted from design descriptions and our unreliable, self-justifying memories. Table 2 will be used in discussing the design.

The initial design theme was to provide a powerful, timeshared machine oriented to scientific use, although it subsequently evolved to commercial use. John McCarthy's definition [McCarthy and Maughly, 1962] of timesharing, to which we subscribed, included providing each user with the illusion of having his own large computer. Thus, our base design provided protection between the users and a mechanism for allocating and controlling the common resources. The machine also had to support a variety of compiled and interpreted languages. The construction was to be modular so that it could evolve and users could build large systems including multiprocessors. It was intended to enhance the top of DEC's existing line of 12- and 18-bit computers. It was designed to be simple, buildable, and supportable by a small organization. Thus it should use as much DEC hardware technology as possible.

THE INSTRUCTION SET PROCESSOR

Our goals for an ISP were: to efficiently encode the various programs using both compiled and interpreted languages; to be understandable and remembered by its users; to be buildable in current technology at a competitive price; and to permit a compiler to provide efficient program production.

Data-Types and Operators

Earlier DEC designs and the then-current six-bit character standard forced a word length that was a multiple of 6, 12, and 18 bits. Thus, a 36-bit word was selected.

The language goals and constraints forced the inclusion of integer and real (floating-point) variables. We chose two's complement integer representation rather than the sign-magnitude representation used on the 7090 or the one's complement representation on PDP-1. The floating-point format was chosen to be the same as the 7090, but with a format that permitted comparison to be made on the number as an integer in order to speed up comparisons and require only a single set of compare instructions.

Special (common) case operators (e.g., $V = 0$, $V = V + 1$, $V = V - 1$) were included to support compiled code. Our desire to execute LISP directly resulted in good address arithmetic. As a result, both LISP and FORTRAN on DECsystem-10 are encoded efficiently.

Since the computer spends a significant portion of its time executing the operating system, the efficient support of operating system data-types is essential. A number of instructions should be provided for manipulating and testing the following data-types:

1. Boolean variables (bits).
2. Boolean vectors.

Table 2. Initial Goals, Constraints, and Basic Design Decisions

User/Language/Operating System

- Cheap cost/user via timesharing without inconvenience of batch processing
- Timeshared use via terminals with protection between users
- Independent user machines to execute from any location in physical memory
- Unrestricted use of devices, e.g., full-duplex use of terminals
- Support for wide range of compiled and interpreted languages
- No special batch mode, batch must appear like terminal via a command file
- Device-independent I/O so that programs would run on different configurations and I/O could be shared among the user community
- Direct I/O for real-time users
- Primitive command language to avoid need for large internal state
- Minimum usable system ⩽16 Kwords
- Modular software to correspond to modular hardware configurations

Instruction-Set Processor (ISP)

- Support user languages by data-types and special operations
  - Scientific (i.e., FORTRAN) ⇛ integers, reals, Boolean
  - List processing (i.e., LISP) ⇛ addresses, characters
  - Support recursive and reentrant programming ⇛ stack mechanism
- Support operating systems
  - Effective as machine language ⇛ Booleans, addresses, characters, I/O
  - Operating system is an extension of hardware via defined operating codes
- Word length would be 36 bits (compatible with DEC's computers)
- Large (1/4 million 36-bit words = 1 million 9-bit bytes) address
- Require minimal hardware ⇛ simple
- General-register based (design decision) with completely general use
- Easy to use and remember machine language
  - Orthogonality of addressing (accessing) and operators
  - Completeness of operators
  - Direct (not base + displacement) addressing
  - Few exceptional instructions
- 2's complement arithmetic (multiple precision arithmetic)

PMS Structure

- Maximum modularity so that users could easily configure any system
- Easy to interface
- Asynchronous operation – system must handle evolving technology
- Multiprocessors for incremental and increased performance (2–4 in design)
- No Pios (IBM channels), use simple programmed I/O with interrupts and direct-memory access for high-speed data transmission

Implementation

- Simple; reliable
- Asynchronous logic and buses for speed in light of uncertain logic and memory speed
- All state accessible to field service personnel via lights
- Use DEC (10 MHz versus 5 MHz) circuit/logic technology (manpower constraint)
- Buildable without microprogramming (no fast, read-only memories in 1963)

Organizational/Marketplace

- Add to high end of DEC's computers
- Use minimal resources, while supporting DEC's minicomputer efforts

3. Arbitrary length field access (load/store only).
4. Addresses.
5. Programs (loops, branching, and subprograms).
6. Ordinary integers.
7. The control of I/O.

A significant number of control instructions were included to test addresses and other data-types. These tests controlled flow by either a jump or skip of the next instruction (which is usually a jump). Loop control was a most important design consideration.

Table 3 gives the data-types and instructions present in the various implementations. The KA10 and PDP-6 processor instruction sets were essentially the same, but differed in the implementation. The PDP-6 had 365 instructions. A double-precision negate instruction in the KA10 improved the subroutine performance for double-precision reals. The instruction, "find first one in a bit vector," was also added to assist operating system resource allocation and to help in a specific application sale (that did not materialize). Finally, double-precision real-arithmetic instructions were added to the KI10 using the original PDP-6 programmed scheme. A few minor incompatibilities were introduced in the KI to improve performance.

With the decision to offer COBOL in 1970, better character and decimal string processing support was required from the intruction set. The initial COBOL performance was poor for character and decimal arithmetic because each operation required: (1) software character by character conversion to an integer, (2) the operation (in binary or double-precision binary), and (3) software reconversion to a character or a decimal number. The KL10 provided much higher performance for COBOL by having the basic instructions for comparing character and decimal strings – where a character can be a variable size. For arithmetic operations, instructions were added to convert between string and double-precision binary. The actual operations are still carried out in binary. For add and subtract, the time is slightly longer than a pure string-based instruction, but for multiplying and dividing, the conversion approach is faster.

Stack Versus General Registers Organization

A stack machine was considered, based on the B5000 and George Interpreter (which later became the English Electric KDF9). A stack with index register machine was proposed for executing the operating system, LISP, and FORTRAN; it was rejected on the basis of high cost and fear of poor performance. The compromise we made was to provide a number of instructions to operate on a stack, yet to use the general registers as stack pointers.

An interesting result of our experience was that one of us (Bell) discovered a more general structure whereby either a stack or general register machine could be implemented by extending addressing modes and using the general registers for stack pointers. This scheme was the basis of the PDP-11 ISP (Chapter 9).

We currently believe that stack and general register structures are quite similar and tend to offer a tradeoff between control (either in a program or in the interpretation of the ISP) and performance. Compilers for general register machines often allocate registers as though they were a stack. Table 4 compares the stack and general register approaches.

A general register architecture was selected with the registers in the memory address space. The general registers (multiple accumulators) should permit a wide (general) range of use. Both 8 and 16 were considered. By the time the uses were enumerated, especially to store inner loops, we believed 16 were needed. They could be used as: base and index, set of Booleans (flags), ordinary accumulator and multiplier-quotient (from 7090), subroutine linkage, fast

Table 3. Data-Types of DECsystem-10/DECSYSTEM-20

Data-Type	Length (bits)	Machine	Operators and [Number of Instructions]	Operator Location
Boolean	1	All	0, 1, 1¬, test by skip [64]	AC ← *f* (AC)
Boolean-vector	36	All	All 16 [64]	AC and/or mem ← *f* (AC, mem)
Characters	0–36 = *v*	All	Load, store [5]	AC ↔ (mem)
Character-string	*v* × *n*	KL	Compare [8]; move [4]	*f* (mem) = *g* (mem); mem *f* (mem)
Digit-string	*v* × *n*	KL	Convert to double integer	*f* (AC) ↔ *f* (mem)
Half word, 2's complement integers = addresses	18	All	Load, store [64]; index loop control	AC ↔ *f* (mem); AC ← *f* (AC)
Full word, 2's complement integers (and fractions)	36	All	Load, store, abs., –(negate) [16] +, –, ×, +1, –1,×,rotate,test (by skip & jumps)	AC and/or mem ← *f* (AC, mem)
Double word, 2's complement integers (and fractions)	72	KL	Load, store, –(negate) [4]; +, –, ×, [4]	AC ↔ *f* (mem); AC ← *f* (AC, mem)
Real	9 (exponent) +27 (mantissa)	All	Load, store, abs., –(negate), +, –, ×, /, × [35]; test (by skip, jump) [16]	AC and/or mem ← *f* (AC, mem) immediate mode was added in KA
Double real	9 + 54 9 + 63	KI, KL KI, KL	Load, store, abs., negate, +, –, ×, / [8]	KA provided negate instruction
Word stack	36	All	Load, store, call, return [4]	Stack ↔ Memory
Word vector	36 × *k*	All	Move [1]	Mem[*a*:*a*+*k*] ← mem[*b*:*b*+*k*]
I/O program	36	All	Short call/return; UUO	AC, memory

access for temporary and common subexpressions, top of stack when accessed explicitly, pointer-to-control stacks, and fast registers to hold small programs.

Since the ACs were in the address space, ordinary memory could be used in lieu of fast registers to reduce the minimal machine price. In reality, nearly all users bought fast registers. Eight registers may have been enough. A small number would have provided more rapid context switching and assisted the assembly language programmer who tried to optimize (and

Table 4. Comparison of Stack and General Register Architectures

	Stack	General Register
Number of Registers	Approximately the same	
Register use	Fixed to stack operation	Can be arbitrary
Control	Built-in hardware (implicit)	Simple, explicit in program when used as a stack
Access to local variables	1 or 2 elements at top of stack	Full set in general registers
Compiler	Easy (no choice)	An assignment (use) problem
Program encoding	Fewer bits	More bits give access to registers for intermediate and index values
Performance	High if element on stack top	High if in general registers (performs relatively better than stack)

keep track of) their use. In fact, Lunde [1977] has shown that eight working registers would be sufficient to support the higher level language usage. Multiple register sets were introduced in the KI10 to reduce context-switching time.

Instruction-Set Encoding and Layout

The ease-of-implementation goal forced an instruction set design style that later turned out to be easy to fabricate with the KL10 microprogram implementation. This also simplified the fabrication of compilers. In fact, of the 222 instructions useful for FORTRAN data-types, the earliest compiler used 180 of them and the current compiler uses 212. We used three principles, we now understand, for the ISP design:

1. **Orthogonality.** An address (with index and indirect control fields) is always computed in the same way, independent of the data-type it references. Indirect addressing occurs as long as the instruction addressed has an indirect bit.
2. **Completeness and symmetry.** Where possible, each arithmetic data-type should have a complete and identical set of operations.
3. **Mapping among data-types.** Instructions should exist to convert among all data-types. Several data-types were incomplete (characters, half-words), and these should be converted to data-types with a complete operator set.

The instruction is mapped into the 36-bit word as follows:

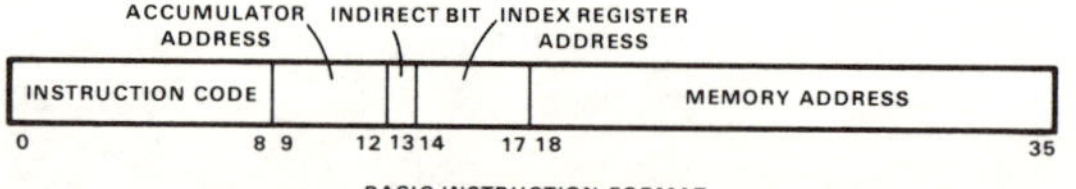

BASIC INSTRUCTION FORMAT

ACCUMULATOR ADDRESS IS 1 OF 16 ACCUMULATORS (GENERAL REGISTERS)
INDEX REGISTER ADDRESS IS INDEX DESIGNATOR TO 1 OF 15 ACs
BIT 13 IS INDIRECT ADDRESS BIT
MEMORY ADDRESS IS ADDRESS OR LITERAL

The entire instruction set fits easily within a single figure (Figure 2). The boldface letters denote instruction mnemonics. The data-types and operations are generally deducible by the instruction names: operator names (e.g., ADD) for word (or integer); D double integers; H half-world; BL vector; 16-operator names (e.g., AND) for Boolean vectors, Test-Boolean (bits); J jump/skip for program control; F floating; DF double floating. The I/O and interrupt instructions are described in the PMS section.

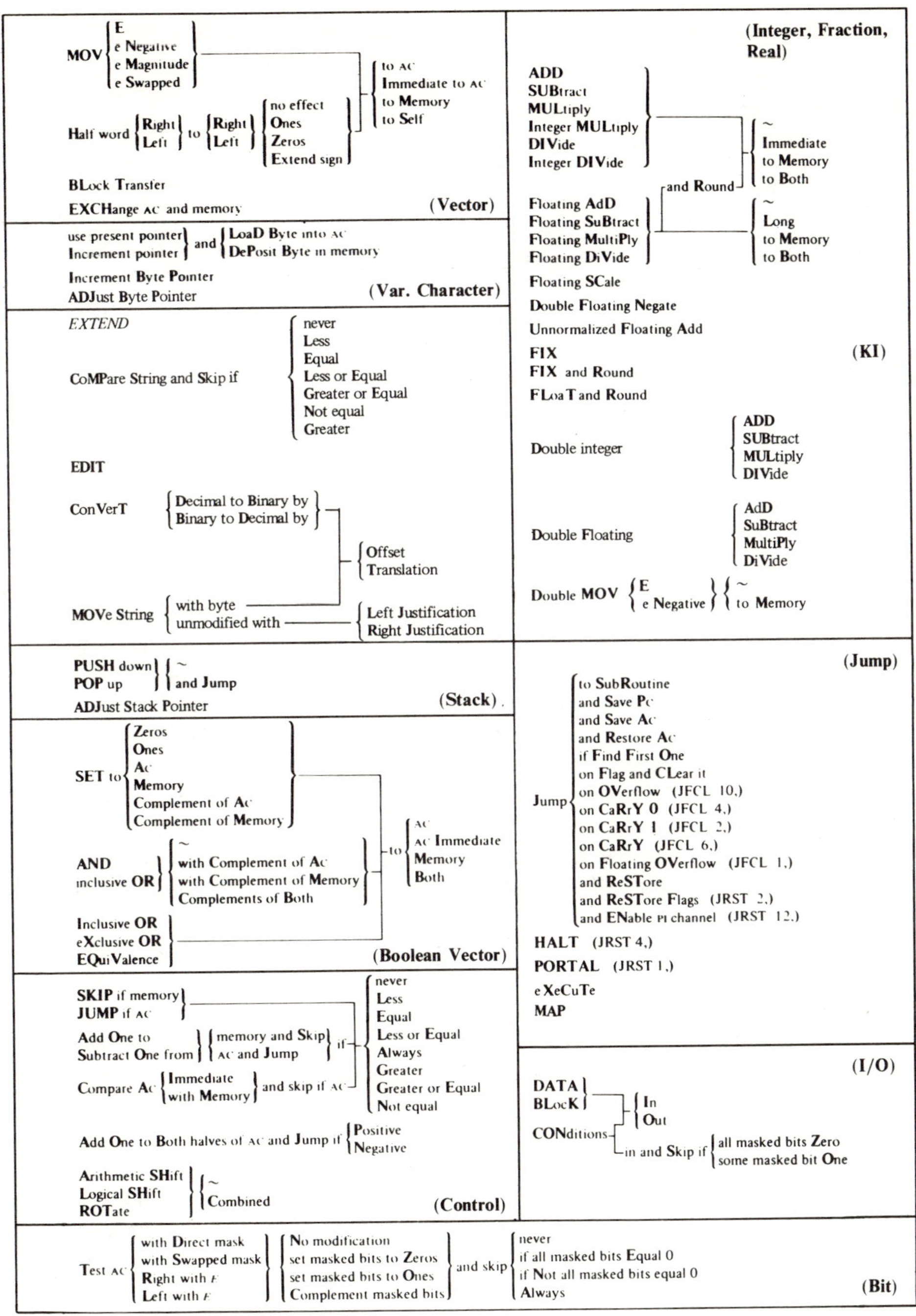

Figure 2. Instruction set.

Multiprogramming/Monitor Facilities

The initial constraint (circa 1963) of a time-shared computer with a common operating system led to several hardware facilities:

1. **Two basic machine modes.** User and Executive (each with different privileges).
2. **Protection.** Protection against operations to halt the computer or operations that affect the common I/O when in User mode.
3. **Communication.** Communication between the user and operating system for calling I/O and other shared functions.
4. **Memory mapping.** Separation of user programs into different parts of physical memory with protection among the parts and program relocation beyond the control of user.

An Executive/User mode was necessary for protection facilities in a shared operating system while providing each user with his own environment. Although there was a temptation (due to having a single operating system) to eliminate or make optional the Executive mode and the general registers, we persevered in the design and now believe this to be an essential part of virtually every computer! (The only other necessary ingredient in every computer is adequate error detection, such as parity.) Separation into at least two separate operating regions (user and executive) also permits the more difficult, time-constrained I/O programs to be written once and to have a more formal interface between system utilities and user.

The Unimplemented User Operation (UUO) is an instruction like the Atlas Extracode and IBM 360 SVC to call operating system functions and common user-defined functions. It also calls functions not present in earlier machines. Thus, a single operating system could be used (by selecting the appropriate options) over several models. This use appears to be more extensive than it is in the IBM System 360/370.

The goals of low cost hardware and minimal performance degradation constrained the protection facilities to a single pair of registers to relocate programs in increments of 1 Kwords. Two 8-bit registers (base and limit registers) with two 8-bit adders were required for this solution. Thus, each user area was protected while running, and a program could be moved within primary or secondary memory (and saved) because user programs were written beginning at location 0. This is identical to the CDC 6600-7600 protection/relocation scheme.

In the KA10, a second pair of registers were added so that the common read-only segment of a user's space could be shared. For example, this enabled one copy of an editor, compiler, or run-time system to be shared among multiple users. Programs were divided into a 128 Kword read-write segment and a 128 Kword read-only segment. Since each user's shared segment had to occupy contiguous memory, holes would develop as users with different shared segment requirements were swapped. This led to "core shuffling," and, in a busy system, up to 2 percent of the time might be spent in this activity. The operating system was modified in the early 70s at the Stanford Artificial Intelligence Laboratory so that the high, read-only segment could share common, global data. In this way, a number of separate user programs could communicate to effectively extend the program size beyond the 256 Kword limit. In retrospect, instructions to move data more easily between a particular user region and the operating system would have been useful; this was corrected in KI10 and is described below.

With the availability of medium-scale integrated circuits, small (32 word) associative memories could be built. This enabled the introduction of a paging scheme in the KI10. Each 512-word page could be declared sharable or private with read-only or read-write access. The basic two-mode protection facility was expanded to four modes: Supervisor, Kernel, Public, and Concealed. There are two monitor modes: Kernel mode provides protection for I/O and system functions common to all users, and Supervisor mode is specialized for a single user. The two user modes are: Concealed for proprietary programs, and Public for shared programs. For protection purposes, the modes are only changed at selected entry portals. The page table was more elaborate than that of the Atlas (circa 1960) whose main goal was to provide a one-level store whereby large programs could run on small physical memories. In fact, the first use of KI10 paging required all programs to be resident rather than having pages being demand driven. A gain over the KA10 was realized by not requiring programs to be in a single contiguous address space. The KI10 design provided more sharing and increased efficiency over the KA10. The KL10 extended KI10 paging for use in the TOPS-20 operating system to be described later.

PMS* STRUCTURE

Table 2 gives the major goals and constraints in the PMS structure design. This section describes system configurations, the I/O system, the memory system, and computer-computer communication structures.

System Configurations

We wanted to give the user considerable freedom in specifying a system configuration with the ability to increase (or decrease) memory size, processing power, and external interfaces to people, other computers, and real-time equipment. Overall, the PMS structure has remained essentially the same as in the PDP-6 design, with periodic enhancements to provide more performance and better real-time capability. (A PDP-6 memory or I/O device could be used on a KI10 processor, and a PDP-6 I/O device can be used on today's KL10 systems.) A radical change occurred with the KL20 to a more integrated, less costly design for the processor, memory, and minicomputer I/O preprocessors.

The PMS block diagram of a two-processor PDP-6 is given in Figure 3. But for simple uniprocessor systems, the PMS structure was quite like that of our small computers with up to 16 modules on both the I/O and Memory Buses (Figure 4).

Interestingly, a unified I/O memory bus like the PDP-11 Unibus was considered. The concept was rejected because a unified bus designed to operate at memory speed would have been more costly.

The goal to provide arbitrary, modular computing resources led to a multiprocessor structure with shared memory. The interconnection between processors and memory modules was chosen to be a cross-point switch with each processor broadcasting to all memory modules.

An alternative interconnection scheme could have been a more complex, synchronous, message-oriented protocol on a single bus. More efficient cable utilization and higher bandwidth would have resulted, but physical partitioning into multiple processor/memory subsystems for on-line maintenance would have been precluded. All in all, the cross-point switch decision was basically sound although more expensive.

Figure 5 shows a PMS block diagram for the KA10 and KI10. There can be up to 16, 65 Kword, 4-port memory modules, giving a total of one Mword of memory. (Each processor addressed four Mwords.) With high speed disk and tape units (e.g., 250 Kwords/second) a program-controlled I/O scheme would place too much of a burden on the central processor.

*See Appendix 2.

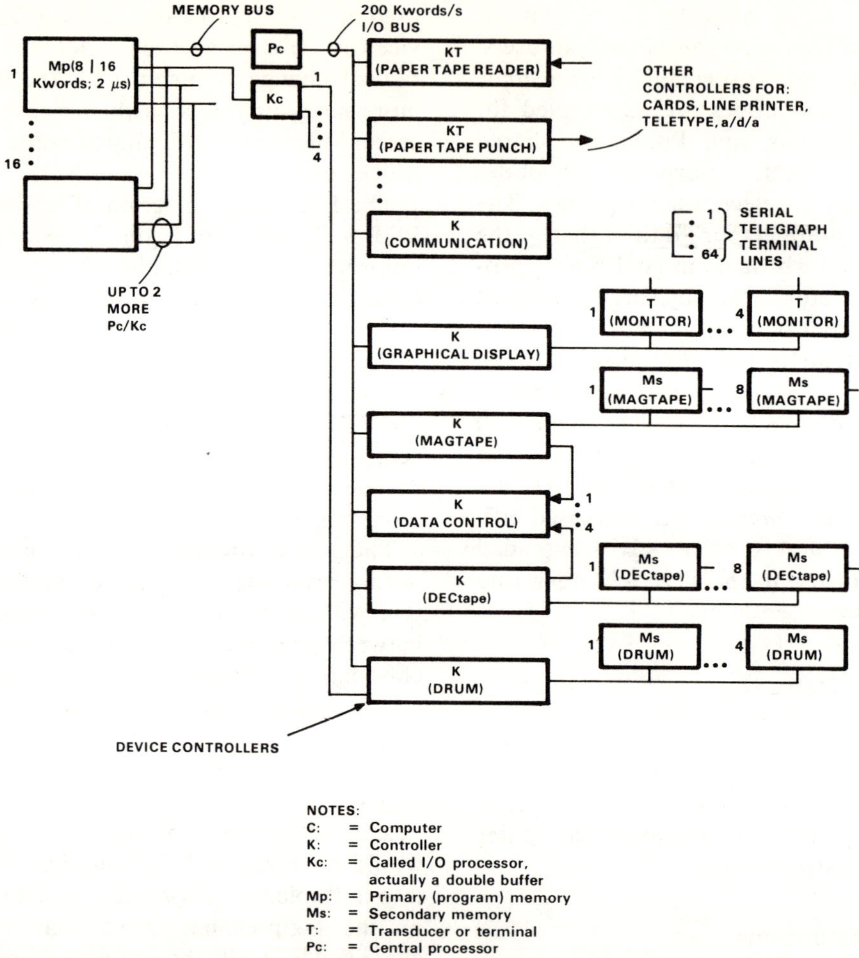

Figure 3. PMS diagram for PDP-6 system.

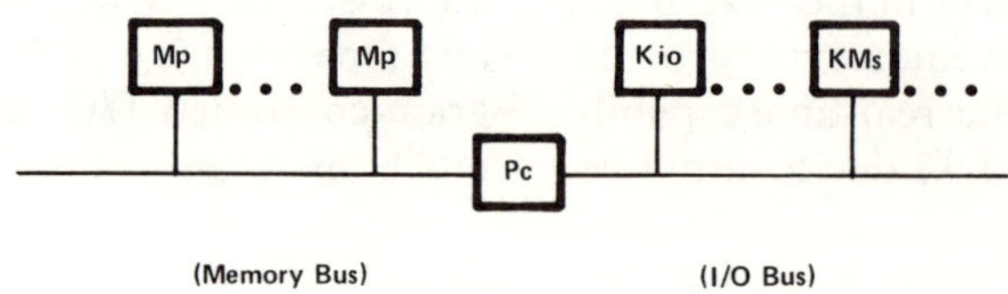

Figure 4. PDP-6 Memory Bus and I/O Bus.

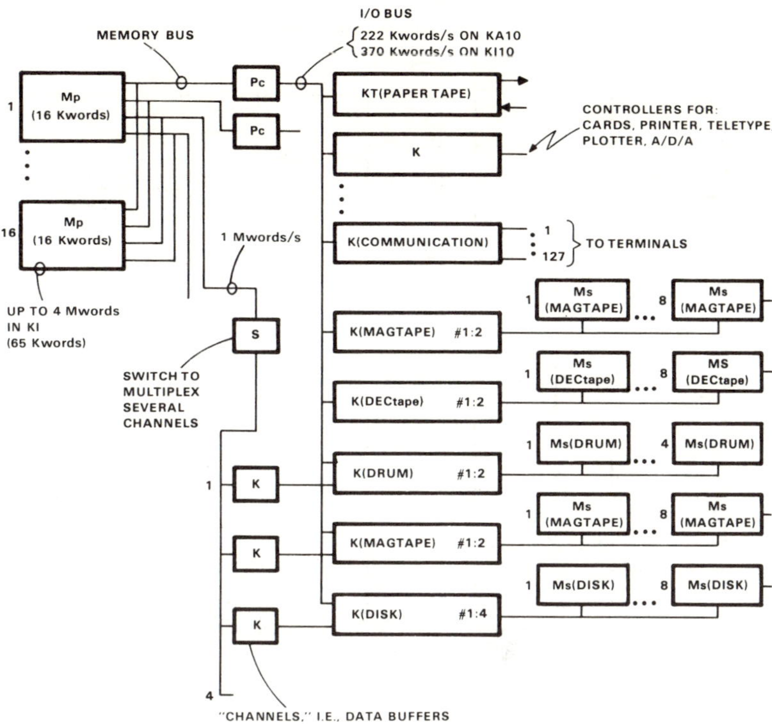

Figure 5. PMS diagram for KA10 and KI10 processor-based system.

Therefore, a direct port to memory was provided as in the PDP-6. In the KA10/KI10 systems, a switch (called a multiplexer) was introduced to expand the number of ports into memory to four for each Memory Bus used. The communications controllers were also expanded to handle more asynchronous and synchronous lines.

The KL10 was, by comparison, a radical departure from previous PMS structures (Figure 6). In order to gain more performance, four words from four low-order interleaved memory modules were accessed in each cycle. The effective processor-memory bandwidth was thus over four Mwords/second. The processor also connects to as many as four PDP-11 minicomputers [shown as *C* (11) in the figure]. Most of the I/O is handled by these front-end computers.

Each PDP-11 can access the KL10 memory via indirect address pointers and transfer data in much the same manner as the peripheral processing units of a CDC 6600. Notice also that the KL10's console is tied to a PDP-11. This PDP-11 can load the KL10 microprogram memory, run microdiagnostics, and provide a potential remotely operated console. Each of the PDP-11s can achieve a word rate of 70 Kchar/second.

Up to eight DEC Massbus controllers are integrated into the processor. The Massbus is an 18-bit data width bus for block-transfer-oriented mass-storage devices such as disks and magnetic tapes. Each Massbus can transfer 1.6

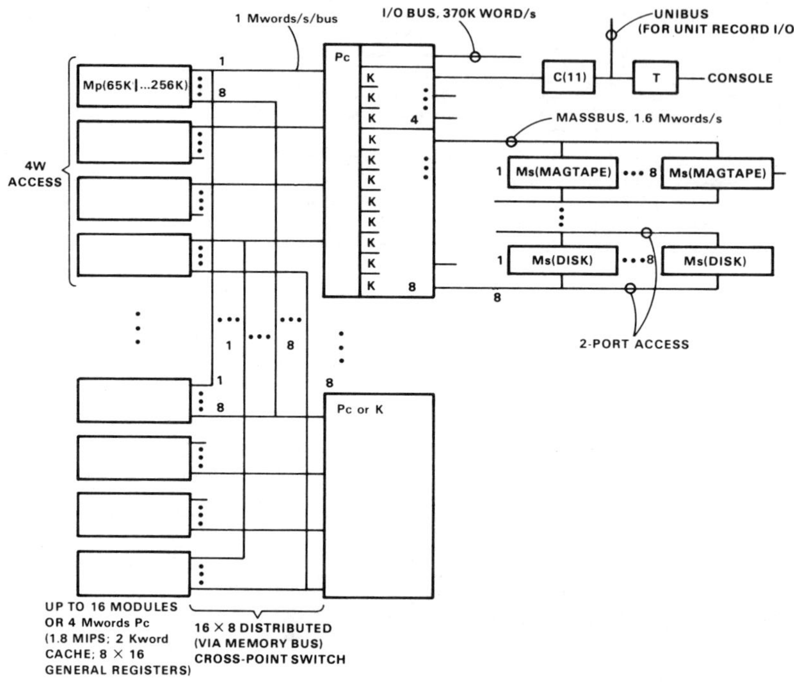

Figure 6. PMS diagram for KL10 processor-based system.

Mwords/second yielding a maximum 12.8 Mwords/second transfer rate for all channels. However, contemporary disks need about 250 Kwords/second so that all eight channels only require 2.0 Mwords/second of the 4 Mword/second memory bandwidth of four modules. Individual disks and tapes can be connected to a second port for increased concurrency. For larger memory configurations, a memory bandwidth of 16 Mwords/second is not uncommon. A 2 Kword processor cache provides roughly a 90 percent hit rate and reduces memory bandwidth demand by nearly a factor of ten.

The cost-reduced KL20 evolved by integrating the Massbus controllers and PDP-11 interfaces onto a single high-speed, synchronous bus. The model 2040 and 2050 computers are based on the KL10 processor and integrate 256 Kwords of memory in a single cabinet with the processor (thereby eliminating the external Memory Bus). The I/O Bus is also eliminated, and all I/O transfers are either via the Massbuses or the PDP-11 I/O computers. (It must be noted that the 2040 structure is possible only because of the drastic increase in logic and memory density!)

I/O System

Relatively, low speed I/O (200 Kwords/second) in the PDP-6 was designed to be under central processor programmed control rather than via specialized I/O processors (IBM System 360/370 Channels). This method had proven effective in our minicomputers and was extended to handle higher data rates with lower overhead than specialized I/O processors.

The decision not to use the IBM-type channel structure was based on high overhead (cost) in both programming and hardware. Because I/O record transmission usually caused a central processor action, we felt the processor might as well transfer the data while it had access to it. This merely required a good interrupt and context switching mechanism, not another specialized processing entity. However, when an inordinately high fraction of the processor's time went to I/O processing, a second, fully general processor was added – not a processor that was fundamentally only capable of data transmission.

The PDP-6 interrupt scheme was based on our previous experience with a 16-level and 256-level interrupt mechanism for PDP-1. The PDP-1 scheme was an extension of the Lincoln Laboratory TX-2 [Clark, 1957]. The PDP-6 had a 7-channel interrupt system, and each device on the I/O Bus could be programmed to a particular level. Hence, a programmer could change the priority of a particular device that caused interrupts on the basis of need or urgency. The PDP-6 also had an I/O instruction ("block input" or "block output") to transfer a single data item between a block (vector) in primary memory and an I/O device. Thus, as each word was assembled by a controller, an interrupt occurred; the block transfer was executed for one word, taking only three memory references (to the instruction, to increment the address pointer and block counter, and to transfer data). Most of the hardware to control the count and address pointer was already part of the processor logic.

In applications requiring higher data transmission (e.g., swapping drums, disks, TV cameras), a controller with a data buffer (erroneously called an I/O Processor) and link to memory was provided. This controller required only a single memory reference per data transfer with the address pointer and block counter in hardware. In the KA10, the name was changed to Channel, and parameters for transferring contiguous records into various parts of memory were part of the channel's control. The device control was via the I/O Bus; hence, we ended up with a structure for high speed device control not unlike the IBM channels we originally wanted to avoid.

Competitive pressure from the Xerox Sigma series caused a change in the way interrupts were handled beginning with the KI10. Although the Xerox scheme had many priority levels, its main utility was derived from rapid dispatch to attend to a particular interrupt signal. We kept compatibility with the 7-channel interrupt by using a spare wire in the bus and adding the ability to directly dispatch to a particular program when a request occurred. At the interruption, the processor sent a signal to requesting devices and the highest priority device responded with a 33-bit command (3-bit function, 18-bit address, 12-bit data). The functions were: (1) execute the instruction found at addressed location, (2) transfer a word to/from addressed location, (3) trap to addressed location, and (4) add data to addressed location. Little use was made of these functions (especially number 4), since only a small number of devices were typically connected to a large system, thus relaxing the requirement of rapid dispatch. Summarily, the problem of competition was resolved when Xerox left the competitive scene. In systems that had a large number of devices, a front-end I/O processing minicomputer was more cost-effective than central processor controlled I/O.

Memory System

Because it was unclear how memory technology would affect memory speed, a completely asynchronous, interlocked Memory Bus was designed. Thus, the 16 fast general registers, the initial 5-microsecond memory, and the next generation 2 microsecond memory could all operate on a single system. (Most memories are now less than 1-microsecond cycle time.)

The asynchronous bus avoided the problem of distributing a single high-speed clock and allowed interleaved memory operation.

Modularity was also introduced to clarify organizational boundaries within the company and to make possible low cost, special purpose production and engineering testers for the memory and I/O equipment. We believe that the concept of well defined modules was relatively unique, especially for memory, and was the basis for the formation of third party add-on memory vendors. MIT and Stanford University purchased memories from Fabritek and AMPEX, respectively, in the mid-1960s to start this trend. (Note that this design style differed from the IBM System/360 design with its relatively bounded configurations and integrated memory. Add-on memory did not appear until the early 70s for the IBM machines because, we believe, of the difficulty of the interface definition.)

The KI10 memory system was improved by assigning signals to request multiple, overlapped memory accesses and to increase the address size from 18 bits to 24 bits. The additional physical memory addresses are mapped into a program's 18-bit addresses via the core-held page table.

The KL10 processor-memory organization was a significant departure from the KI10 as previously discussed. The KL20 eliminated the original Memory Bus to provide an integrated system. It should be noted that this evolution was based on the drastic size reduction (a factor of about 300) from a single cabinet (6 ft × 19 in × 25 in or about 34,000 in^3) for 16 Kwords to a single logic module for 16 Kwords (15 in × 8 in × 1 in or about 120 in^3).

PMS Structures for Computer-Computer Intercommunication

Throughout the evolution, a number of schemes have been used to interconnect with other (usually smaller) computers. The schemes are given in Table 5. Note that the first four

Table 5. Computer Interconnection Structures

Scheme	Data Rate	Structure	Models	Examples
Standard communication link	110, 300 1200, 4800, 9600, 50 Kbits/sec	Network	All	
Special parallel, block transfer via hardware or software	100 Kwords 1 Mwords/sec	Tightly coupled	All	
Multiprocessors	At memory access rate	Multiprocessor	All	2 Pc 16 Pc, proposed
Access into mini address space with interruption	At memory access rate	Multiprocessor shared memory	PDP-6	The large computer accesses data in the small computer
The mini can transfer data into large machine via special control	At memory access rate	Tightly coupled	KA10-KL10	Scheme used to interconnect minis to do I/O Multiple logical channels are provided

schemes were conventional, while the last scheme was used in the KL10/20 structure so that an attached PDP-11 minicomputer could transmit data directly into the memory of the KL10. This scheme was first used in the early 1970s for handling multiple communication lines.

OPERATING SYSTEM

PDP-6 Monitor Design Goals and Philosophy

The initial goals and constraints for the user environment are summarized in Table 2. The most important goal was to provide a general-purpose timesharing system. The Monitor was to allow the user to run in the mode most suited to his requirements, including interactive timesharing, real-time, and batch. In timesharing, there was no requirement for a human operator *per se*. Instead, the operator's console was a user terminal with special privileges. Real-time programs had to be able to operate I/O directly, locked in core, and batch was to be provided as a special case of a terminal job.

Because of the modular expandability of the hardware structure, the software system had to be equally modular to facilitate varying system configurations and growth. The core resident timesharing monitor was only fixed at system generation (i.e., IBM's SYSGEN) time when software modules could be added to meet the system requirements. The core space required for monitor overhead had to be minimized. Thus, job-specific functions were placed in the user area instead of in the Monitor. The first 96 locations of each user job contained pertinent information concerning that job. A temporary area (stack) for monitor operations was also included. In this way, the Monitor was not burdened with information for the inactive jobs. This structure permitted the entire job state to be moved easily.

Adequate protection was to be given to each user from other nonmalicious users. However, the user was not protected against himself because various user status information in the job area could be changed to affect his own job. Because common system resources were allocated upon demand and deadlocks could occur, the term "Gentlemen's Timesharing" was coined for the first monitor.

The UUO or "system call" instruction, provided both Monitor-user communication and upward hardware compatibility. In the latter case, the instruction would use the hardware if available; otherwise, the instruction would trap to the Monitor for execution. For example, double-precision hardware was available on later CPU models. The number of UUOs implemented in the Monitor for Monitor-user communication has been significant. The initial use of UUOs included requests for: core, I/O assignment, I/O transmission, file control, data and time, etc.

PDP-6 Monitor

Monitor was the name given to a collection of programs that were initially core resident and provided overall coordination and control of the operating environment. A nonresident part was later added with the advent of secondary program swapping and file memories (i.e., drum and disk). The Monitor did not include utilities, languages, and their run-time support.

The PDP-6 Monitor was constrained to run in a 16 Kword (minimum) machine with console printer, paper tape reader (for maintenance) and two DECtape units. DECtape was a 128-word/block, block-addressable medium of 450 Kcharacters for which a file system was developed. Memory minimizing led to very sparing use of shared tables. The key global variable data was restricted to: core allocation table, clock queue, job table, linked buffers for Teletype and other buffered I/O devices (e.g., DECtape directory), and a directory of system programs and Monitor facilities.

The original PDP-6 Monitor was less than 6 Kwords. The Monitor has increased at about 25 percent per year with the KA10 at 30 Kwords, KI10 at 50 Kwords, and KL10 at 90 Kwords (Figure 7). This increase provided increased functionality (e.g., better files, batch, automatic spooling), larger system configuration size, more I/O options, increased number of jobs, easier system generation, and increased reliability (e.g., checking, retries, file backup).

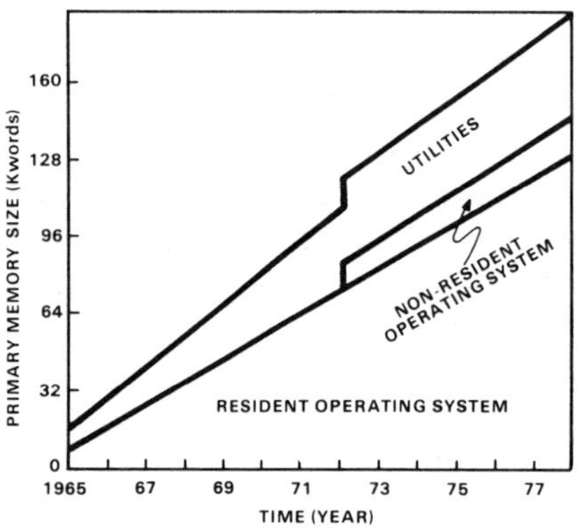

Figure 7. Monitor and main utilities program size versus time.

Note that with a 16 Kword memory, a 9 Kword FORTRAN compiler with 5 Kword run-time package, and 1 Kword utility programs, two users could simultaneously reside in PDP-6 memory and use the machine for program creation and checkout. By keeping the Monitor program size small, subsequent functionality increases kept the Monitor module sizes in bounds such that program swapping was reduced. This provided high performance for a given configuration with little Monitor overhead.

Monitor Structure

Table 6 summarizes the development of the Monitor with the various systems. The facilities are arranged beginning with basics. The following sections deal with the various facilities, in turn.

Memory Protection Swapping. The basic environment was discussed in the ISP section on Multiprogramming/Monitor Facilities.

Facilities Allocator. The Facilities Allocator was a module called from a console or program for an I/O device or memory space request. This module would attach (or assign) a given peripheral or contiguous physical memory area to a given job. Although this module was relatively trivial initially, it evolved to a more complex module because improper resources allocation caused deadlocks.

The KA10 generation software introduced queued operation. A line printer (output), paper tape (input/output), and a card reader (input) spooler were implemented. These spoolers ran as timeshared jobs, accepted requests from other user jobs, and managed the input/output operation.

Program Scheduler. The scheduler was invoked by line frequency (50 or 60 Hz) interrupts to examine run queues and to determine the next action. The first Monitor employed a round-robin scheduling algorithm. At the end of a given time quantum of 500 milliseconds, the next job was run. A job was runnable if it was not stopped by the console and was not waiting for I/O.

Because terminal response time is the user's measure of system effectiveness, subsequent scheduler improvements have favored interactive jobs. With the KA10, separate priority queues were added so that jobs with substantial computation were placed in the lowest priority and then run the longest without interruption. This, in effect, approximated batched operation; for example, jobs from a card reader would operate as a batch stream. Later, batch operation was added for interactive users.

The introduction of disk/drum swapping caused additional complexities since runnable jobs might be located in secondary memory.

Table 6. Monitor Functions Evolution

Facility	PDP-6 (1964)	KA10 (1967)	KI10 (1972)	KL10 (1975)
Protection	One segment per user	Two segments with shared program segment (required for reentrant programs)	Four modes for shared segments	Virtual machine with shared segments
Program swapping	Core shuffling	Core shuffling; with swapping (via drum disk)	Paging used for core management	Demand paging (job need not be wholly resident to run)
Facilities allocator	Devices assigned to users upon request (deadlocks possible ⇒gentlemen's time-sharing)	Spooling of line printer and card reader	Spooling of all devices	
Scheduler	Round-robin scheduler	Scheduler to favor interactive jobs using multiple queues	Fairness and swapping efficiency considerations	Parameters for scheduling set by system manager; priority job classes and "pie-slice" schedule
User files	User files on DECtape, cards, and magnetic tape	Significant enhancement of file function; on-line, random-access disk-based files	Improved file structure reliability, error recovery, protection and sharing; mountable structures	Disk head movement optimization
Command control program	Simple (to implement) requiring little state	Evolution to more powerful, easier to use command language	Common Command Language (CCL)	Extensions to CCL
Batch	No real batch	Remote and local single-stream batch	Multiprogramming batch	Improved multiprogramming batch
Terminal handling and communications	Asynchronous task-to-task communications (for interactive terminals) as monitor module	Synchronous communications for remote job and concentrator stations; "birth" of networks with simple topologies; ARPA network	Synchronous communications in complex topologies; new protocol; IBM BISYNC for 2780 emulation/termination	DECnet communications*
Multiprocessing		Dual processor support (master/slave)	High availability through bus switching hardware	Symmetric multiprocessing

*DECnet is DEC's computer network protocols and functions.

The concept of "look-ahead" scheduling was required, and a more complex queuing mechanism was implemented. As the Monitor selected the next job to be run, it would "look ahead" to determine future queues and invoke the swapping module if required to move a runnable job into core. Because of the higher swapping overhead, it was essential to run large jobs longer and less often. A "fairness" consideration also assured that each job, whatever its size, received enough run time to maintain responsiveness.

Recent enhancements permitted a Systems Manager to set scheduling parameters including established priorities of job classes. A "pie-slice" scheduler is used where classes of users are guaranteed fixed parts of the machine time and resources.

User Files and I/O Device Independence. In the initial PDP-6 design, resources such as magnetic tapes, unit record devices (e.g., card readers, line printer, paper tape reader/punch) and DECtapes (which were file structured) were requested by each user as they were required. The Monitor allocated the device to a requesting given job until released.

I/O calls were evoked by the UUO call instructions. A particular device program call could specify the number of I/O buffers to be provided so that arbitrary amounts of overlapped I/O and computing could be realized.

In order to realize the goal of modularity, each I/O device handler was implemented as a separate module. These modules used a common set of subroutines. The device tables were made as identical as possible to help achieve the device independent goal. Thus, a user specified an I/O channel, not a specific I/O device. The channel-to-name assignment could take place at various times from log-on to program run time.

In the original Monitor, a user was allowed to assign file devices to his job and read and write named files with the devices. Permanent, on-line user files with automatic backup were not implemented until the KA10-generation Monitors. The concept of project/programmer number was adopted (after MIT's CTSS) in order to provide increased file security and sharing. A user was required to enter a project/programmer number with his associated password. This not only established a job, but identified the user to the Monitor. In addition to having resource privileges associated with better ID numbers, the user received a logical disk area for files. File access can be allowed (by the creator of the file) to any of the following levels with decreasing protection (increasing privileges): no access, execute only, plus read, plus append, plus update, plus write, plus rename, and plus alter protection.

Significant evolution occurred in the user file facility. Improved file structure reliability and error recovery (such as writing pointer blocks twice) were achieved. With moving head disk availability, disk head movement optimization for file transfers on single or multiple drives was added. The concept of "mountable" structures was implemented to allow disk packs to be mounted and dismounted during a timesharing operation as well as allowing a user to have a "private" pack mounted. As the number of users supported on the system and the diversity of their applications grew to include "business data processing," both hardware and software allowed expansion of the number and capacity of on-line disks.

Command Control Program. This program processes all commands addressed to the system from user terminals. Thus, terminals served to communicate Monitor commands to the system and to the user programs, and served as an I/O device for user programs. Terminal handling routines were an integral part of the PDP-6 Monitor. The original commands were designed to minimize the amount of state in the Monitor. As a result, users had to type several commands to control programs. A much more powerful command language evolved.

Batch Processing

Batch processing has evolved from the original, fully interactive PDP-6, where a user was expected to interactively provide commands for each step in the generation/execution of a program. The first batch on the KA10 was based on a user-built command file that mimicked his terminal actions. The user invoked this command file to execute his programs. Later, a multiprogrammed batch system was added, and the job control syntax evolved to provide more functions per command. However, batch/interactive command commonality has been preserved through the current Monitor versions. Still, batch control ran as a timeshared job using queued batch control files. Thus, the ability to log in a job, run to completion, and log off is accomplished from a card reader or any other storage or file device. Symbiant (queued) operation allowed control of card readers, line printers, etc., by the batch control program so that the machine could be scheduled more effectively. During this batch evolution, little Monitor enhancement was necessary to specifically address the batch environment. Modules to improve efficiency (by multiple strands and better scheduling) and increase functionality were implemented as "user" jobs and interprocess queuing allowed communication between the "user" modules.

A line printer spooler, for example, was run as one of many jobs by the operator – a notion that evolved beginning with the KA10. If a special form was required for a print job, the operator would be notified and act accordingly. The user was relieved of this responsibility. Operator allocation, control, and media loading of the card reader, magnetic tape, private disk pack, DECtape, and plotter were provided in the KI10.

Terminal Handling and Communications. We believe the users' perception of system effectiveness related directly to his feeling that he was interacting and was in control. The requirement to communicate effectively with the user via the terminal was one of the most difficult design constraints. The very first version of the Monitor used half-duplex communication for simplicity. But finally we decided to pay the additional price to gain the benefit of full-duplex communication, i.e., being able to continuously input and output independently of system load. These philosophies have guided subsequent Monitor generations.

A hardware module was constructed to facilitate terminal communication. This hardware was called the scanner because it looked at all the interface lines connected to Teletypes and interrupted the software when a character was received or needed to be transmitted. These line units, which we built on a single card, formed the basis of the Universal Asynchronous Receiver/Transmitter (UART) LSI chip. A software monitor, called Scanner Service (SCNSER) handled interrupts from the hardware. SCNSER provided the important function of logically coupling a physical terminal with a job running under timesharing. The user was never burdened with attempting to relate his terminal with his job. This software module, by far the most logical complex part of the Monitor, has been rewritten twice to increase terminal functionality.

Later, the KA10 terminal interface was implemented via a "front-end" concentrator PDP-8 computer for large numbers of terminals – particularly where variable line speeds were involved (up to 300 baud). This implementation allowed some off-loading of the processor. Characters were assembled (serial parallel conversion) in the front-end PDP-8 and communicated with the KA10 via the I/O Bus on an interrupt basis.

In 1971, a front-end PDP-11 provided direct-memory access over the I/O Bus. This connection provided high speed, full-duplex, synchronous communications and was the prototype for the current KL10/PDP-11 front-end computer. Software modules were added to the Monitor to allow these synchronous lines to terminate remote PDP-8 and communication concentrator stations in simple point-to-point topologies. A remote station (e.g., line printer) is viewed by the user in the same manner as is a local printer.

With the KI10, a second front-end was produced which allowed BISYNC protocol of the IBM 2780 terminal to be used. However, most of our users were laboratory-oriented and wanted greater performance and functionality. Thus, concentrator/remote station capability including route-through (i.e., communication via multiple concentrators), and multiple hosts were added. These formed the basis of some of our understanding for subsequent DECnet protocol standards and functions. The use of DECsystem-10 in the Advanced Research Projects Agency (ARPA) funded projects formed another key base for our DECnet protocols and functions [Roberts, 1970].

DECnet-10 now provides the capability of having processes in different computers (including PDP-8s and PDP-11s) communicate with each other. These jobs appear to each other as I/O devices in the simplest applications.

Throughout all of this communication functionality evolution, the goal has been to free the user from concern with the link, communication mode, hardware location, and protocol.

Multiprocessing

Although we predicated the original PDP-6 hardware on multiprocessing, the Monitor was not designed explicitly for it. Lawrence Livermore Laboratory did build a two-processor system with their own operating system and special segmentation hardware. To meet the needs of the predominately scientific/computation marketplace in achieving higher processor throughput, a dual-processor KA10 was implemented using a master/slave scheme with wholly shared memory and one Monitor. The slave CPU scanned the queue of runnable jobs, selected one, and ran it. If a Monitor call was encountered, the job was placed in the appropriate queue and the Monitor located another runnable job. The "master" handled all I/O and privileged operations. In a CPU-bound environment, the dual processor provided approximately a 70 percent increase in system throughput.

An offshoot (and evolved design goal) of the dual-processor implementation was high availability. Monitor reconfigurability and bus-switching hardware allowed redundant components to be fully utilized during normal operation and, in the case of a hardware malfunction, to be separated into an operating configuration (with all available I/O) and a maintenance configuration (consisting of CPU, memory, and the faulty component).

At Carnegie-Mellon University (CMU), we proposed to build a 16 to 32 PDP-10 structure [Bell *et al.*, 1971]. It would have 16 Mwords of primary memory available via 16 ports at a bandwidth of 2.1 to 8.6 gigabits/second. With the use of processors larger than those of the KL10, performance would have been over 50 million instructions per second (MIPS). The 16 processor, C.mmp [Wulf and Bell, 1972], based on PDP-11s at CMU, is a prototype of such a system.

Languages and Utilities

Monitor commands called the utilities and languages. The utilities, called CUSP (for Common User System Program), and languages included: EDIT, an editor for creating and editing a file from a user console; PIP, the peripheral interchange program to convert information among the I/O media and files; LOADER to load object modules; DESK, an interactive calculator; MACRO, an assembler; and FORTRAN II. Figure 1 shows these programs at various times, together with their origins.

Utilities and languages have taken advantage of the interactive, terminal-oriented environment. Thus, highly interactive editing/debugging facilities have evolved in terms of the program's own symbols. The file/data transfer utility, PIP (for Peripheral Interchange Program) is still in existence today, although in a much enhanced form. It has since been expanded to support the peripheral devices and the data formats encountered in the DECsystem-10 memory and I/O devices. Such a utility eliminated the need for a "library" of utilities and conversion programs to transfer data between devices. Such tasks as a card-to-disk, card-to-tape, tape-to-disk, etc., conversion are controlled by a terminal using common PIP commands. PIP evolved in a somewhat *ad hoc* fashion from a 1 Kword or 2 Kword size in 1965 to 10 Kwords with substantial generality.

A powerful and sophisticated text editor, TECO (Text Editor and Corrector) was initially implemented at MIT using a graphics display. TECO is character-string oriented and requires a minimal number of keystrokes to execute commands. It included the ability to define programs to do general string substitution. As the sophistication of users was later perceived to decline, the powerful editor created training and use problems. Thus, a family of line- and character-oriented editors evolved which was easier to learn and remember. These were based on other line-oriented editors, but especially Stanford's SOS, which replaced the initial DECline editor in 1970.

Many of the higher level languages were initially produced by non-DEC groups and made available through the DEC User Society (DECUS). For example, APL, BASIC, DBMS, and IQL (an interactive query language) were purchased from outside sources and are now standard, supported products.

BLISS (Basic Language for Implementing System Software), developed at Carnegie-Mellon University, became DEC's systems programming language [Wulf *et al.*, 1971b]. A cross-compiler was subsequently developed for the PDP-11. Its use as a systems programming language has been due to the close coupling it provides to the machine, its general syntactic and block structures, and its high-quality code generator. BLISS has been used for various diagnostic programs, the BLISS Compilers, the PDP-10 APL Interpreter, recent FORTRAN-IV compilers for both PDP-10 and PDP-11, and the BASIC PLUS TWO system. BLISS has also been used extensively within DEC for computer-aided design programs.

Tenex and the TOPS-20 Operating System

Bolt, Beranek, and Newman started a project in 1969 to build an advanced operating system called Tenex which was based on a modified KA10 (including rather elaborate paging hardware). This work was influenced by both the Berkeley SDS 940 and the MIT Multics systems. Subsequently, Tenex influenced and improved the KI10 design which became the base of TOPS-20. The system was described by Bobrow *et al.* [1972], and the three major goals stated in the reference were:

I. State-of-the-Art Virtual Machine
   a. Paged virtual address space equal to or greater than the addressing capability of the processor with full provision for protection and sharing.
   b. Multiple process capability in virtual machine with appropriate communication facilities.
   c. File system integrated into virtual address space, built on multilevel symbolic directory structure with protection, and providing consistent access to all external I/O devices and data streams.
   d. Extended instruction repertoire making available many common operations as single instructions.

II. Good Human Engineering Throughout Systems

a. An executive command language interpreter which provides direct access to a large variety of small, commonly used system functions, and access to and control over all other subsystems and user programs. Command language forms should be extremely versatile, adapting to the skill and experience of the user.

b. Terminal interface design should facilitate intimate interaction between program and user, provide extensive interrupt capability, and full ASCII character set.

c. Virtual machine functions should provide all necessary options, with reasonable default values simplifying common cases, and require no system-created objects to be placed in the user address space.

d. The system should encourage and facilitate cooperation among users as well as provide protection against undesired interaction.

III. The System must be Implementable, Maintainable, and Modifiable

a. Software must be modular with well defined interfaces and with provision for adding or changing modules clearly considered.

b. Software must be debuggable and reliable, allowing use of available debugging aids and including internal redundancy checks.

c. System should run efficiently, allow dynamic manual adjustment of service if desired, and allow extensive reconfiguration without reassembly.

d. System should contain instrumentation to clearly indicate performance.

Dan Murphy (one of Tenex's designers/implementers) came to DEC and led the architecture and development effort that produced TOPS-20. The effort at DEC has been to increase the performance of TOPS-20 to be competitive with the highly tuned Monitor while not losing its generality. The TOPS-20 structure does provide increased reliability and modifiability.

HARDWARE IMPLEMENTATION

While logic and memory technology are often considered the prime determinant of the performance and cost of a computer system, fabrication and packaging technology are equally important. This section surveys logic, manufacturing, and packaging technology as it affected the various DECsystem-10 models. Table 7 summarizes those various logic and packaging technologies.

Logic

The PDP-6 used a set of logic modules that evolved from the earlier PDP-1, which in turn were derived from the Lincoln Laboratory circuits developed for the TX-0 [Mitchell, Olsen, 1956] and TX-2 [Clark, 1957] (Chapter 4) computers as part of the air defense program. These circuits were direct-coupled transistor logic and included both series and parallel transistor circuits to give great flexibility in designs. The PDP-1 circuits operated at a 5 MHz clock, and new transistors enabled the PDP-6 circuits to operate at 10 MHz. The computer's clock was based on a delay line which carried pulses generated by a pulse amplifier using pulse transformers (this too came from Lincoln Laboratory via the early work at MIT on radar and pulse transformers) The pulses were used for register transfer operations (i.e., moving data among the registers) and some logic gating.

Instead of using a small number of lines in a fixed, synchronous clock, many delay lines were used. The route through the control path determined the state of the machine. At each decision point, the next line or chain (set of lines) was selected. Hardware subroutines were also unique with this implementation. A control sequence consisting of a set of delay lines was defined as a subroutine, and a calling module marked the calling site (e.g., add, subtract, and complement are at the lowest level). The basic multiply subroutine used add or subtract; finally, floating multiply used the normalize and multiply subroutines. In this way, the implementation was kept structured and turned out to be quite straightforward. The flowcharts for the PDP-6 were only 11 pages, where each page has about 25 unique statements (actions), yielding a total of only 250 microsteps (each step causes 1 to 6 operations and corresponds roughly to current microprogram statements). The asynchronous adder was designed so that on completion of all the carries, the sequence would restart. Thus, we took advantage of the observation made by von Neumann *et al.* in 1946, [Bell and Newell, 1971, ch. 4] that the average number of carries is $\log_2 36$ or slightly over 5, versus the worst case of 36. An average delay time of about 20 nanoseconds per carry reduced the average add time to only 100 nanoseconds versus 720 nanoseconds, yielding a very simple and fast circuit.

The KA10 used essentially the same circuitry but with significantly better packaging so that automatic wire-wrap backpanels could be used. Note that in Table 7, the existence of certain semiconductors was the basis of new machines. The TTL/H series logic appeared about 1969 and formed the basis of a machine (the KI10) with roughly the same power dissipation and physical size as a KA10, but with a factor of 2.2 more performance. In scientific applications requiring double-precision computation, this performance differential is much greater. Ironically, the TTL/Schottky (TTL/S) series was first available in production quantities at about the time of the KI10. The KI10 design was started earlier and design options chosen so as to preclude the subsequent advances in speed, power, and density that the TTL/S gave.

The other important logic advances employed in the KI10 were the MSI register file and associative memory packages. The register file provided four sets of accumulators and thus decreased the context switching time. (This probably had a higher psychological than real value but was useful where special devices were operated on a high speed, real-time basis.) The associative memory package permitted the construction of a 32-word associative memory to support a paged environment.

The KL10 provides almost a factor of 5 performance improvement over the KA10 for programs using the basic instruction set. An even larger performance improvement is realized for COBOL or extended precision scientific programs. The organization and much of the base work for the KL10 was done by Dave Poole, Phil Petit, John Holloway, and Jack Wright at the Stanford Artificial Intelligence Laboratory.

The KL10 is microprogrammed using a memory based on the 1 Kbit bipolar RAM. A cache memory is also constructed from the 1 Kbit chips. The KL10 is implemented in the emitter coupled logic (ECL) 10K series rather than in the TTL/Schottky of the original Stanford design. It was felt that the ECL speed advantage with 3 nanoseconds gate delay versus 7 nanoseconds for Schottky was worth the extra design effort especially because the ECL required more power and care to lay out the board and backplane.

Fabrication

The Gardner-Denver automatic Wire-wrap machine represented a significant advance in the manufacture of machines. Automatic Wire-wrap economically provided accurately wired

Table 7. Implementations for DECsystem-10 Hardware

Processor	PDP-6	KA10	KI10	KL10
Design start	3/63	1/66	12/69	1/72
First ship	6/64	9/67	5/72	6/75
Logic	Germanium, silicon transistors	Discrete silicon transistors and diodes	TTL/H (MSI) registers; associative memory	ECL 10K; fast, 1 Kbit memories
MIPS (avg.)	0.25	0.38	0.72	1.8
Packaging (slice of processor)	1 bit of AR, MB, MQ, AD:88 transistors, 2-sided PC etch; 2-18-pin and 2-22-pin connectors (11 × 9 inch boards)	Implemented in *R, S, W* series flip-chip (discrete) modules (5-1/2 × 5-1/4 boards)	Implemented in *R, S, W, M* series flip-chip (discrete + MSI) modules 5-1/2 × 5-1/4 boards	6 bits of AR, ARX, MQ, BR, BRX, AD, ADX:70 MSI ECL per module: 216 pin connector: (8 × 16 inch boards)
Processor size	2 bays	2 bays	2+ bays	1/2 bay (including internal channels)
Processor price	$120K	$150K	$200K	$250K
Control design	Asynchronous and subroutine logic	Same as PDP-6	Clocked synchronous	KL20 is clocked synchronous; microprogrammed
Module size	Large modules	Small modules wire-wrap	Same	Large modules (16 Kword core memory module)
Registers	16	16	4 × 16	8 × 16
I/O calls	Prog. interrupts UUO traps	Same	Vectored interrupts	Integrated controller for Massbus; I/O via PDP-11 computers
I/O transmission	I/O and Memory Bus	Added channels	–	
Memory management	18-bit phys. addr. protection and relocation registers	2 protection and relocation registers for shared program segments	22-bit phys. addr; paged using 32-word associative memory	22-bit phys. addr. paged, using associative memory via cache

Table 7. Implementations for DECsystem-10 Hardware (Cont)

Processor	PDP-6	KA10	KI10	KL10	
ISP	See Table 3 (integers, floating)	Conversion to assist d.p. float	Hardware d.p. float	String and conversion for d.p. integers	
Parallelism	–	Simpler (faster) data path	Instruction look-ahead (4-word) fetch	Instruction look-ahead: 2 Kword cache memory	
Fabrication	(Too) large modules	Gardner-Denver automatic Wire-wrap for backpanel interconnection	Semiautomatic wire-wrap for twisted pair	Large (hex) modules with many pins: low-cost minis front-end	(KL20) integrating Pc and Mp together – eliminating Memory Bus ⇒ high-density core memory modules
Consequences	Served as PDP-10 production prototype	Buildable in production	More performance (scientific and real-time); and paging for operating systems	More performance via cache; microprogramming for better COBOL ISP: I/O computers	Lower cost

backpanels. As a more important side effect, it made the high-volume, low-cost fabrication of minicomputers possible! Some backpanel wiring on the KI10 and KL10 processors using twisted pairs cannot be done using the Gardner-Denver machinery. For this, DEC developed a semiautomatic wire-wrap machine which locates the pins and selects the wire length for an operator.

Computer design aids have evolved to support computer implementations on an "as-needed" basis, barely keeping ahead of the implementations. These have included printed circuit board layout/routing, backplane layout/routing, circuit/logic simulation, wire length/logic delay checking, and various manufacturing aids. One notable exception to this trend has been the Stanford University Drawing System (SUDS) developed by the Standard Artificial Intelligence Laboratory. SUDS was used for drawing the entire KL10 design. The design time and cost would have been significantly greater if SUDS had not been available.

Packaging

Semiconductor density is a major determinant of the system size, and size in turn is a major determinant of speed (e.g., shorter interconnection paths). Seymour Cray stated in a lecture given at Lawrence Livermore Laboratory (December 1974) that for each generation of his large computers, the density has improved by a factor of 5.

The packaging for the PDP-6 was identical to that of the PDP-1, 4, and 5 and used a board area of about 40 in^2 with a 22-pin connector. A logic density improvement of 2 was achieved over the previous designs by using 6 special function modules. However, this density turned out to be too high for the number of pins. A natural extension was a board twice as large with 44 pins. The most interesting module was the bit-slice of the working registers: Accumulators, Multiplier-Quotient, and Memory Buffer. This module required more than 44 pins, so the extra signals were bused across the back of the module. This busing increased module swap time, and the mechanical coupling increased the probability that fixing one fault would cause another. Because of this, the designers of the KA10 and KI10 became fearful of large boards. Only with the KL10 in 1972 were large boards reintroduced into the DECsystem-10. On the other hand, large boards had been used in DEC minicomputers since 1969. Multilayered boards were required for the KL10 ECL logic. These boards were adapted from the multilayered boards developed for the TTL/S PDP-11/45 (1972).

Price/Performance

Surprisingly, over time, the various models of the DECsystem-10 have been implemented at an essentially constant cost. The option to apply technology at constant performance with reduced price was never examined as an alternative strategy. In the minicomputer part of the company, both alternatives were vigorously pursued in order to provide a growing business and stimulate design alternatives. The relatively static DECsystem-10 strategy with constant price stems, no doubt, from the highly coupled interaction of: builders (wanting to go on to provide the next highest level of performance which was the founding principle of the group); the salespeople (many of whom came from other companies and are only used to working with a particular user class), users (who want more performance so as to reduce their overall cost/performance ratio), and marketing (which integrates needs and alternatives). This is illustrated in Figure 8. Here we give the performance in terms of the number of general-purpose users versus the system price.

Figure 9 gives a single price of the system for each generation, together with the percentages going of each for the system components. The best cost/performance systems are shown (except, in the case of the minimal PDP-6). Figure 10 gives the price of the various processors ver-

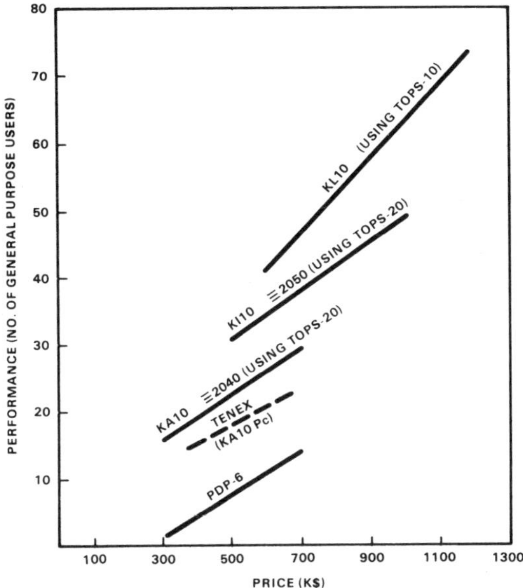

Figure 8. Performance (in general purpose users) versus price for each generation.

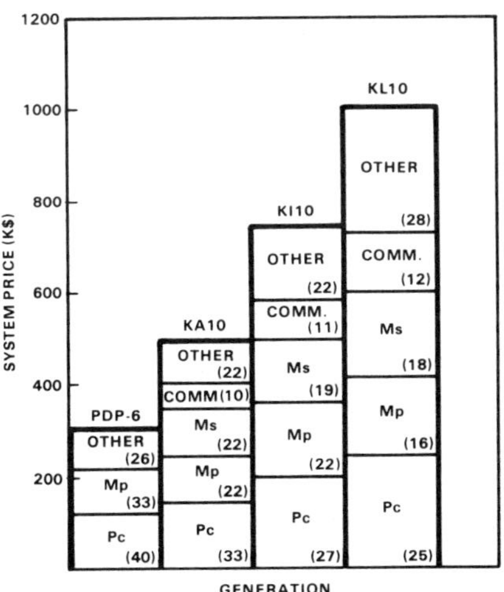

Figure 9. System component price versus generation.

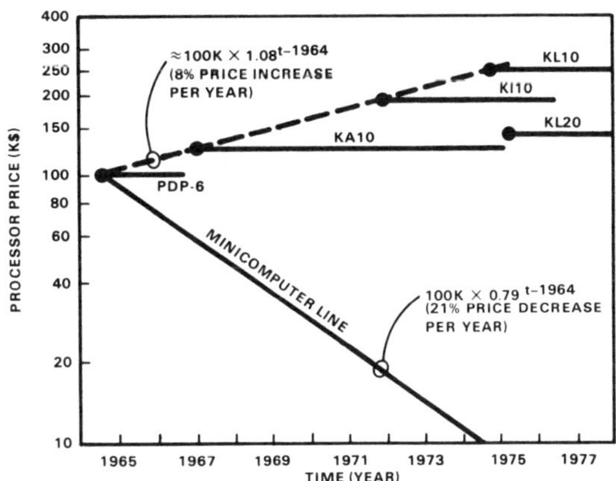

Figure 10. DECsystem-10 processor price versus time.

sus time for the family; note that the processor price has been increasing roughly at the inflation rate, suggesting a manpower intensive (or service-type) market structure. Note that since the performance (Table 7) has improved at roughly a factor of 10 in 10 years, the increase in performance/cost is nearly 20 percent per year. In contrast, a minicomputer line (constant performance) is plotted which shows the price decreasing at 21 percent per year, with a factor of 10 price decline in ten years. We should ask: "Could a PDP-6 level processor be built in 1975 to sell for $10K?"

Clearly it could, and such a system has been built as an advanced development project. This small 10 has a unified bus structure like the PDP-11 with a connection to use the Unibus family I/O devices. A system with 512 Kwords and the performance of greater than that of a KA10 occupies a cabinet somewhat smaller than a PDP-11/70 minicomputer.*

Figure 11 shows how the price of memory has decreased with time. Note that even though there was growth in the memory size of the

*The computer called the 2020 was introduced in May 1978.

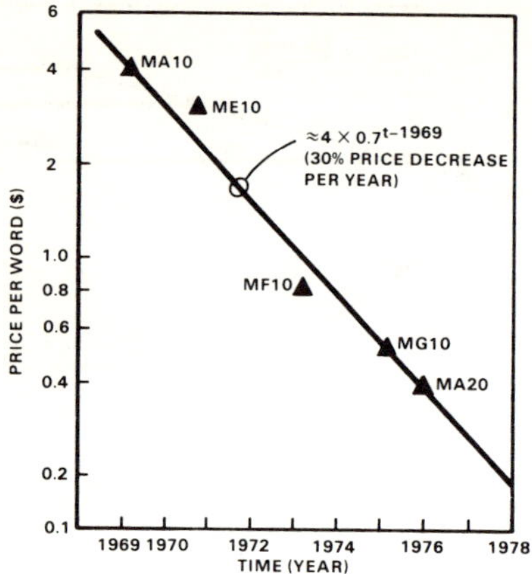

Figure 11. DECsystem-10 primary memory price per word versus time.

monitor of 25 percent per year, there was a positive improvement in the memory price performance. In reality, many functions for which the user was explicitly responsible were moved to the Monitor as basic operations. A similar plot for secondary memory prices is given in Figure 12.

CONCLUSIONS

We believe the existence of the DECsystem-10 has been beneficial to the many environments for which it has provided real-time and interactive computation, including the computer science and computer engineering communities. In turn, we have tried to respond to the needs of these users. Its existence has also been a positive force in encouraging alternative, competitive products in what otherwise might have been a dull, batch environment. The system has also been used by and influenced minicomputer (and now microcomputer) development, including: hardware technology (e.g., wire-wrap), support for machine development (including simulation), and exemplary design leading to timesharing systems (e.g., DEC's TSS/8, RSTS) and user environments (e.g., RT-11 and microcomputer systems).

We believe the key to the 10's longevity is its basically simple, clean structure with adequately large (one Mbyte) address space. In this way, it has evolved easily with use and with technology. An equally significant factor in its success is a single operating system environment enabling user program sharing among all machines. The machine has thus attracted users who have built significant languages and applications in a variety of environments. These user-developers are, therefore, the dominant system architects-implementors.

In retrospect, the machine turned out to be larger and further from a minicomputer than we had expected. As such, it could easily have died or destroyed the tiny DEC organization that started it. We hope that this paper has provided insight into the interactions of its development.

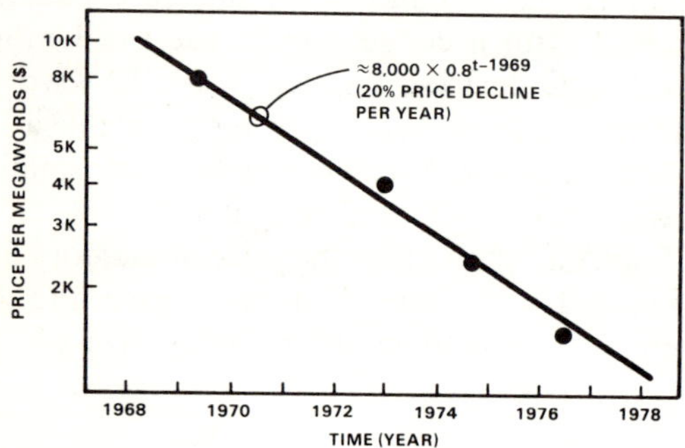

Figure 12. DECsystem-10 secondary memory price per Mwords versus time.

ACKNOWLEDGEMENTS

Dan Siewiorek deserves our greatest thanks for helping with a complete editing of the text. The referees and editors have been especially helpful. The important program contributions by users are too numerous for us to give by name but here are most of them: APL, BASIC, BLISS, DDT, LISP, Pascal, Simula, SOS, TECO, and Tenex. Likewise, there have been so many contributions to the 10's architecture and implementations within DEC and throughout the user community that we dare not give what would be a partial list.

APPENDIX 1

An ISPS Primer for the Instruction Set Processor Notation

MARIO BARBACCI

This appendix introduces the reader to the ISPS notation. Although some details have been excluded, it covers enough of the language to provide a "reading" capability. Thus, although the primer by itself might not be sufficient to allow writing ISPS descriptions, it should be detailed enough to permit the reading and study of complex descriptions. We use the PDP-8 ISPS description as a source of examples.

In the presentation of the PDP-8 registers and data-types the following conventions are used: (1) names in upper case correspond to physical components on the PDP-8 (e.g., program counter, interrupt lines, etc.); (2) names in lower case do not have correspondent physical components (e.g., instruction mnemonics, instruction fields, etc.).

INSTRUCTION SET PROCESSOR DESCRIPTIONS

To describe the instruction set processor (ISP) of a computer, or any machine, the operations, instructions, data-types, and interpretation rules used in the machine need to be defined. These are introduced gradually as the primary memory state, the processor state, and the interpretation cycle are described. Primary memory is not, in a strict sense, part of the ISP, but it plays such an important role in its operation that it is typically included in the description. In general, data-types (integers, floating-point numbers, characters, addresses, etc.) are abstractions of the contents of the machine registers and memories. One data-type that requires explicit treatment is the instruction, and the interpretation of instructions are explored in great detail.

Memory State

The description of the PDP-8 begins by specifying the primary memory that is used to store data and instructions:

```
M\Memory[0:4095]<0:11>,
```

The primary memory is declared as an array of 4,096 words, each 12 bits wide. The memory has a name (M) and an alias (Memory). These aliases are a special form of a comment and are useful for indicating the meaning or usage of a register's name. As in most programming languages, ISPS identifiers consist of letters and digits, beginning with a letter. The period character (.) is also allowed, to increase the readability. The expression [0:4095] describes the structure of the array. It declares the size (4,096 words) and the names of the words (0,1,..., 4094,4095).

The expression <0:11> describes the structure of each individual word. It declares the size (12 bits) and the names of the bits (0,1,...,10,11).*

Memory is divided into 128-word pages. Page zero is used for holding global variables and can be accessed directly by each instruction. Locations 8 through 15 of page zero have the special property called auto indexing: when accessed indirectly, the content of the location is incremented by 1. These regions of memory can be described as part of M as follows:

```
P.0\Page.Zero[0:127]<0:11>        := M[0:127]<0:11>,
A.I\Auto.Index[0:7]<0:11>         := M[8:15]<0:11>,
```

The word (and bit) naming conventions on the left-hand side of a field declaration are independent from the word (bit) names used on the right-hand side. A.I[0] corresponds to M[8], A.I[1] corresponds to M[9], and so on.

Processor State

The processor state is defined by a collection of registers used to store data, instructions, condition codes, and so on during the instruction interpretation cycle.

The PDP-8 has a 1-bit register (L) which contains the overflow or carry generated by the arithmetic operations, and a 12-bit register (AC) which contains the result of the arithmetic and logic operations. The concatenation of L and AC

---

*It should be noted that bit and word "names" are precisely that, i.e., identifiers for the subcomponents of a memory structure. These "names" do not necessarily indicate the relative position of the subcomponents. Thus, R<7:3> is a valid definition of a 5-bit register. The fact that the five bits are "named" 7,6,5,4, and 3 should not be confused with the 7th, 6th, etc., positions inside the register. Thus, bit 7 is the leftmost bit, bit 6 is located in the next position toward its right, etc., while bit 3 is the rightmost bit.

constitutes an extended accumulator LAC. The structure of the extended accumulator is shown below:

```
LAC<0:12>,
   L\Link<>                      := LAC<0>,
   AC\Accumulator<0:11>          := LAC<1:12>,
```

The expression < > indicates a single, unnamed bit (L is only one bit long and there is no need to specify a name for it.)

The Program Counter (PC) is used to store the address of the current instruction being executed as the machine steps through a program:

```
PC\Program.Counter<0:11>,
```

Twelve bits are needed in the PC to address all 4,096 locations of primary memory.

In the PDP-8, I/O devices are allowed to interrupt the central processor. When a device requires service from the central processor, it emulates a subroutine call, forcing the processor to execute an appropriate I/O subroutine. The presence of an interrupt request is indicated by setting the INTERRUPT.REQUEST flag. The processor can honor these requests or not, depending on the setting of the INTERRUPT.ENABLE bit:

```
INTERRUPT.ENABLE< >,
INTERRUPT.REQUEST< >,
```

There are 12 console switches which can be read by the processor. These switches are treated as a 12-bit register by the central processor:

```
SWITCHES<0:11>,
```

Instruction Format

As is the case with most data-types and registers on the PDP-8, instructions are 12 bits long:

```
i\instruction<0:11>,
```

An instruction is a special kind of data-type. It is really an aggregate of smaller information units (operation codes, address modes, operand addresses, etc.). The structure of the instructions must be exposed by describing the format. Most PDP-8 instructions contain an operation code and an operand address:

```
   op\operation.code<0:2>        := i<0:2>,
   ib\indirect.bit< >            := i<3>,
   pb\page.0.bit< >              := i<4>,
   pa\page.address<0:6>          := i<5:11>,
```

The abstractions op, ib, pb, and pa allow the treatment of selected fields of the PDP-8 instructions as individual entities.

PARTITIONING THE DESCRIPTION

In ISPS, a description can be divided into sections of the form:

```
** section.name **
<declaration>,
<declaration>,
. . .

** section.name **
<declaration>,
<declaration>,
. . . . .
```

Each section begins with a header, an identifier enclosed between ** and **. A section consists of a list of declarations separated by commas. Section names are not reserved keywords in the language; they are used to convey to the users of the description some information about the entities declared inside the section. The register and memory declarations presented so far could be grouped into the following sections:

```
** Memory.State **

M\Memory[0:4095]<0:11>,
   P.0\Page.Zero[0:127]<0:11>                 := M[0:127]<0:11>,
   A.I\Auto.Index[0:7]<0:11>                  := M[8:15]<0:11>,

** Processor.State **

LAC<0:12>,
   L\Link<>                   := LAC<0>,
   AC\Accumulator<0:11>       := LAC<1:12>,
PC\Program.Counter<0:11>,
RUN< >,
INTERRUPT.ENABLE< >,
INTERRUPT.REQUEST< >,
SWITCHES<0:11>,
```

```
** Instruction.Format **

i\instruction<0:11>,
   op\operation.code<0:2>        := i<0:2>,
   ib\indirect.bit<>             := i<3>,
   pb\page.0.bit<>               := i<4>,
   pa\page.address<0:6>          := i<5:11>,
   IO.SELECT<0:5>                := i<3:8>,           ! device select
   io.control<0:2>               := i<9:11>,          ! device operation
         IO.PULSE.P1< >          := io.control<0>,
         IO.PULSE.P2< >          := io.control<1>,
         IO.PULSE.P4< >          := io.control<2>,

   sma< >                        := i<5>,             ! skip on minus AC
   spa< >                        := i<5>,             ! skip on positive AC
   sza< >                        := i<6>,             ! skip on zero AC
   sna< >                        := i<6>,             ! skip on AC not zero
   snl< >                        := i<7>,             ! skip on L not zero
   szl< >                        := i<7>,             ! skip on L zero
   is< >                         := i<8>,             ! invert skip sense
   group< >                      := i<3>,             ! microinstruction group
   cla< >                        := i<4>,             ! clear AC
   cll< >                        := i<5>,             ! clear L
   cma< >                        := i<6>,             ! complement AC
   cml< >                        := i<7>,             ! complement L
   rar< >                        := i<8>,             ! rotate right
   ral< >                        := i<9>,             ! rotate left
   rt< >                         := i<10>,            ! rotate twice
   iac< >                        := i<11>,            ! increment AC
   osr< >                        := i<9>,             ! logical or AC with
                                                      ! SWITCHES
   hlt< >                        := i<10>,            ! halt the processor
```

A few more field declarations have been added. These are used to interpret the I/O and Operate instructions. The PDP-8 I/O instruction uses the 9 bits of addressing information to specify operations for the I/O devices. These 9 bits are divided into a device selector field (6 bits, IO.SELECT<0:5>) and a device operation field (3 bits, io.control<0:2>). Note that several alternate field declarations may be associated with the same portion of a register or data-type, thus adding flexibility to the description. Comments can be used to provide additional information to the reader. A comment is indicated by an exclamation point (!), and all characters following (!) to the end of the line are treated as commentary and not as part of the description. The PDP-8 Operate instruction's address field is not interpreted as an address but as a list of suboperations. (Additional details can be found in the DEC PDP-8 processor manuals.)

EFFECTIVE ADDRESS

The effective address computation is an algorithm that computes addresses of data and instructions:

```
** Effective.Address **

last.pc<0:11>,

eadd\effective.address<0:11>    := Begin
   Decode pb => Begin
      0                          :=Begin
         eadd ='00000 @ pa,                    ! Page Zero
         End
      1                          :=Begin
         eadd = last.pc<0:4> @ pa              ! Current Page
         End
      End Next
   If Not ib => Leave eadd Next
   If eadd<0:8> Eqv #001 =>   Begin
      M[eadd] = M[eadd] + 1 Next               ! Auto Index
      End
   eadd = M[eadd]
   End,
```

Since the memory of the machine is 4096 words long, addresses have to be 12 bits long. Of the 12 bits in an instruction, 3 bits have been allocated for the operation code (op), and there are only 9 bits (ib, pb, and pa) in the instruction register left for addressing information. These bits, together with some other portions of the processor state, are interpreted by the algorithm to yield the necessary 12 bits of addressing.

Address Computation

Instructions and data tend to be accessed sequentially or within address clusters. This property is called locality. The PDP-8 memory is logically divided into 32 pages of 128 words each. The concept of locality of memory references is used to reduce the addressing information by assuming that data are usually in the same page as the instructions that reference them. The pa portion of an instruction is the address within the current page. The pb portion on an instruction is used as an escape mechanism to indicate when pa is to be used as an address within page 0 (M[0:127]) instead of the current page. The address of the current instruction is contained in last.pc and is used to compute the current page number.

The first step of the algorithm,

```
Decode pb => Begin
  0                          :=Begin
    eadd ='00000 @ pa,*                          ! Page Zero
    End
  1                          :=Begin
    eadd = last.pc<0:4> @ pa                     ! Current Page
    End
  End Next
```

indicates a group of alternative actions, to be selected according to the value of the expression following the Decode operator. The alternatives appear enclosed between Begin and End and are separated by the comma character (,). The expressions (0 :=) and (1 :=) are used to label the statements with the corresponding value of pb. The alternative statements can be left unnumbered, in which case they are treated as if they were labelled (0:=), (1:=), (2:=),..., etc.

The effective address (eadd) is built by concatenating a page number with the page address (pa). The at sign character (@) of the operator is used to indicate concatenation of operands. If pb is equal to 0, page 0 is used in the computation. If pb is equal to 1, the current page number is used instead.

Constants prefixed with the single quote character (') represent binary numbers. For example, '00000 represents a 5-bit string which is concatenated with the 7 bits of pa to yield the 12 bits needed.

The expression <0:4> is used to select bits 0,..,4 of last.pc. These 5 bits contain the current page number, and, together with the 7 bits of pa, yield the necessary 12 bits.

Indirect Addresses

A full 12-bit target address can be stored in a memory location used as a pointer, and the instruction only needs to specify the address of this pointer location. Indirect addresses are specified via a bit in the instruction register (ib) that indicates whether the address is direct (ib=0) or indirect (ib=1).

The second step of the algorithm,

```
If Not ib => Leave eadd Next
```

is separated from the previous by the operator Next. The statement(s) preceding Next must be completed before the statement following it can be executed. The

---

*The transfer operator (=) modifies the memory or register specified on its left-hand side. If the right-hand side has more bits than the left-hand side, the right-hand side is truncated to the proper size by dropping the leftmost extra bits. If the right-hand side is shorter, enough 0 bits are added on its left until the length of the left-hand side is matched. Thus, the first conditional statement can be written as 0 := eadd = pa.

first step computed a preliminary effective address. The second step tests the value of ib and if it is equal to 0, then the preliminary effective address is used as the real effective address. If ib is equal to 1, the preliminary effective address is used to access a memory location which contains the real effective address. In the former case, the expression Leave eadd is used to indicate the termination of the procedure (this is similar to a RETURN statement in many programming languages).

Auto Indexing

Constants prefixed with the number sign (#) represent octal numbers. For example, #001 represents the following 9-bit string: '000000001. The procedure treats indirect addresses as special cases. If a preliminary effective address in the range #0010:#0017 (8:15) is used as an indirect address (ib = 1), the memory location is first incremented and the new value used as the indirect address:

```
If eadd<0:8> Eqv #001 => Begin
   M[eadd] = M[eadd] + 1 Next              ! Auto Index
   End
eadd = M[eadd]
```

By comparing the high order bits of eadd with #001 and ignoring the lower 3 bits, we are in fact specifying a range of addresses (#0010, #0011, #0012,..., #0017). Memory locations #0010:#0017 constitute the auto indexing registers.

Regardless of whether auto indexing takes place or not, the last step of the algorithm uses the preliminary effective address (which could have been modified by auto indexing) as the address of a memory location which contains the real effective address: eadd = M[eadd].

INSTRUCTION INTERPRETATION

The instruction interpretation section describes the instruction cycle, i.e., the fetching, decoding, and executing of instructions.

```
** Instruction.Interpretation **

interpret                    := Begin
   Repeat                       Begin
      i = M[PC]; last.pc = PC Next
      PC = PC + 1 Next
      execute( ) Next
      If INTERRUPT.ENABLE And INTERRUPT.REQUEST => Begin
         M[0] = PC Next
         PC = 1
         End
      End
   End,
```

The instruction cycle is described by a loop. The Repeat operator precedes a block of statements that are to be continuously executed. The instruction cycle of the machine consists of four steps:

1. A new instruction is fetched (i = M[PC]).
2. The program counter is incremented (PC = PC + 1). It now points to the next instruction. Under normal circumstances (i.e. unless a Jump takes place), this will be the instruction to be executed next.
3. The instruction is executed (execute( )).
4. Interrupt requests, if allowed, are honored. The cycle is then repeated.

The semicolon (;) separator is used to indicate concurrency, i.e., two statements separated by (;) are executed concurrently:

```
i = M[PC]; last.pc = PC Next
```

Notice how the value of the program counter is saved in last.pc before it is incremented. The effective address procedure relies on the fact that last.pc contains the address of the current instruction.

The execute procedure describes the individual instructions:

```
execute                       := Begin
   Decode op => Begin
      #0\and                  := AC = AC And M[eadd( )],
      #1\tad                  := LAC = LAC + M[eadd( )],
      #2\isz                  := Begin
         M[eadd] = M[eadd( )] + 1 Next
         If M[eadd] Eql 0 => PC = PC + 1
         End,
      #3\dca                  := Begin
         M[eadd( )] = AC Next
         AC = 0
         End,
      #4\jms                  := Begin
         M[eadd( )] = PC Next
         PC = EADD + 1
         End,
      #5\jmp                  := PC = eadd( ),
      #6\iot                  := input.output( ),
      #7\opr                  := operate( )
      End
   End,
```

Instruction mnemonics can be specified as aliases for the constants used to specify the operation codes:

```
#3\dca                          := Begin
    M[eadd( )] = AC Next
    AC = 0
    End,
```

Operation Code 0\and: Logical And

If the operation code is equal to 0, the contents of the Accumulator (excluding the L bit) are replaced by the logical product of the Accumulator and a memory location. To indicate that the effective address computation must be executed in order to obtain the memory address, eadd( ) is used.

Operation Code 1\tad: Two's Complement Add

The tad instruction follows the pattern of the previous instruction. Notice, however, that the complete Accumulator (including the L bit) is involved in the operation. The L bit contains the overflow or carry out of the sign position of AC.

Operation Code 2\isz: Increment and Skip if Zero

This instruction is described in two consecutive steps. The first step indicates that some memory location, specified by the effective address computation, will be incremented by 1. Notice the different uses of eadd in the statement:

```
M[eadd] = M[eadd( )] + 1 Next
```

The effective address is computed once, eadd( ), and is used to fetch the memory location, M[eadd( )]. The result of the addition must be stored back in the same memory location. This is indicated by using the effective address register, eadd, on the left-hand side, M[eadd]. The eadd already contains the correct address, and there is no need to recompute it. In fact, because of the auto indexing operations performed during the effective address computation, the effective address must be computed precisely once.

The second step of the instruction,

```
If M[eadd] Eql 0 => PC = PC + 1
```

tests the result of the addition. If the result is equal to 0, the program counter is incremented by one, thus in effect, skipping over the next instruction in sequence. Once again, eadd is used instead of eadd( ) to avoid undesirable side-effects.

Operation Code 3\dca: Deposit and Clear Accumulator

This instruction deposits the Accumulator in a memory location and then clears the Accumulator (excluding the L bit).

Operation Code 4\jms: Jump to Subroutine

This instruction alters the normal sequence of instructions by modifying the Program Counter so that the next instruction will not be the one following the current instruction, but the one located at a memory location specified by the effective address. The Program Counter is stored into the location preceding the subroutine code (the result of eadd( )). The Program Counter is then modified to point to the first instruction of the subroutine (eadd + 1).

Operation Code 5\jmp: Jump

This instruction also modifies the normal sequence of instructions. It can be used to jump to disjoint pieces of code. If we use ib=1 and specify the address of the location preceding the subroutine, the result of the effective address computation yields the return address that was stored by the subroutine call.

Operation Code 6\iot: Input/Output

The input.output procedure describes two specific cases of I/O instruction, namely, those used to control the interrupt mechanism:

```
input.output                    := Begin
   Decode i<3:11> => Begin
      #001\ion                  := Begin          ! turn Interrupt ON
         INTERRUPT.ENABLE = 1 Next
         Restart interpret
         End,
      #002\iof                  := Begin          ! turn Interrupt OFF
         INTERRUPT.ENABLE = 0
         End,
      Otherwise                 := No.Op( )       ! not implemented
      End
   End,
```

The Otherwise operation can be specified in a Decode operation to indicate a default action to be executed if none of the explicitly named cases (#001 or #002) apply. All other I/O operations default to a predefined ISPS procedure (No.Op( )). This is done simply to keep the examples within the space limitations of this appendix.

I/O operation #002 disables interrupts. It typically occurs as the first instruction of an interrupt handling routine. I/O operation #001 enables interrupts. It typically occurs at the end of an interrupt handling subroutine. Its effect is delayed for one instruction (the return from the subroutine) to avoid losing the return address if an interrupt were to occur immediately. This is achieved by skipping over the last portion of the instruction interpretation cycle:

```
If INTERRUPT.ENABLE And INTERRUPT.REQUEST => ....
```

The Restart interpret operation is used to indicate a return from the input.output procedure, not to the place from were it was invoked (inside execute), but to the beginning of the interpret procedure, thus bypassing the interrupt trapping for one instruction.

Operation Code 7\opr: Operate

The Operate instruction encodes a large number of primitive micro-operations in the address bits of an instruction. Some bits (e.g., cla) represent a micro-operation by themselves. Others (e.g., rt and ral) jointly represent a micro-operation. There are several conditional skip micro-operations. These are grouped in a separate procedure for readability:

```
skip< >,

skip.group                    := Begin
   skip = 0 Next
   Decode is => Begin                              ! invert skip condition
      0                       := Begin
         If snl And (L Eql 1) => skip = 1;
         If sza And (AC Eql 0) => skip = 1;
         If sma And (AC Lss 0) => skip = 1
         End,
      1                       := Begin
         IF szl@sna@spa Eql 0 => skip = 1;
         If szl And (L Eql 0) => skip = 1;
         If sna And (AC Neq 0) => skip = 1;
         If spa And (AC Geq 0) => skip = 1
         End
      End Next
   If skip => PC = PC + 1                          ! Skip
   End,
```

```
operate                              := Begin
  Decodc group => Begin
    0                                := Begin          ! group 1
      If cla => AC = 0;
      If cll => L = 0 Next
      If cma => AC = Not AC;
      If cml => L = Not L Next
      If iac => LAC = LAC + 1 Next
      Decode rt => Begin                               ! rotate once or twice
        0                            := Begin          ! once
          If ral => LAC = LAC Slr 1;
          If rar => LAC = LAC Srr 1
          End,
        1                            := Begin          ! twice
          If ral => LAC = LAC Slr 2;
          If rar => LAC = LAC Srr 2
          End
        End
      End,
    1                                := Begin          ! groups 2 and 3
      Decode i<11> => Begin
        0                            := Begin          ! group 2
          skip.group( ) Next
          If cla => AC = 0 Next
          If osr => AC = AC Or SWITCHES;
          If hlt => RUN = 0
          End,
        1                            := Begin          ! group 3
          If cla => AC = 0 Next
          No.Op( )                                     ! eae group
          End
        End
      End
    End
  End
```

Several micro-operations can appear in the same instruction. Not all combinations are legal or useful. Micro-operations are executed at different points in time thus allowing sequences of transformations applied to the Accumulator and/or link bit. For instance, in the group 1 micro-operations, clearing AC/L is done before complementing them; this is done before incrementing the combined L@AC (LAC) register; and this in turn precedes the rotation of L@AC.

OTHER FEATURES OF ISPS

Not all the features of the notation have been presented in the example. This section attempts to provide a list of the missing operations to aid understanding of the larger descriptions in the book. A detailed explanation of the complete language is in the reference manual [Barbacci *et al.*, 1977].

Constants

In general, a constant is a sequence of characters drawn from some alphabet determined by the base of the constant. The base of a nondecimal constant is given by a prefix character. The alphabets for the predefined bases in ISPS are:

Base	Prefix	Alphabet
2	‘	0,1,?
8	#	0,1,2,3,4,5,6,7,?
10		0,1,2,3,4,5,6,7,8,9,?
16	“	0,1,2,3,4,5,6,7,8,9,A,B,C,D,E,F,?

The question mark character (?) can be used to specify a "don't care" digit. Its presence stands for any digit in the corresponding alphabet.

The length of a constant is measured in bits. Decimal constants are one bit longer than the smallest number of bits needed to represent its value (beware that the use of "don't care" (?) decimal digits results in constants of unspecified length). Binary constants have one bit for each digit explicitly written. Octal constants have three bits for each digit explicitly written. Hexadecimal constants have four bits for each digit explicitly written:

Example	Length	Bit Pattern
“1000	16	0001000000000000
15	5	01111
#17	6	001111
0	2	00
‘0?101	5	0?101
#?2	6	???010

Arithmetic Representation

ISPS allows the user to specify arithmetic operations in four different representations: two's complement, one's complement, sign magnitude, and unsigned magnitude (the default is two's complement). To specify a different representation, the following modifiers can be used:

{TC}	two's complement
{OC}	one's complement
{SM}	sign magnitude
{US}	unsigned magnitude

In all the signed representations, the sign bit is the leftmost position of the operand (1 for negative numbers, 0 for positive numbers). The above modifiers can be attached to any arithmetic or relational operator to override a default. They can also be attached to a procedure declaration to set a default throughout the body. When attached to a section name the default applies to all the declarations in the section:

```
test    := Begin {OC}                ! Default for the body
           .....
           End,

** Section.1 ** {TC}                 ! Default for the section

..........

X = Y + {SM} Z                       ! Instance
```

Always remember that the arithmetic representation is a property of the operator, not the operand. Thus, the same bit pattern can be treated as a two's complement or an unsigned integer depending on the arithmetic context in which it is used.

Sign Extension

All ISPS data operators define results whose length is determined by both the lengths of the operands and the specific operator. Some operations require that their operands be of the same length. This is usually accomplished by sign-extending the operands. In the context of unsigned magnitude arithmetic, sign-extension is interpreted as zero-extension (i.e., padding with 0's on the left). In one's and two's complement arithmetic, the expansion is done by replication of the sign bit. In sign magnitude arithmetic, the expansion is done by inserting 0s between the sign bit and the most significant bit of the operand.

Data Operators (in order of precedence)

Negation and Complement: –, NOT

Unary – generates the arithmetic complement of the operand (the operation is invalid in unsigned arithmetic). The result is one bit longer than the operand. The NOT operator generates the logical complement of the operand. The result has the same length as the operand.

Concatenation: @

The @ operator concatenates the two operands. The length of the result is the sum of the lengths of the operands.

Shift and Rotate: Sl0, Sl1, Sld, Slr, Sr0, Sr1, Srd, Srr

These operators shift or rotate the left operand the number of places specified by the right operand. The result has the same length as the left operand.

The operators have the format Sxy where x is either l(eft) or r(ight) to indicate the direction of movement. The y is either 0, 1, d(uplicate), or r(otate), to indicate the source of bits to be shifted in. Sx1 shifts its left operand, inserting 1s in the vacant positions. Sx0 is similar to Sx1, but inserts 0s. Sxd inserts copies of the bit leaving the position to be vacated (not the bit being shifted out). Sxr inserts copies of the bit being shifted out (i.e., rotates the left operand).

Multiplication, Division, and Remainder: *, /, MOD

These operators compute the arithmetic product, quotient, and remainder of the two operands, respectively. The lengths of the results are:

Operation	**Length of Result**
*	Sum of lengths
/	Left Operand (dividend)
MOD	Right Operand (divisor)

Addition and Subtraction: +, −

The + and − operators compute the arithmetic sum and difference of the two operands, respectively. The shortest operand is sign-extended, and the result is one bit longer than the largest operand.

Relational Operations: Eql, Neq, Lss, Leq, Gtr, Geq, Tst

These operations perform an arithmetic comparison between the two operands. The shortest operand is sign-extended, and the result is either 1 or 2 bits long. The first six operators (i.e., all except Tst) produce a 1-bit result indicating whether the relation is True (1) or False (0). The Tst operator produces a 2-bit result indicating whether the relation between the left and right operands is Lss (0), Eql (1), or Gtr (2).

Conjunction and Equivalence: And, Eqv

These operators produce the logical product and coincidence operations of the two operands. The shortest operand is zero-extended, and the result is as long as the largest operand.

Disjunction and Nonequivalence: Or, Xor

These operators produce the logical sum and difference operations of the two operands. The shortest operand is zero-extended, and the result is as long as the largest operand.

Logical and Arithmetic Assignment: =, ←

The logical assignment operator (=) truncates or zero-extends the source (right operand) to match the length of the destination (left operand). The arithmetic assignment operator (←) truncates or sign-extends the source to match the length of the destination.

APPENDIX 2

The PMS Notation

J. CRAIG MUDGE

The PMS notation provides a structural representation of a digital computer system as a graph which has the system's components as the nodes and information flows along the branches. These aspects of a digital computer system level provide a description of the gross structure, including the amounts of information held in various components, the distribution of control that accomplishes these flows, and other interesting parameters (e.g., technology, function, cost, reliability). Only those aspects of the notation that are used in this book are described; a complete description is given in Bell and Newell [1971].

PMS PRIMITIVES

In PMS there are seven basic component types, each distinguished by the kinds of operations it performs:

Memory, M. A component that holds or stores information (i.e., *i*-units) over time. Its operations are reading *i*-units out of the memory and writing *i*-units into the memory. Each memory that holds more than a single *i*-unit has associated with it an addressing system by means of which particular *i*-units can be designated or selected. A memory can also be considered as a switch to a number of submemories. The *i*-units are not changed in any way by being stored in a memory.

Link, L. A component that transfers information (i.e., *i*-units) from one place to another in a computer system. It has fixed ports. The operation is that of transmitting an *i*-unit (or a sequence of them) from the component at one port to the component at the other. Again, except for the change in spatial position, there is no change of any sort in the *i*-units.

Control, K. A component that evokes the operations of other components in the system. All other components are taken to consist of a set of discrete operations, each of which, when evoked, accomplishes some discrete transformation of state.

With the exception of a processor, P, all other components are essentially passive and require some other active agent (a K) to set them into small episodes of activity.

Switch, S. A component that constructs a link between other components. Each switch has associated with it a set of possible links, and its operations consist of setting some of these links and breaking others.

Transducer, T. A component that changes the *i*-unit used to encode a given meaning (i.e., a given referent). The change may involve the medium used to encode the basic bits (e.g., voltage levels to magnetic flux, or voltage levels to holes in a paper card), or it may involve the structure of the *i*-unit (e.g., bit-serial to bit-parallel). Note that T's are meaning-preserving (in number of bits), since the encodings of the (invariant) meaning need not be equally optimal.

Data-operation, D. A component that produces *i*-units with new meanings. It is this component that accomplishes all the data-operations, e.g., arithmetic, logic, shifting, etc.

Processor, P. A component that is capable of interpreting a program in order to execute a sequence of operations. It consists of a set of operations of the types already mentioned (M, L, K, S, T, and D) with the control necessary to obtain instructions from a memory and interpret them as operations to be carried out.

Each component has a set of attributes and associated values and takes on the form:

$$X(a_1{:}v_1;a_2{:}v_2;\ldots).$$

There are alternative, shorthand ways of saying the same thing when the attribute names are clear. For example:

M(function:primary)	Complete specification.
M(primary)	Drop the attribute name function, since it can be inferred from the value.
M.primary	A value can be concatenated with a component name using a dot convention.
M.p	Use an explicitly given abbreviation, namely, primary\p (only if it is not ambiguous).

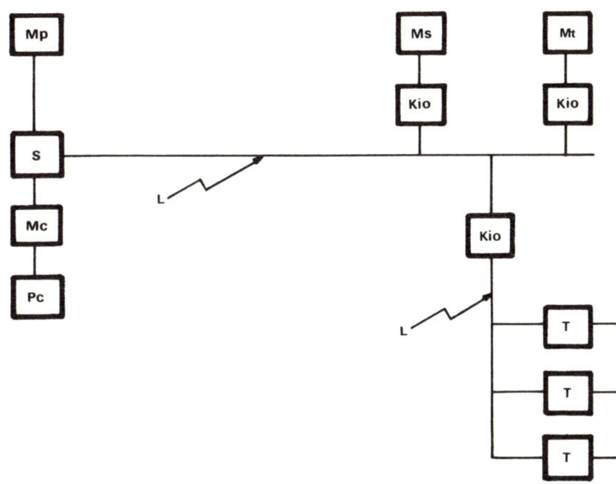

WHERE:

L\ Link (e.g., Unibus)
Kio\I/O Controller
Mc\M.cache\cache memory
Mp\M.primary\primary or program memory (e.g., core)
Ms\M.secondary\secondary memory (e.g., disk)
Mt\M.tertiary
Pc\P.central\central processor
S\Switch (e.g., multiplexer)
T\Transducer (e.g., typewriter)

Figure 1. An example of a PMS diagram of a computer, C.

Mp Drop the concatenation if it is not needed to recover the component name.

Components of the seven types can be connected to make stored program computers, abbreviated by C, as shown in Figure 1.

APPENDIX 3

Performance

C. GORDON BELL, J. CRAIG MUDGE
and JOHN E. McNAMARA

Performance parameters are a combination of architecture (the ISP), hardware implementation, and resources (the PMS structure) being acted on by programs (the use). Simplistic hardware measures, such as instruction times, can be used to characterize machine performance for many cases. However, the ultimate performance parameters have to be based on actual use parameters, otherwise there is no way to correlate the primitive hardware measures to real performance. Benchmarks of synthetic or real workload provide the only real test by which performance can be compared. These might include standardized benchmarks such as Whetstones for the algorithmic scientific languages and COBOL benchmarks for commercial applications.

When one measures performance, there is a tacit assumption that sufficient software exists to exploit a hardware structure, and that the transformation from the basic hardware machine (the macromachine) to the user machine (as provided by a language such as COBOL or FORTRAN) is relatively constant across various architectures. As each level is crossed, a transformation requiring computational work takes place. The form of the work with compiled languages is direct execution via the processor and run-time support program. With interpreted languages, the processor executes an interpretation program which indirectly interprets the data (i.e., final program).

At the lowest level, the internal micromachine provides the architectural facade, the ISP, operating at roughly 10 times the speed of the macromachine. Thus, a macromachine executing 1 million instructions per second may have an effective microcycle time of 100 nanoseconds for executing 10 million microinstructions per second. At the next level, a macromachine (ISP) executing 1 million instructions per second is capable of perhaps 0.1 to 0.25 million higher level FORTRAN language statements (instructions) per second depending on the mix of built-in functions and external functions called.

It is difficult to use the simplistic constant ratio measures across each level-of-interpretation when comparing machines of differing classes (e.g., micro to super) because there is no consistency of data-types (e.g., micros started out with no built-in real arithmetic at a time when minis included them). However, for machines within a class (e.g., mini) where the data-types are implied by the class name, simplistic comparison is probably all right, since the two machines most likely have about the same data-types. Hence a count of the number of data-types reflecting the built-in operations is one of the more significant architectural performance indicators, whether it be for a micromachine, macromachine, or a language machine.

PMS (RESOURCES) PERFORMANCE PARAMETERS

The PMS structure, with the corresponding attributes determining performance (memory cycle time, processor execution rate), provides the basis for understanding machines and comparing them with each other. Figure 1 gives a PMS diagram of a basic computer, with the parameters that, to a first approximation, characterize performance. Alternatively, one might use a more descriptive, or tabular, form; but the goal is to provide a structural/performance basis for defining parameters and comparing and specifying the finite resources of the computer so that performance can be determined against actual workload.

It is imperative to consider the resource constraints and the effect of their interaction as each layer of a machine is designed. For example, a certain line printer requires buffer space (memory size) and central processing time which is then unavailable at the next machine level (e.g., FORTRAN).

Bell and Newell [1971:52] argued that a machine (at any level) can be described with any number of parameters, and carried out the exercise for up to five parameters (Table 1).

Information rate between the processor and memory is used as the processor speed indicator instead of the more conventional instructions per second. Compound indicators such as the product of processor speed times memory size to indicate basic computational performance were not allowed.

The example in Table 2 shows three different architectures with two implementations of a stack architecture. One has the stack in the primary memory (Mp), and the other assumes the stack is in the processor (Pc), using fast registers. The hardware implementations are held roughly constant (the processor to primary memory data rate) and the architecture is varied in order to compare the effect on performance. Note the difference in the various measures in what should fundamentally be about the same performance for a simple benchmark problem.

The statement execution rate (the actual performance) is the highest for the 3-address machine. In contrast, the conventional instructions per second measure shows the 3-address machine to have the lowest performance (by a factor of 4). A more subtle measure, operation rate, is correlated with the true benchmark statement execution rate. It should be noted (ignoring the first machine, a stack machine with stack top in primary memory) that the information rate is a good performance indicator compared to the conventional, but poor, instruction rate measure. For more unconventional machines, instructions per second tends to become a significantly poorer measure. The various vector/array machines (e.g., ILLIAC IV, CDC STAR, CRAY-1) have single instructions to operate on at least 64 operands per instruction; hence instructions per second would be a poor measure. Hand-held calculators have single instructions such as Sin, Polar-to-Cartesian coordinate conversion; using anything but a final benchmark problem would be unfair. Accesses per second used here are as a processor performance measure.

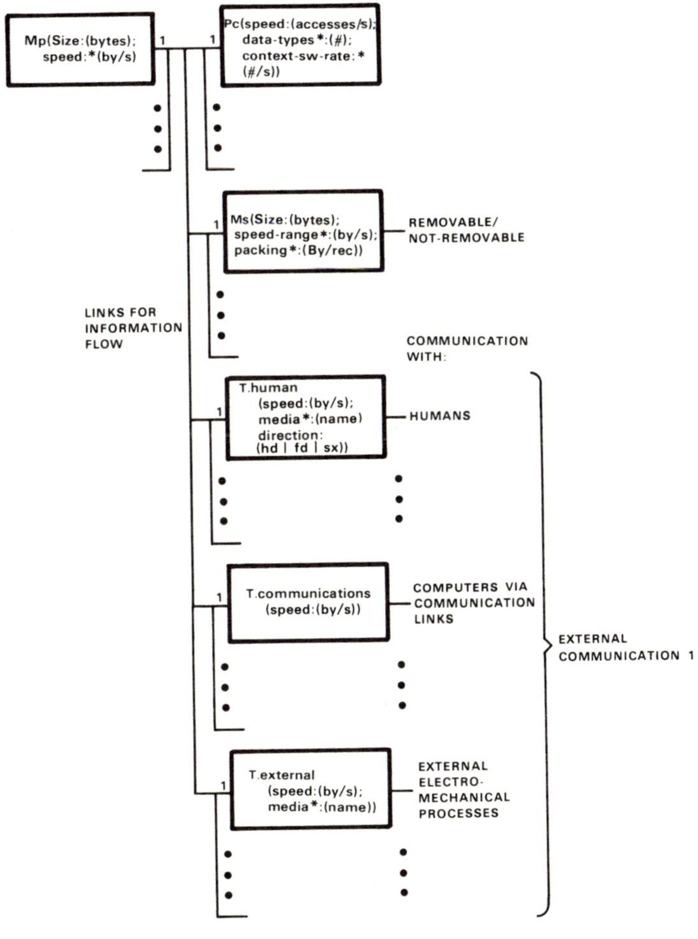

Figure 1. Basic PMS computer structure model with six relevant performance/structure dimensions.

Table 1. Characterizing Computer Systems With 1, 2, 3, 4, or 5 Parameters

Number of Parameters Allowed	1	2	3	4	5
1	Processor information rate	–	–	Processor operation rate	–
2		Primary memory size	–	–	–
3	–	–	Secondary memory size	–	–
4	–	–	–	Processor word length	–
5	–	–	–	–	Number of terminals

THE MULTIPROCESSOR CASE

For multiprocessors the number of processors times the memory accesses per second gives an approximate total. Processor speed can be computed more precisely by using the number of primary memory (Mp) modules and their data rate. For a system where the memory access time and the memory rewrite time equal the time for a processor to operate on a word, the performance is roughly [Strecker, 1970]:

$$\text{Processor speed (in accesses per second)} = (m/t) \times (1 - (1 - 1/m)^{p})$$

where m = number of memory modules, p = number of processors, and t = the access time of a memory module.

Note that when $p = m =$ large, the performance reaches an asymptote:

$$= m/tc \times (1/e)$$

In the case of multiprogramming systems (e.g., real-time, transaction, and time-sharing), the time to switch from job to job is important if there is a high context switching rate.

The memory sizes (in bytes) for both primary and secondary memory give the memory capability. The memory transfer rates are needed as secondary measures, especially to compute memory interference when multiple processors are used. This measure also permits system performance to be computed by subtracting the

Table 2. Performance Metrics for Various Machines Interpreting the Expression, A ← B + C

	Stack (top in Mp)	Stack (top in Pc)	1-Address or General Registers	3-Address
Program	PUSH B PUSH C ADD POP A	PUSH B PUSH C ADD POP A	LOAD B ADD C STORE A	ADD B,C,A
Number of Instructions	4	4	3	1
Accesses	4op + 3a + 6d	4op + 3a +3d	3op + 3a + 3d	1op + 3a + 3d
Program size (bits*)	64	64	72	60
Bits accessed*	16 + 48 + 192 = 266	16 + 48 + 96 = 160	24 + 48 + 96 = 168	12 + 48 + 96 = 156
Time to execute† (microseconds)	0.5 + 1.5 + 6 = 8	0.5 + 1.5 + 3 = 5	0.75 + 1.5 + 3 = 5.25	0.37 + 1.5 + 3 = 4.87
Statement execution rate (actual performance)	1/8 = 0.125M	1/5 = 0.2M	1/5.25 = 0.19M	1/4.87 = 0.21M
Operation rate	2/8 = 0.25M	2/5 = 0.4M	2/5.25 = 0.38M	2/4.87 = 0.42M
Instruction rate	4/8 = 0.5M	4/5 = 0.8M	3/5.25 = 0.57M	1/4.87 = 0.21M
Processor instruction rate/word length	32M = 1M	32M = 1M	32M = 1M	32M = 1M

* Assumes address (a) = 16 bits; data (d) = 32 bits; operation code (op) = 4, 4, 8, and 12 bits.
† Assumes a memory limited processor which can access 32 bits per microsecond.

secondary memory transfers and external interface transfers. For file systems which require multiple accesses to secondary memory for single items, the file access rate capability is needed in order to compute performance. Similarly, for multiprogrammed systems which use secondary memory to hold programs, the access rate is needed.

Communications capability with humans, other computers, and other electronically encoded processes are equally important structure and performance attributes. Each channel (e.g., a typewriter) has a certain data rate and direction (full duplex for simultaneous two-way communication). Collectively, the data rates and the number of channels connected to each of the three different environments (people, computers, electronically encoded processes) signify quite different styles of computing capability, structure, and, ultimately, use.

ISP (ARCHITECTURE) PARAMETERS

While the hardware structure and operation rates are the principal performance determinants, the architecture is also important. Within a given machine class (say minis), architecture has little effect on performance if the data-types are embedded. The values for the data-types dimension in order of increasing complexity are roughly:

word
integer
bit vector
instruction
character
floating or character string (depending upon scientific or commercial use)
program (including lists, stacks)
word vector
arrays

However, it is difficult to order the dimensions, except by complexity, because performance is determined by whether a given problem requires the embedded data-type.

In the U. S. Defense Department's Computer Family Architecture (CFA) study [Barbacci *et al.*, 1977a; Burr *et al.*, 1977; Fuller *et al.*, 1977a; Fuller *et al.*, 1977b] which leads to the selection of the PDP-11 as the standard architecture, benchmarking was used to compare several architectures.

The measures were the number of bits statically required to encode the algorithm (S measure) and the number of bits that dynamically flow between the processor and primary memory (M measure). A third measure gave the activity of the internal register processor (R measure).

The benchmarks (see Table 3; from Fuller *et al.* [1977b:149]), oriented to real-time use were each programmed with assembly languages. The resultant programs were run on a simulator (instrumented to provide the S, M, and R measures) that interpreted the formal ISPS descriptions of the machines.

Table 3. Test Programs

1. **I/O kernel, four priority levels**. Requires the processor to field interrupts from four devices, each of which has its own priority level. While one device is being processed, interrupts from higher priority devices are allowed.
2. **I/O kernel, FIFO processing**. Also fields interrupts from four devices, but without consideration of priority level. Instead, each interrupt causes a request for processing to be queued; requests are processed in FIFO order. While a request is being processed, interrupts from other devices are allowed.
3. **I/O device handler**. Processes application programs' requests for I/O block transfers on a typical tape drive, and returns the status of the transfer upon completion.
4. **Large FFT**. Computes the Fast Fourier Transform of a large vector of 32-bit floating-point numbers. This benchmark exercises the machine's floating point instructions, but principally tests its ability to manage a large address space.
5. **Character search**. Searches a potentially large character string for the first occurrence of a potentially large argument string. It exercises the ability to move through character strings sequentially.
6. **Bit test, set, or reset**. Tests the initial value of a bit within a bit string, then optionally sets or resets the bit. It tests one kind of bit manipulation.
7. **Runge-Kutta integration**. Numerically integrates a simple differential equation using third-order Runge-Kutta integration. It tests floating-point arithmetic.
8. **Linked list insertion**. Inserts a new entry in a doubly linked list. It tests pointer manipulation.
9. **Quicksort**. Sorts a potentially large vector of fixed-length strings using the Quicksort algorithm. Like FFT, it tests the ability to manipulate a large address space, but it also tests the ability of the machine to support recursive routines.
10. **ASCII to floating point**. Converts to ASCII string to a floating-point number. It exercises character-to-numeric conversion.
11. **Boolean matrix transpose**. Transposes a square, tightly packed bit matrix. It tests the ability to sequence through bit vectors by arbitrary increments.
12. **Virtual memory space exchange**. Changes the virtual memory mapping context of the processor.

The CFA project also developed a single architectural measure based on a weighted average of various ISP parameters. The weightings were determined by the CFA user community, and each parameter was evaluated in comparison with several competitive architectures. The parameters and their weights are given in Table 4 from [Fuller *et al.*, 1977a:140–144].

The measures are defined so that computer architectures maximize some and minimize others. The measures that an architecture should maximize are V_1, V_2, P_1, P_2, U, K, B_1, B_2, and D; the measures that should be kept to a minimum are CS_1, CS_2, CM_1, CM_2, I, L, J_1, and J_2. In the composite measures, a maximal measure, the inverses of those measures to be minimized were used.

Lloyd Dickman, of DEC, calculated the measures for four DEC computers as follows:

VAX-11	1.23	PDP-11	1.03
PDP-8	1.09	PDP-10	0.66

Table 4. Criteria for CFA Evaluation

Absolute Criteria

1. **Virtual memory support**. The architecture must support a virtual-to-physical translation mechanism.
2. **Protection**. The architecture must have the capability to add new, experimental (i.e., not fully debugged) programs that may include I/O without endangering reliable operation of existing programs.
3. **Floating-point support**. The architecture must explicitly support one or more floating-point data-types with at least one of the formats yielding more than 10 decimal digits of significance in the mantissa.
4. **Interrupts and traps**. It must be possible to write a trap handler that is capable of executing a procedure to respond to any trap condition and then resume operation of the program. The architecture must be defined such that it is capable of resuming execution after any interrupt.
5. **Subsetability**. At least the following components of an architecture must be able to be factored out of the full architecture:
   Virtual-to-physical address translation mechanism
   Floating-point instructions and registers (if separate from general-purpose registers)
   Decimal instructions set (if present in full architecture)
   Protection mechanism
6. **Multiprocessor support**. The architecture must allow for multiprocessor configurations. Specifically, it must support some form of "test-and-set" instruction to allow the implementation of synchronization functions such as *P* and *V*.
7. **Controllability of I/O**. A processor must be able to exercise control over any I/O processor and/or I/O controller.
8. **Extendability**. The architecture must have some method for adding instructions to the architecture consistent with existing formats. There must be at least one undefined code point in the existing operation code space of the instruction formats.
9. **Read-only code**. The architecture must allow programs to be kept in a read-only section of primary memory.

Quantitative Criteria	**Weight (%)**
1. **Virtual address space.**	
V_1: The size of the virtual address space in bits.	4.3
V_2: Number of addressable units in the virtual address space.	5.3
2. **Physical address space.**	
P_1: The size of physical address space in bits.	6.1
P_2: The number of addressable units in the physical address space.	5.1
3. **Fraction of instruction space unassigned.**	6.0
4. **Size of central processor state.**	
CS_1: The number of bits in the processor state of the full architecture.	4.9
CS_2: The number of bits in the processor state of the minimum subset of the architecture (i.e., without Floating-Point, Decimal, Protection, or Address Translation Registers)	3.7

Table 4. Criteria for CFA Evaluation (Cont)

Quantitative Criteria	Weight (%)
CM_1: The number of bits that must be transferred between the processor and primary memory to first save the processor state of the full architecture upon interruption and then restore the processor state prior to resumption.	6.0
CM_2: The measure analogous to CM_1 for the minimum subset of the architecture.	4.5
5. **Virtualizability**.	
K is unity if the architecture is virtualizable as defined in Popek and Goldberg [1974]; otherwise K is zero.	5.6
6. **Usage base**.	
B_1: Number of computers delivered as of the latest date for which data exists prior to 1 June 1976.	3.1
B_2: Total dollar value of the installed computer base as of the latest date for which data exists prior to 1 June 1976.	2.5
7. **I/O initiation**.	
I: The minimum number of bits which must be transferred between main memory and any processor (central or I/O) in order to output one 8-bit to a standard peripheral device.	12.4
8. **Direct instruction addressability**.	
D: The maximum number of bits of primary memory which one instruction can directly address given a single base register which may be used but not modified.	10.2
9. **Maximum interrupt latency**.	
Let L be the maximum number of bits that may need to be transferred between memory and any processor (CP, IOC, etc.) between the time an interrupt is requested and the time that the computer starts processing that interrupt (given that interrupts are enabled).	9.2
10. **Subroutine linkage**.	
J_1: The number of bits that must be transferred between the processor and memory to save the user state, transfer to the called routine, restore the user state, and return to the calling routine, for the full architecture. No parameters are passed.	6.3
J_2: The analogous measure to CS1 above for the minimum architecture (e.g., without Floating-Point registers).	4.5

ACTUAL (COMPOUND PMS/ISP) PERFORMANCE MEASURE

In order to measure the performance of a specific computer (e.g., a PDP-11/55), it is necessary to know the ISP, the hardware performance, and the frequency of use for the various instructions. The execution time T is the dot product of the fractional utilization of each instruction Ui times the time to execute each instruction Ti.

There are three ways to estimate the instruction utilization U and, hence, obtain T – each providing increasingly better answers. The first defines either a typical or average instruction. The second uses standard benchmarks to characterize a machine's performance precisely. In this way, machines can be compared with an absolute measure. Finally, since the actual use has not been characterized in terms of the standard benchmark (and may even be difficult to characterize in terms of it), a specific unique benchmark may be necessary. Such a characterization is quite possibly needed for real-time and transaction processing where computer selection and installation is predicated on the job.

TYPICAL INSTRUCTIONS

The simplest, single parameter of performance is the instruction time for some simple operation (e.g., add). These were used in the first two computer generations when high level languages were less used. Such a metric is an approximation to the average instruction time and assumes that all machines have about the same ISP and thus there is little difference among instructions, or that a specific data-type is used more heavily than another, or that a typical add time will be given (e.g., the operand is in a random location in primary memory call rather than being cached or in a fast register).

Although it is possible to take the average instruction time by executing one of every possible instruction, since the instruction use depends so much on the data interpreted, this average is relatively meaningless. A better measure is to keep statistics about the use of all programs and to give the average instruction time based on use on all programs. Again, such a measure, while useful for comparing two machines' implementations of models of the same architecture, is relatively useless for particular practices.

Many years ago, there were attempts to make better characterizations by weighting instruction use (i.e., forming a typical U) as to what each one did (e.g., floating point versus indexing and character handling) to give a better performance measure. Instruction mixes were developed that began to better evaluate performance. These mixes, from Bell and Newell [1971:50], are given in Table 5.

The Gibson mix, best known, is still used even today. It has a decidedly commercial flavor and quite possibly reflects the proportion of machines executing commercial, as opposed to scientific, mixes with character operations, switching, and control, where proportionally more integer and floating-point data-types are used. Such mixes are still better approximations than a single instruction average, because use enters in. Note that if the data-type operation is not present in the machine, the programmed subroutine time must be given – typically a factor of 10-20 times greater than for built-in operations.

STANDARD BENCHMARKS

The best estimate of real use comes from carefully designed standard benchmarks that are understood and that are used by other machines. Several organizations, particularly those that purchase or use many machines extensively, have one or more programs that they believe characterize their own workload. Whether a standard benchmark can be of value in characterizing performance depends on the degree that it is typical of the actual use of the computer. A further advantage of benchmarks is that they are the language that the computer is to use, and, hence, reflect the application and characterize the language machine architecture. To illustrate the variability in the scientific FORTRAN benchmark metrics, the performance of a number of machines (VAX-11/780 with floating-point accelerator option, PDP-11/70, and DECSYSTEM 2060), executing about a dozen such benchmarks, is compared in Figure 2. Two scientific benchmarks of the National Physical Laboratory in the United Kingdom [Curnow and Wichmann, 1976] are often singled out as being the most useful benchmarks because of the extensive effort that was put into designing them as typical scientific programs. Several factors, such as the frequencies of the trigonometric functions, frequencies of subroutine calls, and characteristics of the I/O, were considered. The performance of computers executing these benchmarks is expressed in Whetstones per second.

Table 5. Instruction-Mix Weights for Evaluating Computer Power

	Arbuckle[1966]	Gibson*	Knight (scientific)	Knight (commercial)
Fixed +/–	–	6	10 (25)†	25 (45)†
Multiply	–	3	6	1
Divide	–	1	2	–
Floating +/–	9.5	–	10	–
Floating multiply	5.6	–	–	–
Floating divide	2.0	–	–	–
Load/store	28.5	25 (move)	–	–
Indexing	22.5	–	–	–
Conditional branch	13.2	20	–	–
Compare	–	24	–	–
Branch on character	–	10	–	–
Edit	–	4	–	–
I/O initiate	–	7	–	–
Other	18.7	–	72	74

*Published reference unknown.
†Extra weight for either indirect addressing or index registers.

There are similar benchmarks for commercial processors that generally use the COBOL language.

EXACT USE CHARACTERIZATION

If a machine has to be fully characterized before installation, there is no alternative to running the exact problem which will be run on the final system. This is the most expensive alternative to characterize performance and should be avoided because of the dynamic nature of use. Showing that an application yields a given performance on a particular machine is a weak guarantee of performance if any part of the problem changes.

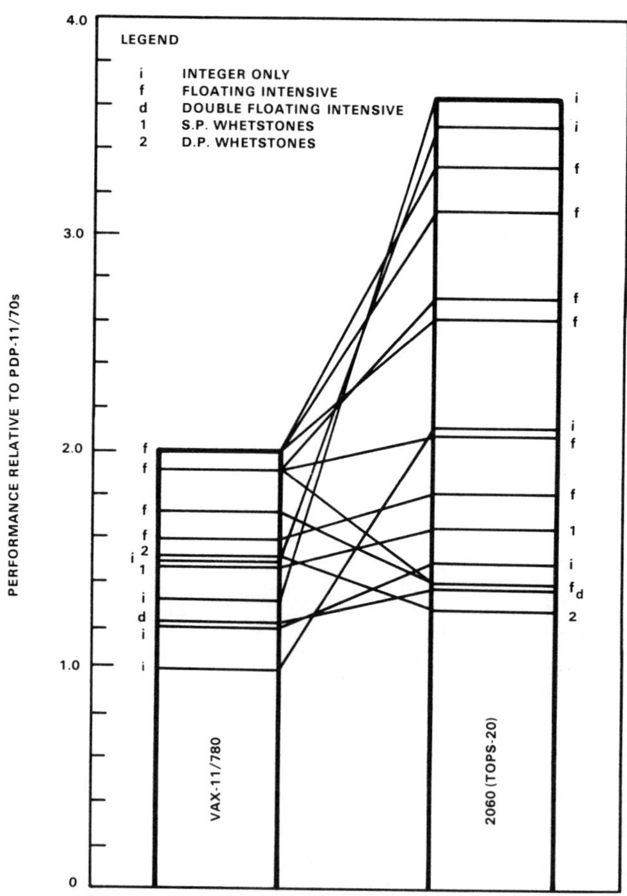

Figure 2. Relative performance for various FORTRAN benchmarks run on VAX-11/780 and DECSYSTEM 2060.

BIBLIOGRAPHY

[Advanced Micro Devices, Inc., 1975] AM 2900 Bipolar Microprocessor Circuits. Advanced Micro Devices, Inc., Sunnyvale, Calif. 1975.

[Advanced Micro Devices, Inc., 1977] AM 2900 Bipolar Microprocessor Family. Advanced Micro Devices, Inc., Sunnyvale, Calif. 1977.

[Allmark and Lucking, 1962] Allmark, R.H., and J.R. Lucking: Design of an Arithmetic Unit Incorporating a Nesting Store. *Proc. IFIP Congr.* pp. 694–698, 1962.

[Almes *et al.*, 1975] Almes, G.T., P.J. Drongowski, and S.H. Fuller: Emulating the Nova on the PDP 11/40: A Case Study. *Proc. IEEE Compcon* 11:53–56, Sept. 1975.

[Amdahl *et al.*, 1964] Amdahl, G.M., G.A. Blaauw, and F.P. Brooks, Jr.: Architecture of the IBM System/360. *IBM J. Res. Dev.* 8(2):87–101, April 1964.

[Arbuckle, 1966] Arbuckle, R.A.: Computer Analysis and Thruput Evaluation. *Comput. Automat.* 15(1):12–15 and 19, Jan. 1966.

[Asimow, 1962] Asimow, M.: *Introduction to Design.* Englewood Cliffs, N.J., copyright © Prentice-Hall, Inc., 1962.

[Balas and Padberg, 1976] Balas, E., and M. Padberg: Set Partitioning – A Survey. *SIAM Rev.* 18(4):711–760, Oct. 1976.

[Barbacci *et al.*, 1977] Barbacci M.R., G.E. Barnes, R.G. Cattell, and D.P. Siewiorek: The ISPS Computer Description Language. Carnegie-Mellon University, Department of Computer Science, Pittsburgh, technical report, August 14, 1977.

[Barbacci *et al.*, 1977a] Barbacci, M.R., D. Siewiorek, R. Gordon, R. R. Howbrigg, and S. Zuckerman: An Architectural Research Facility – ISP Descriptions, Simulation, Data Collection. *Cont. Proc. AFIPS NCC,* pp. 161–173, 1977.

[Barnes *et al.*, 1968] Barnes, G., R. Brown, M. Kato, D. Kuck, D. Slotnick, and R. Stokes: The ILLIAC IV Computer. *IEEE Trans. Comput.* C-17:746–757, Aug. 1968.

[Bartee *et al.*, 1962] Bartee, T.C., I.L. Lebow, and I.S. Reed: *Theory and Design of Digital Machines.* New York, McGraw-Hill, 1962.

[Baskett and Smith, 1976] Baskett, F., and A.J. Smith: Interference in Multiprocessor Computer Systems with Interleaved Memory. *Commun. ACM* 19(6):327–334 June, 1976.

[Baudet, 1976] Baudet, G.: Asynchronous Iterative Methods for Multiprocessors. Carnegie-Mellon University, Department of Computer Science, Pittsburgh, technical report, Nov. 1976.

[Beckman *et al.*, 1961] Beckman, P.S., F.P. Brooks, Jr., and W.J. Lawless: Developments in the Logical Organization of Computer Arithmetic and Control Units. *Proc. IRE* 49(1):53–66, Jan. 1961.

[Bell *et al.*, 1969] Bell, C.G., A.N. Habermann, J. McCredie, R. Rutledge, and W. Wulf: Computer Networks. *Computer Science Research Review.* Pittsburgh, Carnegie-Mellon University, 1969.

[Bell *et al.*, 1970] Bell, C.G., R. Cady, H. McFarland, B. Delagi, J.F. O'Loughlin, and R. Noonan: A New Architecture for Minicomputers – The DEC PDP-11. *Conf. Proc. AFIPS SJCC* 36:657–675, 1970. Reprinted as Chapter 9 of this text.

[Bell and Newell, 1970] Bell, C.G., and A. Newell: The PMS and ISP Descriptive Systems for Computer Structures. *AFIPS Conf. Proc. SJCC* 36:351–374, 1970.

[Bell and Freeman, 1971] Bell, C.G., and P. Freeman: Cai–A Computer Architecture for AI Research. *AFIPS Conf. Proc. SJCC.* 38:779–790, Spring 1971.

[Bell and Casasent, 1971] Bell, C.G., and D. Casasent: Implementation of a Buffer Memory in Minicomputers. *Computer Design,* pp. 83–89, Nov. 1971.

[Bell and Grason, 1971] Bell, C.G., and J. Grason: Register Transfer Module Design Concept. *Computer Design,* pp. 87–94, May 1971.

[Bell and Newell, 1971] Bell, C.G., and A. Newell: *Computer Structures: Readings and Examples.* New York, McGraw-Hill, 1971.

[Bell and Newell, 1971a] Bell, C.G., and A. Newell: A Panel Session – Computer Structure – Past, Present and Future, Possibilities for Computer Structures. *AFIPS Conf. Proc. FJCC* 39:387–396, 1971.

[Bell *et al.,* 1971] Bell, C.G., P. Freeman, M. Barbacci, S. Bhatio, and W. Broodle: A Computing Environment for AI Research – Overview, PMS, and Operating System Considerations. Carnegie-Mellon University, Department of Computer Science, AD-737 531, Pittsburgh, technical report, May 1971.

[Bell *et al.,* 1972] Bell, C.G., J. Grason, S. Mega, R. Van Naarden, and P. Williams: The Description and Use of the DEC Register Transfer Modules (RTMs). *IEEE Trans. Comput.,* pp. 495, May 1972.

[Bell *et al.,* 1972a] Bell, C.G., J. Grason, and A. Newell: *Designing Computers and Digital Systems Using PDP-16 Register Transfer Modules.* Maynard, Mass., Digital Press, 1972.

[Bell *et al.,* 1972b] Bell, C.G., R. Chen, S. Rege: Effect of Technology on Near-Term Computer Structures. *IEEE Comp. 5(2):29–38,* March–April, 1972.

[Bell, J., 1973] Bell, J.R.: Threaded Code. *Commun. ACM* 16(6):370–372, June 1973.

[Bell, *et al.,* 1973] Bell, C.G., R.C. Chen, S.H. Fuller, J. Grason, S. Rege, and D.P. Siewiorek: The Architecture and Applications of Computer Modules: A Set of Components for Digital Design. *IEEE Compcon* 73:177–180, March 1973.

[Bell *et al.,* 1974] Bell, J., D. Casasent, and C.G. Bell: An Investigation of Alternative Cache Organizations. *IEEE Trans. Comput.* C-23(4):346–351, April 1974.

[Bell and Strecker, 1976] Bell, C.G., and W.D. Strecker: Computer Structures: What Have We Learned from the PDP-11? *Proc. Conference: 3rd Annual Symposium on Computer Architecture,* IEEE and ACM, 1976.

[Bell Laboratories, 1975] Bell Laboratories: The Safeguard Data-Processing System: An Experiment in Software Development. *Bell Syst. Tech. J.,* special supplement, 54:S199–S210, 1975.

[Best, 1957] Best, R.L.: Memory Units in the Lincoln TX-2, *Proc. WJCC,* pp. 160–167, 1957.

[Bhandarkar, 1978] Bhandarkar, D.P.: Dynamic MOS Memories: Serial or Random Access? *IEEE Compcon Digest of Papers,* pp. 162–164, Feb. 1978.

[Blaauw, 1970] Blaauw, G.A.: Hardware Requirements for the Fourth Generation. In *Fourth Generation Computers: User Requirements and Transition,* F. Gruenberger (ed.), Englewood Cliffs, N.J., Prentice-Hall, pp. 155–168, 1970.

[Blaauw and Brooks, in preparation] Blaauw, G.A., and F.P. Brooks, Jr.: *Computer Architecture,* in preparation.

[Bobrow *et al.,* 1972] Bobrow, D.G., J.D. Burchfiel, D.L. Murphy, and R.S. Tomlinson: TENEX, A Paged Time Sharing System for the PDP-10. *Comm. ACM* 15(3):135–143, March 1972.

[Buchholz, 1962]Buchholz, W. (ed.): *Planning a Computer System.* IBM Corp. New York, McGraw-Hill, 1962.

[Bullman, 1977] Bullman, D.M. (ed.): Stack Computers. *IEEE Comput.* 10(5):14–52, May 1977.

[Burks *et al.,* 1962] Burks, A.W., H.H. Goldstine, and J. Von Neumann: Preliminary Discussion of the Logical Design of an Electronic Computing Instrument, pt. II. *Datamation* 8(10):36–41, Oct. 1962.

[Burr *et al.*, 1977] Burr, W.E., A.H. Coleman, and W.R. Smith: Overview of the Military Computer Family Architecture Selection. *AFIPS Proc. Conf. NCC*, pp. 131–137, 1977.

[Case and Padegs, 1978] Case, R.P., and A. Padegs, Architecture of the IBM System/370. *Commun. ACM*. 21(1):73–96, Jan. 1978.

[Chaney and Molnar, 1973] Chaney, T.J., and C.E. Molnar, Anomalous Behavior of Synchronizer and Arbiter Circuits. *IEEE Trans. Comput.* C-22(4):421–422, April 1973.

[Chu, 1970] Chu, Y.: *Introduction to Computer Organization*. Englewood Cliffs, N.J., Prentice-Hall, 1970.

[Clark, 1957] Clark, W.A.: The Lincoln TX-2 Computer Development. *Proc. WJCC*, pp. 143–145, 1957.

[Clark and Molnar, 1964] Clark, W.A., and C.E. Molnar: The LINC: A Description of the Laboratory Instrument Computer. *Ann. N.Y. Acad. Sci.* 115:653–668, July 1964.

[Clark and Molnar, 1965] Clark, W.A., and C.E. Molnar, A Description of the LINC. In *Computers in Biomedical Research*. (ed.) B.D. Waxman. New York, Academic Press, 1965. Vol. II, Chapter 2.

[Clark, 1967] Clark, W.A.: Macromodular Computer Systems. *AFIPS Conf. Proc. SJCC* 30:335–336, 1967.

[Coleman *et al.*, 1977] Coleman, V., M.W. Economidis, and W.J. Harmon, Jr.: The Next Generation Four-Bit Bipolar Microprocessor Slice – The AM 2903. *Westcon*, Session 16–4, p. 1, 1977.

[Conti *et al.*, 1968] Conti C.J., D.H. Gibson, and S.H. Pitowsky: Structural Aspects of the System/360 Model 85. I. General Organization. *IBM Syst. J.*, 7(1):2–14, 1968.

[Conti, 1969] Conti, C.J.: Concepts for Buffer Storage. *IEEE Comput. Group News* 2(8), March 1969.

[Conway, 1971] Conway, M.: A Multiprocessor System Design. *Proc. IFIP Congr.*, Yugoslavia, 1971.

[Cooper and Chow, 1976] Cooper, A.E., and W.T. Chow: Development of On-Board Space Computer Systems. *IBM J. Res. Dev.* 20(1):5–19. Jan. 1976.

[Corbato *et al.*, 1962] Corbato F.J., M. Merwin-Dagget, and R.C. Daley: An Experimental Time-sharing System. *AFIPS Conf. Proc. SJCC*, pp. 335–344, 1962.

[Curnow and Wichmann, 1976] Curnow, H.J., and B.A. Wichmann: A Synthetic Benchmark. *Comput. J.* 19(1):43–62, Feb. 1976.

[Data General, 1974] Eclipse Computer Systems. Westboro, Mass., Data General Corp., 1974.

[Davidow, 1972] Davidow, W.H.: The Rationale for Logic from Semiconductor Memory. *AFIPS Conf. Proc. SJCC*, pp. 353–358, 1972.

[DEC, 1972] DEC PDP-11 documents, Programmer Reference Manual and Unibus Interface Manual. Maynard Mass., Digital Equipment Corporation, 1972.

[DEC, 1973] PDP-11 Peripherals Handbook. Maynard, Mass., Digital Equipment Corporation, 1973.

[DEC, 1973a] PDP-11/05/10/35/40 Processor Handbook. Maynard, Mass., Digital Equipment Corporation, 1973.

[DEC, 1974] DDCMP – Digital Data Communications Message Protocol. Maynard, Mass., Digital Equipment Corporation, 1974.

[DEC, 1974a] Introduction to Minicomputer Networks. Maynard, Mass., Digital Equipment Corporation, 1974.

[DEC, 1974b] PDP-11 FORTRAN Compiler Functional Specification. DEC-11-LFSCA-A-D. Maynard, Mass., Digital Equipment Corporation, 1974.

[DEC, 1974c] PDP-11 FORTRAN Object Time System Functional Specification. DEC-11-LFSOA-A-D. Maynard, Mass., Digital Equipment Corporation, 1974.

[DEC, 1975] PDP-11/70 Processor Handbook. Maynard, Mass., Digital Equipment Corporation, 1975.

[DEC, 1975a] LSI-11, PDP-11/03 Processor Handbook. Maynard, Mass., Digital Equipment Corporation, 1975.

[DEC, 1975b] LSI-11 – PDP-11/03 User's Manual (EK-LSI11-TM-001), Maynard, Mass., Digital Equipment Corporation, 1975.

[DEC, 1976] MACRO-11 Reference Manual. DEC-11-OMMAA-B-D, Maynard, Mass., Digital Equipment Corporation, 1976.

[DEC, 1977] Logic Handbook, 1977–78. Maynard, Mass., Digital Equipment Corporation, 1977.

[DEC, 1977a] PDP-11/60 Processor Handbook. Maynard, Mass., Digital Equipment Corporation, 1977.

[Denning, 1968] Denning, P.J.: The Working Set Model for Program Behavior. *Commun. ACM.* 11(5):323–333, May 1968.

[Denning, 1970] Denning, P.J.: Virtual Memory. *Computing Surveys,* pp. 153–189, Sept. 1970.

[Dennis, 1964] Dennis, J.B.: A Multiuser Computation Facility for Education and Research. *Commun. ACM,* 7(9):521–529, Sept. 1964.

[Dijkstra, 1968] Dijkstra, E.W.: Cooperating sequential processes. In *Programming Languages.* F. Genuys (ed.), New York, Academic Press, pp. 43–112, 1968.

[Dijkstra, 1969] Dijkstra, E. W.: Structured programming. In *Software Engineering: Concepts and Techniques.* Peter Naur, Brian Randell, and J.N. Buxton (eds.), New York, Petrocelli/Charter, 1969.

[Eckhouse, 1975] Eckhouse, R.H.: *Minicomputer Systems: Organization and Programming (PDP 11).* Englewood Cliffs, N.J., Prentice-Hall, 1975.

[Eichelberger and Williams, 1977] Eichelberger, E.B., and T.W. Williams: A Logic Design Structure for LSI Testability. *Proc. 14th Design Automation Conference.* June 20–22, 1977.

[Elliott *et al.,* 1956] Elliott, W.S., C.E. Owen, C.H. Devonald, and B.G. Maudsley: The Design Philosophy of Pegasus, a Quantity-Production Computer. *Proc. IEEE* 103:188–196, pt. B, supp. 2, 1956.

[Everett, 1951] Everett, R.R.: The Whirlwind I Computer AIEE-IRE Conference, pp. 70–74, 1951 (reprinted in Bell and Newell, *Computer Structures,* chap. 6, pp. 137–145).

[Fairchild Camera and Instrument Corp., 1976] Macrologic Bipolar Microprocessor Databook. Fairchild Camera and Instrument Corporation, Mountain View, Calif., 1976.

[Farber, 1975] Farber, D.J.: A Ring Network. *Datamation* 21(2):44–46, Feb. 1975.

[Flynn, 1966] Flynn, M.J.: Very High Speed Computing Systems. *Proc. IEEE* 54:1901–1909, Dec. 1966.

[Flynn, 1977] Flynn, M.J., The Interpretive Interface: Resources and Program Representation in Computer Organization. In *High Speed Computer and Algorithm Organization.* Kuck, Lawrie, and Sameh (ed.). New York, Academic Press, 1977.

[Forbes, 1977] Forbes, B.E.: Silicon-On-Sapphire Technology Produces High-Speed Single-Chip Processor. *Hewlett-Packard J.,* pp. 2–8, April 1977.

[Forgie, 1957] Forgie, J.W.: The Lincoln TX-2 Input-Output System. *Proc. WJCC,* 1957.

[Forgie, 1965] Forgie, J.W.: A Time- and Memory-Sharing Executive Program for Quick-Response, On-Line Applications. *Proc. FJCC* 11:127–139, 599–610, 1965.

[Forrester, 1951] Forrester, J.W.: Digital Information Storage in Three Dimensions Using Magnetic Cores. *J. Appl. Phys.* 22:44–48, 1951.

[Frankovich and Peterson, 1957] Frankovich, J.M., and H.P. Peterson: A Functional Description of the Lincoln TX-2 Computer. *Proc. WJCC,* pp. 146–155, 1957.

[Fraser, 1975] Fraser, A.G.: A Virtual Channel Network. *Datamation* 21(2):51–53, Feb. 1957.

[Friedman and Yang, 1969] Friedman, T.D., and S.C. Yang: Methods Used in an Automatic Logic Design Generator (ALERT). *IEEE Trans. Comput.* C-18:593–614, July 1969.

[Fuller, 1976] Fuller, S.H.: Price/Performance Comparison of C.mmp and the PDP-10. *IEEE/ACM Symposium on Computer Architecture,* pp. 195–202, Jan. 1976.

[Fuller and Oleinick, 1976] Fuller, S.H., and P.N. Oleinick: Initial Measurements of Parallel Programs on a Multi-Mini-processor. *13th IEEE Computer Society International Conference,* Washington, D.C., pp. 358–363, Sept. 1976.

[Fuller and Siewiorek, 1973] Fuller, S.H., and D.P. Siewiorek: Some Observations on Semiconductor Technology and the Architecture of Larger Digital Modules. *IEEE Comput.* 6(10):14–21, Oct. 1973.

[Fuller *et al.*, 1976] Fuller, S.H., T. McWilliams, and W. Sherwood: CMU-11 Engineering Documentation. Department of Computer Science, Carnegie-Mellon University, Pittsburgh, Technical report, 1976.

[Fuller *et al.*, 1977 Fuller, S.H., A.K. Jones, and L. Durham (eds.): Cm* Review, June 1977. Department of Computer Science, Carnegie-Mellon University, Pittsburgh, Technical report, June 1977.

[Fuller *et al.*, 1977a] Fuller, S.H., P. Shaman, and D. Lamb: Evaluation of Computer Architectures via Test Programs. *AFIPS Conf. Proc. NCC*, pp. 147–160, 1977.

[Fuller *et al.*, 1977b] Fuller, S.H., H.S. Stone, and W.E. Burr: Initial Selection and Screening of the CFA Candidate Computer Architectures. *AFIPS Conf. Proc. NCC*, pp. 139–146, 1977.

[Fusfeld, 1973] Fusfeld, A.R.: The Technological Progress Function. *Technol. Rev.* 75(4)29–38, Feb. 1973.

[Gaskill *et al.*, 1976] Gaskill, J.R., J.H. Flint, R.G. Meyer, L.J. Micheel, and L.R. Weill: Modular Single-Stage Universal Logic Gate. *IEEE J. Solid-State Circuits* SC-11(4):529–538, 1976.

[Gear, 1974] Gear, C.W.: *Computer Organization and Programming*. 2d ed. New York, McGraw-Hill, 1974.

[Gibson, 1967] Gibson, D.H.: Considerations in Block-Oriented Systems Design. *AFIPS Conf. Proc. SJCC* 30:69–80, 1967.

[Gibson, 1974] Gibson, D.H.: The Cache Concept for Large Scale Computers. In *Rechnerstrukturen*. H. Hasselmeier and W.G. Sprath (eds.). New York, Springer-Verlag, 1974.

[GML Corp, 1977] Computer Review. Lexington, Mass., GML Corp., vol. 1, 1977.

[Grant, 1972] Grant, E.L.: *Statistical Quality Control*. 4th ed. New York, McGraw-Hill, 1972.

[Grason and Siewiorek, 1975] Grason, J., and D.P. Siewiorek: Teaching with a Hierarchically Structured Digital Systems Laboratory. *IEEE Comp.* 8(12):73–81, Dec. 1975.

[Grason *et al.*, 1973] Grason, J., C.G. Bell, J. Eggert: The Commercialization of Register Transfer Modules. *IEEE Comput.* Oct. 6(10):23–27, 1973.

[Haney, 1968] Haney, F.M.: Using a Computer to Design Computer Instruction Sets. Thesis, College of Engineering and Science, Department of Computer Science, Carnegie-Mellon University, Pittsburgh, May 1968.

[Hansen, 1975] Hansen, P.B.: The Programming Language Concurrent Pascal. *IEEE Trans. Software Eng.* SE-1(2):199–207, June 1975.

[Harbison and Wulf, 1977] Harbison, S., and W.A. Wulf: Reflections in a Pool of Processors. Department of Computer Science, Carnegie-Mellon University, Pittsburgh, technical report, Nov. 1977.

[Heart *et al.*, 1973] Heart, F.E., S.M. Ornstein, W.R. Crowther, and W.B. Barker: A New Minicomputer/Multiprocessor for the ARPA Network. *AFIPS Conf. Proc. NCC*, 42:529–537, 1973.

[Hibbard, 1976] Hibbard, P.: Parallel Processing Facilities, New Directions in Algorithmic Languages, *Operating Systems*, Rocquencourt, France, Institut de Recherche d'Informatique, pp. 1–7, 1976.

[Hibbard *et al.*, 1978] Hibbard, P., A. Hisgen, and T. Rodeheffer: A Language Implementation Design for a Multiprocessor Computer System. *ACM IEEE 5th Annual Symposium on Computer Architecture*, pp. 66–72, April 1978.

[Hobbs and Theis, 1970] Hobbs, L.C., and D.J. Theis: Survey of Parallel Processor Approaches and Techniques. In *Parallel Processor Systems, Technologies and Applications*, L.C. Hobbs et al. (eds.). New York, Spartan, pp.3–20, 1970.

[Hodges, 1975] Hodges, D.A.: A Review and Projection of Semiconductor Components for Digital Storage. *Proc. IEEE* 63(8):1136–1147, Aug. 1975.

[Hodges, 1977] Hodges, D.A.: Progress in Electronic Technologies for Computers. National Bureau of Standards Report T73219, March, 1977.

[Intel, 1975] Intel Schottky Bipolar LSI Microcomputer Set: 3001 Microprogram Control Unit, 3002 Control Progressive Element, and 3003 Carry Lookahead Generator, Intel Corporation, Santa Clara, Calif., 1975.

[Intel, 1977] Intel SBC 80/05, Single Board Computer Hardware Reference Manual. Intel Corporation, Santa Clara, Calif., 1977.

[Jensen and Anderson, 1975] Jensen, E.D., and G.A. Anderson: Computer Interconnection Structures: Taxonomy, Characteristics and Examples. *Computing Surveys* 7(4):197–213, Dec. 1975.

[Jones *et al.,* 1977] Jones, A.K., R. Chansler, Jr., I. Durham, P. Feiler, and K. Schwans: Software Management of Cm* – A Distributed Multiprocessor. *AFIPS Conf. Proc.* 46:657–663, 1977.

[Jones *et al.,* 1978] Jones, A.K., R.J. Chansler, Jr., I. Durham, P. Feiler, D. Scelza, K. Schwans, and S.R. Vegdahl: Programming Issues Raised by a Multiprocessor. *Proc. IEEE,* 66(2):229–237, Feb. 1978.

[Juran, 1962] Juran, J.M.: *Quality Control Handbook.* 2d ed. New York, McGraw-Hill, 1962.

[Kahn, 1972] Kahn, R.E.: Resources-Sharing, Computer Communication Networks. *Proc. IEEE* 60(1):1397–1407, Nov. 1972.

[Kilburn *et al.,* 1962] Kilburn, T., D.L.G. Edwards, M.J. Lanigan, and F.H. Sumner: One-level Storage System. *IRE Trans.* EC-11 (2):223–235, April 1962.

[Knight, 1966] Knight, K.E.: Changes in Computer Performance: A Historical Review. *Datamation* 12(9):40–54, Sept. 1966

[Knudsen, 1972] Knudsen, M: PMSL: A System for Understanding Computer Structures, Ph.D. Thesis, Computer Science Department, Carnegie-Mellon University, Pittsburgh, 1972.

[Knuth, 1971] Knuth, D.E.: An Empirical study of FORTRAN Programs. *Software Prac. Exper.* 1(2):105–133, April–June 1971.

[Krutar, 1971] Krutar, R.: personal communication, 1971.

[Kuck *et al.,* 1972] Kuck, D.J., Y. Muraoka, and S.C. Chen: On the Number of Operations Simultaneously Executable in Fortran-Like Programs and Their Resulting Speed-up. *IEEE Trans. Comput.* C-21 (12):1293–1310, Dec. 1972.

[Landman and Russo, 1971] Landman, B.S., and R.L. Russo: On a Pin Versus Block Relationship for Partitioning of Logic Graphs. *IEEE Trans. Comput.* C-20(12)1469–1479, Dec. 1971.

[Lee, 1969] Lee, F.F.: Study of 'Look-Aside' Memory. *IEEE Trans. Comput.* C-18(11):1062–1064, Nov. 1969.

[Levy, 1974] Levy, J.V.: Software Structures: Levels of Interpreters. Unpublished manuscript, July 6, 1974.

[Liptay, 1968] Liptay, J.S.: Structural Aspects of the IBM System/360 Model 85. II. The Cache. *IBM Syst. J.* 7(1):15–21, 1968.

[Logue *et al.,* 1975] Logue, J.C., N.F. Brickman, F. Howley, J.W. Jones, and W.W. Wu: Hardware Implementation of a Small System in Programmable Logic Arrays. *IBM J. Res. Dev.* 19(2):110–119, March 1975.

[Lonergan and King, 1961] Lonergan, W., and P. King: Design of the B5000 system. *Datamation* 7(5):28–32, May 1961.

[Lowerre, 1976] Lowerre, B.: The HARPY Speech Recognition System. Ph.D. Thesis, Department of Computer Science, Carnegie-Mellon University, Pittsburgh, April 1976.

[Louie *et al.,* 1977] Louie, G., Wipfli, J., Ebright, A.: A Dual Processor Serial Data Central Chip. *Digest of International State Circuits Conference,* Philadelphia, IEEE, pp. 144, 145, 1977.

[Luecke, 1976] Luecke, J.: Overview of Semiconductor Technology Trends. *Digest of Papers.* 13th IEEE Comp. Soc. Internat. Conf., Washington, D.C., pp. 52–55, 1976.

[Lunde, 1977] Lunde, A.: Empirical Evaluation of Some Features of Instruction Set Processor Architecture. *Commun. ACM* 20(3):143–153, March 1977.

[Marathe and Fuller, 1977] Marathe, M., and S.H. Fuller: A Study of Multiprocessor Contention for Shared Data in C.mmp. *ACM SIGMETRICS Symposium,* pp. 255–262, 1977.

[Marill and Roberts, 1966] Marill, T., and L.G. Roberts: Toward a Cooperative Network of Time-shared Computers. *AFIPS Conf. Proc. FJCC* 29:425–432, 1966.

[Maurer, 1966] Maurer, W.D.: A Theory of Computer Instructions. *J. ACM* 13(2):226–235, April 1966.

[McCarthy and Maughly, 1962] McCarthy, J., and J.W. Maughly: Time Sharing Computer Systems. In *Management and the Computer of the Future.* M. Greenberger (ed.). Cambridge, MIT Press, pp. 221–248, 1962.

[McCarthy *et al.,* 1963] McCarthy, J., S. Boilen, E. Fredkin, and J.C.R. Licklider: A Timesharing Debugging System for a Small Computer. *AFIPS Conf. Proc. SJCC* 23:51–57, 1963.

[McCracken and Robertson, 1971] McCracken, D., and G. Robertson: C.ai (L*) – An L* Processor for C.ai. Department of Computer Science, Carnegie-Mellon University, Pittsburgh, technical report, 1971.

[McCredie, 1972] McCredie, J.: Analytic Models as Aids in Multiprocessor Design. Department of Computer Science, Carnegie-Mellon University, Pittsburgh, technical report, 1972.

[McLean, 1977] McLean, J.: Univac Disbanding Future Systems Plan. *Electronic News* 12:1-28, Dec. 1977.

[McWilliams *et al.*, 1977] McWilliams, T.M., S.H. Fuller, and W.H. Sherwood: Using LSI Processor Bit-Slices to Build a PDP-11 – A Case Study. *AFIPS Conf. Proc. NCC*, pp. 243–253, 1977. Reprinted as Chapter 19 of this text.

[Meade, 1970] Meade, R.M.: On Memory System Design. *AFIPS Conf. Proc. FJCC* 37:33–43, 1970.

[Meade, 1971] Meade, R.M.: Design Approaches for Cache Memory Control. *Comp. Des.* 10(1):87–93, Jan. 1971.

[Metcalfe and Boggs, 1976] Metcalfe, R.M., and D.R. Boggs: Ethernet: Distributed Packet Switching for Local Computer Networks. *Commun. ACM* 19(7):395–404, July 1976.

[Mitchell and Olsen, 1956] Mitchell, J.L., and K.H. Olsen: TX-0: A Transistor Computer. *AFIPS Conf. Proc. EJCC* 10:93–101, 1956.

[Moore, 1976] Moore, G.E.: Microprocessors and Integrated Electronic Technology. *Proc. IEEE* 64(6):837–841, June 1976.

[Morris and Mudge, 1977] Morris, L.R., and J.C. Mudge: Speed Enhancement of Digital Signal Processing Software Via Microprogramming a General Purpose Minicomputer. *Conference Record*, IEEE Internat. Conf. Acoustics, Speech, and Signal Processing, May 1977.

[Mudge, 1977] Mudge, J.C.: Design Decisions Achieve Price/Performance Balance in Mid-Range Minicomputer. *Comp. Des.* 16(8):87–95, Aug. 1977. Reprinted as Chapter 13 in this text.

[Murphy, 1972] Murphy, D.L.: Storage Organization and Management in Tenex. *Proc. AFIPS FJCC*. Vol. 41, pt. 1, Montvale, N.J., AFIPS Press, pp. 23–32, 1972.

[Myers, 1977] Myers, G.J.: The Case Against Stack-Oriented Instruction Sets. *ACM Sigarch News*, Aug. 1977.

[Myer and Sutherland, 1968] Myer, T.H., and I.E. Sutherland: On the Design of Display Processors. *Commun. ACM* 11(6):410–414, June 1968.

[Nakano *et al.*, 1978] Nakano, T., O. Tomisawa, K. Anami, M. Ohmore, I. Okkura, and M. Nakaya: A 920 Gate Masterslice. *Digest of Technical Papers*, IEEE Solid-State Circuits Conference, pp. 64–65, 1978.

[Needham, 1972] Needham, R.M.: Protection Systems and Protection Implementations. *AFIPS Conf. Proc. FJCC*. pt. 1, 41:571–578, A720, 1972.

[Needham and Walker, 1977] Needham, R.M., and R.D.H. Walker: The Cambridge CAP Computer and its Protection System. *Proc. Sixth Symposium on Operating Systems Principles*, 1977.

[Noyce, 1977] Noyce, R.N.: Large Scale Integration: What is Yet to Come? *Science* 195:1102–1106, 1977.

[Noyce, 1977a] Noyce, R.N.: Microelectronics. *Sci. Am.* 237(3):62–69, Sept. 1977. Copyright © 1977 by *Scientific American Inc.* All rights reserved.

[Nussbaum, 1975] Nussbaum, E.: New Technologies and the Local Telephone Companies. *National Electronics Conf. Proc.*, p. 42, 1975.

[Oleinick, 1978] Oleinick, P.N.: The Implementation of Parallel Algorithms on a Multiprocessor. Ph.D. Thesis, Computer Science Department, Carnegie-Mellon University, Pittsburgh, 1978, in preparation.

[O'Loughlin, 1975] O'Loughlin, J.F.: Microprogramming a Fixed Architecture Machine. *Microprogramming and Systems Architecture*. Maidenhead, Infotech State of the Art Report 23, pp. 205–221, 1975.

[Organick, 1972] Organick, E.I.: *The Multics Systems: An Examination of Its Structure*. Cambridge, M.I.T Press, 1972.

[Ornstein *et al.*, 1967] Ornstein, S.M., M.J. Stucki, and W.A. Clark: A Functional Description of Macromodules. *AFIPS Conf. Proc. SJCC* 30:337–355, 1967.

[Ornstein *et al.*, 1972] Ornstein, S.M., E.E. Heart, W.R. Crowther, H.K. Rising, S.B. Russell, and A. Michael: The Terminal IMP for the ARPA Computer Network. *AFIPS Conf. Proc. SJCC* 40:243–254, 1972.

[Parke, 1978] Parke, N.G.: Personal Communication, 1978.

[Parnas, 1971] Parnas, D.L.: On the Criteria to be Used in Decomposing Systems Into Modules. Department of Computer Science, Carnegie-Mellon University, Pittsburgh, technical report, 1971.

[Patil, 1978] Patil, S.S., and T. Welch : An approach to Using VLSI in Digital Systems. *In 5th Annual Symposium on Computer Architecture.* New York, ACM, pp. 139–143, April 1978.

[Phister, 1976] Phister, M.: *Data Processing Technology and Economics.* Santa Monica Publishing Co., Santa Monica, Calif., 1976.

[Popek and Goldberg, 1974] Popek, G.J., and R.P. Goldberg: Formal Requirement for Virtualizable Third Generation Architectures. *Commun. ACM* 17(7):412–421, July 1974.

[Rajchman, 1961] Rajchman, J.A.: Computer Memories: A Survey of the State-of-the-Art. *Proc. IRE,* pp. 104–127, Jan. 1961.

[Redmond and Smith, 1977] Redmond, K.C., and T.M. Smith: Lessons from "Project Whirlwind." *IEEE Spectrum* 14(10):50–59, Oct. 1977.

[Roberts, 1970] Roberts, L.G. (ed.): Computer Network Development to Achieve Resource Sharing. *AFIPS Conf. Proc. SJCC* 36:543–549, 1970.

[Rossman *et al.,* 1975] Rossman, S.E., C.G. Bell, M.J. Flynn, F.P. Brooks, Jr., S.H. Fuller, H. Hellerman: A Course of Study in Computer Hardware Architecture. *IEEE Comput.* pp. 44–63, Dec. 1975.

[Rothman, 1959] Rothman, S.: R/W 40 Data Processing System. *International Conference on Information Processing and Auto-Math.* Los Angeles, Ramo-Wooldridge, 1959.

[Scarott, 1965] Scarott, G.G.: The Efficient Use of Multilevel Storage. Washington, D.C., Spartan, p. 137, 1965.

[Scelza, 1977] Scelza, D.: The Cm* Host Users Manual. Department of Computer Science, Carnegie-Mellon University, Pittsburgh, July 1977.

[Schroeder and Saltzer, 1971] Schroeder, M.D., and J.H. Saltzer: A Hardware Architecture for Implementing Protection Rings. Proceedings, 3rd Symposium on Operating System Principles. *Commun. ACM* 15(3):157–170, 1972.

[Shannon, 1948] Shannon, C.E.: A Mathematical Theory of Communication. *Bell Syst. Tech. J.* 27:379–423, 623–656, 1948.

[Sharpe, 1969] Sharpe, W.F.: *The Economics of Computers.* New York, Columbia University Press, 1969.

[Siewiorek and Barbacci, 1976] Siewiorek, D.P., and M.R. Barbacci: The CMU RT-CAD System – An Innovative Approach to Computer-Aided Design. *AFIPS Conf. Proc. NCC* 45:643–655, 1976.

[Siewiorek *et al.,* 1976] Siewiorek, D.P., M. Canepa, and S. Clark: C.vmp: The Analysis, Architecture and Implementation of a Fault Tolerant Multiprocessor. Computer Science Department, Carnegie-Mellon University, Pittsburgh, technical report A038633, Dec. 1976.

[Signetics, 1975] Introducing the Series 3000 Bipolar Microprocessor. Sunnyvale, Calif., Signetics Corporation, 1975.

[Simon, 1969] Simon, H.A.: *The Sciences of the Artificial.* Cambridge, M.I.T Press, 1969.

[Singleton, 1969] Singleton, R.C.: Algorithm 347: An Efficient Algorithm for Sorting with Minimal Storage. *Commun. ACM* 13(3):185–187, March 1969.

[Sklaroff, 1976] Sklaroff, J.R.: Redundancy Management Technique for Space Shuttle Computers. *IBM J. Res. Dev.* 20(1):20–28, Jan. 1976.

[Soha and Pohlman, 1974] Soha, Z., and W.B. Pohlman: A High Performance, Microprogrammed NMOS-LSI Processor for 8- and 16-bit Applications. *NEREM* pt. 2, 16:10–19, Oct. 1974.

[Spencer, 1978] Spencer, R.F.: VLSI and Minicomputers. *IEEE Compcon,* Spring 1978.

[Stone, 1971] Stone, H.S.: Parallel Processing with the Perfect Shuffle. *IEEE Trans. Comput.* C-20(2):153–161, Feb. 1971.

[Stone and Siewiorek, 1975] Stone, H.S., and D.P. Siewiorek: *Introduction to Computer Organization and Data Structures: PDP-11 Edition.* New York, McGraw-Hill, 1975.

[Strachey, 1960] Strachey, C.: Timesharing in Large Fast Computers. *Proceedings of the International Conference on Information Processing,* 15–20 June 1959, Paris, UNESCO, pp. 336–341, 1960.

[Strecker, 1970] Strecker, W.D.: Analysis of the Instruction Execution Rate in Certain Computer Structures. Ph.D. Thesis, Carnegie-Mellon University, Pittsburgh, 1970.

[Strecker, 1976] Strecker, W.D.: Cache Memories for PDP-11 Family Computers. *Proceedings of the 3rd Annual Symposium on Computer Architecture,* pp. 155–158, 1976. Reprinted as Chapter 10 in this text.

[Strecker, 1976a] Strecker, W.D.: personal communication, 1976.

[Strecker, 1978] Strecker, W.D.: Optimal Design of Memory Hierarchies. *Proceedings of the 11th Hawaii International Conference on System Sciences,* Western Periodicals Co., p. 78. 1978.

[Swan *et al.,* 1977] Swan, R.J., S.H. Fuller, and D.P. Siewiorek: Cm* – A Modular, Multi-Microprocessor. *AFIPS Conf. Proc.* 46:637–644, 1977.

[Swan *et al.,* 1977a] Swan, R.J., A. Bechtolsheim, K.W. Lai, and J.K. Ousterhout: The Implementation of the Cm* Multi-Microprocessor. *AFIPS Conf. Proc.* 46:645–655, 1977.

[Sweeney, 1965] Sweeney, D.W.: An Analysis of Floating-Point Addition. *IBM Syst. J.* 4(1)31–42, 1965.

[Sutherland, 1963] Sutherland, I.E.: Sketchpad: A Man-Machine Graphical Communication System. M.I.T. Lincoln Lab., Cambridge, technical report 296, May 1965. Abridged version *AFIPS Conf. Proc. SJCC* 23:329–346, 1963.

[Tandem, 1977] Tandem 16 System Introduction. Cupertino, Calif., Tandem Computers, 1977.

[Thomas and Siewiorek, 1977] Thomas, D.E., and D.P. Siewiorek: Measuring Designer Performance to Verify Design Automation Systems.*Design Automat. Conf. Proc.* 14:411–418, 1977.

[Toombs, 1977] Toombs, D.: personal communication, 1977.

[Turn, 1974] Turn, R.: *Computers in the 1980s.* New York, Columbia University Press, 1974.

[Vacroux, 1975] Vacroux, G.: Microcomputers. *Sci. Am. 232(5)32–40, May 1975.*

[van de Goor *et al.,* 1969] van de Goor, A.D., C.G. Bell, and D.A. Witcraft: Design and Behavior of TSS/8: A PDP-8 Based Time-Sharing System. *IEEE Trans. Comput.* C-18(11):1038–1043, Nov. 1969.

[von Hippel, 1977] von Hippel, E.: The Dominant Role of the User in Semiconductor and Electronic Subassembly Process Innovation. *IEEE Trans. Engineer. Management* EM-24(2):60–71, May 1977.

[Wilkes, 1949] Wilkes, M.V.: A personal communication from M.V. Wilkes to S.H. Fuller Jan. 13, 1977, which confirmed that the quote (Chapter 1) which appeared in a British Computer Society's History of Computing in 1949 was accurate.

[Wilkes, 1953] Wilkes, M.V.: The Best Way to Design an Automatic Calculating Machine. Report of Manchester University Computer Inaugural Conference, July 1951, Manchester, 1953.

[Wilkes and Stringer, 1953] Wilkes, M.V., and J.B. Stringer: Microprogramming and the Design of the Control Circuits in an Electronic Digital Computer. *Proc. Cambridge Phil. Soc.,* pt. 2, 49:30–38, April 1953.

[Wilkes, 1965] Wilkes, M.V.: Slave Memories and Dynamic Storage Allocation. *IEEE Trans. Comput.,* pp. 270–271, April 1965.

[Wirth, 1977] Wirth, N.: Towards a Discipline of Real-time Programming. *Commun. ACM* 20(8):577–583, Aug. 1977.

[Wulf, 1971] Wulf, W.: Programming Without the Goto. *Proc. IFIP Congr.,* Yugoslavia, 1971.

[Wulf *et al.,* 1971] Corbin, K., W. Corwin, R. Goodman, E. Hyde, K. Kramer, E. Werme, and W. Wulf: A Software Laboratory: Preliminary Report. Department of Computer Science, Carnegie-Mellon University, 1971.

[Wulf *et al.,* 1971a] Apperson, J., R. Brender, C. Geschke, A.N. Habermann, D. Russell, D. Wile, and W.A. Wulf: Bliss Reference Manual. Department of Computer Science, Carnegie-Mellon University, Pittsburgh, technical report, 1971.

[Wulf *et al.,* 1971b] Wulf, W.A., D. Russell, and A.N. Habermann: BLISS: A Language for Systems Programming. *Commun. ACM* 14(12):780, Dec. 1971.

[Wulf and Bell, 1972] Wulf, W.A., and C.G. Bell: C.mmp – A Multi-Mini-Processor. *AFIPS Conf. Proc. FJCC* pt. II, 41:765–777, 1972.

[Wulf *et al.,* 1975] Wulf, W.A., Levin, R., and Pierson, C.: Overview of the Hydra Operating System Development. *Proc. Fifth Symposium on Operating System Principles,* New York, ACM, 1975.

INDEX

C

R